The Essex Genealogist

Index to Volumes 16-20

(1996-2000)

Essex Society of Genealogists, Inc.
Essex County, Massachusetts

HERITAGE BOOKS
2011

HERITAGE BOOKS
AN IMPRINT OF HERITAGE BOOKS, INC.

Books, CDs, and more—Worldwide

For our listing of thousands of titles see our website
at
www.HeritageBooks.com

Published 2011 by
HERITAGE BOOKS, INC.
Publishing Division
100 Railroad Ave. #104
Westminster, Maryland 21157

Copyright © 2002 Essex Society of Genealogists, Inc.

Other books by the author:
*Essex County Deeds, 1639–1678, Abstracts of Volumes 1–4
Copy Books, Essex County, Massachusetts*
CD: The Essex Genealogist, Volumes 1 and 2 (1981–1982)
The Essex Genealogist, Volumes 1–27 (1981–2007)
The Essex Genealogist, Index to Volumes 1–15 (1981–1995)
The Essex Genealogist, Index to Volumes 16–20 (1996–2000)
The Essex Genealogist, Index to Volumes 21–25 (2001–2005)

All rights reserved. No part of this book may be reproduced or transmitted in any form or by any means, electronic or mechanical, including photocopying, recording or by any information storage and retrieval system without written permission from the author, except for the inclusion of brief quotations in a review.

International Standard Book Numbers
Paperbound: 978-0-7884-2032-0
Clothbound: 978-0-7884-8843-6

The following guidelines have been observed for the indexing of these five volumes of The Essex Genealogist, 1996-2000:

> All titles such as Dr. and Rev. have been eliminated except where there is no given name provided.
>
> All variant spellings of given names have been consolidated under one common spelling (e.g., Rebeckah, Rebekah, Rebecka will appear as "Rebecca."
>
> Wherever possible, married women have been listed under both their maiden names and under their married names, with maiden names in parentheses.
>
> Names appearing in Society related articles and of no particular genealogical significance, have not been included.
>
> Names with page numbers followed by an "a" will be found on the back covers of the original volumes. They will be found on the last pages of the reprinted volumes.

The index was compiled and edited by Nancy C. Hayward and proofread by Shirley Davenport Learned.

Essex Society of Genealogists, Inc.
P. O. Box 313
Lynnfield, MA 01940-0313
www.esog.org

SUBJECT INDEX

FAMILY GENEALOGIES

List Of Genealogies From *The Essex Genealogist*
1981-1998 .... 18:132

Abbott, George - Andover	20:19
Aborn, Samuel - Salem	16:88
Aborn/Ebourne Family - Salem, Lynn	16:30
Alley, Hugh - Lynn	18:17
Angier, Sibyl	16:104
Armitage, Joseph & Godfrey - Boston	18:229
Armitage, Rebecca	18:234
Baker, Edward - Lynn	18:147
Ballard, William - Lynn	16:71
Ballards Of Andover	16:65
Bancroft Family - Lynnfield	20:33
Bancroft, Thomas - Lynnfield	19:211
Barker, Richard - Andover	20:164
Bassett, William - Lynn	18:28
Bennett, Samuel - Lynn, Rumney Marsh	17:87
Bessom/Dennis/Tyler/Harwood Connections	19:230
Blaney Family - Lynn, Salem	16:23, 78
Boynton, Nathaniel - Lynn	20:106
Bradley, Judith - Haverhill	19:234
Brewer, Crispus - Boston, Lynn	19:77
Briant, James, Capt. - Beverly	20:150
Browne, Joseph - Lynn	18:222
Carr, Anne (Cotton)	17:193
Cheever, Ezekiel, Rev.	19:36, 98
Choate - Essex	17:75
Cleaves, William	17:112
Coates, Robert - Lynn; Stonington, Ct.	19:162
Coates, Thomas - Lynn	19:154
Cummings, Isaac - Ipswich, Topsfield	20:174
Dane Family	19:221
Dennen Family - Gloucester	17:220
Derby Family - Salem	17:225
Divan, John - Lynn	18:114
Dubois Family	20:169
Eaton, Jacob - Wells, ME	19:165
Eaton, Theophilus - Salisbury	18:219
Edmands, John - Malden, Saugus	17:25
Edmonds, William - Saugus	16:202
Edwards, Martha - Beverly	17:112
Estes, Matthew - Lynn, Salem	18:90
Farnham, Hiram Putnam - Andover	19:21
Farnum, Daniel - Newburyport	16:104
Farr, George - Lynn	19:25
Farrar, Thomas - Lynn	17:171
Farrington, Edmund	17:142
Fraile, George - Lynn	17:17
Friend, John - Salem	16:138, 212; 17:32, 102, 161
Fuller, John - Lynn	17:154
Gaffney, Michael - Gloucester	17:136
Garcelon, James - Gloucester	19:110
Graves, Mark - Andover	20:204
Graves, Mary Ann	20:227
Graves, Samuel - Ipswich	20:204
Graves, Thomas - Lynn	20:204
Gray, Robert - Lynn	20:102
Hackett, Jabez - Lynn, Taunton	18:79
Hackett, William	16:17
Haddock, Charles - Haverhill	16:146
Hale, John - Boxford, MA; Nova Scotia	18:106
Hammond, Lawrence	16:229
Hardy Family - Groveland	18:9
Hart, Isaac & Samuel - Lynn	18:40
Hood Family - Lynn	18:51
Hutchinson, Joseph - Salem, Danvers	17:14
Ingalls Sisters	19:219
Ingalls, Edmund - Lynn	19:43, 105
Jones, Thomas - Gloucester	18:83
Kelley, Hannah Upton Goodale - Danvers	20:228
Kirtland, Philip & Nathaniel - Lynn	18:109
Knight, William - Lynn	18:71
Larrabee Family	19:224; 20:44, 111
Laughton, Thomas - Lynn	17:45
Longfellow, Franklin Davis	16:48
Marland, Abraham - Andover	19:17
Marshall, Thomas	16:158, 233
More, Richard	16:220a
More, Richard, Capt. - Salem	16:200
Mower, Richard - Lynn	16:195; 17:40
Moy, Alice Rosina	16:48
Needham, Margaret - Danvers	20:24, 91
Newhall Family - Lynn	16:44
Newhall, Anthony - Lynn	17:215
Northey, John	19:81, 169
Norwood, Francis - Gloucester	18:198
Norwood, Thomas - Lynn	18:208
Osborn Family	17:183
Osborn, William - Peabody	17:195
Parker, James - Groton	16:225
Parker, Joseph - Andover	18:154, 235
Parker, Joseph - Groton	17:78
Parker, Nathan - Andover	19:30, 87
Parker, Thomas - Reading, Mass.	16:38
Parsons, Eben - Gloucester	17:224
Pemberton, James	19:206
Perkins - Solving A Problem	16:113
Phillips, Walter - Lynn, Salem	16:153, 221
Pike, Dorothy (Daye)	20:101
Potter, Nicholas - Lynn	19:142
Proctor - Essex	17:75
Purchase, Thomas & Aquilla	17:229
Richards, John - Lynn	16:95
Richards, Joseph	16:69

SUBJECT INDEX

Rogers, Elizabeth	17:114
Silsbee, Henry - Salem, Lynn	18:99
Smith, James - Woolwich, ME	17:202
Smith, Joseph F. - Lynnfield	17:202
Spofford Family - Georgetown	17:140
Tarbox, Cornelius - Biddeford, ME	20:145
Tarbox, George Edward, Jr.	20:146
Tarbox, John - Biddeford, ME	20:144
Tarbox, John - Lynn	20:132
Tarr Family	19:235
Trevitt - Marblehead, Lynn	17:96
Twain, Mark - Connection to Haverhill	19:139
Wallis, Joshua	17:233
Webber/Bowden - Kennebunk, ME	20:145
Whitman, Francis	17:115
Wiborn Family	20:30
Wise - Essex	17:75
Witt, John - Lynn	18:164
Yeaton, Jacob - Marblehead	19:165

ESSEX COUNTY ARTICLES

Ancestry Braintree & Saugus Ironworkers	20:63
Andover - Inhabitants 1692	16:68
Babson Papers - Cape Ann Hist. Assoc.	20:17
Beverly - Oath Of Fidelity	20:198
Beverly Church Records	19:204
Beverly, Town Of	16:136
Boxford - Old Graveyards	19:168
Burlingame, Susan Emiline	20:162
Chebacco, Hog Island Early Families	17:75
Collins, Samuel - Indenture	20:78
Conant, Roger - Salem, Beverly	16:903
Danvers - Washington News Room	20:89
Endicott, John	18:195
Essex County In Revolutionary Times	17:3
Essex County Land Bank Stockholders 1740	18:240
Essex County Post Offices	20:82
Essex County Riches Of Nature	18:902
Gloucester - Oath Of Fidelity	20:200
Gloucester Deaths Not Recorded In VR	16:63, 133; 17:11
Gloucester's Early Settlement	17:904
Graves, Thomas	20:904
Hamilton, MA	18:69
Haradan, Mary	18:145
Haverhill, MA	18:140
Indian Deeds To Lynn & Salem	18:901
Ipswich	18:192
Land Bank & Manufactory Company	18:904
Lawrence	19:13
Lynn - Oath Of Fidelity	20:196
Lynn - Tale Of Two Taverns	19:75
Lynn Town Book 1638	20:194
Lynnfield	19:135
Lynnfield's Old Meeting House	19:903
Manchester	19:201
Manchester - Oath Of Fidelity	20:197, 199
Marblehead Looks Back 350 Years	20:14
Methuen & Its Petitions	20:130
Middleton	20:201
Mill English	16:3
Murray, Judith Sargent - Gloucester	17:191
Nahant - Early Resident	18:14
Northey Silversmiths - Salem	19:198
Nurse, Rebecca	17:901
Old Planters Of Beverly	19:123
Peaslee, Joseph Of Amesbury	16:14
Pickering House - Salem	20:901
Quaker Marriage - Hood/Breed	16:16
Quaker Meetings In Essex County	18:11
Reading & Lynnfield	20:183
Richardson, Thomas - Indenture	20:78
Rotten Rye Bread - Salem Witch Trials	20:902
Salem Deeds - 1640	19:188
Sargents Of Merrimac	20:80
Sheldon, Asa - Apprentice	17:902
Sidney Perley's Boxford	16:193
Tobacco In Mass. Bay Colony	19:901
Voyage Of Massachusetts To Nagasake	17:131
Winter Of 1718/1717	19:904
Witchcraft Trials	18:139

RESEARCH ARTICLES

American Immigrants - Late 19th 20th Cen	17:63
Boston Record Commissioners Reports	19:131
Canadian Census Records After 1901	19:73
Compiling A Family History	18:903
Computers And Genealogy	16:183
Danvers Archival Center	19:15
Essex County Probate Records	16:54
Essex County Vital Records On CD-ROM	18:118
Essex Probate Records	16:169
First Congregational Churches In Mass.	19:902
French-Canadian Genealogical Research	18:3
Haverhill Public Library	18:143
Italian Research	16:123
James, Warren - State Hospital Records	19:86
Jewish Genealogical Research	17:63
Lesson Learned	19:183
Massachusetts Church Records	16:189
Massachusetts State Archives	19:3
Migrations Out Of New England	18:183

SUBJECT INDEX

Noodling With Numbers 18:139
Passenger Lists Port Of Boston 1848-1891 ... 20:123
Preparing Lineages 18:63
Quaker Ancestry - RI Historical Society 19:63
Quaker Meetings - Essex County 19:70
Resources For Newfoundland & Labrador 17:189
Revolutionary War Records 17:9
Umbilical Lines & MTDNA Analysis 17:123
Understanding Tombstones 18:123
Using Census & City Directories 20:3

OUTSIDE ESSEX COUNTY

Ancient & Honorable Artillery Co., Mass. 19:72
Banished From Massachusetts 16:901
Halifax Explosion 17:903
Indian Captives In Canada 20:12
Massachusetts Military Museum 16:135
Maypole Incident 20:903
Tewksbury Warnings Out 1756-1781 .... 16:131
Voyage Of The Arabella 16:902

CORRECTIONS AND REMARKS

Aborn/Nick 20:52
Archbell 16:111
Ayer 19:174
Baker 19:174
Bassett 18:117
Bassett/Derich 16:232
Breed 16:171, 173
Breed/Carlat 16:111
Breed/Miner 17:51
Breed/Wiborn 20:53
Chandler/Goldthwaite 19:56
Cheever 19:173
Clark/Ives/Thayer 16:110
Clemens/Clement 19:237
Collins/Newhall 20:116
Collins/Wiswall 16:109
Essex County Deeds Online 20:53
Farr/Farnsworth 19:117
Farr/McCall 19:117
Garcelon 19:236
Gerry 16:109
Hackett 18:117
Haddock 16:232
Haraden 20:117
Harnden/Horndale/Harndel/Hamden 16:111
Hart 18:117
Hood - Coats 18:117
Hopkinton, MA 19:54

Ingalls 19:173
Ingalls/Allen;Carrier/Toothaker 19:115
Ingalls/Dane/Allen 19:115
Ingalls/Dane/Allen/Toothaker 19:116
Ingalls/Witham 19:115
Johnson 16:173
Kidder, George Sanford 19:55
Kimball Genealogy 20:16
King/Tuttle 16:174
Knight/Cole 18:174
Kretschmar 19:174
Land Bank 1740 .... 19:54
Larrabee, Benjamin 20:176
Larrabee, John 20:176
Larrabee/Parker 20:52
Larrabee/Tibbetts 20:116
Laughton - Lenthall - Eells 17:234
Law/Green 16:110
Manchester-By-The-Sea Historical Society 19:55, 117
Marshall 18:174
Marshall, Thomas 16:231
McKeen/McKean Family 19:55
More 17:51
More, Richard - Salem 17:50
Needham 16:171
Newhall 16:43, 232
Newhall/Bott 16:109
Northey 19:237
Norwood/Butman 19:54
Parker 19:174
Potter 19:237
Potter/Hart/Fuller 19:236
Potter/Roach 19:236
Pray/Thayer 16:175
Pulsifer - Ipswich 17:51
Rhodes 20:52
Rhodes/Howard 19:116
Richards/Williams 16:171
Saunders 16:112
Silsbee, Samuel 18:174
Silsbee/Marsh 18:174
Silsby/Geer 18:174
Tarbox 20:237
Tarbox - Ellsworth, ME 20:238
Tarbox/Brean/Gray/Hiller 20:237
Tarbox/Edwards 20:238
Tarbox/Larrabee 20:237
Tarbox/Nealey/Blaisdell 20:237
Tarbox/Stevens/Parsons/Hull 20:237
Tilton 17:234
Townsend 16:172, 173, 232; 19:175
Waldron/Knight 19:175
Wallingford 17:177
Warren 17:177

3

SUBJECT INDEX

Webber 20:238
Whiting 17:234
Whitney Family 20:117
Williams Family 17:113
Wise 17:177

AUTHORS

Adams, Clayton 20:176
Allen, Nancy Edmands 17:25
Apitz, Joseph 19:17, 81, 169
Arbeiter, Nancy, C.G.R.S. 17:63
Arthaud, John Bradley, M.D. ... 17:233; 19:204
Baker, Nelson M. 18:147, 180a
Bardes, Bruce & Eleanor 17:96
Barnard, Jeanette T.P. 19:206
Barton, Dorothy (Wood) 20:169
Berry, Rebecca 17:171; 18:229
Blaney, Chuckie 16:23, 78
Bowman, Robert E. 20:63
Buxton, John O. 17:195
Chaplin, Duncan D., III 18:63
Connolly, Doris R. 17:225
Cox, Robert A. 16:135
Coyle, James J. 17:17
Cummings, David Butler 20:174
Dearborn, David Curtis, F.A.S.G. ... 16:3; 18:183
Doliber, Donald A. 19:183
Drew, Hannah Bartlett 18:51
Duffy, Janis 20:123
Dunn, Alexander 19:36, 98
Eastmen, Richard W. 18:118
Eaton, Priscilla J. 19:165
Ebens, Mary Jean 19:165, 234; 20:24, 91, 228
Ebens, Richard F. 19:86
Edmands, Theodore 16:202
Emerson, Frank 19:139
Emonds, Walter L. 20:162
Estes, Charles 18:90
Farlow, Charles Frederick 16:71
Farnham, Russell C., C.G. 16:48, 104; 19:21
Fitzpatrick, Marilyn R. 16:38; 17:78; 18:154, 235; 19:30, 87; 20:16
Foster, Robert Nathan 20:150
Fowler, Samuel 19:901
Fullerton, John H. 17:220
Garland, Sally 19:168
Garrett, Nancy (Westcoat) (Harwood) ... 19:230
Goss, David 19:123
Gottwald, Arthur Pratt 16:95
Hale, Roger Conant 18:106
Hanscom, Constance R. 19:110
Hart, James Morrison 18:40
Hawkes, Nathan Mortimer 18:195
Henderson, Robert F. 17:193
Holden, Barbara R.   16:14, 65, 136, 193; 17:14, 75, 140, 191; 18:9, 69, 140, 192; 19:13, 201; 20:14, 80, 102, 130
Holman, Winifred Lovering 19:77
Hovanec, Beverly J. Francis, C.G. ... 16:17; 18:79, 219
Howard, Loea Parker 20:183
Howe, Shirley Tarr 19:235
Hudson, Capt. Henry A., Jr., USNR-Ret. ... 20:82
Kane, Patricia E. 19:198
Kenney, Donald S. 17:112
Kippen-Smith, Priscilla W. 18:145
Kyner, Stephen B. 16:183
LaBelle, Robert 20:24, 91
Laing, Gregory 16:146; 18:143
Lainhart, Ann S. 16:131, 189; 19:131
Lawrence, Roger W., Prof. 18:3; 20:12
Lindberg, Marcia Wiswall, C.G.   16:30, 54, 71, 88, 95, 153, 158, 169, 221; 17:45, 87, 142, 154, 202, 229; 18:17, 28, 114, 164, 198, 208, 222; 19:25, 43, 105, 135, 154, 211, 224; 20:34, 44, 111, 132, 204, 227
MacDonald, Marion A. 16:44, 195; 17:40, 215
Marshall, Sherry Schaller 16:229; 17:114, 115
Melnyk, Marcia 16:123; 18:123; 20:3
Merrill, Madeline Osborne 17:183
Miles, Nancy 17:189
Miller, June (Butler) 19:142
Millhouse, William T. 19:3
Morison, Samuel Eliot 16:902
Nowers, Deborah K. 20:106
Otten, Marjorie Wardwell 19:219; 20:19, 164
Pike, Allen R. 20:101
Pringle, James R. 17:904
Reilly, John C. 16:63, 133; 17:11
Ripley, Donald 18:83
Robertson, Irene P. 19:75
Roderick, Thomas H., Dr. 17:123
Sanderson, Howard Kendall 16:69
Schmid, Jean Parker 16:225
Schmid, John Carolus 16:225
Sibbalds, Mary 17:136; 20:17
Smith, Carole 20:201
Smith, Myron C. 17:131
Sparks, Caroline Massey 16:113
Stattler, Richard 19:63, 70
Stearns, Peter Pindar 16:212, 138; 17:32, 102, 161
Strople, Mary 20:17
Tagney, Ronald 17:3
Tarbox, George Edward 20:146
Taylor, Robert L. 20:144, 145
Tibbetts, Charles S. 18:71

SUBJECT INDEX

Trask, Richard B. 19:15
White, Victoria 17:9
Whittier, John Greenleaf 16:901
Wiborn, John 20:30
Wills, Arline K. 20:903
Wilson, Fred A. 18:14
Wood, Leslie A. 20:169
Wood, Robert A. 20:169
Wood, William 18:902
Worthley, Harold Field 19:902
Wyland, Florence E. Bates 19:162

EVERY NAME INDEX

ABBAGADUSSET, 17:202
ABBE
  Abigail (Goodale), 20:233
  Ebenezer, 20:233
  Elizabeth, 16:119
  Hannah (Silsbee), 18:101
  John, 20:232
  Mary, 20:230, 232
  Mary (Knowlton), 18:101; 20:232
  Samuel, 18:101; 20:232
ABBOT/ABBOTT/ABBOTTS/ ABBUTE/ ABITT, 18:132; 19:59
  ___, Capt., 19:93
  ___, Goodwife, 20:19
  Abigail, 16:218
  Abigail (Lovejoy), 20:23
  Abigail (Myrick), 20:23
  Amelia Lois, 17:58
  Ben Naomi, 20:20
  Benjamin, 16:68; 17:54; 19:94; 20:19-21
  Betsey (Brown), 16:47
  C. H., 20:168
  Charlotte, 16:231
  Charlotte H., 19:116
  Charlotte Helen, 19:21
  Daniel, 19:34; 20:216
  Dorcas, 20:216
  Dorcas (Graves), 20:21, 216
  Dorcas (Hibbard), 20:21
  Ebenezer, 17:152; 20:213
  Edward, 20:21
  Elizabeth, 19:120; 20:21, 216
  Elizabeth (___), 20:20
  Elizabeth (Ballard), 20:22, 23
  Elizabeth (Estey), 20:23
  Elizabeth (Gerry), 20:21
  Ephraim, 19:42
  George, 16:68; 17:55, 58; 19:34, 46, 94, 115, 116, 222; 20:19-23, 165, 167, 216
  Hannah, 16:220; 19:46, 95; 20:21-23, 216
  Hannah (Allen), 20:216
  Hannah (Chandler), 17:55; 19:115, 116, 219, 222; 20:19, 20, 165, 216
  Hannah (Graves), 20:21, 216
  Hannah (Gray), 20:21
  Hannah (Newell), 16:210
  Henry, 18:163; 19:94; 20:216
  Hepsebah (Fry), 18:156
  Isaac, 18:162, 163; 20:82, 216
  Jemima (___), 20:23
  John, 16:68; 18:162; 19:92; 20:19, 21-23, 165, 199
  John A., 18:156
  Jonathan, 17:54
  Joseph, 18:162; 20:19, 21, 216
  Joyce (Rice), 20:23
  Lydia, 20:22, 23
  Lydia (Farrington), 17:152
  Margaret, 18:101
  Mary, 16:101; 20:22, 23, 119, 167
  Mary (Foster), 19:95; 20:216
  Mary (Platts), 20:216
  Mehitabel, 20:23
  Nathan, 20:216
  Nathaniel, 16:68; 20:20, 21
  Nehemiah, 16:68; 19:34, 92, 221; 20:21-23
  S. L., 20:217
  Salome Jane, 19:19
  Samuel, 19:13; 20:22, 23
  Sarah, 20:21-23, 216
  Sarah (Barker), 20:21, 165
  Sarah (Cheever), 19:42
  Sarah (Farnum), 17:54; 19:46, 222; 20:21-23, 167
  Sarah (Graves), 20:213
  Susan, 17:152
  Temperance (Baker), 20:146, 147
  Thomas, 16:68; 19:88; 20:20-22
  Timothy, 16:68; 19:95; 20:19-21, 216
  William, 16:68, 210; 18:163; 20:19, 21
  Zerviah, 17:54
  Zerviah (Holt), 17:54
ABORN/ABORNE see also EBORNE, 18:132; 20:52
  Aaron, 16:94
  Abigail, 16:35; 19:137, 218; 20:33, 37
  Abigail (___), 16:34
  Abigail (Gilbert), 16:31; 17:211, 218; 20:38
  Abraham, 16:88
  Benjamin, 16:92
  Betsy (Alley), 16:94; 18:25
  Betsy/Betty, 16:93
  Catherine (Smith), 16:30
  Catherine/Katherine (Jemmeny), 16:93
  Eben, 19:137
  Ebenezer, 16:35; 20:37
  Elizabeth, 16:89; 19:137, 218
  Elizabeth (Pedrick), 16:36
  Elizabeth (Perkins), 16:36
  Elizabeth (Whittemore), 16:37
  Hannah, 16:30; 17:211
  Hannah (Dove), 16:94
  Isaac, 16:88
  James, 16:30; 17:211; 18:25
  Jane, 16:88
  Jane (Pickering), 16:88
  John, 16:35; 19:218; 20:37, 39
  Joseph, 16:35; 17:206
  Lavina (Gilbert), 16:90
  Lydia, 16:94
  Lydia (Nurse), 16:94
  Margaret, 16:93
  Margaret (Masury), 16:88
  Margaret (Moulton), 16:37
  Martha, 19:137
  Martha (Bancroft), 16:37; 19:217, 218
  Mary, 16:30; 17:211; 19:217; 20:52
  Mary (Goodale), 16:93
  Mary (Sheldon), 16:93
  Mary (Tarbox), 16:36
  Mary (Whittemore), 16:89
  Mary/Polly (Flint), 16:94
  Mehitable, 16:94
  Mehitable (___), 16:94
  Mercy, 16:88
  Moses, 16:30; 17:211; 19:137, 216, 218; 20:38
  Patty, 16:94
  Phebe, 16:94
  Phebe (Pope), 16:94
  Rebecca, 16:30; 17:211
  Rebecca (Bancroft), 16:94; 20:39
  Samuel, 16:30; 17:209, 211; 19:137, 218; 20:48, 52
  Sarah, 16:30; 17:211
  Sarah (___), 16:33
  Sarah (Bell), 16:89
  Sarah (Derby), 16:88
  Sarah (Haines), 16:31; 17:211
  Sarah (Masury), 16:88
  Sarah (Needham), 16:37
  Sarah (Silver), 16:94
  Susanna, 16:31
  Susanna (Trask), 16:31; 17:211
  Thomas, 16:30; 19:137
  Union, 16:35
  Union (Kettle), 16:37
  William, 16:33
ABRAHAM/ABRAHAMS, 17:13
  Woodward, 20:83, 221
ABSON, 20:18
ACERRA
  Elsie Rankin (Friend), 17:164
  Marino, 17:164
ACKLEY
  Ruth, 18:87
ACKROYD see also AKROYD, 16:13
ACTON
  Benjamin, 18:30
ADAM/ADAMS, see also ADDAMS, 17:140, 191; 20:153, 157
  Abbie D. (Noyes), 19:238
  Abigail (___), 18:126
  Abigail (Pierce), 19:240a
  Abraham, 19:240a
  Anna (Stevens), 17:129
  Benjamin, 18:44, 168; 19:148
  Bethiah (___), 19:148
  Catherine (Ford), 19:225-227
  Charles, 20:171
  Charles A., 17:221
  Charles Marble, 20:58
  Charlotte (Holbrook), 19:238
  Clayton, 18:134; 20:176, 177
  Clayton R., 18:136, 137; 20:115, 116
  Clayton Rand, 18:59, 137
  Elijah, 18:126
  Eliza, 17:129
  Ernest Clayton, 18:59
  Fannie B., 20:171
  Gertrude, 16:111
  Hannah (White), 19:238
  Harriet, 17:162
  Harriet (Tarr), 17:162
  Harriet Moulton (Pettingell), 18:59
  Harriet N. (Goldsmith), 20:58
  Henry, 18:126
  Isaac, 18:115
  J., 20:90
  Jacob, 20:220
  James, 19:226, 238
  James Truslow, 18:184
  Jane, 20:220
  John, 16:105; 17:100; 20:115
  John Quincy, 16:106
  Jonathan, 17:129
  Joseph, 20:58
  Josiah, 17:22
  Lemuel, 19:238
  Lucy, 18:168, 170
  Lydia, 19:226; 20:46
  Margaret, 18:19, 21
  Margaret (Watts), 18:21
  Mary, 16:172; 18:224
  Michael Trevitt, 17:100
  Nathan, 16:93
  Nathaniel, 16:93
  Nehemiah, 17:162
  Persis (Potter), 18:168; 19:148
  Rachel, 20:239
  Richard, 19:190
  Robert, 19:192
  Ruth, 17:82
  Sam, 17:7
  Samuel, 18:156, 210, 240a
  Samuel R.T., 17:100
  Sarah, 20:103

Sarah (___), 20:58
Sarah (Larrabee), 20:115
Sarah (Sabin), 18:156
Sarah Frances, 19:237
Susannah, 18:88
Susannah (Trevitt), 17:100
Thomas, 18:21; 19:148; 20:103
Virginia A. (___), 20:171
William, 18:240
William A., 19:238
ADAMSON, 17:134
   Agnes (Rae), 17:56
   Elizabeth Jane, 17:55
   John, 17:56
ADDAMS see also ADAM/ADAMS
   Aphra (___), 17:91
   John, 17:91
   Jonathan, 17:91
ADKINS see also ATKINS
   Elizabeth (___), 16:17
   Mary, 16:17
   Thomas, 16:17
ADSIT
   Abigail (Graves), 20:218
   Betsey (Alger), 20:218
   Ebenezer, 20:218
   John, 20:218
   Mary, 20:218
   Mary (___), 20:218
   Molly, 20:218
   Robert J., 20:222
   Sarah, 20:218
   Tamar (Holdridge), 20:218
AELWELL
   Thomas, 19:136
AGAR, 18:240a
AGGAWAM, 20:50, 51
AINGER
   Bethiah (Liscom), 19:80
   John, 19:80
AINSWORTH, 16:13
AKELEY
   Aline Louise (Fuller), 20:56
   Ansel Davis, 20:56
   Archibald Douglas, 20:56
   Geraldine Agnes, 20:56
   Lydia Violet (___), 20:56
AKER
   Annie, 20:127, 128
   Mary (___), 20:127
   William, 20:127, 128
AKROYD see also ACKROYD, 16:4
ALBEE
   Eleazer, 20:40, 41
   Hepsibah (Bancroft), 20:40, 41
   Julia, 20:41
ALBREE
   Elizabeth, 18:59
   Elizabeth (Green), 18:59
   John, 18:59
ALCOCK
   George, 17:75
   Robert, 16:84
   Ruth (Blaney), 16:84
ALCOTT
   Jane, 16:148
ALDEN
   Anna, 17:148
   Anna (Brame), 16:95
ALDERMAN
   Alice (Williams), 16:118
   Elizabeth, 16:118
   John, 16:118

ALDON
   Anna, 18:50
ALDRICH
   David, 19:150
   Hannah, 18:93
   Hannah (___), 18:31, 95
   Lydia, 18:31
   Miriam, 19:150
   Moses, 18:31
ALEE/ALLEE/ALLY see also
   ALEY/ALLEY, 18:17
ALEIN
   Samuel, 20:197
   William, 20:197
ALEXANDER
   James, 19:55
   John, 17:79; 20:26
   Margaret, 19:55, 59
   Molly (Winn), 20:26
   Randall, 19:55
   Winthrop, 16:29
ALEXANDRA
   Czarina, 17:125
ALEY see also ALEE
   Solomon, 18:54
ALFORD
   Benjamin, 16:90
   Margaret, 17:139
ALFRIDGE
   Edward, 20:198
ALGER
   Betsey, 20:218
   James, 18:96
   Vienna (Estes), 18:96
ALICE
   Lawrence, 16:240
   Mary, 16:240
ALLAN see also ALLEN
   Morton, 17:74
ALLARD
   Andrew, 17:23
   Zurviah/Zeruiah (Haven), 17:23
ALLEN see also ALLAN, ALLIN, 19:55;
   20:18, 80
   ___, Capt., 17:12
   ___, Mrs., 16:68
   "Child", 17:13
   Abigail, 16:27; 18:31; 20:238
   Abigail (Snelling), 16:236
   Abraham, 16:221; 18:31, 52, 117; 20:208, 210
   Ada, 19:119
   Andrew, 19:34, 45, 115, 116, 220, 223; 20:214, 215
   Be Sargent, 17:191
   Benjamin, 16:44; 20:48
   Bethia, 16:40
   C. E., 17:27
   David, 18:39
   Delphina M. (Ward), 20:57
   Dorothy, 16:21
   Eileen, 17:180
   Elizabeth, 20:105
   Elizabeth (Osborn), 17:200
   Elizabeth (Richardson), 19:45, 223
   Eunice, 19:173
   Ezekiel, 20:25
   Faith (Ingalls), 19:45, 115, 116, 220, 223
   Fanny, 19:42
   Florence, 17:180
   Florence C., 16:53
   Francis, 17:200
   Frank, 16:119

   George H., 20:57
   Hannah, 18:38; 19:45, 223; 20:216, 220
   Harry, 16:119
   Hope, 17:89
   J. K., 19:215; 20:34, 40
   Jacob, 17:173
   John, 16:18; 17:120;18:31, 235; 19:45, 115, 116, 220, 223
   John Kermott, 16:37; 18:41; 19:136, 211
   Joseph, 16:132; 17:240; 18:31; 19:42; 20:200
   Katheryn, 18:81
   Kathleen, 17:180
   Kay, 20:77
   Lydia (Aldrich), 18:31
   Mabel Josephine (Pease), 20:57
   Mark, 19:119
   Martha, 19:45, 115, 220, 221, 223
   Martha (Merchant), 19:119
   Mary, 16:59; 18:39, 218; 19:45, 115, 116, 220, 221, 223; 20:166, 233, 234
   Mary (Cheever), 19:42
   Mary (Dane), 19:45
   Mary (Needham), 20:25
   Mary Ann, 17:201
   May (___), 17:120
   Mercy (Peters), 19:115, 116, 220, 223
   Meriam/Miriam, 16:119
   Moses Hooper, 16:236
   Myron O., 20:141
   Nancy, 17:120
   Nancy Edmands, 17:25
   Nathaniel, 17:11
   Onesiphorus, 20:197
   Rachel, 17:236
   Rachel (___), 17:89
   Rebecca (Thompson), 18:39
   Richardson B., 18:133, 135
   Robert, 16:119; 19:202
   Ruth, 18:31, 92; 19:41; 20:171
   Ruth (Bassett), 18:31, 52
   Ruth (Cheever), 19:42
   Samuel, 19:202; 20:171
   Sarah, 16:85; 17:179; 18:19; 19:42, 45, 220, 223; 20:13, 210, 211
   Sarah (___), 16:119
   Susan (Cann), 20:171
   Tabitha, 19:108; 20:213
   Thomas, 19:220
   William, 16:64; 19:124, 201, 202; 20:57
ALLERTON
   Isaac, 19:132; 20:14, 15
   Remember, 20:14
ALLEY see also ALEE, 18:117
   "Daughter", 18:22
   "Son", 18:22
   Abigail, 18:27
   Abigail (___), 18:25
   Abigail (Bassett), 18:21, 26, 32, 52, 53; 19:107
   Abigail (Hood), 18:27, 32, 54
   Abigail (Killam), 18:17
   Abigail (Witt), 16:46; 18:24, 173
   Abner, 16:45; 18:23-27
   Abraham, 18:117
   Adam, 18:17
   Alice, 18:27
   Alice (Phillips), 16:224
   Amos, 18:27
   Ann, 18:16
   Anna, 18:21-23
   Ann/Anna (Legaree/Legery), 18:21, 22, 113
   Anna (Johnson), 18:53

Anna (Tarbox), 20:143
Anna/Ann, 16:45
Anne/Anna (Phillips), 16:224
Benjamin, 16:16; 18:20-25, 37, 47, 53;
    19:107; 20:100
Benjamin B., 18:16
Bethia (Howard), 16:46
Bethiah (Hayward/Howard), 18:24
Bethiah (Ramsdell), 18:25, 26
Betsy, 16:94; 18:25
Betsy (Witt), 18:24
Content, 18:22, 25
Daniel B., 18:25
Deborah (Breed), 18:27, 32
Easter/Esther, 17:49; 20:206
Edward Stoddard, 18:17
Eleazer, 16:45; 18:21, 23-25, 53; 19:107
Elizabeth, 16:96; 18:17, 23-26
Elizabeth (___), 16:45; 18:25
Elizabeth (Lewis), 18:22
Elizabeth (Newhall), 16:46; 18:21, 23, 47,
    53; 19:107; 20:100
Enos, 18:27
Ephraim, 18:22, 23
Esther (Bradley), 18:25
Hannah, 16:45; 18:19-25, 53; 19:107
Hannah (Batcheller), 18:22
Hannah (Hanson), 18:26
Hannah (Hart), 18:21, 23, 47, 53
Hannah (Stacey), 18:25
Hannah Sketh, 18:25
Hepzibah, 18:22; 20:171
Hepzibah (___), 16:45
Hepzibah (Lewis), 18:22
Hepzibah (Newhall), 18:21, 22, 53; 20:100
Hugh, 17:216; 18:14-21, 23, 26, 27, 29, 32,
    53, 54, 72, 92, 132; 20:133, 196
Huldah (___), 18:22
Huldah (Newhall), 16:46; 18:24, 173
Huldah (Purinton), 18:25
Jacob, 16:45; 18:19, 21-24, 53, 173
Jacob/Faroh, 18:21
James, 16:16; 18:24, 93
Jedediah, 18:24
Jerusha, 16:46; 18:24
Joanna, 18:19; 19:155
Joanna (Furnall/Furnald/Furnill), 18:14, 15,
    17-19; 19:155
Joanna (Proctor), 18:25
John, 16:45; 18:17-19, 21-25, 35, 36, 55;
    19:155; 20:197
Joseph, 16:45; 18:20-23, 25, 53, 113;
    20:100, 143
Lois, 18:27
Lois (___), 16:224
Lois (Breed), 18:25, 93
Lydia, 18:22, 25
Marcy/Mercy (Buffum), 18:22
Margaret (Adams), 18:19, 21
Martha, 18:15, 18; 20:44
Mary, 16:45; 18:15, 18, 19, 22, 23; 10:163;
    20:171, 205
Mary (Alley), 18:22
Mary (Fullerton), 18:24
Mary (Graves), 18:14, 15, 17, 18, 53
Mary (Provender), 18:24
Mehitable (Hallowell), 18:22, 23
Mercy/Marcy (Buffum), 18:25
Micajah, 16:16; 18:25
Moses Breed, 16:224
Nancy (Watts), 18:26
Nathan, 18:22
Patience, 18:25; 20:26
Patty (Newhall), 18:24
Peter, 18:22
Polly, 18:26
Rachel (Berry), 16:46; 18:24; 20:43
Rebecca, 18:19, 22, 26, 27, 32; 20:44,
    208-210
Rebecca (Hall), 18:22
Rebecca (Hood), 17:216; 18:15, 16, 19, 20,
    24, 32, 53, 54
Richard, 18:20, 21, 25, 27, 53
Rufus, 18:26
Ruth (Bassett), 18:117
Ruth (Breed), 18:25
Samuel, 16:97; 17:173; 18:17, 20-22, 26,
    27, 32, 52-54; 19:107
Sarah, 16:45; 18:17-22, 25-27, 32, 36, 117;
    19:107, 144; 20:100
Sarah (___), 18:22
Sarah (Bassett), 18:25, 36, 55
Sarah (Graves), 16:46; 18:24
Sarah (Hood), 18:25, 35, 55
Sarah (Silver), 18:17
Sarah (Stebbins), 18:21
Sarah (Webber), 18:25
Seth, 18:27
Shadrach, 18:22
Solomon, 16:45; 18:19, 20, 23-25, 53;
    20:43
Stephen, 18:27
Susanna (Brown), 18:27
Tabitha (Ingalls), 18:25; 19:107
Theodate, 18:25, 27
Thomas, 18:17
Timothy, 16:46; 18:24, 173
William, 16:45; 18:19, 21, 22, 24-26
Zacheus, 18:27
ALLIN/ALLINE/ALLYN see also ALLEN
Edward, 17:229
Henry, 20:79
Hope, 16:164
John, 20:199
Mary, 20:94
Robert, 16:116
Sarah, 16:116
Sarah (___), 16:116
ALTMAN
Carol Tapley (Wiswall), 17:174
Roger William, 17:174
Tara Bea, 17:174
ALVORD
Ebenezer, 18:148
Ruth (Baker), 18:148
AMBROSE
Dorothy, 17:52; 20:178
Henry, 17:53
Susanna (___), 17:53
AMERIGE
Mary, 19:177
Morris, 19:177
Sally (Brown), 19:177
AMES, 18:63
Aaron, 19:111
Almira, 19:21-24
Annis G., 19:111
Charlton, 19:21
Daniel, 19:111
Diademia, 19:111
Ebenezer, 19:111
Elizabeth, 19:111
Elizabeth (Hall), 19:111, 113
Ezra, 19:111
Hannah, 19:111, 113, 114
Isaac, 19:111
James, 19:111, 113
James G., 19:111
John, 17:86; 18:155
Lucy (Garcelon), 19:111
Nathan, 19:87
Ruth, 19:38
Ruth (Estes), 18:94
William, 19:38
AMILS
Anna, 17:31
AMORY
Thomas C., 17:132
AMSBURY
Doris M., 17:18; 18:132, 136
AMY
Ella, 18:239
ANCHISES, 18:240a
ANDERSON
Arzbell, 18:114
Bob, 17:50
Clara P., 17:164
Clara P. (Saville), 17:164
Hannah (Bessom), 19:230
John, 19:132
John N., 17:164
Judy, 20:16
Marion, 18:133
Robert, 19:210
Robert Charles, 16:228; 17:177; 18:67,
    190; 19:176, 211
Thomas, 19:230
Virginia DeJohn, 16:225
ANDREW/ANDREWS/ANDRES, 16:13;
17:139; 20:18
___, Miss, 20:132, 133, 146
___, Mr., 19:160; 20:223
___, Mrs., 17:13; 20:148
Abigail, 16:25; 18:33; 20:94
Abigail (Bassett), 18:32, 33
Abigail (Very), 16:180
Ann (Cross), 18:33
Anna, 18:205
Anna (___), 18:205
Betsey Bardley, 20:239
Deborah (Bassett), 18:32, 33
Deborah (Frye), 16:120
Deborah (Sargent), 17:179
Dorcas, 17:179
Dorcas (Daniels), 20:239
Edward Deming, 16:189
Elizabeth, 17:179; 18:200, 201, 205;
    19:144
Elizabeth (___), 16:120; 17:179
Elizabeth (Hill), 20:221
Elizabeth (Storey), 19:179
Francis, 18:33
George, 18:33
Hannah, 20:135, 141
Hepzibah, 16:176
Huldah, 17:179
Jacob, 18:39
James, 16:120; 18:238
James H., 16:239
Jane (___), 17:229
Jerusha, 17:179
John, 16:40, 164; 17:76; 18:55; 17:76, 179;
    19:151, 179
Jonathan, 18:205; 20:239
Joseph, 16:27, 68; 17:76; 18:39
Katherine, 16:81
Latty, 19:57
Lois (Nicholson), 19:151
Margaret (Woodward), 18:201

Mary (Burnham), 20:239
Mary (Clark), 18:116
Mary (Coates), 19:160
Michael, 18:33; 20:239
Nathaniel, 18:101
Nicholas, 18:33
Peggy/Margaret (Parker), 16:40
Phebe (Copperwaite), 18:39
Phillippe, 16:26
Rachel, 19:179
Ralph, 16:180; 20:200
Robert, 16:120
Ruth, 18:204
Ruth (___), 16:27
Ruth (Riggs), 18:204, 205
Samuel, 17:229
Sarah, 18:33, 81; 20:36
Sarah (Hood), 18:55
Stephen, 17:179
Thomas, 16:27; 17:76; 18:33, 158
William, 16:63; 17:76; 18:33, 201, 204, 205; 20:221

ANDROS, 18:240a
___, Gov., 18:14
Edmond/Edmund, 16:229; 17:155; 20:22, 205

ANGELL
Perce, 20:199
Phillip, 20:199

ANGIER, 18:132
Dorothy (___), 16:104
Edmund, 16:34; 19:38
Mary, 20:233
Ruth, 19:37, 38
Ruth (Ames), 19:38
Samuel, 16:104
Sibyl, 16:104; 18:134

ANNABLE
Sarah, 19:82

ANNIS
Deliverance, 19:110, 111
Experience (Harraden), 18:200; 19:110
Isaac, 18:200; 19:100
Jacob, 16:132
Rachel, 17:219

ANTHONY
Elizabeth (Rowe), 19:226
Margaret, 19:171

ANTOINETTE
Marie, 18:189

ANTROBUS
Joan, 16:174

APITZ
Albert Frederick, 19:20
Joe, 19:17, 198
Joe M., 18:35
Joseph, 19:81, 169
Sarah Dorothy (Marland), 19:20

APPLEBY
Anna, 19:150

APPLETON
Hannah (Gott), 18:205
John, 17:214; 20:225
Martha Ellen, 16:102
Nathan, 19:14
Samuel, 16:206
William, 18:205
William S., 19:134

APPLIN
Hannah, 19:29

ARBEITER
Nancy, 17:63

ARCHAMBAULT
Harry D., Mrs., 16:41

ARCHARD
Samuel, 19:196, 197

ARCHBEL, 18:132
John, 16:111

ARCHER
Jonathan, 17:231
Samuel, 19:201, 202

ARDIOLI
A. (___), 16:124

ARMITAGE
Abigail, 18:116
Bishop, 16:108
Charlotte (Lombard), 16:108
Eleazer, 18:115, 232, 233
Elizabeth, 18:232, 233
Elizabeth (___), 18:232, 233
Esther, 18:232
Godfrey, 18:229, 230, 233, 234; 19:44, 138; 20:134, 184, 194
Hannah, 18:115, 232, 233
Hannah (Foy), 18:233
Hannah (Needham), 18:115, 116, 232, 233
Isabella, 18:232
Isabella (Tilly), 18:232
Jane, 18:232
Jane (___), 16:162; 18:109, 147, 229, 232, 234; 19:197
Joanna (Richardson), 18:232
John, 18:234
Jonathan, 18:232, 233
Joseph, 16:72; 17:88; 18:14, 71, 72, 79, 114, 115, 147, 229-234; 19:44, 45, 75, 132, 138, 142, 162, 188, 190, 193, 194, 197; 20:184, 194, 214, 215
Mary (Cogswell), 18:233, 234
Rebecca, 18:232-234; 20:133-135, 146
Rebecca (Webb), 18:234
Samuel, 18:233, 234; 20:134
Sarah (Webb), 18:233, 234; 20:134
Thomas, 18:233
Timothy, 18:232

ARMSTRONG
Agnes (___), 17:103
Eleanor, 19:239
Frances Augusta (Goodridge), 17:103
James, 17:103
Margaret, 18:138
William, 17:103

ARNOLD
Abigail, 16:237
Benedict, 19:64; 20:31
George, 18:95
Jacob, 18:95
Mary, 17:179
Sarah, 20:56

ARONDALE, 16:13

ARRINGTON
Benjamin, 16:101
Deborah (Richards), 16:101
Elizabeth R., 16:102
George S., 16:101
James, 16:101
Jane M. (Harris), 16:101
Joseph, 16:102
Katherine (Richards), 16:102
Lydia, 16:101
Mary (Abbott), 16:101
Mary (Pickering), 16:101
Mercy/Elizabeth, 16:101
Mercy/Elizabeth (Arrington), 16:101
Polly, 16:101

ARROGINA
Alice, 16:50

ARTHAUD
John, 16:177
John Bradley, 17:233; 18:132, 137-139; 19:204

ARTIOLI
Augusto, 20:5

ARTRIDGE
George, 17:81
Lydia (Parker), 17:81

ARVEN
Abiel, 20:49

ASH
Judith, 18:219

ASHBEE/ASHBY
Edmund, 20:224
Elizabeth, 19:153
Fanna, 16:100
Mary, 16:177

ASHFIELD
Hannah, 19:224, 226
Jane/Jean (Larrabee), 19:224-226
William, 19:226

ASHMONT
Ruth, 17:110

ASHTON, 16:4
Elizabeth, 19:53
Jacob, 16:81

ASHWORTH, 16:13

ASKLING
Helen, 20:148

ASLEBE/ASLEBEE/ASLEBY/ASSALBEE
J., 18:155
John, 16:68; 18:158, 160; 19:30, 32

ASLET/ASLETT
Rebecca, 19:175, 221
Rebecca (Ayer), 19:175
Sarah, 19:175, 221

ASPINALL/ASPINWALL, 16:13
Mary, 18:149
Peter, 18:149

ASSALBEE see ASLEBEE

ASTEN, 18:163
Thomas, 16:68

ATCHINSON
Bazaliel, 17:152
Elenor (Farrington), 17:152

ATHERTON
Hope, 18:149
Sarah (Hollister), 18:149

ATKINS see also ADKINS
Eunice, 20:56
Mary, 16:18; 19:177
Rachel, 16:18
Thomas, 16:18

ATKINSON
Hannah, 16:233
Mary, 17:185

ATTO
Alice, 16:48

ATWATER
Rachel, 18:25

ATWELL/ATWILL
Benjamin, 18:227
Hannah (Browne), 18:226, 227
Joanna, 18:212
Joanna (Mansfield), 18:212
Joseph, 18:227
Louis H., Mrs., 16:111
Lydia, 20:143
Nathan, 16:70
Pan (___), 18:227

Sarah (Rhodes), 18:227
Thomas Hicks, 18:212
William, 18:212
ATWOOD, 18:157
Abigail, 18:160
Experience, 18:178
H. Marion (Sargent), 17:170
John, 19:101
Joseph, 16:146
Margaret, 16:76
Martha (Cheever), 19:101
Martha (Pike), 20:56
Sarah, 20:55
Sarah (Collins), 20:55
Stephen, 20:55, 56
Thomas, 16:159
AUBE
Andre, 20:13
AUCHMATZ/AUCHMUTY
Robert, 18:209, 240a
AUDLEY
Edmond, 18:230
AUSTIN
Abiel, 17:117
John, 17:116; 18:162
John D., 19:176
Leonard, 20:198
Mary, 17:117
Nellie R., 17:165
Patience (Stevens), 17:116
Rachel, 17:116
Samuel, 16:68; 18:160
Sarah (Moulton), 17:117
Sarah A. (Mead), 17:165
Thomas, 20:130
William, 16:63; 17:134
William R., 17:165
AVERILL
Daniel, 18:56
Dorothy, 20:236
Joanna (Hood), 18:56
Samuel, 16:133
AVERY, 16:111
___, Mr., 17:13
Alden, 17:28
Betsy, 17:221
Elisha, 17:26
Elizabeth, 18:89
Elizabeth/Eliza (Edmands), 17:26
Ephraim, 17:26
Harriet (___), 17:28
Harriet (Upham), 17:28
Idella, 17:28
James, 17:28
John Quincy Adams, 17:28
Kittridge, 17:27
Leander, 17:28
Lydia, 18:96
Maria (___), 17:28
Martha (___), 17:28
Mary, 20:179
Mary (Lane), 20:179
Melzar, 17:28
Sally/Sarah, 16:118; 18:178
William, 20:179
AVIS
Samuel, 18:203
Sarah (Goodwin), 18:203
AWTY
Brian, 20:69, 71
Brian G., 20:67
AXEY
Francis, 20:134

James, 16:164; 18:17, 72, 230; 19:138; 20:134, 195
AYER/AYERS/AYRES/HEIRS/EAYRE/ EAIERS/EIRE/EYRE, 19:31
Abigail Greenleaf (Gott), 16:118
Betsey, 18:180
Gardner, 18:180
Gilbert, 16:133
Hannah (___), 19:175
Jabez, 18:168
James, 16:146
John, 16:118; 19:30, 174, 175
Lewis T., 18:180
Louisa, 18:180
Mae C. (Williams), 18:180
Mary, 19:30, 31, 174, 175, 221; 20:166, 168
Mary (Murray), 18:180
Mary (Wells), 18:180
Mary Ann (Hovey), 18:180
Mary Hale (Carlton), 18:180
Matilda (Lanphire), 18:180
Mehitable (Graves), 20:219
Nathaniel, 19:30, 175
Nora E. (Wallace), 18:180
Osgood, 18:180
Persis (Stewart), 18:168
Peter, 19:30, 175
Rebecca, 19:175
Rebecca (___), 19:30
Richard, 20:219
Robert, 19:30, 175
Rosina (Davis), 18:180
Roxana, 18:180
Samuel, 18:180
Sarah, 18:49; 19:149
Sylvia (Wright), 18:180
Thomas, 17:12; 18:180; 19:30, 175
Wilder, 18:180
Willard, 18:180
Winfield Scott, 18:180

BABB
Alexander, 16:240
Elizabeth (___), 16:240
Esther (Wescott), 16:240
Hannah (___), 18:76, 77
James, 18:76, 77
William, 16:240
BABBIDGE
Abigail, 18:221
BABBIGS
Francis, 20:160
BABCOCK
Abigail, 19:164
Dorothy, 19:164
Elizabeth (___), 19:164
Hannah (Coates), 19:164
James, 19:164
John, 19:164
Joseph, 19:164
Molle, 18:77
BABSON, 19:41, 118
___, Capt., 17:12
___, Mrs., 17:11
Amanda (Stanwood), 17:108
Edward, 17:108
Elinor (Hill), 17:236
Emeline (Rogers), 17:163
Emeline Rogers, 17:163
Fanny Gilman, 17:108
Fitz James, 17:167
George Friend, 17:108

Gorham, 18:145, 146
Grace Gordon, 17:167
Hannah, 17:236
James, 17:236
Jho., 17:11
John J., 16:216, 17:11; 20:17
Julia (Friend), 17:108
Martha, 17:135
Mary, 17:167; 20:240
Mary (___), 17:12
Mary (Butman), 19:119
Mary (Dolliver), 17:236
Mary (Haradan), 18:145, 146
Mary/Polly (Griffin), 17:108
Nathaniel, 17:163
Nathaniel Haradan, 18:145
Philip, 17:12
Richard, 17:236
Sarah Elizabeth (Proctor), 17:167
Solomon, 16:133
Thomas, 20:200
William, 16:133; 17:108
BACHELDER/BACHELLER/ BACHELLOR/BACHILLOR see also BATCHELDER
Abigail, 18:76
Edith (Brown), 17:240
Hepsibah, 17:240
John, 16:163; 19:214, 216; 20:190
Joseph, 17:240; 20:83
Phebe, 17:240
Rebecca, 16:82
Sarah, 17:152
Theophilus, 16:70
William, 17:240
BACKUS
Dana Convers, 16:158; 20:91
Mary, 20:91
Mary E. N., 16:158
BACON/BEACON
Alice, 19:211, 214; 20:33
Benjamin, 17:134
Daniel, 16:116; 18:169
Dorothy, 16:115
Dorothy (Bradhurst), 16:116
Elizabeth, 16:25
Elizabeth (Griggs), 16:206, 209
Elizabeth (Knight), 16:116
Ephraim, 16:209
Freeman, 19:177
George Allen, 19:177
Hannah (Higgins), 19:177
Hulda (Holbrook), 19:177
Isabella, 19:177
Jacob, 16:116
Joanna (Lanman), 19:177
John, 18:50; 19:177
Louisa Jane (Lynde), 19:177
Mary (Read), 16:116
Mary (Taylor), 16:26
Michael, 19:211
Mihil, 16:26
Nancy Ann (Hart), 18:50
Oliver, 18:126
Olivia (Campbell), 18:169
Rebecca, 20:94
Rebecca (___), 18:126
Sarah, 17:204
Susannah, 20:94
BADCOCK
Mary (Cheever), 19:42
Thomas, 19:42

BADGER
Judith, 19:17
BAGLEY
Eliza (Bickford), 16:239
John, 16:239
BAGNALL, 16:13
BAILEY/BAILY/BAYLEY/BALEY
Abiah (Haseltine), 17:116
Alonza F., 17:207
Anna, 18:171
Anne (Memoy), 17:239
Asa, 16:131
Benjamin, 17:116
Benoni, 18:171
Bertha S., 17:207
Caleb, 18:81
Caroline B. (Smith), 17:207
Cora (Wood), 20:171
David, 17:116; 19:178
Elizabeth, 17:239; 19:178
Experience (Putnam), 19:178
Frederick W., 17:175
George, 17:239; 20:171
Hannah M. (Cluff/Clough), 17:116
Hannah/Joannah, 19:93
Isaac, 19:178
Jeremiah, 17:116
Jesse, 17:239
John, 17:239; 18:11; 19:52; 20:130, 221
Jonathan Parker, 16:180
Joseph, 19:22
Lydia, 20:50
Marguerite, 17:31
Mary, 17:239
Mary (Clark), 16:180
Mary (Godfrey), 18:81
Medora E., 17:116
Mehitable (Johnson), 17:116
Mercy (Burbank), 17:116
Nancy, 16:239
Nathaniel, 16:180
Rosalie Fellows, 19:174
Sarah, 19:120; 20:180, 218, 221
Sarah (Clark), 16:180
Sarah (Emery), 19:178
Sarah (Ingalls), 19:52; 20:221
Sarah Loring, 16:67; 19:35, 20:19, 167, 168, 217
Stephen, 17:116
Theophilus, 17:147
BAKCG
Mary (Conant), 16:60a
BAKE see also BALKE
Hannah (Jenkins), 17:78
BAKER, 16:13; 20:153, 157
___, Cpl., 18:147
___, Mrs., 19:42
Abigail, 16:39; 18:149-151, 153
Abigail (Fisher), 18:149
Abraham, 20:26, 28, 96
Alexander, 20:141
Alice (___), 20:95
Anna, 16:176; 17:236; 18:153
Anne (___), 18:153
Anne (Perkins), 18:153
Barbara, 19:164
Benjamin, 16:40
Christine (Otis), 18:149
Clotilda (Daniels), 19:174
Cornelius, 17:236
Daniel, 18:149, 153; 20:28, 95
Daniel C., 18:12
Deliverance, 18:149
Dinah, 20:25-28
Ebenezer, 18:21, 152, 153
Edmand, 16:207
Edmonds, 16:206
Edward, 16:164; 17:90; 18:114, 115, 132, 147-149, 151-153, 167, 180a, 199, 230; 19:138, 149, 174, 213; 20:195, 197
Eleanor Johnson, 18:156
Elijah, 16:217; 20:179
Elisha, 20:95
Elizabeth, 16:167;17:118; 18:25, 30, 115, 116, 149, 152, 166; 20:96
Elizabeth (Baker), 20:96
Elizabeth (Chase), 20:28, 95
Ellen Frye, 19:33
Eunice, 17:163
Francis, 20:95
Grace, 18:149
Grace (Marsh), 18:149
Hannah, 16:137; 17:150; 18:48, 150; 20:28, 96, 179
Hannah (Jones), 16:172; 18:149
Hannah (Munn), 18:149
Hannah (Poland), 16:141
Hannah (Puffer), 20:179
Hannah (Winn), 20:97
Hannah (Withington), 20:179
Hannah (Woodbury), 17:236
Hannah/Hana, 18:148
Isabel (Sherman), 20:95
Isabel (Twining), 20:95
Isacher, 16:240
Jabez, 17:236; 18:204
James, 18:153
Joan/Jane (___), 18:115, 147, 167
John, 16:33; 18:147, 149, 151, 153, 217, 240; 19:42; 20:179
John Kelsey, 18:153
Joseph, 16:167; 18:147-149, 152, 204; 20:95, 96
Juliette (Friend), 16:217
June (Longfellow), 16:53
Marshall, 16:167; 18:152; 19:174
Martha, 20:95
Martha (Baker), 20:95
Martha (Sherman), 20:96
Mary, 16:167; 18:147-153; 19:40, 99, 101; 20:45, 138, 142
Mary (___), 18:204
Mary (Alice), 16:240
Mary (Aspinwall), 18:149
Mary (Earle), 20:95
Mary (Hathaway), 20:28
Mary (Hayward), 19:174
Mary (Lewis), 16:166; 17:150; 18:149, 150
Mary (Marshall), 16:167; 18:149, 151, 152, 199, 204; 19:149
Mary (Norwood), 18:204
Mary (Quincy), 18:149
Mary (Tarbox), 20:141
Mehitable (Sherman), 20:26, 28, 96
Moses, 19:174
Nathaniel, 20:96
Nelson, 18:147; 19:102
Nelson M., 16:167;18:115, 167, 180a
Patience (Ryder), 20:95
Polly (Hopkins), 20:95
Preserved (Trott), 20:179
Prudence, 18:149
Rachel (Allen), 17:236
Rebecca, 16:167; 18:152, 153, 199; 19:149; 20:27, 28
Rebecca (___), 18:149
Rebecca (Clark), 18:149
Rebecca (Kelsey/Kellse), 18:151, 153
Richard, 16:162
Robert, 19:216
Ruth, 16:167; 18:148, 151, 152
Ruth (Holton), 18:148
Samuel, 18:148, 149; 20:95, 97
Sarah, 16:167; 18:21, 149, 152
Sarah (Baker), 18:152
Sarah (Chase), 20:95
Sarah (Hollister), 18:149
Sarah (Whiting), 18:149
Sherebiah, 19:174
Stephen, 18:132; 20:28
Susanna, 20:28
Susanna (Mitchell), 20:45
Susannah (Aborn), 16:33
Susannah (Whipple), 19:174
Tabitha, 20:96
Temperance, 20:146, 147
Thankful, 20:28, 96
Thankful (Ward), 19:174
Theodore Michael, 16:53
Thomas, 16:141;17:150;18:56, 147-153, 240; 19:159, 164; 20:197, 198
Thomas Marshall, 19:174
Timothy, 18:147, 149
William, 18:153
BALBONI
Angelina, 20:4
Charles, 20:4
Luigi, 20:4
BALCH/BOLCH, 19:126, 205
Eunice (Kimball), 20:136
Freeborn, 19:128
John, 16:136; 19:123, 124, 127, 128; 20:136, 198
Margaret (___), 19:127, 128
Mary (Conant), 16:136
Samuel, 16:89; 20:198
William, 18:9
BALCOMB
Frank W., 16:102;18:149, 164
BALDRIDGE
Mary, 20:176
BALDWIN
Caroline, 16:238
Clarissa B. (Parker), 19:97
Effie, 20:9
Elaine, 20:148
Hannah, 19:203
Hannah (Norman), 19:203
Henry P., 16:108
John, 19:97, 203
Joseph, 18:152
Mary (Potter), 18:152
Sibyl (Lombard), 16:108
Stewart, 19:176
Susanna (Wilson), 16:82
William, 16:82
BALE
H. G., 17:164
BALEY see BAILEY
BALKE/BAKE/BARKE/BULKE
John, 17:78
BALL
Eleazer, 16:209
Sarah, 20:174
BALLANTINE
John, 20:79
BALLARD/BALLORD see also BULLARD, 16:231; 18:137, 209
Abigail, 16:67

Abigail (___), 16:76
Abigail (Worden), 16:77
Abigail/Jemima, 16:74
Alice, 16:77
Amy Cutler (Green), 16:77
Ann/Anne, 16:67
Anna (Raymond), 16:76
Ann/Anna (Sprague), 16:75; 20:43
Annie (Marshall), 16:76
Benjamin, 16:77
Betsey (Valentine), 16:77
Beulah, 16:76
Beulah (Ballard), 16:76
Deborah (Ivory), 16:74
Deborah (Tobey), 16:75
Dorcas (Cressey), 16:77
Dorothy, 16:73
Ebenezer, 16:75; 18:215
Elizabeth, 16:67; 17:54; 18:170, 171; 20:22, 23, 135
Elizabeth (___), 16:66;18:71
Elizabeth (Phelps), 16:67; 20:22, 23
Elizabeth (Pickering), 16:76
Elizabeth (Potter), 17:146
Elizabeth (Stoneman), 16:75
Elizabeth (Valentine), 16:77
Elizabeth Gooch, 16:77
Ella Mortimer, 19:139
Ephraim, 16:65
Ester/Hester, 16:71
Fear (Freeman), 16:76
Grace (Berwick), 16:67; 17:54
Hannah, 16:67
Hannah (___), 16:66
Hannah (Hooper), 16:67
Hannah (Kidder), 16:67
Hannah (Pierce), 16:76
Henry Clay, 19:139
Hephzibah (Hemenway), 16:76
Jane, 16:73;18:208
John, 16:66, 167; 17:134; 18:30, 71, 72, 231; 19:158, 159; 20:196, 217
John Lynde, 16:77
Jonathan, 16:66
Joseph, 16:66; 18:215; 20:22, 23
Joshua, 16:76
Judith, 16:77
Judith (Boyden), 16:77
Keziah, 16:77
Keziah (Ballard), 16:77
Lucy, 16:67
Lydia, 16:67
Margaret (Atwood), 16:76
Martha, 16:75
Martha (Moore), 16:65
Mary, 16:74
Mary (___), 16:71
Mary (Hunting), 16:75
Mary (Newhall), 16:75; 19:159
Mary (Norwood), 18:215
Mehitable, 16:77
Molly, 16:76
Molly (Bates), 16:77
Nancy/Anna, 16:77
Nathaniel, 16:71; 17:157; 18:71, 72; 20:135, 196
Priscilla, 16:73
Rebecca, 16:72; 18:116, 208
Rebecca (___), 16:66
Rebecca (Horn), 16:67
Rebecca (Hudson), 16:72; 17:157
Rebecca (Minzies), 16:76
Rebekah (Hooper), 16:67

Robert, 17:89
Samuel, 16:75
Sarah, 16:67; 17:54; 18:73; 20:43
Sarah (Burrill), 16:74
Sarah (Cressey), 16:77
Sarah (Fear/Sears), 16:76
Sarah (Stocker), 16:73, 167
Sarah Pleasant (Pollard), 19:139
Stephen, 16:76
Susan (Haven), 16:77
Susanna (Story), 16:72
Susannah, 16:74; 17:144
Sylvanus, 16:77
Timothy, 16:76
William, 16:65; 17:46; 18:71, 132, 213; 19:138; 20:43, 194
Zaccheus, 16:77
BALUGANI
Generosa, 19:178
BAMFIELD
___, Mrs., 19:143
BAMFORD
James, 18:132
Robert E., 18:132
BAMMAN
Gale Williams, 18:68
BANCROFT/BARCROFT, 16:4; 18:104; 19:105; 20:48
___, Capt., 18:44, 217, 218; 19:120a
___, Ens., 20:189, 193
___, Mrs., 19:138; 20:184, 188, 194
"Daughter", 20:38
Abigail, 20:34, 35, 40, 41
Abigail (Aborn/Aborne), 16:35; 19:218; 20:33, 37
Abigail (Eaton), 19:214, 215; 20:33, 34, 37, 38
Abigail (Taylor), 20:33, 41
Alice (Bacon), 19:211, 214; 20:33
Angeline (Matthews), 20:38
Anna (Lawrence), 20:33
Anne, 19:211
Asenath (___), 20:38
Benjamin, 16:40; 20:33, 41
Betsy, 20:43
Bridgett, 20:43
Caleb, 20:33
Charles, 20:40, 171
Charles N., 20:38
Chloe, 20:40
Cora (Wood), 20:171
David, 20:33, 37
Ebenezer, 16:36; 19:137, 213-217; 20:33-40, 42, 43, 48
Elijah Newhall, 20:38
Elisabeth (Nichols), 20:33
Elizabeth, 17:172; 19:137, 213-215, 217, 218; 20:36-38, 40, 41, 48
Elizabeth (Coburn), 20:38
Elizabeth (Damon), 20:33
Elizabeth (Eaton), 16:37; 19:215, 216, 218; 20:33
Elizabeth (Farwell), 20:33, 35, 39, 40
Elizabeth (Gerry), 19:218; 20:33, 38
Elizabeth (Ives), 20:43
Elizabeth (Metcalf), 19:211, 214, 215, 217; 20:33
Esther, 20:42
Esther (Smith), 20:42
Eunice, 20:33, 37, 43
Eunice (Bancroft), 20:33, 37
Eunice (Doolittle), 20:41
Eve (Hawkes), 20:33, 37, 42, 43

Fanny (Kendall), 20:40
George, 20:184
George Washington, 20:24
Hannah, 19:217, 218, 239; 20:37, 43, 48
Hannah (___), 20:33
Hannah (Hasey), 20:33
Hannah (Parker), 20:33
Hannah (Towne), 20:40
Hannah (Wayte), 19:215
Hannah/Susannah (Fletcher), 20:40
Hepzibah, 19:218; 20:40, 41
Herodata/Rhoda, 20:42
Isaac, 20:41
Jacob, 20:33, 37, 43
James, 18:215; 20:33-35, 37, 39, 40, 42
Jane (___), 19:211
Jeremiah, 20:33
Joan, 20:37
Job, 20:42
Job/John, 20:43
Joel, 20:41
Joel Clark, 20:41
John, 16:34; 19:135, 137, 211-218; 20:33, 34, 36-38, 40, 42, 43, 48, 140, 184, 188
Jonathan, 16:88; 19:214; 20:33, 41
Joseph Farwell, 20:40
Joshua, 20:33
Judith, 19:214
Julia (Albee), 20:41
Lois, 20:34, 35, 39-41
Lucinda, 20:41
Lucy, 20:40
Lucy (Day), 20:41
Lucy (Whitney), 20:33, 40
Lydia, 20:29. 42
Lydia (Deane), 20:33
Lydia (Parker), 20:33
Martha, 16:37; 19:217, 218; 20:41
Martha (Green), 20:33, 41
Mary, 19:137, 213-215; 20:37, 41-43
Mary (Benighton), 20:33, 36, 37
Mary (Clark), 19:218; 20:33, 36, 37
Mary (Harriman), 20:33, 38
Mary (Lamson), 20:33
Mary (Newhall), 20:33, 35, 38, 39, 41
Mary (Pierpont), 20:33
Mary (Taylor), 20:33, 37, 43
Mary (Walton), 20:43
Mary (Webster), 19:214; 20:33
Mary Dandridge, 20:40
Mary/Polly, 20:40
Matilda (Rand), 20:38
Mehitable, 19:214; 20:34, 35, 38
Mehitable (Fitch), 19:214; 20:33
Mercy (Coburn), 20:41
Molley, 20:38
Nancy B. (Davis), 20:41
Nathaniel, 16:44; 20:33, 37, 39, 42, 43
Onesimus, 20:38
Patience, 19:137; 20:34-36
Perkins, 20:37
Phebe (McIntire), 20:38
Polly, 20:38, 40
Rachel, 20:40-43
Raham, 16:37; 19:214, 215, 217, 218; 20:33, 36-38
Ralph, 19:215
Rebecca, 16:94; 20:39, 40
Rhoda, 20:43
Ruth, 20:39, 42, 48
Ruth (Boutwell), 16:94; 20:33, 35, 39
Ruth (Kendall), 19:214; 20:33
Ruth (Newhall), 20:33, 37, 42

Sally (Preston), 20:40
Samuel, 19:211, 214; 20:33
Sarah, 19:213-215; 20:34, 35, 40-42
Sarah (Ballard), 20:43
Sarah (Lampson/Lamson), 19:214; 20:33
Sarah (Leathe), 19:214; 20:33
Sarah (Needham), 20:24
Sarah (Parker), 20:33
Sarah (Pierson), 20:33
Sarah (Poole), 19:214; 20:33
Sarah (Taylor), 20:41
Sarah (Temple), 20:33
Sarah (Upton), 20:43
Sarah Tyng (Farwell), 20:40
Sophronia, 20:38
Susanna, 20:37, 40
Susannah (Fletcher), 20:33
Tabitha, 19:218
Thomas, 16:37; 17:20; 18:41; 19:136, 211-217; 20:33-40, 42, 43, 184, 185, 188, 189, 197
Thomas Boyington, 20:43
Timothy, 19:217, 218; 20:33-41, 48
Wealthy (Davis), 20:38
Wilder, 20:38
William, 19:211; 20:33, 42
Zebiah (Russell), 20:43
BAND
Lucy, 17:212
BANGS
Desire, 16:87
BANKS see also MILLBANK
Charles C., 17:45
Charles E., 19:236; 20:36
Charles Edward, 16:23; 17:87; 18:17, 29, 40, 43, 71, 110; 19:154
Ruth, 18:106
William, 16:161
BANNISTER
Bertha (Witt), 18:169
Edward, 18:169
Sarah, 18:171
BARBER
Anna, 18:203
Anna (Baker), 16:176; 17:236
Charlotte, 20:163
Daniel, 16:176; 17:236
Francis E., 20:109
Martha E. (Boynton), 20:109
Mary, 16:176
Mollie, 19:235
Peter, 19:133
Rachel, 17:236
BARCLAY
John E., Mrs., 16:21
BARCROFT see BANCROFT
BARDES
Bruce, 17:96; 18:138
Eleanor, 17:96; 18:138
BARDLEY/BARDSLEY, 16:13, 18:132
BARE
Anne, 16:99
BAREBON DE WYNSDON
Henricus, 20:69
BARGE
Giles, 20:18
BARKE see BALKE
BARKER, 18:162; 20:131, 168
___, Capt., 18:214
"Child", 20:217
Abiel, 20:217
Abigail, 20:167
Abigail (Wheeler), 20:166-168

Alice, 19:58
Ann (___), 20:217
Benjamin, 18:159, 163; 20:165, 167
Bethia (Bodwell), 18:161
Ebenezer, 16:68; 20:130, 165-167
Ellen Frye, 18:156
Esther, 20:119, 165, 166
George, 19:160
Hannah, 18:157; 19:113; 20:165
Hannah (___), 18:159
Hannah (Foster), 19:57
Hannah (Kimball), 20:119, 167
Hannah (Marston), 20:167
Jacob, 19:57
James, 20:130
Joanna (___), 20:21, 23, 164, 165, 167
John, 16:68; 20:20, 119, 165-167, 217
Joseph, 20:222
Margaret, 20:119
Margaret (Hyde), 20:119
Martha, 18:161
Martha (___), 20:167
Mary, 20:166, 167
Mary (___), 20:119
Mary (Abbot), 20:22, 23, 119, 167
Mary (Dix/Mix), 20:58, 167
Mary (Stevens), 20:167, 217
Mary S., 19:172
Mehitable, 17:56
Nathan, 18:161, 163
Philemon, 18:162
Polly/Mary, 19:97
Richard, 16:68; 18:160, 161; 19:95; 20:21, 23, 119, 164, 165, 167, 217
Ruth, 20:221
Samuel, 19:33
Sarah, 20:21, 165
Sarah (Bessom), 19:230
Sarah (Graves), 20:217
Sarah (Roberts), 20:119
Stephen, 16:68; 18:161; 20:22, 23, 119, 130, 165, 167
Susan (Coates), 19:160
Susanna, 17:205
William, 16:68; 20:58, 165-167
Zebediah, 20:130
BARLOW
Edward, 19:209
Mary (Pemberton), 19:209
BARNARD/BARNERD
Edward T., 18:138
Eleanor (___), 16:17
James, 18:163, 237; 19:91
Jeanette (Tenney), 19:210
Jeanette T. P., 19:206
John, 16:19; 18:158; 19:38
Jonathan, 17:93
Ruth, 16:15
Sarah, 16:17; 17:95
Sarah (Peasley), 16:15
Stephen, 16:68; 18:157
Thomas, 16:15; 18:132; 19:34; 20:165, 166
BARNES see also BARROW
Elisha, 19:150
Elizabeth, 19:153
Freelove, 19:149
Joanna (Sprague), 18:75
Joseph, 18:75
Lydia (Potter), 19:150
Mary (Henchman), 17:100
Rachel, 17:52; 20:178
Ruth, 19:149
Thomas, 20:83

BARNET
Abigail (Norwood), 18:215
Jacob, 17:14
Joseph, 17:134
William Reynolds, 18:215
BARNEY/BARNITT
Abigail, 18:165
Ann (Witt), 16:237; 18:164, 165
Anna, 16:237
Constance (Davis), 18:165
David, 18:206
Dorcas, 18:165
Elizabeth (___), 16:237; 18:165, 206
Elizabeth (Barrett), 18:165
Hannah, 18:165
Hannah (Johnson), 18:165
Israel, 18:165
Jacob, 16:237; 18:165
John, 16:237; 18:165
Jonathan, 18:165
Joseph, 18:165
Lydia, 18:206
Mary (Thorp/Throop), 16:237; 18:165
Mary (Toogood), 18:165
Ruth, 18:165
Samuel, 18:165
Sarah, 17:203; 18:165
Sarah (Griffin), 18:165
BARNITT see BARNEY
BARNS
Elisha, 19:149
William, 19:149
BARR
Helen N., 17:208
BARRACLOUGH, 16:13
BARRELL
Hannah, 20:179
Hannah J., 17:228
BARRENTYNE
William, 20:73
BARRET/BARRETT/BERRIT
Abigail Beals (Hart), 18:50
Charles, 18:50
Dinah (Brigham), 18:170
Edward, 17:148
Elenar, 17:80
Elizabeth, 18:165
Ezekiell, 17:80
Increase, 20:221
Israel, 17:44
John, 17:79; 20:221
Joseph, 18:227
Josiah, 20:221
Lucy (Mower), 17:44
Margaret (Parker), 17:79
Martha (Burrill), 17:148
Richard, 19:142
S. (Longley), 17:177
Samuel, 20:217
Sarah, 17:80; 20:216-218
Sarah (Browne), 18:227
Timothy, 18:170
BARRON
Abigail (Woods), 16:41
Isabella (Larrabee), 20:49
Jonathan, 20:40
Lydia, 19:112
Mary Dandridge (Bancroft), 20:40
Rebecka (Parker), 16:41
Silas Parker, 16:41
Stephen, 16:41
Sybil (Parker), 16:41
William, 20:49

BARROW/BARROWS see also BARNES
  Hannah, 20:55
  John, 20:56
  Sarah (___), 17:44
  Sarah (Briggs), 20:56
  Teague, 17:90
  Rufus S., 18:105
BARRY
  Thaddeus, 18:226
BARSTOW
  Mary, 16:236
BARTHOLOMEW
  Abigail, 17:49; 20:140
  Henry, 16:27; 19:196, 197
  William, 17:89; 18:110, 193; 19:194
BARTLET/BARTLETT, 20:80
  ___, Dea., 16:106
  Abigail, 16:178
  Abigail H., 17:235
  Albert Leroy, 18:140
  Ann Hoyt, 17:239; 20:120
  Anna (Longley), 17:83
  Azubah, 18:171
  Bailey, 16:146
  Betsey Norton, 19:240
  Challis, 17:239
  Comfort Philbrook, 19:240
  Daniel, 18:112; 20:103
  Denk, 20:199
  Dorcas Priscilla, 16:142
  Edmund, 19:13
  George, 18:112
  Hannah (Philbrick), 17:57; 18:177; 19:240; 20:240
  James Philbrook, 19:240
  John, 16:221
  John H., 17:235
  Joseph Gardner, 17:157
  Josiah, 16:156
  Lawrence, 19:53
  Lucy J., 18:178
  Mary, 16:81
  Mary (___), 17:235
  Mary (Chittenden), 18:112
  Mary (Currier), 17:58
  Mary (Ingalls), 19:53
  Mary Ann, 19:240
  Mary Jane (___), 17:239
  Mary Jane (Gould), 17:239; 20:120
  Mary Jane (Townsend), 17:58
  Molly, 17:83
  Moses Norton, 19:240
  Perley, 17:57; 18:177; 19:240; 20:240
  Richard, 19:58
  Robert, 17:214; 20:15, 199
  Rosina (Northey), 19:172
  Ruth, 16:213
  Ruth (Phillips), 16:221
  Samuel, 17:83
  Sarah (___), 16:221
  Sarah (Purchase), 17:230
  Susanna (Collins), 18:112
  Susannah (___), 20:103
  Tirzah, 16:223
  William, 17:58; 19:172; 20:120
BARTOL/BARTOLL
  ___ (Codner), 20:15
  ___, Mrs., 17:214
  Abigail (Bartlett), 16:178
  Joana, 20:16
  John, 17:210; 19:169; 20:15, 199
  Margaret, 20:55
  Mercy (Northey), 19:169
  Robert, 18:225
  Sally (Trevitt), 17:100
  Samuel, 19:169; 20:199
  Sarah, 18:225
  Sarah/Margaret (Beckett), 18:225
  Tabitha (Rockwood), 19:169
  Thomas, 16:178
  William, 17:214; 20:15, 16
BARTON
  Abigail Wood (Northey), 19:171
  David Wood, 20:172
  Dorothy (Wood), 20:169
  Dorothy May (Wood), 20:172, 173
  Edward, 16:117
  Elizabeth (___), 16:117
  Henry, 20:172
  Lydia, 18:205
  Margaret, 17:227
  Margaret (Gardner), 17:227
  Mary, 16:117
  Nancy Joan, 20:172
  Samuel, 17:227; 18:208; 19:171
  Sarah, 17:227
  Susanna, 18:95
BARTRAM/BARTROM/BARTRUM/BARTHRUM
  Ellen, 18:28
  Esther, 19:144
  Gollood, 20:198
  Hannah (___), 18:28
  Sara (Johnson), 19:144
  Sarah (___), 18:74
  William, 17:146; 18:28, 74, 132; 19:144
BARWICK see also BERWICK
  Margaret (Potter), 19:153
  William, 19:153
BARZINI
  Luigi, 16:128
BASKEN
  Paul, 17:177
  Virginia, 17:56
  Virginia (Corkum), 17:53
  Virginia May (Bernklow), 17:177
BASS/BAS
  Ann (Kirtland), 18:113
  Edward, 20:199
  Lillian Janette, 19:232
  Samuel, 18:113
BASSET/BASSETT, 16:96; 18:105, 117
  ___, Goodman, 19:214
  "Child", 18:39
  Abigail, 18:21, 26, 31-33, 36, 39, 52, 53, 55; 19:107
  Abigail (___), 17:173; 18:52
  Abigail (Berry), 17:172; 18:31, 35, 52, 53, 55; 20:92
  Abigail (Davis), 18:33, 38
  Abigail (Fern), 18:35
  Alice, 18:37, 55
  Amy, 18:39
  Ann, 18:39
  Ann (Burt), 18:29, 117
  Ann (Holland), 18:28
  Ann (Morris), 18:39
  Anna (Holder), 18:37
  Beulah, 18:39
  Charity, 18:37
  Charity (Curtis), 18:33, 37
  Christopher, 18:37
  Content, 18:37, 55
  Daniel, 16:85; 18:25, 33, 35-37, 39, 54, 55
  David, 18:39
  Davis, 18:39
  Deborah, 18:32, 33, 39
  Deborah (Dunn), 18:39
  Deliverance, 17:216; 18:15, 16, 30, 31, 36, 37, 52, 53, 104
  Desire, 18:27, 35, 36, 53
  Edward, 18:36
  Elisha, 18:28-30, 33, 38, 39
  Elizabeth, 16:222; 17:76; 18:25, 28, 29, 33, 34, 38, 39, 55
  Elizabeth (Collins), 18:30, 33
  Elizabeth (Darling), 18:38, 55
  Elizabeth/Rebecca, 18:35
  Eunice, 18:35
  Eunice (Hacker), 18:35
  Grace, 18:39
  Hannah, 16:16, 80; 18:28-33, 35, 37-39, 52, 55, 91-93, 105, 132, 210; 20:212
  Huldah, 18:37, 55
  Huldah (Hood), 18:33, 38, 55
  Isaac, 16:16, 224; 18:35, 39, 102
  Isaiah, 18:34, 36
  John, 16:79; 17:172; 18:28-33, 35-39, 41, 52, 53, 55, 92; 20:92, 199
  Joseph, 16:16; 17:207; 18:31, 34, 35, 39, 52, 177
  Joseph Smethurst, 18:38
  Josiah, 18:39
  Louisa (___), 17:207
  Lydia, 18:36, 37, 55
  Lydia (Hood), 18:25, 36, 55
  Margaret, 18:37
  Mary, 16:222, 224; 17:41; 18:28-31, 34-39, 52, 53, 55
  Mary (___), 18:30, 32, 33, 37, 55
  Mary (Allen), 18:39
  Mary (Bubier), 18:37
  Mary (Burch), 18:36
  Mary (Collins), 18:35, 102
  Mary (Griffin), 18:34
  Mary (Haines), 18:39
  Mary (Lawrence), 18:33, 39
  Mary (Linch), 18:39
  Mary (Lippincott), 18:39
  Mary (Woodnutt), 18:39
  Mary Louisa, 17:207
  Mercy, 18:34
  Mercy (Bell), 18:36
  Michael, 18:32, 33, 37, 38, 55
  Miriam/Merriam, 18:28-30, 32-35; 19:83, 84, 198, 200
  Morris, 18:39
  Nancy Pote, 18:38
  Nathan, 18:39
  Nehemiah, 18:34, 35
  Paul, 18:39
  Phebe (Copperwaite), 18:39
  Rachel, 18:29, 30, 39, 102
  Rachel (Hews), 18:39
  Rebecca, 18:29, 30, 35, 37, 39; 19:237
  Rebecca (___), 17:173; 18:52
  Rebecca (Berry), 17:172; 18:31, 34, 52, 55; 19:84; 20:92
  Rebecca/Elizabeth (Berry), 18:35
  Reuben, 18:39
  Richard, 18:36
  Roger, 18:28
  Ruth, 18:11, 31, 52, 117
  Ruth (Newhall), 18:36, 55
  Samuel, 18:28-30, 39; 19:216
  Samuel Pote/Pato, 18:38
  Sara (Hood), 17:216
  Sarah, 18:25, 28, 29, 31-33, 35-39, 52, 55; 19:213

Sarah (Browne), 18:226
Sarah (Burt), 18:28, 52, 102, 117
Sarah (Ellet), 18:39
Sarah (Hood), 18:15, 16, 26, 29, 30, 52, 53, 92
Sarah (Sanders), 18:39
Tabby, 18:38
Tabitha (Smethurst), 18:38, 55
Thomas, 18:36
Timothy, 20:37
William, 16:95, 156; 17:46; 18:15, 18, 19, 26, 28-35, 37-39, 52, 53, 55, 60a, 92, 102, 103, 117, 132; 19:47, 84, 145, 213; 20:92, 132, 135, 196, 197
Zebedee, 18:39
Zephaniah, 18:35, 36
BATCHELDER/BATCHELER/
BATCHELLER/BATCHELOR see also
BACHELDER, 18:187
Abigail (Buzzell), 16:57
Abraham, 16:57
Ann (Sleeper), 20:239
Anne (Taylor), 16:57
Benjamin, 20:136
Betsy, 18:16
D. H., 17:162
David, 20:188
Dorcas Priscilla (Bartlett), 16:142
Ebenezer, 18:234; 20:135
Edward, 16:111
Elizabeth, 16:38; 20:136
Elizabeth (___), 20:136
Elizabeth (Davis), 16:57
Esther Ross (Worth), 17:59
Experience, 20:136
Fanny (Ober), 17:162
Florence, 19:232
George Otis, 17:59
Hanna (___), 16:38
Hannah, 18:22, 46; 20:136
Hannah (Hale), 20:136
Hannah (Tarbox), 20:136
Hannah (White), 20:136
Hannah C., 16:57
Henry, 18:22
Huldah, 19:109
Increase, 16:57
Jerusha (Breed), 18:22
John, 16:38, 142; 20:136, 185, 188, 200
Joseph, 20:198
Josiah, 19:159; 20:136
Lucy W., 17:162
Lydia, 16:47; 20:239
Mark, 16:142; 20:136
Mary, 16:57
Mary (Batchelder), 16:57
Mary (Carter), 16:57
Mehitable, 20:136
Nathaniel, 16:57
Rebeckah, 20:136
Samuel, 16:57, 142; 20:136
Sarah, 16:142; 19:51; 20:136
Sarah (Drake), 16:57
Sarah (Friend), 16:142; 20:136
Sarah (Tarbox), 18:234; 20:135
Theophilus, 20:239
BATE
Kerry William, 20:91
BATEMAN
Bridget, 16:59
BATES, 18:132, 135, 137
Albert C., 16:186
James, 16:77

John, 19:169
Joseph, 20:48
Martha (Ballard), 16:77
Mehitable (Ballard), 16:77
Molly, 16:77
Obadiah, 16:77
Robert, 17:20; 19:136, 213, 216, 217
Sally (Northey), 19:169
Samuel A., 19:117
BATH
William, 19:143; 20:198
BATT
Ann, 17:52; 20:178
Thomas, 16:203
BATTELLE
Adeline, 17:59
BATTEN
Mary, 19:177
BATTER
___, Mr., 18:231; 19:143, 192, 195
Edmond, 19:197
Nicholas, 20:194
BATTERSBY
Dorothea, 17:54
BATTES
Ruth, 17:206
BATTLES
Elizabeth, 18:96
Jeremiah, 18:96
BATTY
Nicholas, 16:71; 19:138
BAWLER
S. E., 16:51
BAXTER
Abigail, 20:137
Elizabeth (Smith), 20:205
Ruth (Onthank), 20:137
Samuel, 20:137, 205
BAYFORD
Annis, 19:116, 120, 222; 20:20
BAYLES
John, 19:193
BAYLEY/BAYLIE/BAYLY see also
BAILEY
___, Rev., 17:15
Abner, 18:236
Anna (Richardson), 16:59
Benona, 18:169
Dorothy (___), 20:216
Elizabeth, 17:99; 19:52
Elizabeth (Witt), 18:169
Harriet E., 17:55
Henry, 20:216
James, 17:16
Joanna, 17:55
John, 17:99; 18:210; 19:51, 52
Joshua, 16:59
Nathaniel, 16:133
Olive (Leavens), 16:59
Samuel, 16:59
Sarah, 17:99; 19:52
Sarah (___), 19:51
Sarah (Ingalls), 17:99
Stephen, 16:59
Theophilus, 16:73; 20:204
Thomas, 16:24
BEACH
John, 19:101
BEADLE
Nathaniel, 19:143
BEAL/BEALE/BEALL
James, 20:199
John, 20:199

Mary (Whitridge), 18:46
Samuel, 20:199
Thomas, 20:67, 196
William, 18:46
BEAMSLEY
Anne (___), 20:223
Grace, 20:223-226
Mercy, 19:223
William, 20:223
BEAN
Augusta, 16:149
Elizabeth, 20:217, 220
Increase Robinson, 19:58
Joanna (Thompson), 19:58
Joanna (Treethy), 20:220
John, 16:17
Joseph, 19:58; 20:220
Madeline Mae, 16:52
Sarah (Evans), 19:58
BEARD
Agnes, 19:153
Anne (___), 18:51
Thomas, 18:51
BEAUCHAMP
Elizabeth, 20:234
BEAUDET
Genevieve (Gruren), 20:170
Joseph, 20:170
Maroailine, 20:170
BEAUPRE
Walter, 18:133
BECK
Eliz (Stone), 17:120
John, 20:204
Mary, 20:119
Samuel, 17:120
BECKET/BECKETT
John, 17:231
Sarah, 19:160
Sarah/Margaret, 18:225
BECKFORD, 18:132, 139
John, 18:231
BECKS see also BECX
John, 18:231
BECKWITH
Betsey (Northey), 19:169
William, 19:169
BECROFT
Elizabeth Westbrook, 17:127
BECX see also BECKS, 20:77
BEDAT/BEDATE
Antoine, 19:110
Jeanne, 19:110
Petronille (Leger), 19:110
BEDELL
Anna (Carr), 17:194
Robert, 17:194
BEDFORD
Deborah, 17:237; 20:146
Jane (___), 20:174, 175
Nathan, 20:146
BEEBE, 20:183, 190
BEECHEN, 20:165
BEEDE
Abigail, 18:11
Emma Frances (Wood), 20:171
Moses, 18:11, 12
William D., 20:171
BEEKMAN
William, 17:94
BEENS
Hanna, 16:198
BEERS
Joseph Spencer, 17:174

Lydia (Frothingham), 17:174
Mary Ann, 20:227
Mary Ann Nichols, 17:174
BEGOOD
Lettice, 18:57
BEIDER
Alexander, 17:73
BELCHER
___, Gov., 18:240a; 20:47, 49
Andrew, 16:36; 17:93
Ebenezer, 16:204
Gregory, 17:157
Hannah (___), 19:100
Jeremiah, 19:159; 20:98
Jeremy, 18:193
Joseph, 17:157; 19:100
Mary, 20:139
Ranis (Rainsford), 17:157
Rebecca, 17:144
Ruth (Hutchins/Hitchings), 16:204
Samuel, 18:193
BELDEN
Lydia, 18:113
BELKNAP/BELNAP
Abraham, 19:138; 20:184, 195
Elizabeth, 18:57
Henry Wyckoff, 19:148
Joseph, 17:147; 19:44
Lydia (Ingalls), 19:44
Sarah, 20:211
BELL
Abigail, 18:179
Alexander Graham, 16:185
Ann Maria, 17:32
Augusta, 17:32
Betsy (Friend), 17:32
Caroline, 17:32
Deborah, 16:56
Elizabeth, 17:32
Elizabeth (___), 16:32
George, 16:32
John, 17:32
Mary, 17:32; 20:143
Mary (James), 16:32
Mercy, 18:36
Raymond, 19:141
Raymond M., 19:140
Rebecca (Aborn), 16:31; 17:211
Samuel, 16:32; 17:32; 18:179
Sarah, 16:89
Thomas, 16:31; 17:211; 19:132
William Henry, 17:32
BELLAMY
Hannah, 19:58
BELLINGHAM
___, Gov., 19:209; 20:183
___, Mr., 18:196
Richard, 16:71; 18:196; 20:201
BELLOWS
Abigail (Liscom), 19:80
Moses, 19:80
Persis, 20:212
BELNAP see BELKNAP
BEMIS
Elizabeth, 17:44
Samuel, 17:44
BENIGHTON/BONYTHON, 18:132
Mary, 19:145; 20:33, 36, 37, 102
BENIT/BENNIT/BENNET/BENNETT
___, Capt., 18:151
___, Mr., 20:120
"Son", 17:94
Abigail (Lane), 18:202

Anthony, 20:198
Aphra (___), 17:91
Aron, 20:197
Benjamin, 17:85
Charles Frederic, 20:152
Dorcas, 18:202, 180
Dorothy, 17:95
Dorothy (___), 17:91
Edward, 17:213; 20:199
Elijah, 19:179
Elisha, 17:89; 18:153, 226
Ellis, 17:89
Francis, 17:161
Fred, 19:180; 20:120
Isabelle, 17:161
John, 16:64; 17:89; 20:198
John Corliss, 17:161
Katherine, 17:161
Lydia, 16:235
Lydia (Longley), 17:83
Martha (Proctor), 17:161
May Friend, 17:161
Moses, 20:197
Nathaniel, 18:202
Patience, 17:12
Paulina (Webber), 19:180; 20:120
Roberta (___), 17:161
Samuel, 16:165; 17:87; 18:132, 231;
  19:138, 189, 195, 212; 20:189, 191-193,
  195
Sarah, 17:89; 18:37
Sarah (___), 17:87
Sarah (Barnard), 17:95
Sarah (Hargraves), 17:91
Sarah Ellen (Briant), 20:152
Sophia Mary (Wallis), 19:179
Thomas, 17:83
Victoria (Friend), 17:161
Will, 19:180
William, 19:202; 20:197
BENNER
Mary, 17:59
BENSON
Abigail, 17:232
Benjamin, 18:204
Hannah (Norwood), 18:204
John, 17:232
Mary (Williams), 17:232
Ruth, 20:60a
BENT
Caroline, 20:41
BENTINGA
Leslie Ann (Wood), 20:173
Victor D., 20:173
BENTLEY, 19:42
William, 18:95; 19:125, 198, 199
BENTON
Josiah Henry, 17:137
BEOMONT
Ann, 19:153
BERNAP
Lydia, 20:234
BERNARD
Robert, 19:32
BERNKLOW
Frederick Alton, 17:177
Marjorie Elizabeth (Corkum), 17:177
Virginia May, 17:177
BERRY, 17:173
___, Gov., 18:143
Abigail, 17:172; 18:31, 35, 52, 53, 55;
  20:92
Alinda, 17:38

Anna (Merriam), 16:75
Athelred, 17:172
Benjamin, 17:22
Bethia (Burrage), 18:116
Catherine, 18:227
Daniel, 17:172; 20:92
David A., 19:71
Divan, 18:116
Elizabeth, 16:75; 17:172; 18:116; 20:92
Elizabeth (___), 16:75
Elizabeth (Divan), 17:159; 18:116; 20:92
Ellen T., 19:71
Ephraim, 18:116
Ethelred, 20:92
George, 20:220
Georgianna, 20:108
Hannah, 16:26; 17:159; 18:52, 53;
  20:25-27, 91, 92
Hannah (Farrar), 17:172; 18:34, 35, 53,
  116; 20:27, 92
James, 17:159; 18:228
Jane, 20:221
Jerusha, 17:172; 20:92
Joanna (Riddan), 17:159
John, 17:22; 19:50; 20:43, 91, 180
Jonathan, 17:159
Joseph, 20:43
Lucy, 20:43
Martha, 16:75
Mary, 17:158; 18:81, 116
Mary (Clark), 18:116
Mary (Fuller), 17:158; 18:116
Mary (Johnson), 18:116
Mary (Mayor), 17:172; 20:92
Mary (Stocker), 17:159
Mary (Stowers), 17:159
Mehitable, 17:172; 20:92
Moriah (Ingalls), 19:50
Nancy, 17:36
Polly (Brimblecom), 20:43
Priscilla (Smith), 17:204
Rachel, 16:46; 18:24; 20:43
Rachel (Atkins), 16:18
Rachel (Bancroft), 20:42, 43
Rachel (Leach), 17:172; 20:180
Rebecca, 16:75; 17:171; 18:31, 34, 52, 55,
  134; 19:84; 20:92
Rebecca (Ballard), 16:75; 18:116
Rebecca (Yale), 18:116
Rebecca/Elizabeth, 18:35
Ruth, 19:50
Ruth (Ingalls), 19:50
Samuel, 17:20; 18:116; 19:50; 20:92
Sarah, 16:167; 17:159; 20:43, 92, 232
Sarah (___), 20:43
Sarah (Leach), 20:92
Sarah/Betsey, 20:239
Thaddeus, 17:90; 18:34, 35, 53, 116, 132,
  216; 20:26, 27, 43, 92
Thomas, 16:75; 17:22; 18:115, 116, 150;
  20:92
BERTHOFF
Rowland T., 16:10
BERWICK see also BARWICK
Ann (___), 16:67
Grace, 16:67; 17:54
Thomas, 16:67
BESOM/BESOME see also BESSOM,
BISSON
Hannah, 20:222
Miriam Lewis, 20:222
Philip, 16:84
Ruth, 16:84

Sarah, 20:221
Sarah (Bubur), 16:84
BESSEL
   John, 19:239
BESSENS, 17:97
BESSOM see also BESOM, BISSON
   Abigail Lewis, 19:231
   Anna (Harris), 19:230
   Betsy Lewis, 19:231
   Charlotte Woodruff, 19:231-233
   Edmund Lewis, 19:231
   Elizabeth, 19:230, 231
   Elizabeth (Laskey), 19:230
   Elizabeth (Lewis), 19:230, 231
   George Washington, 19:231
   Grace, 19:230
   Hannah, 19:230, 231
   Hannah (Blaney), 19:231
   Hannah Phillips, 19:231
   Jane, 19:230
   Jean, 19:230
   Jennie (Hood), 17:217
   John, 17:212; 19:230
   John Russell, 19:231
   Joseph, 19:230
   Margaret, 19:230
   Martha, 19:231
   Mary, 19:230
   Miriam Lewis, 19:231
   Nicholas, 19:230
   Phillip, 19:230-233
   Rebecca (Chin), 19:230
   Rebecca Cleaves (Smith), 19:230, 231
   Richard, 19:230
   Ruth, 19:230
   Ruth (Collyer), 19:230, 231
   Ruthy, 19:231
   Sarah, 19:230, 231
   Sarah (Bubier), 19:230
   Sarah (Gale), 19:230
   Sarah E., 19:231
   Susannah, 19:230
   Tabitha Lewis, 19:231
   William, 19:230
   William Gray, 19:231
BEUMER
   Hal, 19:81
BEVERSTOCK
   Francis Palace, 18:59
   Laura Ann (Wheeler), 18:59
BEVINS
   Elisha M., 17:102
   Isabel E. (Friend), 17:102
   Sophia (___), 17:102
BIBLER, 19:240
BICKFORD
   Eliza, 16:239
   James, 19:109
   Mary (Ingalls), 19:109
   Sarah, 20:43
BICKNAL
   Benjamin, 19:212
   Martha (Metcalf), 19:212
   William, 19:212
BICKNESS
   William, 18:79
BIDLATHE
   Christopher, 20:223
BIGELOW
   Abigail (Witt), 18:170
   Francis Hill, 19:200
   Jason, 18:170
   Mary (Gleason), 18:170

   Samuel, 18:170
BIGSBY
   Haskell G., 20:89
BILES see BYLES
BILL
   Beulah, 19:164
   Charles, 16:74; 17:157
   Deliverance, 19:40
   Francis, 19:40
   Hannah, 19:164
   Hannah (Bellamy), 19:58
   James, 19:39, 40
   Jonathan, 19:40, 58
   Joseph, 19:40
   Lydia, 20:146, 147
   Mary, 19:120
   Mehitable, 19:40
   Ruth (Fuller), 16:74; 17:157
   Sarah, 19:38-40; 20:147
BILLIAS
   George Athan, 19:166
BILLING
   Philomela, 16:212
BILLINGHAM
   ___, Dep.Gov., 20:187
   Richard, 17:209
BILLINGS
   Abigail (Eaton), 18:220
   Elijah, 18:87
   Hannah (Farrar), 18:220
   James, 19:163
   John, 18:87, 220
   Mary (Jones), 18:87
   Solomon, 18:220
   William, 19:163
BILLINGTON
   Thomas, 16:175; 20:67
BING
   Benjamin, 17:11
BINGHAM
   Catherine (Potter), 19:153
   Delucena, 20:83
   Delucena Lathrop, 17:39
   Louisa (___), 17:39
   Lucy Huntington, 17:39
   Thomas, 19:153
BIRD
   Daniel, 16:79
   Sarah (Blaney), 16:79
BIRDSALL
   Henry, 19:194
BIRDSEYE
   Hannah, 16:212
BIRMINGHAM
   Lydia (Rhodes), 17:157
   Richard, 17:157
BISHOP
   ___, Mr., 19:191
   Clare (Wiswall), 16:240
   Clifton Reynes, 17:215
   Clinton, 16:240
   Dulzebella (King), 17:139
   Edward, 16:137; 17:16
   Eleanor (Crafts), 16:240
   Eleanor C., 18:133
   Lydia, 17:139
   Lydia (Norman), 17:139
   Martha, 16:73
   Nathaniel, 19:197
   Persis, 18:180
   Richard, 17:139
   Samuel, 16:133
   Thomas, 17:139; 20:197

   Townsend, 19:190; 20:235
BISSON see also BESOM, BESSOM, 18:132, 139
   Elizabeth (Noe/Noot), 19:230
   Jean, 19:231-233
   Jean LeGros, 19:230
BITFIELD
   Elizabeth, 17:55; 20:58
   Elizabeth (___), 20:58
   Mary, 20:58
   Samuel, 20:58
BITNAR
   Sarah (Ingalls), 19:45, 46
   William, 19:45, 46
BIXBY, 18:132
   Abigail (Rogers), 17:114
   Daniel, 16:68; 18:56
   George, 19:179; 20:180
   James, 16:174
   Joseph, 16:193; 17:157; 19:33
   Nathan, 17:114
   Rebecca (Porter), 19:179; 20:180
   Sarah (Rhodes), 17:157
BLACK, 18:132, 139
   Daniel, 16:193
   Freegrace, 16:137
   James, 20:89
   John, 16:137; 19:201, 202
   Moses, 20:89, 90
   Tom, 20:158
   William, 20:89, 90
BLACK WILLIAM, 19:162
BLACKADER
   Christopher Charles, 16:83
   Ruth Catherine (Tardy), 16:83
BLACKLER
   Martha, 16:179
   Ruth, 19:230
   William, 20:199
BLACKSTONE
   Patience, 17:179
BLAGUE see BLAKE
BLAISDELL/BLASDELL/BLESDELL, 20:80
   ___, Mrs., 18:230; 19:197
   Abigail, 17:238
   Charles, 20:59
   Elizabeth, 18:230
   Harriet M. (Hamblon), 20:59
   Henry, 16:180; 18:230
   James, 20:237
   Lydia (Parker), 16:180
   Sarah, 16:238
   Sarah (Holmes), 16:59
   William, 16:59
BLAISE, 20:68
BLAKE/BLAGUE/BLAQUE
   Abigail, 16:52; 20:220
   Deborah, 19:206, 208, 209
   Dorothy, 16:117
   George, 16:193
   Joseph, 18:113
   Martha (Kirtland), 18:111-113
   Rebecca, 20:166, 168
   Sally, 18:171
   Samuel, 16:173
   Susanna (Newhall), 17:219
   William, 17:219
BLAKEWAY
   Jacob, 16:120a
BLANCHARD
   Deliverance (Parker), 17:81
   Elizabeth (___), 16:204

Elizabeth (Merriam), 16:205
Jonathan, 16:68
Joshua, 16:204
Lucy, 17:205; 18:45
Mehitable (___), 16:204
Nathaniel, 17:82
Olive, 17:82
Ruth (Adams), 17:82
Samuel, 16:68; 20:214
Thomas, 17:82
William, 17:81
BLANCHETTE
Samuel, 20:215
BLAND
John, 19:120
**BLANEY/BLANER/BLAYNEY/BLANO/
BLANY**, 16:96; 18:137
___, Lord, 16:23
___, Miss, 20:26
___, Mr., 19:217
Aaron, 16:86
Abigail, 16:28; 18:23; 19:151
Abigail (Andrews), 16:25; 20:94
Abigail (Browne), 16:81
Abigail (Bucknam), 16:29
Abigail (Yeoman), 16:85
Alice, 16:78; 20:26
Alice (Peasley), 16:27
Alice E., 17:31
Ambrose, 16:28
Andrews, 16:23
Andros, 16:87
Ann Mears, 16:87
Ann Mears (Blaney), 16:87
Anna, 19:108
Anna (Cox), 16:86
Anna (Potter), 16:29
Anna/Nancy (Curtis), 16:86
Anna/Nanny, 16:86
Anne, 16:86
Arnold, 16:87
Asa, 16:79
Benjamin, 16:23
Benjmain Sharpe, 16:86
Bethia, 16:83
Bethia (Cogswell), 16:29
Betsey (Dennis), 16:87
Betsey (Grant), 16:84
Beulah (Brown), 16:83
Caroline, 16:86
Caroline (Blaney), 16:86
Catherine (Mears), 16:86
Charles C., 16:23; 20:27
Chloe (Green), 16:82
Christopher, 16:84
Chuckie, 16:23; 18:132
Daniel, 16:25; 20:93
David, 16:26; 18:98; 20:211
Desire (Dean), 16:27; 18:94
Dinah, 16:84
Dorothy, 20:148
Elizabeth, 16:24; 20:94
Elizabeth (Andrews), 17:229
Elizabeth (Cogswell), 16:29
Elizabeth (King), 17:229
Elizabeth (Mackworth), 16:23
Elizabeth (McLeod), 16:86
Elizabeth (Purchase), 16:25; 17:229; 19:147; 20:93
Elizabeth (Waite), 16:82
Elizabeth (Williams), 17:230
Elizabeth K. (Trask), 16:84
Elizabeth/Betsey, 16:83

Elizabeth/Betsey (Ingalls), 16:86; 19:108
Emma (Roundy), 16:79
Eunice, 16:87
Eunice (Segar), 16:87
George A., 16:23
Grace Bessom, 16:84
Hannah, 16:24; 19:151, 231; 20:93, 210
Hannah (___), 16:86; 20:211, 215
Hannah (Gray), 16:29
Hannah (King), 16:23; 20:27, 93
Hannah (Osgood), 16:82
Hannah (Rand), 16:27; 20:210
Hannah (Winship), 16:83
Henry, 16:25; 19:147; 20:93, 210
Huldah, 16:82
Ivory, 16:79; 20:211
Jedediah, 16:28
Joanna (Pearce), 16:79
John, 16:23, 153; 17:229; 20:27, 93, 196, 215
Jonathan, 16:28; 19:108
Jonathan Chapell, 16:84
Joseph, 16:25, 155; 20:94, 103
Judah (Curtis), 16:29
Katherine (Walker), 16:27
Liddie, 16:27
Lidia/Elizabeth, 16:95
Lois, 16:79
Lois (Ivory), 16:27; 19:147
Lucinda, 16:87
Lydia, 16:79
Lydia (Sargent), 16:82
Martha, 16:80; 18:31, 93, 98; 19:108
Martha (Mansfield), 16:27
Mary, 16:79; 17:101; 19:52
Mary (___), 20:211
Mary (Browne), 16:79
Mary (Chapell), 16:84
Mary (Estes), 16:78; 18:93, 94
Mary (Gridley), 16:86
Mary (Marston), 16:81
Mary (Pedrick), 16:84
Mary/Polly (Seccomb), 16:83
Mercy (Marston), 16:84
Nancy (Williston), 16:84
Nehemiah, 16:28
Penelope, 16:26
Philip, 16:84
Robert, 16:78
Ruth, 16:83
Ruth (Besome), 16:84; 19:230
Ruth (Phillips), 16:86
Ruth M., 17:57
Sally Avis (Leach), 16:87
Samuel, 16:86
Sarah, 16:24, 26; 20:25, 27, 93, 94
Sarah (___), 16:81
Sarah (Browne), 16:84
Sarah (Speer), 16:86
Sarah (Whitcomb), 16:87
Stephen, 16:83
Susannah, 16:81
Susannah M., 16:84
Thomas, 16:26; 18:94
William, 16:81; 19:230
BLAQUE see BLAKE
BLASDELL see BLAISDELL
BLASHFIELD
Thomas, 20:198
BLATCHFORD
John, 16:133
BLATT
Warren, 17:68

BLAYNEY see BLANEY
BLESDELL see BLAISDELL
BLIGH
Mary, 20:100
BLISS/BISS
Lydia, 19:226
BLODGETT/BLODGETTE
___ (Bancroft), 20:40
George, 20:98
George B., 19:210
William, 20:40
BLOOD
Abigail, 17:82
Abigail (Parker), 17:82
Charles, 20:188
Edmund, 17:82
Eunice, 17:82
Hannah, 17:79
Hannah (Jenkins), 17:78
Isabel (___), 17:80
John, 17:82
Maria, 16:238
Mary (Parker), 17:86
Nehemiah, 17:82
Richard, 17:80
Robert, 17:78; 18:71, 72
Sarah, 17:82
BLOSSE
Catherine, 20:169
BLOTT/BLOTTS
Elizabeth (___), 19:212
William, 19:212; 20:189
BLUNDEL
___, Col., 18:78
BLUNT/BLUNTS
___ (Ballard), 16:66
Elizabeth (Ballard), 16:67; 17:54
Ephraim, 17:54
Isaac, 19:35
John, 17:178
Martha (Ordway), 17:54
Moses, 17:54
Sally (Gilpatrick), 17:178
Sarah (___), 17:54
Sarah (Foster), 17:54
William, 16:66-68; 17:54
Zerviah (Abbot), 17:54
BLYTH/BLYTHE
Benjamin, 16:46; 18:113
Hitty, 18:218
Judith, 17:32
Mary (Legree), 16:46; 18:113
BOADEN see BODEN, BOWDEN, 20:146
BOARDMAN, 18:132, 136
Aaron, 17:89; 19:100
Abiah (Sprague), 19:100, 147
Abigail (___), 18:227
Eunice (Cheever), 18:215
Eunice (Ivory), 19:100, 147
John, 18:215, 236, 240; 19:100, 147
Jonathan, 18:214
Lydia, 19:100
Mary, 18:152; 19:53, 100
Mary (___), 19:100
Mary (Cheever), 19:100
Rachel (Browne), 18:226, 226
Samuel, 18:227
Sarah (Wait/Waite), 19:100
Susanna (Norwood), 18:214, 215
Thomas, 20:224, 225
William, 18:213; 19:100, 147
BODEN/BOADEN see also BOWDEN
Ambrose, 20:146

Benjamin, 16:156; 17:101
Lydia (___), 18:38
Mary, 16:29; 17:101; 19:53
Ruth (James), 16:29
Samuel, 16:29
BODGE
George Madison, 16:138; 17:19; 18:41, 150, 167; 19:145, 163, 210, 214; 20:135, 207
Sarah Adaline, 20:147
BODIER
Edward, 20:199
BODKIN
___, Dr., 17:125
BODWEL/BODWELL, 19:95; 20:131
Abigail, 18:159
Abigail (Ladd), 18:159
Bethia, 18:161
Bethiah (Emery), 18:159
Daniel, 18:159; 20:130
Elizabeth, 18:159
Elizabeth (Bowers), 18:159
Elizabeth (Mansur), 18:159
Elizabeth (Messer), 18:159
Elizabeth (Parker), 18:159
Elizabeth (Roberts), 18:159
Hannah, 18:159; 20:207
Henry, 16:68; 18:159; 19:96; 20:130
James, 18:159; 20:130
John, 18:159; 20:131
Mary, 18:159
Mary (Parker), 18:159
Parker, 18:159
Ruth, 18:159
Ruth (Gutterson), 18:159
Samuel, 18:159
Sarah (Lancaster), 18:159
Stephen, 18:159
Tiffen, 18:159
BOGERT
Bruce, 17:126
BOIT see BOYT
BOKESON
Susanna, 16:193
BOLAND
W., 17:133
BOLCH see BALCH
BOLES
E. C., 17:102
BOLTON
John, 20:54
Margery, 20:54
Margery (Pratt), 20:54
BOMER see also BROWN
Abigail, 16:144
John, 16:144
Nabby/Abigail (Friend), 16:144
BOND
Aaron, 16:133
Abigail, 16:63
Abigail (Rogers), 19:177
Amy (Graves), 20:216
Charles Henry, 19:177
Charles Lawrence, 19:177
Charles Milton, 19:177
Charles W. M., 19:177
Edward, 20:216
Elizabeth, 20:216
Elizabeth (Coy), 20:216
Henry, 18:40, 158; 19:157
Isabella (Bacon), 19:177
John, 16:112; 18:237; 19:177; 20:216, 218
Jonathan, 19:177

Judith (Dow), 19:177
Martha, 20:216
Martha (Hall), 20:218, 219
Mary (Amerige), 19:177
Nathaniel, 19:177
Robert, 20:199
Sally (Sweetser), 19:177
BONDS
William, 17:25
BONIGHTON
Richard, 19:236
BONYON
William, 20:145
BONYTHON see also BENIGHTON, 18:132
John, 20:36
Mary, 20:36
Richard, 20:36
BOODRY
Bethia L. (Reed), 17:59
Dennis Sylvester, 17:59
BOOKER
Mary, 20:57
BOOTH, 16:13
Alice, 18:100
Eleanor, 16:119
Elizabeth, 17:18
George, 16:157
John, 18:101
Mary, 20:142
Mary (Manning), 18:101
BOOTHBY
Foster, 17:170
Norma Austin (Friend), 17:170
BOOTMAN/BUTMAN
Betsey, 16:215, 220, 17:32
Elizabetn (Harrander), 16:215
Jonathan, 16:215
Polly, 16:214
BORDEN
Asahel, 18:88
Jemima (Jones), 18:88
BORDMAN
Joseph, 17:26
Mary, 19:40, 99
Sarah (___), 19:99
William, 19:99
BOREMAN/BORMAN
Hannah, 19:98
Mary, 18:239; 20:120
BORENE
Lawrence, 20:199
BORGIALLI
Vincent, 19:57
BORODELL
Ann, 16:55
BORON
William, 20:199
BOSSON, 18:132
Jennie (Hood), 17:173
Jennie Hood, 16:221; 18:51
BOSTWICK
Gideon, 16:190
BOSWORTH
Alice, 17:16
Hannah, 16:72
Helen P., 18:133
Ruth, 16:172
BOTETOURT
John, 16:120a
BOTHAM
___, Mrs., 17:12
BOTT
Dorothy/Dolly (Newhall), 16:44

Elizabeth (Haskell), 17:108
Emma Francis (Friend), 17:108
Frances, 16:45
Hannah, 16:45
Hannah (___), 16:109
James, 16:44; 17:108
James L., 17:108
John, 16:45
Linch, 16:45
Mary, 16:45
Mary (Cummings), 16:45
Phebe (___), 16:45
Phebe (Lindsey), 16:45
Priscilla (Clark), 16:109
Ruth (Hathorne), 16:44
Ruth S., 16:239
Sally, 16:45
Stacy Read, 16:45
BOUDE, 18:132
BOULDER
Hattie, 17:238
BOUND
Ruth, 20:234
BOURNE, 19:174
___, Judge, 20:50
Abigail, 19:165, 167, 168
Katherine (Wheelwright), 19:165
Martha, 16:172
Ruth (Bosworth), 16:172
Samuel, 19:165
Shearjashub, 16:172
BOUTEL/BOUTWELL see also BOWTELL
Elizabeth (Frothingham), 20:39
James, 18:74, 147; 19:142; 20:39, 194
John, 20:193
Mary, 19:137
Ruth, 16:94; 20:33, 35, 39
BOWDEN see also BOWDOIN, BODEN, BURDEN, 20:149
Almira (Hutchins), 19:239
Barbara/Barberry (Hood), 18:55
Benjamin, 18:33, 55
Damaris, 20:145, 146, 238
Elizabeth, 17:99; 19:52
Elizabeth (Holder), 16:236
Francis, 18:32
Mary, 20:222
Michael, 17:213; 18:103; 19:105, 155
Oliver, 19:239
Samuel, 16:236
Sarah, 16:236; 18:103
Susannah, 19:159
BOWDER
Benjamin, 20:221
Elizabeth (Graves), 20:221
BOWDITCH
Daniel, 20:42
Ebenezer, 20:42
George, 20:42
Jane, 20:42
Joseph, 20:42
Lucy (Mansfield), 20:42
Nathaniel, 17:227
Nathaniel Ingersoll, 19:133
Richard, 20:42
Sarah, 20:42
Sarah (Bancroft), 20:42
Thomas, 20:42
William, 20:42
BOWDOIN see also BOWDEN, BODEN, BURDEN, 18:132
James, 17:95

BOWDY
　Betsy, 19:238
BOWEN, 17:139; 20:90
　Abigail (Estes), 18:96
　Clarence, 20:216
　Clarence Winthrop, 17:23
　Hannah (Harris), 17:101; 19:53
　James, 18:96
　Johanna (Gaffney), 17:139
　John, 17:139
　Lovice (Gaskill), 18:97
　Lydia, 16:73
　Martha (Trevitt), 17:101; 19:52
　Mary (Blaney), 16:87
　Mary (Boden), 17:101; 19:53
　Nathan, 16:96; 17:101; 19:38, 52
　Nathaniel, 16:97
　Nathaniel A., 18:97
　Samuel, 16:87
　Sarah (___), 17:101
　Thomas, 20:15
　Tom, 20:16
　William, 19:38
BOWERS
　Elizabeth, 18:159
　Jonathan, 18:158
　Nehemiah, 20:49
　Sarah (Larrabee), 20:49
BOWIN
　John, 20:199
BOWLER
　___, Mr., 17:41
BOWMAN, 20:120
　Alvira/Elvira W. (Paige), 19:59
　Elias, 20:239
　Horace S., 19:59
　Martha (___), 20:239
　Mary Ann (Ross), 20:239
　Nancy Marie, 20:239
　Phebe (___), 19:59
　Phillip, 19:59
　Robert E., 18:135, 137, 138; 20:63
　Samuel, 18:158
　Thomas, 20:239
　Thomas Jefferson, 20:239
BOWTELL see also BOUTEL
　James, 19:138
BOYCE
　Abigail (___), 20:94
　Benjamin, 20:94
　David, 20:94, 111, 112
　Dinah (Baker), 20:25-28
　Dorothy, 20:240
　Ebenezer, 20:27, 28
　Eliza, 18:11, 12
　Elizabeth, 20:94
　Ellenor (Plover), 20:94
　Esther, 16:211; 17:197; 19:37; 20:94
　Hannah, 20:24-26
　John, 18:96
　Jonathan, 17:198; 18:25; 20:25-28, 94, 95
　Joseph, 19:145; 20:27, 94
　Lydia, 20:27
　Mary, 20:95
　Mary (Allin), 20:94
　Nicene, 18:96
　Patience, 17:198; 20:27
　Patience (Alley), 18:25; 20:26
　Patience (Gaskill), 20:26, 27, 94, 95
　Paul, 18:96
　Polly (Estes), 18:96
　Rebecca (Baker), 20:27, 28
　Rebecca (Trask), 19:145; 20:94

　Samuel, 18:11, 12
　Sarah, 20:94
　Sarah (Meacham), 20:27, 94
　Susannah (Bacon), 20:94
BOYD see BOYT
BOYDELL
　John, 17:94
BOYDEN
　Joanna (Mower), 17:44
　Joseph, 16:77
　Judith, 16:77
　Martha, 20:41
　William, 17:44
BOYER, 17:14; 19:116, 220
　Carl, 18:67
　Paul, 20:168
BOYINTON
　Caleb, 16:19
BOYLE/BOYLES
　Catharine, 19:179
　Jonathan, 20:198
　Robert, 20:64
BOYLSTON
　Abigail, 19:103
　Jerusha (Minot), 19:157
　Mary (Coates), 19:157
　Thomas, 19:157
　Zabdiel, 19:157
BOYNTON, 17:141; 18:132
　___, Mrs., 17:11
　Altaserah (Goodwin), 20:107
　Ann Lummas, 20:108
　Asa, 16:211
　Benjamin, 17:12
　Benjamin Franklin, 20:108
　Caroline, 20:107, 108
　Caroline Augusta, 20:108
　David, 20:108
　Elesibeth (Wood), 17:152
　George Pickering, 20:108
　Georgianna (Berry), 20:108
　Hannah, 17:83
　Hannah (Barney), 18:165
　Hannah (Collins), 20:106, 107
　Hannah (Humphries), 20:106-108
　Harriet J. (Hutchings), 20:108
　Johannah, 17:83
　Jonathan, 17:152
　Joseph, 17:12
　Joshua, 18:165
　Josiah C., 20:108
　Lucy Ann (Noyes), 20:107, 108
　Martha E., 20:109
　Martha Ellen, 20:108, 109
　Mary, 16:180; 20:106, 107
　Mary (Edmunds), 16:211
　Mary R., 20:108
　Nathaniel, 20:106-109
　Pickering, 20:106, 107
　Pickering Collins, 20:108
　Richard, 20:106-108
　Richard M., 20:108
　Sally, 20:106, 107, 109
　Sarah (___), 20:221
　Sarah D. (Thompson), 20:108
　Susan, 20:106, 107
　Susan (___), 20:107
　Susannah (Williams), 20:106
　William, 20:107
　William Pickering, 20:108
BOYT/BOIT/BOYD
　John, 18:75
　Rebecca (Peck), 18:75

BRACKENBURY
　Ellen, 16:137
　Richard, 16:137
BRACKETT
　Abigail (___), 20:176
　Herbert I., 20:176
　Joshua, 20:176
　Mary Jane, 17:120
　Sarah Weeks, 20:176
BRADBURY see also BREDBURY, 16:13
　Charles, 20:145
　George T., 19:19
　Helen (Marland), 19:19
　Mary, 20:45
　Mary (Perkins), 16:17
　Paul, 17:58
　Ruth (Ware/Weare), 17:58
　Theophilus, 19:161
BRADDRICK
　Martha, 16:132
BRADFORD
　___, Gov., 16:200
　Charity, 18:105; 19:148
　John, 17:20
　Rachel, 18:85
　Robert, 20:198
　Samuel, 20:201
　Sarah (Henley), 19:103
　Thomas, 17:11
　William, 19:103, 126; 20:198
BRADHURST
　Dorothy, 16:116
　Hannah (Gore), 16:116
　Ralph, 16:116
BRADLEY
　Abbey/Abina/Gobinet, 18:177
　Anna (How), 19:234
　Apphia, 17:152
　Benjamin, 17:152; 19:234
　Daniel, 16:75; 17:55; 19:234
　Esther, 18:25
　Isaac, 19:234
　Jeremiah, 19:234
　Jonah, 18:25
　Jonathan, 19:96
　Joseph, 19:234
　Judith, 19:234
　Mary, 17:54
　Mary (Williams), 17:55
　Nehemiah, 19:234
　Rachel (Atwater), 18:25
　Rebecca (Berry), 16:75
　Sarah, 19:234
　Sarah (Noyes), 19:234
BRADSHAW
　Elizabeth, 18:151
　George D., 20:40
　Mary/Polly (Bancroft), 20:40
　Stephen, 17:113
BRADSTREET, 18:134; 19:94
　___, Col., 19:34
　___, Dr., 19:32
　___, Gov., 19:75
　___, Mr., 16:72; 18:231; 19:34
　Anne (___), 16:65
　Anne (Dudley), 17:193; 18:193
　Dorothy, 17:193
　Dudley, 16:65, 66, 68; 18:157; 20:164, 168, 214
　James Dudley, 16:209
　Mary, 17:80
　Sarah, 18:193

Simon, 16:65, 164, 166, 168; 17:193; 18:193, 230; 19:188, 191, 192, 197, 202; 20:19, 23, 189, 214
BRAGDON
Alice (Parson), 17:223
Blanche, 17:223
Daniel, 19:165
Fred, 17:223
Hannah, 16:104
Lester MacKenzie, 16:104
Sally (Hatch), 19:165
Sarah Ann, 19:165
BRAGG
Ann (Parker), 19:91
Anne (___), 19:91
Catherine, 19:150
Edward, 18:164; 19:91
Elizabeth (Roberts), 18:164
Joab, 20:239
John, 19:91
Lydia (Brann), 20:239
Mary (Bridges), 19:91
Rebekah (___), 20:47
Sarah (___), 18:164
Sarah (Shores), 20:239
Sarah Shores, 20:239
Timothy, 20:142
William, 20:239
BRAILSFORD, 16:13
BRAINERD
Lawrence, 16:174
BRAME
Anna, 16:95
BRAN see also BRANN
Sarah, 20:48
BRAND
Harriet, 17:107
Thaddeus, 19:145
BRANDON
John C., 20:94
BRANN see also BRAN
Lydia, 20:239
BRANSON
George, 18:230
BRANT
___, Chief, 17:127
BRATTLE
Edward, 17:214; 20:15
Mary, 17:214
Mary (Legg), 17:214
Sarah, 18:225
Thomas, 17:91; 19:133; 20:97
BRAUER
Robert John, 20:148
Shirley Anne (Tarbox), 20:148
BRAULT
Anne, 20:169
Claude (De Cheorainville), 20:169
Henri, 20:169
BRAY, 17:220
Betsey, 18:205
Eli, 17:221
Enoch, 17:223
Hannah, 17:56; 20:119
John, 18:37, 179; 20:200
Lucy (Tilton), 17:223
Mary (Lewis), 18:37
Mary (Wilson), 17:236
Nathaniel, 20:200
Rachel, 20:59
Sarah, 17:236; 20:43
Sarah E. (Dennen), 17:221
Thomas, 17:11

BRAZIER
J., 16:43
BREAD see also BREED
Allin, 19:138
BREADAN see also BREEDEN, BREDON, BREADDINE
Mary, 19:37
BREADDINE see also BREADAN, BREDON, BREEDEN
Elizabeth (Marshall), 19:82
Joseph, 19:82
BREAM
John, 20:199
BREAN see also BREEN
Mary, 17:21; 20:134, 137, 237
BRECKENBANK
Elizabeth, 20:212
BREDANE
Brian, 17:89
BREDBURY see also BRADBURY, 16:13
BREDEAN
Samuel, 18:115
BREDON see BREADDINE, BREADAN, 19:80
BREED see also BREAD, 18:132, 133, 135, 210
Abigail, 16:96; 17:150; 18:32, 36, 53
Abigail (Allen), 16:236
Abigail (Alley), 18:27
Abigail (Blaney), 16:236
Abigail (Breed), 18:32, 36
Abigail (Collins), 16:224; 18:36
Abigail (Hodgdon), 16:224
Abigail (Lindsey), 16:29
Abigail Phillips, 16:224
Abraham, 18:35
Alice, 18:36
Allen, 16:29, 163; 17:19; 18:23, 36, 53, 71-73, 132, 137, 147, 170, 171; 19:25, 29, 108; 20:30, 31, 53, 100, 103, 132, 134, 135, 137, 194, 196
Allen Blaney, 16:236
Amos, 16:16; 18:36, 53, 97; 20:212
Amy, 18:11
Andrews Blaney, 16:23
Anna, 18:31, 36, 53
Anna (Hood), 18:31, 36
Anna (Rolls), 17:218
Anna (Smith), 18:105
Anne/Anna (Hood), 17:216; 18:53
Annie (Hood), 18:15, 16
Archer F., 16:111
Barney, 20:31
Benjamin, 16:16; 18:27, 31, 53, 54, 92
Benjamin, 18:92
Bevil, 20:31
Christopher, 20:31, 53
Cornelia, 16:224
Daniel, 16:224; 18:15, 36
Deborah, 18:27, 32, 97
Delia, 20:53
Deliverance, 17:149
Deliverance (Bassett), 18:15, 16, 31, 36, 52, 53, 104
Desire, 18:93
Desire (___), 18:27, 93
Desire (Bassett), 18:27, 35, 36, 53
Dorothea, 16:111
Ebenezer, 16:16; 18:35, 37, 53, 55, 93, 97, 98; 19:47
Edith H. (Gove), 18:15
Elizabeth, 16:16; 17:145; 18:11, 105, 149, 168, 170, 171; 19:27

Elizabeth (___), 16:71; 18:71-73
Elizabeth (Ballard), 17:146; 18:170, 171, 20:135
Elizabeth (Phillips), 18:36
Elizabeth (Sunderland), 18:53
Elizabeth (Wheeler), 16:173
Emma Bell, 16:171
Enoch, 18:36
Ephraim, 18:24, 173
Eunice, 17:160; 18:93, 98; 19:237
Eunice (Souther), 17:218
Evelyn Augusta, 16:236
Ezra, 18:32, 36, 214
Francis, 19:47
Frederick, 16:70; 19:76
Geoffrey R., 17:86
George, 16:171; 20:53
George Herbert, 18:15
George Herschel, 16:111
Gershom, 16:171; 20:30, 31, 53
Hannah, 17:41; 18:11, 36, 93, 97; 20:30, 53
Hannah (___), 20:30
Hannah (Alley), 18:22, 25
Hannah (Bassett), 18:35
Hannah (Estes), 18:31, 36, 93
Hannah (Palmer), 20:31, 53
Hannah (Wing), 16:224
Hannah N., 20:53
Henry, 20:31
Hepzibah, 16:47; 19:107, 148
Hulda (___), 16:45
Hulda (Newhall), 20:100
Huldah, 16:29; 18:32, 36
Huldah (Breed), 18:32, 36
Huldah (Newhall), 16:47; 17:145
Isaac, 20:31
Isabella, 16:111
Isaiah, 18:12, 31, 36, 93
J. Howard, 20:53
Jabez, 16:16; 18:15, 27, 36, 53, 93
James, 16:16; 18:11, 22, 25, 35; 19:237; 20:53
Jane, 17:145; 20:42
Jane (Newhall), 16:47
Jerusha, 18:22
John, 16:47; 17:51; 18:36, 54, 75, 111, 113; 20:31, 135, 196
Jonathan, 16:224; 18:172, 210
Joseph, 16:101; 17:145; 18:213, 226; 19:148; 20:196
Josiah, 18:172
Kezia (___), 18:22
Kezia/Keziah, 16:16; 17:172; 18:53, 54, 97, 98
Kezia/Keziah (Buxton), 18:25, 27, 36, 105
Leroy, 20:31
Liddia (Gott), 20:135
Lois, 18:25, 93
Lydia, 16:97
Lydia (Bassett), 18:37, 55
Lydia (Johnson), 16:224
Lydia (Mower), 18:93; 19:107
Lydia N., 20:53
Martha, 16:47
Martha (Newhall), 19:148
Mary, 16:29; 17:42; 18:36, 93, 98, 173; 20:42, 53
Mary (___), 17:218; 18:53, 98
Mary (Bassett), 16:222; 17:41; 18:35, 36, 53
Mary (Kirtland), 17:47; 18:111, 113
Mary (Newhall), 19:148
Mary (Sargent), 18:132, 137

Mary (Stocker), 17:145
Mary E., 18:11, 12
Mary Elizabeth (Osborne), 16:236
Mathew, 17:145
Mehitable, 17:145; 18:23
Mercy, 17:145; 19:148
Mercy (Palmer), 16:171; 17:51
Molly (Chase), 16:224
Moses, 18:11, 93
Nancy, 16:171
Nathan, 16:16; 17:41; 18:11-13, 21, 22, 25, 27, 32, 36, 53, 105
Nathaniel, 18:21; 19:67
Nehemiah, 16:16; 18:15, 32, 35, 36
Newhall, 18:11
Noyes, 20:53
Palmer, 20:53
Rebecca, 18:97, 149, 168, 171
Rebecca (Bassett), 18:35; 19:237
Rebecca (Phillips), 16:156; 18:35, 53
Richard, 18:105; 19:47
Robert Thompson, 16:111
Robert Thomson, 17:86
Ruth, 16:16; 17:145; 18:25, 53, 92, 97, 172, 227
Ruth (___), 18:54, 210
Ruth (Allen), 18:31, 92
Ruth (Estes), 18:97; 20:212
Ruth (Haynes/Hooper), 18:172
Ruth (Newhall), 18:36
Ruth (Phillips), 16:224; 18:36
Samuel, 17:216; 18:15, 16, 29, 31, 36, 52-54, 92, 108; 19:237
Sarah, 16:16; 17:51; 18:11, 31, 36, 38, 53, 54, 104, 105, 113; 29:226; 20:48, 205
Sarah (Alley), 18:27, 32, 36
Sarah (Bassett), 18:35
Sarah (Bran), 20:48
Sarah (Farr), 19:29
Sarah (Farrington), 17:145; 19:148
Sarah (Hathorn), 18:54, 113
Sarah (Newhall), 17:218
Sarah (Norwood), 18:210
Sarah Ellen, 16:111
Scotty, 20:53
Shubael, 16:171
Susannah (Newhall), 17:145
Theodate, 18:36
Theophilus, 17:158; 18:11; 19:148
Thomas, 19:29; 20:31, 53
Timothy, 17:217; 19:29; 20:48, 196
Van Rensselaer, 20:53
Walter, 18:97
William, 17:151; 18:11, 15, 32, 35, 97; 20:31, 53
William N., 18:15
Zephaniah, 16:224; 18:36
BREEDEN/BRIDEAN see also BREADAN
Elizabeth (Edmunds), 16:211
Elnathan, 17:25
Samuel, 16:211
BREEN see also BREAN, 20:137
Helen, 18:135, 136, 138
Helen Gallagher, 18:136
Mary, 20:105
BREHAUT
Ellerton J., 19:16
BRENNER
William, 17:64
William/Wolf, 17:66
BREWER/BREUR
___, Col., 18:106
Abigail, 19:77-79
Anna, 19:77
Crispus, 19:48, 77-80; 20:135, 206, 207
Daniel, 19:120
Elizabeth, 19:77, 79, 106, 239; 20:207, 210
Elizabeth (Graves), 19:79, 156, 20:206
Hannah, 19:47-49, 79, 120; 20:21, 23
Hannah (Perkins), 17:148
John, 19:79, 156; 20:206
Margaret, 18:173
Mary, 19:77, 79; 20:206
Mary (___), 19:48, 77, 79, 80; 20:207
Mary (Coats), 19:79, 155, 156; 20:206
Rebecca, 19:79, 80; 20:206
Sarah, 16:156; 19:77, 79, 156; 20:205, 207
Susanna, 16:171
Thomas, 19:77-79, 156; 20:196, 206
BREWSTER
William, 16:120a; 19:175
BRIAN
Lydia (Herrick), 20:152
BRIANT see also BRYANT
Abigail, 17:59
Alice (___), 17:59
Anna, 20:151
Benjamin, 20:150, 151, 155
Betsey, 20:151
Caroline (Johnson), 20:153
Charlotte (Safford), 20:153
Edward Payson, 20:153
Elizabeth (Ober), 20:150
Emily Judson, 20:153, 158
James, 20:150-158, 161
John, 17:59; 18:216; 20:58, 150
John Groves, 20:151
John Ober, 20:153, 159
Jonathan, 20:151
Lydea (English), 20:151
Lydia (Herrick), 20:151, 153, 154, 157
Margaret (Smith), 20:58
Mary (Herrick), 20:151, 153, 154
Mehitable, 19:214
Nancy, 16:100
Rebecca, 20:151
Samuel I., 20:154
Samuel Ingersoll, 20:150, 153, 154, 156, 158, 159, 162
Sara (Hoyt), 20:151
Sarah, 20:154, 155, 157
Sarah (Bancroft), 19:214
Sarah (Strickland), 20:151, 152, 157
Sarah Ellen, 20:152, 156
William, 20:151
BRIARS
John, 20:199
BRICK
Elinor, 18:38
BRICKETT
James, 16:146
Susannah, 16:146
Susannah (Pillsbury), 16:146
BRIDEAN see BREEDEN
BRIDGE
Francis, 18:107
BRIDGES, 19:154
___, Capt., 18:114, 115, 147; 19:44, 192; 20:187, 188, 191
___, Mr., 17:213
___, Mrs., 20:188
Alice (Milinton), 17:178
Daniel, 16:235; 18:219
Edmond/Edmund, 17:178; 19:30; 20:195
Edward, 19:138
Eleanor, 19:35
Elizabeth (___), 17:178
Elizabeth (Kingsbury), 18:155, 157
Hannah (___), 16:85
James, 16:68; 18:155, 159, 161, 162; 19:32
John, 16:68; 17:80; 18:163
Mary, 18:41; 19:91, 221
Mary (Langton), 17:178
Mary (Tyler), 19:221
Moody, 18:163
Obadiah, 18:157
Patience, 16:235; 18:219, 220
Robert, 16:162; 17:89; 18:40, 230; 20:187, 188, 191
Sarah, 17:22; 19:221
Sarah (___), 18:159
Sarah (Estabrook), 17:80
Sarah (Towne), 19:221
Thankful (Jellison), 16:235; 18:219
BRIDGMAN
Lewis F., 17:225
Thomas, 17:87
BRIDLEY
John, 20:42
Sarah (Bowditch), 20:42
BRIER
Jacob, 16:133
BRIERLEY, 16:13
BRIGGS
Aroline (Haddock), 16:148
Ebenezer, 16:148
George W., 17:110
L. V., 18:90
Sarah, 20:56
BRIGHAM
Dinah, 18:170
Edward, 19:80
John, 18:175
Mercy, 18:175
Sarah (Davis), 18:175
Sarah (Liscom), 19:80
BRIGHT
Nathaniel, 18:158, 237
BRIMBLECOM/BRIMBLECOMB
Polly, 20:43
Sarah, 16:81
BRIMSDILL
Dinah, 18:213
BRINEY
M. E., Mrs., 16:49
BRINSDELL
Dinah, 18:177
BRINSDON/BRONSDON, 18:133, 137
Robert, 16:28; 17:92; 18:74, 76
BRINTNALL
Abigail, 16:237
Esther (___), 16:237
Hester (Carpenter), 16:237
James, 18:34
John, 16:208; 18:34, 209; 19:228; 20:103, 113
Mary (Bassett), 18:34
Phoebe (Smith), 18:34
Samuel, 16:237
Thomas, 16:237
BRINTNESS
George, 16:91
Mary (Wellman), 16:91
BRISCOE
Mary, 18:101
BRISCOMB
Eliza, 18:237
BRISTO, 17:42

BRISTOL
   Theresa Hall, 18:190
BRITON/BRITTAN/BRITTON
   Edward, 16:26
   Hannah (Felt), 16:26
   Lydia, 18:81
   Phillip, 20:103
   Ruth (Parker), 16:38
   Samuel, 16:38
BROADBENT, 16:13
BROCK
   ___, Rev., 20:192
   Albie E., 17:170
   Edward, 17:159
   Elizabeth, 18:41
   Ellen (Friend), 17:170
   Esther (Newhall), 17:159
   John, 16:64; 18:41
   Margaret (Larrabee), 20:46
   Walter Adams, 17:170
BROCKETT
   Hannah Sketh (Alley), 18:25
   Munson, 18:25
BROCKLEBANK
   John, 17:140
   Samuel, 16:199; 17:140
BROCKWAY
   Abigail, 18:88
   Asa, 17:116
   Chloe (Giddings), 18:88
   Elice, 17:116
   Hebsibah (Hodgman), 17:116
   Jonathan, 17:116
   Lorany, 18:88
   Phebe (Smith), 17:116
BRODERICK, 19:162
   Carlfred/Calfred B., 18:48; 19:154
BROGIS
   Edward, 19:30
BRONSDEN/BRONSDON see BRINSDON
BROOK/BROOKE
   ___, Lord, 20:98, 183, 194
   Robert, 20:187
BROOKHOUSE
   Jn. F., 20:158
   R., 20:157-159
   Robert, 20:161
BROOKINGS
   Abner, 17:119
   Anna (Reeves/Revis), 17:119
   Fanny, 17:119
   Henry, 17:119
   James, 17:119
   John, 17:119
   Josiah, 17:119
   Lucy, 17:119
   Luther, 17:119
   Lydia, 20:145, 149
   Molly, 17:119
   Samuel, 17:119
   Sarah, 17:119
   Susanna, 17:119
BROOKS
   ___, Lord, 19:138; 20:187
   Abigail, 18:205
   Abigail (Boylston), 19:103
   Ann (Dixey), 16:119
   Benjamin, 20:40
   Ebenezer, 19:103
   Edmund, 16:58
   Edward, 16:151
   Eleazar, 16:144
   Elizabeth, 18:148

Esther (Stetson), 17:59
Eunice, 16:225
Hannah, 17:84; 19:41, 103, 104
John, 16:119; 20:221
Martha/Patty, 18:205
Mary (Norwood), 18:207
Mary (Pearce), 16:58
Mary (Skilling), 16:119
Mary Dandridge (Bancroft), 20:40
Mary White (Carstairs), 16:151
Nathan, 20:99
Noah, 17:59
Olive Hodgdon, 20:149
Reuben, 18:207
Richard, 19:138; 20:195
Ruth, 16:83
Sarah (Wyman), 20:99
William, 16:119
BROUGHALL
   John, 17:58
   Mary (___), 17:58
BROUGHTON
   ___, Mr., 20:187
   Thomas, 16:163
BROUNAFF
   Bridget, 19:153
BROWN see also BROWNE, BOMER,
   18:184; 20:118
   ___, Capt., 19:217
   Abigail, 16:59; 17:180; 18:43, 45, 117, 215
   Abigail (Brown), 16:59; 17:180
   Abigail (Davis), 17:180
   Abigail (Kimball), 18:166
   Abigail H., 17:162
   Abigail Hinds (Reed), 17:38
   Abraham, 17:53
   Aileen May (Longfellow), 16:51
   Andrew, 20:145
   Ann Louise (Smith), 17:208
   Anna, 16:221; 17:44
   Anna (Burnap), 19:148
   Aphia, 17:240
   Augustus, 19:120
   Benjamin, 17:158; 18:226, 228; 19:120
   Bert, 16:51
   Betsey, 16:47
   Betty, 19:83, 169
   Beulah, 16:83
   Beulah (Bassett), 18:39
   Bridget (Bateman), 16:59
   Caleb, 17:235
   Catherine (Parker), 16:40
   Charles Erastus, 17:117
   Cyrus Henry, 18:222
   Daniel, 18:47, 70, 225, 228; 19:177; 20:82, 103
   David, 17:178
   Deborah, 16:82
   Deborah (Holdredge), 16:55
   Deborah (Tarbox), 20:146
   Dorcas, 18:42, 43; 19:35
   Dorcas (___), 18:43
   Dorcas (Prisbury), 18:227
   Dorothy, 16:55
   Dorothy (Davis), 16:59
   Ebenezer, 16:40; 18:212, 223, 225
   Edith, 17:240
   Edmond, 16:221
   Edward, 17:47; 20:89
   Eleazer, 17:101; 18:240
   Eli, 20:221
   Elijah, 19:170
   Elisha, 17:11

Eliza, 16:47
Elizabeth, 17:139; 18:166; 19:144
Elizabeth (Bancroft), 19:213
Elizabeth (Shepherd), 17:53
Ellen/Helen (O'Connor), 18:177
Ephraim, 16:209; 18:226; 19:106
Esther (Merriam), 18:228
Ezekiel, 17:180
Ezra, 16:99; 18:226; 19:106
Frances J. (Edmands), 17:30
George, 18:156
Ginger (Osborn), 17:199
Goold, 18:11
Hannah, 16:117; 17:199; 18:44, 206; 19:31, 151, 161; 20:219
Hannah (___), 16:216
Hannah (Collins), 16:55
Hannah (House), 20:240
Hannah (Ramsdell), 19:177
Hannah (Scott), 16:209
Harriett (Shorey), 19:120
Herbert, 20:172
Hulda, 18:220
Ira, 20:31
Isaiah, 16:59; 17:180
James, 17:134; 18:177, 206, 226; 20:146, 240
James Phillips, 16:224
Jane, 20:46
Jeremiah, 19:148
Jerusha, 18:228
John, 16:93; 17:19; 18:39, 76, 225, 226, 240; 19:32, 106, 216; 20:36, 111-113, 190, 218, 240
John H., 18:177
Jonathan, 16:44; 17:118; 18:218, 226
Joseph, 16:133; 17:101; 18:43; 221, 227, 228; 19:177, 213, 214; 20:48, 113
Josephine Ann Hurin (Edwards), 17:27
Josiah, 19:137; 20:36, 199
Judith, 16:57
Lemuel, 18:70
Lucy, 17:227
Luna (Howes), 20:172
Luther, 18:177
Lydia, 17:177
Lydia (___), 19:106
Lydia (Buckland), 18:112
Lydia (Mansfield), 18:212
Lydia (Phillips), 16:221
Margaret, 17:28
Margaret (___), 18:78
Margaret (Hayward), 17:139
Margaret (Smith), 18:225, 228; 19:177
Marion, 18:177
Marjorie E., 20:171, 172
Martha, 16:72; 20:240
Martha (___), 18:227
Martha (Gray), 16:83
Martha (Mansfield), 18:227
Mary, 16:156; 17:53; 18:36, 55, 225; 19:31, 145; 20:46, 113
Mary (___), 19:148
Mary (Fellows), 17:19
Mary (Huse), 16:222
Mary (Mason), 17:235
Mary (Newhall), 16:56
Mary (Paul), 20:113
Mary (Phillips), 16:224
Mary (Porter), 16:179; 17:240
Mary (Webber), 20:145
Mary Friend (Marchant), 17:34
Mary Jane, 17:235

Mary/Polly, 20:145
Massa, 18:96
Mehitable, 20:229, 233
Mercy, 20:240
Mercy P., 19:170, 172
Miriam, 16:222
Miriam (___), 16:222
Nathan, 16:79
Nathaniel, 16:72; 17:199
Nicholas, 20:184, 186, 191, 194
Paliatiah, 16:216
Peter, 18:226
Phoebe, 18:112
Rachel, 16:176; 19:102
Rachel (___), 17:178
Rebecca (Hoyt), 17:235
Rebecca Elizabeth (Symonds), 17:117
Rebeckah (White), 16:79
Richard, 16:99; 18:235, 236
Rufus, 18:226; 19:106
Ruth, 16:179
Ruth Burrill, 17:41
Sally, 17:33; 18:212; 19:177
Sally (Burnham), 17:36
Sally (Northey), 19:170
Sally/Sarah (Peabody), 18:177
Samuel, 16:179; 17:240; 18:78; 19:148
Sarah, 17:47; 20:35, 178
Sarah (___), 19:32
Sarah (Bartol), 18:225
Sarah (Brattle), 18:225
Sarah (Dix), 17:47; 18:102
Sarah (Graves), 20:221
Sarah (Ingalls), 17:47; 19:106
Sarah (Jenks), 16:72
Sarah A., 19:238
Sarah Collins (Hill), 17:118
Sarah Elizabeth, 17:117
Sarah/Sally, 16:216
Simeon, 20:117
Stephen, 16:222; 17:36
Stephen B., 18:134, 135
Susan (Norwood), 18:206
Susannah, 17:240; 18:27, 78; 19:109, 148
Thankful (___), 17:44
Theodore, 17:34
Theophilus, 17:235
Thomas, 16:55; 18:166, 225, 227; 19:120; 20:113
Timothy, 16:59
Walter E., 17:208
William, 16:83; 17:15; 19:120, 143
BROWNE see also BROWN, 20:48
  "Child", 18:228
  "Son", 19:215
  Abigail, 16:81; 19:48
  Ann, 17:47; 18:224
  Ann (Pendleton), 18:224
  Anna (Downing), 18:228
  Anna (Twiss), 18:226
  Anne, 18:40
  Augustus, 17:157
  Benjamin, 16:153; 18:227, 228
  Catharine (Winthrop), 16:81
  Catherine (Berry), 18:227
  Christopher, 20:198
  Daniel, 18:223, 224
  Dorcas (Gould), 19:215
  Dorcas (Prisbury), 18:225, 228
  Dorothy, 17:143
  Dorothy (Pike), 19:48
  Easter, 19:48
  Ebenezer, 18:223, 224, 227, 228; 19:215
  Edith (___), 19:32
  Edward, 17:48; 19:48; 20:140
  Eleazer, 16:79; 18:222-224
  Elizabeth, 17:157; 18:228; 19:215
  Elizabeth (___), 19:215
  Elizabeth (Bancroft), 19:215
  Elizabeth (Hutchinson), 18:227
  Elizabeth (Miner), 18:224
  Elizabeth (Young), 18:228
  Eme, 17:220
  Ephraim, 18:225-227
  Ester, 18:228
  Grace, 18:224
  Hannah, 17:41; 18:226, 227; 19:32
  Hannah (Collins), 18:224
  Hannah (Ramsdell), 18:228
  Hephsabeth, 19:215
  James, 16:91; 18:227, 228
  Jane (Stocker), 18:227
  John, 17:151; 18:60a, 222-228, ; 19:213; 20:214
  Jonathan, 18:224, 227
  Joseph, 18:222-225; 19:215; 20:196
  Lydia (Burrill), 18:227
  Margaret, 18:228
  Martha, 17:147; 18:73
  Martha (___), 18:225
  Martha (Mansfield), 18:228
  Mary, 16:79; 18:199, 208, 224-228; 19:32, 229
  Mary (Hull/Hall), 18:225
  Mary (King), 18:227
  Mary (Mansfield), 18:227
  Mary (Newhall), 18:208, 222, 223
  Mary (Paul), 18:225
  Mary (Rhoads), 18:228
  Mary (Salter), 18:224
  Nathan, 19:48
  Nathaniel, 18:208
  Nicholas, 16:71; 17:48; 18:41, 133, 230; 19:48, 138, 215; 20:183, 189, 190
  Peter, 18:227
  Rachel, 18:226, 227; 19:48
  Rebecca (Morse), 19:48
  Rebecca (Nichols), 19:215
  Richard, 18:227; 19:32
  Rufus, 18:226
  Sally, 18:228
  Sally (___), 18:226
  Samuel, 16:81; 18:90, 208, 228
  Sarah, 16:84; 18:224-228; 19:48
  Sarah (Dix), 17:48; 19:48
  Sarah (Ingalls), 17:48; 19:48
  Sarah (Jones/Joans), 18:224, 225
  Sarah (Putnam), 16:79
  Sarah (Stocker), 18:228
  Solomon, 18:228
  Tabitha, 19:215
  Thomas, 17:17; 18:208, 222-228; 19:211, 215; 20:196
  William, 17:89; 18:93, 227, 228; 19:190; 20:15, 204, 205
  William B., 19:160
BROWNELL
  Joseph, 18:91, 92
  Ruth (Cornell), 18:91
BRUCE
  David, 16:83
  Elizabeth, 19:158
  Hannah, 16:83
  Hannah (Blaney), 16:83
  Jane, 16:83
  John, 18:168; 19:147
  Jonathan, 16:83
  Mary (Potter), 18:168; 19:147
  Robert, 17:134
  Ronald, 16:83
  Sarah (Chapman), 16:83
  William, 16:83
BRUEN
  Obadiah, 20:18
BRUER see BREWER
BRUIJN
  Elise De, 18:133
BRUMMAGE
  Katherine, 18:16
BRUNO, 16:123
BRUSH
  John Woolman, 16:189
BRY
  Alfred, 16:152
BRYANT see also BRIANT
  Abraham, 19:214; 20:150
  Anna, 18:212
  Calvin S., 19:178
  Elizabeth (___), 16:120; 18:227
  James, 18:226; 20:113
  John, 16:94; 18:212, 216
  Jonathan, 18:212
  Joseph, 18:227
  Mabel (Russell), 19:178
  Margaret (Smith), 18:212
  Mary (Larrabee), 18:226
  Mary (Whitney), 16:120
  Mary Frances (Zecchini), 19:178
  Mercy, 19:156
  Mercy (___), 20:213
  Richard, 16:120
  Russell E., 19:178
  Sally (Brown), 18:212
  Sarah, 18:97, 212
  Sarah (Norwood), 18:212
  Thomas, 19:156; 20:206, 213
BUBIER
  Christopher, 18:212; 19:230, 233
  Joanna (Bubier), 18:212
  Margaret (Levallier), 19:230
  Mary, 18:37
  Sarah, 19:230
BUBUR
  Sarah, 16:84
BUCK
  Abigail (Wyman), 20:99
  Azuba, 19:178
  Isaac, 20:208, 209, 211
  Mehitable, 20:26
  Ruth (___), 20:208, 209
  Ruth (Graves), 20:211
  Samuel, 20:99
  Susanna, 18:158
BUCKINGHAM
  Temperance, 18:113
BUCKLAND
  Lydia, 18:112
BUCKLEY, 16:4
  John, 16:132
  Mary, 20:29, 99, 100
  Michael, 20:128
  Sarah (Smith), 20:100
  William, 20:100
BUCKMAN
  Benjamin, 18:228
  Ester (Browne), 18:228
  Hannah (Wayte), 19:215
  William, 19:215

BUCKMINSTER
Joseph, 16:75
BUCKNAM
Abigail, 16:29
Abigail (Cheever), 19:104
Deborah (Sprague), 16:81
Elizabeth, 16:172
Isaiah, 18:169
Mary (Dike), 18:169
Samuel, 16:81
William, 19:104
BUCKNELL
Sarah, 16:120
Sarah (Whidden), 16:120
William, 16:120
BUEL
Rosaling Hannett, 16:110
BUFFAM see BUFFUM, 17:183; 18:93
BUFFINGTON
Benjamin, 20:93
Hannah, 18:100
Hannah (Buffum), 20:93
BUFFUM/BUFFAM
Abigail, 17:199
Anna (___), 18:22, 25
Benjamin, 17:198; 20:93
Caleb, 16:26, 117; 17:186, 197; 18:90, 91, 96; 20:27, 92, 93
David, 17:198
Deborah, 20:99
Elizabeth, 17:200; 20:27
Elizabeth (Burrell), 16:26; 20:27, 93
Elizabeth (Buxton), 17:198; 20:93
Elizabeth (Estes), 17:197
Elizabeth (Farrar), 16:26; 17:173; 20:27, 93
Hanna (Breed), 18:11
Hannah, 16:117; 17:186, 198; 20:27, 93
Hannah (Gaskill), 18:96
Hannah (Pope), 16:26, 117; 20:27, 92, 93
Israel, 16:47
James, 16:26; 17:198; 20:27
Jedediah, 17:198; 18:97
John Henry, 19:171
Jonathan, 16:78; 17:198; 18:11, 22, 25, 94, 218; 20:93, 95
Joseph, 18:11; 17:198; 20:27, 93
Joshua, 17:197; 18:218, 240; 19:216; 20:78, 79
Marcy, 18:22
Margaret, 16:155; 17:198
Margaret (___), 18:11
Margaret (Osborn), 17:198
Mary (Gaskill), 20:93, 95
Mercy, 18:25
Mercy (Thrasher), 20:93
Moses, 18:96
Olive (Gaskill), 18:97
Rebecca Maria (Northey), 19:171
Richard, 17:198
Robert, 16:26, 117; 17:173; 20:25, 27, 78, 79, 92-94
Ruthy (Oliver), 16:47
Samuel, 16:88
Sarah, 16:26; 18:53; 10:25, 27
Sarah (Blaney), 16:26; 20:25, 27, 93, 94
Sarah (Gaskill), 18:96
Sarah (Hacker), 20:27
Susanna, 17:200
Susanna (Southwick), 16:26; 20:93
Tamer (Gaskill), 18:96
Tamoson, 20:93
Thomasine (Ward), 16:117; 20:92
William, 17:198

BULBIE
Richard, 20:199
BULKE see BALKE
BULKLEY
Mary, 16:42
BULL, 16:36
Elizabeth (Pedrick), 16:36
Mary (Cheever), 19:37
Thomas, 19:37
BULLARD see also BALLARD
Sybil, 16:236
BULLOCK
Henry, 19:197
John, 17:196; 18:133
Mary (___), 18:133
Richard, 20:124
BULLY
Elizabeth, 16:211
BULMORE
Mary, 17:175
Mary (Godfrey), 17:175
Patrick, 17:175
BULOW
Sarah, 18:201
BUNKER
Betty (Lewis), 18:221
Patience (Eaton), 18:221
Thomas, 18:221
BURACK/BURAK
Chana (___), 17:67
Morris, 17:67
Samuel, 17:67
BURBANK, 17:140
Ebenezer, 18:10
Hannah, 18:10
Mary, 18:10
Mercy, 17:116
Sarah (Hardy), 18:10
BURCH
Mary, 18:36, 203
BURCHAM
Edward, 16:163; 18:72; 19:45, 138; 20:190, 194
BURCHSTEAD/BURCHSTED, 18:104
___, Dr., 16:79; 18:16, 36, 97; 20:211
Anna, 16:97
Anna (___), 17:219
Anna (Brame), 16:95
Anna (Potter), 16:29; 19:150, 151
Benjamin, 18:226
Benjamin B., 18:26
Benjamin Brame/Bream, 16:95; 17:41; 18:21, 24, 214
Elizabeth (Newhall), 16:47; 19:151
Frederick, 19:151
Henry, 16:29, 78; 17:147; 18:21; 19:150, 151; 20:140
Joanna, 16:95
Joanna (Newhall), 16:47
John H., 18:14, 15
John Henry, 16:29; 18:112, 133
Katherine, 16:95, 96, 221
Mary, 17:219; 19:151
Mary (Rand), 18:112
Rebecca, 16:95
Ruthey, 16:16
Sarah, 16:96; 19:151
Sarah (James), 16:95; 19:151
Winthrop Alexander, 18:133
BURDEN see also BOWDEN
George, 18:230
Joseph, 19:149
Lidia (Collins), 19:149

BURDETT, 18:197
BURDICK
Lucinda, 20:219
BURDITT
Jemima, 19:178
BUREK
Catherine, 19:57
BURGER
Robert, 20:196
BURGES/BURGESS/BURGIS, 16:175
Anna (Richards), 16:99
Betty, 16:9
Elizabeth, 16:204
James, 16:99
Margaret, 16:9
Robert, 16:164, 196; 18:222; 19:146; 20:133
Sarah (___), 16:206
BURGOYNE, 17:5
BURILL see BURRELL
BURK/BURKE see also BURT
Anna, 17:103
Martha, 16:232
BURLEIGH, 19:44, 106
Charles, 16:103; 17:47; 18:211; 19:43
BURLEY
Andrew, 18:240
Giles, 18:133
Harriet (Eastman), 18:178
James, 18:178
Justin, 18:133
Sarah, 18:179; 20:16
BURLINGAME
Mary, 19:150
Stephen, 19:150
Susan, 20:163
Susan Emiline, 20:162
BURLOW
Sarah, 18:210
BURNAP/BURNAPP see also BURNET, 18:133
Anna, 19:148
Hezekiah, 19:148
Isaac, 20:188
Joseph, 18:42; 19:217; 20:37
Rebekah, 19:148
Robert, 16:163; 18:41; 20:185, 188, 187, 190, 191
Ruth, 19:148
Sarah, 19:148
Sarah (Potter), 19:148
Susanna, 17:116
Thomas, 19:148
Timothy, 19:148
BURNELL see also BURRELL
Cassandra, 20:94
John, 16:206
Mehittebel (Edmunds), 16:206
Roberd, 16:206
Sarah (Chilson), 16:206
BURNET/BURNETT see also BURNAP
Deborah, 17:202
Israel, 16:136
Joseph, 16:36; 20:188
BURNHAM see also BURNUM, 17:139
Almira (Currier), 17:36
Andrew H., 17:36
Betsey (Norwood), 18:204
Caroline S., 17:36
Daniel, 18:204
Edward, 17:36
Francis, 17:36
Henry, 17:36

Henry A., 17:221
James, 18:239; 20:120
James F., 17:36
Joanna, 18:239
Jonathan, 17:36
Joshua, 18:239
Martha (Garfield), 17:36
Martha F., 17:36
Mary, 17:120; 18:239; 20:239
Mary (___), 18:239
Mary (Kinsman), 18:239; 20:120
Mary (Knight), 18:77
Ruth (Haskell), 17:36
Sally, 17:36
Sally (Friend), 17:36
Sarah, 18:239
Sarah A. (Proctor), 17:36
Simeon, 17:36
Simeon A., 17:36
Solomon, 18:77
Susan P. (Davenport), 17:36
Thomas, 18:239

BURNILL/BURNULL see also BURRELL
John, 16:206
Mary, 16:206
Mehitabell, 16:206

BURNS
Elias, 16:217
Elizabeth, 18:180
Judith Elaine, 19:93
Martha (Friend), 16:217
Mary, 20:115
Reuben, 17:134
Winifred, 18:58

BURNUM see also BURNHAM
John, 17:76

BURPEE
Rebecca Jewett, 19:208

BURR
Elizabeth Amelia (Hunt/Hart), 17:119
George Washington, 17:119
Harriet (Brand), 17:107
Helen K. (Friend), 17:107
Lemuel G., 17:107
Washington, 17:119
William E., 17:107

BURRAGE
Ann, 18:172
Bethia, 18:116
Elizabeth, 20:205
John, 16:75; 18:172, 213, 214; 19:51, 105, 155; 20:103, 140
Lydia, 18:211, 213-215
Mary, 16:233
Mary (___), 16:233
Mehitabel (Sargent), 18:213
Sarah (Newhall), 17:172
Thomas, 16:73; 17:172; 18:103, 213; 20:112, 140

BURRALL/BURREL/BURRELL/ BURRILL/BURILL see also BURNELL, BURNIL, 16:97; 18:133
Abigail, 16:25
Ann (Thompson), 18:92
Anna, 16:85; 17:156; 19:41, 103, 104
Anna (___), 16:75
Anna (Alden), 17:148; 18:50
Anna (Breed), 18:36
Anna (Mansfield), 17:159
Benjamin, 20:211
Cornelius VanBuren, 16:151
Ebenezer, 16:28; 17:41;18:26, 102, 103, 208, 211, 213; 19:49, 106, 159, 227; 20:210
Elizabeth, 16:26; 19:27, 29; 20:27, 93, 210
Elizabeth (___), 19:29
Elizabeth (Baker), 18:25
Elizabeth (Collins), 20:211
Elizabeth (Mansfield), 18:36
Esther, 17:27
Eunice, 17:148; 18:50
Ezra, 18:36, 227
Francis, 16:164; 17:46; 18:18; 19:25, 29, 255; 20:132, 133, 135, 196
George, 16:196; 17:46; 18:111; 19:138; 20:193, 194
Hannah, 18:208; 20:209
Hannah (Linsdey), 16:29
Helen Burton (Carstairs), 16:151
Isaiah, 20:143
Jarvis, 17:159
John, 16:29; 17:28; 18:29, 60a, 75, 92, 100, 111, 116, 223; 19:29, 145, 150, 163; 20:103, 133, 135, 196, 218
Joseph, 17:173; 20:134, 196
Liddi, 18:28
Lois, 17:148
Lois (___), 20:103, 111, 112
Lois (Ivory), 17:148; 19:150
Lydia, 17:41; 18:227; 20:137
Margaret (Brown), 17:28
Margaret (Ruck), 17:159
Martha, 16:69; 17:148
Martha (Farrington), 17:41
Mary, 16:198; 17:40; 18:31, 36, 54, 92, 150; 19:163; 20:103, 211
Mary (Hill/Hills), 16:69; 17:148
Mary (Mansfield), 17:148
Mary (Tarbox), 20:143
Micajah, 17:206
Nathan, 17:217
Rebecca (Mansfield), 17:159
Ruth, 16:25; 17:100; 19:147, 150
Ruth (Farrington), 17:206
Sally, 19:107
Sally (Curtin), 18:105
Samuel, 16:96; 17:148; 18:50, 150; 19:103, 108; 20:140
Sarah, 16:74;17:148; 18:153; 20:60a
Sarah (Farrington), 17:147
Sarah (Graves), 20:210
Susanna, 19:108
Theophilus, 16:69; 17:145; 18:47, 90, 208, 213; 19:216, 217; 20:102, 103, 112, 137, 206, 208, 210, 211
Thomas, 18:47; 19:28

BURRELL-BROWN
Ruth, 16:102; 17:159

BURROUGHS/BURROWS
___, Rev., 17:15
George, 20:138
Hannah, 20:138
Hubbard, 18:239
Mary (Wilkins), 18:239
Sarah (Scales), 20:138

BURT/ BURTT see also BURK
___, Goody, 17:171
Abigail (Cheever), 19:40
Ann, 18:29, 117, 166
Ann (Holland), 18:28, 29
Azubah, 16:120
Benjmain, 16:91
Edward, 18:29
Eunice (Murry), 16:238
Gorge, 16:132
Hugh, 17:88; 18:28, 29, 74; 19:138; 20:184, 190, 195
Huldah, 20:230
James, 16:120
John, 19:40, 199, 200
Jonathan, 18:25
Mary, 16:120; 18:28, 74
Mehitable (Spalding), 16:91
Ruth (___), 16:132
Ruth (Pearse), 16:238
Ruth Pierce, 16:238
Samuel, 16:163
Sarah, 16:71; 18:28, 52, 73-75, 102, 117
Sarah (Webber), 18:25
Thomas, 16:132
William, 16:238

BURTON, 17:183
Boniface, 17:87; 18:80, 230; 19:138; 20:189, 190, 194
Francis (___), 17:87
Hannah, 16:117; 17:186; 20:120
John, 16:117; 17:186; 19:193
Phoebe, 16:198

BURTS
___, Goodman, 18:41

BURTT see BURT

BUSH
Ann (___), 20:220
Marcia Ellen, 17:169

BUSHNELL
William, 20:154

BUSSELL
Samuel, 16:68

BUSWELL
Mary, 16:58
Samuel, 16:193

BUTLER, 19:116
Adele P., 17:166
Amos, 16:94
Caleb, 16:225
Charles, 20:58
Elizabeth, 17:237; 20:58
Elizabeth (Needham), 20:27
George, 17:240
Hannah, 17:206
John, 20:27, 58
Jonathan, 20:58
Jonathan B., 17:224
June, 19:142
Martha (Storey), 19:179
Mary (Aborn), 16:94
Mary (Ingalls), 19:46
Mary (Marshall), 16:160
Mary E. (Parsons), 17:166
Philip, 20:58
Ralph, 16:160
Samuell, 20:58
Sarah, 19:41, 42
Sarah (Pigeon), 20:58
Susanna, 17:240; 19:42, 173
Thomas, 19:179
William, 17:76; 19:46
William H., 17:166

BUTMAN see also BOOTMAN, 20:18
Abigail, 18:201; 19:54
Abigail (Norwood), 18:201; 19:54; 20:118
Hannah, 18:201; 19:54
Hannah (Smith), 20:59, 180
Jeremiah, 18:201, 206, 207; 19:54; 20:117, 118, 198
Jerusha, 18:207
John, 19:119; 20:117

Lucy (___), 18:207
Lucy (Norwood), 18:206
Martha (Harris), 18:201
Mary, 19:119
Paul A., 19:54
Richard, 20:59, 180
Sarah, 18:201; 19:54; 20:117, 118
Sarah (Robinson), 19:119
William, 18:201; 19:54
BUTOLPH
Thomas, 18:233
BUTTER
Stephen, 16:58
BUTTERFIELD
Ann (Ballard), 16:67
Elizabeth (Bancroft), 20:40
Joseph, 16:67; 20:40
Lydia (Ballard), 16:67
Samuel, 16:67
BUTTERWORTH, 16:13
Mary, 16:72
BUTTON
___, Mr., 19:194
BUXTON, 17:183
Abigail (Breed), 18:53
Amos, 17:198
Anthony, 18:44
Dorcas (Osborn), 17:199
Eleanor (Osborn), 17:198
Elizabeth, 17:198; 18:97; 20:93, 99
Elizabeth (Buffam), 17:200
Esther, 17:198
Esther (Southwick), 17:198
Hannah, 20:26
Henry, 17:198
James, 17:198; 18:53
Jane (Hutchinson), 16:155
John, 17:200; 20:234
John O., 17:188; 18:136
Jonathan, 16:155
Joseph, 17:199
Keziah, 18:25, 27, 36, 105
Lydia, 16:43
Lydia (Osborn), 17:198
Mary, 16:236; 17:200; 20:213, 231, 234, 235
Mary (Small), 20:234
Mercy, 17:200
Mercy (Osborn), 17:200
Patience (Osborn), 17:198
Samuel, 16:26
Sarah, 17:198
Sarah (Hart), 18:44
Thomas, 19:193
BUZZELL
Abigail, 16:57
Eliz (Stone), 17:120
John, 16:57
Samuel, 16:57
Sarah (___), 16:57
Sarah (Keyes), 16:57
Sarah (Wibird), 16:57
BYARD
John, 18:221
Judith (Eaton), 18:221
BYHAM
Johanna, 20:225, 226
BYLES/BILES, 17:220
Jonathan, 17:113
Margaret (Corey), 17:113

CABOT
Francis, 16:93

George, 16:136
John, 19:123
Rebecca, 17:26
CADBURY
Henry J., 19:71
CADE, 17:139
CAESAR
The Ethiopian, 18:127
CAFASSO
Kathleen, 18:145
CAFFAREEN
Abigail (Norwood), 18:202
Joseph, 18:202
CAILEY
James, 16:132
CAIRS/CAVIES/CAVIS
Elizabeth (Silsbee), 18:101
John, 18:101
CALDER
William, 20:82
CALDWELL
Mary, 20:225
CALEB
Downing, 18:226
CALEF, 19:16
CALENDAR see CALLENDER
CALL, 18:133
Arthur E., 17:111
Elizabeth (Bessom), 19:230
Henry P., 19:230
Joanna, 19:48
Mary Story (Sayward), 17:111
Paul, 19:230
Philip, 18:133
Sarah (Trussell), 18:133
CALLENDER/CALENDAR
John, 16:73
Mary Russell, 18:215
Priscilla (Ballard), 16:73
CALLEY
John, 17:97
Thomas, 20:15
CALLUM see also COLLUM
Anne, 16:37
Bethiah (Gaskill), 20:95
Caleb, 20:95
Lydia, 16:37
CALQUETTE
Suzanne, 18:7
CAMBEL
James, 16:132
CAME
Arthur, 19:226
Mary, 19:225, 226
Violet (___), 19:226
CAMMEL
James, 16:131
CAMP
Anthony, 16:8
Anthony J., 16:13
CAMPBEL/CAMPBELL
Deborah (Norwood), 18:203
Elisabeth, 17:152
Mary McBell, 18:67
Michael, 18:72
Olivia, 18:169
Robert, 18:203
Thomas, 16:81
Winifred A., 17:188
CAMPION
Clement, 18:230
CANDAGE
Elizabeth, 16:235

Elizabeth (Millett), 16:235
James, 16:235
Joseph, 16:213
Ruth L., 20:176
Sarah (Friend), 16:213
CANDIDE
Alexander, 20:198
CANE
___, Mrs., 17:13
"Son", 17:13
CANES
Shedrick, 17:134
CANN
Susan, 20:171
CANNELL
William, 18:134, 137
CANNEY
Robert Sayward, 18:133
Samuel, 16:18
Sarah (Hackett), 16:18
Thomas, 18:133
CAPEN/CAPIN
Alexander, 20:176
Bernard, 17:229
E. H., 17:37
Jane (___), 20:176
Joan (Purchase), 17:229
CARD
Huldah (Soule), 20:145
Joel, 20:145
Lucy, 20:145
Rebecca Wallis, 19:235
CARDER see also CHARDER
John, 18:238
CAREY
Charles, 18:40
CARIER see CARRIER
CARKIN
Alice (Barker), 19:58
Jonas, 19:58
Joseph, 18:239
Sybil (Littlehale), 18:239
CARLAT
Blanche (Ridenour), 16:111
Claude, 16:111
Emyle Louise, 16:111
CARLETON/CARLTON, 18:220
Asa, 19:92
Batchelder, 20:239
Benjamin, 20:37
Betsey Bradley (Andrews), 20:239
Eben, 20:131
Elizabeth, 20:213
Elizabeth (Bancroft), 20:37
Ezekiel, 19:91
Flora Ann, 20:239
John, 16:68
Joseph, 16:68; 20:239
Lydia (Batchelder), 20:239
Mary Hale, 18:180
Mehitabel (Head), 20:239
Moses, 16:236
Obadiah, 20:38
Polly (Bancroft), 20:38
Reuben, 20:239
Richard A., 20:180
Sally, 16:236
Sybil (Bullard), 16:236
CARLISLE
Lester, 17:157
CARLSON
Anna C. (___), 20:126
Olga, 20:126

CARLTON see CARLETON
CARLYLE
Elizabeth (Peck), 18:75
John, 18:75
CARMACK
Sharon DeBartolo, 20:11
CARNES
John, 16:96
CARNEY
John B., 19:31
CARON-LAGASSE
Lucille, 18:8
CARPENTER
Abigail (Arnold), 16:237
Abigail (Briant), 17:59
Alma (Varney), 18:125
Calvin, 18:125
Eliphalet, 16:210
Frank, 18:132
Hester, 16:237
Joseph, 16:237
Malona (___), 18:125
Margaret (Sutton), 16:237
William, 16:237; 17:59
CARR see also CORR
Agnes D., 18:135
Ann, 19:178
Anna/Anne, 17:194
Anne (Cotton), 17:193
Annie, 16:120
Bridget, 18:177
Catherine (___), 18:177
Dorothy, 17:194
Dorothy (Boyce), 20:240
Elizabeth, 18:166; 19:17; 20:180
Elizabeth (___), 19:178
Elizabeth (Chase), 17:194
George, 17:193; 19:178
Grace Alice (Farr), 16:151
James, 16:57; 17:194
Jemima (Osborn), 17:184
John, 17:179
Mary, 17:179
Mary (___), 17:179
Mary (Sears), 16:57
Moses, 17:194
Richard, 17:19; 20:180, 240
Sarah, 16:57
Sarah (Bailey), 20:180
Thady, 18:177
William Wilkins, 16:151
CARRELL see CARROLL
CARRIAGE
John, 18:238
Mary, 18:58
CARRIER/CARIER
___, Mr., 19:45
Andrew, 19:220, 221, 223
Martha (Allen), 19:45, 115, 220, 221, 223
Martha (Dane), 19:116
Richard, 19:220, 221, 223
Sarah, 19:219-221, 223
Thomas, 16:68; 219-221, 223
CARROLL/CARRELL
Anne, 19:180
Joseph W., 16:101
Mary, 17:18
Mary (___), 17:19
Mary (Ballard), 16:77
Nathaniel, 16:77; 17:11
Ruth Tarbox, 17:221, 223
Sally, 18:205
Susan Ingraham (Tufts), 16:101

CARSTAIRS
Belle Wolf (Wilson), 16:151
Charles Stewart, 16:151
Daniel Haddock, 16:150
Emily Frances, 16:151
Esther Holmes (Haseltine), 16:151
Helen Burton, 16:151
James, 16:150
John Haseltine, 16:151
Lena Farr, 16:151
Louise (Orne), 16:151
Lucy Haddock, 16:150
Mary White, 16:151
Mary White (Haddock), 16:150
Priscilla Moore (Taylor), 16:151
CARTER
___, Mr., 19:42
Benjamin, 19:173
Betsey (___), 17:178
Daniel, 17:185
Elizabeth (Chinn), 20:58
Elizabeth (Edes), 20:47
Eme/Emma, 18:71; 19:142, 144, 153
Eunice (Allen), 19:173
Eunice (Brooks), 16:225
Eunice (Flanders), 18:175
Hannah, 19:97
James, 20:47
Jeremiah Jaquith, 16:179
John, 20:13
Joseph, 19:217
Lucy Wilder, 20:42
Mary, 16:57; 17:185; 19:153; 20:99
Mary (Atkinson), 17:185
Melinda, 18:175
N. F., 19:95
Obed, 19:173; 20:58
Phebe (Wright), 16:179
Plats/Plato, 18:175
Sally, 19:173
Samuel, 16:225
Sarah (Cheever), 19:42
Sarah (Davis), 19:173
Thomas, 19:81
William, 16:208
CARTERET
___, Gov., 16:18
CARVER
Elizabeth, 18:40
Grace (___), 18:40
John, 16:120a
Richard, 18:40, 41
Susanna, 18:40
CARY
John, 19:161
CASE
Charlotte, 16:59
David, 16:238
Henry, 16:59
Julia, 19:55, 117
Lyman, 16:238
Margaret, 17:42
Maria (Blood), 16:238
Martha (Corwin), 16:59
Mary (Estes), 18:95
CASH
Rebecca, 20:221
CASHMORE
Lucy (___), 17:12
CASS/CASSE
Ebenezer, 18:200
Elizabeth, 16:209
John, 18:97

Keziah, 18:97
Lydia (Sargent), 18:200
CASTELL
Christina, 19:141
CASWELL
Elizabeth, 16:237
Thomas, 16:237
CATE
Catherine (Kendall), 18:175
Charles Giles, 18:175
Laura Hannah, 18:175
CATHERINE
The Great, 17:125
CAVE
Thomas, 20:202
CAVERLY
Hannah (Johnson), 16:239
Moses, 16:239
CAVIES/CAVIS see CAIRS
CELUCCI
___, Gov., 19:5
CENTER see also SENTER
Addison, 17:110
Alice (Cowdery), 20:28
Bessie E., 17:170
Bill, 20:28
Charlotte A., 17:110
Cotton, 20:28
Edward B., 17:170
Eleanor, 20:98
Elizabeth, 20:98
Elizabeth (Hartley), 17:170
Hannah (Evans), 20:28
James, 20:28
Jeremiah, 20:26, 28, 98, 99
John, 20:28, 98
Jonathan, 20:98
Mary, 20:25, 26, 28
Mary (___), 20:98
Mary (Wyman), 20:26, 28, 98, 99
Mary P. (Currier), 17:110
Mehetabel, 20:98
Ruth, 20:98
Ruth (___), 20:98
Ruth (Todd), 20:28, 98
Ruth (Wright), 20:98
Sarah, 20:98
CERNY
Johni, 17:73; 18:65
CHACKSFIELD see also CHAXFIELD
John, 18:231
CHADBOURNE
Alice, 18:202
CHADWELL, 18:133
___, Wid., 18:209
Anna, 19:164
Benjamin, 16:73, 74, 196; 18:47; 20:134, 208
Elizabeth (Howe), 16:74; 18:172
Hannah, 17:159
Harris, 16:70; 18:172
Margaret (___), 20:91
Mary (Newhall), 17:219
Moses, 17:19; 18:74, 172; 20:196
Richard, 17:88
Ruth, 18:46, 47, 53; 19:157; 20:26, 91
Ruth (Witt), 18:172
Sarah (Croft), 17:147
Sarah (Ivory), 18:47
Thomas, 17:88; 18:71, 99, 172; 19:47, 51, 138; 20:91, 103; 20:194
CHADWICK, 16:13, 175
___, Capt., 18:106

"Infant", 20:125
Elizabeth, 20:125
Frederick, 20:125
John, 19:89
Margaret, 20:125
Martha, 17:96
Martha (___), 20:125
Mary, 19:93
Sarah, 19:33, 89, 90
CHAFFEE
A. B., 19:22
Experience, 16:73
CHAFFIN
A. W., 17:102
CHALLEN
W. H., 20:75
CHALLIS
Gideon, 17:58
Lucy (Stanwood), 17:58
CHALMERS
Anthony, 20:56
Phyllis Ann (Southard), 20:56
CHAMBER, 19:160
CHAMBERLAIN/CHAMBERLIN, 17:89;
19:103, 206
___, Judge, 17:88
Ann, 19:157
Charles P., 20:59
Dorothy, 16:44
Edmond, 16:225, 226
Edward, 16:211
Esther (Hammond), 19:157
Experience, 16:116
Experience (___), 16:117
George Walter, 16:226; 17:43; 20:95
Hannah (Edmunds), 16:211
Hannah (Hasey), 19:145
Henry, 20:59
Jacob, 16:117
John, 19:145
Mary (___), 20:59
Mary (Parker), 16:228
Mary (Tibbetts), 16:117
Mellen, 16:160; 17:88; 18:211, 226; 19:39,
  207, 210; 20:98
Polly, 19:167
Samuel, 19:157
Sarah, 19:145
Sarah D. (Winder), 20:59
Thomas, 16:225, 226, 228
William, 16:117, 225, 226
CHAMBERS
Abigail, 17:175
David, 16:131
James, 16:131
John, 16:131
Joseph, 16:131
Margaret, 19:137
Martha, 16:131; 19:137
Mary (Bulmore), 17:175
Mary Jane, 16:178
Sarah, 16:131
Thomas, 17:175
William, 16:131
CHAMBLESS
Mary, 18:38
Sarah, 18:38
CHAMBLETT
William, 17:134
CHAMLET
Moris, 20:199
CHAMPLAIN
Samuel, 19:123

Samuel De, 19:13
CHAMPNEY, 17:82
Elizabeth, 17:41
Israel, 17:41
Joseph, 17:41
Richard, 17:41
Sarah, 17:41
Thankful (Mower), 17:41
Thomas, 17:41
CHANDLER, 16:76
___, Capt., 16:68; 20:221
___, Goody, 19:30
Abigail, 16:132
Annis (___), 19:115
Annis (Bayford), 19:116, 120, 222; 20:20
Catherine, 18:29
Catherine Soleman, 18:28
Charles Chauncey, 18:133
Eleanor, 16:118
Elizabeth, 19:97
Ella (Pfeiffer), 19:56
Emma, 19:56
George, 19:93, 116
Hannah, 16:132; 17:55; 19:93, 95, 115,
  116, 219, 222; 20:19, 20, 165, 216
Hannah (___), 19:30
Hannah (Abbot), 20:21
Hannah (Brewer), 19:120; 20:21, 23
Hannah (Ford), 17:180
Henry, 16:68; 19:34; 20:23
Henry Lucius, 19:56
John, 16:68, 132; 19:34, 93; 20:21
Joseph, 16:68
Josiah, 18:240; 19:89, 90
Lucius H., 19:56
Lydia (Abbot), 20:23
Mary, 20:120
Mary (Fowler), 19:119
Mary (Simonds), 16:59
Molley, 16:132
Nathan, 19:94
Philemon, 17:180
Rebecca, 19:111
Rebecca (Lovejoy), 19:93
Roger, 16:59
Samuel, 16:210; 17:11; 20:17
Sarah, 16:233; 19:119
Sarah (___), 16:132
Sarah (Abbott), 20:216
Sarah (Ballard), 16:76
Sarah (Chadwick), 19:89, 90
Seth, 16:225; 17:83
Thomas, 16:68; 132; 18:155; 19:30, 34,
  120; 20:19-21, 23
William, 16:68, 132; 19:93, 115, 116, 119,
  120, 222; 20:19, 20
Zebadiah, 20:216
CHAPELL
Mary, 16:84
CHAPIN
Ann B., 20:109
Benjamin, 20:34
CHAPLIN, 17:140
Ann, 16:81
Benjamin, 16:36; 19:137, 216, 217; 20:89
Charles, 20:90
Duncan D., 18:63
Martha, 16:116
William, 20:89
CHAPMAN
___, Rev., 17:184
Edward, 20:16
Elizabeth, 16:25

Elizabeth L., 17:32
Emma, 17:157
Emme (Devereaux), 18:179
Hannah (Davis), 18:179
Hannah (Devereux), 16:25
Joana (Bartoll), 20:16
Johnny "Appleseed", 18:133
Lydia (Wells), 16:237
Mary, 16:237
Ralph, 16:237
Ruth (Ingalls), 19:46
Samuel, 18:126, 179; 19:46, 218
Sarah, 16:83; 18:113
Stephen, 16:25
William, 18:179
Zerviah, 19:150
CHAPPEL
Sarah (___), 16:84
William, 16:84
CHARDER see also CARDER
Elizabeth (Stevens), 18:238
CHARDON
Peter, 18:210, 240a
CHARLEMAGNE, 16:120a
CHARLES
King, I, 19:72; 20:192
King, II, 17:125; 18:195
Prince, 17:125
CHARNOCK
Mary, 16:25
CHARPENTIER
Catherine, 19:26
CHASE
Abigail, 17:199
Abigail (Buffam), 17:199
Aquilla, 16:86
Benjamin, 18:93, 98
Charles, 18:11
Daniel, 16:86; 17:159
Dolly, 18:239
Elizabeth, 17:194; 20:28, 95
Enoch, 18:239
Eunice (Breed), 18:93, 98
George Wingate, 16:141
Jacob, 18:11; 20:43
Jane, 20:37
Jane (Rundlet), 16:86
Jerusha (Tarbox), 20:144
John, 20:144
John B., 18:11
John Carroll, 20:95
Joseph, 20:96
Judeth (___), 18:239
Lucy (Berry), 20:43
Lydia (Hacker), 18:98
Mary, 16:119, 224; 18:105
Molly, 16:224
Peggy (Fuller), 16:86
Peggy (Mansfield), 17:159
Philip, 18:98
Rebecca, 16:86, 91; 17:160; 18:98; 20:212
Samuel, 16:99; 17:199
Sarah, 20:95
Sarah (Bailey), 20:180
Sarah (Sherman), 20:96
Stephen, 20:36
Wells, 20:81
William, 20:95
CHATTO
Annie Lewis, 18:176
Castillia Lacoste (Fullerton), 18:176
John Roundy, 18:176

CHAXFIELD see also CHACKSFIELD
    John, 16:72
CHEATHAM see CHEETHAM
CHECKLEY
    Samuel, 18:236; 20:47
CHEESMAN
    Elizabeth (Phillips), 16:221
    George, 16:221
CHEETHAM/CHEATHAM/CHEATMAN
    Mary, 16:8, 9
CHEEVER
    "Daughter", 19:99
    Abigail, 19:38-40, 98, 102, 104
    Abigail (Eustis), 19:104
    Abigail (Jarvis), 19:38-40
    Abigail (Lippingwell), 19:38. 39, 98
    Abijah, 18:152, 214; 19:100-103, 159
    Abner, 17:160; 18:152, 214, 227; 19:99-101, 103;
    Abraham, 19:36
    Ames, 19:36, 38, 41, 42
    Amos, 19:42, 98
    Ann, 19:101, 102
    Ann (Roby), 18:152; 19:101
    Anna, 19:38, 41, 104
    Anna (___), 19:101
    Anna (Burrill), 19:41, 103, 104
    Anna (Gerrish), 19:38, 41
    Anna (Ropes), 19:42
    Anne, 19:42
    Bartholomew, 19:36
    Benjamin, 19:36, 39, 98, 99, 101
    Betsy (Morse), 19:42
    Betty, 19:98
    Charles Augustus, 19:102
    Daniel, 19:36
    David, 19:102, 103
    Dorcas (Cook), 18:152; 19:101
    Ebenezer, 19:39, 98
    Edward, 18:15; 19:40, 100, 101
    Edward Maxim, 19:101
    Eleanor, 19:101
    Eleanor (Platts), 19:104
    Elizabeth, 17:226; 18:173; 19:37, 98, 101-104
    Elizabeth (Foster), 19:103
    Elizabeth (Gage), 19:99
    Elizabeth (Gill), 19:41, 102, 103
    Elizabeth (Gray), 19:103
    Elizabeth (Huxford), 19:104
    Elizabeth (Jenner), 19:41, 102
    Elizabeth (Lee), 19:42
    Elizabeth (Newhall), 18:152; 19:101
    Elizabeth (Scott), 19:102
    Elizabeth (Senter), 19:38, 39
    Elizabeth (Tuttle), 19:104
    Ellen (Lathrop), 19:36-38
    Eunice, 18:215
    Eunice (Ivory), 19:100, 147
    Ezekiel, 18:152, 192, 193; 19:36-42, 98-103, 173; 20:16
    Fanny (Allen), 19:42
    Grace, 19:102
    Hannah, 19:38, 98, 99, 104
    Hannah (Brooks), 19:41, 103, 104
    Hannah (Clark), 19:42
    Hannah (Perkins), 18:152; 19:101
    Hannah (Phillips), 19:39, 99
    Hannah Hilton (Crombie), 19:42
    Hepzibah (Alley), 20:171
    Humphrey, 19:101
    Israel, 19:98
    Jacob, 19:42, 104
    John, 18:152; 19:41, 42, 99, 101
    Jonathan, 19:102, 103
    Joseph, 19:41, 104; 20:171
    Joshua, 18:152, 226; 19:40, 41, 100-104, 108, 159; 20:48
    Josiah, 19:42
    Juliana (Corey), 19:104
    Lois, 19:104
    Lot, 19:102
    Lydia, 19:99
    Marcy (Newhall), 17:160
    Margaret, 19:104
    Margaret (___), 19:36
    Margaret (Ives), 20:42
    Martha, 19:101
    Martha (Collins), 19:98
    Martha (Hall), 19:99
    Martha (Wigglesworth), 18:152; 19:101
    Mary, 18:152; 19:37, 38, 42, 98, 100, 101, 103; 20:38
    Mary (___), 19:36, 159
    Mary (Baker), 18:152; 19:40, 99, 101
    Mary (Boardman), 18:152; 19:40, 99, 100
    Mary (Emerson), 18:152; 19:40, 99, 100
    Mary (Giles), 19:101
    Mary (Richards), 19:39, 98
    Mary (Saunders), 19:38, 41
    Mary Barry, 20:170, 171
    Mary Saunders, 19:42
    Mehitable, 17:160; 19:98, 102
    Mehitable (Newhall), 19:100
    Mercy (Newhall), 19:101
    Mercy (Wilkins), 19:39, 99
    Nancy (Hassam), 19:42
    Nathan, 17:159; 19:40, 41, 98, 103, 104
    Nathaniel, 19:38, 39, 99
    Patty, 19:99
    Peter, 19:36
    Polly, 19:104
    Priscilla (Crafts), 19:42
    Rachel (Brown), 19:102
    Rachel (Greely), 18:152; 19:101
    Rachel (Stacey), 19:39, 99
    Rebecca (Weston), 18:152; 19:101
    Relief, 19:103
    Rhoda, 19:99
    Richard, 19:36
    Robert, 20:45
    Ruth, 19:38, 41, 42
    Ruth (Allen), 19:41
    Ruth (Angier), 19:37, 38
    Ruth (Perkins), 19:98
    Sally (Williams), 19:102
    Samuel, 18:193; 19:36-39, 41, 42, 51, 98, 101, 104; 20:15, 16
    Sarah, 18:152; 19:38-40, 42, 98, 100-104, 173
    Sarah (Bill), 19:38-40
    Sarah (Butler), 19:41, 42
    Sarah (Choate), 19:38, 41
    Sarah (Davis), 19:38, 41, 42
    Sarah (Jenkins), 19:40
    Sarah (Low), 19:104
    Sarah (Lynde), 19:41, 102
    Sarah (Phillips), 19:102
    Sarah (Warren), 19:40
    Sarah (Weaver), 19:102
    Sarah (White), 19:39, 98
    Solomon, 19:99
    Susan, 19:42
    Susanna, 19:37, 38
    Susanna (Butler), 19:42, 173
    Thankful (Hammond), 19:101
    Thomas, 17:173; 18:152, 208, 210, 225, 226, 240, 240a; 19:36-42, 99-104, 147, 158, 159, 228
    William, 19:36, 38, 100, 101, 104, 173; 20:89, 90
CHENEY
    Abigail (Davis), 16:40
    Bethiah, 16:40
    Deborah (Parker), 16:40
    Hannah, 17:119
    Martha, 19:208
    Mary, 16:40
    Thomas, 16:40
    Timothy, 16:40
    William, 16:40
CHESTERFIELD
    Clemens, 20:103
    Priscilla (___), 20:103
CHEVALIER
    Marie-Josephine, 20:170
CHEW
    Nathaniel, 18:230
CHICK
    Edson, 19:18
    Mary Alice (Peirce), 19:18
CHICKATAUBOTT, 18:240a
CHICKERING
    ___, Mr., 18:166
    Samuel, 18:162; 19:91
CHILD
    Betsey, 17:238
    Elijah, 18:125
CHILLE
    Hannah, 16:197
    Mary (Mower), 16:197
CHILSON
    Jane (Rhodes), 19:155
    John, 20:197
    Sarah, 16:206
    William, 18:95; 19:155
CHILTON
    James, 19:236
CHIN/CHINN
    Elizabeth, 20:58
    Mary (Bessom), 19:230
    Rebecca, 19:230
    Samuel, 19:230
CHIPMAN
    Anna (Lurvey), 20:58
    Anthony, 20:58
    John, 16:136; 17:101; 19:38, 84
CHISEMORE
    Abigail, 19:180
CHITTENDEN
    Mary, 18:112
CHOATE/CHOTE, 18:133; 20:223
    Abigail Patch, 18:205
    Adaline Augusta, 18:207
    Ann (___), 20:224
    Anne (___), 17:75
    Dudley, 20:82
    Elizabeth (___), 16:234; 20:224
    Elizabeth (Graves), 16:234; 20:224
    Francis, 17:75; 18:240
    Henry, 18:207
    Hepsiba (___), 18:207
    John, 16:159, 234; 17:75, 76; 18:210, 240a; 19:41; 20:224
    Mary (Varney), 17:75; 19:41
    Prudence (Woodward), 16:233, 234
    Robert, 17:75
    Sarah, 19:38, 41
    Sarah (___), 17:75

Sarah (Perkins), 16:160
Thomas, 16:160; 17:75; 18:240; 19:41
CHOQUET
Mark, 19:174
CHORLEY, 16:13
CHOTE see CHOATE
CHRISTENSON
Wenlock, 19:64
CHUB/CHUBB, 19:201
___, Mrs., 16:64
Pasco, 16:68
William, 20:198
CHURCH
Daniel, 20:119
Elizabeth (Gage), 20:119
Eunice (Winter), 20:119
Gideon, 20:119
Mary (Edwards), 20:119
Ruth, 20:119
Ruth (Bosworth), 16:172
Samuel, 20:119
Sarah, 16:231
CHURCHILL
Ann (Northey), 18:35; 19:84, 85
Joseph, 18:35; 19:84, 85
Sarah (Stacy), 18:133
CHURCHMAN
___, Goodman, 18:41
CHURCHWELL
Arthur, 20:199
CHUTE, 19:148
James, 20:223
Lionel, 18:192
CICELY
a/k/a Su George, 19:145
CIMINO, 20:5
CLAIRBORNE-FITZHUGHS, 19:140
CLAP/CLAPP
Aaron, 17:115
Abigail (Whitman), 17:115
Albert C., 16:118
Ebenezer, 17:115
George H., 16:118; 18:178
Louisa A. (Rollins), 16:118
Mary, 19:41; 20:179
Mary (Gordon), 18:178
Mary (Wales), 18:178
Sally, 19:170, 172
Sarah, 20:179
Thomas, 18:178
CLARE see also CLERE
Arthur J., 16:53
Emily May (Longfellow), 16:53
CLARK/CLARKE/CLEARKE, 17:202;
 18:105, 133
___, Mr., 19:149, 189
Abigail, 17:236; 18:200
Abigail (Renew), 20:240
Abraham, 17:197
Adam, 17:214
Agnes, 19:55, 59
Agnes (Tybbot), 17:139
Alice, 16:60a
Alice (Pepper), 16:59
Alice A., 20:171
Amasa, 19:18
Anna (Leach), 18:77
Azuba (Buck), 19:178
Benjamin, 17:138; 18:77
Caroline, 16:110
Deliverance, 18:91
Ebenezer, 20:58, 240
Edmund, 17:135; 18:76

Edward, 18:205, 240
Elizabeth, 18:49, 50, 112, 113
Elizabeth (___), 18:235
Elizabeth (Pierce), 17:139; 18:76
Elizabeth Frances (Farnum), 16:240
Elizabeth M., 16:102
Emeline (Shedd), 19:178
Ephraim, 19:112; 20:130
Eunice, 17:135
Eunice (Potter), 19:150
Francis, 19:18
Francis Darracott, 19:18
Gertrude, 20:172
Grace M., 16:39
Greenleaf, 19:18
Hannah, 17:226; 19:42
Hannah (___), 18:91
Hannah (Davis), 17:139
Hannah (Lee), 20:58
Henry, 20:83
Isaac, 18:29, 92
J. Richard, 20:129
James, 18:49
Jemima, 18:86, 87
Jerusha (Norwood), 18:205
John, 16:133; 17:93; 18:229, 235; 20:196
John Lewis, 16:240
Joseph, 16:59; 17:139; 18:49; 20:200
Joseph S., 16:189
Joshua, 20:58
Josiah, 16:180; 17:179
Julia (Cogswell), 19:18
Lydia, 17:138; 19:119; 20:141
Margaret, 18:159, 235
Martha, 16:234
Martha (Farr), 19:27
Martha (Lyon), 16:110
Mary, 16:180; 17:198; 18:116; 19:26, 27,
 218; 20:33, 36, 37
Mary (Allen), 16:59
Mary (Boynton), 16:180
Mary (Collins), 19:149
Mary (Johnson), 19:221
Mary (Kirtland), 18:112
Mary (Swaine), 20:36
Mary Frances, 19:178
Mathew, 20:199
Mehitable (Lambert), 18:49, 50
Nannie (Hollyday), 19:18
Nicholas, 19:150
Patience (Blackstone), 17:179
Priscilla, 16:109
Prudence (Hill), 18:49
Rebecca, 18:23, 149
Ruth, 17:138
Samuel, 18:112; 19:178; 20:111, 178
Sarah, 16:64; 17:54, 138
Sarah (Lurvey), 20:58
Sarah (Peacock), 16:180
Sarah E., 17:222
Sarah Fisher (Marland), 19:18
Sarah Francis, 19:18
Thomas, 16:110; 20:36, 190, 192
Walter, 18:91
William, 16:180; 17:18; 18:50, 87; 19:119,
 176; 20:198
CLATTENBURG
Catharine Elizabeth, 19:238
CLATTERIE
Richard, 20:199
CLAYTON, 16:13
CLEARKE see CLARK

CLEASBIE
Anne, 19:43
Henry, 19:43
CLEAVE
Margaret, 16:213
CLEAVELAND
N., 20:83
Richard, 16:187
CLEAVES/CLEEVES
Benjamin, 17:113
Ebenezar, 17:113
Eleanor, 17:112
Eleanor (Gardner), 18:81
Emery N., 17:112
Hannah, 17:113
John, 17:112
Lidea, 20:151
Margaret (Corey), 16:180; 17:112
Martha, 17:112
Martha (Corey), 16:179; 17:112
Martha (Edwards), 17:112; 18:133, 134
Robert, 17:113
William, 16:179; 17:112; 18:81, 133, 134;
 20:198
CLEEVER
Samuel, 16:218
Susan Hannah (Friend), 16:218
CLEEVES see CLEAVES
CLEMENS/CLEMENT/CLEMENTS/
CLEMONS, 19:139
Abraham, 19:141
Adam, 19:139, 140
Christina (Castell), 19:141
Elizabeth, 18:148
Elizabeth (Bancroft), 20:41
Elizabeth (Fawne), 19:141
Elizabeth (Moore), 19:140, 141
Elizabeth Moore, 19:139, 141
Ezekiel, 19:141
Fawne, 19:141, 160
Gershom, 19:140
Hannah (Gove), 19:141
Hannibal, 19:140
James Newton, 19:140
Jane (Lampton), 19:139, 141
Jeremiah, 19:140, 141
Job, 18:140
John, 17:96; 19:141
John Marshall, 19:139-141
Jonathan R., 19:140
Lydia (___), 19:141
Mary, 19:115; 20:22, 166
N. E., Mrs., 19:140
Olivia (Langdon), 19:237
Olivia Louise (Langdon), 19:141
Parmelia (Goggin), 19:139, 141
Percival W., 19:141
Philip, 20:41
Robert, 18:140, 141; 19:141
Samuel, 19:141, 237
Samuel B., 19:139-141
Samuel Langhorne, 19:139, 141
Sarah (Hoyt), 19:141
William, 17:112; 19:212; 20:197
William H., 19:139
CLERE see also CLARE
Elizabeth, 19:179
John, 19:179
CLEVELAND
Edmund James, 20:25
Ephraim, 17:25
Horace Gillette, 20:25
Samuel, 17:132

William, 17:132
CLEVERLY
Elizabeth, 17:53
Esther (Minor), 17:54
Joseph, 17:54
CLOAK
Anna Eliza, 16:236
CLOON
John C., 19:231
Tabitha Lewis (Bessom), 19:231
CLOSE
John, 17:134
CLOUDMAN
Abigail (___), 19:106
CLOUGH see also CLUFF
___, Mrs., 17:13
Abigail (Shore), 17:232
Abraham, 17:188
Benjamin, 17:116; 20:219
David, 17:188
Elbridge G., 17:239
Elizabeth (Thompson), 17:235
Florinda M., 17:239
Hannah, 17:116
Hannah (___), 17:117
Hannah (Clough), 17:116
Hannah (Scales), 17:187
Henry C., 17:239
Isaac, 17:117
James M., 17:239
James S., 17:239
Jonathan, 17:188
Joseph, 17:13; 20:143
Lydia, 17:239
Mary, 20:141
Mary (Austin), 17:117
Moses, 20:220
Nathan, 17:187
Nathan Henry, 17:235
Olive, 18:239
Olive (Graves), 20:219
Rachel (Austin), 17:116
Rebecca (Graves), 20:220
Samuel, 16:19; 17:188
Sarah, 17:188
Susanna (Palmer), 17:239
Susanna F., 17:239
Thomas M., 17:239
William, 17:116
CLOUSTON
John, 19:166, 167
Lois (___), 18:48
CLOYCE
Sarah (Towne), 19:221
CLOYES
John, 16:177
Mary, 16:177
Susannah (Lewis), 16:177
Thomas, 16:177
CLUB
Thomas, 20:198
CLUFF see also CLOUGH
Hannah M., 17:116
COALE see also COLE
John, 20:197
COAS
Jeremiah, 16:133
Samuel, 16:133
William, 17:13
COATES/COATS see also COOTES/
COOTS, 18:133; 19:154
"Child", 19:160
"Daughter", 19:160

Abigail, 17:157; 18:30, 102; 19:155-157, 162, 164
Abigail (___), 19:159
Abigail (Sargent), 19:157
Abraham Titcomb, 19:160
Alice, 19:157
Alse (Henley), 20:213
Amos, 19:164
Ann (Chamberlain), 19:157
Ann (Edmands), 17:27
Ann (Titcombe), 19:156, 160
Anna (Gray), 19:164
Anne, 19:161
Ballard, 19:159
Bartholomew, 19:163, 164
Benjamin, 18:226; 19:155, 156, 158-161; 20:48, 113
Benjamin Newhall, 19:158
Beulah (Bill), 19:164
Caleb, 19:163, 164
Christopher, 19:164
Daniel, 19:163
David, 19:160, 161, 163
Deborah, 19:159
Deborah (Jenks), 19:159
Desire, 19:164
Dorothy, 19:163, 164
Dorothy (Coates), 19:163, 164
Eals/Alse (Henley), 18:48; 19:155, 156
Eleanor (___), 19:163
Eleazer, 19:78, 162
Elizabeth, 16:207; 19:155, 159-161
Elizabeth (___), 19:159, 160
Elizabeth (Bruce), 19:158
Elizabeth (Flood), 19:154
Emily, 19:159
Eunice, 19:158
Eunice (Newhall), 18:48; 19:158
Experience, 19:164
Ezra, 19:159
Freelove (Frink), 19:164
Grace, 19:164
Hannah, 19:164
Hannah (Bill), 19:164
Harriet, 19:159
Hezekiah, 19:163, 164
Hopestill (Eliot), 19:164
James, 19:155
Jane, 19:154, 156
Jane (Sumner), 19:162
Jemima (Harthorn), 19:156, 158
John, 16:156; 18:48; 19:155-160, 162-164; 20:133, 196, 213
Jonathan, 19:160
Joseph, 19:154, 164
Lucy, 19:158
Lydia, 19:159, 160
Margaret (Tink), 19:158
Margarit (Ramsdell), 19:164
Mariah (Howe), 19:159
Martha, 19:155, 156, 160, 163; 20:208, 213
Martha (Gay), 19:156
Mary, 19:79, 155-158, 160, 161, 163, 164; 20:206
Mary (Alley), 19:163
Mary (Garns/Garney), 19:158
Mary (Hodgkins), 19:162
Mary (Keys), 19:164
Mary (Kimball), 19:158, 159
Mary (Pinson), 19:156, 157
Mary (Wait), 19:161
Mary (Witherdin/Witherington), 19:155

Mehitable (Thurston), 19:160, 161
Mercy (Hunstable), 19:157
Nabby (King), 19:159
Nancy (Edmands), 17:26
Nancy Elizabeth, 19:160
Naomi (___), 19:155
Obadiah, 19:154, 163, 164
Phillip, 19:151, 156, 161
Pynson, 19:157
Robert, 19:154, 162-164; 20:196
Ruth, 18:48; 19:158, 161
Ruth (Hart), 18:48; 19:156, 157
Ruth (Potter), 19:151, 161
Ruth (Pratt), 19:151, 161
Samuel, 18:48; 19:155-159
Sarah, 18:48, 117; 19:156, 158, 160, 161
Sarah (Becket), 19:160
Sarah (Stone), 19:161
Stephen, 17:26; 19:161
Susan, 19:160
Susannah, 19:163
Tabitha, 19:156
Thankful, 19:163
Thankful (Pendleton), 19:164
Thomas, 18:99; 19:154-158, 160-162
Victoria, 19:163
William, 19:157, 161, 163, 164
Zebulon, 19:164
COBB
Ebenezer, 18:81
Edward, 18:81, 82
Francis Davis, 16:108
Irene, 20:172
John, 18:81
Kathrine H., 16:108
Lucy, 18:173
Matthew, 16:108
Mehitable (Robinson), 18:81
Olivia, 16:47
Phebe Bliss (Farnum), 16:108
Rhoda (Smith), 18:81
Sarah (Hackett), 18:81
Wealthy, 18:170
COBBET/COBBETT/COBBITT/COBITT
___, Mr., 17:88; 19:45, 154
Samuel, 17:151; 18:114; 20:134, 196, 216
Thomas, 18:147, 230; 19:138; 20:193, 195
COBBY
William, 16:149
COBORN/COOBORN/COBURN
Dolly (Varnum), 19:35
Elizabeth, 20:38
Elizabeth (Southworth), 18:129
George, 18:129
Hezekiah, 19:96, 97
Joanna (Wood), 20:38
John, 20:41
Josiah, 20:38
Lydia (Parker), 19:96, 97
Mercy, 20:41
Peter, 19:35
Robert, 20:198
Sarah (Richardson), 20:41
COCHRANE
Jennie, 19:180
COCK
Thomas, 20:198
William, 20:199
COCKCROFT, 16:13
COCKS see also COX
Thomas, 17:41
CODDINGTON
John Insley, 18:190; 19:90

CODNER, 19:201
  Gregory, 17:212
  Joana (Bartoll), 20:16
  Joanna, 20:15
  John, 20:15, 16, 199
  Lucy (Band), 17:212
  Rachel, 17:232
  Susanna, 17:200
CODY
  Buffalo Bill, 20:120
COES
  Elizabeth (Hawkins), 20:233
  Samuel, 20:233
COFFIN/COFFYN, 19:240a
  Anna, 16:120
  Benjamin, 16:120
  Charles, 18:11
  Eleanor, 17:227
  Elizabeth, 16:238
  Eunice (Legro), 16:33
  Experience (Hillard), 16:33
  Henry, 16:33
  Joshua, 19:210
  Martha, 17:227
  Mary, 16:33
  Miriam (Woodman), 16:120
  Peter, 16:64
  Sarah (Aborn), 16:33
  Tristram, 18:140, 141
  William, 16:33
COFFRAIN
  Archeleus, 20:89
  Edward, 20:89
  Joseph, 20:89
COGAN/COGGEN
  Eleanor, 16:237
  John, 17:88
  Mary, 16:132
  William, 16:237
COGGESHALL
  John, 16:202
COGGINS
  ___, Mr., 19:78
COGSWELL, 18:133, 134
  Abigail (Goodwin), 18:203
  Benjamin Punchard, 19:17
  Bethia, 16:29
  Elizabeth, 16:29; 18:31, 53, 92
  Esther (Merrill), 19:17
  Francis, 19:17
  Georgiana (McCoy), 19:17
  Hannah (Goodhue), 16:80
  Joan (Antrobus), 16:174
  John, 16:80; 18:192, 194, 203, 233
  John Francis, 19:17
  Jonathan, 17:76
  Joseph, 16:28
  Joseph Badger, 19:17
  Judith (Badger), 19:17
  Julia, 19:18
  Leander, 18:59
  Mary, 16:174; 18:233, 234
  Mary Marland, 19:17
  Mary Sykes (Marland), 19:17
  Susan Louisa (Holt), 19:17
  Thomas Marland, 19:17
  William, 17:76; 19:17
  William Abraham, 19:17
COHEN
  Abraham, 17:67
COIT/COITT
  Elizabeth, 18:88, 86
  Nathaniel, 20:200

COKER
  Anne, 18:235, 236
  Anne (Price), 18:235
  Benjamin, 18:235
  Hannah, 16:194
  Hathorne/Harthorn, 16:223
  Johan, 16:227
  Jonathan Phillips, 16:223
  Mary (Phillips), 16:222
  Miriam (Collins), 16:223
  Robert, 19:179
  Samuel, 16:173
  Sarah, 17:52; 20:178
  Sarah (Greenleaf), 16:223
  Thomas, 16:223
  Tirzah (Bartlett), 16:223
COLBURN
  Elizabeth, 16:56
  Sarah, 19:178
COLBY, 18:133; 20:80
  Allen, 20:89
  Charles, 16:179
  Dorothy (Ambrose), 17:52; 20:178
  Elbridge Gerry, 17:57
  Elizabeth (Sargent), 17:53
  Jacob, 16:179
  John, 20:13
  Samuel, 16:15; 17:52; 20:178
  Susanna, 17:52; 20:178
COLCARD
  ___, Mr., 20:127
COLCOTT
  Edward, 18:230
**COLDAM/COLDUM/COLDHAM/
  COLDOM/COLDUM**, 18:198
  Clement, 18:47, 198, 199, 208
  Elizabeth, 18:198, 208, 224; 19:149
  Mary (Pierce), 18:198, 208
  Peter Wilson, 18:228
  Thomas, 16:196; 17:18; 18:72; 19:138;
    20:134, 195
COLE see also COALE, 16:126
  Abigail (Blaisdell), 17:238
  Alexander, 18:101
  Anna, 18:101
  Bethia (Pitman), 18:101
  David W., 17:238
  Deborah, 20:13
  Donald B., 16:10
  Elizabeth (Tarbox), 20:140, 144
  Eunice, 19:240
  George, 20:133
  James, 17:202
  Jannet, 18:101
  John, 18:174; 19:217
  John S., 17:238
  Mary, 20:13
  Mary (Knight), 18:174
  Mercy, 17:168
  Mercy E., 17:167
  Nathaniel, 20:139
  Sarah (Aslet), 19:175, 221
  Sarah (Davis), 19:221
  Solomon, 20:198
  Sophia (Tarbox), 20:139
  Sybell B., 17:170
  Thomas, 19:196
  Trafford, 16:124
  Trafford R., 16:128
  William, 20:140, 144
COLEMAN/COLMAN
  John, 16:111
  William, 17:240

COLES
  James A., 18:16
  John, 19:212
COLESWORTHY
  ___, Capt., 17:134
COLKERT
  Meredith B., 18:67
COLLETTA
  John P., 16:128; 17:73
COLLICOTT/COLLICUT/COLLICUTT
  Elizabeth, 17:53
  Elizabeth (Hoagg/Hogin), 17:53
  Firzwid/Fredisweed, 17:195
  George, 17:53
COLLIDGE
  Richard, 18:237
COLLIER see also COLLYER
  Elizabeth, 18:113; 19:167
  Joseph, 17:204
  Mary (Smith), 17:204
  Rand, 20:221
COLLINGS
  Ebenezer, 17:13
COLLINS, 18:99, 111
  ___, Goodman, 19:212, 214
  ___, Mrs., 17:12
  "Child", 18:112
  Abigail, 16:56; 17:113; 18:30, 36, 102-105;
    19:50, 106; 20:211
  Abigail (Johnson), 17:171; 18:33
  Abigail (Richards), 20:211
  Abijah, 18:105
  Ann, 18:100; 19:212, 216
  Ann (___), 19:215
  Ann (Ryall/Royal), 18:100
  Ann S., 17:38
  Anne (___), 18:112
  Azuba, 20:55
  Barbara, 18:101
  Benjamin, 16:109; 18:14, 101, 112;
    19:216; 20:82, 103, 196, 206, 208
  Bethia (Mansfield), 19:98
  Betsy, 16:16
  Caleb, 16:79; 18:209, 213; 20:112, 210
  Charity, 20:106
  Charity (Bradford), 18:105; 19:148
  Charity (Morgan), 20:107
  Clarissa, 20:147
  Content, 16:16
  Content (Hood), 18:55
  Daniel, 17:11; 16:133; 18:200
  Dorothy, 18:100; 20:103, 104, 137, 138
  Dorotie, 20:102
  Ebenezer, 16:33; 18:103
  Edward, 16:229; 17:115
  Eleazer, 17:218; 18:103, 167; 19:108
  Elias, 19:149
  Elizabeth, 17:41; 18:26, 30, 33, 101;
    20:206, 208, 211
  Elizabeth (___), 18:102
  Elizabeth (Leach), 18:101, 112
  Elizabeth (Phillips), 16:223; 18:105
  Elizabeth (Rhodes), 20:205
  Elizabeth (Sawyer), 18:55; 19:169, 198
  Elizabeth/Tibiah, 17:218
  Ephraim, 18:102
  Ester, 18:100
  Eunice, 18:101; 19:149, 235; 20:208
  Eunice (Atkins), 20:56
  Eunice (Mathews), 20:208
  Ezekiel, 16:133; 18:103; 20:208
  Ezra, 19:106
  Frederick, 20:211

Hannah, 16:55; 17:39; 18:11, 102, 224; 20:106, 107
Hannah (Doane), 20:56
Hannah (Lamson), 19:148
Hannah (Mansfield), 18:102
Hannah P., 17:38
Helen, 19:20
Henry, 16:28; 17:20; 18:17, 28, 49, 71, 99, 100, 102, 103, 112, 133; 19:20, 25, 27, 45, 46, 79, 138, 148, 149, 163, 212, 213, 215-217; 20:132, 194, 196, 205-208
Hepzibah (Hardy), 20:208
Hezekiah, 18:103
Jacob, 16:79; 18:102, 103, 172, 209, 213, 224; 20:112, 208-210
James, 18:103
James P., 17:38
Jane, 20:55
Jedediah, 16:96; 18:35, 102, 104, 105
Jerusha, 17:218
Joanna, 20:116, 117
Joanna (___), 20:116
Job, 16:96; 17:113; 20:209, 211
John, 16:155; 17:171; 18:29, 33, 92, 103; 19:98, 148; 20:56, 132
Jonathan, 16:96l 18:103; 19:149; 20:205
Joseph, 16:109; 18:14, 30, 35, 54, 100, 102, 103, 209, 213, 224; 19:78; 20:56, 102, 111, 132, 235, 196, 204, 205, 208, 209, 211
Joshua, 18:30, 102, 103
Judith, 16:16
Judith (Dow), 18:102
Keziah, 17:218; 18:167
Lansberry, 16:221
Lemuel, 16:133
Lidia, 19:149
Lois, 16:16
Lucretia, 16:16
Lydia, 20:112
Lydia (Blaney), 16:79
Margaret (Downing), 18:30, 102, 103, 209, 224
Mariah (Smith), 20:208, 211
Marilyn M., 18:133
Mark, 20:208
Martha, 18:105, 98, 148, 149
Mary, 16:81; 17:147; 18:35, 102; 19:149
Mary (___), 16:56
Mary (Burrill), 20:211
Mary (Nichols), 20:208
Mary (Norwood), 18:200, 209, 215, 224
Mary (Rand), 16:80; 18:209
Mary (Silsbee), 18:30, 101, 102
Mary (Tolman), 17:218
Mathias, 18:102
Meriah, 20:208
Meriah (Collins), 20:208
Micajah, 18:11, 105;
Michael, 20:116
Miriam, 16:223
Miriam (Silsbee), 18:92, 104, 105; 19:148
Moses, 18:213
Nathaniel, 16:223; 18:101, 103, 105; 19:148, 216
Nehemiah, 16:223; 18:92, 105; 19:148
Peace, 16:47
Pickering, 20:107
Priscilla, 16:109
Priscilla (Kirtland), 18:111, 112
Rebecca, 16:16; 17:149; 18:35, 208; 19:50, 85, 108, 169, 198, 199
Rebecca (___), 20:208
Rebecca (Graves), 20:207, 208
Rebecca (Hussey), 18:54
Rebecca (Newhall), 17:21; 18:167; 19:108
Rebecca (Phillips), 16:80
Rebecca (Sparrow), 20:56
Rebeckah (Potter), 19:149
Richard, 18:103
Ruth, 18:92, 105; 20:208, 211
Ruth (Potter), 19:148
Samuel, 16:19; 17:239; 18:11, 29, 54, 92, 105, 208; 20:78, 79, 103, 211
Sarah, 16:27; 18:100, 167, 211, 224; 20:55, 211
Sarah (___), 20:103
Sarah (Ayers/Heirs), 18:49; 19:149
Sarah (Graves), 17:113; 20:210, 211
Sarah (Silsbee), 18:100; 20:102
Solomon, 20:56
Susanna, 17:47; 18:111, 112, 208
Tabitha, 17:160; 18:48, 49
Tamar (Graves), 20:210, 211
Theodate, 16:221; 18:15, 24, 27, 54, 104
Theophilus, 19:149
Unis/Eunice, 19:149
William, 16:90; 17:158; 18:24, 34, 36, 55, 92, 102-104, 172, 210, 213, 215; 19:50, 105-108, 155, 229; 20:48, 105, 112, 113, 208-211
Z., 17:157; 18:19, 55, 102, 228
Zaccheus, 16:80; 17:41; 18:23, 24, 26, 30, 34, 35, 38, 52, 54, 55, 57, 90, 98, 103-105, 209, 210, 212; 19:49, 105, 169, 175, 198, 229; 20:102, 104, 111, 113, 138, 208, 209
Zachariah, 16:79
Zachary, 16:85; 17:158; 18:36, 104; 19:50, 105, 108; 20:48

COLLUM see also CALLUM
Arthur, 16:118
John, 16:118
Mary (___), 16:118
Scott, 18:136
Scott W., 16:43

COLLY see CORLIS

COLLYER see also COLLIER
John, 19:230
Ruth, 19:230, 231
Ruth (Blackler), 19:230

COLMAN see COLEMAN

COLNER
Samuel, 18:238

COLSON/COLSTON
Adam, 18:43
Eliza, 20:221
Elizabeth, 18:42, 43
Mary (Dustin), 18:43

COLWELL
Arthur, 18:96
Rhoda (Estes), 18:96
Wynneth, 16:51

COMB
Henry, 19:192

COMBS
Elizabeth, 20:233

COMEAU, 18:6
Michael, 20:128

COMEE
David, 16:171
Martha, 16:171; 17:25
Sarah (Johnson), 16:171

COMER/COOMER
Martha (Gilbert), 16:34
Richard, 16:34

COMEY/COMIN/COMINS/COMMI/ COMMIN/COMMING/COMMN/ COMYNS see also CUMMINGS
___, Goodman, 20:175
Abraham, 20:175
Doris Ruth, 17:228
Elizabeth, 16:236
Izahk, 20:175
John, 17:134, 20:175
Mary, 20:175
Ursely, 20:175

COMPTON
John, 19:132

COMSTOCK
George, 18:95

COMYNS see COMEY, CUMMINGS

CONANT, 19:125, 126, 128
___, Mr., 16:136
Abial, 17:233
Alice (Clarke), 16:180
Anna (Tarbox), 20:141
Bethia, 16:58, 213
Caleb, 16:201; 19:124
Christian (More), 16:201
Daniel, 16:143; 20:141
Elizabeth, 16:60a
Elizabeth (___), 16:180
Elizabeth (Dodge), 16:143
Elizabeth (Walton), 16:180
Exercise, 16:137
Hannah, 17:50
Joanna, 16:155
John, 16:201; 20:15
Joshua, 16:180
Keziah, 16:201
Lot, 16:60a
Margaret (Layton), 17:48
Martha, 16:143
Mary, 16:136
Nathaniel, 17:48; 20:198
Richard, 16:180
Robert, 16:136
Roger, 16:137; 17:240; 18:133; 19:123-125, 127-129, 201
Sarah, 16:180
Sarah (___), 16:180
Sarah (Horton), 16:180; 19:124, 127
Sarah (Newcomb), 16:201
Seeth (Gardner), 16:180

CONARY
Eleanor, 18:135

CONCKLIN/CONKLIN
Ananian, 17:195
Ananias, 17:183
Cornelius, 16:32; 17:211; 20:52
Henry N., Mrs., 20:47
Joseph, 18:113
Lydia (Kirtland), 18:113
Mary (Aborn), 16:32; 17:211; 20:52

CONNOLLY
Doris R., 17:225; 18:133
Doris Ruth (Comey), 17:228
John, 17:228

CONNOR see O'CONNOR, 18:177

CONOPEHIT
James, 19:145
Mary (___), 19:145

CONROY
Thomas E., 18:139

CONSTANTIA, 17:192

CONVERSE, 16:225
Adeline (Battelle), 17:59
Allen/Alin, 16:225

Ann (Long), 16:228
Benjamin, 17:59
Edward, 16:225
Elisha S., 16:202
James, 16:225
James W., 16:202
John, 16:228
Josiah, 16:226
Sarah (Parker), 16:228
COOBORN see COBORN
COOK/COOKE
   ___, Mr., 17:224
   Abigail, 18:48; 19:119
   Abigail (___), 18:93
   Benjamin C, 17:165
   Benjamin F., 17:165
   David N., 17:165
   Deborah, 20:56
   Dorcas, 18:152; 19:101
   Elijah, 18:95
   Elisha, 18:49
   Elizabeth, 16:118; 20:29, 99
   Elizabeth (Buxton), 20:99
   Elizabeth (Cheever), 19:104
   Elizabeth (Newhall), 16:44
   Elizabeth (Wilson), 20:99
   Esek, 18:96
   Genevieve, 17:165
   Gregory, 16:118
   Hannah, 17:230
   Hannah (Dearing), 16:238
   Hannah (Estes), 18:96
   Harriet (Tarr), 17:165
   Harriet Ruth (Waters), 19:145
   Helen M., 17:31
   Henry, 19:192, 194
   Hephzibah (Bancroft), 20:41
   Isaac, 18:58; 20:99
   J. Russell, 17:165
   Jacob, 16:238
   Jeremiah R., 17:165
   Joanna, 20:138
   Joanna (___), 18:95
   John, 18:93; 19:104
   Julia Franklin (Friend), 17:165
   Kate W., 17:165
   Margaret (Ives), 20:42
   Mary, 17:201
   Mary (___), 18:58
   Mary (Carriage), 18:58
   Mary (Hathorn), 16:238
   Mary (Wilson), 20:29
   Patience, 20:232
   Rachel (___), 17:237
   Richard, 19:81
   Ruth, 17:149
   Samuel, 18:93; 20:29, 41, 42, 99
   Sarah (Masury), 18:58
   Stephen, 16:44; 18:58
   Susanna, 17:56
   Susannah (Goodwin), 16:118
   Thomas, 16:80
COOL
   John, 20:199
COOLEY
   Abi (Jones), 18:89
   Emmaline Hadin, 17:30
   George, 18:89
COOLIDGE
   Richard, 18:158
COOMBS
   Betsey (Lewis), 16:100
   Frederick, 20:89
   Joann, 18:132
   John M., 16:100
   Lydia, 17:178
COOMER see COMER
COONS
   David, 16:49
COOPER, 17:154, 18:99
   Abigail, 18:239
   Abigail (Lowell), 18:239
   David, 18:239
   Elizabeth, 19:179
   Elizabeth (Goodridge), 19:179
   Hannah, 19:179
   Hannah (Rogers), 18:239
   John, 16:34; 19:138, 179; 20:194
   Lydia, 18:206, 239
   Mary, 19:179
   Mary/Polly, 18:120
   Moses, 18:239; 19:179
   Rebecca, 18:239
   Robert, 19:179
   Ruth, 18:156
   Sarah, 17:52; 19:179; 20:178
   Sarah (Salmon), 19:179
   Simeon, 18:239
   Thomas, 16:31
   Thomas W., 17:142; 18:109
   Timothy, 18:28, 133, 156, 167; 19:138, 179; 20:195
   William, 17:154; 19:131, 179
COOS
   Stephen, 20:225
COOTES/COOTS see also COATS
   Jane (Witherdin), 19:155
COPELAND
   John, 19:64
   Lawrence, 19:58
   Leanora Allen, 17:180
   Lydia (Townsend), 19:58
   Mary (Kingman), 19:236
COPLEY, 20:77
   John Singleton, 17:191
   Lydia, 17:55
COPPERWAITE
   Phebe, 18:39
CORBETT see CORBITT
   Samuel, 17:147
CORBIN
   James, 16:208
CORBITT/CORBETT
   Caroline, 19:238
   Elizabeth (Fairn), 19:238
   Ichabod, 19:238
CORDES
   Charles Frederick, 19:118
   Virginia (Woodman), 19:118
CORDWELL
   William, 16:133
COREY/CORY
   Amy (Green), 16:77
   D. P., 19:102, 103
   Deloraine P., 16:82; 19:210
   Deloraine Pendre, 17:25; 19:224
   Elijah, 19:104
   Elizabeth, 16:92
   Giles, 16:92; 17:14, 112; 18:133; 19:16
   Joseph, 16:77
   Juliana, 19:104
   Margaret, 16:180; 17:112
   Martha, 16:179; 17:112; 19:39; 20:93
   William, 18:239
CORKER
   Edward, 20:134
   Thomas, 20:134
CORKUM
   Ann, 17:53
   Carrie (Mann), 17:53
   Carrie Cutter (Mann), 17:177
   Dorothea (Pentz), 17:53
   Elizabeth (Collicutt), 17:53
   George, 17:53
   George Edward DeLacy, 17:177
   George Henry, 17:53
   John, 17:53
   Joseph, 17:53
   Marjorie Elizabeth, 17:53
   Martha (Etter), 17:53
   Virginia, 17:53
CORLIS/CORLISS/COLLY, 20:45, 115, 177
   Augustus W., 19:224
   Benjamin H., 17:36
   Ebenezer, 17:237
   Jonathan, 18:240
   Lydia, 18:56
   Lydia (Elwell), 17:237
   Martha F. (Burnham), 17:36
   Sarah/Sally, 17:237
CORNEAL
   Johana (Marshall), 16:233
   Peter, 16:233
CORNELISON
   Ann, 16:128
CORNELL
   Deliverance (Clark), 18:91
   George, 18:91
   Philadelphia (Estes), 18:91
   Ruth, 18:91
   Thomas, 18:91
CORNEY see also CURNAY/CURNEY
   Abigail, 19:118
   Abigail (Skilling), 19:118
   John, 19:118
CORNING
   Elizabeth, 16:137
   Samuel, 16:137; 18:76; 20:198
CORNKIDG
   Thomas, 20:199
CORR see also CARR
   Ella Mortimer (Ballard), 19:139
   Helen Pleasants, 19:139
   Thomas Read, 19:139, 140
CORSER
   Jane (Nichols), 16:59
   John, 16:59
   Tabitha (Kenney), 16:59
CORTLAND
   Nathaniel, 18:111
CORWIN
   George, 17:212; 19:143; 20:188
   Jonathan, 17:60; 18:90; 20:134
   Margaret (Shatswell), 16:59
   Martha, 16:59
   Matthias, 16:59
   Samuel, 19:192
CORWITHIN
   David, 19:193
CORY see COREY
COSEN
   ___, Goodman, 19:30
COTHRAN
   Alice, 20:145
COTTER
   Elizabeth (___), 17:56
   John Patrick, 17:55
   Margaret Annie (Rae), 17:55

Mary Ethel, 17:55
Nancy (Fraser), 17:56
Patrick, 17:56
William L.M., 17:56
COTTLE
Edward, 20:80
Sarah (___), 16:18
William, 16:18
COTTON
Alvah, 18:133
Anne, 17:193
Dorothy (Bradstreet), 17:193
Hannah, 19:160
John, 17:193; 18:233; 20:187
Leonard, 19:160
Seaborn, 17:193; 18:233
COUGHLAN
Sarah, 20:60a
COUSENS
A. M., 16:50
Clara, 16:49
COUTURE
M.H., 19:76
COWAN
Relief, 18:212
COWDECK
Richard, 20:197
COWDEN
Clarissa, 18:179
Clarissa (Gates), 18:179
Jeremiah, 18:179
Katherine, 18:179
Marcus, 18:179
Mary, 18:179
Olive, 18:179
Orilla, 18:179
Samuel, 18:179
Sophrona, 18:179
Truman, 18:179
Wealthy, 18:179
COWDERY/COWDREY/COWDRY
Alice, 20:28
Jeremiah, 18:41
Nathaniel, 20:186, 190
William, 18:41, 230; 19:138, 212; 20:183-186, 190-192, 194
COWELL
Elizabeth (___), 18:227
Pan (___), 18:227
COWPER
Elizabeth (Potter), 19:153
John, 19:153
COX see also COCKS, 20:183, 184, 189
___, Mr., 18:214
Abigail, 20:137
Anna, 16:86
Anne, 20:138
Benjamin, 16:101; 20:118
Bob, 19:55
Catherine (Daland), 16:101
Edward, 17:20
Grover, 16:51
Hannah, 16:96; 18:44
John, 17:158
Leah, 20:218
Lemuel, 16:136
Mary, 18:16
Mary (Burchstead), 19:151
Mary/Polly, 18:180
Mehitable S., 20:60a
Robert A., 16:135
Thomas, 18:214; 19:151

COY
Elizabeth, 18:56; 20:216
Elizabeth (Edwards), 17:112
Hannah, 18:76
John, 17:112; 18:76; 20:198
Mary, 18:76
Sarah, 18:76
Sarah Emma (Knight), 18:76
COYLE
Anna C., 17:163
James J., 17:17; 18:134; 19:55
COYT
John, 19:193
CRABTREE, 16:4
Benjamin, 19:45
Elizabeth (Ingalls), 19:45
CRADDOCK/CRADOCK
___, Gov., 19:25
___, Mrs., 17:12
Abigail, 17:12
Matthew, 19:125
CRAFT see also CROFT, 18:167
William, 18:164
CRAFTS
___, Col., 16:97
Emma Stowe (Friend), 17:103
Harriet E. (Morse), 17:103
Mansfield Meader, 17:103
Priscilla, 19:42
William, 17:103; 18:112; 20:135
CRAIG
Edith Mae, 19:235
CRAN
Mary A., 17:105
CRANE
Eliza/Betsy, 20:147
Henry, 18:81
Keziah, 17:51
Mary, 18:81, 82
Richard, 17:75
Tabitha (Kingsley/Kinsley), 18:81
CRANSHAW, 16:13
CREEGER see also KRIEGER
Bluma/Bloomer, 17:64
CREESY/CRESSEY/CRESSY/CRESY
___, Capt., 19:186
Anna (Davis), 16:77
Benjamin, 18:240
Dorcas, 16:77
Edward, 17:56, 222
Eliza C. (Jones), 17:56
Jonathan, 16:77, 220
Joseph, 18:240
Lucy, 16:220
Marietta, 17:56
Ruth (___), 16:220
Sarah, 16:77; 17:203
William A., 17:102
CRISSY
Ann Eliza, 17:119
Benjamin, 17:119
Cornelius, 17:119
George, 17:119
Lyman, 17:119
Marcellus, 17:119
Mary Jane, 17:119
Susannah (Gillen), 17:119
William, 17:119
CROAD/CROADE
Frances (___), 18:90
John, 16:154
Richard, 18:90, 91

CROCKER
Peletiah, 19:137
Richard, 20:199
CROFT/CROFTS see also CRAFT, 18:164
Ann, 18:167
Ann (___), 17:147
Sarah, 17:147
William, 18:28, 51, 167
CROLL
Aaron, 19:84
CROMBIE
Hannah Hilton, 19:42
CROMMETT
Jeremiah, 18:77
Judith (Knight), 18:77
CROMWELL, 16:162, 20:184
Dorothy (Kenniston), 19:195
Elizabeth (Larrabee), 20:44
Grace (Hodgkins), 20:44
Hannah (Barney), 18:165
Jane, 16:118; 18:101
John, 16:68; 18:165
Joshua, 20:44
Lydia (___), 20:44
Oliver, 16:165; 18:195; 19:75
Philip, 19:190, 195, 196
CROOM
Emily, 20:11
CROSBEY/CROSBIE/CROSBY
Anthony, 16:203
Dexey, 16:150
Gert, 17:190
Susannah, 16:132
Timothy, 16:132
CROSE
Mary, 16:131
CROSS/CROSSE
___, Goodman, 20:195
Abigail (Selman), 16:236
Ann, 18:33
Ann E., 17:167
Anna (Jordan), 16:116
Carrie Selman, 16:236
Cicely, 19:174
Deborah, 19:58
Elizabeth (Graves), 20:225
Hannah (Preston), 20:230
James, 16:58
John, 16:236; 20:130
John Lewis, 16:236
Joseph, 16:118
Martha (Hibbard), 19:58, 120
Mary, 16:55; 19:169, 170; 20:225, 240
Mary (Graves), 20:225
Mary (Phillips), 18:160
Mary Abigail (Dennis), 16:236
Mary Susan (Ramsdell), 16:236
Michael, 16:118
Moses, 20:225
Peter, 20:230
Philip, 18:160
Ralph, 20:225
Robert, 16:116; 20:225
Samuel, 19:58, 120; 20:225
Sarah, 18:56
Stephen, 20:135
William, 20:130
CROSSMAN
Anne (___), 17:56
Elizabeth (Graves), 20:218
John, 20:218
CROSTE
Goodman, 19:138

CROSWELL
Mary/Polly (Whitman), 17:115
Nathaniel, 17:115
CROUNWELL
Maude (___), 18:17
Richard, 18:17
CROW/CROWE
___, Mr., 20:233
Elizabeth Powell, 16:187
Hannah (___), 18:91
John, 20:197
Joseph, 18:91
Sarah (Goodale), 20:233
CROWELL
Fred E., 18:190
CROWN
Frances C. (Friend), 17:167
James E., 17:167
James W., 17:167
Mercy E. (Cole), 17:167
CROWNINSHIELD
Anstis (Williams), 17:226
Elizabeth, 17:226
George, 17:226
John, 17:226; 18:93, 94
Mary (Derby), 17:226
CROWTHER, 20:82
CRUMPTON
Jane (___), 16:200
Samuel, 16:200
CRUMWELL
Philip, 19:143
CUE
Huldua, 16:212
Mary, 20:141
Mary (Porter), 20:141
Robert, 20:141, 198
CULLEN
Florence, 16:52
CULVERWELL
Eekiel, 19:36
CUMBEE/CUMBEY/CUMBY
Rebecca, 17:217; 18:53, 57
Robert, 18:57
CUMMINGS/CUMMINS see also COMEY, COMYNS
Abbott Lowell, 17:89; 20:174
Amy (Green), 20:174
Clarissa (Read/Reed), 16:179
David Butler, 20:174
Deborah (Larrabee), 20:44
Edward M., 16:179
Elizabeth, 19:240
Isaac, 20:174
John, 16:193; 19:229; 20:13, 174
Lola (___), 20:174
Margaret (___), 19:167
Mary, 16:45
Mary (Larrabee), 19:228
Mary/Mercy (Larrabee), 19:229
Molly, 18:96
Samuel, 18:56
Susannah (Hood), 18:56
Thomas, 19:167; 20:44
Walter H., 16:179
CUNLIFFE, 16:13
CUNNINGHAM
Effie Fettyplace (Lefavour), 20:156
John, 17:240
Sarah, 16:177
Susanna (Butler), 17:240
CURIER see CURRIER

CURLEY
William T., 20:43
CURNAY/CURNEY see also CORNEY
___, Capt., 17:13
John, 17:240; 20:200
CURRAN
Susannah, 18:206
CURRELL
Thelma, 17:208
CURRIE
Nancy, 17:37
CURRIER/CURIER
Alice, 16:78
Almira, 17:36
Anna, 20:219
Benjamin Hallowell, 16:102
Edward H., 17:110
Elizabeth M. (Clark), 16:102
Elizabeth Tweed, 16:102
George, 16:102
Georgiana, 17:110
Jemima (Rand), 16:102
John J., 16:67; 19:210
Jonathan, 20:219
Joseph, 16:102
Joseph Richards, 16:102
Lydia (Richards), 16:102
Martha, 16:66
Martha Ellen (Appleton), 16:102
Mary, 17:58
Mary P., 17:110
Nathaniel, 16:110
Rebecca (Estes), 16:102
Richard, 16:15
Sarah (Graves), 20:219
Susan M. (Trask), 17:110
Warren Heading, 16:102
CURTAIN see also CURTIN
Mary (___), 18:103
Eunice, 16:46
Ezra, 18:104
John, 18:103, 104
Mary (Silsbee), 18:104
CURTICE see also CURTIS
Anne, 17:201
Elizabeth (Fraile), 17:22
Rebekah, 20:232
Thomas, 18:160
William, 17:22
Zacheus, 16:32
CURTIN see also CURTAIN
Abigail, 16:224
Abigail (Silsbee), 18:105
James, 18:105
John, 19:149; 20:208
Kate A., 20:147
Lydia, 18:105
Martha (Collins), 19:149
Mary (___), 18:103
Sally, 18:105
CURTIS see also CURTICE
Abigail, 17:42
Abigail H. (Bartlett), 17:235
Allen, 18:95
Anna/Nancy, 16:86
Bethia (Parker), 16:40
Carl O., 17:188
Charity, 18:33, 37
Charles Bartlett, 17:188
Dana, 19:168
Daniel, 16:86; 17:147
Dorothy Lucille, 17:188
Ebenezer, 20:55

Effie Gertrude (Osborn), 17:188
Elizabeth, 18:213
Elizabeth (Estes), 18:95
Elizabeth (Scadlock/Scarlet), 16:86
Eunice, 18:44
Fear, 20:55
Fear (Dunham), 20:55
Francis, 19:168
Geraldine Adele, 17:188
Hannah, 20:236
Jacob, 20:55
Joseph, 16:40
Judah, 16:29
Judith (Needham), 20:91
Katharine (Parker), 16:40
Kenneth Greeley, 17:188
Lois (Estes), 18:96
Love (Rogers), 17:114
Lydia, 18:44
Madeline Osborn, 17:187
Mary, 18:213; 19:227
Mary (Tinkham), 20:55
Mary Ann (Sheridan), 17:188
Molly (___), 19:168
Nathaniel, 19:131
Perley Osborn, 17:188
Rachel, 16:180
Rebecka (Farrington), 17:147
Sally, 17:44
Samuel, 16:40; 18:96
Sarah, 17:204
Stephen Winslow, 17:188
William, 16:86; 17:217; 18:72, 208, 209, 213; 19:100; 20:91
William H., 17:235
Zaccheus, 16:193
Zachariah, 17:114
CURWEN/CURWIN, 18:93
Elizabeth (___), 18:17
George, 20:187
George A., 17:98
Jonathan, 18:91
Mehitable, 17:98
Roger, 18:17
CUSHING
Elizabeth (Gray), 20:139
Ezekial, 20:139
John, 16:234
Sarah, 18:31
CUSHMAN
Sara E., 18:83
Sarah, 16:156
CUTHERILL
Robert, 19:232
Saydee Jefferson (Harwood), 19:232
CUTLER, 17:21
___, Capt., 19:225
___, Mr., 17:82
Abigail, 16:111
Cornelius, 17:20
Daniel, 17:20
David, 16:111
Ezekiel, 17:20
Hannah, 20:235
John, 16:93; 20:89
Lucy, 18:178
Manasseh, 18:69, 70, 133
Samuel, 17:20
CUTTER
Ammi, 17:53
Artemas, 17:53
Ebenezer, 18:100
Hannah (Holden), 17:53

John, 17:54
Lydia (Harrington), 17:54
Martha, 17:53
Martha Wise, 17:177
Mary (Marsh), 18:100
Samuel, 16:96; 17:20
Sarah (Eaton), 17:53
William R., 19:210
William Richard, 16:224; 17:224
CUTTIN/CUTTING
___, Mr., 19:159
David, 16:208, 209
Deborah (Coates), 19:159
Dorothy (Sabin), 16:209
John, 16:209
Lydia, 18:168
Mary, 16:209
Sarah, 16:209
Sarah (Edmands), 16:209
William, 16:209
CUTTS
Ann (___), 18:180
Edward, 18:180
Frances Ann, 18:180
Robert, 18:180
CYCKINS
Alice, 19:153

D'AILLEBOUST
Louis, 18:124
DACRE
___, Baroness, 20:70
DAGGITT
Susanna, 20:234
DAILEY
Abigail (James), 16:29
Mary (Boden), 16:29
Peter, 16:29
DAKIN, 18:72
Thomas, 18:107
DALAND, 18:152; 19:41; 20:36
Ben, 16:88
Catherine, 16:101
Geneva, 16:80; 17:149; 18:212
John, 19:199
Sarah, 19:171
DALE
Netta Wier, 16:51
DALLAIRE
Emma, 16:119
Georganna, 16:119
Lowell, 16:119
DALTON
Beatrice Savage, 18:137
DAM
Mary, 19:160
DAMON
___, Miss, 18:205
Abiah, 18:205
Abigail (Sherman), 20:179
Daniel, 18:199, 200; 19:150
Deborah, 20:179
Deliverance (Potter), 19:150
Ebenezer, 16:42
Edward, 20:199
Elijah, 19:150
Elizabeth, 20:33, 38
Elizabeth (Kingsbury), 20:179
Elizabeth (Potter), 18:199
Frank, 20:203
Hepzibeth, 17:116
John, 20:179, 185
Joseph, 18:149; 20:179

Lucretia (Gardner), 18:205
Lydia (___), 16:42
Mary, 19:150
Mary (Baker), 18:149
Rebecca (Bancroft), 20:39
Tama, 18:46
Thomas, 20:39
DAMPNEY
Elizabeth, 16:27
Elizabeth (Wiley), 16:27
John, 16:27
Joseph, 16:27
Mary, 16:27
Penelope (Blaney), 16:27
William, 16:27
DAMROSCH
Clara, 17:170
DANA
Hannah, 20:119
Jacob, 20:119
Patience (___), 20:119
Richard, 19:203
DANE
___, Mr., 17:13
"Child", 17:13
Abigail, 19:115, 219, 221, 222; 20:166
Annis (Bayford), 19:116
Deliverance, 19:219
Deliverance (Haseltine), 19:115, 116, 219, , 221, 222
Elizabeth, 19:115, 219, 221, 222
Elizabeth (Ingalls), 19:45; 115, 219, 221, 222
Esther (Kimball), 16:142
Francis, 16:68; 19:45, 115, 116, 219-222; 20:19, 20, 22, 165
Hannah (Chandler), 19:115, 116, 219, 222; 20:20
Hannah (Poor), 19:45, 115, 116, 222
John, 19:116, 222; 20:19
Martha, 19:116
Mary, 18:149, 167, 168; 19:45, 116
Mary (___), 19:219, 222
Mary (Thomas), 19:45
Nathan, 18:133
Nathaniel, 16:68; 19:115, 116, 219, 222
Phebe, 19:115
DANFORD
Betsy, 16:99
DANFORTH see also DAVENPORT, 19:136; 20:43
___, Gov., 19:225, 228
Agnes, 17:164
David, 16:132
Edward F., 17:164
Hannah (Bancroft), 20:43
Hannah (Marston), 16:85
John, 16:132; 20:34, 43
Joshua, 16:85; 19:177
Kezia (Reed), 19:177
Louisa M. (___), 17:164
Lucinda, 16:85
Lucy, 19:177
Lydia (___), 16:85
Samuel, 16:132
Sarah (___), 16:132
DANIELS
Clotilda, 19:174
Dorcas, 20:239
George F., 16:90
Reuben, 20:239
Sally (Philbrick), 20:239

DANKLE/DUNKLE
John, 16:132
DARBIE/DARBY
Anne, 17:218
John, 16:94; 20:141, 199
Rebekah (Tarbox), 20:141
DARCEREAU
E. J. (Sueet), 16:0
DARLING
Abigail (Read/Reed), 18:179
Benjamin, 18:38, 55, 132, 133
Bethsheba (Inman), 18:96
Daniel, 19:144, 236
Ebenezer, 18:95
Elizabeth, 18:38, 55; 19:29
Ellen, 16:110
George, 16:24; 18:114, 179
Hannah, 18:132, 133, 138
Hannah (___), 18:133
Hannah (Bassett), 18:38, 55, 132
Hannah (Florance), 18:38
Hannah (Potter), 19:236
Hannah (Roach), 19:144
Henry, 18:38
John, 18:38; 19:137
Joseph, 18:96
Kate (___), 18:114
Lois (Gowen), 18:38
Mary (Severy), 18:38
Phebe, 18:96
Sally, 19:97
DARRACOTT
Elizabeth Marland, 19:18
Franklin, 19:18
Franklin Marland, 19:18
George, 19:18
Julia Maria (Marland), 19:18
Julia Marland, 19:18
DART
Jerusha, 18:96
DAVENPORT see also DANFORTH, 18:233
David Paul, 18:190
John, 19:173
Richard, 19:188
Robert R., 18:65
Susan P., 17:36
DAVES see also DAVIES, DAVIS
Esther, 18:162
DAVID, 17:92
Fannie E. (Hart), 17:164
Mildred R., 17:164
Thomas F., 17:164
DAVID I, 16:240
DAVIDSON
J., 17:132
Phoebe A., 20:147
DAVIES see also DAVES, DAVIS
Allison C., 20:172
Arthur Charles, 20:172
Chloe (Molyneaux), 20:172
DAVIS see also DAVES, DAVIES, DENNIS, 16:153; 17:45; 18:49, 133; 19:118; 20:17, 36, 44, 115, 146
Aaron, 20:216
Abigail, 16:40; 17:148; 18:33, 38, 39; 19:49
Abigail (Sargent), 18:200
Alice, 20:114
Alice (Newman), 17:139
An (___), 16:63
Anna, 16:77
Anne (Coates), 19:161
Benjamin, 18:177; 18:240

Betsey, 20:57
Bridget (Loker), 18:175
Charles, 18:39; 19:204
Constance, 18:165
Crafts, 16:77
Cumningham, 19:42, 173
Daniel, 16:132
Deborah (Martin), 17:148
Dorothy, 16:59
Ebenezer, 16:64
Eck, 16:53
Edward, 16:210
Elinor, 18:39
Elinor (Brick), 18:38
Elisha, 18:39
Eliza, 17:111
Elizabeth, 16:57; 17:42; 18:39, 200, 202-204
Elizabeth (___), 18:38
Elizabeth (Bassett), 18:38
Elizabeth Brewster, 18:176
Emme (Devereux), 16:25
Ephraim, 16:68
Esther, 16:132
George, 16:163
Hannah, 16:132; 17:139; 18:179
Hannah (Haskell), 20:216
Hannah (Scott), 18:39
Harold R., 16:53
Hester/Esther (Scott), 18:39
Isaac, 18:38, 39; 20:198
Jacob, 16:40; 17:240; 20:223, 224
James, 16:133; 17:240; 18:140; 20:130
Jedediah, 16:64
Jenkin, 17:46; 19:138; 20:195
Joanna, 17:42
John, 16:132; 17:139; 18:20, 38, 39, 110; 20:131, 134, 196, 200
John D., 18:177
John J., 17:221
Jonathan, 20:50
Joseph, 16:65; 18:202
Judith (Brown), 16:57
Katherine, 18:81
Kinnikum, 16:133
Leona, 19:180
Lucinda, 17:139
Margaret, 18:206
Margaret (Grover), 18:206
Mark, 17:42
Mark Winslow, 18:176
Martha (Lambert), 16:53
Mary, 16:56; 17:42; 18:211; 19:147
Mary (Johnson), 19:221
Mary (Mower), 17:42
Mary Margaret (Longfellow), 16:53
Moley, 16:132
Moses, 16:132; 18:200
Nancy B., 20:41
Nancy Constance (Hanscom), 18:176
Oliver, 18:202
Polly (Kench), 18:177
Rachel, 16:40; 18:202
Rachel (Norwood), 18:202
Rebecca (Larrabee), 20:50
Rebecca (Scott), 18:39
Robert, 18:175; 19:161, 168
Rosina, 18:180
Sally, 19:57, 118
Sally (Day), 19:118
Sally (Rich), 18:177
Samuel, 18:206; 19:118

Sarah, 16:132; 18:20, 39, 175, 202; 19:38, 41, 42, 173, 221; 20:216
Sarah (Cheever), 19:42, 173
Sarah (Kirtland), 18:110
Susanna, 16:132; 18:202
Thomas, 17:148; 18:38, 39, 141
Walter A., 17:78
Walter Goodwin, 16:21; 17:202; 19:224; 20:229
Wealthy, 20:38
William, 16:25; 18:177
William T., 19:116
Zachary, 16:57
DAWES see DAWS
Thomas, 19:131
DAWN
Armand, 17:166
DAWS/DAWES
Abigail (Reed), 19:119
Elizabeth (___), 19:119; 20:59
John, 19:119; 20:59
Jonathan, 20:59
Lois (___), 19:119
Peggy, 20:59
DAWSON
James, 17:95
DAY/DAYE
Abigail, 19:89
Abigail (Leach), 19:119
Abraham, 18:162
Ada, 16:171
Anthony, 17:240
Benjamin, 18:77
Clarissa, 16:92
Dimock, 19:118
Dorothy, 20:101
Edwin F., 20:109
Elizabeth (Candage), 16:235
Emma Merriam (Sprague), 16:171
Hannah (Wright), 16:171
Hannah Ellen (Withey), 20:109
Isaac, 16:133
James, 16:235
Joan (Morris), 20:101
John, 16:171; 18:184; 19:119; 20:200
John Warren, 16:171
Jonathon, 16:235
Joseph, 16:133; 17:134
L. P. O., 17:26
Lucy, 20:41
Lydia (Bennett), 16:235
Martha (Knight), 18:77
Mary Catherine (Eaton), 16:235
Nancy (Yates), 16:235
Nathaniel, 16:64
Nellie Etta, 16:235
Sally, 19:118
Sally (Hale), 16:235
Sally/Sarah (Ingersoll), 19:118
Thomas, 20:101
Timothy, 20:200
Willard, 16:235
William, 17:134
DEACON/DEAKIN
___ (Allin), 16:164
___, Mr., 16:164
Elizabeth (Alderman), 16:118
John, 16:118; 18:72; 19:138; 20:195
Phebe, 18:164
DEAL
Abigail, 18:42, 43
James, 17:132

DEAN/DEANE
___, Rev., 16:105
Abigail (Brintnall), 16:237
Ann/Anna, 16:179
Bethiah (Edson), 16:237
Catherine, 16:237; 17:59
Deborah, 19:149
Desire, 16:27, 78; 18:94
Eleanor (Cogan), 16:237
Elizabeth, 19:149
Elizabeth (Flint), 16:78
Ezra, 16:237
George, 18:90
John, 19:212; 20:197
Jonah, 19:149
Jonathan, 18:76
Joseph, 16:78; 18:90
Josiah, 19:150
Lois, 19:149
Lydia, 20:33
Lydia (Leonard), 16:237
Martha, 19:119
Mary, 19:149
Mary (___), 19:150
Mary M., 18:79
Nancy J., 17:104
Rachael, 19:149
Sarah (Potter), 19:149, 150
Thomas, 18:90; 19:155
Timothy, 19:149, 150
Walter, 16:237
William, 16:237
DeANGELIS
Priscilla Grindle, 16:128
DEARBERG
Beatrice, 16:151
DEARBORN, 18:189
Amelia A. (Foisie), 19:180
Anne (Carroll), 19:180
Arthur Grant, 19:180
Cyrus, 20:82
David, 19:54
David Curtis, 16:3; 18:183
John J., 16:147
Leona (Davis), 19:180
Melvina (Jeanotte-Brodeur), 19:180
Nathaniel, 18:187
Sherburn, 18:187
Wayne Rodman, 19:180
DEARING
Elizabeth, 17:119
Hannah, 16:238
Henry, 18:232
DEATH
Lydia, 19:149
DEBELL
Zachery, 20:223
DECAINE
Nicholas, 17:212
DeCHEORAINVILLE
Claude, 20:169
DECKER
Eliza, 17:167
DeCOSTER
Isaac, 17:148; 18:48
Martha (Hart), 17:148; 18:48
DeCUMBERMERE
Dorothy, 20:238
DEER see also DOOR
Elizabeth, 16:75
DeFOREST
L. Effingham, 16:158
Louis Effingham, 19:36

DEFT see also TUFT
   Elizabeth (Jenks), 16:72
   Samuel, 16:72
DeJERSEY
   Eliza (Briscomb), 18:237
   John, 18:237
   Margaret, 18:237
   Margaret (Parker), 18:235, 237
   Mary, 18:237
DeKOSENKO
   Mary White (Carstairs), 16:151
   Stephen, 16:151
DeKOVEN
   Helen (Haddock), 16:150
   John, 16:150
DeLaGARIGE
   Marie, 19:110
DELAND
   Bethia, 16:178; 20:120
   Philip, 20:198
DELANO
   Sally (Hart), 18:50
   Sarah (Northey), 19:83
   Thankful, 19:112
   William, 18:50
   Zebedee, 19:83
DELAWARE
   Anna, 19:179; 20:180
DELONG
   H. C., 16:220
DELOREY
   Janet, 18:136
   Janet I., 18:134
   Janet Ireland, 18:132, 136, 138; 20:94
DEMING
   William, 19:132
DEMPSEY, 18:211
   James G., 17:99; 18:198
   Miriam, 20:140
DEMPSTER
   Adeline Florella, 20:32
DENIS see DENNIS
DENISON/DENNISON
   ___, Maj., 17:141
   ___, Maj. Gen., 20:202
   Ann, 16:55
   Ann (Borodell), 16:55
   Daniel, 18:192, 193
   Edward, 20:223
   George, 16:55
   Patience (Dudley), 18:193
   Sarah, 16:113
DENMARK
   Abigail, 17:172
   Patrick, 16:111
DENNAN/DENNEN, 18:133
   Agnes, 17:223
   Betsy (Avery), 17:221
   Eme (Browne), 17:220
   Emma Marie (Parsons), 17:55
   Francis, 17:220
   Frank R., 17:222
   George, 17:56
   George Albert, 17:55
   Hannah, 17:220
   Hannah (Dike), 17:220
   James, 16:133; 17:220
   James A., 17:224
   James Albert, 17:55
   Job, 17:220
   John, 17:222
   Joseph, 17:220
   Lyda, 17:222
   Marietta, 17:223
   Marietta (Cressy), 17:56
   Mary (Eveleth), 17:220
   Mary (Haskell), 17:220
   Mary Ethel (Cotter), 17:55
   Molly (Haskell), 17:220
   Nicholas, 17:220
   Olive Lois, 17:55
   Peter, 17:222
   Peter Robert, 17:56
   Sadie, 17:222
   Sara E., 17:221
   Sarah, 17:223
   Sarah (Paine), 17:220
   Sarah E., 17:222
   Sarah E. (Clark), 17:222
   Simeon, 17:220
   Susan Roberts (Stanwood), 17:56
   Will, 17:222
   William, 17:220
DENNETT see also DENNITT
   Samuel, 16:179
   Sarah (Frost), 16:179
DENNING
   ___, Mrs., 17:11
DENNIS/DENIS see also DAVIS, 17:204; 19:52
   Ann, 19:53
   Archibald Selman, 16:236
   Benjamin, 19:231, 232
   Betsey, 16:87
   Charlotte, 19:231
   Charlotte Woodruff (Bessom), 19:231
   David, 16:87
   Edward Haskins, 19:232
   Eleanor, 19:232
   Elizabeth, 18:37
   Elizabeth (Farr), 19:28, 29
   Elizabeth (Smith), 17:203
   Elizabeth (Terry), 19:232
   Florence (Batchelor), 19:232
   Florence B., 19:233
   Florence H., 19:231
   Giley, 19:232
   Hannah/Annie (Rogers), 16:236
   James, 17:203
   John, 17:203; 19:28
   Joseph, 19:28, 29
   Lawrence, 17:203
   Maria Threse, 19:231
   Marietta Jane, 19:231-233
   Mary Abigail, 16:236
   Nathan, 19:28
   Rebekah (Martyr/Martry/Martyn), 19:231
   Samuel Clune, 19:231
   Sarah, 20:135
   Sarah/Mary, 17:203
   Susannah (Kinsman), 16:87
   Thomas, 20:223
   William, 17:203
DENNISON see DENISON
DENNITT see also DENNETT
   George, 17:207
   Phebe (Smith), 17:207
DENOME
   Judith Angelique, 20:170
DENT
   Francis, 18:109
DERBY, 18:133
   Anna (Williams), 17:113; 19:50
   Anstis, 17:227
   Betsy, 17:226; 18:212
   Bridget (Newhall), 16:43
   Charles, 17:226
   Eleanor (Coffin), 17:227
   Elias Hasket, 17:225
   Eliza G. (Fletcher), 17:228
   Elizabeth, 17:227
   Elizabeth (Cheever), 17:226
   Elizabeth (Crowninshield), 17:226
   Elizabeth (Hasket), 17:198
   Elizabeth Laura, 17:228
   Ezekiel Hersey, 17:227
   Francis Coffin, 17:228
   George, 17:228
   Hannah, 18:94
   Hannah (Brown), 17:227
   Hannah (Clark), 17:226
   Hannah (Young), 16:43
   Hannah J. (Barrell), 17:228
   John, 17:225; 18:212; 20:156
   John Barton, 17:228
   John Hasket, 17:226
   Jonathan, 17:226
   Louisa (Lear), 17:227
   Lucretia, 20:232
   Lucy (Brown), 17:227
   Lucy (Smith), 17:226
   Lydia, 17:226; 18:212
   Lydia (Buxton), 16:43
   Lydia (Gardner), 17:226
   Margaret, 17:197
   Margaret (Barton), 17:227
   Martha, 17:226, 227
   Martha (Coffin), 17:227
   Martha Coffin, 17:228
   Mary, 17:226
   Mary (Hodges), 17:225
   Mary (Townsend), 17:228
   Mary Jane, 17:228
   Nathan, 17:26
   Nathaneil Foster, 17:228
   Polly, 18:212
   Rachel (Codner), 17:232
   Rebecca, 18:212
   Richard, 17:225
   Roger, 16:43; 17:198
   Sally, 18:212
   Samuel, 16:43; 17:113; 19:50
   Sarah, 16:88; 17:226
   Sarah (Barton), 17:227
   Sarah (Langley), 17:225
   Sarah (Norwood), 18:212
   Sarah Ellen, 17:228
   William, 18:212
DeRICH/DERICH/DERICK/DURICK/DEUTCH/DOICH/RUCK
   Herbert, 16:48
   John, 16:232
   Martha (Foster), 16:232
   Mary (Basset), 16:232, 238; 18:29, 30
   Mary (Hood), 17:216
   Michael, 16:232, 238; 17:216; 18:30
DERICK see RUCK
DERRENBERGER
   Missy, 19:240
DesROSIERS/DESROSIER, 18:7
   Marie, 20:169
DEUTCH see DeRICH
DEVEREAUX/DEVEREUX/DEVERIX/DEVEROUX
   Abigail (Burrill), 16:25
   Benjamin, 19:151
   Elizabeth, 16:167; 17:42
   Elizabeth (Bacon), 16:25
   Elizabeth (Chapman), 16:2

Elizabeth (Gatchel), 19:151
Elizabeth (Riddan), 16:25
Emme, 16:25; 18:179
Hannah, 16:25; 18:160; 19:151
Hannah (___), 16:25
Hannah (Blaney), 16:25; 19:151; 20:93
Humphrey, 16:25; 17:214; 20:199
James, 17:132
John, 16:23; 17:210, 214; 18: 158; 19:167; 20:15
Joseph, 16:25; 18:160
Lois, 19:151
Lois (Hibbert), 19:151
Lydia (Newhall), 17:219
Mary (Charnock), 16:25
Mary (King), 19:151
Potter, 19:151
Ralph, 16:25; 19:150, 151
Robert, 16:25; 19:151; 20:93
Ruth, 19:151
Ruth (Potter), 16:25; 19:150, 151
Sarah, 16:25
Susanna (Hartshorn), 18:158
Susannah (Phillips), 18:160

DEVINE
Lawrence, 17:58
Lawrence H., 19:57
Mary, 17:58
Mary (Floyd), 17:58
Patrick, 17:58
Sarah F. (Gannon), 19:57

DEWEY
Betsey, 16:92
Betsey (Tarbox), 20:138
Charles, 20:138
Deborah (York), 19:163
George, 16:175
Jabez, 19:163
Louisa/Catherine Louisa (Farnum), 16:108
Mary/Mercy, 17:152
Orville, 16:108

DEWHURST, 16:13

DeWITT see WITT, 18:169

DEWOLF/DEWOLFE
Balthazar, 18:112
Mary, 18:112
Phebe (Marvin), 18:113

DEXTER, 16:175; 19:209
Alice (Smith), 16:72
Benjamin, 20:55, 56
Catherine, 18:170
Ebenezer, 20:55
Hannah (Barrows), 20:55
Hannah (Godfrey), 20:55
Lydia (Rider), 20:55
Mary, 16:138
Polly, 19:172
Samuel, 20:55
Sarah (Arnold), 20:56
Suzannah, 20:55
Thomas, 16:138; 17:88; 19:26, 138, 162, 188, 189; 20:193, 195

DEYARMOND
Alexander, 17:56
Elizabeth, 17:55
Isabell (Dickson), 17:56

DI FRANCO
J. Philip, 16:128

DIAMOND see also DIMOND
Aholiab, 18:105
John, 16:196; 18:105
Joseph, 19:53
Lydia (Silsbee), 18:105

Mary, 18:105
Richard, 18:105
Samuel, 18:105
Sarah, 19:53
Sarah (Ingalls), 19:53

DIANA
Princess Of Wales, 16:174; 17:125

DICER
Elizabeth, 19:235

DICKASON see also DICKSON
Edward, 20:171
Mary (Alley), 20:171
Mary Frances, 20:170, 171

DICKEY
Adam, 19:119
James, 19:119
John, 19:119
Mathew, 19:119

DICKORE
Marie, 18:190

DICKSON see also DICKASON
Isabell, 17:56

DIETERICH/DIETRICH
Harriet, 16:34; 18:138
Harriet Hall, 18:134

DIGBY
Kenelm, 20:64

DIKE
Abigail (Jennison), 18:169
Alice (Ballard), 16:77
Ann (Jennison), 18:169
Anthony, 16:141; 18:169
Benjamin, 16:132
Daniel, 18:169
Hannah, 17:220; 18:169
John, 16:132
Joseph, 16:77
Lidea, 16:132
Margery (___), 16:141
Mary, 18:169
Mary (Witt), 18:169
Rebecah, 18:169
Rebecca (Doliver), 17:220
Rhoda, 18:169
Richard, 17:220
William, 18:169

DILL/DILLE
John, 20:223
Mary (Smith), 17:213

DIMMICK
Temperance, 16:76

DIMAN see DIVAN

DIMON
Aholiab, 18:104
Mary, 19:120

DIMOND see also DIAMOND
Israel, 20:120
Lydia (Silsbee), 18:104
Mary (Chandler), 20:120
Mary (Stevens), 20:120

DINSMORE
Fanny, 20:221
Mary, 20:221

DINSOMER
___, Capt., 20:24

DISPAW
Edward, 20:197
Henry, 20:197

DIVALL
Mary, 18:59

DIVAN/DIVEN/DIMAN, 18:72
___, Mrs., 18:26
"Child", 18:116

Eliezer, 18:116
Elizabeth, 17:116; 18:114, 116, 166; 20:92
Elizabeth (Baker), 18:115, 116
Ezekell, 18:116
Hannah (Needham), 18:115, 116, 232
Hester/Esther (___), 18:114-116
Hester (Marshall), 18:166
Jno., 16:197
John, 16:164; 18:114-116, 133, 166, 167, 232; 20:140, 197
Mary, 18:114, 115, 165-167

DIVANS, 19:158

DIX/DIXE/MIX
Andrew Newton, 16:178
Anna, 18:46
Betsey (___), 16:178
Delia, 16:178
Eason, 16:131
Esther (___), 17:48
Hannah (Batchelder), 18:46
Joel H., 16:178
John, 17:116; 18:158, 237
John Adams, 16:178
John T., 16:178
Jonathan W., 16:178
Joseph, 16:178
Mary, 20:58, 167
Mary (___), 17:116
Mary Ann, 16:178
Ralph, 16:178; 17:48
Samuel, 18:46
Sarah, 17:47; 18:102; 19:48
Thomas, 20:199

DIXEY/DIXIE
Ann/Anna, 16:119
Anna (Burke), 17:103
Anna/Nancy, 19:50
Elizabeth C., 17:103
John, 20:15
Margaret, 20:233
Samuel, 20:15
Sargent, 19:201
Thomas, 20:15, 16
William, 16:137; 17:103; 18:14; 19:43, 75, 202; 20:197

DOAKE
Hannah (Devereux), 19:151
James, 19:151

DOANE
Daniel, 17:57
Hannah, 20:56

DOD/DODD
Judith, 19:119
Thomas, 20:199

DODGE
Abigail, 19:119
Abigail (Dodge), 19:119
Abigail (Edwards), 16:142
Abner, 18:221
Andrew, 16:215
Augusta (Bell), 17:32
Bartholemew, 16:213
Bethia (Conant), 16:58
Betty/Elizabeth (Parker), 16:38
Charity, 18:166
Elisha, 18:166
Elizabeth, 16:137; 18:97
Elnathan, 17:32
Elyaphan, 17:32
Emily (___), 19:59
Esther, 16:143
Esther (Friend), 16:142
Eunice, 16:213

Grenville, 19:15
Hannah, 18:98, 178
Hannah (Fowler), 19:239
Hezekiah, 18:220
Israel W., 16:139
Jacob, 16:142; 19:59
James, 16:142
Jemima (Patch), 16:142
Jeremiah, 17:141
Joanna (___), 18:166
John, 16:58; 18:240; 19:239
Jonah, 16:142; 18:220
Jonathan, 16:142; 18:78
Joseph, 16:142
Joseph Thompson, 16:142
Judith, 17:141
Judith (Eaton), 18:220
Judith (Spofford), 17:141
Levina (___), 17:32
Lois, 16:143
Lois (Dodge), 16:143
Lydia (___), 18:221
Lydia (Herrick), 16:235; 18:220
Margaret, 16:213
Margaret (Cleave), 16:213
Martha, 16:213
Mary, 16:137
Mary (Conant), 16:136
Mary (Edwards), 16:142
Mary (Kimball), 18:166
Mary (Tarbox), 20:142
Moses, 16:38
Parker, 18:240
Rebecca L., 18:98
Richard, 16:137
Robert, 20:142
Sarah, 16:142; 17:178; 18:73
Sarah (Eaton), 16:142
Sarah (Friend), 16:142
Simon, 19:119
Susanna, 16:235; 18:220
Uzziel, 16:216
William, 16:136; 19:189; 20:89, 198

DOE
Adda, 17:27
Albert, 17:27
Freddy, 17:27
Lucy, 17:27
Theodora (Edmands), 17:27

DOEFF
Hendrik, 17:133

DOICH see DeRICH

DOLE
George T., 20:154
Hannah (Todd), 20:208, 212
John, 20:212
Moses, 20:212

DOLIBER/DOLLIBER, 18:133; 19:187
Donald, 17:75
Donald A., 16:153; 18:133-139
Donald B., 19:183
Joseph, 16:119; 17:209
Mary (Pousland), 16:119
Mary Caste/Casbe (Peltro), 16:119
Mary/Polly, 16:58
Peter, 20:15
Rebecca (Taylor), 16:119
William, 16:119

DOLITLE see DOOLITTLE
DOLIVER see DOLLIVER
DOLLARHIDE/DOLLARHYDE
William, 18:190; 20:8-11

DOLLIBER see DOLIBER

DOLLIVER/DOLIVER, 18:133
___, Mr., 17:11
Abigail, 19:118
Abigail (Sanders), 19:118
Anna (Higginson), 17:236
Dorothy, 19:175
Elizabeth Ann, 17:162
Elizabeth F. (___), 17:162
John, 20:199
Joseph, 17:12; 20:199
Mary, 17:236
Mary (Elwell), 17:236
Mary (Wallis), 17:236
Paul, 17:236
Peter, 19:118
Rachel, 17:236
Rachel (Barber), 17:236
Rebecca, 17:220
Samuel, 17:236
Sarah, 20:222
William, 17:133
William H., 17:131
William P., 17:162

DONAHEW/DONAHUE/DUMPHY
Catherine, 17:138
Eunice, 17:135, 136
Eunice (Clark), 17:135, 137
John, 17:135, 137
Lydia, 17:138
Philemon, 17:138

DONNEL/DONNELL
Alice, 18:200, 202
Alice (Chadbourne), 18:202
Andrew, 16:17
Lydia, 18:178
Samuel, 18:202

DONOVAN
___, (Mrs.), 19:136
Alfred M., 19:136
Deborah (Larrabee), 20:44
James, 20:44

DOOLITTLE/DOLITLE
Eunice, 20:41
John, 16:164; 18:230; 19:78
Sarah, 19:147

DOOR see also **DEER**
Eleazer, 18:115, 116
Hannah (Armitage), 18:115

DORMAN
Timothy, 16:193

DORMOND
Ebenezer, 16:90

DORR
Esther (Goldthwaite), 19:18
John, 19:18
Lucretia, 19:17, 18
Sarah, 18:171

DORY
Phillip, 20:197

DOTEN
Edward Lewis, 16:180
Lydia Morton (Holmes), 16:180

DOTSON, 19:233

DOTY
Joseph P., 16:180
Sarah (Allen), 16:180
Sarah Lizzie, 16:180

DOUGLAS/DOUGLASS see also **DUGLAS**, 16:231; 18:133
Abigail, 16:75
Abigail (Sharp), 16:75
Alexander, 16:75; 18:46
Daniel, 17:105

Hannah Maria (Friend), 17:105
Sarah, 16:74, 75; 17:198
Sarah (Ballard), 16:75

DOUTEY/DOUGHTY/DOUTIE/DOUTY/DOWTY
Abigail, 16:207
Benjamin, 17:238
Betsey (Child), 17:238
Elizabeth (Bully), 16:211
Joseph, 16:44, 89
Stillman, 17:238
Thomas, 16:211

DOVE
Hannah, 16:94

DOW
Abigail (Phillips), 16:223
Abraham, 16:223; 17:52; 20:178
Benjamin, 16:223; 18:105
George, 19:184
George Francis, 18:218
Goodrich Q., 16:118
Hannah (Phillips), 16:223
Hannah (Silsbee), 18:105
John, 17:52; 18:156; 20:178
John Francis, 18:51, 56
Joseph, 18:59
Judith, 16:223; 18:102; 19:177
Lydia Ropes, 16:200
Martha, 18:156
Mary, 16:223
Mary (Page), 17:52; 20:178
Mehitable, 17:52; 20:178
Mehitable (Haines), 17:52; 20:178
Moses, 19:234
Phebe (___), 16:223
Rebekah, 20:141
Sarah (Bradley), 19:234
Sarah (Brown), 17:52; 20:178
Susannah (Hoyt), 17:52; 20:178

DOWCE see **DOWSE**

DOWDIN
Ann, 18:215

DOWNER
Joseph, 18:174
Mary (Knight), 18:174

DOWNEY/DOWNIE
Elizabeth (Albree), 18:59
James, 20:127
John, 18:59
Matthew, 20:127

DOWNING
___, Mr., 18:195, 196
Abigail (Brown), 16:120
Anna, 18:228
Anstest/Anstis, 16:131
Benjamin, 20:140
Caleb, 18:117, 227
Elizabeth (Knight), 18:75
Emanuel, 17:212; 18:195; 19:132, 188; 20:132
George, 18:195
Hazel, 20:55
Joanna, 17:148; 19:49
John, 18:75
Joseph, 18:227
Macam, 20:197
Margaret, 18:30, 102, 103, 209, 224
Mehitable, 18:75
Richard, 20:199
Sarah (Browne), 18:227
Sarah (Coats), 18:117
Thomas, 16:120

DOWNS
  Jane, 16:239
DOWSE/DOWCE
  ___, Mrs., 16:63
  Abigail, 16:63
  Jane (Aborn), 16:88
  John, 16:63
DOWSETT
  David, 16:133
DOWST
  Jane (Aborn), 16:89
  William, 16:89
DOWTY see DOUTEY
DOYL/DOYLE
  Felix, 16:133
  Frances Ann, 18:136
  Thomas, 17:8
DRAGETT
  Alice (Coates), 19:157
  Isaac, 19:157
DRAKE, 18:187
  ___, Mr., 18:195
  Abigail, 16:57
  Abraham, 16:57
  Francis, 17:115
  Francis S., 19:134
  Isabell, 19:120
  Joseph, 17:238
  Polly (Simonds), 17:238
  Sarah, 16:57
  Sarah (Hobbs), 16:57
  Theodate (Robie), 16:57
DRAPEAU
  David, 16:52
  Marion Zepha (Longfellow), 16:52
  Sepherine (Morin), 16:52
  William J., 16:52
DRAPER
  Abigail (Richards), 17:29
  Benjamin, 16:39
  Ira, 17:29
  Lydia, 17:29
  Mary, 16:39
  Mary (Parker), 16:39
  Thomas, 17:29
DRESER/DRESSER
  Bridget (Pemberton), 19:208
  Daniel, 19:208
  Mary (Pemberton), 19:208
  Thomas, 16:64
DREW
  ___, Capt., 20:158
  Hannah Bartlett, 18:51, 135
  Phineas, 20:83
DREWRY see also DRURY
  Christina Evelyn (Marland), 19:20
  John, 19:20
DRISCOLL
  Charles E., Mrs., 16:152
DRIVER, 18:165
  ___, Goodman, 18:166
  Mary, 18:58
  Phebe (___), 19:145
  Robert, 17:17; 18:99, 172, 230; 19:45, 47, 138, 145; 20:132-134, 195, 196, 207
  Ruth, 18:43, 172, 199; 19:144, 145
DRURY see also DREWRY
  Susanna (___), 16:74
DUBOIS see also WOOD
  Antoinette (Limousine), 20:169
  Catherine (Blosse), 20:169
  Catherine (Jean), 20:169
  Claude Catherine, 20:169
  Dominique, 20:170, 171, 173
  Francis, 20:169
  Francis Xavier, 20:170
  Francoise (Rivard), 20:169
  Genevieve, 20:169
  Henry, 20:170
  Jean, 20:169, 140, 173
  Jean Baptiste, 20:169, 170, 173
  Jeanne (Raoult), 20:169
  Joseph, 20:170
  Joseph-Marie, 20:169
  Judith Angelique (Denome), 20:170
  Julie (Guertin), 20:170
  Louis, 20:170
  Marguerite (Urbain), 20:170
  Marguerite (Vadnais), 20:170
  Marie Anne, 20:169
  Marie Anne (Peradeau), 20:170
  Marie Charles, 20:169
  Marie Genevieve, 20:170
  Marie Genevieve (Dubord), 20:169
  Marie Jeanne, 20:169
  Marie Joseph, 20:170
  Marie Josephine, 20:169, 170
  Marie Josephine (Grignon), 20:169
  Marie Josephte (Frappier), 20:169
  Marie Josette, 20:169
  Marie Marguerite, 20:170
  Marie Veronique, 20:170
  Marie-Joseph (Grignon), 20:170
  Maroailine (Beaudet), 20:170
  Michel, 20:169, 170, 173
  Michelle (Tessier), 20:169
  Olive (Laforme), 20:170
  Pierre, 20:169, 170
  Prosper, 20:170
  Rita I., 20:173
  Sophie (Lessard), 20:170
DUBORD
  Jean Baptiste, 20:169
  Marie (Houray), 20:169
  Marie Genevieve, 20:169
DUCKWORTH, 16:13
DUDLEY, 17:139
  ___, Gov., 16:153; 18:29, 92, 195, 196; 20:183
  Aaron, 17:24
  Anne, 17:193; 18:193
  Benjamin, 17:119
  Daniel, 17:119
  Dorothy (___), 18:193
  Elizabeth, 17:119
  Hannah, 17:119
  Joanna, 17:119
  Joseph, 16:210; 17:119
  Mary, 17:119
  Patience, 18:193
  Paul, 16:208
  Sophia (Frail), 17:24
  Susan (___), 20:189
  Susanna, 17:119
  Susanna (Lord/Ladd), 17:119
  Thomas, 16:226; 17:119; 18:193; 20:189
  W., 20:79
  William, 16:208
DUDY
  Moses, 20:200
DUFFY
  Janis, 20:123
  Mark J., 16:189
DUGGLAS/DUGLAS/DUGLES see also DOUGLAS
  Abigail (Sharp), 16:233
  Alexander, 16:233; 19:78
  Allister, 20:197
DUKESHIRE
  Mary (Kempton), 20:55
DULEY
  Mary, 17:168
DUMMER
  ___, Gov., 20:130, 131
  Stephen, 19:30
DUMPHY see DONAHUE
DUNCAN
  Mary, 17:191
  Mary (Epes), 17:191
  Nathaniel, 17:191
  Peter, 17:191
DUNELL
  Robert, 20:224
DUNHAM
  Bethiah (Friend), 16:213
  Catherine (Potter), 20:221
  Eleazer, 20:56
  Fear, 20:55
  George, 16:213
  Miriam (Phillips), 20:56
DUNIWAY
  David C., 18:191
DUNKLE see DANKLE
DUNKLEE
  Sally, 20:42
DUNN
  Alexander, 19:36, 98
  Clara M., 19:23
  Deborah, 18:39
  Grace E., 19:23
  John E., 19:23
  Leonard, 19:23
  Leslie, 19:21, 23, 24
  Mary (Farnham), 19:22, 23
  Mary Almira (Farnham), 19:21, 23, 24
  Mary Estella, 19:23
  Thomas H., 19:23
  Thomas Henry, 19:23
  Tom, 19:21-23
  Wilford E., 19:23
  William, 19:23
DUNNELLS
  David, 19:164
DUNPHY
  Eunice, 17:139
DUNTON/DUNTTON
  Hannah, 17:113
  John, 16:165; 19:75
  Nathaniel, 20:217
  Samuel, 20:190
  Sarah, 20:216, 217, 219
DUNWELL
  Abigail, 19:150
DUNZACK
  Bathsheba (Norwood), 18:207
  Daniel, 18:207
DUPEE
  Rebecca, 19:240
DURANT
  Hannah (Hanson), 18:26
  Reuben, 18:26
DUREN
  Charles M., Mrs., 16:41
DURGIN
  Edith, 17:186
  Edwina Victoria, 16:52
  Florence (Cullen), 16:52
  Napoleon, 16:52

DURHAM
   Belinda, 17:105
DURICK see DeRICH
DURKEE, 18:133, 136
DURLING
   Anna (Krotzer), 17:56
   George, 17:56
   James Krotzer, 17:55
   Jessamine (Pardee), 17:55
   John Hubbard, 17:55
   Lydia (Copley), 17:55
   Marjorie Hubbard, 17:55
DURRELL, 20:13
   Catherine, 19:227; 20:50
   Lydia, 19:227; 20:50
DUSTIN/DUSTON, 18:133
   Hannah (Emerson), 18:141
   Mary, 18:43
   Saloame, 18:59
DUTCH
   Barbara, 16:201
   Benjamin, 18:240
   Christian, 16:201
   Grace, 19:162
   Grace (Pratte), 16:201
   Hannah, 18:202
   Hester, 17:237
   Osmond, 16:201; 17:237; 20:18
   Samuel, 16:201; 17:50
   Susannah, 16:201; 17:50
   Susannah (More), 16:201; 17:50
DUTTON
   Abigail Coffin, 16:120
   Anna, 16:120
   Anna (Coffin), 16:120
   Benjmain, 16:120
   Elizabeth/Eliza (Robertson), 16:120
   Sarah, 19:206
   Stephen Coffin, 16:120
   Thomas, 16:120
**DWINEL/DWINNEL/DWANIEL/
   DWINILS/DWINNELL**
   Dinah (Brinsdell), 18:177, 213
   H., 20:90
   Jonathan, 18:177
   Mary, 16:217
   Mehitable, 16:194
   Michael, 18:56
   Sally (Hayward), 18:178
   Simeon, 18:178
   Susanna, 18:211, 213
   Thomas, 18:177, 213
DYER
   ___, Capt., 16:150
   Abigail, 20:115
   Elizabeth, 19:111, 112; 20:239
   Lucy, 19:113
   Samuel, 19:112
   Thankful (Delano), 19:112
DYSON, 16:13

EABORN see also ABORN
   Samuel, 17:212
EAGER
   Esther (___), 17:43
   Francis, 17:43
EAIERS see also AYERS, EYRES
   Ralph, 20:199
EAKLE
   Arlene, 17:73; 18:65
EAMES
   Abigail, 18:215
   Amy, 17:177
   Daniel, 16:194; 20:168
   Elizabeth, 18:170
   Lydia (Wheeler), 20:168
   Rebecca (___), 16:194
   Rebecca (Blake), 20:16, 168
   Robert, 16:193
   William, 17:23
EARL/EARLE see also EHRLE
   Alice Morse, 20:52
   Anna (Howard), 19:149
   Elizabeth, 18:199; 19:149, 150
   Mary, 20:95
   Mary (___), 20:91
   Oliver, 20:96
   Rebecca (Sherman), 20:96
   William, 19:149
EASTHAM see EASTMAN
EASMAN see EASTMAN
EASTERBROOK
   Elizabeth (Parker), 17:79
**EASTMAN/EASMAN/ESTMAN/
   EASTHAM/EASTMEN**, 18:119
   Abigail, 16:147
   Abigail (Mellen), 17:177
   Benjamin, 16:19; 17:152
   Clarissa, 18:178
   Dorothy (___), 17:152
   Edmund, 16:19
   Elizabeth, 18:178
   Francis A., 18:178
   Francis Beckett, 18:178
   Harriet, 18:178
   Henry L., 18:178
   Joseph, 16:59; 17:177
   Love (Tuck), 18:178
   Martha, 16:59
   Mary Land, 18:143
   Miriam, 17:152
   Patience (Smith), 16:59
   Richard, 16:187
   Richard W., 18:118
   Sally, 16:236; 17:54
   Tamison (Woodwell), 16:59
EASTWICK
   ___, Mrs., 19:143
   Edward, 19:193
   Esther, 17:20
EATON
   ___, Mrs., 19:137
   Abigail, 18:220; 19:214, 215; 20:33, 34, 37, 38
   Abigail (Bourne), 19:165, 167
   Abigail (Fellows), 16:235; 18:219
   Abigail (Gott), 16:235
   Abigail (Herrick), 18:220
   Amos, 18:221
   Andrew Beattie, 16:239
   Anne (___), 17:56; 19:101
   Audria, 16:229
   Benjamin, 16:32; 18:220; 19:137
   Calvin, 18:221
   Daniel, 19:136, 165, 212, 213, 216; 20:34, 197
   David, 20:34
   Ebenezer, 18:220
   Elizabeth, 16:37; 18:220; 19:91, 165, 215, 216, 218; 20:33
   Elizabeth (Kendall), 19:215; 20:34
   Elizabeth (Reed), 18:221
   Elizabeth (Thorn), 19:167
   Esther, 20:36, 37
   Eunice (Singletary), 17:56
   George F., 17:109
   Grace (___), 18:99
   Hannah (Jordan), 18:220, 221
   Helen/Ellen (___), 17:56
   Hepsibar, 18:43
   Hophni, 19:165
   Hubbard, 18:221
   Irving, 18:221
   Jacob, 17:145; 19:165, 167
   James, 17:27; 18:219-221
   Jeremiah, 19:137, 165, 216; 20:48
   Joanna (Evans), 18:220
   Job, 17:56
   John, 16:58; 17:54; 18:210, 220; 19:46, 165, 173, 215, 216; 20:34
   Jonas, 18:99; 20:185
   Jonathan, 18:219-221
   Joseph, 18:43; 19:137, 165; 20:48, 140, 198
   Joshua, 18:113; 19:213
   Judith, 18:219-221
   Judith (Ash), 18:219
   Lilly, 17:47; 18:41; 20:34
   Lydia, 19:165
   Lydia (Moulton), 19:165
   Martha, 19:59; 20:35
   Mary, 17:204; 20:48
   Mary (___), 16:58
   Mary (Ingalls), 19:46, 173
   Mary (Littlefield), 19:165
   Mary (Simons), 17:56
   Mary (Whitmore), 18:221
   Mary Campbell, 18:221
   Mary Catherine, 16:235
   Mary S. (Thomas), 18:221
   Mehitable (Barker), 17:56
   Mehitable (Breed), 17:145
   Mercy (Horne), 16:32
   Moses, 16:235; 18:219-221
   Nancy, 19:165
   Nathaniel, 19:165
   Olive, 19:165
   Patience, 18:221
   Patience (Bridges), 16:235; 18:219, 220
   Polly (Hackett), 18:120
   Priscilla, 20:24, 91, 228
   Priscilla J., 19:165
   Richard, 17:173
   Ruth, 19:46, 165
   Ruth (Peirce), 18:113
   Sally, 18:221
   Sally (Pickering), 18:220
   Sarah, 16:142; 17:53; 18:220; 19:137
   Sarah (Clark/Clarke), 17:54
   Sarah (Sweetser), 17:27
   Sarah (Young), 17:53
   Sarah Ann (Bragdon), 19:165
   Susanna (Dodge), 16:235; 18:220
   Sylvanus, 18:221
   Theophilus, 16:235; 18:219, 220
   Thomas, 17:53; 18:221; 20:34, 36, 37
   Timothy, 16:90
   W. H., 16:189
   William, 17:158; 18:120; 19:137, 165, 216, 217; 20:34, 185, 190
   William E., 16:158
   William Hackett, 17:57
EAYRE see AYER, 19:175
EBBORN see ABORN, EBOURNE
EBENS
   Mary Jean, 19:234
   Mary Jean (___), 20:175
   Richard F., 19:86

**EBORNE/EBOURN/EBOURNE/EBURN/
EBURNE** see also ABORN, YEBORNE
Hannah, 17:211
James, 17:211
Kathren (Smith), 17:210, 211
Mary, 17:210, 211
Moses, 17:211
Rebecca, 17:211
Samuel, 17:209, 210
Sarah, 17:211
ECCLESTON
Avery Nelson, 17:176
Emeline Augusta, 17:176
Sally Burton (Ray), 17:176
EDDY, 18:133, 137
Richard, 17:136
EDE
John, 20:69
EDELSTEIN
Linda C., 19:117
EDES
Edward, 20:47
Elizabeth, 20:47
Eunice (Lakin), 17:85
Isaiah, 17:85
John, 20:47
Lucretia, 18:205
Rebecca, 20:47
Sarah, 17:204; 20:47
Sarah (Larrabee), 20:47
Thomas, 20:47
EDGAR
Aida, 16:119
Carrie, 16:119
Eugenia, 16:119
Mabel, 16:119
Sybil, 16:119
EDGECOMB
Elizabeth (Tarbox), 20:144
Nicholas, 20:144
EDGERLY
___, Mr., 16:64
___, Mrs., 16:64
EDISON
Thomas, 16:185
EDMANDS see also EDMONDS,
EDMUNDS
Addie E., 17:31
Alice E. (Blaney), 17:31
Allan Christi, 17:31
Alonzo, 17:27
Andrew, 17:27
Andrew J., 17:30
Ann/Nancy, 17:27
Anna (Amils), 17:31
Annie Stewart (Romer), 17:31
Artemus, 17:27
Artemus Seymour, 17:30
Arthur Seymour, 17:30
Benjamin, 16:208
Charles, 17:27
Charles H., 17:29
Clara, 17:27
Consider, 17:27
Cora (___), 17:29
Dorothy M., 17:31
Ebenezer, 16:202; 17:28
Ebenezer P., 17:29
Edith G. (Mansfield), 17:30
Edward, 17:31
Edward Wesley, 17:30
Elbert, 17:31
Elizabeth C., 17:30

Elizabeth/Eliza, 17:26
Ella Josephine (Mansfield), 17:30
Ellis Lincoln, 17:31
Elwood Donald, 17:27
Emma Florence (Pierce), 17:30
Emmeline I. (Ferris), 17:31
Ernest Carl, 17:31
Ernest John, 17:31
Esther, 17:29
Esther (Burrill), 17:27
Ethel Jean, 17:31
Everett V., 17:29
Florence, 17:31
Frances Caroline, 17:31
Frances J., 17:30
George, 17:27
George Draper, 17:29
Hannah, 16:208; 17:27
Hannah (___), 16:208
Hannah (Scott), 16:209
Harriet, 17:27
Helen M. (Cook), 17:31
Helena L. (Moltzen), 17:31
Hellin, 17:27
Ida, 17:27
Imogene, 17:27
Isobel (Hemingway), 17:27
James W., 17:29
Jesse, 17:27
John, 16:209; 17:25; 18:134
John Lincoln, 17:30
Joseph, 16:208
Josephine Ann Hurin (Edwards), 17:27
Lorena, 17:27
Lot/Lott, 17:26
Lucellia, 17:27
Lucy Caroline (Kettell), 17:30
Lydia (___), 17:29
Lydia (Draper), 17:29
Marcellus, 17:27
Margaret (___), 17:27
Margaret Ellen, 17:30
Margaret Lillian, 17:31
Marguerite (Bailey), 17:31
Maria (___), 17:30
Mary, 16:209; 17:26
Mary (Wade), 17:27
Mary Anna (Hawes), 17:31
Mary C. (Findley), 17:31
Mary Francis, 17:29
Mary M. (Hull), 17:30
Mary/Marcy (White), 17:27
Mary/Polly, 16:238; 17:27
Mehitabel, 16:204
Mehitable (Trusdale), 16:209
Melissa, 17:27
Mildred Florence, 17:31
Milton A., 17:31
Nancy, 17:26
Nancy Allen, 18:134
Nathaniel, 17:31
Nelson, 17:31
Nelson W., 17:30
Oscar Melvin, 17:30
Phebe (Terry), 17:29
Ralph, 17:27
Rodney, 17:27
Ruth, 17:30
Ruth (Putney), 16:209
Ruth (Wiley), 17:27
Sally, 17:27
Sarah, 16:209; 17:26

Sarah (Williams), 17:26
Sarah A. (Payne), 17:29
Sarah/Sally, 17:27
Solon V., 17:29
Susan (___), 17:31
Theodora, 17:27
Theodore, 16:202
Wilfred S., 17:31
Willard, 17:27
William, 16:208; 17:26
EDMONDS see also EDMANDS,
EDMUNDS, 20:162
___, Goody, 16:203
Abigail (Doutey/Doughty), 16:207
Ann (Martin), 16:203
Bathsheba (Sanford), 16:208
Daniel, 16:202
Ebenezer, 16:208; 17:25
Elijah, 16:211
Elizabeth, 16:204
Elizabeth (Burgess), 16:204
Elizabeth (Merriam), 16:204
Elizabeth (Rhodes), 16:207
Esther (Boyce), 16:211
George, 16:211
Griffin, 19:29
Hannah (Newell), 17:25
James, 16:202
John, 16:202
Jonathan, 16:207
Joseph, 16:203
Mary, 16:202; 17:99
Mary (___), 16:204
Mary (Pratt), 16:208
Richard, 16:202
Robert, 16:206; 18:240; 19:158, 159
Samuel, 16:202
Sarah, 16:207
Sarah (Berry), 16:207
Sarah (Hallet), 16:207
Sarah (Hudson), 16:204
Sarah (Williams), 17:25
Susanna (___), 16:204
Theodore, 18:134
Thomas, 16:207
Walter, 16:202
William, 16:202; 17:25; 18:134, 231;
  19:138; 20:195
EDMONDSON, 16:13
EDMUNDS see also EDMANDS,
EDMONDS, 18:153
___ (Wheeler), 16:211
___, Goodman, 17:215
Abigail, 16:207
Abigail (Doutey/Doughty), 16:211
Ann (___), 16:202
Bathsheba (Sanford), 16:206
Benjamin, 16:205
David, 16:207
Ebenezer, 16:205
Elijah, 16:211
Elizabeth, 16:205
Elizabeth (Griggs), 16:206
Elizabeth (Rhodes), 19:155
Eunice (Parker), 16:209
George, 16:211
Hannah, 16:205
Hannah (___), 16:210
Hannah (Hinkson), 16:207
Hannah (Newell), 16:210
Hannah (Peake), 16:209
James, 16:211
Jemima, 16:210

John, 16:202; 20:197
Jonathan, 16:206
Joseph, 16:75; 18:150-152, 226; 20:197
Lemuel, 16:209
Martha (Smallidge), 16:207
Mary, 16:205
Mary (___), 16:202
Mary (Fry), 16:211
Mary (Pratt), 16:206
Mary/Molly, 16:209
Mehitable, 16:205
Molly (Gale), 16:210
Moses, 16:210
Nathaniel, 16:206
Rebecca, 16:205
Robert, 16:206; 18:150
Samuel, 16:205; 18:151; 19:155; 20:197
Sara (Kidder), 16:210
Sarah, 16:207
Sarah (Hudson), 16:206
Sarah (Williams), 16:210
Silence (Emerson), 16:209
Stephen, 16:210
Thankful, 16:211
William, 16:203; 18:151

EDSON
___, Mr., 19:159
Bethiah, 16:237
Emily (Coates), 19:159
Olive D., 20:55
Samuel, 16:237
Susanna (Orcutt), 16:237

EDWARD
Benjamin, 20:238
King, I, 16:240
Martha (Gaines), 20:238

EDWARDS, 19:191
Abigail, 16:142
Abigail (Allen), 20:238
Abigail (Lamson), 20:238
Abigail (Ober), 20:238
Abraham, 19:160
Benjamin, 17:112; 20:141, 238
Betsey, 16:48
Edward, 19:160
Eleanor, 20:120
Elisabeth (Coates), 19:160
Elizabeth, 17:112
Elizabeth (___), 19:193
Elizabeth (Emerson), 19:160
Esther, 20:136, 141
Esther (Tarbox), 20:238
Griffin, 17:214
John, 17:112; 18:216; 20:198, 238
Josephine Ann Hurin, 17:27
Martha, 17:112; 18:133, 134
Mary, 16:142, 235; 20:119
Mary (Farrar), 20:238
Mathew, 20:191
Rebecca (Ford), 20:238
Rice, 17:112; 20:198, 238
Ruth (Morrill), 20:238
Ruth (Phillips), 18:160
Sally (Norwood), 18:216
Sarah (Perkins), 20:238
Thomas, 17:112; 19:193; 20:199
William, 17:143

EELLS, 18:134, 135
Ann (Lenthall), 17:234
Myron, 17:234
Samuel, 17:234
William, 17:234

EHRENFRIED
Albert, 16:189

EHRLE see also EARL
Charity, 17:120

EIRE/EYRE see also EAIERS, AYER
Anne (___), 19:174
Cicely (Crosse), 19:174
Hannah (___), 19:174
Richard, 19:174
Robert, 19:174
Thomas, 19:174

ELDER
Janus G., 19:110, 113

ELDERKIN
John, 17:87; 18:79; 19:138, 189, 190; 20:195

ELDERSHAWE
Alice (Potter), 19:153
Francis, 19:153

ELDRIDGE
George N., 17:162

ELIOT see also ELLIOT, ELLIOTT
Abigail, 17:16
Andrew, 17:212; 18:235; 19:131
Hopestill, 19:164
Jacob, 19:212
John, 16:209; 20:95
Mary, 19:212

ELITHORP/ELITHORPE
Mary, 19:226; 20:49
Thomas, 19:162

ELIZABETH
Queen, 17:125

ELKINS
Elizabeth, 17:230
Elizabeth (Gale), 17:230
Jane (Purchase), 17:230
John, 17:179
Mary, 17:230; 18:94
Oliver, 16:153; 17:230
Robert, 17:230
Sarah, 17:230
Sarah/Sally (Nichols), 17:179
Thomas, 17:230; 19:51

ELLENWOOD
Martha, 17:203

ELLERSON
Betsy, 18:212

ELLERY, 20:17, 18
Abigail, 17:37
Abigail (Norwood), 18:200
David H., 17:109
George, 17:109
Georgiana, 17:109
Hannah (Proctor), 17:109
Ida A., 17:109
Mary, 20:237
Nathaniel, 18:200
Sarah E. (Goldsmith), 17:109
William, 17:240

ELLES see also ELLIS
John, 16:240

ELLET
Sarah, 18:39

ELLETRAP see also ELLITROP
Ann (___), 18:238
John, 18:238

ELLINGTON/ELLWYN
Elizabeth, 19:211

ELLINGWOOD/ELLINWOOD
Ebenezer, 16:136
Elizabeth, 16:236
Elizabeth Jane Thompson, 20:238

Ralph, 16:137

ELLIOT/ELLIOTT
Abigail (Edmunds), 16:210
Andrew, 16:218, 220; 18:60a; 20:198
Asahel, 16:210
Benjamin, 16:220
Deborah, 16:55
Deborah (Bell), 16:56
Elizabeth, 18:81
Francis, 20:202
Gemima (Edmunds), 16:210
Henry, 16:56
Jane (___), 18:81
Lucy (Cressy), 16:220
Lydia, 17:32
Mary (Brown), 19:32
Mary A., 17:105
Nathaniel, 16:210
Ruth, 16:218; 17:102
Sarah (___), 16:220; 17:32
Sarah (Rounday), 16:218
Thomas, 18:81
William, 17:32; 19:32; 20:198

ELLIS see also ELLES
___, Rev., 17:104
Betsey (Harraden), 20:118
Elizabeth (Valentine), 16:77
George Sheldon, 17:176
Jonathan, 16:77; 19:97
Joseph, 18:221
Mary (Tetlow), 17:176
Mildred Louise, 17:176
Sally (Eaton), 18:221
Stephen, 20:118
Susanna, 17:100
Susanna (Parker), 19:97
Thomas, 18:134

ELLISON see also ELSON
John, 17:134
Suzanne, 17:189

ELLITROP see also ELLETRAP
John, 20:197

ELLMES/ELMES
Robert, 16:68; 19:83
Sarah (Northey), 19:83

ELLSWORTH
Jonathan, 19:161

ELMES see ELLMES
Robert, 16:68

ELRES
Nathan'l, 16:68

ELSON see also ELLISON
Dinah, 19:46
Mary, 19:144
Mary (Potter), 19:143-145
Samuel, 19:144
Sara, 19:144

ELWEEL
Nehemiah, 17:13

ELWELL, 17:139
___, Mrs., 17:13
Abigail, 18:176
Abigail (Vinson), 17:237
Caleb, 16:133
David, 16:133
Elias, 17:35
Elisha, 18:30
Elizabeth, 18:30
Elizabeth (Butler), 17:237
Hannah (Parker), 19:96, 97
Helen Maria, 17:35
Hester (Dutch), 17:237
Isaac, 17:138; 18:176; 20:200

Jacob, 16:133; 17:237
John, 18:30
Joseph, 17:240
Josiah, 17:240
Lydia, 17:237
Mary, 17:236; 18:30
Mary (Haines), 18:39
Mehitable (Millett), 18:176
Parker, 19:96; 19:97
Payne, 17:237
Rachel, 17:132
Rebecca (Webber), 17:237
Robert, 17:237
Samuel, 17:237; 18:30; 20:200
Sarah, 18:30
Sarah (Bassett), 18:29
Thomas, 17:240; 18:29, 30; 20:200
Thomasin (___), 17:35
William, 16:133; 17:237; 18:30
Zebulon, 17:11

EMERSON, 20:18
Buckley, 20:83
Daniel, 18:232
Elizabeth, 19:160
Frank, 19:139
George Brandon, 19:139
George Franklin, 19:139
Gertrude Mary (Toner), 16:120
Hannah, 18:141
Hannah Bliss, 16:107
Helen Elizabeth (Peters), 19:139
Jane (Armitage), 18:232
John, 17:240; 18:84
Joseph, 16:88; 19:220
Joshua, 16:119
Martha, 16:179
Martha (Toothaker), 19:220, 221, 223
Mary, 18:152, 200; 19:40, 99, 100
Mary (Chase), 16:119
Oliver Waldo, 16:120
Peter, 20:48
Phebe (___), 16:107
Sarah, 18:152
Silence, 16:209
William, 16:107

EMERY
___, Mr., 19:45
Abigail, 19:46; 20:139
Anne, 17:55
Bethiah, 18:159
Caroline (Smith), 16:107
Charity (Nason), 20:139
Eleanor, 16:178
Elizabeth, 17:54; 20:138, 139, 144, 148
Elizabeth (Goodwin), 20:138
Elizabeth (Merrill), 19:93
George, 16:140
Hannah (Morse), 17:52; 20:178
Job, 20:139
John, 17:52; 19:46, 93; 20:178
Jonathan, 17:52; 20:178
Joseph, 16:68; 19:93, 94
Joshua, 17:52; 20:178
Mary, 19:35, 93, 95
Mary (Webster), 19:46
Mary (Woodman), 17:52; 20:178
Molly, 17:52; 20:178
Moses, 16:107
S. H., 18:82
Samuel, 20:138
Sarah, 17:120; 19:178
Sarah (Smith), 17:52; 20:178
Zachariah, 20:138

EMMERTON
James A., 16:223; 18:17, 99
EMMONS/EMONS
Ebenezer, 19:226
Hannah (Cheever), 19:104
William, 19:104
EMONDS
Walter L., 20:162
EMORY
Douglas Wallace, 17:123
___, Mr., 18:166
EMRO
Elizabeth C., 17:208
ENCAS, 18:240a
ENDECOTT/ENDICOT/ENDICOTT, 19:126; 20:180a
___, Col., 17:209
___, Gov., 16:136, 19:43, 60a, 75
___, Maj., 17:143
___, Mr., 17:14, 240; 18:196
Damaris (Osborn), 17:200
Elizabeth (Phillips), 16:157
Grace (Symonds), 18:44
John, 18:42, 44, 195, 197, 231; 19:15, 25, 127; 20:120a, 132, 201
Mary, 16:155; 20:58
Mehitabel, 18:43, 44
Robert E., 16:157
Samuel, 17:200
Sarah, 18:42; 19:151
William, 17:200; 20:89, 90
Zerubbabel, 16:157; 18:44
ENGALS see also ENGOLLS, INGALLS
Lemuel, 16:210
ENGLE
Gideon, 17:31
ENGLISH
Joseph, 19:202
Lydea, 20:151
Philip, 16:89; 20:151
Rebecca (Briant), 20:151
Samuel, 19:202
ENGOLLS see also ENGALS, INGALLS
Eliezer, 20:199
ENOS
Charlotte Kendall (Mooney), 18:175
Eben Francis, 18:175
Elizabeth/Betty Kendall, 17:127; 18:175
ENTWISTLE, 16:13
EPES
Daniel, 16:157
Mary, 17:191
EPHRAIM
Peter, 18:60a
Yawatan (___), 18:60a
ERINGTON/ERRINGTON
Anna, 19:48
Thomas, 16:71; 18:74; 19:196,
ERSKIN
___, Rev., 19:60a
ERVINGTON
Thomas, 20:190
ERWIN
Abigail (Bassett), 18:39
Joseph, 18:39
ESTABROOK
Abraham, 17:79
Benjamin, 17:80
Ellen, 17:80
Hannah, 17:80
Joell, 17:79
John, 17:80
Jonathan, 17:80

Joseph, 17:79
Lemuel, 17:80
Martha (Heald), 17:80
Moses, 17:79
Oliver, 17:80
Robert, 17:79
Samuel, 17:79
Sarah, 17:79
Thomas, 17:79
ESTES
"Child", 18:210
Abigail, 18:96
Abigail (Traft), 18:96
Abijah/Ahijah, 16:78; 18:31, 91-96, 210
Altha, 18:96
Anna, 18:94, 95, 97, 98; 20:212
Anna (Newhall), 16:80; 18:31, 93, 98
Asenath (McArthur), 18:96
Azubah (Hill), 18:96
Benjamin, 17:197
Benjamin Hall, 18:96
Betsey, 18:96
Betsey (Estes), 18:96
Bijah, 18:95
Charles, 16:80; 18:90, 134; 20:212
David, 18:96
Dexter, 18:96
Diantha, 18:96
Dorothy (___), 18:90
Elizabeth, 16:78; 17:197; 18:19, 93-95, 97, 98; 20:212
Elizabeth (___), 18:90
Elizabeth (Battles), 18:96
Elizabeth (Fowler), 18:97; 20:212
Elizabeth (Inman), 18:95, 96
Elizabeth (Knight), 18:95
Elizabeth (Norwood), 18:31, 92, 210
Emeline B. (___), 18:98
Esther, 16:95
Esther (Higley), 18:96
Esther (Osborn), 17:200
Eunice, 18:98
Ezekiel, 18:98
Ezra Baker, 18:98
Freelove, 18:95, 96
Freelove (Estes), 18:95, 96
Freelove (Hill), 18:96
Gulielma, 18:96
Gulielma Maria, 18:98
Hannah, 18:31, 36, 91, 93-96, 98; 20:212
Hannah (___), 18:31, 95
Hannah (Aldrich), 18:93
Hannah (Bassett), 16:80; 18:31, 52, 91-93, 210; 20:212
Hannah (Nichols), 18:98; 20:212
Hannah (Walling), 18:96
Hannah (Wares), 18:96
Huldah, 18:95, 97
Isaac Hacker, 18:98
Isabella, 18:95
Israel, 18:96
Jedediah, 17:200
Jerusha (Dart), 18:96
John, 16:80; 18:11, 29, 31, 52, 91-93, 95-97, 210; 20:212
Joseph, 18:96
Kate (McArthur), 18:96
Lavinia (Wood), 18:96
Lois, 18:96, 98
Lydia, 18:98
Lydia (Avery), 18:96
Lydia (Hawkes), 18:95
Marcus/Mark, 18:95

Mark, 18:96, 97; 20:212
Martha, 18:98
Martha (Blaney), 16:80; 18:31, 93, 98
Mary, 16:78; 18:93-95, 97
Mary (Breed), 18:98
Mary (Larrabee), 18:95
Mary (Orne), 16:78; 18:31, 92, 93
Mary Ann (Peters), 18:96
Mary M. (Patch), 18:98
Mary/Polly (Evans), 18:97
Massa (Brown), 18:96
Matthew, 16:80; 18:11, 31, 52, 55, 90-95, 97, 98, 134, 210; 20:78, 103, 212
Molly (Cummings), 18:96
Naomi, 18:96
Nathan, 18:96
Nathaniel, 18:93-95
Otis, 18:96
Peter, 18:95, 96
Phebe, 18:96
Phebe (Darling), 18:96
Philadelphia, 18:31, 91, 92
Philadelphia (Jenkins), 18:31. 52. 90
Polly, 18:95, 96
Rebecca, 16:102; 18:96-98; 20:212
Rebecca (Chase), 18:98; 20:212
Rebecca (Hill), 18:96
Rebecca L. (Dodge), 18:98
Rhoda, 18:96
Richard, 18:29, 31, 90-93, 95, 96, 103, 105
Robert, 18:90
Russell, 18:96
Russell Abijah, 18:96
Ruth, 18:94, 96-98
Ruth (Gardner), 18:94
Ruth (Graves), 16:156; 18:31, 93, 97; 20:212
Ruth Ames, 18:95
Sally, 18:96
Sally (Thayer), 18:96
Samuel, 18:94-96
Samuel Gardner, 18:94, 95
Sarah, 18:91, 93-95
Sarah (Leet), 18:96
Silas, 18:96
Springett Penn, 18:98
Stephen, 18:95, 96
Susan, 18:95
Thomas, 18:98
Vienna, 18:96
William, 16:96; 18:24, 31, 91, 93, 97, 98; 19:107; 20:212
William Henry, 18:98
Zaccheus, 18:95
ESTEY/ESTY
Hannah, 20:23
Jeffry, 19:197
John, 20:201
Jonathan, 19:239
Mary (Towne), 19:221
Mary Towne, 16:67
Mathew, 19:228
Susannah (Munroe/Monroe), 19:239
William, 20:221
ESTMAN see EASTMAN
ESTRADA
Julie Evelyn (Listernick), 17:175
Nicole Isabella, 17:175
Ruben Fillipe, 17:175
ESTY see ESTEY
ETTER
Elizabeth (Cleverly), 17:53
Franklin, 17:53

Margaretta (Martin), 17:53
Martha, 17:53
Peter, 17:53
EULIN
John, 16:64
EUSTIS/EUSTUS
Abigail, 19:104
Abigail (___), 18:50; 19:104
Abigail (Merriam), 20:42
Betsy, 18:50
John, 16:111
Joseph, 18:50; 20:42
Thomas, 19:104
William, 19:131
EVANS, 19:183
Abigail, 16:116
Amos, 16:81
Barbara Jean, 16:172
Daniel, 19:234
Dorcas (___), 19:227
Edward, 19:226, 227
Elizabeth, 17:149; 20:221
Elizabeth (Blaney), 16:81
Hannah, 20:28, 217, 219
Hannah (Brown), 16:117
Jennifer, 18:139
Joanna, 18:220
John, 19:234
John Quincy, 17:57
Judith (Bradley), 19:234
Mary/Polly, 18:97
Nathaniel, 20:105
Richard, 19:234
Sarah, 19:58
Sarah (Bradley), 19:234
Sarah (Larrabee), 19:227
Tamsin, 16:19
Thomas, 16:117; 19:234
EVE, 17:191
EVELETH, 17:220; 20:18
Abigail, 16:235
Isaac, 17:220
Joseph, 17:76
Mary, 17:220
Sylvester, 17:220
EVERDEEN
"Child", 17:12
Joseph, 17:13
EVERED see also WEBB
John, 19:30, 31, 174, 175
Stephen, 19:174
EVERSFIELD
Nicholas, 20:68
EVERTON
William, 16:230
EWELL
Henry, 19:82
Sarah, 19:82
Sarah (Annable), 19:82
EYLES
Eveline Blancy, 17:56

FAIRBANKS
Adam, 17:24
Comfort, 17:176
George, 17:24
Hannah (Frail), 17:24
Jonas, 20:67
Jonas, 18:109; 20:67
Jonathan, 17:176
Lorenzo S., 17:176
Lucy, 17:24
Lydia (Holbrook), 17:176

Marina (Fuller), 17:24
Mary (Frail), 17:24
Moses, 17:24
Nathaniel, 18:95
Sarah, 17:24
Sarah (Walker), 17:24
FAIRBURN
William Armstrong, 17:134
FAIRN
Elizabeth, 19:238
FAIRWEATHER see also FAYERWEATHER
John, 18:232
Thomas, 19:212
FALES
Anna (Graves), 20:209
John, 20:209
FALINO
Jeannine J., 19:200
FALKNER
John, 19:32
FALLS
John, 16:60
John Q. A., 16:60
Marinda/Martha (Lewis), 16:60
FANCEY/FANCY
Elizabeth (Rayner), 20:225, 226
Thomas, 20:226
FANEUIL, 18:134
Peter, 17:94
FARAOH see FARRAR
FARLEY
C. A., 19:233
Elizabeth, 17:83
Lydia, 16:37
Michael, 20:225
FARLOW
Charles Frederick, 16:67; 17:157; 18:71; 132
FARMER
Elizabeth (___), 16:131
John, 16:138
Paul, 19:131
Thomas, 16:131
William, 18:213
FARNAM/FARNHAM see also FARNUM
Adelbert, 16:51
Almira (Ames), 19:21-24
Donald Henry, 16:51
Emma (Tibbetts), 16:51
Eunice (___), 19:21-24
Hannah, 16:100
Henry, 19:22
Hiram, 19:23
Hiram P., 19:23
Hiram Putnam, 19:21-24
Horace, 19:24
Iva Clara (Longfellow), 16:51
James, 19:24
John, 16:203; 19:21, 22, 24
John Henry, 19:21, 23, 24
Marjorie May, 16:48
Mary, 19:22, 23
Mary Almira, 19:21, 23, 24
Mary C. (Ristine), 19:21
Myrtle, 19:24
Myrtle E., 19:21
Phebe, 19:92
Putnam, 19:24
Ralph, 19:24
Russell C., 16:48; 18:134; 19:21, 54, 135
Sarah, 19:23
Sarah Elizabeth, 19:21, 23, 24

Tabitha, 19:92
William, 19:22, 23
William W., 19:21, 24
FARNSWORTH
   ___, Mr., 19:59
   Aaron, 17:83
   Abigail, 19:26
   Abigail (___), 19:59
   Azubah (Burt), 16:120
   Azyba, 17:83
   Claude Matthias, 19:26
   Elizabeth (Page), 17:83
   Isaac, 17:82
   John, 20:196
   Jonathan, 16:120; 19:26
   Joseph, 19:26
   Josiah, 19:26
   Keziah, 16:120
   Mary, 16:42; 19:26
   Mary (___), 19:117
   Mary (Burt), 16:120
   Mary (Farr), 19:26, 117
   Matthias, 16:120; 18:7; 19:26, 27, 117; 20:13, 196
   Phineas, 16:120
   Samuel, 19:26
   Sarah (___), 19:26
   Sarah (Nutting), 19:26, 117
FARNUM see also FARNAM, 18:132
   Alice (___), 20:21, 23
   Catherine Louisa, 16:108
   Charlotte, 16:108
   Columbus, 16:240
   Daniel, 16:104; 18:134
   Dorothy, 16:104
   Elizabeth, 19:31
   Elizabeth (Holt), 17:55; 20:21
   Elizabeth (Parker), 19:31
   Elizabeth Cordis, 16:108
   Elizabeth Frances, 16:240
   Evelyn (Leonard), 16:108
   Grace (___), 19:222
   Hannah, 16:104; 17:153; 19:31
   Hannah (Bragdon), 16:104
   Hannah Bliss, 16:106
   Hannah Bliss (Emerson), 16:107
   Henry, 16:104
   James, 19:31
   John, 16:68; 19:21, 24, 31-33, 54
   John Hay, 16:107
   Joshua, 16:106
   Katharine, 16:104
   Louisa, 16:108
   Mary (Frye), 19:21, 24
   Mary Bliss, 16:108
   Phebe, 19:31
   Phebe Bliss, 16:108
   Ralph, 16:68; 17:55; 19:21, 54, 222; 20:21-23
   Samuel, 16:107; 19:34
   Sarah, 16:107; 17:54; 19:31, 46, 222; 20:21-23, 167
   Sibyll Ainger, 16:108
   Susan, 19:120
   Susan/Susannah, 19:59
   Sybil, 16:104
   Sybil (Angier), 16:104
   Thomas, 16:68
   William, 16:104
   William Emerson, 16:108
FARR, 16:165
   ___, Corp., 20:102
   Adelaide L. (Jordan), 16:151

   Beatrice (Dearberg), 16:151
   Benjamin, 18:100; 19:25-27, 29, 78; 20:196
   Catharine Lucy, 16:151
   Daniel Haddock, 16:151
   Elizabeth, 19:25-29
   Elizabeth (Burrill), 19:27, 29
   Elizabeth (Stowers), 19:25, 26
   George, 19:25-29, 117, 138; 20:194, 205
   Grace Alice, 16:151
   Hannah, 19:27-29
   Hannah (Applin), 19:29
   Hannah (Walden), 19:27, 28
   Hannah (Walden/Walker), 20:205
   Helena L., 16:146
   Helene Louisa (Haddock), 16:151
   James, 19:117
   John, 19:25-27, 29
   Joseph, 17:151; 18-75, 103; 19:25-29, 175, 227; 20:48, 113, 140, 196, 204, 205
   Lazaras, 19:25, 27
   Martha, 19:25, 27, 28
   Mary, 19:25-29, 117, 163
   Mary (Graves), 20:208
   Naomi, 19:27
   Naomi (Lindsey), 19:28; 20:205
   Nathaniel, 19:27
   Rebecca (Knight), 19:27, 175
   Rebecca (Rea), 18:75; 19:28; 19:175
   Rebecca (Waldron), 19:175
   Robert, 19:25
   Ruth, 19:27, 28
   Sarah, 19:25-27, 29
   Thomasin, 19:27
   William Haddock, 16:151
   William Wilberforce, 16:151
FARRAR /FARAOH/PHAROAH, 18:72; 19:78
   Abigail (Johnson), 17:171
   Elizabeth, 16:26; 17:171; 20:27, 93
   Elizabeth (___), 17:171; 19:144; 20:92
   Elizabeth (Hood), 17:172; 18:52
   Hannah, 17:172; 18-34, 35, 53, 220; 20:27, 92
   Henry, 17:171
   Mary, 20:238
   Mehittabel, 17:173
   Nehemiah, 16:119
   Peleg, 17:173
   Ruth (Simonds), 16:119
   Sarah, 17:171
   Susanna, 17:172; 18:53, 151; 19:144, 148
   Thomas, 16:156; 17:171; 18:11, 28, 52, 103, 134; 19:77, 144; 20:92, 135, 196
FARRELL
   John, 19:59
   Martha (Eaton), 19:59
FARRER
   Samuel, 18:134
FARRINGTON
   ___, Capt., 16:98; 18:16; 19:158
   ___, Lt., 18:208
   Abigail, 16:151; 17:148; 19:49
   Abigail (___), 17:150; 18:48, 151
   Abigail (Breed), 17:150; 18:36
   Abigail (Davis), 17:148; 19:49
   Abigail (Fuller), 16:74; 17:150
   Abigail (Sexton), 17:152
   Amos, 17:206
   Anna (Johnson), 17:153
   Aphia, 17:152
   Apphia (Bradley), 17:152
   Benjamin, 17:152

   Betsey (Woods), 17:153
   Daniel, 17:150; 18:36
   David, 20:210
   Donald G., 17:142
   Dorothy, 17:147; 18:47, 48, 151
   Dorothy (Browne), 17:143
   Ebenezer, 17:148; 19:49; 20:209
   Edmond/Edmund, 17:142, 154; 18:134, 164, 151; 19:138; 20:194
   Edward, 16:68; 17:142; 18:73; 19:34, 221; 20:215, 216
   Elenor, 17:152
   Eliza, 17:148
   Elizabeth, 16:74; 17:142
   Elizabeth (Evans), 17:149
   Elizabeth (Knight), 16:71; 17:143; 18:73; 20:214, 217
   Elizabeth (Newhall), 17:142; 18:73
   Elizabeth (Putnam), 17:152
   Elizabeth (Smith), 17:150
   Esther, 17:152
   Hannah, 17:149
   Hannah (___), 17:145; 19:105
   Hannah (Baker), 17:150; 18:48, 150
   Hannah (Farnum), 17:153
   Hannah (Hawkes), 17:150
   Hannah (Ingalls), 17:148; 19:49, 145
   Hannah (Newhall), 17:149
   Huldah, 17:148; 19:49, 145
   Jacob, 17:146; 18:73
   James, 17:152
   Jeremiah, 17:149
   Joanna, 16:47
   Joanna (Frye), 17:153
   John, 16:71, 74; 17:142, 206; 18:73, 134; 19:28; 20:111, 207, 214, 215
   Jonathan, 17:152
   Joseph, 17:144
   Judith (Ingalls), 17:153
   Liddy (Mansfield), 17:145
   Lucy (Graves), 20:209
   Lydia, 17:149
   Lydia (Hudson), 17:145, 157
   Lydia (Mansfield), 17:149
   Lydia (Newhall), 16:47
   Martha, 17:41, 148
   Martha (Browne), 17:147; 18:73
   Mary, 16:148, 151; 17:147
   Mary (___), 17:145
   Mary (Collins), 17:147
   Mary (Johnson), 17:145; 18:48
   Mary (Stephens), 17:152
   Mary/Margaret (Gloyd), 17:149
   Mary/Mercy (Dewey), 17:152
   Matthew, 16:159; 17:18, 19, 155; 18:29, 48, 52, 60a, 73, 109, 134, , 164, 213, 222; 19:27, 145, 227; 20: 135, 196, 214-216
   Mehetable (Sexton), 17:152
   Mehitable, 17:152
   Miriam (Eastman), 17:152
   Molly (Swan), 17:152
   Nathan, 17:152
   Nathaniel, 16:47
   Patience, 17:152
   Phebe, 17:152; 19:95
   Phebe (Poor), 17:153
   Philip, 17:153
   Phineas, 17:153
   Prudence, 17:147
   Rebecka, 17:147
   Ruth, 17:152
   Ruth (Battes), 17:206
   Ruth (Killum), 17:152

Samuel, 17:147; 19:49, 105, 145
Sarah, 17:142, 152; 18:208; 19:49, 148
Sarah (Bachelder), 17:152
Sarah (Breed), 17:150
Sarah (Franklin), 17:147; 18:73
Sarah (Frye), 17:153
Sarah (Hart), 17:148; 18:48, 151
Sarah (Holton/Houlton), 17:152
Sarah (Newhall), 17:149
Sarah (Potter), 17:145
Sarah (Stocker), 17:150
Sarah (Upham), 17:206
Sisley (___), 17:143
Stephen, 17:144
Susan (Abbott), 17:152
Susanna, 17:149; 18:16
Theophilus, 17:20; 18:48, 150; 20:137
Thomas, 17:143; 19:196
William, 16:69, 97; 17:20; 18:48, 150; 19:105; 20:137

FARWELL, 16:65; 19:174
Elizabeth, 20:33, 35, 39, 40
John, 20:219
Sarah (Hovey), 20:219
Sarah Tyng, 20:40

FAULKNER
Abigail, 19:219, 221, 222
Abigail (Dane), 19:115, 219, 221, 222; 20:166
Ammiruhaman, 19:219
Dorothy, 19:219, 221, 222
Dorothy (Robinson), 20:23
Edmund, 19:219, 222; 20:23
Francis, 16:68; 19:34, 115, 219, 222; 20:167
John, 16:68; 20:22, 23
Sarah (Abbot), 20:22, 23

FAWNE
Elizabeth, 19:141

FAXON
Etta, 17:208
Joanna, 20:179

FAY
Rhoda, 20:212

FAYERWEATHER see also FAIRWEATHER, 19:31

FAYS
Antonio, 20:4

FEAR
Sarah, 16:76

FEARS
___, Mrs., 17:12
Sally, 18:204
William, 16:64; 17:12

FEATHERSTONE
Phebe, 19:177, 178

FEAVER
Hannah, 17:153
Hannah (Farrington), 17:153
Jacob, 17:153
Mary, 17:153
Willebe, 17:153

FEDERHEN
Deborah A., 19:200

FEDRICKS
Joseph, 17:12

FEIRMAYES
___, Mrs., 19:142

FELCH
Daniel, 20:202
Henry, 20:185

FELLOWS
Abigail, 16:235; 17:19; 18:203, 219
Anna (___), 16:159
Benjamin, 17:98
Caleb, 18:203
Cornelius, 18:202
Deborah (Fraile), 17:19
Elizabeth, 18:202
Elizabeth (Norwood), 18:202
Elizabeth (Rust), 17:19
Ephraim, 16:159
Gustavus, 18:202
Hannah (Dutch), 18:202
Hannah (Parker), 18:202
Hannah (Pierpont), 18:202
Israel, 17:50
Jacob, 17:21
John, 17:76
Jonathan, 18:202
Joseph, 17:18
Lydia (Stanton), 18:203
Mary, 17:19
Mercy (Treadwell), 18:202
Nathaniel, 18:203
Ruth, 17:19
Ruth (Fraile), 17:18
Samuel, 18:202
Sarah, 17:19
Sarah (Fraile), 17:21
Sarah (Kimball), 17:19
Sarah (Williams), 18:202
Susanna (More), 17:50
William, 17:18; 20:225

FELMINGAM
___, Mr., 17:209

FELT
Abigail (Blaney), 16:85; 18:23
Elizabeth, 16:26; 19:224, 225
Elizabeth (Blaney), 16:26; 20:94
Elizabeth (Purchase), 16:26
Elizabeth (Wilkinson), 19:224
George, 16:26; 17:231; 19:224
Hannah, 16:26
Hannah (Silsbee), 18:101
John, 16:26
Jonathan, 16:26; 17:231; 18:101; 20:94
Joseph, 16:85; 18:18, 23
Joseph B., 16:139; 17:21
Lydia (___), 18:18
Molly, 16:85; 18:23
Phillippe (Andrews), 16:26
Sarah (Mills), 18:18

FELTON, 16:32
Asa, 17:205
Benjamin, 19:190
Daniel, 17:98; 19:175
David, 17:205
Dorcas (Upton), 20:234
Francis, 20:222
Hannah, 20:234
Hannah (Swinerton), 17:205
John, 16:157
Mary (Epes), 17:205
Mary (Graves), 20:222
Mary (Smith), 17:205
Nathaniel, 16:32
Ruth, 17:205; 18:19
Sally (Gould), 17:205
Sally (Graves), 20:222
Samuel, 17:205
Sarah, 17:205
Sarah (Stephens), 19:175
Stephen, 20:234
Thomas, 19:175
Thomas K., 20:222

FENNELL
Anna Eliza (Cloak), 16:236
Annie Rogers Cross, 16:236
Carrie Selman (Cross), 16:236
Catherine (___), 16:236
Charles, 16:236
James Knox, 16:236
James Porter, 16:236

FENTON
Robert, 20:212
Sarah (Graves), 20:212

FERAN, 19:58

FERGUSON
Catharine (Boyle), 19:179
Emily Frances (Carstairs), 16:151
James, 19:179
James Bott, 16:109
Walter, 16:151

FERMATIC
Gertrude (Nichols), 17:58
Peter, 17:58

FERN/FERNE
Abigail, 18:35
Susanna, 18:14

FERNALD
Margaret, 17:53

FERNE see FERN

FERNS
Elizabeth (Tarbox), 20:137
James, 20:137

FERNSIDE
Elizabeth (Starr), 16:57
John, 16:57; 17:209
Lydia, 16:56

FERREMAN
William, 20:198

FERRIS
Emmeline I., 17:31
Mary Walton, 16:174; 18:109

FESTI
Louise, 17:57

FFRAYER
Nathaniel, 18:85

FIELD
Alexander, 19:193
Donald, 16:126
Elijah, 16:87
Elizabeth (Ross), 19:111, 113, 114
Joan (___), 16:126
Margaret, 20:13
Polly (Gridley), 16:87
Priscilla (Ingalls), 19:53
Samuel, 19:53

FIELDING, 16:13

FIELDS
Donald, 16:123
James T., 19:203
Joan (___), 16:123

FIENNES
Margaret, 20:70

FIFIELD
Gertrude, 20:32
Osgood, 17:57
Rachel, 16:179
Ruth (___), 16:179
Sally O. (Hackett), 17:57
Samuel, 16:179

FILBRICK
Thomas, 18:230

FILLMORE
___, Mr., 16:149

FINCH
George, 19:51

Hannah, 19:51
FINDLEY
Mary C., 17:31
FINLAY
Lydia, 16:195
Lydia Ropes (Dow), 16:200
FINLEY
Florence (Allen), 17:180
Russell, 17:180
FINNEY
Esther (Lewis), 18:148
Jeremiah, 18:148
FINSON
Mary, 18:202
FIRTH, 16:13
Henry, 18:38
Sarah (Fogg), 18:38
FISCHER see also FISHER
Abijah, 16:217
David Hackett, 19:176
Eben, 17:104
Sarah Moar (Friend), 16:217
FISH/FISHE
Betsy, 16:239; 17:51
Francis, 20:147
Fred, 16:152
Grizell, 20:96
Nancy Maria (Tarbox), 20:147
FISHER see also FISCHER
Abel, 20:179
Abigail, 18:149
Abigail (___), 18:149
Abigail (Marriott), 20:179
Anthony, 20:179
Daniel, 18:149; 20:179
Deborah (White), 20:179
Deborah (Witt), 18:169
Eleazer, 20:179
Esther, 20:179
Ezekiel, 20:179
Hannah (Baker), 20:179
James, 20:179
Jeremiah, 20:145
Joanna (Faxon), 20:179
John, 18:169
Mary (___), 20:145
Mary (Avery), 20:179
Nathaniel, 20:179
Susannah (Wadsworth), 20:179
FISK/FISKE
Ebenezer, 16:142
Jane Fletcher, 19:176
John, 17:78, 86
Joseph, 20:197
Martha (Kimball), 16:142
Mary, 17:86
Mary (Parker), 17:86
Nancy, 17:29
Samuel, 17:86; 18:93
Samuel Bartlett, 18:96
Sarah, 17:86
Thomas, 17:86
Vienna (Estes), 18:96
Wainright, 17:86
William, 17:29; 18:158
FITCH, 18:235
Hannah (Brown), 17:227
John, 17:240
Mehitable, 19:214; 20:33
Zachariah, 18:235; 20:190
Zachary, 18:230; 19:138; 20:183, 190, 194
FITTS see also FITZ
___, Rev., 17:184

Jeremy, 19:45
Zachery, 20:191
FITTYPLACE
Rebecca, 16:81
FITZ see also FITTS
Eunice (Baker), 17:163
Eunice Augusta, 17:163
William, 17:163
FITZGERALD
Ezekiel, 17:53
Harriet, 17:53
Margaret (Fernald), 17:53
FITZPATRICK
Marilyn, 16:38; 17:78; 18:133, 136, 154, 235; 20:16
Marilyn R., 19:30, 87
FITZWALTER, 18:76, 78
FLACK
Elsa H., 17:190
FLAGG
___, Mr., 18:78
Charles A., 18:191
Ernest, 18:34
Esther (Ballard), 16:76
John, 16:99; 17:25; 19:101; 20:112
Jonathan, 16:76
Mary/Molly (Hart), 18:44
Theodore, 18:44
FLANDERS
Eunice, 18:175
Jane (Norton), 17:238; 18:175
Katherine (Hackett), 16:19
Sarah, 17:149; 18:151
Thomas, 16:19
Timothy, 17:238; 18:175
FLANNIGAN
Arthur S., 17:207
Cassa Adelaide (Smith), 17:207
FLETCHER
Ebenezer, 18:120
Edward H., 17:228
Edwin J., 16:53
Eliza G., 17:228
Hannah/Susannah, 20:40
Joseph, 20:40, 139
Mammie, 16:53
Margaret, 20:139
Mary P. (Sias), 16:53
Molly (Smith), 20:139
Moses, 17:228
Nathan, 16:133; 20:82
Olive (Lawrence), 18:120
Olive (Proctor), 18:120
Oliver, 18:120
Patience, 17:157
Rachael (Gregg), 17:228
Robert, 17:228
Sarah, 16:59
Susannah, 20:33
FLINT, 20:202
___, Capt., 19:217
___, Lt., 19:137
Abigail, 16:233
Abigail (___), 18:45
Adam, 18:45
Alice, 20:60a
Charlotte, 18:45
David, 16:78
Ebenezer, 19:214
Elizabeth, 16:55; 17:198; 18:45
Eunice, 18:170
George, 16:36
Hannah (___), 16:78

Hannah (Moulton), 16:36
Heman, 19:99
Jacob, 18:45
James, 18:45
Jane (Silsbee), 18:101
John, 18:101; 19:78; 20:203
Jonathan, 17:206; 18:43
Joseph, 16:88
Judith (Bancroft), 19:214
Lydia, 18:43
Mary, 17:206; 18:45
Mary (Hart), 18:43, 45
Mary (Osgood), 18:45
Mary/Polly, 16:94
Olive, 20:213
Rhoda (Cheever), 19:99
Samuel, 20:230
Sarah (Aborn), 16:36
Thomas, 16:36; 17:14; 18:43
William, 18:45
FLOOD see also FLOYD
___, Mr., 19:138
Clara (Edmands), 17:27
Elizabeth, 19:154
Jane (___), 19:154
Joseph, 18:72; 19:154
Mary, 16:131
Obadiah, 19:154
Ruth, 16:223
FLORANCE
Hannah, 18:38
FLOWER
Hannah, 20:179
FLOWERS, 17:57
Ruth Catherine (Tardy), 16:83
Thomas, 16:83
FLOWIN
Thomas, 20:199
FLOYD/FLUD see also FLOOD, 17:92
___, Capt., 16:89
___, Goodman, 18:166
Abigail, 19:104
Abigail (Friend), 16:218
Abigail (Hasey), 18:151
Abigail (Pratt), 18:151
Andrew, 18:151
C. Harold, 18:151; 19:147
Dorothy, 19:147
Elener, 18:151
Elinor (___), 18:151
Elizabeth (Bradshaw), 18:151
Elizabeth (Potter), 19:147
George, 16:218
Hannah, 18:151
Hannah (Bellamy), 19:58
Hugh, 18:151
John, 16:163; 17:88; 18:114, 151, 166, 167, 233; 19:58, 78, 147
Joseph, 19:146, 147; 20:134, 137, 194
Mary, 16:31; 17:58; 18:151
Mary (Baker), 18:150, 151
Mary (Morgan), 18:151
Mary (Tuttle), 18:151
Nathaniel, 19:147
Obadiah, 18:99
Peter, 18:151
Rachel, 18:151
Rachel (Floyd), 18:151
Ruth, 19:147
Samuel, 18:232
Sarah (Bennett), 17:89
Sarah (Doolittle), 19:147
Sarah (Simpson), 18:151

Stephen, 18:151
Susanna, 18:151
Thomas, 18:40
William, 18:151
FLYNN
John J., 20:149
Mary Elizabeth, 20:148
Matthew, 19:57
FOGG
Aaron, 18:38
Charles, 18:38
Hannah (Allen), 18:38
John, 19:195
Lydia (Larrabee), 20:115
Moses, 20:115
Rachel, 18:38
Ralph, 19:189, 190, 195
Sarah, 18:38
Sarah (Bassett), 18:38
FOISIE
Amelia A., 19:180
FOLETTE see FOLLETT
FOLEY, 20:77, 126
___, Mr., 20:73
Mary, 20:125
FOLGER
Dorcas, 16:208
FOLLETT/FOLETTE
Howard J., 20:148
Marie Augusta (Tarbox), 20:148
Mary (Blaney), 16:79
Thomas, 16:79
FOLSOM
George T., 16:52
Sarah Elizabeth, 16:52
Sarah Elizabeth (Kennedy), 16:52
FOOT/FOOTE, 19:201; 20:77
___, Mr., 20:204
Joshua, 19:132
Pasco, 19:202
Samuel, 17:193; 20:80
Sarah, 20:54
Thomas, 19:236
FORBES
Elizabeth (Jones), 18:88
Simon, 18:88
FORD, 17:229
Betty, 18:205
Catherine, 19:225-227
Elizabeth, 17:204
Elizabeth (Smith), 17:204
Elizabeth/Eliza (Robertson), 16:120
Emma (___), 20:176
Hannah, 16:239; 17:180; 19:57
John, 17:214
Joseph, 17:180
Mary (___), 19:226
Mary (Melvin), 17:204
Mary (Rous), 17:204
Rebecca, 20:238
Sarah (Edes), 17:204
Stephen, 17:204
William, 17:204; 19:226
FORMAN
William, 20:199
FORNIS
Alice, 17:102
FORTIN/FORTUNE
Deborah, 18:33
Elias, 20:199
John, 18:33
Rebecca, 18:33
Samuel, 18:33

Sarah, 18:33
Sarah (Bassett), 18:32, 33
William, 18:33
FOSS
Clarissa (Osborn), 17:187
Heman, 20:57
Jeremiah, 17:187
Julia A. (Ward), 20:57
FOSTER, 18:134; 20:156
___, Goodman, 16:175
"Daughter", 17:114
Abigail, 17:197; 18:166
Abigail (___), 16:155
Abigail (Lord), 20:225
Abigail (Smith), 17:205
Abraham, 16:68; 19:33, 34
Amy (Thompson), 18:202
Andrew, 16:68; 17:54
Ann (___), 16:66; 17:55; 20:166
Anne, 20:225
Asa, 17:114; 18:162, 163; 19:94
Bartholomew, 17:240; 20:200
Benjamin, 16:239; 19:57
Bridget (Wood), 19:208
Charles, 17:27; 19:90
Christopher, 19:138, 189; 20:193, 194
Daniel, 17:114
David, 17:196; 19:33
Ebenezer, 18:202
Elinor, 18:201, 202
Elizabeth, 17:205; 19:103, 107
Elizabeth (Berry), 16:75
Elizabeth (Leatherland), 20:225
Elizabeth (Rodgers), 17:114
Elizabeth K., 18:135
Ephraim, 16:68; 18:160; 19:32
Esther, 18:202, 236
Esther (Lathrop), 18:200
Eunice, 20:118
Eunice (Hardy), 18:10
Gideon, 18:217, 218
Hannah, 19:57; 20:118
Hannah (Ford), 16:239; 17:180; 19:57
Hannah (Stone), 18:202
Hannah Ford, 16:239; 17:180
Harriet (Edmands), 17:27
Isaac, 16:131; 17:76
Israel, 18:77
Jacob, 20:118, 225
James, 18:216; 20-83, 118
Jean (Stone), 18:77
Jemima, 18:202
Jeremiah, 19:208
Job, 16:239; 17:180; 19:57
John, 17:205; 18:10, 200, 202; 19:179; 20:118, 180
Jonathan, 16:194; 20:100
Joseph, 16:239; 17:130; 19:57; 20:118
Joshua, 18:163
Lizza B., 17:27
Lydia, 17:199; 20:118
Martha, 16:232; 20:225
Martha (Graves), 20:225
Mary, 16:239; 19:57, 95; 20:166, 167, 216, 240
Mary (___), 16:239
Mary (Caldwell), 20:225
Mary (Foster), 16:239; 19:57
Mary (Frye), 19:57
Mary (Lewis), 19:57
Mary (Russ), 17:54
Mary (Willer), 20:225
Mary Ann (Fry), 17:180

Miriam, 18:202
Miriam (Norwood), 18:202
Moses, 17:114
Nabbe/Abigail, 17:205
Nathan, 17:205; 18:202
Nathaniel, 20:225
Peter, 20:118
Priscilla (Proctor), 20:100
Rachel, 17:197
Rachel (Tarbel), 17:199
Rebecca, 17:205
Rebecca (Rowland), 19:179; 20:180
Rebecca (Wood), 17:205; 19:179
Reinald, 17:76
Robert Nathan, 20:150
Roger, 20:155
Ruth (___), 17:205
Sally, 19:179
Sarah, 17:54; 20:118
Sarah (Grover), 18:202
Sarah (Haraden), 20:118
Simeon, 17:205
Stephen, 17:205; 19:179
Susanna (Barker), 17:205
Susanna (Kinney), 18:202
Susanna (Robinson), 18:202
Susannah (Roberts), 20:118
Thomas, 16:133
Timothy, 16:75
William, 16:193; 18:202, 236
Zabuol, 18:202
FOURNIER
Anoine Theodore, 20:56
Elmire Bordua (Lassonde), 20:56
FOWLE
Ebenezer, 16:32
Elizabeth, 17:172
Hannah, 20:28
Hannah (Holton), 16:32
John, 18:236
Joseph, 16:32
Mary (Carter), 20:99
Peter, 20:97, 99
Polly, 16:101
Sarah (Holton), 16:32
Sarah (Winn), 20:97
Susanna (Nick), 20:52
FOWLER, 20:80
Ann, 20:232
Anna, 17:199
Augustus, 20:89, 90
Dorothy (Farnum), 16:107
Elizabeth, 18:97, 166; 20:212
Elizabeth (Buxton), 18:97
Ezekiel, 16:88; 18:97
Hannah, 16:19; 19:239
Jacob, 19:198
John, 16:107
Joseph, 18:240; 20:120
Margery, 20:165
Martha, 16:194
Martha (Kimball), 20:120
Mary, 18:76; 19:119
Obed, 18:144
Philip, 20:120
Samuel, 19:60a
Thomas, 17:193
FOWLES
Thomas, 17:88
FOX
George, 19:63-65
Hannah (Phillips), 19:99
Joel, 19:99

FOXCROFT
  Thomas, 20:49
FOY/FOYE
  Dorothy (___), 18:233
  Elizabeth, 18:49
  Elizabeth (Hart), 18:49
  Hannah, 18:233
  James, 18:49
  John, 18:49, 233
  Moses, 18:49
  Naomi, 18:49
  Polly (Estes), 18:95
  William, 18:95
FRAIL/FRAILE/FRAILLE/FRAYLE
  Abigail, 17:21
  Ann, 17:21
  Ann (Upton), 17:19
  Anne (___), 20:137
  Asenath, 17:24
  Deborah, 17:18, 19
  Elizabeth, 17:18, 19, 22
  Elizabeth (___), 17:17, 18
  Elizabeth (Frail), 17:22
  Eunice, 17:18
  Experience (Haven), 17:24
  George, 17:17, 18, 215; 18:134, 222; 19:55, 138; 20:132, 195
  Hannah, 17:18, 24
  Hannah (Gibbs), 17:24
  Huldah, 17:22
  Isaac, 17:24
  Jane (Gould), 17:20
  Joseph, 17:22
  Martha (Patte), 17:24
  Mary, 17:20, 23
  Mary (Carrell), 17:18
  Mary (Pease), 17:22
  Patty, 17:24
  Ruth, 17:18, 21; 20:137
  Sally, 17:24
  Sally (Frail), 17:24
  Samuel, 17:18, 23; 20:134, 137
  Sarah, 17:21, 23
  Sarah (Fairbanks), 17:24
  Sarah (Haven), 17:22, 23
  Sophia, 17:24
  Zerviah, 17:24
  Zurviah/Zeruiah (Haven), 17:23
FRANCIS
  John, 20:67
  Judith, 17:199
  William, 20:89, 90
FRANK
  Emory, 17:65
  Fanny (___), 17:65
  Louis, 17:65
  Zelig, 17:65
FRANKLIN
  Ann, 18:48, 50
  Annie Lewis (Chatto), 18:176
  Ben, 19:185
  Bernice Lucretia, 18:176
  Charlotte (Case), 16:59
  Cynthia Ann, 16:59
  David, 18:50
  Dorothy (Hunt), 16:73
  Elizabeth (___), 18:50
  Ernest Lynwood, 18:176
  George, 16:73
  John, 16:59
  Margaret, 16:59
  Otis, 16:59
  Phoebe (___), 17:89

  Samuel, 16:59
  Sarah, 17:147; 18:73
  William, 17:89
FRAPPIER
  Marie Josephte, 20:169
FRASER
  Nancy, 17:56
FRAYLE see FRAILE
FRAZIER
  Albina, 19:20
FRAZIN
  Judith R., 17:73
FREDERICKS
  Betty B. (Lewis), 19:56
FREELAND
  Anna, 20:212
FREEMAN see also FREMAN, 16:175
  Alice, 17:177
  Benjamin, 16:76
  Desire (___), 18:179
  Fear, 16:76
  Temperance (Dimmick), 16:76
  William, 18:179
FREETE
  Francis, 19:230
  Jane (Bessom), 19:230
FREETO
  Grace Bessom (Blaney), 16:84
  James, 16:84
FREEZE
  Dorothy (Carr), 17:194
  George, 17:194
  John, 17:194
FREIBERG/FRIEGBERG
  Malcolm, 16:139
FREMAN see also FREEMAN
  Chester, 16:40
  Rachel (Parker), 16:40
FRENCH, 18:134
  Deborah, 20:13
  Freedom, 20:13
  Lydia, 18:120
  Martha, 20:13
  Roger, 20:118
  Thomas, 20:223
FRIAR
  Miriam (Bassett), 18:33
FRIE/FRYE
  Abiel, 19:92
  Hannah, 19:33, 92
  Samuel, 18:162; 19:94
FRIEDMAN
  Jane, 16:29
  Jane Thayer, 16:173; 17:49; 18:135
FRIEND
  "Daughter", 17:38
  "Infant", 17:33
  "Son", 17:38
  A. Augusta (Tarr), 17:109
  Abbie Davis, 17:110
  Abbie Pedrick, 17:103
  Abigail, 16:215; 17:32
  Abigail H. (Brown), 17:162
  Abigail Hinds (Reed), 17:38
  Abigail Long, 17:36
  Addie L., 17:103
  Addie Pickett, 17:105
  Addison Wonson, 17:35
  Adele P. (Butler), 17:166
  Agnes (Danforth), 17:164
  Albert, 17:37
  Albert Lenox, 17:164
  Alfred, 16:216; 17:33, 170

  Alice, 17:111
  Alice Clementine, 17:162
  Alice P., 17:103
  Alice Porter, 17:102
  Alice Standley (Ward), 17:164
  Alinda (Berry), 17:38
  Alphonse W., 17:110
  Alphonso, 17:36
  Alphonso F., 17:110
  Amanda, 17:37
  Andrew, 17:32
  Andrew J., 17:104
  Angeline (Smith), 17:37
  Ann (Wilson), 17:105
  Ann Calder (Hersey), 17:107
  Ann Ethelyn, 17:161
  Ann Maria, 17:105
  Ann Maria (Trask), 17:38
  Ann Thomas, 17:36
  Anna (Kimball), 16:212
  Anna (Pratt), 16:144; 17:33
  Anna C., 17:107
  Anna C. (Coyle), 17:163
  Anna Maria (Trask), 16:217
  Anna P., 17:39
  Anna Woodbury, 17:103
  Anna/Nancy, 16:144
  Annette (Parsons), 17:38
  Annie, 17:107
  Annie Ellery, 17:168
  Arthur G., 17:166
  Arthur Langdon, 17:104
  Arthur/Archer Proctor, 17:111
  Augusta, 16:215
  Augusta Putnam, 17:35
  Belinda (Durham), 17:105
  Belinda Richmond, 17:105
  Benjamin, 16:140
  Benjamin F., 17:106
  Benjamin Franklin, 17:34
  Bessie E. (Center), 17:170
  Bessie Homer, 17:162
  Bessie K., 17:106
  Bethiah, 16:140
  Betsey, 16:215; 17:32
  Betsey (Bootman/Butman), 16:215; 17:32
  Betsey (Keyser), 16:212
  Betsey (Thomas), 17:33, 105
  Betsy D. (Roper), 17:108
  Caleb, 16:144; 17:32
  Caroline, 17:37
  Caroline (Nichols), 17:168
  Caroline A., 16:220
  Caroline Dolliver (Sayward), 17:36
  Caroline H., 17:110
  Carrie P., 17:110
  Charles, 16:215; 17:33, 180
  Charles F., 17:32
  Charles Henry, 17:32
  Charles Porter, 17:104
  Charles W., 17:102
  Charles Ward, 17:38
  Charlotte A. (Center), 17:110
  Charlotte Augusta, 17:33
  Charlottee, 16:214
  Christiana M. (Swan), 17:33
  Christopher, 16:138
  Clara, 17:168
  Clara A., 17:162
  Clara E., 17:104
  Clara Eve, 17:106
  Clara F., 17:167
  Clara L., 17:164

Clara P. (Anderson), 17:164
Clarence Edward, 17:106
Clarence Howard, 17:102
Clarisa, 16:215; 17:32
Clarissa F. (Larouque), 17:167
Clarissa Ferson (Larouque), 17:106
Daniel, 16:144; 17:39
Daniel Alfred, 17:38
Daniel W., 16:218; 17:39
Donald, 17:169
Dorcas (Hovey), 16:218; 17:38
E. Augusta, 17:163
Edgar N., 17:162
Edgar Roy, 17:164
Edias/Edeth, 16:143
Edith (Fuller), 17:111
Edith (Ober), 16:143
Edmund, 16:220; 17:102
Edmund Gallop, 17:102
Edward, 16:138
Edward E., 17:104
Edward Ellery, 17:109
Edward W., 17:107
Edwin, 17:36
Edwin Kent, 17:163
Elbridge Gerry, 16:218; 17:38
Elbridge Harrison, 17:38
Eleanor Scott, 17:168
Elias, 17:108
Eliza, 16:216; 17:34; 18:207
Eliza S., 17:105
Elizabeth, 16:116; 17:35
Elizabeth (Kimball), 18:207
Elizabeth (Kitchen), 16:138
Elizabeth (Parkhurst), 17:35
Elizabeth (Patch), 16:215; 17:32
Elizabeth Ann (Dolliver), 17:162
Elizabeth C. (Dixey), 17:103
Elizabeth D. (Low), 16:220
Elizabeth L. (Chapman), 17:32
Ella Lane, 17:161
Ella M. (Haynes), 17:104
Ella W., 17:165
Ellen, 17:109
Ellen (Shaw), 17:109
Elsie Jane (Rankin), 17:164
Elsie Rankin, 17:164
Emeline, 16:216
Emeline Rogers (Babson), 17:163
Emiline (Thomas), 17:37
Emily, 17:35
Emily May (Shattuck), 17:102
Emma (Lufkin), 17:167
Emma E. (Porter), 17:102
Emma E. (Smith), 17:103
Emma Francis, 17:108
Emma Stowe, 17:103
Epes E., 17:109
Ernest Rockwell, 17:166
Ernestine Rockwell, 17:180
Erville Lesley, 17:103
Esther, 16:141
Eunice (Dodge), 16:213
Eunice Augusta (Fitz), 17:163
Eva F., 17:165
Eva/Dora P. (Littlefield), 17:167
Eveline, 17:168
Everett Thurston, 17:170
Fannie E., 17:102
Fanny, 16:215; 17:162
Fanny Maria, 17:162
Flora B. (McDonald), 17:104
Flora Eaton, 17:104

Flora T., 17:105
Florance S. (Wilson), 17:168
Florence, 17:37
Frances Augusta (Goodridge), 17:103
Frances C., 17:167
Frances Obena, 17:180
Frances Putnam (Goodale), 17:102
Francis Alinda, 17:107
Frank Bertram, 17:102
Frank E., 17:33
Frank M., 17:106
Frank W., 17:36
Frank Waldo, 17:109
Franklin, 16:217
Franklin Fischer, 17:107
Frederick T., 17:37
Genvieve (Little), 17:170
George F., 16:216; 17:35
George Ferdinand, 17:108
George Franklin, 17:35
George Howard, 17:105
George L., 17:164
George Lincoln, 17:102
George S., 17:109
George W., 17:109
George Warren, 17:38
Georgia H., 17:109
Georgia S., 17:168
Georgiana (Currier), 17:110
Georgiana (Ellery), 17:109
Georgiana Maria, 17:38
Gertrude, 17:163
Gertrude (Weber), 17:169
Grace A. (McCoy), 17:164
Grace F. (Powers), 17:166
Grace Gordon (Babson), 17:167
Grace N., 17:166
Hannah, 16:145
Hannah (Birdseye), 16:212
Hannah (Ober), 16:145; 17:165
Hannah (Palmer), 16:217
Hannah (Wells), 16:212
Hannah E. (Gott), 17:107
Hannah Elizabeth, 17:32
Hannah M. (Haskell), 17:39
Hannah M. (Perkins), 17:170
Hannah Maria, 17:105
Hannah Ober, 17:105
Hannah Ober (Friend), 17:105
Hannah P. (Collins), 17:38
Harriet (Adams), 17:162
Harriet Everett, 17:35
Harriet Kimball, 17:162
Harriet W., 17:107
Helen Augusta, 16:220
Helen D., 17:166
Helen K., 17:107
Helen M., 17:110
Helen M. (Upham), 17:163
Helen Maria, 17:32
Helen Maria (Elwell), 17:35
Helen P. (___), 17:164
Henry, 17:37
Hepsibah A. (Pickett), 17:104
Herman, 17:106
Herman Davidson, 17:108
Hermon D., 17:167
Hester, 16:138
Horace, 17:106
Horace M., 17:167
Horace W., 17:166
Howard M., 17:166
Ida A., 17:109

Ida A. (Ellery), 17:109
Ida M. (Rowe), 17:103
Isaac, 16:212
Isaac P., 17:32
Isabel E., 17:102
Israel, 16:212; 17:35
James, 16:140; 17:32, 102
James Augustin, 17:38
Joan, 16:138
Joanna, 16:216
Joanna (Gallop), 16:220; 17:102
Joanna Elizabeth, 16:220
Joel, 16:216; 17:33
Joel Henry, 17:33
Joel Murray, 17:33
John, 16:138; 17:32, 102; 18:134; 19:202
John Henry, 17:33
John Ingersoll, 17:35
John Kinsman, 17:38
John Kinsman Wells, 16:218
John Knight, 16:218
John L., 17:38
John Palmer, 16:217
Jonathan, 16:145
Joseph, 16:144; 17:33
Joseph E., 17:32
Joseph Putnam, 17:102
Joseph Sayward, 17:35
Josiah, 16:145
Josiah Ober, 16:216; 17:36, 169
Judith (Spofford), 16:213
Julia, 17:35
Julia Ann, 17:105
Julia Franklin, 17:105
Julia Marie (___), 17:162
Juliette, 16:217
Justine, 17:106
Laura Burbank, 17:110
Lemuel, 16:216; 17:33, 170
Lemuel Henry, 17:105
Lena A., 17:163
Lester C., 17:163
Lester Danforth, 17:164
Lewis, 17:164
Lillian Prescott, 17:103
Lillie F., 17:105
Lizzie H., 17:102
Lizzie/Elizabeth O. (Smith), 17:104
Lottie K., 17:111
Louisa, 16:218
Louisa Huntington (Bingham), 17:39
Lucinda (Grosslin), 17:165
Lucretia R. (Nash), 17:162
Lucy, 17:37
Lucy (Cressy), 16:220
Lucy (Groslin), 17:170
Lucy (Knight), 16:218; 17:39
Lucy (Peabody), 16:217; 17:38
Lucy Ann, 16:218; 17:32
Lucy E. (Proctor), 17:168
Lucy Elizabeth (Proctor), 17:111
Lucy Ellery (Ryerson), 17:37
Lucy Steele, 17:106
Lucy W. (Batchelder), 17:162
Luke Elliot, 16:219; 17:102
Lydia (Elliott), 17:32
Lydia Ellen (Pedrick), 17:103
Mabel Collins, 17:163
Mabel D., 17:166
Mabel Laud, 17:163
Margaret, 19:106
Margaret (Dodge), 16:213
Margaret (McDonald), 17:163

Margaret (Shepherd), 16:212
Margaret A., 17:163
Margaret Alice (MacKenney), 17:161
Margaret G., 17:38
Margery (___), 16:138
Maria, 16:215; 17:33
Maria (Haskell), 17:110
Maria G. (___), 16:216
Martha, 16:143; 17:34
Martha (Conant), 16:143
Martha (Dodge), 16:213
Martha (Hardy), 16:217
Martha (Kimball), 16:216; 17:33
Martha A., 17:165
Martha Ann, 17:34
Martha Ann (Stearns), 17:167
Martha H. (McLane), 17:107
Martha Hale, 16:218
Martha Kimball, 17:35
Martha S. (Pierce), 17:39
Mary, 16:141; 17:34
Mary (Babson), 17:167
Mary (Dexter), 16:138
Mary (Dwinils), 16:217
Mary (Mansfield) [Sarah?], 17:105
Mary (Masury), 16:218
Mary (Moulton), 16:140
Mary (Smith), 16:214
Mary (Welch), 17:106
Mary A. (Kenney), 17:167
Mary C., 17:107
Mary C. (Rowe), 17:165
Mary E., 17:32
Mary E. (Pulcifer), 17:109
Mary Elizabeth, 16:217; 17:108
Mary Elizabeth (Kemp), 17:106
Mary Elizabeth (Mansfield), 17:104
Mary Gardiner (Hersey), 17:107
Mary Ingersoll, 17:35
Mary Ingersoll (Sayward), 17:35
Mary Philbrooks (Waite), 17:166
Mary/Nellie E. (Hoy), 17:180
Mattie, 17:166
Mehitable E. (Lee), 17:103
Mildred R. (David), 17:164
Minnie (Rowe), 17:106
Minnie A., 17:165
Moses, 16:212; 17:109
Nabby/Abigail, 16:143
Nancy, 16:214
Nancy (Thomas), 17:36
Nancy F., 17:110
Nancy Jane, 17:104
Nathaniel, 16:143; 17:34
Nellie D., 17:166
Nellie P., 17:103
Nellie R. (Austin), 17:165
Norma Austin, 17:170
Olive (Gilcreast), 16:217
Olive (Keyes), 16:212
Oscar, 17:109
Patty/Martha, 16:214
Pelatiah, 16:216
Perley B., 17:166
Phebe, 16:213
Phebe Kimball, 17:34
Philomela (Billing), 16:212
Phineas, 16:213
Phineas H., 17:162
Phineas Hovey, 17:38
Polly, 16:214
Polly (Bootman/Butman), 16:214
Preston, 17:39

Priscilla, 16:143; 17:168
Ray Garland, 17:168
Ray Scott, 17:109
Richard, 16:143; 17:33, 105; 18:207
Roger Berry, 17:163
Roscoe Hill, 17:180
Roy, 17:33
Ruth, 17:111
Ruth (Bartlett), 16:213
Ruth (Elliot), 16:218; 17:102
Ruth Cole, 17:168
Sally Peabody, 16:217
Samuel, 16:140; 17:38; 19:202; 20:197
Samuel A., 17:163
Samuel Kimball, 16:216; 17:37
Samuel Thomas, 17:36
Sarah, 16:141; 20:136
Sarah (Dodge), 16:142
Sarah (Wallace/Wallis), 16:212
Sarah A. (Patterson), 17:104
Sarah Clementina, 17:38
Sarah Elliot, 16:219; 17:102
Sarah Hovey, 16:218
Sarah Moar, 16:217
Sarah Pratt, 16:144
Sarah Scott, 17:35
Sarah/Sally, 16:216; 17:33, 36
Sarah/Sally (Brown), 16:216; 17:33
Sarah/Sally (Friend), 16:217; 17:35, 107
Seth, 16:215; 17:102
Seth Louis, 17:103
Sidney, 17:36
Simeon, 16:212
Solomon, 16:216
Solomon A., 17:105
Solomon Augustus, 17:105
Sopha, 16:217
Susan Hannah, 16:218
Susanna (___), 16:144
Susanna (Johnson), 16:212
Suzie A. (Mace), 17:37
Suzie Babson, 17:167
Tammy Gilford, 17:162
Thaddeus Edwin, 17:38
Thomas, 16:212
Victoria, 17:37
Walter, 17:111
Walter Carroll, 17:103
Walter M., 17:168
Walter Ober, 17:166
Weston U., 17:163
William, 16:144; 17:32
William A., 17:32
William E., 17:107
William H., 17:104
William Henry, 17:34
William Hovey, 17:38
William K., 17:165
William Murray, 17:165
William Nat, 17:163
William Preston, 17:104
William Sayward, 17:36
William Scott, 16:216; 17:36
Winslow G., 17:162
Winthrop, 16:145
FRIESEL
Evyatar, 17:69
FRIGA, 19:68
FRIND
Thomas, 20:199
FRINK
Andrew, 16:149
Betsy (Roff), 16:148

Freelove, 19:164
Nancy, 16:147
Samuel, 16:148
FRITH
Joseph, 20:37
FRITOCCI
"Pappy", 16:124
Frank, 16:124
Leo, 16:124
Randolph, 16:124
FRIZELL
Hannah (___), 20:179
FROST
Abigail, 17:119
Anna, 16:132
Betty Kendall (Enos), 17:127
Edmund, 16:34
Elizabeth Kendall (Enos), 18:175
J. O. J., 20:14
John Eldridge, 16:104
Lydia, 16:132
Raymond Harry, 18:175
Samuel, 16:132
Sarah, 16:179; 19:137; 20:220
Thomas, 20:199
William, 19:91
FROTHINGHAM
Charles, 17:174
Elizabeth, 20:39
Jonathan, 20:25
Lydia, 17:174
Lydia (Kidder), 17:174
Richard, 16:225
Sarah, 17:157
Sarah (Needham), 20:25
Thomas, 20:221
FRY/FRIE/FRYE
___, Capt., 19:34
___, Dea., 16:68
Altaserah (Goodwin), 20:107
Ann (___), 18:156
Anne, 18:156
Benjamin, 16:68; 18:156
Daniel, 16:214
David, 19:92
Deborah, 16:120
Dorcas (Parker), 19:92
Ebenezer, 19:34
Esther, 18:156; 19:46
Hepsebah, 18:156
Isaac, 20:216
James, 16:68; 17:153; 18:152, 157; 19:33, 101
Joanna, 17:153
John, 18:156; 19:34, 92
Jonathan, 17:153
Joseph, 16:44; 17:180; 18:156, 163; 19:57
Joshua, 19:35
Lydia, 19:31, 33
Lydia (Osgood), 19:33
Mary, 16:211; 18:156; 19:21, 24, 57
Mary (Lewis), 17:180; 19:57
Mary (Parker), 18:155, 156
Mary Ann, 17:180
Mehitable, 18:156
Nathaniel, 18:156
Naomi (Haskell), 20:216
Pamelia, 19:178
Samuel, 16:68, 120; 18:162
Sarah, 17:153
Sarah (Cheever), 18:152; 19:101
Sarah (Wilson), 17:153
Tabitha (Farnam), 19:92

Tabitha (Parker), 19:92
FRYAR
    Miriam (Bassett), 18:32
FRYER
    Thomas, 18:33
FUCILLA
    Joseph, 16:128
FUERMAN
    Isaac, 20:221
FULFORD
    Annis Augusta, 16:60
FULLARTON see also FULLERTON
    Fergus, 17:56
    Mary, 17:56
    Mary (Fullarton), 17:56
FULLER, 18:213; 20:104, 165
    "Son", 17:144
    Abigail, 16:74; 17:150; 19:108
    Abigail (Gustin), 17:156
    Alice, 17:159
    Alice (Gray), 17:160
    Aline Louise, 20:56
    Almira (Lawson), 20:56
    Alonzo Lorenzo, 20:56
    Anna (Burrill), 16:85; 17:156; 19:41, 103, 104
    Anna (Johns), 16:86
    Anna (Reed), 17:159
    Anthony T., 20:56
    Benjamin, 16:74; 17:144; 18:209; 19:227; 20:137, 209
    Betsey, 17:160
    Daniel, 16:86
    Deborah, 20:179
    Deborah (Damon), 20:179
    Deborah (Whipple), 16:86
    Dorothy, 17:157
    Edith, 17:111
    Edward, 16:166; 17:143; 19:150, 178; 20:135, 196
    Elisha, 17:144; 20:196
    Elizabeth, 16:74; 17:143; 18:211; 20:119, 179
    Elizabeth (___), 20:223
    Elizabeth (Farrington), 16:74; 17:143
    Elizabeth (Walden), 17:144
    Esther (Fisher), 20:179
    Esther (Newhall), 17:159
    Eunice (Breed), 17:160; 19:237
    Eunice (Potter), 17:156; 18:49; 19:150, 237
    Fred, 20:57
    Hannah, 16:86; 17:15
    Hannah (___), 17:159; 20:209
    Hannah (Flower), 20:179
    Hannah (Lewis), 16:166; 17:144
    Hannah (Mansfield), 16:85; 17:159
    Hannah (Prince), 17:156
    Hepzibah (Hathorn), 17:156; 18:167
    Ignatius, 17:154
    James, 17:158
    James Prince, 17:159
    Jeremiah, 20:179
    John, 16:72; 17:19, 143, 154; 18:72, 116, 134, 165, 167, 208, 209, 222, 223; 19:27, 142, 146, 150, 157, 159; 20:48, 111, 135, 196, 214, 216
    Jonathan, 16:86; 17:158; 20:202
    Joseph, 16:86; 17:144; 18:49, 161, 208; 19:150, 151, 237; 20:48, 210
    Leola Maud (Pease), 20:56
    Lydia, 17:160; 18:49; 19:150
    Lydia (Potter), 19:150
    Margaret, 17:159

    Marina, 17:24
    Mary, 16:74; 17:154; 18:43, 116
    Mary (Blaney), 16:85
    Mary (Graves), 20:209
    Mary (Martin), 17:159
    Mary (Pedrick), 16:84
    Mary (Wyman), 17:158
    Mehitable (Hering), 17:157
    Milicent, 17:158
    Nathaniel, 16:85; 17:156; 19:103
    Oliver, 17:160
    Peggy, 16:86
    Rebecca, 17:156
    Rebecca (Belcher), 17:144
    Rebecca (Chase), 17:160
    Ruhanas, 17:157
    Ruth, 16:74; 17:157; 18:45
    Ruth (___), 17:159
    Sally, 17:159
    Sally/Sarah, 19:177
    Samuel, 16:74; 17:158; 19:126
    Sarah, 17:157; 19:150
    Sarah (___), 17:159
    Sarah (Bacon), 17:204
    Sarah (Colburn), 19:178
    Sarah (Laith/Lathe/Leathe), 17:160; 19:151, 237
    Sarah (Lewis), 17:158
    Sarah (Newhall), 17:156; 18:116, 167
    Sarah/Sally, 17:160
    Solomon, 17:159
    Susanna, 16:74; 17:157
    Susanna (Ballard), 16:74; 17:144
    Susannah (Maynard), 17:159
    Thomas, 16:84; 17:15; 18:210, 240; 20:103, 179, 201, 202, 209
    Timothy, 18:226; 20:202, 203
    William, 16:86; 17:154
    William Hyslop, 20:209
FULLERS, 20:175, 201
FULLERTON see also FULLARTON
    Albert Louis, 17:55
    Castillia Lacoste, 18:176
    David, 17:55
    David John, 17:55
    Elizabeth Jane (Adamson), 17:55
    George Brinton, 18:176
    John David, 17:55
    John H., 17:220; 18:133
    John Hubbard, 17:55
    Marjorie Hubbard (Durling), 17:55
    Mary, 18:24
    Mary Bell (Rae), 17:55
    Nancy Jane (Higgins), 18:176
    Olive Lois (Dennan), 17:55
FURBUSH
    John, 20:199
FURNALD
    Joanna, 18:17
FURNALL/FURNELL/FURNILL
    Eleanor (___), 18:19
    Joanna, 18:14, 15, 18, 19; 19:155
    Strong, 18:19
    Susanna, 18:14
FURNIVAL, 20:180a
FYRMIN
    Gyles, 18:140

GAFFNEY
    Abigail (Story), 17:139
    Barnabas, 17:138
    Charles, 17:135
    Charlotte (Phillips), 17:139

    Daniel, 17:135
    Eliza (Gardiner), 17:139
    Elizabeth (Story), 17:139
    Eunice (Clark), 17:138
    Eunice (Dumphy/Donahue), 17:135
    Frank, 17:136
    Frank H., 17:131
    Henrietta (Webber), 17:139
    Jefferson, 17:135
    Johanna, 17:139
    Lucinda (Davis), 17:139
    Matthew, 17:135
    Michael, 17:131; 18:134
    Thomas Jefferson, 17:138
    William, 17:135
GAGE
    ___, Gov. Gen., 17:3
    Andrew, 18:57
    Benjamin, 18:73
    Denison, 16:100
    Ebenezer, 20:119
    Elizabeth, 19:33, 87, 88, 99; 20:119
    Elizabeth (Hood), 18:57
    Elizabeth (Northend), 18:73
    Hapzabeth (Lewis), 16:100
    Henry, 18:73
    J. Smith, 18:180
    Johanna/Hannah (Knight), 18:73
    John, 18:73; 20:119
    Minoh G., 17:109
    Moses, 18:73
    Philena (Hovey), 18:180
    Priscilla (Kimball), 20:119
    Sarah (___), 18:73
    Sarah (Dodge), 18:73
    Sarah (Haseltine), 20:119
    Thomas, 18:73
    William, 18:73; 20:89
GAINER
    Thomas, 19:132
GAINES/GAINS see also GEARNES
    Abraham, 16:203
    Alice (Norwood), 18:203
    Daniel, 18:203
    Henry, 18:72; 19:138; 20:195
    Jane, 17:46
    John, 18:203; 20:223, 238
    Judith (___), 18:203
    Martha, 20:238
    Mary (Treadwell), 20:238
GALBREATH
    Mary, 20:55
GALE, 19:201
    Abigail (Burrill), 16:25
    Ambrose, 17:100; 19:202
    Deliverance (Wakefield), 16:146
    Edmund, 16:136
    Elizabeth, 17:230
    Elizabeth (Grant), 18:58
    Harriet (Eastman), 18:178
    Jonathan, 20:48
    Joseph, 16:146
    Mary, 17:118
    Merriam, 18:30
    Molly, 16:210
    Samuel, 16:146
    Sarah, 16:146; 17:100; 19:52, 230
    Stephen, 18:178
    Susanna, 16:212
    William, 18:58
GALEUCIA see GALOSHOE
GALL
    Benieman, 20:199

GALLANT
   Celia/Cecilia Victoria, 18:58
   Elizabeth (___), 18:58
   John, 18:58
GALLEY see also **GALLI, GALLY**
   John, 19:202
GALLI see also **GALLEY, GALLY**
   Jonathan, 16:126
GALLISON
   Caroline, 17:162
   John, 16:96
GALLOP/GALLOPP/GALLOUPE
   August, 19:204, 205
   Augustus A., 17:112
   E. K., 20:161
   Edmund, 16:220
   Joanna, 16:220; 17:102
   John, 19:132
   Love (Rogers), 17:114
   Mahala (___), 16:220
   Thomas, 17:114
GALLY see also **GALLEY, GALLI**
   Elizabeth, 16:55
GALOSHOE/GALEUCIA
   Hannah, 20:210
GALUCIA
   Elizabeth, 17:200
GALVIN
   William Francis, 19:12
GAMAGE/GAMMAGE
   Anne (Gott), 18:201
   Betty, 18:201
   Elinor (Foster), 18:201, 202
   Hannah, 16:177; 18:201
   John, 18:201
   Joshua, 18:201, 202
   Mary, 18:201
   Mary (Norwood), 18:201
   Nathaniel, 18:201
   Rebecca, 18:201, 205
   Ruth, 18:201
   Sarah, 18:201
   Sarah (Platts), 18:201
GAMMON
   Betsey, 18:202
GANNETT
   J. H., 17:166
GANNON
   Ann (Kehoe/Keough), 19:57, 240; 20:120
   Betsey (___), 19:240
   Elizabeth, 19:57; 20:120
   John, 19:57, 240; 20:120
   Mary, 19:57; 20:120
   Richard, 19:240
   Sarah, 19:57; 20:120
   Sarah F., 19:57
   Thomas, 19:57; 20:120
   William, 19:57; 20:120
GARCELON/GARSALON see also
   JOSELING
   Abigail, 19:112
   Alonzo, 19:111
   Anna, 19:114
   Anne (La Rue), 19:110
   Annis, 19:113
   Asa, 19:114
   Daniel, 19:111, 113, 114, 236
   David, 19:112
   Deborah, 19:112
   Deliverance, 19:113
   Deliverance (Annis), 19:111
   Diademia, 19:236
   Ebenezer, 19:236
   Ebenezer A., 19:113
   Elizabeth, 19:112
   Elizabeth (Dyer), 19:111, 112
   Elizabeth (Ross), 19:111, 113, 114
   Esther, 19:112
   Hannah (Ames), 19:111, 113, 114
   Hannah (Barker), 19:113
   Hannah E., 19:114
   Harris, 19:113
   Harvey, 19:113
   Hosea, 19:113
   Isaac, 19:112
   James, 19:110-113, 236
   Jane, 19:113
   Jeanne (Bedat), 19:110
   Jennet (Pettingill), 19:111, 112
   Joseph, 19:112
   Justus Pettingill, 19:112
   Katherine (Millbank), 19:111, 113
   Katy (___), 19:236
   Keziah, 19:236
   Lucy, 19:111, 112
   Lucy M., 19:113
   Lydia, 19:112
   Maria, 19:236
   Maria (Harris), 19:112
   Marie (De La Garige), 19:110
   Mark, 19:111, 113, 114
   Martha (Harris), 19:111
   Moses Harris, 19:112
   Peter, 19:111, 113, 236
   Philip M., 19:113
   Pierre, 19:110, 113
   Polly, 19:113
   Polly (Parker), 19:111, 113
   Sally, 19:110-112
   Samuel Dyer, 19:112
   Seward, 19:114
   Susan, 19:112
   Thankful, 19:113
   Washington, 19:114
   William, 19:111, 112, 236
   William G., 19:114
GARDENER/GARDINER see also
   GARDNER
   ___, Capt., 18:150
   ___, Mr., 19:196
   Christopher, 17:229
   Cyrus, 18:175
   Eliza, 17:139
   Henry Shere, 18:138
   Joanne (___), 20:154
   John, 17:21
   Joseph, 20:207
   Melinda (Carter), 18:175
   Olive A., 18:175
   Samuel, 17:21
GARDNER see also GARDENER, 17:139
   ___, Capt., 16:89; 18:41, 150
   Abel, 17:199
   Anna (Putnam), 18:94
   Anne (Myrick), 19:119
   Benj., 18:45
   Benjamin, 17:205
   Daniel, 18:94, 240
   David E., 16:11
   Eleanor, 18:81
   Elizabeth, 17:226
   Elizabeth (Gardner), 17:226
   Elizabeth (Weld), 17:226
   Frank A., 17:148; 19:150
   George F., 17:31
   James, 17:240
   John, 17:12; 18:240
   Jonathan, 17:226; 18:101
   Joseph, 17:19; 19:159; 20:135
   Lucretia, 18:205
   Lydia, 17:226
   Margaret, 17:227
   Mary, 19:51
   Mildred Florence (Edmands), 17:31
   Molly (Smith), 17:205; 18:45
   Polly (Northey), 19:169
   Reuben, 19:169
   Richard, 17:226
   Ruth, 18:94
   Samuel, 16:31; 18:60a; 19:119; 20:48
   Sarah, 17:197; 19:51, 150
   Sarah (Derby), 17:226
   Sarah (Porter), 17:226
   Seeth, 16:60a, 201
   Susanna, 17:179; 19:119
   Susanna (Smith), 19:119
   Weld, 17:205
   William, 16:133
GARELICK/GARLICK, 16:13
GARFIELD
   Elizabeth, 17:44
   Martha, 17:36
GARFORD
   Gervase, 19:196
GARLAND
   Joseph, 17:222
   Joseph E., 17:37
   Matilda, 17:37
   Sally, 19:168
GARLICK see GARELICK
GARNS/GARNEY
   Mary, 19:158
GARNSEY
   Provided (Gaskill), 18:97
   William, 18:97
GARRETT
   Amanda Marcella, 19:233
   Gregory Ross, 19:233
   James Newton, 19:233
   Melissa Pope, 19:233
   Nancy (Westcoat), 19:230
   Nancy Westcoat (Harwood), 19:233
GARSALON see GARCELON, 19:110
GARSIDE, 16:13
GARTHET
   Elizabeth Jane, 17:56
GARY see also GEARY
   Abigail, 19:148
   Mehitable, 18:85, 87
GASCOIN
   Joseph, 16:98
GASKILL
   Alice (Pickering), 18:96; 20:95
   Bethia (___), 18:134
   Bethiah, 20:95
   Bethiah (Woodin), 20:27, 94, 95
   Content, 20:95
   Deborah (Wing), 18:97
   Ebenezer, 18:97; 20:95
   Estes, 18:97
   Hannah, 18:96, 97; 20:95
   Hannah (Estes), 18:95, 96
   Jonathan, 18:96; 20:95
   Keziah (Cass), 18:97
   Lovice, 18:97
   Mary, 20:93, 95
   Mary (Boyce), 20:95
   Nathan, 20:95
   Nicene (Boyce), 18:96

Olive, 18:97
Patience, 18:97; 20:26, 27, 94, 95
Provided, 18:97; 20:95
Provided (Southwick), 20:94
Samuel, 18:96, 134; 19:216; 20-27, 94, 95
Sarah, 16:16; 18:96; 20:95
Sarah (Varney), 20:95
Silas, 18:97
Tamer, 18:96
Varney, 18:96

GATCHEL/GATCHELL see also
GETCHELL, 18:134
Elizabeth, 19:151
John, 17:212
Johnathan, 20:199
Joseph, 20:199
Susannah, 18:211
Wilbur, 17:212

GATES
Clarissa, 18:179
Susanna, 17:117

GAVET/GAVITT
Katherine, 17:179
Phillip, 20:199

GAY
Lydia (Tyler), 16:115
Margaret (Harden), 16:115
Martha, 16:115; 19:156
Philip, 16:115
Samuel, 16:115
Zebulon, 16:115

GEANS
Henry, 18:230

GEARE/GERE see also GEER
Benjamin, 16:110
Mary, 16:110
Shuball, 16:110
Thomas, 16:110
William, 16:109

GEARNES see also GAINES
Andrew, 18:31
Mary (Bassett), 18:31

GEARY/GEARE see also GARY
John, 17:113
John Thomas, 16:110
Susannah (Williams), 17:113

GEDNEY/GEDNY
Bartholomew, 17:15; 19:143; 20:135
Bethiah, 16:154; 17:16; 19:143
Deborah, 19:47; 143
Eleazer, 19:143
John, 19:142-144, 194, 196
Katharine (___), 19:143
Martha, 16:154
Mary, 18:168; 19:142, 144, 145
Nathaniel, 19:143, 145
Sarah (___), 19:142
William, 18:78

GEE
Hannah, 19:119

GEENEMANS
Leendart, 17:133

GEER see also GEARE
Elizabeth (Herrick), 16:115
George, 16:110, 116
Jonathan, 16:115
Joseph, 18:174
Lucy, 16:115
Mary (___), 16:115
Phebe (Park), 16:115
Sarah (Allen/Allyn), 16:110
Stephen, 16:115
Thomas, 16:110

Walter, 16:110

GEISER
Karl F., 18:191

GELLOM see GILLAM, 19:132

GENTILHOMME
Jane, 17:117

GEORGE
"Sagamore", 18:60a; 19:145
Eliza, 16:205
King, 18:187; 19:239
Mary, 16:179; 17:119
Mary (___), 16:204
Richard, 17:90
William, 19:138; 20:195

GEORGES
Robert, 19:128

GERE see GEARE

GERRISH, 17:51
Anna, 19:38, 41
Anne (Parson), 16:229
Jacob, 16:69; 20:117
Joseph, 19:41
Sarah, 17:51
William, 16:229; 19:192

GERRY/GERY
Benjamin, 20:38
Elbridge, 18:134
Elizabeth, 19:218; 20:21, 33, 38
Elizabeth (Damon), 20:38
Nathaniel, 20:21
Thomas, 16:109; 20:221

GETCHELL see also GATCHEL
Ephraim, 20:229
Isabella Pope (Goodale), 20:229
John, 19:194
Susanna, 17:238

GIBBENS see also GIBBONS
Lillian, 16:11

GIBBON
Edward, 16:138

GIBBONS see also GIBBENS
Elizabeth, 16:56
James, 16:56
Judith (Lewis), 16:56

GIBBS, 20:187
Betsey, 18:179
Elizabeth (___), 17:93
Hannah, 17:24; 18:212
Huldah (Gould), 17:22
Jacob, 17:24
Joseph, 17:22
Mary, 18:212
Mary (Goodwin), 17:24
Robert, 17:93

GIBSON
Isaac, 17:105
Julia Ann (Friend), 17:105
Lucy (Perkins), 17:105
Sam, 17:105
Samuel, 19:209
Sarah (Pemberton), 19:209

GIDDING/GIDDINGE/GIDDINGS
___, Mr., 19:46
___, Mrs., 17:11
Anna (Ingalls), 19:46
Chloe, 18:88
Daniel, 19:87
Elizabeth (___), 16:234; 20:224
Job, 16:176
John, 16:233
Joshua, 18:88
Margaret, 16:176
Margaret (Low), 16:177

Mary, 17:12
Robert, 17:12
Samuel, 17:76
Sarah, 16:177
Sarah (Marshall), 16:233
Submit (Jones), 18:88
Thomas, 20:224

GIFFORD/GIFFORDS, 18:222
___, Mr., 16:175
Hannah, 20:233
John, 16:23; 17:88; 20:193
Mary (Mower), 17:41
Matthew, 17:41
Mehitable, 16:82

GILAM see GILLAM

GILBERT
Abial (Hayward), 18:171
Abigail, 16:31; 17:211; 19:218; 20:38
Addison, 17:221
Benoni (Bailey), 18:171
Eliza Ann, 17:111
Elizabeth (___), 16:34; 18:171
Elizabeth (Graves), 20:222
Elizabeth (Kilham), 16:34
Elizabeth (Witt), 18:171
Eunice, 16:240
Hannah, 16:34
Henry, 18:171
Humphrey, 16:34
John, 16:34; 18:76, 171
Joseph, 18:240
Judith, 18:217
Lavina, 16:90
Lemuel, 18:217
Martha, 16:34
Martha Ann, 18:207
Mary, 16:34
Mary (Coy), 18:76
Ruth (___), 18:217
Samuel C., 18:207
Sarah, 17:92
Thomas, 18:171; 20:222
William, 18:171

GILCHRIST/GILCREAST
Betty (Norwood), 18:205
Olive, 16:217
William, 18:205

GILE/GUILE see also GUIL
___, Dr., 18:27
Clyde Ambrose, 16:53
Daniel, 18:27
Ebenezer, 18:156
Elizabeth, 18:157
Frances (Longfellow), 16:53
James, 18:157, 157
Joseph, 18:156
Judith, 18:157
Lydia (Hawkes), 18:27
Mary, 18:156
Mary (Johnson), 18:156
Mary (Robertson), 16:53
Ruth, 18:156
Ruth (Parker), 18:155, 156
Samuel, 18:140
Sarah, 18:157
Stanley Clyde, 16:53
Vera, 16:108

GILES, 20:68
Ebenezer, 20:42
Eleazer, 20:42
Elizabeth, 17:199; 18:217, 218
Eve (Hawkes), 20:33, 37, 42, 43
John, 16:89; 17:16

Lydia (Grover), 20:42
Mary, 17:205; 18:45; 19:101
Mehitable, 17:117
Mercy (Aborn), 16:89
GILFORD
Mary (Witt), 19:144
Samuel, 19:144
GILKEY
Joseph, 20:114
Phebe (Larrabee), 20:114
GILL
Anna, 18:211
Anna (___), 18:211
Arthur, 19:132
Elizabeth, 19:41, 102, 103
Michael, 19:102
Samuel, 20:13
Suzannah, 18:167; 18:158
William, 18:211; 20:198
GILLAM/GILAM/GELLOM
___, Mrs., 19:133
Benjamin, 17:88; 18:232, 234; 19:132, 133
Edward, 19:131, 133
Joseph, 19:132, 133
Robert, 19:132
GILLEN
Susannah, 17:119
GILLIAM
Benjamin, 19:131
Robert, 19:131
GILLO/GILLOW/GILLOWE
John, 16:196; 17:17; 18:72, 230; 19:145
Rose (___), 17:17
GILLOWAY/GILLOW
John, 17:89
GILMAN
Edward, 18:230; 19:191
Joseph W. B., 19:172
Lucy (Northey), 19:172
Moses, 16:17
Nancy, 20:239
William, 20:239
GILPATRICK
Huldah (Tarbox), 20:140
James, 17:178
Jane, 20:139
Joseph, 20:140
Mary (Tarbox), 20:140
Robert, 17:178
Sally, 17:178
Sarah, 20:139, 140
William, 20:140
GILREIN
John, 18:177
Marion (Brown), 18:177
GINGELL
John, 20:201
GIOVANNI, 16:124
GIRARD
Beatrice Allison (Wood), 20:172
Evelyn (McCaul), 20:172
Richard, 20:172
GIRDLER
Elenor, 18:37
Francis, 20:15
John, 19:52
Mary (Ingalls), 19:52
GIVEN
Jane (Larrabee), 20:50
John, 20:50
Sarah, 20:50
GLADDEN
Sanford Charles, 19:134

GLAS
Richard, 20:199
GLASEY
Sarah, 19:53
GLASS, 19:201
GLAZIER
Ira A., 17:73
Prentice, 16:226; 20:146
GLEASON
Joseph, 17:21; 20:137
Lydia (Tarbox), 17:21; 20:137
Mary, 18:170
Ruth, 17:23
GLIDDENS
Sara (___), 16:204
William, 16:204
GLIDE
John, 20:197
GLOVER
___, Col., 17:6
___, Goody, 18:74
Charles, 16:63
Elizabeth, 16:45
John, 16:119; 17:7; 18:74; 19:165, 166
Jonathan, 16:44
Joseph, 16:44
Martha, 17:13
Mary (Newhall), 16:45
Patty (Friend), 16:214
Sarah, 16:223
William, 16:111
GLOYD
Mary, 19:137
Mary/Margaret, 17:149
GOATEM
Sarah (Franklin), 17:147
Thomas, 17:147
GODDARD
John, 17:148
Samuel, 19:22
Sarah, 17:147
Sarah (Farrington), 17:148
GODFREY
Anne (___), 17:175
Azuba (Collins), 20:55
Christopher, 17:175
Deborah, 16:57
Deborah (Cook), 20:56
Enoch, 20:55
Hannah, 20:55
Hannah (Hackett), 18:81
John, 18:81
Josiah, 18:81
Katherine (Davis), 18:81
Margaret, 19:120; 20:119
Mary, 17:175; 18:81; 19:83
Mary (Berry), 18:81
Mehitable, 18:81
Miriam (Smith), 20:55
Moses, 20:56
Richard, 20:55
Robert, 18:81, 82
Sarah, 18:81
Sarah (___), 18:81
Susannah (Green), 18:81
Thomas, 17:135
William, 18:81
GODFRIE/GODFRY
George, 20:199
John, 19:30; 20:214
GODSOME
Francis, 17:154

GODSON
Francis, 19:138; 20:195
GOFFE
Elizabeth, 16:71
GOGGIN
Parmelia, 19:139, 141
GOLD see GOULD
GOLDSMITH
Harriet N., 20:58
Hutton, 16:142
Lucy (Gould), 20:142
Miriam (Kimball), 16:142
Nathaniel, 20:142
Sarah E., 17:109
GOLDTHWAIT/GOLDTHWAITE
Anne-Scott, 19:56, 59
Benjamin, 20:35
Charlotte, 19:56, 99
David, 18:240
Elizabeth, 19:37
Elizabeth (Cheever), 19:37
Elizabeth A., 17:117
Emma (Chandler), 19:56
Esther, 19:18
Esther (Boyce), 19:37
Evelyn, 19:56
Ezekiel, 19:37
H. Chandler, 19:59
Hannah, 17:200; 19:37
Hannah M. (Lawrence), 17:118
Harriet B. (Scott), 19:56
Henry Chandler, 19:56
James B., 19:56
James Wilburn, 19:56
Leone L. (___), 19:56
Luther, 17:118
Mary (Thomas), 19:37
Patricia, 19:56
Rebecca, 17:200
Samuel, 19:37
Sarah (Gowing), 20:35
Susan (___), 19:56
Thomas, 19:37, 56
Wilburn Scott, 19:56
GOLDWAITE
Esther (Boyce), 20:94
Ezekiel, 20:94
GOOCH
Abigail, 20:51
Elizabeth, 16:77
Harriott (Norwood), 18:203
James, 18:203
John, 19:102
Sarah (Weaver), 19:102
GOOD
Sarah, 17:15
GOODAKER
Adam, 19:212
GOODALE see also GOODELL, 18:134, 137
Abigail, 20:229, 233
Abigail (Eliot), 17:16
Abigail (Needham), 20:233
Abigail Currier (Griffin), 20:228
Abraham, 20:205
Amos, 20:234
Ann (Fowler), 20:232
Augusta (Jocelyn), 20:228
Betsey, 20:229
David, 20:229
Deborah (Hawkins), 20:229, 230, 232, 233
Ebenezer, 20:228-230, 233
Eleazer, 18:169
Elizabeth, 18:167

Elizabeth (Beauchamp), 20:234
Elizabeth (Witt), 18:149, 167
Elizabeth Wallis, 20:229
Emily Hannah Purdy (Sullivan), 20:228
Enos, 20:233
Ezekiel, 20:232
Frances Putnam, 17:102
Grace (Phelps), 20:230
Hannah, 18:169; 20:229
Hannah (Rhodes), 20:205
Hannah (Upton), 20:228, 229, 231
Hannah Upton, 20:228, 229
Hester, 20:232
Hitte, 20:229
Hitty (Preston), 20:228-230
Huldah (Burt), 20:230
Isaac, 17:16; 20:229, 230, 232, 233
Isabella Pope, 20:229
Jacob, 20:229, 231, 233
James, 20:228-231
John, 18:149, 167; 20:234
Jonathan, 20:230, 233
Joshua, 16:88
Keturah, 20:233
Keturah (Goodale), 20:233
Lydia (Lee), 20:232
Maria Preston, 20:228
Mary, 16:93; 20:230, 231, 233, 235
Mary (Abbe), 20:230, 232
Mary (Angier), 20:233
Mary (Buxton), 20:231, 234, 235
Mary (Osborn), 17:198
Mehitable, 20:231
Mehitable (Brown), 20:229, 233
Mehitable White, 20:229
Nathan, 18:167
Nehemiah, 20:196
Patience (Cook), 20:232
Phebe, 20:229, 231, 234
Phebe (Goodale), 20:229
Phebe Ann Putnam, 20:229
Rachel, 20:231, 234, 235
Rebecca (Newhall), 17:16
Rebecca (Witt), 18:169
Rebecca Newhall, 17:15
Rebeckah, 18:169
Richard, 18:154
Robert, 17:16
Ruth (Bound), 20:234
Sally, 20:229
Sally Bodge, 20:229
Samuel, 20:231, 232, 234, 235
Sarah, 20:229, 231, 233
Sarah (Russell), 20:234
Sarah (Whittredge), 20:229, 230
Silas, 18:169
Solomon, 18:167
William, 20:228-230
Zachariah, 20:234
GOODELL see also GOODALE
Elizabeth, 17:120
Enoch, 16:88
Isaach, 17:14
Robert, 17:14
Sarah, 20:213
Zachary, 17:14
GOODHEW/GOODHUE, 17:57
Abigail, 16:178
Bethia, 16:160
Dorothy (Haskell), 20:216
Elizabeth, 16:80; 20:216
Hannah, 16:83
Hannah (Dane), 19:115

Isaac, 17:120
Jacob, 16:145
Jane (___), 19:179
Joseph, 20:216
Marguerite, 17:120
Nicholas, 19:179
Sarah (Kimball), 16:145
Sarah (___), 17:120
William, 16:159; 17:76; 19:115
GOODING
Betsy (Hart), 18:50
James, 20:220
Mary (Jack), 20:220
Richard, 20:200
Thomas, 18:50
GOODMAN
Ernestina, 19:186
Mary/Margaret, 18:100
GOODNOW
Sarah, 18:170
GOODRICH, 17:141
Daniel, 18:204
Mary (___), 18:204
Sarah, 18:201, 204
GOODRIDGE, 18:134, 135
___, Mrs., 16:63
Ann, 16:63
Augusta (___), 17:103
Elizabeth, 19:179
Frances Augusta, 17:103
Hannah (Graves), 20:211
Jane, 20:211
Joanna, 18:59; 19:180
John, 17:12
Joseph, 18:59, 236; 19:180
Mary (Lavenuke), 18:59; 19:180
Nancy (Hackett), 16:239
Samuel, 20:89
Theophilus M., 16:239
William, 17:103
GOODWIN
Abigail, 16:180; 18:203; 20:42
Albert T., 16:103
Alice, 18:203
Altaserah, 20:107
Amasiah, 20:107
Elizabeth, 16:118; 20:138
Freelove, 18:203
Hannah (Graves), 20:219
Hepzibah (Phillips), 18:160
Lydia Mariah (Richards), 16:103
Mary, 17:24
Mary (___), 20:107
Mary (Burch), 18:203
Nathaniel, 16:186; 19:214
Richard, 17:240
Samuel, 18:203; 20:219
Sarah, 16:91; 18:201, 203
Sarah (Norwood), 18:203
Susannah (Stowers), 16:118
Susannah (Wheeler), 16:118
Timothy, 20:48
William, 17:98; 18:32, 33, 160; 19:38
GOOKIN
Daniel, 16:225
Samuel, 17:79
GOOLD see also GOULD
Joseph, 18:42
GOOODING
Luxford, 16:180
GOOSE
Susannah (___), 17:20

GOOTENBERG
John/Yonah, 17:68
Samuel, 17:68
GORD
Allen, 17:23
Margaret/Pegge, 16:131
GORDON
Caroline Parmelia (Norwood), 18:217
Charles M., 17:29
John, 18:217
Mary, 18:178
Mary Francis (Edmands), 17:29
GORE
Abigail (Parker), 16:39
Hannah, 16:116
John, 16:39
Rhoda (___), 16:116
Timothy, 16:39
GORGES
Fernando, 17:155
GORHAM
Abner D., 17:164
GORKUM
Anna Catherine Barbara, 19:238
Johann Wilhelm, 17:53
Sophia Catherine (Speiss), 17:53
GORR
Shmuel, 17:73
GOSLEN, 19:111
GOSLING
Marion, 18:134
GOSS
Betsy, 16:176
Charles Carpenter, Mrs., 16:41
David, 19:123
Deborah, 19:50
Joseph, 16:88
Mary (Tarr), 16:177
Patience (Harraden), 18:200
Richard, 18:134
Thomas, 16:177; 18:200
GOTIER
Anne, 20:73
GOTT, 18:134
___, Mr., 17:209
Abigail, 16:235
Abigail (___), 18:206
Abigail (Morgan), 17:119
Abigail Greenleaf, 16:118
Anne, 18:201
Benjimin, 16:63; 20:135, 141
Betsy, 16:176
Betsy (Goss), 16:176
Charles, 16:34; 17:119; 18:206; 19:119, 188; 20:135, 141
Daniel, 18:205, 222, 223
Deborah (Richardson), 18:205
Ebenezer, 16:176
Eleanor (___), 20:140
Elizabeth, 18:223
Elizabeth (Richardson), 18:205
Elizabeth (Wanson), 16:58
Esther, 18:202, 206
George, 16:176
Hannah, 18:205
Hannah (Andrews), 20:135, 141
Hannah (Gamage), 16:177; 18:201
Hannah (Norwood), 18:205
Hannah (Tarbox), 20:141
Hannah E., 17:107
John, 16:177; 18:166, 201, 234; 20:135, 140, 141
Joseph, 18:205

Judith (___), 17:107
Liddia, 20:135
Lois, 16:58
Lydia, 18:202; 20:141
Lydia (Barton), 18:205
Lydia (Clark), 19:119; 20:141
Martha (Kimball), 18:166
Mary, 16:157; 18:165
Nathaniel, 18:205
Peter, 18:205
Rachel (Littlefield), 18:205
Rebeckah (Tarbox), 18:234; 20:135, 140
Ruth (Ivory), 19:147
Sally (Tarr), 16:176
Samuel, 19:147; 20:135, 141
Sarah (Dennis), 20:135
Sarah (Gammage), 18:201
William, 16:58; 17:107; 18:201

GOTTSCHALL
Patti, 18:137

GOTTWALD
Arthur Pratt, 16:95; 18:137

GOULD see also GOOLD
Abigail (Lamson), 20:142
Andrew, 18:56
Ann M. (___), 20:142
Anne (Mecum), 20:142
Asa, 20:142
B. A., 20:236
Benjamin, 20:226
Benjamin Apthorpe, 17:21; 20:142
Christian (Hill), 17:22
Daniel, 18:57; 19:158; 20:39, 142
Deborah, 17:22
Dorcas, 17:22; 19:215
Elisha, 20:142
Elizabeth, 17:238
Elizabeth (___), 16:117
Elizabeth (Hood), 18:56
Elizabeth (Peabody), 20:142
Elizabeth (Thorndike), 17:22
Eunice (Coates), 19:158
Eunice (Perley), 20:142
Gideon, 17:21
Hannah (Curtis), 20:236
Henry, 17:21
Huldah, 17:22
Huldah (Fraile), 17:22
Jacob, 16:234
James, 16:94
Jane, 17:20
John, 16:131; 20:190, 236
Joseph, 19:158
Lucy, 20:142
Lucy (Tarbox), 18:57; 20:142
Lydia, 17:22; 18:57; 20:142
Martha, 20:232, 236
Mary, 16:117; 18:164
Mary (Booth), 20:142
Mary (Upham), 19:158
Mary Jane, 17:239; 20:120
Miriam, 18:105
Moses, 20:142
Nathan, 16:117
Paul, 17:22
Phebe (Deacon), 18:164
Rebecca, 18:100
Rebecca (Aborn), 16:94
Ruth, 18:57; 19:137; 20:142
Ruth (___), 20:39
Ruth (Bancroft), 20:39
Ruth (Towne), 20:142
Sally, 17:205
Samuel, 17:22; 20:142
Sarah (___), 20:225, 226
Sarah (Ingalls), 19:53
Sarah (Pike), 17:22
Sarah (Ward), 17:21
Thomas, 17:22; 19:53, 137, 216
William, 16:131
Zaccheus, 17:21; 18:164; 20:142, 236

GOULD/GOLD
Jane, 17:21

GOULETTE
Anne (Merrill), 17:188
Anne Merrill, 16:57
Anne O., 17:235

GOVE see also GROVE
Edith H., 18:15
Edmund, 16:224
Edward, 18:37
Florence C. (Allen), 16:53
Florence Vernabelle, 16:53
Hannah, 19:141
Huldah (Bassett), 18:37, 55
Mary (Breed), 16:224
Sarah Elizabeth (Folsom), 16:52
Stephen, 18:37, 55
Willis, 16:52
Willis Ansel, 16:53

GOVER
William, 20:199

GOWDY
Lydia (Stocker), 18:215
Nathaniel O., 18:215

GOWELL
Anna (Graves), 20:220
Charles, 20:220

GOWEN
Abigail (Cook), 18:48
Daniel, 20:197
Elizabeth, 18:48
James, 18:49
Lois, 18:38
Nathaniel, 20:197
Nicholas, 18:48

GOWING, 18:134
Abigail, 19:137
Benjamin, 19:137
Daniel, 16:44; 19:136, 137, 212; 20:36, 188
Deliverance (Wyman), 18:212; 20:98
Elizabeth (Brock), 18:41
Ezekiel, 18:212; 19:137, 218; 20:36, 98
George, 18:42
Hannah, 19:137
Hannah (Bancroft), 19:218
James, 20:35
John, 16:44; 19:136, 216; 20:34, 35, 188
Jonathan, 19:137
Joseph, 16:93; 18:216; 19:218; 20:39
Leonard, 17:206
Lucy Endicott (Hart), 17:206
Lydia (Hawkes), 18:212
Lydia (Wellman), 20:35
Martha, 19:137; 20:35
Mary, 19:137
Mehitable, 20:35
Nathaniel, 18:212; 19:136, 137, 212; 20:34, 36
Patience, 20:35
Patience (Bancroft), 20:35
Robert, 18:41; 19:136, 212, 213; 20:35, 185
Samuel, 19:137; 20:35
Sarah, 20:35

Thomas, 19:137, 216; 20:37, 39

GRADY
Catherine, 17:180

GRAFTON
John, 16:180
Joseph, 17:210; 19:193
Seeth (Gardner), 16:180

GRANBERRY, 18:174

GRANGER
Elizabeth (Baker), 18:25
John, 16:20
Martha (Poor), 16:20

GRANT
Abigail (Whitman), 17:115
Abraham, 19:104
Amos, 19:151
Betsey, 16:84; 17:239
Daniel, 18:58
Dorcas, 17:239
Elijah, 17:239
Elisabeth/Betsey (Horsum), 17:239
Elizabeth, 17:239; 18:58; 20:222
Elizabeth (Estes), 18:93
Francis, 20:15
Frazier J., 20:57
John, 17:239; 19:230
Joshua, 17:239
Lois (Devereux), 19:151
Lucy, 17:239
Lydia, 17:239
Marcy, 17:239
Margaret (Bessom), 19:230
Margaret (Cheever), 19:104
Mary, 16:46
Mary (Driver), 18:58
Nathaniel, 17:239
Patience, 17:239
Patrick, 17:115
Polly, 17:239
Prince, 17:133
Samuel, 17:239; 18:93
Susanna (___), 20:15
Thomas, 16:222

GRAVES, 19:183, 201
___, Left., 20:102
___, Maj., 18:16
"Son", 20:209
Abigail, 16:85; 19:156; 20:209, 210, 213, 218, 219, 225
Abigail (Blake), 20:220
Abigail (Graves), 20:210
Abigail (Green), 20:212
Abigail (Jaques), 20:220
Abigail (Palmer), 20:220
Abigail (Williams), 20:211
Abigail W. (Hodgkins), 20:226
Abraham, 16:68; 20:204, 215-220
Abraham (Allen), 18:31
Allen, 20:210
Amy, 18:18; 19:28; 20:205, 215, 216
Amy (___), 20:21, 214, 216
Andrew, 20:221
Ann, 19:229; 20:205, 220, 224
Ann (___), 20:220
Anna, 20:209, 219, 220
Anna (___), 20:225, 226
Anna (Currier), 20:219
Anna (Freeland), 20:212
Anna (Hayward), 20:216, 217
Beamsley, 20:226
Benjamin, 20:211, 222, 227
Bethia (Jackson), 16:85
Betsy, 18:16

Beula (Grover), 20:212
Catherine (Potter), 20:221
Catherine (Sutherland), 20:220
Charles Johnson, 20:220
Crispus, 16:85; 18:19, 31; 19:79; 20:112, 207-209, 211, 212, 221
Crispus Jacob, 20:210
Daniel, 16:90; 19:79, 156; 20:208, 211-213, 221
David, 20:213, 219
Deborah (Safford), 20:226
Deliverance, 20:222
Dexter, 16:150
Dorcas, 20:21, 216
Dorothy, 20:207
Ebenezer, 16:74; 20:204, 207, 209, 213, 216-222
Edward, 20:216
Eleazer, 19:231; 20:217, 219-222
Eliza (Colson), 20:221
Elizabeth, 16:234; 19:79, 156; 20:21, 205-208, 210, 217, 218, 221, 222, 224, 225
Elizabeth (___), 16:24; 20:215, 216, 224-226
Elizabeth (Bean), 20:217, 220
Elizabeth (Burrill), 20:210
Elizabeth (Collins), 20:206, 208, 211
Elizabeth (Evans), 20:221
Elizabeth (Hill), 20:221
Elizabeth (Jacques), 20:221
Elizabeth (Knight), 17:144; 18:73, 174; 19:27; 20:214, 217
Elizabeth (Lewis), 20:208, 210
Elizabeth (Nicholson), 20:208, 213
Elizabeth (Rayner), 20:225, 226
Elizabeth (Richardson), 20:218, 222
Elizabeth (Sayward), 20:226
Elizabeth (Sinecross/Signcross), 20:221
Elizabeth (Stevens), 20:222
Elizabeth (Stretton/Stratton), 20:216, 217
Esther, 20:217, 218, 220-222
Eunice (Collins), 20:208
Fannie (Jack), 20:220
Fanny (Dinsmore), 20:221
George, 20:222
Grace (Beamsley), 20:223-226
Grace Bubier (Prentiss), 20:221
Hannah, 16:85; 19:79; 20:21, 205, 206, 208, 211, 212, 216, 219, 224, 226
Hannah (___), 16:85; 17:49; 20:204, 205
Hannah (Besom), 20:222
Hannah (Blaney), 16:85; 20:210
Hannah (Brown), 20:219
Hannah (Evans), 20:217, 219
Hannah (Galoshoe/Galeucia), 20:210
Hannah (Perkins), 20:225, 226
Hannah (Rand), 16:27; 20:210
Hannah (Todd), 20:208, 212
Hester, 17:146; 18:73; 20:217
Isabella (Hutchinson), 20:221
Isaiah, 18:134
J. C., 20:226
Jabez, 20:220
Jacob, 18:19; 20:209, 210, 220
James, 17:174; 20:211, 218, 219, 227
Jane (Adams), 20:220
Jane (Berry), 20:221
Jane (Venin), 20:211
Jerusha, 20:210
Joanna, 20:210, 220, 221
Joanna (Byham), 20:226
Joanna (Pearce), 20:224
Johanna (Byham), 20:225
John, 19:79; 20:204, 207-209, 217, 219-226
John Bailey, 20:222
John Card, 20:209, 212, 218, 226
Johnson, 20:221
Jonathan, 20:219
Jonathan Blaney, 16:85
Joseph, 16:85; 17:46; 20:211, 212, 220, 221
Joshua, 20:220
K. V., 20:213, 217
Katy (Hawthorne), 20:221
Kenneth, 17:174
Kenneth Vance, 16:79; 17:146; 18:73; 19:156; 20:204
Levi, 20:221
Louisa, 16:148
Lucy, 20:209, 219
Lydia, 19:156; 20:213, 219
Lydia (Newton), 20:212
Lydia (Wallis), 20:208, 213
Margaret, 17:146; 18:73; 20:217
Margaret (Gray), 20:221
Mark, 16:24; 17:144; 18:31, 73, 97; 19:79; 20:21, 204-206, 208, 210-212, 214-222
Mark Bond, 20:216
Martha, 19:155, 156; 20:212, 213, 219, 225, 226
Martha (Coates), 19:156; 20:208; 20:213
Martha (Hall), 20:218, 219
Martha (Kneeland), 20:224, 225
Martha (Mallett), 20:220
Mary, 18:14, 15, 17, 18, 53; 20:206, 208-211, 213, 215, 216, 219-222, 224-226
Mary (Bowden), 20:222
Mary (Buxton), 20:213
Mary (Dinsmore), 20:221
Mary (Graves), 20:221, 222
Mary (Harris), 20:221
Mary (Hendley), 20:222
Mary (Hopson), 18:73; 20:217, 218
Mary (Jack), 20:220
Mary (Merry), 20:208, 210
Mary (Newton), 20:211, 212
Mary (Smith), 20:207, 109
Mary (Standley), 20:222
Mary (Stevens), 20:222
Mary (Williams), 20:210
Mary Ann, 17:174; 20:227
Mary Ann (Beers), 20:227
Mary Ann Nichols (Beers), 17:174
Mary Elizabeth/Molly, 20:219
Maureen R., 20:222
Mehitable (Hutchinson), 20:220
Miriam Lewis (Besom), 20:222
Moses, 20:220, 225, 226
Nancy (Livermore), 16:85
Nathaniel, 19:79, 156; 20:208, 211-213, 220
Olive, 20:219
Olive (Flint), 20:213
Persis (Bellows), 20:212
Phineas, 20:219
Polly, 20:221
Polly (Paine), 20:221
Prudence (Woodward), 20:224
Rand, 16:79; 20:210, 211, 227
Rebecca, 19:79; 20:207-210, 212, 220
Rebecca (___), 18:73; 20:205, 206
Rebecca (Alley), 18:19; 20:208-210
Rebecca (Cash), 20:221
Rebecca (Sweetland), 20:222
Rhoda (Fay), 20:212
Richard, 16:139
Robert, 20:104
Roland B., 20:219
Ruth, 16:156; 18:31, 93, 97; 20:208-212, 217
Ruth (___), 18:31
Ruth (Barker), 20:221
Ruth (Collins), 20:208, 211
Ruth (Phillips), 16:155; 18:97; 20:208, 212
Ruth (Taylor), 20:208, 211, 219
Ruth (Wadleigh), 20:219
Sally, 20:222
Sally (Hodgdon), 20:219
Sally (Lloyd), 20:222
Samuel, 16:79; 17:49; 18:19, 73, 105; 19:78, 79, 156, 157; 20:196, 204-213, 217-227
Sarah, 16:46; 17:47; 18:24; 20:205, 206, 209-213, 217-222, 224-226
Sarah (___), 18:19; 20:207, 221, 224-226
Sarah (Allen), 16:85; 18:19; 20:210, 211
Sarah (Alley), 18:117
Sarah (Bailey/Bayley), 20:218, 221
Sarah (Barrett), 20:216-218, 221
Sarah (Bessom), 19:231
Sarah (Brewer), 16:156; 19:79, 156; 20:205, 207
Sarah (Dolliver), 20:222
Sarah (Dunton), 20:216, 217, 219
Sarah (Frost), 20:220
Sarah (Jacques), 20:221
Sarah (Muzzey), 20:212
Sarah (Pearce), 18:19
Sarah (Perkins), 20:217, 218
Sarah (Phillips), 16:85
Sarah (Pierce), 20:209
Sarah (Roberts), 20:218
Sarah (Staples), 20:220, 221
Sarah (Upton), 19:156; 20:213
Sarah (Whitmark), 16:85
Sarah B. (Loviss), 20:222
Stephen, 20:212
Susanna (Hobbs), 20:220
Susanna (Marrett), 20:212
Susanna (Merrill), 20:221
Susanna (Millais), 20:212
Susannah, 20:220
Tabitha, 19:156; 20:213, 221
Tamar, 20:210, 211
Thomas, 16:79; 17:49; 18:14, 17, 73, 180a; 19:79; 20:196, 204-214, 217-220, 222, 224, 227, 240a
Tirzah (Newton), 20:212
Ursilla (Wilson), 20:217, 219
William, 16:85; 18:19, 31, 117; 19:79; 20:207-212, 217, 219-221
William Andrew, 20:222
William Dolliver, 20:222
Zerviah (Williams), 20:212
GRAY, 16:111; 20:31
___, Mr., 20:38
Abigail, 20:213
Abigail (___), 20:102, 104, 105
Abraham, 16:85; 18:23
Alice, 17:160
Alice (Breed), 18:36
Anna, 19:164
Anna (Newhall), 20:105
Benjamin, 16:64; 18:213, 214; 19:151
Charles, 16:219
Clarissa (Eastman), 18:178

Daniel, 20:213
Deborah, 20:104, 105, 138, 237
Dorothy, 19:153; 20:104, 105, 137
Dorothy (Collins), 18:100; 20:102-104, 137, 138
Edward, 20:102
Eliza Ellen, 16:219
Elizabeth, 19:103; 20:139
Elizabeth (Allen), 20:105
Elizabeth (Coburn), 20:38
Elizabeth (Curtis), 18:213
Elizabeth (Emery), 20:139
Elizabeth/Betsy (___), 18:45
Hannah, 16:29; 18:54; 20:21, 213
Hannah (___), 20:105
Hannah (Scarlet), 16:85
Harrison, 18:178
Henry, 19:94
Isaac, 18:45
Jane, 16:219
Jeremiah, 18:15, 16, 36, 54
John, 20:102, 139
Joseph, 17:151; 19:101
Josiah, 16:219
Lydia, 20:213
Lydia (Graves), 19:156; 20:213
Margaret, 20:221
Martha, 16:83
Mary, 16:219; 20:139
Mary (Burchstead), 19:151
Mary (Holt), 20:213
Nathaniel, 16:94
Nathaniel Wilder, 16:219
Olive, 20:139
Phebe, 16:219; 20:213
Phebe (Friend), 16:219
Robert, 16:68; 18:100; 19:142; 20:102-105, 137, 138
Sarah, 20:104, 105
Sarah (Hawkes), 19:151
Susanna (___), 18:93
Tabitha (Allen), 20:213
Theodate (Hood), 18:15, 16, 36, 54
Thomas, 17:96; 18:162; 19:92, 156; 20:213
Thomas E., 17:209; 19:81
William, 16:85; 17:151; 18:36, 54, 93; 19:105; 20:102
Winthrop, 16:97; 18:54

GREELEY/GREELY, 19:141
Elizabeth (___), 17:233
Joseph, 17:233; 18:228
Lydia, 19:120
Rachel, 18:152; 19:101
Sarah (Browne), 18:227, 228

GREEN see also GREENE
___, Mr., 17:91
Abigail, 20:212
Amy, 20:174
Amy Cutler, 16:77
Anna, 17:85
Benjamin, 18:105
Beriah, 20:118
Betsy, 17:120
Chloe, 16:82
Daniel, 20:176
David, 17:86
Deborah (Brown), 16:82
Deliverance (Osborn), 17:198
Elbridge, 17:26
Eleazer, 17:84
Eliza E. (Osborn), 17:187
Elizabeth, 16:42; 17:43; 18:59
Elizabeth (Harris), 16:239

Elizabeth (Roads), 16:239
Elizabeth (Whitman), 17:115
Elizabeth Lilly, 16:110
Emma, 16:49
Eunice (Burrill), 17:148
Ezra, 17:148
Hannah, 19:47, 236
Hannah C. (Osborn), 17:187
Henry, 20:176, 185
Isaac, 19:225
J. G., Mrs., 16:49
James, 16:82
Jane (Tibbetts), 16:220
Jerusha (Gross), 18:215
John, 17:89; 18:215; 19:225
Jonathan, 19:103
Joseph, 17:15
Josiah Sawtell, 17:85
Loami, 17:187
Margaret, 17:184
Margaret (DeJersey), 18:237
Martha, 20:33
Martha (Collins), 18:105
Mary, 17:85; 20:98
Mehitable (___), 17:184
Micajah, 17:198
Mildred Gertrude, 20:56
Mira, 16:220
Molly, 17:84
Nathan, 17:184; 18:237
Peter, 16:239
Polly (___), 20:176
Rebecca, 19:144
Rebecca (Hills), 19:144
Russell, 17:187
Ruth, 16:22
Samuel Abbott, 17:78
Samuel H., 16:239
Sarah, 16:56; 17:85
Sarah (Moulton), 16:110
Sarah (Parker), 17:84
Sarah (Wood), 20:176
Susannah, 18:81
Tabitha (James), 17:100
Theophilus, 18:218
Thomas, 17:85; 19:144
William, 16:220; 17:115

GREENAWAY
John, 18:176
Mary, 18:176
Mary (___), 18:176

GREENE/GRENE see also GREEN, 16:175
Amy, 20:175
Benjamin, 18:81
David, 17:50; 18:139; 19:80
David L., 16:174; 18:136, 164; 20:77
Elizabeth Caroline (Marland), 19:18
G. Holden, 17:184
Henry, 16:203; 17:89
Isaac, 20:41
John, 20:175
Joseph Warren, 19:18
Martha, 20:41
Martha (Boyden), 20:41
Mary, 16:203
Mehitable (Hart), 18:44
Phineas, 18:44
Richard, 17:89
Wilma, 16:50

GREENHALGH, 16:13
GREENLAND
John, 19:225

GREENLEAF
Bathsheba, 18:215
David Coates, 19:161
Elias Davis, 17:42
Elizabeth (Coates), 19:160, 161
Ephraim Mower, 17:42
Gardner, 17:160; 18:49
Jane, 18:77
John, 19:160, 161
Lydia Nicholson (Hart), 17:160; 18:49
Margery, 19:119
Mary (Mower), 17:42
Sarah, 16:223; 17:42
Sarah (Turner), 17:179
Stephen, 16:133; 17:42
Thomas, 19:160, 161
Thomasine, 17:42

GREENOUGH
Abigail (Hammond), 16:230
Luke, 16:230
William, 20:82

GREENWOOD
Anna, 20:50
Martha (Patte), 17:24
Miles, 16:69
Nathaniel, 17:91; 18:213; 20:47
Thomas, 19:157
Val, 17:73

GREGERSON
George, 17:135

GREGG
Rachael, 17:228

GREGORY
Hannah (Meadowcroft), 16:5
Howard Mark, 20:172
Isaac, 16:76
Jean Marie (Wood), 20:172
Margaret, 19:116
Molly (Ballard), 16:76

GREN
Charls, 20:199

GRETE
Clara M. (Dunn), 19:23
George L., 19:23

GREVAN/GREVEN
Philip, 16:66
Philip J., 20:20, 168

GRICE
Mary, 17:219
Priscilla (___), 17:219

GRIDLEY
Abigail (Sharpe), 16:86
Charlotte, 16:87
Elizabeth, 16:87
Elizabeth (Woods), 16:87
Francis, 16:87
Lucy, 16:87
Lydia, 16:87
Lydia (Blaney), 16:87
Mary, 16:86
Oliver, 16:87
Polly, 16:87
Polly (Scott), 16:87
Richard, 17:100
Rufus, 16:87
Samuel, 16:86
William, 16:87

GRIEBEL
Dorothea Marion (Ranks), 17:176
Dorothea R., 16:55
Dot, 18:184
Frederick W., 17:176

GRIFFEN/GRIFFIN
  Abigail Currier, 20:228
  Adoniram, 16:133
  Alfred W., 17:104
  Elizabeth, 18:215
  Elizabeth (Ring), 18:31
  Esther, 18:202
  Hannah, 16:132
  John, 18:34
  Joseph, 18:31, 52
  Mark, 17:135
  Mary, 18:34
  Mary (Upham), 18:34
  Mary Esta, 17:187
  Mary/Polly, 17:108
  Nathaniel, 18:31
  Robin M., 20:116
  Samuel, 16:63
  Sarah, 18:165
  Sarah (Bassett), 18:31, 52
GRIFFING
  Lydia (Kirtland), 18:113
  Robert, 18:113
GRIFFITH
  Charlene Emma (Julian), 17:208
  Grace L., 17:208
GRIGGS see also GRIGS, 17:154
  Elizabeth, 16:206
  Elizabeth (Casse), 16:209
  John, 16:209
GRIGNON
  Marguerite-Josephine (Chevalier) 20:170
  Marie Josephine, 20:169
  Marie-Joseph, 20:170
  Pierre, 20:170
GRIGS see also GRIGGS
  Jacob, 20:200
  Steven, 20:199
  William, 20:200
GRIMES
  Evaline P., 17:167
GRIMPSEN
  John, 20:80
GRIMSHAW, 16:13
GRINDLE
  Eliphalet, 16:213
  Elizabeth, 19:239
  Ichabod, 16:240
  Mary (Friend), 16:213
GRISWOLD
  Mary (Dewolfe), 18:112
  Matthew, 18:112
GROOM
  Louise, 20:109
GROSLIN see also GROSSLIN
  Lucy, 17:170
GROSS
  Abigail (Young), 19:177
  Jerusha, 17:99; 18:211, 215
  Laurania, 19:177
  Thomas, 19:177
GROSSLIN see also GROSLIN
  Lucinda, 17:165
GROUER
  Edmund, 16:140
GROUNDELL
  Judith, 17:212
GROUT
  Johannah, 17:83
  Johannah (Boynton), 17:83
  John, 17:83
GROVE see also **GOVE**
  Mary, 17:229

GROVER/GROVVER
  Abigail, 17:54
  Abigail (Parsons), 17:137
  Ann Thomas (Friend), 17:36
  Augusta Putnam (Friend), 17:108
  Betty (Gammage), 18:201
  Beula, 20:212
  Charles E., 17:36
  Daniel, 17:13
  Edith Friend, 17:108
  Edmund, 20:120, 198
  Edward, 17:108; 19:202
  Elizabeth, 18:202, 206
  Esther, 18:205
  Hannah, 17:202
  Harriet (Lufkin), 17:108
  John, 17:203
  Judith, 18:201
  Lydia, 20:42, 120
  Margaret, 18:206
  Margaret (___), 20:120
  Nehemiah, 18:201
  Richard, 17:12
  Sarah, 18:202
  Sarah (Barney), 17:203
  Stephen, 17:240
  William, 17:108
GROVES
  John, 16:177
  Rebecca, 16:177
  Rebecca (Wallis), 16:177
GROVES/LeGROVE
  Hannah (Sallows), 16:177
  Nicholas, 16:177
GROVVER see GROVER
GROW/GROO
  Abigail, 17:153
  David, 17:153
  Elizabeth (Edmunds), 16:210
  Hannah, 17:153
  Jacob, 17:153
  James, 16:210
  John, 17:153
  Jonathan, 17:153
  Mary, 17:153
  Mary (Farrington), 17:153
  Peter, 17:153
  Phebe, 17:153
  Rebeckah, 17:153
  Samuel, 17:153
  Sarah, 17:153
GRUREN
  Genevieve, 20:170
GUDIN
  Phillip, 20:199
GUE
  Francis Chaplin, 16:228
GUERTIN
  Julie, 20:170
GUIL see also GILE
  Ruth, 18:160
GUILD
  Curtis, 20:183, 189
GUILE see GILE
GUILFORD
  Abigail (Marble), 18:117
  Simeon, 18:117
GUILFOYLE
  Catherine, 18:58
  Christine, 18:58
  Ellen G. (___), 18:58
  Francis, 18:58
  George, 18:58

  James L., 18:58
  Joseph T., 18:58
  Peter F., 18:58
  Thomas, 18:58
  William, 18:58
  Winifred, 18:58
  Winifred (Burns), 18:58
GUNDERSON
  Bernice, 18:136
GUPPY
  Henry B., 16:12
GUSS
  Peter, 17:135
GUSTIN
  Abigail, 17:156
  Elizabeth (Browne), 17:157
  John, 17:157
GUTCH
  Robert, 17:202
GUTTEMAN
  Ernestina, 19:186
GUTTERSON
  John, 16:68; 20:130, 131
  Joseph, 20:131
  Ruth, 18:159
  William, 20:131
GUY
  Elizabeth, 16:23; 20:93
  William, 16:24
GUZIK
  Estelle M., 17:73
GWIN
  Joanna (Richardson), 18:232
  Thomas, 18:232
GYBS
  Daniel, 19:110
GYLES
  Beth, 18:202

HABERFULL see HALLOWELL
HACKER
  Anna (Estes), 18:97, 98; 20:212
  Elizabeth, 18:98
  Eunice, 18:35
  Hannah, 18:98
  Isaac, 18:97, 98; 20:212
  Isaiah, 16:16; 18:98
  Jeremiah, 16:88; 18:98
  Lydia, 18:98; 19:171
  Lydia (Smith), 18:98
  Nancy (Shove), 18:98
  Rebecca, 18:98
  Sarah, 20:27
  Spinget Penn, 18:98
  William Estes, 18:98
HACKETT see also HAGGETT, 18:79
  Abel, 18:120
  Abigail (Sinclair), 19:238
  Annis Augusta (Fulford), 16:60
  Asa, 18:120
  Asael/Asahel, 18:120
  Benjamin, 18:120
  Betty, 17:239
  Charlotte (___), 18:120
  Dorothy (Allen), 16:21
  Ebenezer, 16:19; 18:82
  Edward, 18:81
  Eleanor, 18:81
  Eleanor (Gardner), 18:81
  Eliza (Hammond), 18:120
  Elizabeth (Elliott), 18:81
  Elizabeth (Richmond), 18:81
  Emeline, 18:120

Emma Thrasher, 19:237
Ephraim, 16:19
Frances (___), 18:79, 81, 82
Frank O., 17:239
George, 18:81
Hannah, 18:81, 82
Hannah (___), 18:81
Hannah (Fowler), 16:19
Hannah (Ring), 16:19
Hannah (Young), 16:19
Harold E., 16:22
Henry, 18:180
Hiram Abiff, 17:239
Hiram M., 16:60
Jabez, 16:17; 18:79-81, 134, 230
James, 18:120
Joanna (Washburn), 18:82
John, 16:18; 18:80-82; 19:238
Joseph, 16:239; 18:120
Judah/Jude, 16:19
Katherine, 16:19
Lorenzo W., 17:239
Lucius O., 17:239
Lydia, 18:120
Lydia (French), 18:120
Lydia (Martin), 19:238
Lydia (Thomas), 18:81
Malachi, 16:18
Margaret (___), 16:17
Maria (Maryfield), 17:239
Mary, 16:18; 18:81, 82
Mary (___), 18:82, 180
Mary (Adkins/Atkins), 16:17
Mary (Crane), 18:81, 82
Melvina (___), 17:239
Mercy, 18:81
Nancy, 16:239
Nancy (Bailey), 16:239
Olive Jane (Marston), 19:238
Polly, 18:120
Polly (___), 18:120
Rebecca, 16:18
Sally O., 17:57
Samuel, 18:79-82
Sarah, 16:18; 18:81, 120
Sarah (Andrew), 18:81
Sarah (Barnard), 16:17
Stella, 18:120
Tamsin (Evans), 16:19
William, 16:17; 18:79, 117, 120, 134; 19:238
William Roswell, 19:238

HADDOCK/HADDUCK/HAYDOCK, 18:134
"Child", 16:148
"Daughter", 16:147
Abbie M. (___), 16:149
Abigail, 16:148
Abigail (Haseltine), 16:147
Abigail (Webster), 16:147
Adriana, 16:148
Alfred, 16:151
Amelia (Watkins), 16:151
Aroline, 16:148
Augusta (Bean), 16:149
Benjamin Franklin, 16:148
Bert, 16:149
Caroline (Kimball), 16:148
Catherine Lucy (Shinn), 16:148
Charles, 16:146
Charles Brickett, 16:148
Charles F., 16:149
Charles H., 16:149
Charles Leonard, 16:149
Clara P. (Wilson), 16:149
Clarence A., 16:149
Clarence E., 16:149
Daniel, 16:146
Deliverance (Wakefield), 16:146
Dolly, 16:147
Dolly (Hoyt), 16:147
Edward, 16:149
Edward C., 16:149
Edward Hiram, 16:148
Elizabeth (Matthew/Maytham), 16:149
Elizabeth Stanley, 16:151
Emily, 16:148
Emily Frances, 16:151
Florence May, 16:149
Frances, 16:148
Frances Elizabeth, 16:148
George W., 16:148
Harriet Jane (Poole), 16:149
Hazen, 16:148
Helen, 16:150
Helena Louisa, 16:151
Henry, 16:148
James, 16:146; 17:16
Jane (Alcott), 16:148
John, 16:146
John Haseltine, 16:151
John W., 16:146
Josephine (___), 16:152
Leonard, 16:147
Leslie B., 16:149
Leslie Burt, 16:151
Lorenzo Kimball, 16:148
Lorna R. (Smith), 16:149
Louisa (Graves), 16:148
Lucretia (Kimball), 16:147
Lydia, 16:147
Maria Josephine, 16:151
Martha Celia (Marie), 16:149
Mary, 16:147
Mary (Farrington), 16:148
Mary E., 16:151
Mary White, 16:150
Mehitable Wingate, 16:147
Nancy (Frink), 16:147
Nellie (McAdams), 16:149
Oliver J., 16:149
Oscar, 16:149
Rebecca, 16:147
Richard, 16:146
Roderick, 16:148
Roderick R. E., 16:149
Roderick William, 16:149
Roswell Shurtleff, 16:148
Sally Haseltine, 16:148
Sarah (Page), 16:147
Sarah (Whiting/Whitting), 16:146
Sarah A., 16:149
Sarah Ellen (Whitney), 16:150
Sarah F., 16:151
Stanley Brickett, 16:151
Susan Saunders (Lang), 16:148
Susannah, 16:147
Susannah (Brickett), 16:146
Theodore, 16:150
Will Oliver, 16:149
William, 16:146
William Henry, 16:149
William Townsend, 16:147
Wilson Eugene, 16:149

HADEN
Mary, 19:159

HADLEY, 20:80
Annabella (Lucas), 17:166
Deborah (___), 19:118
Elias, 19:53
George, 19:118
Hannah, 19:208
Joseph, 17:166
Joseph Franklin, 17:166
Mary (Friend), 17:166
Samuel, 20:80
Sarah (Ingalls), 19:53
Susanna, 19:169
Susannah, 19:199
Wenda, 16:52

HADLOCK/HADLOCKE
James, 17:14; 18:85
John, 17:16; 18:85
Josiah, 18:85
Nathaniel, 17:240; 18:85; 20:200
Rebecca, 18:85
Remember (Jones), 18:85
Samuel, 18:85

HAGEN, 17:141

HAGGETT/HAGGIT see also HACKETT
Deliverance, 16:20
Hannah, 16:20
Henry, 16:20
Jacob, 16:20
Joanna (Johnson), 16:20
Martha (Poor), 16:20
Mary, 16:20
Moses, 16:20
William, 16:20

HAGGRIT, 18:117

HAIDEN
___, Capt., 20:222

HAINES/HAINS/HYNES, 20:13
James, 16:34
Mary, 18:39
Mehitable, 17:52; 20:178
Sarah, 16:31; 17:211
Thomas, 17:16

HAINSWORTH, 16:13

HALE, 19:16
Albert Brown, 18:108
Amanda, 16:118
Ames, 16:234
Curtis, 16:234
Edmund, 16:235
Eliphalet, 18:106, 107
Elizabeth (Weare), 18:106, 108
Eunice (Silver), 16:235
George, 16:118
Gilbert, 18:107, 108
Hannah, 20:136
Hannah (Pemberton), 19:208
Hazen Goodrich, 18:108
Henry, 16:218; 18:108
James, 18:108
John, 16:118; 18:106-108, 134; 19:129
Joseph, 16:193; 18:106
Joseph William, 18:108
Joshua, 19:208
Lydia Ann (Masury), 16:218
Martha (Sawyer), 16:235
Mary (___), 16:118
Mary (Lyons), 18:106, 108
Mary D. (___), 16:118
Mehitable, 16:212
Moses, 18:106
Muriel, 18:108
Olive, 18:108
Phebe (Herrick), 16:235

Priscilla (Peabody), 18:106
Robert, 16:136; 18:210; 18:240a
Robert S., 18:107
Roger Conant, 18:106, 108, 134
Sally, 16:235
Samuel, 16:235
Samuel Dudney, 18:108
Sara, 20:95
Sarah, 18:108, 205
Sarah (Lord), 18:106-108
Thomas, 18:106, 107

HALEY
Betty (Tarbox), 20:140
Edmund, 17:175
Lucy (Sherwood), 17:175
Mary, 20:139
Paul A., 19:75
Phoebe, 17:175
Rachel, 18:168
Samuel, 20:140

HALL/HALLE/HALLET see also HULL, 18:225
___, Capt., 17:25
Abigail C., 20:54
Anne (___), 18:153
Benjamin, 20:131
Cynthia, 19:120
Daniel, 17:120
David, 19:23
Deborah (Cross), 19:58
Desire (___), 18:179
Dorcas, 18:228
Dorcas (Marble), 19:120
Ebenezer, 19:58
Edith (___), 16:111
Edith B., 16:111
Edward, 19:147
Elijah, 19:120
Elizabeth, 19:111, 113, 147
Ephraim, 17:82; 18:103, 167, 228; 19:99, 103, 147
Ester, 20:56
Eunice (___), 19:99
Frances, 18:205
Frances B. (Lewis), 16:100
Isabella (Shepherd), 18:88
James, 18:228
Jerusha (Brown), 18:228
John, 18:162; 19:58; 20:145, 240
Joseph, 20:196
Lois (___), 17:120
Lydia (Shattuck), 20:54
Martha, 18:168; 19:99, 147; 20:218, 219
Mary (Browne), 18:225, 227, 228
Mary (Cheever), 19:103
Mary (Cross), 20:240
Mary (Witt), 18:172
Mary (Wood), 17:152
Mary Carr, 17:120
Mehitable, 19:239
Nathaniel, 17:152
Oliver, 16:100
Patty (Cheever), 19:99
Phineas, 19:99
Rebecca, 18:22; 19:147
Richard, 16:134; 19:87, 88; 20:218
Samuel, 18:82
Sarah, 16:207; 19:147; 20:136, 142
Sarah (___), 19:147
Sarah (Kimball), 19:58
Sarah Elizabeth (Farnham), 19:21, 23, 24
Steve, 19:123
Thomas, 18:172, 228; 19:212
Tom, 19:21-24
Tom D., 19:23
William, 18:225
Zachariah, 16:206; 20:54

HALLAHAN
Frances Ann (Doyle), 18:136

HALLAWAY see HOLLOWAY

HALLETT see also HALL
Hannah, 18:211

HALLOWELL see also HOLLOWAY, 18:168; 19:144
Benjamin Newhall, 16:102
Bethia, 19:144
Bridget (Newhall), 16:102
Bridget Newhall, 16:102
Charity (Mansfield), 18:23; 19:145
Edward, 17:99; 19:49, 145
Henry, 16:70; 17:148; 18:23
Henry H., 17:99; 18:134
Huldah (Farrington), 17:148; 19:49, 145
John, 17:99
Joseph, 16:204; 17:99; 18:134; 19:145
Lydia Witt, 16:102
Mary (Alley), 18:22, 23
Mary (Hutchings/Hitchings), 16:204; 17:96
Mary (Norwood), 19:145
Mehitable, 18:22, 23
Mehitable (Breed), 18:23
Samuel, 16:86; 17:150; 18:22, 23; 19:145, 148; 20:111
Sarah, 18:23
Sarah (Chamberlain), 19:145
Sarah (Richards), 16:102
Sarah Richards, 16:102
Theophilus, 16:102; 18:23

HALLOWELL/HABERFULL
Mary, 18:208

HALLS
Joseph, 17:151

HALSEY/HALSY/HALSYE
Priscilla, 20:91
Thomas, 19:138; 20:194

HALSTEAD
Levi Warren, 20:40
Lucy (Bancroft), 20:40

HALSY see HALSEY

HAM
Fannie, 17:188

HAMBLON
Benjamin, 20:59
Harriet M., 20:59
Mary (Smith), 20:59

HAMILTON
Alexander, 18:70
Amos, 18:171
Elizabeth (Lees), 16:9
Helen, 18:136
James, 16:9
Miriam (Witt), 18:171

HAMLIN
Martha, 19:58
Mary, 17:57

HAMMATT
Abraham, 19:162

HAMMER
Elsa Margaretha, 16:110

HAMMON
___, Mrs., 19:138

HAMMOND, 17:204
___, Wid., 20:194
Abigail, 16:230; 18:235
Abigail (Collins), 16:56
Anne (___), 16:230
Anne (Parson), 16:229
Asa, 18:206
Audria (Eaton), 16:229
Bethia (Blaney), 16:84
Candace (Norwood), 18:206
Eliza, 18:120
Elizabeth, 16:56
Elizabeth (___), 17:202
Ella, 18:178
Esther, 19:157
Francis, 16:230
Jane, 16:230
Jane (___), 16:229
John, 16:230; 18:158
Lawrence, 16:56; 17:115; 18:134
Lucy J. (Bartlett), 18:178
Margaret (Locke), 16:229
Martha, 16:230
Mary (Smith), 17:203
Richard, 16:84; 17:202
Robert, 18:178
Thankful, 19:101
William D., 18:178

HAMMONS
John, 17:240

HAMOR
David, 17:178
John, 18:176
Mary, 18:176
Mary (Rodick), 18:176
Sally (Gilpatrick), 17:178

HAMPSON
John W., 18:239
Olive (Clough), 18:239

HAMPTON
Henry, 18:165
James, 19:194
Sarah (Barney), 18:165

HAMSON
Lewis E., 19:233

HANCHMAN
Nathaniel, 18:227

HANCOCK
Daniel, 16:184
John, 20:131
Karen, 16:184
Sarah, 16:172

HANDFORD/HANDFORTH see also HANFORD
Nathaniel, 16:72; 17:18; 18:72, 79, 230; 19:138, 190; 20:194

HANDLIN
Oscar, 16:128

HANDY
George, 18:96
John Littlefield, 16:174
Ruth (Estes), 18:96

HANEY
Rebecca (Dupee), 19:240
William, 19:240

HANFORD see also HANDFORD
Hannah (___), 16:86

HANNETT, 20:224

HANOVER
Ebenezer, 16:29

HANRIGHT
Harvey, 17:178
Louisa Albian, 17:178

HANSCOM
Albert Elwin, 18:176
Constance Franklin (Richardson, 18:176
Constance R., 19:110
Nancy Constance, 18:176

Robert E., 18:134
Thomas, 18:134
HANSON
Abigail, 16:47; 20:100
Betfield, 16:100
Chadwick, 20:168
Dorcas, 19:20
Edward W., 18:132, 136
Elizabeth (Boyce), 20:94
Elizabeth (Norwood), 18:206
Hannah, 18:26
Hannah (___), 16:47
John, 18:206
Thomas, 16:17
Tobias, 20:94
HARADAN/HARADEN/HARRIDEN, see also HARRADEN, 20:17
Betsey, 20:118
Betsey (Richmond), 20:118
Edward, 18:145; 20:117
Experience, 19:110
James, 20:118
John, 20:117, 118
Jonathon, 18:145
Mary, 18:145, 146
Mary (Demack), 18:146
Nathaniel, 18:145, 146
Sarah, 20:118
Sarah (Butman), 20:117, 118
HARCHER
William, 20:194
HARDACRE/HARTIKER
George, 20:227
Mary Ann (Graves), 20:227
HARDEN
Margaret, 16:115
Peter, 17:19
Sarah (Fellows), 17:19
HARDESTY, 16:13
HARDIE see also HARDY
Samuel, 18:60a
HARDING
___, Mr., 20:57
Abigail, 20:139, 144
Elizabeth, 20:50
Elizabeth (Eaton), 18:220
Hannah, 19:177
Josiah, 18:220
Mabel Josephine (Pease), 20:57
Mary (___), 18:126
Simeon, 18:126
Steven, 20:145
HARDMAN, 16:112
HARDY see also HARDIE, 18:9, 134
Abigail, 16:64
Anne (Savory), 18:10
Benjamin, 18:10
Claude, 18:10
Daniel, 18:10
David, 16:91
Deborah (Wallingford), 18:10
Edmund, 18:10
Edward, 18:10
Edwin Noah, 18:10
Elizabeth, 20:101
Elizabeth Elaine, 16:53
Esther (___), 18:10
Eunice, 18:10
Hannah (Burbank), 18:10
Hannah (Hardy), 18:10
Hannah (Wooster), 18:10
Harriet, 16:149
Hepzibah, 20:208

Isaac, 18:10
Jacob, 18:10
Joseph, 18:10
Laura Adeline, 17:170
Lydia, 20:54
Martha, 16:217
Mary (Burbank), 18:10
Mehitable, 18:10
Nathaniel, 18:10
Phebe, 17:116
Prudence, 19:87
Rebecca (___), 18:10
Rebecca (Manning), 16:91
Richard, 18:10
Ruth, 18:10
Samuel, 18:10
Sarah, 18:10
Sarah (Hardy), 18:10
Sarah (Walker), 18:10
Thomas, 18:10; 20:80
William, 18:10
HARGRAVES/HARGREAVES/ HARGROVE, 16:13
___, Mrs., 17:90
Sarah, 17:91
William, 17:90
HARIS see HARRIS
HARKER
Elizabeth (___), 19:46
Sarah, 17:47; 19:43-47, 49
William, 18:99, 110; 19:43, 46, 47
HARKNESS
Ebenezer, 18:92
HARMAN/HARMON
___, Capt., 20:114
Elizabeth, 20:70
Lydia, 20:229
HARNDEN see also HORNDALE, 18:134
Benjamin, 16:111
Ebenezer, 16:111
Edward, 16:111
Hepzebah, 16:111
John, 16:111
Mary (___), 16:111
Mary (Jacquith), 16:111
Richard, 16:111
Sarah (Sherman), 16:111
Susanna (___), 16:111
William, 16:111
HAROD
John, 20:199
HARPER
Martha, 18:29
HARRADAN/HAROADON/HARRADEN/ HARRIDEN/HARRADARNE/ HARADEN/ HARRADINE/ HARRENDEN, see also HARADAN, 18:145; 20:118
___, Goodman, 18:84, 145
Andrew, 20:200
Anna (Shaw), 18:200
Belinda, 20:118
Benjamin, 18:199, 200; 20:118
Betsy, 20:118
Caleb, 18:200
Deborah, 18:200
Deborah (Norwood), 18:199, 200
Delphia, 20:118
Ebenezer, 18:200
Edward, 17:240; 18:200; 20:200
Experience, 18:200
Hannah, 17:108
John, 19:54

Jonathan, 18:134
Joseph, 18:200
Moses, 18:200
Patience, 18:200
Rocena, 20:118
Ruell, 18:200
Sarah (___), 18:200
Sarah (Butman), 19:54
Sophia, 20:118
Susanna, 18:200
HARRANDER
Elizabeth, 16:215
HARRIDEN see HARADAN
HARRIGAN
___ (Low), 17:110
Timothy, 17:110
HARRIMAN, 17:140
Elizabeth (Swan), 17:53
Hannah, 17:52; 20:178
Leonard, 18:134
Mary, 20:33, 38
Matthew, 17:53
HARRINGTON
Lydia, 17:54
Mary, 17:149
Priscilla, 16:87
Prudence, 17:149
HARRIS/HARIS, 19:183
Abigail, 18:201
Amos, 20:45
Andrea (Mason), 19:184
Anna, 19:230
Benjamin, 18:201
Charles, 19:184
Deliverance, 18:37
Desire, 19:236
Donald F., 17:50
Elenor (Girdler), 18:37
Elizabeth, 16:239
Elizabeth (Dennis), 18:37
George, 17:209
Griffin, 20:196
Hannah, 17:101; 18:201; 19:53; 20:45
Hannah (Larrabee), 20:45
Isaac T., 17:120
Jane M., 16:101
John, 18:37; 20:45, 199
John Charles, 19:184
Lawrence Jackson, 19:112
Lizzy, 20:9
Lucy (Band), 17:212
Lydia (Barron), 19:112
Lydia (Tuttle), 20:45
Margaret, 20:45
Maria, 19:112
Martha, 18:201; 19:111
Martha (Foster), 20:225
Mary, 16:100; 18:201; 20:45, 221
Mary (Baker), 20:45
Mary (Bradbury), 20:45
Mary (Wheeler), 18:201
Mary Carr (Hall), 17:120
Mason, 18:37
Naomi, 18:201; 20:45
Patience, 18:201
Rachel, 20:45
Rebecca, 18:37, 201
Rebecca (Bassett), 18:37
Rendel, 20:146
Richard, 16:222; 17:212; 20:225
Robert, 18:37
Robert Deane, 17:78
Ruth, 18:201

S. P., 16:49
Samuel, 17:97; 20:198
Sarah, 18:37, 201; 20:45, 236
Sarah (Bennet), 18:37
Sarah (Norwood), 18:201
Stephen Larrabee, 20:45
Thomas, 16:63; 18:201
William, 20:45
HARRISON
   Barbara G., 16:128
   Robert, 19:43
HARRUB
   Ellen, 19:170
HARSHORNE see also HARTSHORN
   Timothy, 20:40
HART/HARTE see also HARTT, 18:117; 19:135, 136
   ___, Mrs., 20:188
   "Daughter", 18:46
   "Sons", 18:46
   Aaron, 17:158, 160; 18:44, 45, 47-49
   Abigail, 17:205; 18:43-46, 49, 117
   Abigail (Brown), 18:43, 45, 117
   Abigail (Deal), 18:42, 43
   Abigail (Lambert), 18:46-48
   Abigail (Lamboard), 17:148; 18:23
   Abigail Beals, 18:50
   Abijah, 17:148; 18-48
   Adam, 18:42, 43, 45
   Adeline, 17:206
   Ann (___), 18:50
   Ann (Franklin), 18:48, 50
   Anna, 18:50
   Anna (Dix), 18:46
   Anna (Noyes), 18:43
   Asa, 18:46
   Benjamin, 18:48, 50
   Betsy, 18:50
   Betsy (Eustis), 18:50
   Burrill, 18:50
   Cassandra, 17:206
   Charlotte, 17:206
   Daniel, 18:44, 46
   Darling (Huntress), 18:49
   David, 18:46, 50
   Deborah, 18:42
   Deborah (Welch), 18:48
   Dorcas (Brown), 18:42, 43
   Dorothy (Farrington), 17:147; 18:47, 48, 151
   Ebenezer, 17:206; 18:42-45
   Edmund, 18:48-50
   Edward, 18:50
   Elias, 18:46, 48, 49
   Elizabeth, 18:42-44, 47, 49; 19:48, 147, 151, 216; 20:187
   Elizabeth (Clark), 18:49, 50
   Elizabeth (Colston/Colson), 18:42, 43
   Elizabeth (Gowen), 18:48
   Elizabeth (Hutchinson), 18:40, 41
   Elizabeth (Ingols), 18:46, 47; 19:48
   Elizabeth Amelia, 17:119
   Elizabeth/Betsy (___), 18:45
   Endicot, 17:206
   Ephraim, 19:49
   Eunice, 18:44, 50
   Eunice (Burrill), 18:50
   Eunice (Curtis), 18:44
   Ezekiel, 18:46
   Fannie E., 17:164
   Hannah, 18:21, 23, 46, 47, 53
   Hannah (Brown), 18:44
   Hannah (Butler), 17:206
   Hannah (Cox), 18:44
   Hannah (Norton), 18:50
   Henry Hunter, 18:50
   Hepsibar (Pearson), 18:43
   Isaac, 18:40-45, 117, 134; 19:136, 151, 212, 217; 20:185, 187-189, 207
   Jacob, 18:44
   James M., 17:149
   James Morrison, 18:40
   Jane (Muzzey/Massey), 18:49
   Jean (Simmons), 18:46
   John, 16:93; 17:147; 18:42-50, 106, 151; 19:137, 216, 227
   Jonathan, 16:33; 17:206; 18:42-45, 209
   Joseph, 18:44, 46-50, 60a, 223; 19:157; 20:111
   Joseph Burrill, 18:50
   Josiah, 17:148; 18:48
   Lois, 18:49
   Lois (Potter), 19:150, 236
   Love, 18:49
   Lucy, 18:50
   Lucy (Merry), 18:50
   Lucy Ann (___), 18:50
   Lucy Endicott, 17:206
   Lydia, 18:44, 49
   Lydia (Curtis), 18:44
   Lydia (Fuller), 17:160; 18:49; 19:150
   Lydia (White), 18:44
   Lydia Nicholson, 17:160; 18:49; 19:151
   Martha, 17:148; 18:48
   Martin, 17:206
   Mary, 17:159; 18-43, 45-47, 49, 117
   Mary (Fuller), 18:43
   Mary (Hawkes), 17:206
   Mary (Needham), 18:46; 19:48
   Mary (Pitman), 18:46
   Mary (Whiteridge), 18:46
   Mary (Whiting), 18:46
   Mary Turner (Tolman), 18:50
   Mary/Molly, 18:44
   Mehitable, 18:44
   Mehitable (Endicott), 18:43, 44
   Mehitable (Lambert), 18:49, 50
   Mercy (Hawks), 18:43-45
   Michael, 17:148; 18:47, 48
   Moses, 17:160; 18:48, 49; 19:151
   Nabby, 17:206
   Nancy Ann, 18:50
   Nathaniel, 18:44
   Nehemiah, 18:45
   Phebe, 18:50
   Phebe (___), 18:45
   Phebe (Ivory), 18:48, 50
   Polly, 17:206; 18:45, 50, 217
   Polly (___), 18:46
   Polly (Smith), 17:206; 18:44, 45
   Prudence Clark, 18:50
   Ralph, 18:47; 19:150, 236
   Rebecca, 18:42, 45, 46
   Ruth, 18:48, 49; 19:156, 157
   Ruth (Chadwell), 18:46, 47; 19:157
   Sally, 18:50
   Sally (Webb), 18:50
   Samuel, 16:73; 17:148; 18:23, 40-50, 117, 134; 19:137, 151, 216; 20:34, 68, 135, 196, 223
   Sarah, 17:148; 18:43-45, 48-50, 151; 19:151, 216
   Sarah (___), 18:48
   Sarah (Endicott), 18:42; 19:151
   Sarah (Hawkes), 18:45
   Tabitha, 18:44
   Tabitha (Collins), 17:160; 18:48, 49
   Tama (Damon), 18:46
   Thomas, 16:89; 18:40, 42-45, 117, 226; 19:137, 216, 217; 20:113
   William, 18:44, 46, 48, 50
   Zerubbabel, 16:93; 18:44
HARTHORN/HARTHORNE see also HATHORN, HAWTHORNE
   Jemima, 19:156, 158
   John, 19:154
   Samuel, 19:158
   Suzanah (Gill), 19:158
HARTIKER see HARDACRE
HARTLEY, 20:67
   E. N., 17:88
   Elizabeth, 17:170
HARTSHORN/HARTSHORNE see also HARSHORNE
   Abigail, 20:35
   Abigail (Bancroft), 20:35
   Derick S., 18:158
   Ebenezer, 20:35
   James, 20:35
   John, 20:35
   Martha (Eaton), 20:35
   Susanna, 18:156, 158, 160
   Susanna (Buck), 18:158
   Susanna (Nichols), 20:35
   Tabitha (Pratt), 20:35
   Thomas, 18:158
   Timothy, 19:136; 20:35
HARTT see also HART
   Abigail (Armitage), 18:116
   Bonino, 18:116
HARTWELL
   Arthur S., 16:151
   Jacob, 18:16
   Josiah, 18:45
   Olive, 18:16
   Phebe (___), 18:45
   Ward, 18:16
HARVEY/HARVIE
   Andrew, 18:58
   Elizabeth, 18:58
   Hannah (Gilbert), 16:34
   Ina Georgia, 17:208
   James, 18:58
   John, 18:58
   Mary, 18:58
   Mary (Stack), 18:58
   Nathaniel, 20:225
   Peter, 16:34
   Richard, 20:199
   William, 18:58
HARWOOD
   Charlotte Woodruff (Tyler), 19:232
   David, 17:20
   Elizabeth Virginia, 19:232
   Ezra, 18:217
   George, 20:240a
   Hannah, 16:37
   Henry, 19:194
   John, 17:20
   John Marshall/Stubblefield, 19:232
   John S., 19:233
   John Stubblefield, 19:232, 233
   Jonathan, 18:169
   Lottie Gay, 19:232
   Mary (Witt), 18:169
   Nancy, 18:217
   Nancy (___), 18:217
   Nancy (Westcoat), 19:230
   Nancy Goffigon (Wescoat), 19:233

Nancy Westcoat, 19:233
Richard Henry, 19:232, 233
Russell Franklin, 19:232
Sarah Jefferson (Wilkins), 19:232
Saydee Jefferson, 19:232
Virginia A. (Stubblefield), 19:232
William Franklin, 19:232

HASCOLE see HASKALL

HASELTINE see also HAZELTINE, 17:140
Abiah, 17:116
Abigail, 16:147
Abigail (Moores), 16:148
Abigail (Winn), 20:28
Ann (___), 19:219, 222
Deborah, 17:52; 20:178
Deliverance, 19:219, 221, 222
Esther Holmes, 16:151
James, 16:148
John, 16:150; 18:9, 141
Maxy, 20:28
Molle, 16:131
Robert, 18:9; 19:219, 222
Sarah, 16:131; 20:119

HASEY
Abigail, 18:151; 19:40
Ebenezer, 18:211
Hannah, 19:145; 20:33
Hannah (Wayte), 19:215
Jacob, 19:40
Joseph, 19:215

HASKALL/HASCOLE see also HASKELL
Ambrose, 17:149
Anna (___), 17:149
Deliverance (Breed), 17:149
Farrington, 17:149
Joseph, 20:216
Margaret, 17:149
Mark, 17:149; 20:198
Mary, 17:149
Mary (Graves), 20:216
Mary (Tybott/Tibbetts), 20:216
Prudence (Farrington), 17:149
Roger, 20:198
William, 17:149; 20:216

HASKEL/HASKELL, 17:220
Adam, 17:221
Ambrose, 17:147
Amy (Graves), 20:216
Asa, 17:221
Benjamin, 20:216
Bess (Kellogg), 16:118
Charles, 17:39
Charles S., 16:118
Daniel, 20:216
Dianna (___), 17:39
Dorcas, 20:216
Dorothy, 20:216
Ebenezer, 20:216
Edith, 16:64
Elizabeth, 16:137; 17:107; 20:216
Elizabeth (Goodhue), 20:216
Eps, 18:172
Esther, 18:77
Hannah, 17:13; 20:216
Hannah M., 17:39
Harriet, 19:97
Harriet Booth (Tremere), 16:118
Hubbard, 17:13
Ignatius, 17:178
Ira J., 20:216
John, 20:200
John W., 17:110
Joseph, 17:240; 20:200, 216
Josiah, 20:200
Judith, 20:143
Lucy, 18:207
Lydia (Witt), 18:172
Maria, 17:110
Mark, 20:108, 200
Mary, 16:64; 17:220; 20:216
Mary R. (Boynton), 20:108
Molly, 17:220
Nabby D., 16:103
Nathaniel, 16:64
Naomi, 20:216
Prudence, 16:235
Prudence (Farrington), 17:147
Rebecca, 17:34
Rebecca (Witt), 18:172
Ruth, 17:36; 19:97
Ruth (Ashmont), 17:110
Sarah, 16:176; 18:201; 20:216
Sarah (Davis), 20:216
Sarah (Haskell), 20:216
Stephen, 16:64
Theodore, 16:118
Thomas, 17:178
Walter, 20:216
William, 16:64; 17:224; 18:172
Winthrop A., 18:134

HASKET
Elizabeth, 17:198

HASKIN/HASKINS
___, Mrs., 16:136
Hannah (Newell), 16:119
John, 20:199
Roger, 20:198
Rogers, 16:136

HASSAM, 19:99
Elizabeth (___), 19:42
John T., 18:152; 19:36
Jonathan, 19:42
Nancy, 19:42
Sarah (Cheever), 19:42
William, 19:42

HASSEY
___, Miss, 18:205

HASTINGS
Abigail, 17:116
Bethia (Hallowell, 19:144
George, 17:117
Mary (Green), 17:117
Samuel, 19:144

HASTY
Elizabeth (Larrabee), 20:115
Robert, 20:115

HATCH
Abigail (Cheever), 19:104
Elizabeth C. (Edmands), 17:30
Lester C., 17:30
Mary, 20:31, 53
Mary (Northey), 19:83
Michael, 18:75
Nehamiah, 19:83
Priscilla (Sprague), 18:75
Reuben, 19:104
Sally, 19:165

HATCHER
Patricia Law, 18:40

HATFIELD
Edwin F., 16:21

HATHAWAY
Lozarus, 18:173
Mary, 20:28
Patty, 18:173

HATHER
Margaret, 18:226; 20:112

HATHORN/HATHORNE see also
HARTHORN, HAWTHORNE, 19:198
___, Capt., 19:190
___, Mr., 16:71; 19:159; 20:137
Ann, 16:164
Benjamin, 18:94
Ebenezer, 16:198; 17:158; 18:114, 115, 167; 20:196
Ester (Witt), 17:158; 18:166
Hannah (___), 18:94
Hannah (Derby), 18:94
Hannah (Estes), 18:93, 94
Hepzebeth, 18:167
Hepzibah, 17:156
Hester (Witt), 18:115, 167
James, 16:44
John, 16:23; 17:15, 20, 232; 18:17, 52, 114, 135, 167, 229, 230; 20:132, 134
Joseph, 18:94
Keziah (Collins), 17:218; 18:167
Mary, 16:238; 17:20; 18:41, 167
Nathaniel, 17:20; 20:134, 137, 196
Priscilla, 17:232
Rebecca (Stocker), 16:167; 18:167
Ruth, 16:109
Ruth (___), 16:44
Samuel, 16:156; 18:167, 225
Sarah, 18:54, 113, 167
Sarah (___), 18:167
Suzannah (Gill), 18:167
William, 16:165, 202; 17:146; 18:232, 234; 19:81, 190, 192, 195; 20:132

HAUGH
___, Rev., 16:162
Samuel, 18:41; 20:190-192

HAVEN, 18:47
Amariah, 17:24
Anna (Stow), 16:74
Asa, 17:24
Benjamin, 17:23
Daniel, 16:74
Elizabeth (Frail), 17:24
Esther (Graves), 20:218
Experience, 17:24
Hannah (Walker), 16:74
Jane (Gould), 17:24
Jedediah, 17:23
Jesse, 17:23
Joseph, 16:74; 19:228
Lydia (Whitney), 16:74
Martha (Walker), 16:74
Mary, 16:74; 20:133, 148
Mary (Ballard), 16:74
Mary Ann, 16:87
Mehitable, 16:74
Mehitable (Haven), 16:74
Moses, 16:74; 17:22
Nathaniel, 20:218
Richard, 16:74; 17:18; 18:222, 223, 231; 20:133, 196
Ruth (Frail), 17:24
Ruth (Gleason), 17:23
Sarah, 16:74; 17:22
Sarah (Bridges), 17:22
Susan, 16:77
Susanna (___), 16:74
Susanna (Newhall), 20:133
Susannah, 16:74
Zedekiah, 17:24
Zurviah/Zeruiah, 17:23

HAVENS
  Elizabeth, 20:96
  James, 19:34
  William, 18:81
HAWARD see also HAYWARD
  Ruth (Jones), 18:84
HAWES
  David, 16:41
  Mary Anna, 17:31
  Rebekah (Parker), 16:41
  Susanna, 16:32
HAWKE
  John, 20:191
HAWKES/HAWKS, 18:213
  ___, Mr., 18:52
  Abigail, 18:27
  Abigail (Bancroft), 20:41
  Abigail (Farrington), 17:150
  Abijah, 19:50
  Adam, 17:47, 89; 18:27, 31, 40, 41, 80, 135, 212, 222, 224; 19:138; 20:41, 191, 195, 196, 212; 20:184, 192
  Ahijah, 18:27
  Anna, 18:27
  Anna (Breed), 18:53
  Anne (Browne), 18:40
  Caroline (Bent), 20:41
  Charles Warren, 19:59
  Deliberance, 18:92
  Dolly Carter (Mansfield), 20:41
  Ebenezer, 16:156; 17:173; 18:27, 31, 32, 53, 92, 210; 19:51; 20:212
  Eliza, 20:41
  Elizabeth, 18:27, 213
  Elizabeth (Cogswell), 18:31, 53, 92
  Elizabeth (Wellman), 20:41
  Elkanah, 18:240
  Eunice, 19:50
  Eve, 20:33, 37, 42, 43
  Hannah, 17:150; 18:92, 173
  Hannah (Blaney), 16:82
  Hannah (Hitchings), 19:50
  Hannah (Pickering), 19:59
  Jerusha (Merriam), 18:92
  John, 16:156; 18:31, 41, 92, 208-210, 212, 222, 224, 240; 19:137, 212, 227; 20:41, 42, 48, 192, 197
  Jonathan, 17:150
  Joseph, 18:92, 228
  Joshua, 20:41
  Lois, 19:50
  Lois (Wheeler), 20:41
  Lydia, 18:27, 95, 209, 212, 224; 20:41
  Lydia (Burrill), 17:98
  Lydia (Wiley), 20:41
  Mary, 17:41; 18:210, 227
  Mary (___), 20:42
  Mary (Burrill), 18:92
  Mary (Whitford), 18:212, 224
  Matthew, 16:16; 18:92, 105
  Mercy, 18:43-45
  Mortimer, 17:89
  Moses, 18:226, 240; 19:212, 228, 229; 20:48, 113, 197
  Narcissa, 20:41
  Nathan, 19:50
  Nathan M., 17:28
  Nathan Mortimer, 17:29; 18:134, 195; 19:76
  Pamela, 20:41
  Pamela Andrews, 20:41
  Patience, 18:92
  Philadelphia, 18:92
  Philadelphia (Estes), 18:31, 92
  Polly, 20:41
  Rachel, 20:41
  Rachel (Bancroft), 20:41
  Rebecca, 18:27
  Rebecca (Alley), 18:27, 32
  Ruth (Breed), 18:92
  Ruth (Collins), 18:92, 105
  Ruth (Phillips), 16:156; 18:31
  Ruth (Purchase), 20:212
  Sally, 20:41
  Sally (Sargent), 20:41
  Samuel, 18:31, 92
  Sarah, 18:45, 92, 135; 19:30, 151
  Sarah (Bassett), 18:31, 52
  Sarah (Cushing), 18:31
  Sarah (Cushman), 16:156
  Sarah (Hitchings), 19:50
  Smith Adam, 17:150
  Susanna, 17:30; 18:80
  Thomas, 18:42; :137
  Timothy, 20:41
  William, 16:82; 18:27
HAWKINS
  Abigail, 20:233
  Agnes (Stilson), 20:233
  Annis, 20:233
  Annis (___), 20:233
  Deborah, 20:229, 230, 232, 233
  Elizabeth, 20:233
  Elizabeth (Humphreys), 20:230, 233
  George, 19:189
  Hannah (Giffords), 20:233
  James, 20:230, 233
  John, 20:233
  Margaret (Dixey), 20:233
  Rebecca, 20:233
  Robert, 20:233
  Tabitha (Homan), 20:233
  Thomas, 18:230; 20:199, 233
HAWKS see HAWKES
HAWTHORN/HAWTHORNE see also HARTHORN, 18:135, 136; 19:158
  John, 17:215; 20:37
  Katy, 20:221
  Nathaniel, 18:53
HAY
  John, 16:104
  Katharine (Farnum), 16:104, 106
  Peter, 18:113
HAYDEN
  Barbara (Collins), 18:101
  Betty (Potter), 19:148
  Richard, 16:78; 18:101
  Tibudah, 18:168; 19:148
  William, 19:148
HAYES
  A. D., 17:108
  Abigail (Evans), 16:116
  Comfort, 16:116
  Edward, 18:90
  Elizabeth, 18:88
  Enoch, 16:116
  Ichabod, 16:116
  John, 16:63
  Louisa M., 17:102
  Lyman, 20:41
  Mary (Horne), 16:117
  Moses, 16:116
  Peter, 19:135
  Philadelphia (Jenkins), 18:31, 52, 90
  Steve, 16:188
  Susannah (Knowles), 16:116
HAYNES
  ___, Gov., 18:196
  Ella M., 17:104
  Emma (___), 17:104
  Hannah (Harriman), 17:52; 20:178
  Jonathan, 17:53
  Joseph W., 17:104
  Richard, 19:191, 192; 20:198
  Robert, 20:197
  Ruth, 18:172
  Sarah (Moulton), 17:53
  Thomas, 17:52; 20:178, 197
  William, 19:191, 193
HAYWARD/HAWARD/HAYWOOD see also HOWARD
  Abial, 18:171
  Abigail (Graves), 20:213
  Adam, 16:77
  Anna, 20:216
  Anna (Snell), 18:178
  Anne, 20:217
  Bethiah, 18:24
  Dorothy Flynn, 17:28
  Edmond, 18:178
  Elizabeth, 17:203
  Elizabeth (Niles), 19:174
  Freda, 20:125
  Isaiah, 18:178
  Jabez, 20:213
  John, 19:78
  Jonathan, 16:77
  Joseph, 20:125
  Joshua, 19:174
  Judith, 16:59
  Judith (Ballard), 16:77
  Kathrine H. (Cobb), 16:108
  Lena (___), 20:125
  Margaret, 17:139
  Mary, 19:174
  Mary (Ballard), 16:77
  Sally, 18:178
  Sarah (Ingalls), 19:45
  William, 19:45
HAZELTINE see also HASELTINE
  Charles F., 19:43
  Deliverance, 19:116
  Samuel, 17:52; 20:178
  Sarah (Cooper), 17:52; 20:178
HAZELTON/HEASLETINE
  Abiah (___), 17:117
  Abigail (Hastings), 17:116
  Deliverance, 19:115
  Nathaniel, 17:116
  Samuel, 17:117
HAZELWOOD
  Earle, 19:168
  Janet (___), 19:168
HAZEN
  H. H., 19:210
  Henry A., 16:225
  Thomas, 16:193
HAZLEHURST, 16:13
HE TU
  Agathe, 20:170
HEAD
  ___, Gov., 18:143
  Mehitabel, 20:239
HEALD
  Hannah, 16:40
  Martha, 17:80
HEALY see HENLY
HEAP, 16:13

HEARD
Hannah, 20:13
HEATH
Bartholomew, 17:54
Elias, 18:178
Elizabeth, 17:54
John, 17:55; 18:156, 160
Jonathan, 16:52
Joseph, 18:156
Lucy (Cutler), 18:178
Martha (Dow), 18:156
Mary (Bradley), 17:54
Nathaniel, 19:167
Sarah (Partridge), 17:55
W., 18:106
William, 17:7
HEAZLETINE see also HASELTINE
Mary (Graves), 20:226
Stephen, 20:226
HEBB
Raymond, 19:142, 152
HEBERD see HUBBARD, 20:215
HEDGES
William, 16:164
HEINES
Samuel, 18:206
Sarah (Norwood), 18:206
HEIRS see AYERS
HELM
Mathew, 16:187
HEMENWAY
Abigail (Morse), 16:76
Hephzibah, 16:76
Joshua, 16:76
Ralph, 16:74
Sarah (Haven), 16:74
Susannah, 20:38
HEMINGWAY
Charity, 19:57
Elizabeth, 17:114
Isobel, 17:27
John, 17:114
Mary (Trescott), 17:114
HENCHMAN
___, Mr., 18:23
Deborah (Wager), 18:113
Lydia, 17:100
Mary, 17:100
Nathaniel, 16:75; 18:113, 172, 213, 224;
   19:101, 159; 20:48, 103, 104, 112, 113
Peter, 19:217
HENDERSON
Benjamin, 17:89
David, 19:29
Elizabeth (Darling), 19:29
Hannah (Farr), 19:28, 29
John, 19:28, 29
Margaret, 19:29
Martha, 18:202; 19:29
Robert F., 17:193; 20:179
HENDIE
Orrin, 20:199
HENDLEY/HENDLY
Benjamin, 18:32, 33
Elias, 19:51
Mary, 17:98; 19:48, 51; 20:222
Samuel, 19:157
Sarah (___), 19:51
HENDRICK
Daniel, 19:46
Sarah, 19:46
HENFIELD
Hannah (Hutchinson), 16:155

William, 16:155
HENGEL
Susan, 20:77
HENLEY/HENLY/HEALY
Ann (___), 19:103
Benjamin, 17:98
David, 19:103
Eals/Alse, 18:48; 19:155, 156; 20:213
Elizabeth, 19:103
Elizabeth (Cheever), 19:103
Ezekiel, 19:103
Katharine (Russell), 19:103
Mary, 19:103
Samuel, 19:103, 155
Sarah, 19:103
Sarah (Hesilrige), 19:103
Thomas, 19:103
HENRY, 19:233
Elizabeth (Hart), 18:44
Esther (Parker), 19:93
Hugh, 19:137
John, 18:44; 20:158
King, VII, 20:66
Lucy, 17:178
Mary, 19:137
William, 19:93
HENSHAW, 19:69
___, Mr., 19:65
HENVILL/HENVILLE
Elizabeth, 19:59; 20:59
HEREDGES
John T., 19:95
HERICKE see HERRICK
HERING
Mehitable, 17:157
HERRICK/HERICKE
___, Lt., 17:5
Abigail, 16:55; 18:220
Abigail (Eveleth), 16:235
Barnabas, 16:178; 20:120
Benjamin, 19:151
Bethia (Deland), 16:178; 20:120
David, 16:58
Dorcas (Punchard), 19:173
Ebenezer, 16:235; 20:131
Ede, 16:137
Edith, 20:234
Edith (Laskin), 16:116
Eliza (Friend), 17:105
Eliza A., 16:178
Eliza Ann, 17:106
Elizabeth, 16:115
Elizabeth (___), 16:180
Elizabeth (Trask), 16:55
Emeline Friend, 17:106
Ephraim, 16:55
George, 17:60
Henry, 16:116, 140; 20:120, 198
Hulda (Brown), 18:220
Isaac A., 17:34
John, 18:166; 20:136, 198
Jonathan, 16:143; 20:152-154
Joseph, 16:155; 17:16; 20:58
Joseph Franklin, 17:105
Josephine, 17:106
Joshua, 18:220
Judith (Woodbury), 16:116
Lydia, 16:137; 18:220; 20:151-154, 157
Lydia (___), 16:178; 20:120, 152
Lydia (Grover), 20:120
Lydia (Woodbury), 20:120
Martha, 20:154
Martin, 16:90; 19:137

Mary, 16:137; 20:151, 153
Mary (Buswell), 16:58
Mary (Conant), 16:155
Mary (Cross), 16:55
Mary (Dodge), 16:143
Mary (Endicott), 16:155; 20:58
Mary (Friend), 17:34
Mehitable (Tarbox), 20:136
Oliver, 19:173
Phebe, 16:235
Prudence (Haskell), 16:235
Rebecca (Stanley), 16:235
Rufus, 16:155
Ruth (___), 16:180
Samuel, 16:180
Sarah (Carter), 19:173
Sarah (Kimball), 18:166; 20:136
Sarah (Phillips), 16:155
Sarah (Potter), 19:151
Stephen, 16:55
Thankful, 17:106
Thankful (___), 17:105
Thomas, 16:235; 19:96, 173
William, 16:178; 20:120
Zachariah, 20:198
HERRIDEN see HARRADEN, 20:118
HERSEY
Abel, 17:107
Ann Calder, 17:107
Elizabeth (Haskell), 17:107
Ezekiel, 17:225
Mary Gardiner, 17:107
Sarah (Langley), 17:225
William, 18:60a
HERSGER
John, 18:201
Miriam (Pool), 18:201
HESILRIGE
Sarah, 19:103
HETHERD
William, 20:198
HEWES
David, 18:135
Eliza (Hawkes), 20:41
James, 20:41
Matilda (Norwood), 18:206
Samuel, 18:206
HEWETT/HEWIT/HEWITT
John, 20:138
Joseph, 20:53
Nathan, 19:163
Sarah (Tarbox), 20:138
Susannah (Coates), 19:163
HEWS
Rachel, 18:39
HIBBARD
Abigail (Whittier), 20:207
Augustine George, 20:207
Daniel, 20:207
Dorcas, 20:21
Dorothy, 20:207
Dorothy (Graves), 20:207
Ebenezer, 20:207
Elizabeth, 20:207
Elizabeth (Graves), 20:21
Hannah (Bodwell), 18:159; 20:207
Hepsibah (Sawyer), 20:207
John, 18:159; 20:207
Joseph, 20:21, 131, 197, 207
Martha, 19:58, 120; 20:207
Mary, 20:207
Ruth, 20:207
Ruth (Huse), 20:207

Ruth (Walden), 20:207
HIBBERT
John, 17:19
Lois, 19:151
Robert, 18:111
HIBBINS
William, 19:132
HICKEY
Walter, 20:10
HICKMAN
Mary, 19:109
HICKS, 17:139
Elizabeth (Baker), 18:235
Louise Marshall, 18:117
Zechariah, 18:235
HIDDEN
___, Mrs., 17:12
John, 20:53
Sarah, 18:178
HIGGINBOTTOM, 16:13
HIGGINS
Benjamin Swett, 16:103
Eleazer, 19:177
Ellen/Nell Louise, 19:57
Enoch, 19:177
Hannah, 19:177
Joseph Richards, 16:103
Laurania (Gross), 19:177
Louise (Rich), 19:57
Mary (Atkins), 19:177
Nancy Jane, 18:176
Noah S., 16:103
Rebecca (Richards), 16:103
Sarah (Hodgkins), 18:176
Theophilus, 18:176
William P., 19:57
HIGGINSON, 20:240a
Anna, 17:236
Francis, 19:127, 201
John, 16:33; 17:15; 18:60a, 210; 19:105, 196
Sarah (Whitfield), 17:236
Stephen, 17:132
HIGH
W. C., 17:167
HIGLEY
Dudley, 18:96
Esther, 18:96
Esther (___), 18:96
HILDRETH
Alvin A., 20:153
Ephraim, 17:79
Mary (Herrick), 20:151, 153
Mercy, 19:171
Polly (Dexter), 19:172
Prudence, 19:35
Urbane, 19:171
HILL, 20:18
___, Mr., 18:31, 52
Abigail, 16:137
Abigail (Bell), 18:179
Abraham, 19:82
Annette, 17:110
Azubah, 18:96
Christian, 17:22
Dolly R., 20:143
Eben, 18:179
Ebenezer, 20:40
Edwin A., 16:195
Elinor, 17:236
Eliza, 16:239
Elizabeth, 19:20; 20:221
Freelove, 18:96

Hamilton A., 19:210
Hanna (Beens), 16:198
Hannah (Stowers), 19:82
Isaac, 20:38
J. B., 20:40
Jethro, 20:55
John, 16:137; 18:60a, :240
Joseph, 18:36; 19:229
Lydia, 16:131
Lydia (___), 16:131
Mary, 16:69
Mary (Bassett), 18:31, 52
Mary (Breed), 18:36
Mary (Mower), 16:198
Mehitable (Bancroft), 20:38
Mehitable (Jewett), 20:55
Prudence, 18:49
Rachel, 20:54
Rebecca, 18:96
Rebecca (Bancroft), 20:40
Richard, 16:198
Ruth (Graves), 20:212
Sarah, 16:176; 18:172; 19:82, 198
Sarah (Larrabee), 19:229
Sarah Collins, 17:118
Shadrach, 20:212
Tamzen, 19:148
Valentine, 17:88
William, 16:198
William G., 16:202
HILLARD
David, 19:163
Experience, 16:33
Jonathan, 19:163
HILLER
Abigail (___), 20:138, 237
Joseph, 17:95; 20:103, 138, 237
HILLIARD
Israel, 19:163
Victoria (Coates), 19:163
HILLMAN
Paul A., 18:138
HILLS
Abigail Knapp, 19:238
Deborah, 19:206
Elizabeth (Knapp), 19:238
John, 19:238
Mary, 16:102; 17:148; 19:215
Rebecca, 19:144
Sarah (Burrill), 17:148
Thomas, 17:148; 20:83
HILTON
Hannah, 16:99
Hannah (Joy), 18:211; 19:50
Joseph, 18:211; 19:50
Miriam, 18:77
Ruell (Harraden), 18:200
William, 18:200
HINCHLIFFE, 16:13
HINCHMAN
Elizabeth, 18:226; 19:229; 20:113
HINCKLEY
Elizabeth, 19:96
HINCKSMAN
Thomas, 19:31
HINDS
Benjamin, 17:50
James, 19:194
Rhoda (More), 17:50
HINES
James, 19:194
John, 20:15
Susannah, 19:83, 84

HINKSON
Hannah, 16:207
Naomi, 18:18; 20:44
HINMAN
Eunice, 20:51
HIRST
William, 18:60a
HITCHCOCK
Enos, 17:7
HITCHENS see also HITCHINS
Bethia, 19:155
Daniel, 19:212
Hannah (Ingalls), 19:50
HITCHING
Daniel, 18:223
Ruth, 18:215
Ruth (___), 18:215
Thomas, 18:215
HITCHINGS see also HUTCHINS/ HUTCHINGS
Abijah, 19:51
Anna, 19:51
Anna/Nancy (Dixey), 19:50
Benjamin, 17:26
Daniel, 17:29; 18:135; 19:50, 159
Eunice (Hawkes), 19:50
Hannah, 19:50
Hannah (Ingalls), 19:50
James, 19:50
John, 19:50
Joseph, 17:99; 18:135; 19:50
Lois (Hawkes), 19:50
Mary, 17:96; 19:50
Mary (Edmonds), 17:99
Mary (Gardner), 19:51
Mary (Vickery), 19:51
Nathan, 17:29; 19:50
Nathaniel, 19:50
Sarah, 19:50
Sarah (Gardner), 19:51
William, 19:51
HITCHINS see also HITCHENS
Daniel, 18:240; 19:100
Keturah, 16:47
Lois, 16:47
HOAG/HOAGG/HOGIN
Elizabeth, 17:53
Lindley, 18:12
Mary, 16:222
HOALLMAN
Edward, 20:199
HOAR/HOARE
William, 19:197; 20:198
HOBB, 20:201
HOBBS
Abigail, 16:194
Abraham, 16:214; 19:240
Benjamin, 16:145
Daniel, 16:145
Dinah, 20:141
Eliza, 19:240
Elizabeth (Cummings), 19:240
Elizabeth (Graves), 20:207
Foster, 17:221
Hannah, 19:240
Hannah (Friend), 16:145
Jonathan, 19:240; 20:207
Mary (___), 16:145
Mary (Friend), 16:214
Mary Marland (Cogswell), 19:17
Mary/Polly (Pierce), 19:240
Polly (___), 19:240
Sarah, 16:57

Sarah (___), 16:214
Susanna, 20:220
William, 19:17; 20:202
HOBBY
Jane, 16:88
HOBERT
Dorothy (Sprague), 18:75
James, 18:75
HOBES
Thomas, 16:34
HOBS
Robert, 20:199
HODGDON/HODGEDON see also HOGDON
Abigail, 16:224
Almira (Osborn), 17:187
Bethiah (Tarbox), 20:145
Charles, 17:187
Cora, 17:187
Elizabeth, 20:139
Nellie, 17:187
Rebecca (Norwood), 18:206
Sally, 20:219
Samuel, 18:206
Sarah, 18:206
Thomas, 20:145
HODGES
Almon D., 17:225
Gamaliel, 17:225; 18:93; 20:103
Mary, 17:225
Sarah (Williams), 17:225
HODGKIN
Thomas, 19:111
HODGKINS
Abigail W., 20:226
Edward, 18:176
Eliza (Adams), 17:129
Elizabeth, 18:22
Ezekiel, 17:129
Grace, 20:44
Grace (Dutch), 19:162
Hannah (Gee), 19:119
J. L., 17:129
Jerusha, 17:129
John, 16:64
Mary, 19:162
Mary (Hamor), 18:176
Samuel, 19:119
Sarah, 18:176
Thomas, 20:225
William, 19:162
HODGMAN
Abigail, 19:137
Abigail (Gary), 19:148
Elizabeth, 19:148
Hebsibah, 17:116
John, 17:116
Lois (Parlin), 17:116
Thomas, 19:137, 148
HOFF
James, 17:58
Mary (Devine), 17:58
HOFFMAN
William, 16:128
HOGDON see also HODGDON
___, Mrs., 17:13
HOGG
Sophronia (Bancroft), 20:38
HOGGIT
Abigail, 16:131
Joseph, 16:131
Lydia, 16:131
Mary, 16:131

Susanna, 16:131
Thomas, 16:131
William, 16:131
HOGIN see HOAG
HOGKINS
John, 20:225
HOIELL
John, 20:199
HOLBROOK, 20:118
Anna (Wild), 19:238
Charlotte, 19:238
Hannah (Harding), 19:177
Hulda, 19:177
Jay, 19:4
John, 19:238
Lydia, 17:176
Mary, 20:179
Mary (___), 17:176
Steward H., 18:191
Stewart, 18:183
Thomas, 17:176; 19:177
HOLDEN see also HOLDIN
Abigail (Grover), 17:54
Anna, 19:226; 20:47
Asa, 17:84
Barbara, 16:65; 19:237
Barbara A., 16:14; 17:14; 18:132-135, 137-139; 20:130
Barbara R., 18:9, 69, 140, 192; 19:13, 201; 20:14, 80, 102
Elizabeth, 16:100; 17:82
Elizabeth (___), 16:115
Hannah, 17:53
Hannah (Lawrence), 16:115
Hannah (Parker), 17:82
Hannah (Woods), 16:115
Jonathon, 16:115
Joseph, 17:82
Josiah, 17:82
Martha, 17:82
Sibel (Parker), 17:84
Simon, 17:54
Stephen, 16:115
William, 16:115
HOLDER
Anna, 18:37
Barbara (Collins), 18:101
Bathsheba (Needham), 18:53, 54; 20:27
Christopher, 19:64
Daniel, 18:54
Elizabeth, 16:236; 20:95
Hannah, 20:240
Hannah (___), 17:49
Hannah (Hood), 18:54
Jessie, 16:111
Mary (Breed), 18:93
Rachel, 18:11
Richard, 18:93
Thomas, 18:53, 54, 101; 19:82; 20:27
HOLDIN see also HOLDEN
Hannah (Parker), 17:83
Josiah, 17:83
Simon, 17:82
HOLDREDGE/HOLDRIDGE
Deborah, 16:55
Deborah (Elliott), 16:55
Lydia (Quimby), 16:56
Tamar, 20:218
William, 16:55
HOLGRAVE
___, Mr., 19:188
HOLLAND
Ann, 18:28

Elizabeth, 16:176
Lydia (Potter), 19:151
Michael, 16:239
Richard, 16:177
Samuel, 19:151
Sarah (Cunningham), 16:177
Susanna (Ingersoll), 16:239
HOLLINGSOWTH
Amanda Marcella, 19:233
Kendall Osbin, 19:233
Revell Carter, 19:233
Thomas Christopher, 19:233
HOLLINGSWORTH/HOLLINGWORTH, 16:13
Richard, 16:200
Susanna, 16:32
HOLLISTER
Abel, 17:175
Abigail (Chambers), 17:175
John, 18:149
Lucy, 17:175
Sarah, 18:149
HOLLOWAY/HALLOWAY see also HALLAWAY, HALLOWELL
Bethia (Potter), 18:168; 19:144
Joseph, 18:168, 231; 19:144; 20:197
Mary, 18:211, 224
HOLLOWELL see also HALLOWELL
Mary (Alley), 18:22
HOLLYDAY
Nannie, 19:18
HOLLYOKE see HOLYOKE
HOLMAN
Huldah (___), 16:78
John, 16:78
Lydia, 18:35; 19:19, 171
Mary Lovering, 16:202; 18:175; 20:16
Winifred L., 18:71
Winifred Lovering, 16:95; 18:72, 133, 137, 157; 19:48, 77; 20:207
HOLMES/HOLMS
___, Mr., 19:26
Bathsheba (Sanford), 16:206
David, 16:208; 18:125
Gladys, 20:171
Hester (Wormwell), 20:55
John, 17:214; 19:26, 27
Lucy, 18:170
Lydia Morton, 16:180
Mary, 20:55
Obediah, 17:183
Richard, 20:55
Robert, 20:225
Sarah, 16:59
Sarah (Estes), 18:93
Sarah (Farr), 19:27
Temperance (___), 18:125
Thomas, 18:93
HOLT see also HOULT, 16:4
Brooks Frye, 19:178
Edith (Parker), 19:97
Elizabeth, 17:55; 20:21
Elizabeth (Russell), 16:233
Elizabeth (Short), 17:55
Hannah (Allen), 19:45, 220, 223
Hannah (Martin), 19:239
Hannah (Russell), 16:233
Henry, 16:67; 17:54; 18:159; 19:239
Humphry, 16:131
James, 19:45, 220, 223
Jonas, 19:178
Joshua, 18:163
Martha (___), 18:159

Mary, 16:233; 19:46; 20:112, 213
Mary (Russell), 16:233
Mary Eleanor, 19:178
Mary Frances (Clark), 19:178
Moses, 16:233
Nicholas, 16:65; 17:55; 18:231; 19:239
Oliver, 16:233; 19:239
Pamelia (Frye), 19:178
Robert J., 18:136
Samuel, 19:30, 45, 223
Sarah, 16:120; 19:220
Sarah (Allen), 19:45, 223
Sarah (Ballard), 16:67; 17:54
Sarah (Wright), 16:120
Stephen, 19:94, 97
Susan Louisa, 19:17
Uriah, 16:120
William, 19:239
Zerviah, 17:54

HOLTEN/HOLTON/HOULTON see also HOULTON
Benjamin, 16:157; 17:152
Ebenezer, 18:101
Eunice (Collins), 18:101
Hannah, 16:32
Hannah (Aborn), 16:31
James, 18:19
Joseph, 16:31
Lydia (Leach), 17:152
Mary (___), 18:148
Mary (Lindsey), 18:19
Ruth, 18:148
Ruth (Felton), 18:19
Samuel, 19:15
Sarah, 16:32; 17:152
Sarah (Ingersoll), 16:32
Susanna (Hawes), 16:32
William, 18:148

HOLYOKE see also HOLLYOKE
___ (Pynchon), 20:188
___, Mr., 17:46; 19:136, 212; 20:183, 189
Ann, 19:178
Anne, 20:97
Edward, 17:97; 18:99, 230; 19:138; 20:98, 132, 187, 188, 194
Eliezer, 19:77, 78, 212; 20:188
John, 19:78
Samuel, 18:135

HOMAN
John, 17:97
Nathaniel, 17:101
Tabitha, 20:233

HOMANS
Charles Stephen, 16:214
Charlottee (Friend), 16:214
Maria Theresa, 16:214
Stephen, 16:214
William, 16:214

HONEYWOOD
John, 18:152; 19:149
Ruth (Potter), 18:152; 19:149

HOOD, 18:117, 135
___, Goodman, 18:166
___, Mr., 20:102
"Child", 18:54, :57
"Daughter", 18:57
"Son", 18:56, 57
"Twins", 18:56
Abigail, 18:27, 32, 54, 56
Abigail (Ingalls), 19:108
Abigail (Potter), 18:56
Abner, 16:16; 18:15, 16, 54
Agnes (Snow), 18:54
Amos, 18:56
Anna, 18:31, 35, 36, 55
Anna/Anne, 18:53
Anne, 17:216; 18:51, 52
Anne (___), 18:51
Anne (Kimball), 18:57
Annie, 18:15, 16
Avese, 18:51
Barbara/Barberry, 18:55
Benjamin, 16:222; 17:217; 18:25, 35, 52-56
Breed, 18:55
Catherine, 18:51
Charlotte (___), 16:238
Content, 16:27; 18:35, 36, 54, 55, 104
Cumbey, 18:57
Daniel, 18:54, 56
David, 16:238
Deborah (___), 17:216; 18:53, 56
Dorcas (Hovey), 18:56
Elizabeth, 17:172; 18:35, 51-57
Elizabeth (___), 17:216; 18:51
Elizabeth (Bassett), 16:222; 18:25, 34, 55
Elizabeth (Coy), 18:56
Elizabeth (Palmer), 18:56
Elizabeth (Reddington), 18:57
Elizabeth/Rebecca (Bassett), 18:35
Esther, 18:56, 57
Eunice, 18:57
George, 18:12
Grace, 18:51
Hannah, 17:216; 18:52-54
Hannah (___), 18:57
Hannah (Berry), 16:26; 17:172; 18:52, 53; 20:92
Huldah, 18:33, 38, 55-57
Jane, 18:51
Jedediah, 18:54
Jennie, 17:173
Joanna, 18:56
Joanna (Dwinnell), 17:216; 18:53, 56
John, 17:173; 18:11, 20, 21, 29, 35, 36, 38, 51-54, 56, 57, 92; 19:45; 20:136, 142
Joseph, 17:216; 18:52, 53, 56, 57, 93
Keziah (Breed), 16:16; 18:54
Lettice (Begood), 18:57
Lydia, 18:25, 36, 55
Lydia (___), 18:55
Lydia (Corliss/Colly), 18:56
Lydia (Gould), 18:57; 20:142
Lydia (Tarbox), 18:57; 20:142
Marcy, 18:57
Mary, 17:216; 18:51, 52, 54, 56
Mary (___), 17:147
Mary (Hubbard), 18:56
Mary (Kimball), 18:57; 20:136
Mary (Newhall), 17:173; 18:20, 30, 51, 52
Mary (Perkins), 18:56
Mehitable, 18:56
Nathan, 18:56
Nathaniel, 17:216; 18:52, 53, 56, 57
Patience, 18:54, 104
Rebecca, 16:222; 17:216; 18:15, 16, 19, 20, 24, 32, 35, 52-55, 57
Rebecca (Cumbey), 17:217; 18:53, 57
Richard, 16:16; 17:17; 18:15, 16, 20, 24, 27, 28, 30, 35, 51-54, 56, 57, 60a, 103, 104; 19:29; 20:92, 141, 142, 196
Robin, 17:202
Rose, 18:51
Ruth, 17:216; 18:52, 53
Ruth (Gould), 18:57; 20:142
Ruth (Towne), 18:56
Samuel, 17:173; 18:52-54, 56, 57, 103, 104, 208; 20:142
Sarah, 17:216; 18:15, 25, 26, 29, 30, 35, 52-57, 92, 105
Sarah (Breed), 17:216; 18:36, 38, 53, 54
Sarah (Cross), 18:56
Sarah (Nolens), 18:57
Sarah (West), 18:54
Susanna, 18:56
Theodate, 18:15, 16, 36, 54, 103
Theodate (Collins), 16:221; 18:15, 24, 27, 54, 104
William, 18:56
Zebuion, 18:54

HOOKER
___, Capt., 20:222
Henry, 16:209
Mary (Edmunds), 16:209
Thomas, 18:186

HOOLE
Thomas, 18:135

HOOPER
Abigail (Blaney), 16:80
Agnes, 20:139
Elizabeth (___), 16:231
Elizabeth (Lee), 19:42
Elizabeth (Trevitt), 17:100
Elizabeth (Vickery), 16:81
Elizabeth (Whittaker), 16:81
Eunice (Collins), 18:101
Francis, 16:231
Greenfield, 17:97; 18:32
Hannah, 16:67
Henry, 16:81
Joseph, 16:81
Katherine (Andrews), 16:81
Lydia (Richards), 16:99
Mary (Bartlett), 16:81
Mary (Collins), 16:81
Mary (Ingalls), 19:53
Mary (Larrabee), 20:46
Mary (Poland), 20:46
Mary (Stickney), 16:81
Nathaniel, 16:58
Polly (Noyes), 16:81
Rebecca (Fittyplace), 16:81
Rebekah, 16:67
Robert, 16:81; 17:98; 18:33, 160; 19:53; 20:221
Ruth, 18:172
Ruth (Swett), 18:160
Sally (Northey), 19:169
Samuel, 16:99; 17:100; 18:101
Sarah, 20:119
Sarah (Brimblecomb), 16:81
Sarah (Weber), 16:58
Thomas, 16:68
Vashti (Mann), 16:81
William, 16:81; 19:169; 20:46, 198
William R., 17:106

HOPER
John, 20:199
Robert, 20:199

HOPKE
Henrietta, 18:177

HOPKINS
Anna (Stover), 17:178
Betsey (___), 18:178, 179
Constance, 17:57
Elisha, 18:179
Elizabeth (Stretton/Stratton), 20:216, 217
Hannah, 18:166
Joseph, 18:179

Polly, 20:95
Sarah, 16:37
Simeon, 17:178
Stephen, 17:57
HOPKINSON, 17:140
HOPSON
Mary, 18:73; 20:217, 218
HOPWOOD, 16:13
HORAN
Mary, 17:179
HORICE
Edward, 20:83
HORMAN
Nathaniel, 20:221
HORN see HORNE
HORNDALE see also HARNDEN
HORNE/HORN see also ORNE
Benjamin, 16:31; 17:211
Elizabeth (King), 16:32
John, 16:32; 19:188
Margarett, 16:32
Mary, 16:117
Mercy, 16:32
Rebecca, 16:67
Sarah (Aborn), 16:31; 17:211
Timothy, 19:137
HORRID
Thomas, 20:199
HORRIGAN
Janice, 19:5
HORSUM
Elisabeth/Betsey, 17:239
John, 17:239
Olive (___), 17:239
HORTIN
Peter, 20:199
HORTON, 19:125
Jonathan, 18:178
Lydia (Donnel), 18:178
Mary (Shepard), 18:178
Sarah, 16:60; 19:124, 127
Thomas, 18:178
William, 20:223
HOSKINS
Jacob, 18:82
Mary (Hackett), 18:82
HOSLEY
Aaron, 17:81
HOSMER
Abel, 17:178
George L., 18:220
James, 16:202
Lucy (___), 17:178
HOTCHKISS, 18:135
Abigail (Douglas), 16:75
David, 16:75
HOUARD see HOWARD
HOUGH/HOWE
Benjamin, 17:138
Benjamin K., 17:138
Bridget (Carr), 18:177
Eben, 17:135
Ebenezer, 18:153
John, 18:177
Joseph, 17:142
HOUGHTON
Benjamin, 20:116
Hannah (Newhall), 20:116
Thomas, 20:132
HOULT see also HOLT
Hannah (___), 16:68
Henry, 16:68
Nicholas, 16:68

Samuel, 16:68
HOULTON see also HOLTON
Benjamin, 16:155; 17:16
Hannah (Aborn), 17:211
Henry, 17:16
James, 16:155
John, 17:16
Joseph, 17:14
HOURAY
Marie, 20:169
HOUSE
Hannah, 20:240
HOUSTON
___, Mr., 18:221
Judith (Eaton), 18:221
HOVANEC
Beverly, 18:134
Beverly J. Francis, 16:17; 18-79, 219
HOVEY, 19:86
Abigail (Hood), 18:56
Abijah, 20:219
Anne (___), 18:56
Chauncey, 18:180
Daniel, 19:93
Dorcas, 16:218; 17:38; 18:56
Ebenezer, 18:180
Hannah (Preston), 16:218
Ivory, 18:56
John, 18:56, 180
Joseph, 19:93
Luke, 16:193
Lydia (Graves), 20:219
Mary, 19:93
Mary (Chadwick), 19:93
Mary Ann, 18:180
Mary/Polly (Cox), 18:180
Persis (Bishop), 18:180
Philena, 18:180
Phineas, 16:218
Sarah, 20:219
Stephen, 18:56
HOW see also HOWE
Abraham, 16:176
Anna, 19:234
Daniel, 19:138
Edward, 19:138
Eliakim, 17:116
Frances (Willey)), 16:160
Hepzibah (Andrews), 16:176
Joseph, 16:160; 18:109
Rebecca, 17:116
Rebecca (How), 17:116
HOWARD/HOUARD see also HAYWARD, 16:13
___, Mrs., 17:11
Anna, 19:149
Bethia, 16:46
Charles, 18:216
Daniel, 20:140
Edward, 16:115; 18:219; 20:140
Eleanor (Tarbox), 16:115; 20:140
Ellener, 20:140
Ezekiel, 18:227
Huldah, 19:116
Jean, 20:140
Jeminer, 20:140
Jerusha (___), 16:45
Jerusha (Newhall), 20:100
John, 16:4; 18:85, 216; 20:221
Jonathan, 17:199; 20:140
Joseph, 18:216; 20:221
Judith, 20:46
Judith (Eaton), 18:219

Loea Parker, 17:45; 18:40; 19:135, 136; 20:183
Lois, 16:46; 20:29
Lydia, 18:216
Lydia (Norwood), 18:216
Martha, 16:115; 20:140
Mary (Tapley), 20:140
Mary (Tarbox), 16:89
Mary Elizabeth (Meadowcroft), 16:4
Nathaniel, 20:198
Priscilla (Jones), 18:85
Rachel (Osborn), 17:199
Rebecca (Bancroft), 20:40
Rebecca (Sprague), 18:216
Robert, 16:89
Ruth (Jones), 18:85
Samuel, 20:40
Thomas, 18:85
Timothy, 16:45; 18:23, 24; 20:100
HOWARTH, 16:13
HOWE see also HOW, HOUGH, 18:177
___, Capt., 20:202
Abraham, 18:168; 19:148
Daniel, 20:195
Edward, 20:194
Elizabeth, 16:74
Elizabeth (Jackson), 19:220, 221
Ephraim, 19:138; 20:195
Eunice (White), 20:236
Harlan Lewis, 19:235
Jeremy, 20:195
John, 20:202
Joseph, 18:46; 19:159
Josiah, 19:148
Julia Ward, 18:11
Mariah, 19:159
Mark, 20:236
Martha (Potter), 18:168; 19:147, 148
Mary (Needham), 18:46; 19:48
Moses, 20:83
Patty (Hathaway), 18:173
Persis, 17:116
Sarah, 16:176
Sarah (___), 19:148
Shirley (Tarr), 19:235
Shirley Alma (Tarr), 19:235
William S., 18:135
HOWELL
___, Mr., 20:183
Edward, 20:192, 194
King, 19:44
Sarah (Barrett), 20:216-218
Titus, 17:208
HOWES
___, Rev., 16:191
Luna, 20:172
HOWLAND
Dorothy (Ballard), 16:73
Lydia, 16:27
Mary (Kimball), 20:227
Rebecca (Hussey), 18:54
Richard C., 18:133, 137, 138
Samuel, 16:73
Sarah, 17:117
Thomas, 20:227
HOWLETT
Mary, 16:193
HOY
Catherine (Grady), 17:180
George W., 17:180
Mary/Nellie E., 17:180
HOYT, 16:223, 20:80
David, 16:78

David W., 16:189; 17:154; 18:31, 82, 154, 219; 19:30, 210
David Webster, 16:21
Dennis, 19:238
Dolly, 16:147
Elizabeth, 19:58
Elizabeth (Huntington), 17:52; 20:178
Ezekiel, 19:48
Frances (___), 17:55
George W., 19:238
Jacob, 20:81
Jane (Wentworth), 19:238
John, 16:19; 17:55; 19:238
Mary, 17:54
Mary (Brown), 17:53
Mary Richardson (Leighton), 19:238
Micah, 17:52; 20:178
Naomi, 20:20
Rebecca, 17:235
Rebecca (Browne), 19:48
Sarah, 19:141; 20:151
Sarah (Rowe), 19:238
Susanna (Colby), 17:52; 20:178
Susannah, 17:52; 20:178
Thomas, 17:52; 20:178

HUBBARD/HEBERD
Aaron, 18:56
Dorcas (Haskell), 20:216
Eliezer, 20:216
Elizabeth (___), 20:215
Esther (Larrabee), 20:51
James, 18:230
John, 20:7, 215
Lucretia, 16:172
Mary, 18:56
Mary (___), 18:56
Moses, 20:51
Philip, 18:49
Sarah (Bradstreet), 18:193
William, 17:203; 18:193

HUBLEY
Aaron, 19:238
Anna Catherine B. (Gorkum), 19:238
Catherine Matilda (Spurr), 19:238
Claire (Wardwell), 20:54
Elmer Adams, 19:237
Ferdinand/Frederick, 19:238
George Jacob, 19:238H
James William, 19:237
Mabel Sarah (Montgomery), 19:237
Richard Elmer, 19:237
Sarah Frances (Adams), 19:237
Sophia Elizabeth (Rafuse), 19:238

HUCHESON see also HUTCHESON
Thomas, 18:231

HUCHINGS
Sarah, 18:208

HUCHINS see also HUTCHENS
___, Mr., 17:91
Elizabeth, 19:27
Elizabeth (Farr), 19:27
John, 19:27
Nicholas, 19:26, 27

HUCKSTON
Christover, 20:199

HUDSON, 18:132, 135, 137
Abigail (Shore), 17:232
Diana/Dinah, 20:42
Elizabeth (___), 16:73; 17:149
Esther (Graves), 20:218
Francis, 17:232
Henry, 20:82
John, 19:192

Jonathan, 16:73; 17:147; 18:167
Lydia, 17:145
Mary (Hathorn), 18:167
Moses, 16:197; 18:167, 211, 224, 225; 20:102, 140, 196
Rebecca, 16:72; 17:157; 19:80
Samuel, 17:232
Sarah, 16:204; 18:170, 209, 211, 224
Sarah (Collins), 18:167, 211, 224
Thomas, 17:158; 18:230; 19:138; 20:194, 218

HUGHES
Hannah (Page), 18:39
John, 18:39
Lora Smith, 17:175
William, 20:164

HUITT
William, 20:199

HULBERT
Jonathan, 17:149
Susanna (Farrington), 17:149

HULL see also HALL
Ann (Tyler), 17:30
George, 17:30
Isaac, 20:198
John, 18:240a; 20:15
Mary, 18:225
Mary M., 17:30
Sarah, 20:237

HULLING
Ray G., 18:191

HUMBER
Edward, 17:212

HUMFREY/HUMPHRY, 16:35
John, 20:189

HUMPHERY-SMITH
Cecil R., 16:12

HUMPHREY, 19:49; 20:48, 184
___, Mr., 16:89; 17:240; 18:79; 19:47, 189; 20:189
___, Mrs., 18:52
Ann, 18:30
John, 18:17, 30; 19:25, 29, 135, 188, 189; 20:183

HUMPHREYS/HUMPHRIES, 19:217
___, Mr., 17:213
Abigail (Bassett), 18:39
Anne, 17:214
Clement, 18:39
Edward, 20:233
Elizabeth, 20:230, 233
Elizabeth (Combs), 20:233
Hannah, 20:106-108
John, 17:214; 20:132

HUMPHRY see HUMFREY

HUNSTABLE
Mercy, 19:157
Mercy (Sharp), 16:56
Samuel, 16:56
Samuel Livingston, 16:56
Sarah (Green), 16:56
Sarah (Whitman), 16:56; 17:115
Thomas, 16:56; 17:115
William, 16:56

HUNT
___, Dr., 20:90
Abiah, 16:73
Abiah (Hunt), 16:73
Benjamin, 16:73
Daniel, 16:73
Dorothy, 16:73
Dorothy (Ballard), 16:73
Eben, 20:89

Edward, 17:55
Elizabeth, 17:53
Elizabeth Amelia, 17:119
Ephraim, 16:73
Experience (Chaffee), 16:73
Freeman, 17:225
Hannah (Peck), 16:73
Harold Conrad, 20:32
Hazel Adeline (Smith), 20:32
Joan, 20:238
Lydia (Bowen), 16:73
Margaret Alice, 20:32
Martha (Bishop), 16:73
Mary (___), 16:73
Oliver, 16:73
Priscilla, 16:73
Rebecca, 16:73
Ruth (Todd), 20:98
Samuel, 17:5; 20:98
Sarah (Jackson), 16:73
Susannah (___), 20:98
Thos. D., 20:159
Virginia, 20:32
William, 16:73

HUNT/HUNTER
Christian, 16:200; 17:50

HUNTER
John, 18:171
Susanna (Witt), 18:171

HUNTING
Abigail (Blaney), 16:86
Asa, 16:86
Jane (Ballard), 16:75
Joseph, 16:75
Mary, 16:75

HUNTINGTON
Anne, 17:54
Benjamin, 18:180
Elizabeth, 17:52; 20:178
Elizabeth (Hunt), 17:53
Elizabeth (Martin), 17:54
Joanna (___), 18:180
Joanna (Bayley), 17:55
John, 16:173; 17:53; 18:180
Molly (Rowell), 18:180
Samuel, 17:54
Sarah, 18:180
Timothy, 18:180
William, 17:55

HUNTRESS
Darling, 18:49
George, 18:49

HUNTS
Jeremiah, 19:93

HURD
D. Hamilton, 16:22; 18:80, 82

HURTIL
Elizabeth (___), 19:59

HUSE
Anna (Graves), 20:219
John, 16:133
Mary, 16:222
Ruth, 20:207
Thomas, 20:219

HUSSEY, 16:65
Alice, 18:54
Christopher, 18:140
Lydia (___), 16:100
Rebecca, 18:54
Silvanus, 16:16; 18:214

HUTCHENS see also HUCHINS
Nicholas, 20:196

HUTCHESON see also HUCHESON
   Ann (Browne), 17:47
   Benjamin, 19:135
   Elisha, 16:210
   Francis, 17:47
   Hannaniah, 19:135
   Martha (Stearns), 17:47
   Sarah (Laughton), 17:47
   Thomas, 17:47
HUTCHIN
   Samuel, 20:207
HUTCHINGS/HUTCHINS/HITCHINGS
   ___, Mr., 20:204
   Almira, 19:239
   Betsey (Davis), 20:57
   Daniel, 16:203; 20:193, 197
   Elizabeth, 16:204
   Elnathan, 16:204
   Harriet J., 20:108
   Hugh, 20:57
   Ida Florence, 20:57
   Isaac, 20:57
   Jack Randolf, 20:57
   Joseph, 16:202-204; 20:197
   Martha, 16:204
   Mary, 16:204
   Mary (Edmonds), 16:202
   Olive A. (Ward), 20:57
   Rachel (Elwell), 17:132
   Rebecca, 16:204
   Ruth, 16:204
   Sally (Sawyer), 20:219
   Samuel, 16:203, 204
   Sarah, 16:204
   William, 17:132
   William V., 17:132
   William Vinson, 17:132
HUTCHINSON see also HITCHINS, 18:157, 197; 19:55
   ___, Capt., 19:133
   ___, Mrs., 16:160
   Abigail (___), 16:155; 17:20
   Abigail (Eliot), 17:16
   Alice (___), 17:14
   Alice (Bosworth), 17:16
   Ann, 16:203
   Anne, 20:96
   Anne (Browne), 18:40
   Bartholomew, 16:155
   Benjamin, 16:154; 17:16
   Bethiah, 16:155
   Bethiah (Gedney), 16:154; 17:16
   Betsey (Russell), 17:16
   Edward, 16:210; 18:41, 42; 19:135
   Elizabeth, 18:40, 41, 227
   Elizabeth (Kingsbury), 18:157, 160
   Elizabeth (Parker), 18:157, 158
   Elizabeth (Swinnerton), 17:16
   Francis, 19:137, 212, 217; 20:197
   Hannah, 16:155; 19:30; 20:232
   Hannah (Fuller), 17:15
   Hannah (Johnson), 20:214
   Hannah (Richardson), 17:16
   Isabella, 20:221
   Israel, 16:144; 17:6; 18:217; 19:167
   Jane, 16:155
   Jane (Phillips), 16:154
   Joanna (Conant), 16:155
   John, 17:14; 18:218
   Joseph, 16:154; 17:14; 18:135
   Levi, 17:16
   Lydia (___), 17:15
   Mary, 16:44

   Mary (Cummings), 16:155
   Mehitable, 16:119; 20:220
   Mercy, 19:217
   Nathaniel, 16:155; 18:228; 19:137, 216, 217
   Rebecca, 17:15
   Rebecca (King), 17:15
   Rebecca (Newhall), 17:16
   Rebecca Newhall (Goodale), 17:15
   Richard, 17:14; 19:191, 193
   Ruth, 18:218
   Samuel, 16:68; 17:15; 18:41, 157, 158; 19:33, 138; 20:195
   Sarah, 16:155
   Sarah (Tarbell), 16:155
   Thomas, 16:159; 17:47; 18:41, 209; 19:137, 212, 217, 229
   Timothy, 19:229
HUTTON
   Elizabeth (Killam), 16:201
   Richard, 16:34
   Susannah (More), 16:201
HUXFORD
   Elizabeth, 19:104
HYDE
   Comfort (Hayes), 16:116
   Eliza C., 16:116
   Elizabeth (Fuller), 20:119
   Hannah (Dana), 20:119
   Jacob, 16:116
   Job, 20:119
   Jonathan, 20:119
   Margaret, 20:119
   Mary (Beck), 20:119
   Mary (Davis/Dennis), 16:116
   Samuel, 16:116; 20:119
HYNES see HAINES

IANIZZI, 16:123
   Bruno, 20:8
IERSTON/IRESON
   Edward, 16:164
ILLINGWORTH, 16:13
ILSLEY
   Enoch, 19:96
   John, 18:154
   Mary (Parker), 19:96
   Parker, 19:96
INERSOL, 20:18
INGALLS/INGHALLS/INGALS see also ENGALS, INGOLLS, INGULLS
   ___, Mrs., 19:154
   "Daughter", 19:50
   "Son", 18:22
   Abiah, 19:108
   Abigail, 16:103; 19:49, 108, 109
   Abigail (___), 19:106
   Abigail (Emery), 19:46
   Abigail (Fuller), 19:108
   Abigail (Stocker), 16:86; 19:108
   Abner, 19:108
   Agnes, 19:53
   Amos, 16:96; 19:51, 109
   Ann (___), 19:44, 49, 222, 223
   Ann (Collins), 18:100
   Ann (Dennis), 19:53
   Anna, 19:46, 108, 109
   Anna (Ingalls), 19:109
   Anna (Parker), 17:47; 19:48
   Anne, 19:108
   Anne (___), 18:211; 19:48, 105
   Annis/Ann (Telbe), 19:173
   Benjamin, 19:96, 108

   Charles A., 19:115
   Collins, 19:109
   Daniel, 19:106
   David, 19:49, 105
   Deborah, 19:51
   Deborah (Goss), 19:50
   Dinah (Elson), 19:46
   Edmond/Edmund, 17:47; 19:43-48, 51, 53, 75, 105, 106, 108, 109, 115, 116, 173, 219, 222, 223; 20:194, 204, 214
   Edmund/Edward, 19:109
   Edward, 19:43, 138
   Eleazer, 16:103; 17:98; 18:23, 180; 19:47, 49, 51-53, 109; 20:15
   Eleazer Collins, 19:108, 109
   Elijah, 19:105
   Elizabeth, 16:80; 17:47; 18:167; 19:45, 46, 48, 51, 52, 106-109, 115, 116, 173, 210, 221, 222
   Elizabeth (___), 19:43, 109
   Elizabeth (Ashton), 19:53
   Elizabeth (Barrett), 19:45
   Elizabeth (Foster), 19:107
   Elizabeth (Lewis), 18:23; 19:106
   Elizabeth (Strouthers), 19:50
   Elizabeth/Betsey, 16:86
   Elmira Prindall, 19:115
   Esther (Fry), 18:156; 19:46
   Eunice (Ludden), 19:46
   Faith, 19:45, 115, 116, 173, 220, 222, 223
   Francis, 19:43-46, 75, 138, 220; 20:194
   George Warren, 16:103
   Hannah, 17:148; 18:22, 25; 19:47, 49-51, 106, 107, 145
   Hannah (Abbott), 19:46; 20:23
   Hannah (Alley), 18:22, 23, 25; 19:107
   Hannah (Brewer), 19:47-49
   Hannah (Joy), 18:211; 19:50
   Hannah (Marshall), 18:180
   Hannah (Perkins), 17:148
   Hannah (Strouthers), 18:211
   Henry, 16:68; 18:155; 19:35, 43-46, 50, 109, 115, 173, 212, 215, 222; 20:22, 23
   Hepsibah, 19:105, 106, 108, 109
   Hepzebah (Ingalls), 19:109
   Huldah (Batchelder), 19:109
   Isaac, 19:115
   Jacob, 19:50, 51, 106, 109, 115
   James, 17:47; 19:35, 46, 48, 105-107; 20:23, 131
   Joanna (Call), 19:48
   John, 16:68; 18:22, 23, 25, 180; 19:45, 46, 51-53, 107-109, 173, 192; 20:196
   John N., 19:50
   Jonathan, 18:211
   Jonathan Norwood, 19:50
   Joseph, 17:98; 18:46; 19:46, 50-53, 108, 173
   Josiah, 18:156; 19:46, 91
   Judith, 17:153
   Kay Germain, 20:11
   Leah (Stuart), 19:115
   Lydia, 16:97; 19:44, 105, 106, 108, 19
   Lydia (Lewis), 19:106, 108
   Marcy (Pratt), 19:107
   Margaret, 19:53
   Margaret (Friend), 19:106
   Martha (Blaney), 16:86; 19:108
   Martha (Lewis), 19:51
   Mary, 19:44-46, 49, 51-53, 105, 109, 173
   Mary (___), 19:44
   Mary (Boardman), 19:53
   Mary (Hendley), 17:98; 19:48, 51

Mary (Hickman), 19:109
Mary (Holt), 19:46
Mary (Ingalls), 19:51, 109
Mary (Lane), 19:53
Mary (Merritt), 19:53
Mary (Osgood), 19:46; 20:23
Mary (Trevitt), 17:97; 19:53
Mary (Tucker), 19:51, 53, 109
Mercy (Pratt), 19:107
Moriah, 19:50
Moses, 19:46
Nabby, 16:224
Naby/Abigail (Richards), 16:103
Nathaniel, 18:22, 25, 100, 211; 19:46-53, 105-109, 212; 20:196, 210
Phebe, 19:33, 91
Priscilla, 19:53
Rebecca, 17:47; 19:48, 51, 107-109
Rebecca (Collins), 17:218; 19:50, 108
Rebecca (Leighton/Laughton), 17:46; 19:47, 48
Rebeckah (___), 19:96
Robert, 16:196; 17:47; 19:43-49, 51, 105, 106, 108., 109, 173; 20:196
Ruth, 19:46-48, 50, 51, 105, 106, 148
Ruth (Eaton), 19:46
Sally, 20:109
Samuel, 16:68; 17:148; 18:34, 100, 103, 150; 19:45-50, 52, 53, 105-108, 148, 173, 216; 20:196
Sarah, 16:224; 17:47; 18:103; 19:45-50, 52, 53, 105, 106, 148, 173; 20:221
Sarah (___), 18:180; 19:53
Sarah (Alley), 16:85; 18:22, 25; 19:107
Sarah (Diamond), 19:53
Sarah (Farnum), 19:46, 222; 20:22, 23
Sarah (Glasey), 19:53
Sarah (Harker), 17:47; 19:43-47, 49
Sarah (Hendrick), 19:46
Sarah (Ingalls), 19:49, 50, 105, 148
Sarah (Richards), 19:50, 109
Sarah (Russell), 16:233; 19:46
Sarah (Summer), 19:45
Sarah (Thomson), 19:46
Stephen, 19:46
Susanna (Brown), 19:109
Susanna (Burrill), 19:108
Tabitha, 18:25; 19:50, 107
Tabitha (___), 20:210
Tabitha (Lewis), 18:22, 25; 19:50, 106, 107
Thomas, 19:53, 107, 108
William, 18:209, 211; 19:50-53, 96
Zacheus, 18:21
Zerviah (Norwood), 18:211; 19:50
Zibiah, 16:86
INGERSOL/INGERSOLL
___, Mrs., 16:64; 17:12
Abigail (Doliver), 19:118
David, 17:12
Deborah, 19:226; 20:44
Deborah (___), 20:44
John, 17:20; 18:179; 19:118; 20:44
Mary, 16:179; 19:229; 29:114
Nathaniel, 17:14; 19:215
Richard, 19:189
Sally/Sarah, 19:118
Samuel, 17:11; 19:94
Sarah, 16:32, 64
Sarah (Larrabee), 19:229
Susanna, 16:239
William, 17:135
INGHAM
Norman W., 19:176

INGLE, 16:13
INGLEBY, 16:13
INGOLLS/INGOLS see also INGALLS
Abigail, 19:79
Ann (___), 17:113
David, 19:79
Hannah, 19:79
Hannah (Brewer), 19:79
Isaac, 18:163
Mary, 19:79
Samuel, 19:79
INGOLLSBEE
Elizabeth, 18:200
INGOLS see INGOLLS
Elizabeth, 18:46, 47
Nathaniel, 17:113
Robert, 18:46
Tabitha, 16:199; 17:133
INGRAHAM
Duncan, 17:219
Susanna (Newhall), 17:219
INGULS see also INGALLS
Abigail (Mansfield), 17:159
Abner, 17:159
Hannah, 19:107
Hipzebeth, 19:107
Sally (___), 18:226
INIUS, 18:240a
INMAN
Abigail, 20:227
Bethsheba, 18:96
Elizabeth, 18:95, 96
Huldreth (___), 18:96
Jeremiah, 18:96
IREDALE, 16:13
IRELAND
William, 20:201
IRESON, 18:135
Abiah (Ingalls), 19:108
Anna, 19:108
Anna (Blaney), 19:108
Anna/Nanny (Blaney), 16:86
Benjamin, 17:151; 19:47, 108, 216; 20:216
Edward, 17:46; 18:99; 19:105, 106, 108, 138; 20:132, 195
Edwin, 20:132
Hannah (Mansfield), 19:108
Hepsibah (Ingalls), 19:105, 106, 108
John, 16:86; 19:106, 108
Joseph, 19:108
Mary, 19:216
Samuel, 16:86; 19:108
Sarah (Sargent), 19:108
Susanna (Burrill), 19:108
Tabitha (Allen), 19:108
Zibiah (Ingalls), 19:86
Zibiah/Abiah (___), 19:106
ISBELL
Robert, 19:197
ISCHEN
Norman, 19:128
ISHERWOOD, 16:13
IVES, 18:135
Benjamin, 18:240
Caroline (Clark), 16:110
Elizabeth, 20:43
James, 16:110
Margaret, 20:42
Robert Hale, 20:43
Sarah (Bray), 20:43
IVORY, 19:138
Benjamin, 16:75; 18:169; 19:147
Deborah, 16:74

Deborah (Tobey), 16:75; 18:169
Elizabeth, 19:147
Eunice, 19:100, 147
Hannah/Anna, 20:138
John, 16:79; 18:54, 171; 19:100, 147
Lois, 16:27; 17:148; 19:147, 150
Mary, 16:102; 18:168, 171-173; 19:144, 147
Mary (Davis), 19:147
Phebe, 18:48, 50
Ruth, 19:147
Ruth (Ivory), 19:147
Ruth (Potter), 16:79; 18:171; 19:100, 147
Sarah, 18:47, 169
Thomas, 17:147; 18:169; 19:147; 20:195, 196
William, 16:75; 17:87; 18:135, 169

JACK
Fannie, 20:220
John, 18:128
Joseph, 20:220
Mary, 20:220
Susannah (Graves), 20:220
JACKMAN
Joseph, 20:82
JACKSON/JACSON, 16:111; 19:48
___, Goodman, 19:214
"Child", 17:13
Alice (Goodwin), 18:203
Amelia Lois (Abbott), 17:58
Barbara (Sinclair), 17:117
Bethia, 16:85
Eben, 17:117
Ebenezer, 17:117
Edmund, 19:132
Elizabeth, 19:220, 221
Elizabeth (Dane), 19:221
Ervin Randall, 17:117
George, 16:31; 17:211; 20:52
Jane (Downs), 16:239
Jane (Gentilhomme), 17:117
John, 16:38; 17:97; 18:84, 158; 19:221; 20:198, 200
Joseph, 17:13; 19:131
Lillian Alberta (Randall), 17:117
Lupira Spaulding (Newbegin), 17:117
Margaret (___), 17:97
Martha, 17:96; 19:52, 53
Mary, 17:174
Mary (___), 17:97
Mary (Aborn), 16:31; 17:211; 20:52
Mehitable (Giles), 17:117
Michael, 17:25
Oscar Ervin, 17:117
Patty/Martha, 17:179
Phebe (Patten), 17:174
Priscilla, 17:117
Rebecca, 16:55
Robert, 16:239
Samuel, 17:117
Sarah, 16:73
Susanna (Jones), 18:84
William, 17:58; 18:203
JACOB
Joseph, 19:49
JACOBS
Abel, 16:77
Abigail (Trask), 17:212
Alice (Ballard), 16:77
George, 16:154
John, 16:77
Joseph, 17:48; 18:15, 18; 103; 19:105, 217

Judith, 19:214
Nancy/Anna (Ballard), 16:77
Sarah, 19:217
Sarah (Lindsey), 18:15, 18
William, 17:212
JACOBUS, 19:211
Donald Lines, 16:75; 17:175; 18:25, 67; 19:176; 20:70, 75, 219
JACQUES see also JAQUES
Elizabeth, 20:221
Sarah, 20:221
JACQUITH
Mary, 16:111
JAFFREY
George, 18:237
JAGGER, 16:13
JAMES
___, Goodwife, 17:96
Abigail, 16:29
Ambrose, 16:29; 17:99; 19:52
Benjamin, 16:29; 17:99; 18:19; 20:112
Elizabeth (Bowden), 17:99
Erasmus, 17:210; 19:82
Goody, 16:31
Hannah, 16:29
Hannah (Blaney), 16:28
Jonathan, 16:29
Joseph, 16:29
King, 20:12
King, I, 20:175
King, II, 16:197; 17:125
Mary, 16:32, 17:99
Mary (Breed), 16:29
Mary (Rowland), 17:212
Mary (Trevitt), 17:99; 19:52
Molly Trevitt, 17:100
Rebecca (___), 17:100
Rebecca Trevitt, 17:100
Ruth, 16:29
Sarah, 17:219; 19:151
Sarah (Lindsey), 16:29; 17:99; 18:19
Tabitha, 16:29; 17:99
Tabitha (Procter), 17:100
Warren, 19:86
William, 17:99
JAMESON/JAMISON
Charles, Mrs., 16:111
E. O., 19:41; 20:223, 224
Holden, 16:111
JANE
Peter, 18:127
JANES
Katherine, 16:58
JANKES see JENKS
JANNEY
Francis A., 16:151
Lena Farr (Carstairs), 16:151
JAQUES see also JACQUES
Abigail, 20:220
Ann (Graves), 20:220
Annie Laurie, 17:170
Benjamin, 20:221
Daniel, 20:218
Elizabeth (Graves), 20:221
Isaac, 20:220
JAQUISH
Ruth, 16:178
JARVICE/JARVIS
___, Mrs., 16:63
Abigail, 19:38-40
Elias, 17:93
Elizabeth, 16:85
Elizabeth (Stratton), 16:172

Joseph, 16:63
Leonard, 18:237
William, 16:172
JAYNES
___, Mr., 16:154
JEAN
Catherine, 20:169
Dennis, 20:169
Marie (Pelletier), 20:169
JEANOTTE-BRODEUR
Melvina, 19:180
JEARNS
Andrew, 18:52
Mary (Bassett), 18:52
JEFFARDS
___, Mr., 18:231
JEFFERSON
Thomas, 16:108
JEFFORD
Mary (___), 18:46
JEFFREY
Joseph, 20:36
Priscilla (___), 20:36
JEFFREYS/JEFFRIES
John, 18:232
William, 19:201
JEFTS, 18:138
JELLISON
Elizabeth (Milliken), 20:238
John, 20:238
Thankful, 16:235; 18:219
JEMMENY
Catherine/Katherine, 16:93
JENCKES/JENCKS/JENKES see also JENKS
Elizabeth, 18:151
John, 16:207; 18:240; 19:158; 20:197
Joseph, 17:91
Nathan, 18:240
Samuel, 16:165; 18:151, 240; 20:197
JENKINS
Ann (___), 18:90
Caleb M., 19:172
Content (Alley), 18:25
David, 19:40
Hannah, 17:78
Jabez, 18:29, 92
Jane Parsons (Northey), 19:172
Joel, 17:78
Joseph, 18:25; 19:177, 178
Mary, 17:59; 20:47
Nancy, 19:177
Obadiah, 17:82
Patrick, 19:14
Phebe (Featherstone), 19:177, 178
Philadelphia, 18:31, 52, 90
Reginald, 18:90
Sarah, 19:40
JENKS/JANKES see also JENCKES, 19:160
Abigail, 16:72
Alice (Smith), 16:72
Deborah, 19:159
Ebenezer, 16:72
Elizabeth, 16:72
Elizabeth (Berry), 18:116
Elizabeth (Potter), 19:147
Esther, 16:72
Hannah (Bosworth), 16:72
Hester/Esther (Ballard), 16:71
Joanna, 16:72
John, 18:116; 19:159, 164
Jonathan, 18:226
Joseph, 16:71; 18:231; 19:147; 20:68

Margaret, 18:124
Martha (Brown), 16:72
Mary (___), 16:72
Mary (Butterworth), 16:72
Mary (Haden), 19:159
Nathaniel, 16:72
Patience (Sprague), 16:72
Samuel, 19:164
Sarah, 16:72
Sarah (Merriam), 18:116
William, 16:72
JENNER
Elizabeth, 19:41, 102
JENNINGS
Rebecca (Hutchins/Hitchings), 16:204
William, 16:204
JENNISON
Abigail, 18:169
Ann, 18:169
William, 18:94
JEROME
Mary (Graves), 20:222
Stephen, 20:222
JESSEMAN
Chloe, 19:170, 171
JEWET/JEWETT/JEWIT
Alice (Cothran), 20:145
Ann, 18:239; 19:208
David, 16:63
Elizabeth, 18:239
Faith, 18:239
Francis, 18:10
Hannah, 18:239
Hepsebah, 18:239
J., 16:43
James, 20:145
Jeremiah, 18:239
John, 16:132
Joseph, 16:131
Martha, 17:201
Maximilian, 18:239; 19:179
Mehitable, 20:55
Noah, 20:223
Ruth (Hardy), 18:10
Ruth Riggs, 20:145
Samuel, 18:10
Sarah, 18:239
Sarah (___), 18:239
Sarah (Hardy), 18:10
Sarah (Storey), 19:179
Seth, 18:239
JIPSON
Deborah (Newton), 19:180
Micah, 19:180
JOANES/JOANS see also JONES
Eprin, 20:199
Griffin, 20:199
Hannah (Tolman), 18:225
Hugh, 18:225
Michael, 18:46
Richard, 20:199
JOCELIN/JOCELYN
Augusta, 20:228
Bella, 18:184
Henry, 17:229
Roger, 18:183
Thomas, 18:183, 184
JOHANSON
Maria, 20:128, 129
JOHNS
Anna, 16:86; 17:159
JOHNSON see also JONSON, 16:96; 18:133; 19:47

___, Capt., 18:161
___, Mr., 16:175
Abby, 16:111
Abigail, 17:171; 18:33; 19:219, 221, 222
Abigail (___), 20:114
Abigail Lewis (Bessom), 19:231
Abigail Phillips (Breed), 16:224
Alice (___), 17:171
Andrew, 16:132
Ann, 18:21
Ann (Alley), 18:16
Ann (Legery/Legaree), 16:97; 18:21, 113
Anna, 17:153; 18:53
Anna (Burchsted), 16:97
Anne (Cotton), 17:193
Arabella (___), 20:189
Benjamin, 16:47; 18:16, 21; 19:33
Bethia, 17:49
Bethia (Newhall), 19:148
Betsy (Batchelder), 18:16
Betsy (Graves), 18:16
Caleb, 18:16
Caleb Hervey, 18:16
Caroline, 20:153
Catherine (Sprague), 19:93
Charles Warren, 18:16
Clara, 18:16
Damaris (___), 16:232
Daniel, 17:49; 18:11; 19:29; 20:134, 196
Daniel Alfred, 18:16
Daniel W., 18:16
David, 16:16; 17:49; 20:105
Dolly Madison, 18:16
Dorothy, 17:118
E. J., 18:14, 15
Ebenezer, 20:120
Edith (Durgin), 17:186
Edmund, 16:224; 18:135
Edmund Buxton, 18:16
Edward, 18:16; 19:148
Edward Augustus, 18:16
Edward Kirke, 18:16
Eleanor (Edwards), 20:120
Eliza, 18:16
Elizabeth, 18:48; 19:158, 218, 219, 221, 222
Elizabeth (Dane), 19:115, 219, 222
Elizabeth (Newhall), 16:46
Ephraim, 16:132
Esther/Easter (Laughton), 17:49
Francis, 16:68; 17:210; 18:16; 19:34, 192
Frank, 17:186
Frank, Mrs., 17:183
Franklin Everett, 18:16
Frederick Henry, 18:16
George, 19:231
George L., 18:16
Hannah, 16:16; 17:49; 18:165; 20:214
Hannah (___), 17:49; 19:94
Hannah (Barker), 18:157
Hannah (Newhall), 16:46
Hannah (Sawyer), 16:173
Hannah (Tenney), 18:156
Helen D. (Friend), 17:166
Holton, 16:29
Irene Sanders, 18:136
Isaac, 19:43; 20:189
James, 16:68; 18:116
Jerusha (Newhall), 16:47
Joanna, 16:20
John, 16:68; 19:33; 20:82, 214
John Legree/Legery, 16:97
Jonas, 20:198

Jonathan, 16:99; 18:15, 16
Joseph, 16:97; 18:16, 21, 113, 156, 157; 19:51
Josiah, 16:131; 19:34
Katherine (Brummage), 18:16
Lettice, 20:116
Lydia, 16:224; 17:49
Lydia (___), 16:173
Lydia (Breed), 16:97
Lydia (Newhall), 17:49
Lydia (Richards), 16:69
Martha, 18:212; 19:35, 93-95
Mary, 16:15; 17:49; 18:16, 48, 116, 156; 19:221; 20:94, 100
Mary (___), 16:132
Mary (Berry), 18:116
Mary (Briscoe), 18:101
Mary (Cox), 18:16
Mary (Holt), 16:233
Mary (Mansfield), 17:159
Mary Graves, 18:16
Mehitable, 16:239; 17:116
Miriam Breed, 18:11, 12
Nathaniel, 18:156
Nehemiah, 16:16; 17:49
Olive (Hartwell), 18:16
Pamela, 18:16
Pharaoh, 16:173
Phebe (Hardy), 17:116
Phoebe (Burton), 16:198
Rachel, 17:160
Rachel (Roberts), 16:97
Rebecca, 19:175, 221
Rebecca (Aslett), 19:175, 221
Rebecca (Ingalls), 19:51
Richard, 16:156; 17:46; 18:52, 55, 72, 99, 102, 135, 227, 230, 231; 19:28, 51, 138, 155; 20:105, 140, 195
Richard B., 16:24
Richards, 16:46
Ruhamah, 16:116
Ruth, 16:16
Ruth (Gile), 18:156
Ruth (Lindsey), 16:29
Sally (Foster), 19:179
Samuel, 16:96; 17:5; 18:23, 29, 60a, 103, 172; 19:49, 91, 93, 96, 105, 106, 145, 213; 20:102, 103, 114, 134, 135, 196
Sarah, 16:171; 19:144, 229; 20:114, 115
Sarah (___), 20:120
Sarah (Mansfield), 16:198; 18:16
Sarah (Rogers), 16:97
Stanley C., 16:10
Stephen, 19:179, 219, 221, 222
Susanna, 16:177
Susanna (Farrington), 18:16
Susanna (Mower), 16:167
Susanna (Waters), 16:177
Thomas, 16:68; 17:116; 19:34, 93
Tillman B., 17:180
Timothy, 16:146; 18:155, 163; 19:33, 89, 93
Walter, 18:16
Washington Harlow, 18:16
Welcome J., 18:16
Welcome William, 18:16
William, 16:46; 17:159; 18:156
William Frederick, 18:16
William S., 17:166
JOHNSTON
Harry F., 16:106
JOLL
Albert P., 17:207

Annie E. (Smith), 17:207
JONES see also JOANES, 16:111
"Child", 18:87, 89
Abbott, 19:59
Abi, 18:86, 89
Abigail, 18:87, 88
Abigail (Brockway), 18:88
Alice, 16:71
Alice (Friend), 17:161
Ambi, 18:89
Amos, 18:89
Ann (Prior), 18:85, 86
Anna (Pease), 18:87, 89
Annah, 18:89
Annah/Hannah (___), 18:86, 89
Anne, 18:85, 86
Asabel W., 18:83
Bathsheba, 18:86
Benjamin, 18:11, 83-89; 20:28
Bethia, 18:85
Betsy, 19:59
Catherine, 17:119
Charlotte Augusta (Friend), 17:104
Chloe (Giddings), 18:88
Clinton, 17:161
Damaris, 16:117
Daniel, 18:89
David, 18:88
Dina (Philips), 18:88
Ebenezer, 17:119; 18:85, 87, 89; 19:59, 120
Edward W., 17:104
Eleazer, 18:85, 87, 89
Eliza C., 17:56
Elizabeth, 17:119; 18:85-88
Elizabeth (___), 18:85-89; 19:59
Elizabeth (Abbott), 19:120
Elizabeth (Avery), 18:89
Elizabeth (Coit), 18:86, 88
Elizabeth (Hayes), 18:88
Elizabeth (Maloon), 17:119
Elizabeth (Wild), 18:85
Ephraim, 18:85, 87, 89
Esther, 18:89
Evelyn, 18:236
Eviah, 18:89
Ezra, 19:58
Francis, 18:85
Gersham, 18:85, 87, 89
Giles, 18:88
Gustavus, 19:58
Hannah, 16:172; 17:119; 18:85, 87, 149
Hannah (Wellman), 19:58
Hannah (Wheeler), 19:58
Hezekiah, 19:59, 120
Irena, 18:86
Isaac, 18:86, 88
Isabella (Shepherd), 18:88
Israel, 18:83, 86-88
Issecher, 18:88
Jacob, 19:59
James, 20:131
Jemima, 18:88
Jemima (Clark), 18:86, 87
Jerusha, 18:86
Jewett, 19:59
Joanna (Osgood), 16:117
John, 16:173; 17:23; 18:85
John S., 17:104
Joseph, 16:117; 18:86, 88
Judah, 18:89
Lemuel, 18:89
Levi, 18:86

Lois (Wadsworth), 18:88
Lorany (Brockway), 18:88
Lucean/Lucena/Lucrann, 18:86
Maldwyn A., 16:10
Margaret, 17:119
Maria F. (___), 17:104
Mary, 18:84-87; 19:59
Mary (___), 18:85
Mary (Gould), 16:117
Mary (Meacham), 18:85, 86
Mary Baker (Norwood), 18:204
Mary/Marie (North), 18:83
Maryan, 18:87
Mehitabel, 18:89
Mehitable (Gary), 18:85, 87
Mercy (___), 18:87, 89
Michael, 17:119
Nabbe/Abigail (Foster), 17:205
Naomy, 18:86
Nathan, 20:41
Nellie A., 20:147
North, 18:84
North/Nathaniel, 18:85
Priscilla, 18:85, 87
Priscilla (Kirtland), 18:113
Priscilla (Smith), 18:85, 87
Rachel (Bradford), 18:85
Rebecca (___), 18:87, 89
Rebecca (Rolland), 18:88
Remember, 18:84, 85
Rhoda (Parsons), 18:88
Richard, 17:119
Robert, 16:117; 17:119
Russell, 17:205
Ruth, 18:84, 85
Ruth (Ackley), 18:87
Samuel, 18:84-87
Samuel York, 18:204
Sarah, 16:173; 18:224, 225
Sarah (Bancroft), 20:41
Sarah (Bill), 20:147
Sarah (Parsons), 18:86
Sarah (Wood), 18:86, 88
Sibil, 18:12
Silas, 18:89
Simeon, 17:119
Stephen, 18:88
Submit, 18:88
Susan (Farnum), 19:120
Susanna, 18:84
Susanna (Baker), 20:28
Susannah (Adams), 18:88
Thomas, 17:240; 18:83-89, 113, 135
Tryphena, 18:89
William, 17:119; 18:85
William Clark, 18:87, 88
William Haslet, 17:234
Zebulon/Zebblon, 18:86, 89
Zerviah, 18:87
JONSON see also JOHNSON
Anna, 16:173
Samuel, 16:173
JORDAN, 20:144
Adelaide L., 16:151
Anna, 16:116
Ebenezer, 20:144
Elizabeth, 19:226; 20:46
Hannah, 18:220, 221
James, 18:220
Lucy (Tarbox), 20:144
Mehitable (___), 18:220
Robert, 20:46
William B., 20:176

JORLIN see also JOSLIN
Constantine, 17:12
JOSE
Joanna, 20:239
JOSELING
James, 19:112
**JOSELING/JOSLIN/JOSLYN/
JOSELING/JOSELYN/JOSLYN/
JOSLAN/JOSSELYN** see also JORLIN,
GARCELON, 19:60a, 111, 113
Florence I., 20:171
John, 20:171
Roger, 20:71
Roger D., 16:230
Sarah E., 17:111
William, 19:112
JOY
Caroline, 17:178
Hannah, 18:211; 19:50
JOYCE
Dorothy/Dottie, 16:52
JUDD
David, 16:157
JUDKIN
Thomas, 17:240
JUDSON
William, 17:209
JULIAN
Charlene Emma, 17:208
JUMPER
Abigail (Wise), 19:235
Edward, 16:64; 19:235
Susannah, 19:235
Susannah (Parsons), 19:235
William, 19:235

KANAI
Madoka, 17:132
KANE
A. H., 16:50
Martha E. (Longfellow), 16:50
Patricia E., 19:198
KARDELL
Caroline Lewis, 18:66
KEANE see also KEAYNE, KEEN
___, Capt., 17:91
KEARNS
Addie M. (Osborn), 17:187
Timothy L., 17:187
KEASAR/KEASER
___, Mr., 18:222
George, 16:72; 17:20; 18:72, 164
John, 18:222
KEAYNE see also KEANE, KEEN
___, Capt., 16:161
___, Mr., 16:160
R., 19:209
Robert, 19:72, 206-208
KEEN/KEENE see also KEANE, KEAYNE
Avis, 18:12
Elizabeth (Bassett), 18:39
Lois, 18:11
Peter, 18:39
KEHOE
Ann, 19:240; 20:120
KEINE see also KENNY
___, Mr., 19:132
Henrie, 17:14
KELLEY see also KELLY
___, Mr., 17:13
___, Mrs., 17:13
Abiel, 18:240
Anna (Norwood), 18:205

Charles Franklin, 20:228
David, 20:228
David Brainad, 20:228
Elizabeth Wallis (Goodale), 20:229
George Kurd, 20:228
Hannah (Richardson), 20:228
Hannah Upton (Goodale), 20:228, 229
James, 18:205
James Henry, 20:228
John, 18:120
John Bodge, 20:228, 229
John H., 20:228
Lizzie (Rundlett), 20:228
Louise (Festi), 17:57
Louise (Young), 20:228
Marietta, 20:228
Nancy (Munsey), 20:228
Richard, 18:240
Samuel Willey, 20:229
Sarah, 18:120
Sarah (___), 18:120
Sarah Frances, 20:228
Thomas H., 17:57
KELLOGG
Bess, 16:118
Dale C., 17:78
David, 18:86
Elizabeth, 16:178
Elizabeth (Jones), 18:86
Lucy Mary, 18:191; 20:232
Nathaniel, 16:109
Priscilla (Collins), 16:109
KELLY see also KELLEY
Bathsheba (Needham), 20:24
Hannah (Needham), 20:24
James, 20:24
John Henry, 18:58
Margaret (___), 18:58
Michael, 18:58
Moses, 20:24
KELSEY/KELLSE
Rebecca, 18:151, 153
KELTY
Matthew, 16:100
Pamelia (Tufts), 16:100
KEMBALL see also KIMBALL
Sarah, 16:145
KEMP
John, 17:106
Maria (McIntire), 17:106
Martha, 16:42
Mary Elizabeth, 17:106
KEMPTON
Fear (Curtis), 20:55
John, 20:55
John Winslow, 20:55
Margaret (Bartol), 20:55
Mary, 20:55
Mary (Holmes), 20:55
Richard, 20:55
Sarah (Snow), 20:55
Suzannah (Dexter), 20:55
Thomas, 20:55
KENCH
Polly, 18:177
KENDALL
___, Goodie, 17:127
Asa, 18:175
Catherine, 18:175
Elizabeth, 19:215; 20:34
Elizabeth (___), 17:127
Ezekiel, 16:77
Fanny, 20:40

Polly (Worcester), 18:175
Rebecca (Ballard), 16:77
Ruth, 19:214; 20:33
Sarah (Cheever), 19:40
Tabitha, 17:113
Thomas, 16:111; 19:40; 20:185, 190
KENISTON
Allen, 19:196
Mildred, 16:52
KENNAN
Ann, 17:161
KENNEDY
Sarah Elizabeth, 16:52
KENNEY
Deborah (___), 17:43
Dinah, 20:232, 235, 236
Donald S., 17:112; 18:133, 134
Henry, 17:16; 20:235, 236
Israel, 18:56
Josiah, 17:43
Mary, 17:43
Mary A., 17:167
Priscilla (Lewis), 20:235
Susannah (Hood), 18:56
Tabitha, 16:59
KENNISTON
Dorothy, 19:195
KENNY see also KENNEY, KEINE
Ebenezer, 17:98
Joanna, 17:52; 20:178
KENT, 18:85
Anna, 17:83
George W., 20:89
Hannah, 19:178
Herman, 19:170
Josiah, 20:200
Mary (Toogood), 18:165
Mary Alice (Northey), 19:170
Penelope, 18:204
Shirley, 17:208
Thomas, 17:240
KEOUGH
Ann, 19:57
KEPPEL
Mary, 19:107
KERIVAN/KEROVAN, 17:239
KERSHAW, 16:13
KERTLAND
Nathaniel, 18:75; 20:196
Philip, 16:164; 20:195
KESAR/KESER see KEYSER
KESSICK
Elizabeth (Whitman), 17:115
William, 17:115
KETOVER
Karen Sherman, 20:176
KETTELL/KETTLE
Hannah (Kidder), 16:90
James, 17:30
Lucy Caroline, 17:30
Richard, 17:30
Mary (Paine), 17:30
Nathaniel, 16:90
Union, 16:37
KEY
Elizabeth (Marshall), 16:231
John, 16:231
Sarah (Church), 16:231
William, 16:231
KEYES/KEYS
Mary, 19:164
Mary/Polly (Mansfield), 18:212
Olive, 16:212

Sarah, 16:57
Solomon, 18:212
KEYSER/KEYSAR/KEYZER/KEZAR
Abigail (Mitchell), 20:54
Abigail C. (Hall), 20:54
Betsey, 16:212
Charles W., 20:54
Ebenezer, 19:216
Eleazer, 19:216
Flora Etta, 20:54
George, 16:233; 17:147; 18:72, 109, 148, 230; 19:162
John, 20:54
Olive (Scribner), 20:54
William, 20:54
KIDD
___, Capt., 16:229
KIDDER
Aaron, 19:56
Abigail, 16:131
Calvin, 19:55, 56, 59
Clarissa (Wilkins), 19:56
Clarissa Adelaide, 19:55
Clinton, 19:56
Clinton Wellington, 19:55
Ephraim, 16:131
Evelyn (Lewis), 19:56
George Sanford, 19:55, 56, 59
Hannah, 16:6
James, 19:56
John, 17:174; 19:56
Joseph, 19:56
Joseph Calvin, 19:56
Louise, 19:56
Louise (Rice), 19:55, 56
Luther M., 16:111
Lydia, 17:174
Mary (___), 19:56
Mary (Jackson), 17:174
Mary (Wilkins), 19:56
Reuben, 19:56
Samuel, 16:210
Sarah, 16:131
Tabitha, 16:131
Thomas, 19:56
William M., 16:111
KILBURN
Abigail, 17:205
KILCUP
Abigail, 19:37
KILGON
Elizabeth, 18:49
Hannah, 18:49
KILHAM see also KILLAM, KILLUM
Daniel, 16:34
Elizabeth, 16:34
Mary (Safford), 16:34
KILLAM see also KILHAM, KILLUM, 16:63
Abigail, 18:17
Carrie B., 19:168
Daniel, 17:209
Elizabeth, 16:201
John, 19:168
Joseph, 16:63
Priscilla (___), 19:168
Samuel H., 19:168
William H., 19:168
KILLET
Charles, 20:158
KILLUM see also KILHAM, KILLAM
Abigail, 18:169
James, 17:152
Ruth, 17:152

KIMBALL/KIMBEL see also KEMBALL, 17:140; 18:184
Abigail, 18:166
Abigail (Foster), 18:166
Abigail (Inman), 20:227
Abner, 18:240
Anna, 16:212
Anne, 18:57
Anne (Mitchell), 20:227
Anne (Quarles), 18:166
Benjamin, 18:166
Caleb, 16:147
Caroline, 16:148
Catherine (Larrabee), 20:51
Charity (Dodge), 18:166
Daniel, 20:16, 59
Deborah (Bassett), 18:33
Deborah (Pemberton), 19:208; 20:119
Ebenezer, 18:166
Edith, 16:145
Eliphalet, 20:83
Elizabeth, 16:142; 18:207
Elizabeth (___), 16:34; 20:227
Elizabeth (Brown), 18:166
Elizabeth (Carr), 18:166
Elizabeth (Fowler), 18:166
Ephraim, 16:141; 20:136
Esther, 16:142
Eunice, 20:136
Ezra, 16:142
Francis Orville, 20:228
Hannah, 20:119, 136, 167
Hannah (Burton), 20:120
Hannah (Farrington), 17:152
Hannah (Hopkins), 18:166
Hannah (Kimball), 20:136
Hannah (Potter), 20:136
Hannah (Preston), 20:230
Hannah/Joanna, 17:52; 20:178
Henry, 16:34
Huldau (Cue), 16:212
Jacob, 18:57; 20:136
James, 16:142
Jerusha, 18:166
Joanna (___), 18:166
Joel, 20:229
John, 16:143; 17:152; 18:166, 240; 19:87; 20:120
Jonathan, 18:166
Joseph, 20:226, 227
Joshua, 18:33; 20:221
Lois, 18:183
Lucretia, 16:147
Lucy, 16:145
Martha, 16:142; 17:33; 18:166; 20:16, 59, 120
Mary, 16:142; 18:57, 166, 179; 19:158; 20:16, 59, 136, 227
Mary (Friend), 16:141
Mary (Gott), 18:165
Mary (Graves), 20:219, 226
Mary (Ingalls), 19:53
Mary (Lovering), 16:142
Mary (Ober), 19:158
Mary (Tarbox), 16:142; 20:136
Mary (Wentworth), 16:142
Mary (Witt), 18:165
Mehitable, 20:59
Mehitable (Hutchinson), 16:119
Meriam (Stone), 20:227
Miriam, 16:142
Moses, 20:230
Nathan, 16:144

Nathaniel, 16:216; 20:226
Nehemiah, 16:142
Oliver, 19:158
Phebe (___), 16:216
Phebe Ann Putnam (Goodale), 20:229
Philip, 20:218
Priscilla, 16:145; 20:119
Priscilla (___), 18:57
Richard, 16:149; 18:165, 166, 179; 20:16, 51, 59, 120, 136
Samuel, 16:156; 18:165, 166; 20:59
Sarah, 16:145; 17:19; 18:166, 179; 19:58; 20:59, 136, 227
Sarah (___), 20:59, 120
Sarah (Burley), 18:179; 20:16
Sarah (Friend), 16:144
Sarah (Spofford), 20:59
Sarah Frances (Kelley), 20:228
Solomon, 20:219
Stephen, 20:227
Thomas, 18:158, 166; 19:38, 53, 208; 20:119, 136
William, 16:119

KING, 18:36, 138
___, Capt., 17:151
___, Mr., 16:165; 18:164; 19:45
Abigail (Rogers), 16:174
Amos, 17:15
Benjamin, 18:35; 19:84, 85
Daniel, 16:23; 18:94, 99, 135; 19:189, 192; 20:93
Dulzebella, 17:139
Elizabeth, 16:32; 17:229
Elizabeth (___), 16:28
Elizabeth (Guy), 16:23; 20:93
Elizabeth (Marsh), 18:100
Elizabeth (Tuttle), 16:174
Hannah, 16:23; 18:100; 20:27, 93
John, 17:135
Marquis F., 20:176
Mary, 18:227; 19:151
Mary Claire, 17:123
Nabby, 19:159
Ralph, 16:24; 17:46; 18:29, 30, 60a; 19:78, 145; 20:93, 135, 197, 215
Rebecca, 17:15
Rebecca (Hutchinson), 17:15
Richard, 16:174
Rufus, 16:174
Sally G., 19:170
Sally Gerrish, 18:35; 19:171
Samuel, 18:100; 19:171
Sarah (___), 16:166
Sarah (Northey), 18:35; 19:84, 85
Susan, 16:188
Tabitha (___), 19:47
William, 16:140; 18:199, 230; 19:51, 132

KINGMAN
Desire (Harris), 19:236
John, 19:236
Mary, 19:236

KINGSBURY
Abigail (Baker), 18:149
Charlotte (Dennis), 19:231
Chester L., 17:111
Elizabeth, 18:155, 157, 160; 20:179
Elizabeth (Fuller), 20:179
Harry F., 17:111
Henry, 18:157, 161
John, 20:179
Lottie K. (Friend), 17:111
Nathaniel, 18:149
Sarah E. (Joslin), 17:111

Susanna (___), 18:157
KINGSLEY/KINSLEY
Sarah, 19:120
Tabitha, 18:81
KINGSMAN
William, 17:138
KINNEY
Elizabeth, 18:67
Eunice (White), 20:236
Israel, 20:236
Susanna, 18:202
KINSLEY
John, 19:120
Mary, 19:190
Nancy (___), 19:120
Nellie, 19:120
KINSMAN
Farley, 18:207
Jerusha (Norwood), 18:207
Mary, 18:239; 20:120
Mary (Boreman), 18:239; 20:120
Nathaniel, 16:63
Robert, 18:239; 20:120
Susannah, 16:87
KINVILLE
Dorothy M. (Edmands), 17:31
Ronald George, 17:31
KIPPEN-SMITH
Priscilla W., 18:145
KIRBY
John Vernon, 18:135
Sally, 17:29
KIRST
Michael, 16:188
KIRTLAND/KIRKLAND
Alice (___), 18:110
Ann, 18:113
Barbara (___), 18:109
Daniel, 18:113
Ebenezer, 18:110
Elizabeth, 18:111-113
Elizabeth (___), 18:113
Hannah, 18:110-113
John, 17:47; 18:109-113; 19:217
Lydia, 18:113
Lydia (Belden), 18:113
Lydia (Marvin), 18:113
Lydia (Pratt), 18:113
Martha, 18:111-113
Martha (Whittlesey), 18:113
Mary, 17:47; 18:20, 110-113
Mary (Perkins), 18:113
Mary (Rand), 18:112
Nathaniel, 16:24; 17:18; 18:109-113, 135, 164, 167, 231; 19:48; 20:133, 191
Parnell, 17:146; 18:113, 164
Parnell (___), 17:47; 18:110, 113
Phebe (Marvin), 18:113
Phillip, 16:196; 18:72, 109-113, 135; 19:138
Priscilla, 18:73, 109, 111-113; 19:27, 217
Richard, 18:109
Rose (___), 18:109
Ruth (Peirce), 18:113
Samuel, 18:113
Sarah, 18:110-113
Sarah (Chapman), 18:113
Susanna, 18:109-113
Temperance (Buckingham), 18:113
KITCHEN, 18:93
Bethiah (___), 18:91
Edward, 16:208; 17:21
Elizabeth, 16:138

John, 19:191
Robert, 16:138; 18:90, 91
KNAPP
___, Capt., 20:158
Elizabeth, 19:238
Hannah, 16:100
Martha G., 16:100
Mary (Jenkins), 17:59
Samuel, 17:59
KNEELAND see also NEELAND/NELAND
David, 16:179
Edward, 20:225
Joanna (Murch), 16:179
Martha, 20:224, 225
Martha (___), 20:225
KNIGHT/KNIGHTS/NITE/NIGHT, 18:71
Abigail, 18:77
Amery, 19:98
Ann, 18:72, 73
Benjamin, 18:76, 95
Betsey, 18:77
Betsey (Gibbs), 18:179
Charlotte, 20:221
Daniel, 16:71; 18:73, 75-78, 112, 174; 19:27
Elizabeth, 16:71; 17:143; 18:73, 75-78, 95, 174; 19:27; 20:28, 141, 214, 217
Elizabeth (___), 16:71; 18:71-74, 76; 20:214
Elizabeth (Ballard), 17:146
Elizabeth (Pitman), 16:71; 18:73, 75
Elizabeth (Potter), 17:146
Eme/Emma, 19:142, 144
Emma, 18:71, 74, 78
Emma/Eme (Wellman), 18:72, 74
Esther, 18:75
Eunice (Larrabee), 20:114
Francis, 18:72, 74, 78
Grace (Tucker), 18:76
Hannah, 18:72, 75-78
Hannah (___), 18:76, 77
Hannah (Rand), 16:71; 18:73, 75
Hannah (York), 18:76
Jacob, 16:71; 17:19; 18:72-75, 174; 19:27, 175; 20:135, 196, 215
Joanna, 18:77
Job/Jacob, 17:151
Joel, 18:179
Johanna, 18:78
Johanna/Hannah, 18:73
John, 16:116; 18:28, 71-74, 76-78; 19:27, 136, 196; 20:198
Jonathan, 17:14
Joseph, 18:74, 76-78; 19:42, 98
Judith, 18:77
Lucy, 16:218; 17:39
Lucy (___), 18:76
Lucy (Knowlton), 18:76
Lydia, 18:76
Lydia (___), 18:76
Lydia (Libby), 18:77
Lydia (White), 20:232
Margaret Alice (Hunt), 20:32
Martha, 18:74, 77, 78
Martha (Patashall), 18:77
Mary, 16:71; 18:73, 77, 78, 174; 19:27; 20:145
Mary (Fowler), 18:76
Mary (Richards), 19:98
Mary (Winslow), 18:77
Nathan, 20:114
Nathaniel, 18:95
Nehemiah, 20:232

Pattishall, 18:77, 78
Philip, 17:14; 19:98
Priscilla, 18:75
Priscilla (Kirtland), 18:112
Ralph, 20:32
Rebecca, 18:76, 77; 19:27, 175
Rebecca (Rea), 18:73, 75; 19:27, 28
Rebecca (Stevens), 16:71
Rebecca (Waldron), 19:175
Rebecca (Wharton), 18:74
Robert, 20:199
Ruhama, 18:77
Ruhamah (Johnson), 16:116
Ruth, 18:76, 77
Samuel, 18:77
Samuel Patashall, 18:77
Sarah, 18:75, 77
Sarah (Burt), 16:71; 18:73-75
Sarah Emma, 18:76
Susanna, 18:77
Susanna (Barton), 18:95
Susanna (Brown), 18:78
Walter, 19:124
William, 16:71; 17:18; 18:71-74, 76-78, 109, 135, 164; 19:142, 196; 20:193, 194, 214
Winthrop, 18:77
KNIGHTS/KNITES see also KNIGHT
Benjamin, 16:133
Esther, 19:175
John, 18:240; 19:175; 20:197
Joseph, 18:240
Sarah, 19:175
Stephens, 19:175
Thomas, 19:175
KNOLLES see also KNOWLES
Eleanor, 20:69, 76
KNOLTON
Mary, 18:101
KNOTT, 16:13
___, Miss, 19:81
Desmond O'Malley, 17:169
Hannah, 17:98
Margaret Lamar (Middleton), 17:169
KNOW
Elizabeth, 18:172
KNOWLES see also KNOLLES
___, Mr., 16:165; 17:90
Elizabeth (Hart), 20:187
Experience (Chamberlain), 16:116
James, 16:116
John, 16:116; 17:123; 20:187
Martha, 20:96
Samuel, 17:123
Susannah, 16:116
Susannah (Lawrence), 16:117
Tryphena (Locke), 16:116
KNOWLTON
___, Capt., 16:234
Abigail (Bachelder), 18:76
Benjamin, 16:201
Daniel, 16:209
Ebenezer, 18:240
Frances A., 17:106
Jane/Jenny (Parker), 19:90
John, 17:112; 18:76; 19:202
Joseph, 19:119
Lavinia, 18:205
Lucy, 18:76
Martha (Dean), 19:119
Mary, 20:232
Mary (Edmands), 16:209
Nathaniel, 20:225, 226

Susanna, 17:50
Susannah (Dutch), 16:201; 17:50
KNOX
___, Gen., 18:186
Henry, 19:166
KREIS
Herschell, 16:188
KRETSCHMAR
Burton George, 18:176
Elizabeth Bixby, 18:132
Ida (Smith), 18:135, 175
Ida Louise (Smith), 18:176
Randi Susan, 18:176
KRIEGER see also CREEGER
Jacob, 17:64
KROTZER
Anna, 17:56
KUETVIL
Nicholas, 16:133
KUNKSHAMOOSHAW
Abigail (___), 18:60a; 19:145
David, 18:60a; 19:145
KURZWEIL
Arthur, 17:74
KYNER
Stephen B., 16:183

LaBELLE
Robert, 20:24, 91
LACEY/LACY, 16:67
Ephraim, 17:152
Hannah (Gray), 20:213
John, 20:213
Lawrence, 16:68; 20:214
Martha (Wood), 17:152
Mary, 16:66, 194
Mary (Foster), 16:66; 20:166, 167
LACKEY
Richard S., 18:66
LACOUNT/LAVANT
Mary, 19:87
LACY see LACEY
LADD see also LORD
Abigail, 18:159
Abigail (Bodwell), 18:159
Caroline Colburn, 17:175
Daniel, 18:140
Nathaniel, 18:159
Phoebe (Haley), 17:175
Wesley Charles, 17:175
LAFORME
Olive, 20:170
LAIGHTON see LAUGHTON
LAING
Gregory, 16:146; 18:134, 143
LAINHART
Ann, 20:6
Ann S., 16:36; 17:74; 18:137, 138; 19:131; 20:11
Ann Smith, 18:139
LAIS see LAW, 16:0
LAITH/LAITHE/ LATHE/LAYTHE/ LEATHE
Ebenezer, 20:113
Elizabeth (Larrabee), 20:112, 113
Sarah, 17:160; 19:151, 237
LAITON see also LAUGHTON, LEIGHTON
John, 17:45, 48; 18:111
Parnell (___), 18:111
Richard, 17:45
LAKE, 17:202
LAKEMAN
Annette (Hill), 17:110

James, 20:41
John L., 17:110
John W., 17:110
Nancy F. (Friend), 17:110
Rachel (Hawkes), 20:41
LAKEN/LAKIN, 17:78
David, 17:82
Elizabeth (Robertson), 17:81
Eunes (Lakin), 17:85
Eunice, 17:82, 85
Grace (McGill), 16:53
Hannah, 17:81
Harold, 16:53
Jacob, 17:85
John, 17:81
Joseph, 17:82
Lydia, 17:81
Lydia (Parker), 17:81
Mary, 16:115
Nathaniel, 17:82
Shirley R., 16:53
Sibyl, 17:81
Syble (Parker), 17:82
William, 17:81
LAMAR, 17:161
Agnes, 17:169
LAMB
Abigail, 17:200
Jonathan, 19:149
Joseph W., 18:139
Kay, 16:83
Kay (Parkman), 17:180
Lydia, 18:199; 19;149
Lydia (Death), 19:149
LAMBERT
Abigail, 18:46, 47; 19:48
Daniel, 16:32
Eleanor/Ellen, 18:18
Jenny, 16:119
John, 17:212; 18:15; 20:198
Margarett (Horne), 16:32
Martha, 16:53
Mary (Fullerton), 18:24
Mehitable, 18:49, 50
Michael, 18:15, 46, 79
LAMBOARD
Abigail, 17:148
LAMPSON see also LAMSEN/LAMSON, 16:35
Joseph, 20:136
Mehitable (Tarbox), 20:136
Sarah, 19:214
LAMPTON
Jane, 19:139, 141
LAMSEN/LAMSON see also LAMPSON, 19:203
Abigail, 20:142, 238
D. F., 17:39
Elizabeth (Bancroft), 19:214
Hannah, 19:148
Jonathan, 18:70
Mary, 20:33
Naomi (Witt), 18:170
Reuben, 18:170
Sarah, 20:33
LANCASTER see also LANKESTER
Sarah, 18:159
LANDER see also LOUDER
Jonathan, 17:205
Margaret (Henderson), 19:29
Sarah (Felton), 17:205
William, 19:29

LANDRY
  Paul, 16:194
LANE, 20:18
  ___, Mrs., 17:13
  Abigail, 18:202
  Abigail (Norwood), 18:202
  Ada (Allen), 19:119
  Ammi, 18:202
  Andrew, 16:176
  Beth (Gyles), 18:202
  Betsey (Gammon), 18:202
  Betsy (Green), 17:120
  Clara A.(Friend), 17:162
  Deborah (Harraden), 18:200
  Dorcas (Bennett), 18:202
  Ebenezer, 17:120
  Eliza (Perkins), 17:120
  Elwin Dexter, 17:162
  Esther, 19:57
  Esther (Gott), 18:202
  Esther (Griffin), 18:202
  Francis, 18:202
  Hannah (Robinson), 18:202
  Hannah (Wyman), 18:202
  Henry L., 19:119
  Isaac, 18:202
  James, 17:184; 18:202
  Jane (Sullivan), 17:120
  Jerusha (___), 18:202
  Jerusha (Stevens), 18:202
  Job, 16:177
  John, 17:120
  Joseph, 18:169, 200
  Josiah, 18:202
  Judith, 18:202
  Judith (Woodbury), 18:202
  Leah (Prescott), 17:184
  Levi, 18:202
  Margaret, 16:234
  Mark, 18:202
  Mary, 17:184; 19:53; 20:179
  Mary (Ashby), 16:177
  Nancy, 16:176
  Paul C., 17:120
  Rebecca (Witt), 18:169
  Ruth, 18:202
  Samuel, 17:13
  Sarah, 19:119
  Sarah (Story), 16:176
  Susanna, 19:119
  Susannah (Davis), 18:202
  Theophilus, 18:202
  William, 17:184
LANG
  Nancy, 17:201
  Richard, 16:149
  Susan Saunders, 16:148
LANGDON
  Jervis, 19:237
  John, 17:20; 20:46
  Olivia, 19:237
  Olivia Louise, 19:141
  Sarah (___), 17:20
LANGKSFORD
  Sarah, 16:63
LANGLEY
  Esther, 16:87
  Hannah (Vickery), 17:225
  John, 17:225
  Sarah, 17:225
  William, 16:196
LANGLY
  Richard, 19:138

LANGMAID
  Bela, 18:180
  Betsey (Ayer), 18:180
LANGTON
  Mary, 17:178
LANKESTER see also LANCASTER
  Joseph, 20:80
LANMAN
  Joanna, 19:177
LANPHIRE
  Matilda, 18:180
LAPHAM
  Lydia, 20:54
LAREBY/LARRABY see also LARRABEE
  Benjamin, 19:224
  Elizabeth (Felt), 19:225
  Isaac, 19:224
  Jane, 19:224
  John, 19:224
  Samuel, 19:224
  Stephen, 19:225
  Thomas, 19:224
  William, 19:225; 20:155
LARKUM
  Cornelius, 20:198
  Mordecai, 20:198
LAROUQUE
  Benjamin, 17:106
  Clarissa F., 17:167
  Clarissa/Clara Ferson, 17:106
  Lydia (Truebody), 17:106
**LARRABEE/LARRABE/LARRA BY/
LEATHERBEE/WETHERBEE** see also
LAREBY, 18:209; 19:224; 20:52
  ___ (Main/Mains), 19:225
  "Child", 19:227, 228
  Abiel (Arven), 20:49
  Abigail, 19:226; 20:46, 49, 50, 115
  Abigail (Dyer), 20:115
  Abigail (Gooch), 20:51
  Abigail (Pitman), 19:229; 20:114
  Alice (Davis), 20:114
  Amy (Pride), 20:44, 115, 116, 176
  Anna, 20:49, 115
  Anna (Greenwood), 20:50
  Anna (Holden), 19:226; 20:47
  Anna (Williamson), 20:49
  Anthony, 19:229
  Benjamin, 18:226; 19:226, 228, 229; 20:44, 46, 49-51, 112, 114, 176, 177
  Bethiah, 19:226, 227
  Catherine, 20:51
  Catherine (Durrell), 19:227; 20:50
  Catherine (Ford), 19:225-227
  Catherine (Tibbetts), 20:115, 116, 177
  Daniel, 20:47, 48, 112
  David, 20:49, 112, 113
  Deacon John, 20:46
  Deborah, 18:18; 20:44, 114
  Deborah (Ingersoll), 19:226; 20:44
  Deborah (Larrabee), 20:114
  Easter/Esther, 19:226
  Ebenezer, 20:42, 47-49
  Eleanor, 19:228, 229; 20:111
  Eleanor (___), 18:226; 19:225, 227, 228
  Elizabeth, 18:226; 19:229; 20:44, 47-50, 112, 113, 115, 177
  Elizabeth (Felt), 19:224
  Elizabeth (Harding), 20:50
  Elizabeth (Hinchman), 18:226; 19:229; 20:113
  Elizabeth (Jordan), 19:226; 20:46
  Elizabeth (Newman), 19:229; 20:113

  Elizabeth (Rowe), 19:226, 229; 20:114
  Elizabeth (Trask), 20:112
  Elizabeth (Wakefield), 20:51
  Elizabeth (Wesson/Weston), 20:47
  Elizabeth (Winter), 20:114
  Ephraim, 19:225, 226; 20:46, 47, 50
  Esther, 20:51; 19:227
  Eunice, 20:114
  Eunice (Hinman), 20:51
  Ezekiel, 20:114
  Hannah, 16:47; 18:226; 19:229; 20:45, 49, 50, 112, 113, 115
  Hannah (___), 20:176
  Hannah (McKenney), 20:114
  Hannah (Newhall), 20:42
  Hannah (Stone), 20:177
  Hannah H. (Skillings), 20:115
  Hepzibah, 20:47, 48
  Isaac, 19:217, 225-229; 20:48, 111-114
  Isabel (___), 20:49
  Isabella, 20:49, 50
  Isabella (___), 19:225, 226
  James, 20:46, 50, 112
  Jane, 19:225, 229; 20:50, 176
  Jane (Brown), 20:46
  Jane (Rogers), 20:50
  Jane/Jean, 19:226
  Jesse, 20:51
  Joanna, 19:228, 229; 20:205
  Joanna (Littlefield), 20:51
  Joanna (Milbury), 19:225-227
  Joel, 20:51
  John, 18:226; 19:225, 226, 228, 229; 20:45-50, 111, 113-115, 176
  Jonathan, 20:46, 112, 114, 115
  Joseph, 19:228; 20:111-114, 177
  Joshua, 20:177
  Judith (Howard), 20:46
  Lettice (Porterfield), 20:50
  Lucy (Stone), 20:115
  Lydia, 20:46-48, 50, 51, 115
  Lydia (Adams), 19:226; 20:46
  Lydia (Bailey), 20:50
  Lydia (Bliss/Biss), 19:226
  Lydia (Collins), 20:112
  Lydia (Durrell), 19:227; 20:50
  Lydia (Mitchell), 20:115
  Lydia (Wakefield), 20:51
  Margaret, 20:45, 46
  Margaret (___), 19:229
  Margaret (Hather), 18:226; 20:112
  Margaret (Paine), 19:226; 20:45
  Margaret (Wellington), 20:115
  Margaret (Williamson), 20:49
  Martha (Towne), 19:229; 20:111
  Mary, 18:95; 226; 19:228, 229; 20:46, 50, 51, 113-115, 176
  Mary (___), 20:237
  Mary (Baldridge), 20:176
  Mary (Brown/Browne), 18:226; 19:229; 20:46, 113
  Mary (Burns), 20:115
  Mary (Came), 19:225, 226
  Mary (Elithorpe), 19:226; 20:49
  Mary (Holt), 20:112
  Mary (Ingersoll), 19:229; 20:114
  Mary (Jenkins), 20:47
  Mary (Pomeroy), 20:46
  Mary (Simonds), 19:226; 20:48, 49
  Mary (Stevens), 20:111, 112
  Mary/Mercy, 19:229
  Mehitable, 20:46-48
  Mehitable (___), 16:94

Miriam, 20:115
Miriam (Lord), 20:51
Molly (Merrill), 20:46
Nathaniel, 20:50, 114
Olive, 20:114
Phebe, 20:114
Philip, 20:114
Priscilla (Townsend), 19:229; 20:111
Rachel, 18:226
Rebecca, 20:49, 50
Rebekah (___), 20:47
Robert, 20:47
Rubin, 20:111
Sally (Smith), 20:114
Samuel, 18:226; 19:225, 226, 228, 229; 20:36, 44, 46, 48-50, 112, 113
Sarah, 18:226; 19:226-229; 20:44, 47, 49, 51, 113, 115
Sarah (___), 20:112
Sarah (Breed), 19:226; 20:48
Sarah (Given), 20:50
Sarah (Johnson), 19:229; 20:114, 115
Sarah (Wallis), 20:47
Sarah Weeks (Brackett), 20:176
Solomon, 20:114
Stephen, 18:226; 19:224, 226-229; 20:44-46, 48-51, 111, 113-115, 177
Temperance (Walker), 20:51
Thomas, 19:225, 226, 229; 20:44, 114, 177
Timothy, 20:49
William, 19:224, 226, 227; 20:46-51, 115, 176

LARRAME
___, Mrs., 16:64

LARRIMORE
Abigail (Trask), 17:212
Thomas, 17:212

LaRUE
Anne, 19:110

LASKEY/LACHEY
Alice, 19:156
Benjamin, 19:156
Deborah Peach (Northey), 19:171
Elizabeth, 19:230
Jean, 19:156
John C., 19:171
Robert, 19:156
Samuel, 19:156
Samuel Hendley, 19:156
Tabitha, 19:155, 156
Tabitha (Coates), 19:156
Thomas, 19:156
William, 19:156

LASKIN
Anna, 16:119
Edith, 16:116

LASSAR
Marcia G., 20:154

LASSONDE
Elmire Bordua, 20:56

LATHE
Francis, 18:56
Mary (___), 18:56

LATHERBEE see also LARRABEE, LEATHERBEE
Samuel, 19:137

LATHROP see also LOTHROP
Ellen, 19:36-38
Esther, 18:199, 200
Thomas, 19:36, 37

LATTAMORE
___, Mr., 17:96

LATTINE
John, 20:199

LAUD
Archbishop, 18:197

LAUGHTON/LAIGHTON/ LEIGHTON/ LAITON/LIGHTON/LAYTON, 17:45, 18:23, 99, 134; 19:227
___, Mr., 19:155; 20:133, 135, 196
Abigail, 17:46; 18:102
Easter/Esther (Alley), 17:49; 20:206
Elizabeth, 17:47; 20:206
Esther/Easter, 17:46; 18:102
Hannah, 17:46; 18:102; 20:140, 146
Hannah (Silsby), 17:47; 18:102
Hepsibah (Stimson), 17:49
Jacob, 17:49
James, 17:49; 20:206
Jemima, 17:49; 18:102
John, 17:46; 18:100, 102; 20:140
Joseph, 17:48; 18:102
Margaret, 17:48; 18:102
Mary, 17:49
Parnall (___), 17:47
Rebecca, 17:46; 20:206
Samuel, 17:46; 20:133, 196, 206
Sarah, 17:47; 18:102
Sarah (___), 17:45; 18:102, 231; 20:140, 206
Sarah (Dix), 17:47; 18:102
Sarah (Graves), 17:47; 20:206
Sarah (Lenthall), 19:48
Sarah (Redknap), 17:47; 18:102
Sarah (Swayne), 17:48
Thomas, 16:71, 164; 17:17; 18:19, 72, 99, 102, 135, 222, 230; 19:48, 138, 162; 20:133, 134, 140, 194, 196, 206
Thomas, Mrs., 17:234

LAURENCE see also LAWRENCE
Elizabeth, 16:95

LAVANT see LACOUNT

LAVENUKE, 18:134, 135
Mary, 18:59; 19:180
Mary (Divall), 18:59
Stephen, 18:59

LAVERANC
Robert, 20:199

LAVIGNE
Charles, 16:49

LAW, 18:135
Daniel W., 16:110
Elizabeth Lilly (Green), 16:110
Elizabeth Little (Newhall), 16:110
Elsa Margaretha (Hammer), 16:110
Emma Belle (Upton), 16:110
Henry, 16:110
Hubert Newhall, 16:110
Peter, 16:110
Susan/Sukey (Wellman), 16:110
William Bancroft, 16:110

LAWLER
Phyllis, 17:228

LAWNSDALE, 16:13

LAWRENCE see also LAURENCE
Abbott, 19:14
Agatha (___), 18:7
Anna, 20:33
Cecil, 17:31
Cordelia A. (Ward), 20:57
Daniel, 18:21
E., 16:43
Ebenezer, 16:44
Emmeline I. (Ferris), 17:31
George, 18:237
Hannah, 16:115; 17:82
Hannah M., 17:118
Jean Baptiste, 18:7
Margaret (Adams), 18:21
Mary, 18:33, 39
Olive, 18:120
Philip, 18:95
Polly (Estes), 18:95
Roger W., 18:3; 20:12
Samuel, 19:13
Sarah, 16:43; 17:83; 18:112
Susannah, 16:117
William, 16:133; 17:81; 20:57

LAWSON, 19:16
___, Rev., 17:15
Almira, 20:56
Ann, 20:91
Christopher, 17:202

LAWTON, 18:219
Martha, 19:17
Rebecca, 20:96

LAYCOCK, 16:13

LAYTHE see LAITH, 20:113

LAYTON see also LAUGHTON
Abigail, 17:48
Easter, 17:48
Hannah, 17:48
John, 17:48
Margaret, 17:46
Moses B., 19:240
Sarah, 17:48
Thomas, 16:164; 17:45

LEA
J. Henry, 19:211

LEACH
Abigail, 19:119
Anna, 18:77
Arabella (Norman), 19:203
Benjamin, 19:42
Charles, 18:77
Daniel, 18:77
Desire (Bangs), 16:87
Elizabeth, 16:55; 18:101, 112
Elizabeth (___), 19:202
Elizabeth (Flint), 16:55
Elizabeth (Wellman), 20:41
Hannah (Baldwin), 19:203
Jenny (___), 17:178
Joan, 19:153
John, 16:55; 17:14
Joseph, 18:218; 20:116
Lawrence, 16:140; 19:202, 203
Lydia, 17:152
Mary, 20:235
Miriam (Hilton), 18:77
Molle (Babcock), 18:77
Nancy Ann, 17:44
Nathaniel, 17:178
Paul, 18:77
Phelps, 19:203
Rachel, 17:172; 20:180
Rebecca (Knight), 18:77
Richard, 17:14; 18:112
Robert, 19:202, 203; 20:197
Robert J., 16:189
Sally Avis, 16:87
Samuel, 19:202, 203; 20:197
Sarah, 20:92
Sarah (Conant), 16:60a
Sarah (Lawrence), 18:112
Susan (Cheever), 19:42
Susannah (Newhall), 20:116
Thomas, 16:87

LEADBETTER
　Thomas, 17:219
LEADER
　___, Mr., 17:88; 19:45
　Richard, 17:46; 19:189, 195
LEAMING see also LEEMING
　Harriet (Meadowcroft), 16:4
　John, 16:4
LEAMON
　David, 17:190
LEAR
　Louisa, 17:227
LEARNED/LARNED, 16:65
　Catherine, 18:203
　Comfort, 17:43
　Deborah (___), 17:43
　Ebenezer, 17:43
　Isaac, 16:226
　Shirley, 16:8; 17:8
　Shirley D., 20:3
LEATHE
　Sarah, 19:214; 20:33
**LEATHERBEE/LEATHERBY/
　LETHERBEE**, see also LATHERBEE,
　LARRABEE, 20:176
　Ephraim, 16:44
LEATHERLAND
　Elizabeth, 20:225
LEAVENS
　Olive, 16:59
LEAVERMORE
　William, 20:198
LEAVITT see also LOVETT
　Emily, 17:176
LEAZING/LEESONE
　Joan, 18:46, 115, 148, 232; 20:91
LeBLANC
　Steve, 18:6
LECHFORD
　Thomas, 17:88; 19:210
LeCLAIR
　Cherie Ann, 20:56
　Judith A. (Southard), 20:56
　Mildred Gertrude (Green), 20:56
　William Alexander, 20:56
　William Alfred Harry, 20:56
LeCLER, 18:4
LeCLERC
　Michael, 19:176
LeCRAW/LECROIX
　Mercy, 19:84, 169
　Philip, 18:160
LEDDEL
　Henry, 18:237
LEDDEN
　Larry, 16:185
LEE, 18:111; 19:117
　___, Mrs., 19:202
　"Child", 18:112
　Ann, 18:112
　Anna, 18:203
　Anna (___), 19:42
　Benjamin, 19:55
　Downing, 18:77
　Ed, 18:135
　Elizabeth, 19:42
　Hannah, 20:58
　Hannah (Hilton), 16:99
　Hannah (Stone), 18:77
　Henry F., 16:99
　Huldah, 16:100
　James, 17:103
　John, 18:112; 19:202

　Joseph, 19:92
　Lydia, 20:232
　Mary (Dewolfe), 18:112
　Mary (Stevens), 19:55
　Mehitable E., 17:103
　Nancy (___), 17:103
　Phoebe (Brown), 18:112
　Richard, 16:159; 17:112
　Ruth, 19:151
　Samuel, 19:202; 20:199
　Sarah, 18:112
　Sarah (Kirtland), 18:111, 112
　Seward, 20:153, 157
　Thomas, 18:111, 112
　William, 18:57
　William E., 18:138
LEE see LEES
LEECH/LEACH
　Asa, 20:82
　Sarah, 16:137
　Sarah (___), 17:43
LEEDS
　Rachel, 18:39
LEEHEY
　Patrick, 18:132, 134, 137
LEEMING see also LEAMING
　Harriet (Meadowcroft), 16:9
　John, 16:9
LEES/LEE, 16:13
　Daniel, 16:8
　Elizabeth, 16:5
　Hannah (Meadowcroft), 16:4
　James, 16:8
　Jonathan, 16:7
　Lydia (___), 16:9
　Margaret (___), 16:8
　Margaret (Burgess), 16:9
　Mary, 16:5
　Raymond, 16:4
LEESONE see LEAZING
LEET
　Sarah, 18:96
LeFABVRE
　Marie Antoinette, 20:169
LEFAVOR
　George, 20:89
LEFAVOUR, 18:135
　Amos, 19:179; 20:180
　Anna (Delaware), 19:179; 20:180
　Effie Fettyplace, 20:156
　John, 20:154
LEFF
　John, 17:212
LEFFINGWELL/LEFFINWELL see also
　LIPPINGWELL, 19:39
　Michael, 19:39
LEGAGE
　Caroline, 16:53
LEGARE/LEGAREE
　Ann, 18:113
　Daniel, 18:111
　Elizabeth (Kirtland), 18:111, 113
　Francis, 18:111, 113
　Mary, 18:113
LEGER/LEGERE/LEGERY see also
　LEGREE
　Ann, 16:97
　Anna, 18:21
　Petronille, 19:110
LEGG, 16:77
　Elizabeth, 17:96
　John, 17:213; 19:82; 20:187
　Keziah (Ballard), 16:77

　Mary, 17:214
LEGREE see also LEGER
　Mary, 16:46
LEGRO
　Eunice, 16:33
　John, 20:199
LEIGHTON see also LAUGHTON, LAITON
　___, Mr., 19:25
　Elizabeth (___), 17:45
　Elizabeth (Nutter), 17:45
　Hazen, 20:57
　Joanna (___), 17:45
　Levi, 19:238
　Mary Richardson, 19:238
　Olive (Lord), 20:57
　Rebecca, 19:47, 48
　Samuel, 18:78; 20:44
　Sarah (Peavey), 19:238
　Thomas, 17:45
LELAND
　Jerusha, 19:174
LELAR
　Henry, 17:132
LEMIRE/GOUCHER
　Marguerite, 20:170
LEMMON/LEMON
　Hannah (Swett), 18:160
　Joseph, 18:160; 19:84
　Martha (Blackler), 16:179
　Neil C., 16:179
LEMORINER
　John, 20:199
LENARD/LENARDE/LENNARD see also
　LEONARD
　Elizabeth (Harman), 20:70
　James, 20:70
　John, 20:70
　Jordaine, 20:70
　Jordam, 20:70
　Margaret (Fiennes), 20:70
　Martin, 20:70
　Sampson, 20:70
LENER
　Dewayne J., 16:128
LENTHAL/LENTHALL, 18:134, 135
　Ann, 17:234
　Ciceley (___), 17:234
　Nan, 17:234
　Robert, 17:234
　Sarah, 17:45; 19:48
LENTZ
　Cindy Pulsifer, 18:137
LEONARD/LYONARDE see also LENARD,
　20:63, 70, 74, 77
　___ (White), 16:237
　Anna (Barney), 16:237
　Charlotte (Farnum), 16:108
　Elizabeth (Caswell), 16:237
　Etta May (Longfellow), 16:51
　Evelyn, 16:108
　George, 18:210; 18:240a
　George W., 16:108
　Henry, 16:175; 18:80, 230; 20:67, 71, 76
　James, 16:237; 18:80; 20:67, 71, 76
　Jonathan Stewart, 17:50
　Lydia, 16:237
　Margaret (___), 16:237
　Sarah (More), 17:50
　Thomas, 16:237; 18:80, 82
　Uriah, 16:237
　Walter Leroy, 16:51
　William, 16:237
LESLIE, 17:8

LESSARD
  Marguerite (Lemire/Goucher), 20:170
  Noel, 20:170
  Sophie, 20:170
LETHERBEE/LETHERBY see also LEATHERBEE
  ___, Mr., 18:210
  Deborah, 18:20
LEVALD
  Rosette, 17:169
LEVALLIER
  Margaret, 19:230
LEVERETT/LEVERIT
  Benjamin, 19:103
  Hudson, 17:91
  John, 16:201; 17:88; 19:132; 20:78
  Thomas, 18:80
LEVITT
  William, 20:71
LEWIS, 16:153; 17:45; 18:214, 231; 19:29, 69, 145, 173; 20:192
  ___, Mr., 17:215
  "Baby", 19:55
  Abigail, 16:166
  Abigail (___), 18:213
  Abigail (Blaney), 16:85; 18:23
  Abigail (Kilcup), 19:37
  Abraham, 19:146
  Alonzo, 16:71; 17:18; 18:14, 18, 28, 47, 51, 60a, 109; 19:43, 100, 136, 162; 20:194, 195
  Ann, 20:59
  Ann Collins (Ingalls), 18:23
  Anna (Ingalls), 19:109
  Benjamin, 16:99
  Benjamin Richards, 16:100
  Betsey, 16:100
  Betsey (Tarbox), 18:23
  Betty, 18:221; 19:55
  Betty (___), 19:56
  Betty B., 19:56
  Bonnie, 19:55
  Catherine (___), 16:100
  Charity, 18:37
  Clarissa Adelaide (Kidder), 19:55
  Daniel Day, 17:75
  David, 17:160
  Deborah, 18:148
  Deliverance, 18:37
  Ebenezer, 16:166
  Edmond/Edmund, 16:85; 17:41; 18:22, 34-36, 102, 103, 148; 19:50, 79, 105-107, 148, 230; 20:210
  Edward, 18:148
  Elizabeth, 18:22, 23, 148; 19:79, 106, 230, 231; 20:208, 210
  Elizabeth (___), 16:166
  Elizabeth (Brewer), 19:79, 106, 239; 20:210
  Elizabeth (Brooks), 18:148
  Elizabeth (Marshall), 20:180
  Elizabeth (Newhall), 16:100; 18:22; 19:106, 148
  Elizabeth (Thomas), 18:23
  Esther, 18:148
  Evelyn, 19:55, 56
  Ezekiel, 19:37
  Fanna (Ashbee), 16:100
  Frances B., 16:100
  G. H., 18:149
  George, 16:177; 19:136
  George Harlan, 16:100; 17:41; 18:22, 148; 19:106
  Hanna (Marshall), 17:156
  Hannah, 16:85; 17:144; 18:148; 19:79
  Hannah (___), 18:151
  Hannah (Baker), 18:148
  Hannah (Farnham), 16:100
  Hannah (Hallett), 18:211
  Hannah (Knapp), 16:100
  Hannah (Marshall), 16:166; 18:149
  Hannah (Richards), 16:100
  Hepsebah (Breed), 16:85; 18:22; 19:107, 148
  Hepzibah, 16:100; 18:22, 148
  Hepzibah (Tarbox), 18:23
  Isaac, 18:151, 211
  J. W., 16:65; 17:140; 20:131
  James, 18:22
  Jane (Ballard), 16:75
  Joan (Leazing), 18:148
  John, 16:74, 164; 17:41; 18:14, 18, 23, 26, 135, 149, 213, 224; 19:27, 79, 106, 148, 213, 228, 239; 20:196, 210, 217
  John Richards, 16:100
  John Stanley, 19:55
  Jonathan, 16:166
  Jonathan Blaney, 16:85
  Joseph, 16:85; 18:22, 148; 19:107
  Judith, 16:56
  Lois, 17:41
  Louisa G., 16:119; 17:59
  Louise, 19:55
  Lucy Ann, 16:100
  Lydia, 16:100; 19:106, 108; 20:221
  Lydia (Lewis), 16:100
  Lydia (Newhall), 17:160
  Marcus W., 18:191
  Marinda/Martha, 16:60
  Martha, 19:51
  Martha G. (Knapp), 16:100
  Mary, 16:58; 17:42; 18:37, 75, 148-150; 19:57
  Mary (Breaden/Breedan), 19:37
  Mary (Breed), 17:42
  Mary (Burrill), 17:41
  Mary (Cheever), 19:37
  Mary (Davis), 18:211
  Mary (Harris), 16:100
  Mary (Newhall), 18:151
  Mary Jane (Todd), 16:100
  Molley (Felt), 16:85; 18:23
  Nabby (Ingalls), 16:224
  Nancy (Briant), 16:100
  Nathan, 18:151
  Nathaniel, 16:85; 18:23; 19:79, 212; 20:197
  Nelson, 17:180
  Persithe/Persis, 18:148
  Philip, 18:37
  Polly (Alley), 18:26
  Priscilla, 20:235
  Rebecca, 16:100; 18:37; 19:79
  Rebecca (Clark), 18:23
  Rebecca (Lewis), 16:100
  Rebecca (Lummus), 16:100
  Rebecca (Mansfield), 16:100
  Rebekah (Richards), 16:100
  Richard, 16:100
  Samuel, 16:166; 18:26, 148
  Sarah, 17:158, 219; 18:37; 19:79
  Sarah (___), 16:166
  Sarah (Alley), 16:85; 18:22; 19:107
  Sarah (Bassett), 18:37
  Sarah (Glover), 16:223
  Sarah (Hudson), 18:211
  Sarah (Weaver), 17:180
  Silas Dean, 19:55
  Stanley, 19:56
  Susanna, 16:177; 20:180
  Susanna (Meacham), 18:26
  Susannah (Gatchell), 18:211
  Tabitha, 18:22, 25; 19:50, 79, 106, 107
  Tabitha (Russell), 19:230
  Thomas, 16:75; 17:42; 18:22, 26, 116, 148, 150; 19:79, 106, 159; 20:48, 180
  William, 18:23, 37; 19:37, 109
LIBBEY/ LIBBY, 16:153; 17:45; 18:49; 19:118; 20:36, 44, 115, 146
  Aaron, 20:239
  Betsey Elizabeth, 20:239
  Charles T., 19:224
  Charles Thornton, 16:21; 17:202; 19:224
  David, 20:239
  David Freeman, 20:239
  Deborah (Larrabee), 20:44
  Ebenezer, 20:115
  Edna Mertelle (Maloon), 20:239
  Elizabeth (McKinney), 20:239
  Emily (Woodsum), 20:239
  Everett Ethelbert, 20:239
  Hannah (Larrabee), 20:115
  Henry, 20:34
  Joanna (Jose), 20:239
  John, 18:77; 20:44
  Joshua, 20:115
  Lydia, 18:77
  Mary, 20:239
  Mary (Larrabee), 20:114
  Mary (Miller), 18:77
  Miriam (Larrabee), 20:115
  Nancy Marie (Bowman), 20:239
  Shuah, 20:144
  Thomas, 20:114
LIFFORD see also LYFORD
  John, 19:124
LIGHTFOOT/LIGHTFOOTE
  ___ (Bartoll), 20:15
  Francis, 18:230; 19:138; 20:195
  John, 17:230
  Mary (Elkins), 17:230
  William, 20:15, 16
LIGHTNING, 17:204
LIGHTON see LAUGHTON
LILLE/LILLEY/LILLIE/LILLY
  George, 18:101; 19:216, 227
  Hannah, 18:30
  Hannah (Bassett), 18:29, 30
  John, 16:208; 18:30
  Phebe, 18:30
  Rebecca, 18:30
  Sarah, 18:30
  Sarah (Silsbee), 18:101
  Susanna, 18:30
LIMEBURNER
  Grace, 16:41; 19:97
LIMOUSINE
  Antoinette, 20:169
  Hilarie, 20:169
  Marie Antoinette (LeFabvre), 20:169
LINANE
  Michael, 20:56
  Phyllis Ann (Southard), 20:56
LINCH
  Sarah, 18:39
LINCOLN
  ___, Earl, 20:187, 189
  Amasa, 17:120
  Betsy (Stacy), 17:120

Mary, 20:55
Molly (Richmond), 20:118
Nathaniel, 17:120
Susan (Wilbur), 17:120
Zerviah, 18:162
LINDALL
Timothy, 18:60a
LINDBERG
___, Mrs., 16:43
M. W., 16:207
Marcia, 16:8, 26, 29, 71, 74, 92, 95, 199; 17:41; 18:45, 132-134, 136-139; 19:81, 210; 20:52
Marcia (Wilson), 17:174; 20:227
Marcia W., 16:204; 18:133, 135, 164, 208, 222; 19:25, 43, 135, 154, 224; 20:44, 111, 132
Marcia Wiswall, 16:10, 30, 88, 153, 158, 169, 198, 221; 17:45; 18:17, 28, 114, 198; 19:105, 211; 20:26, 34, 204
LINDSAY/LINDSEY/LINDZEY/LINSEY/LINZEY/LYNSEY, 18:14, 23
___, Goodman, 18:166
Abigail, 16:29; 17:159; 18:19, 21, 23, 24; 19:144; 20:29, 100
Abigail (Blaney), 16:29; 19:151
Amy (Graves), 18:18; 19:28; 20:205
Anna (Potter), 19:151
Benjamin, 16:29
Bennony, 18:18
Christopher, 18:15, 18, 135; 19:28; 20:205
Daniel, 19:51
Deborah (Ingalls), 19:51
Eleazer, 16:154, 156; 17:150; 18:18-20, 46; 19:47, 106, 144, 162; 20:111, 112, 134, 196, 197
Eliazer, 20:100
Elizabeth, 18:19
Elizabeth (Maule), 18:19
Elizabeth (Munroe), 18:18
Hannah, 16:29; 18:19
Huldah (Breed), 16:29
John, 16:45; 17:49; 18:17-20; 19:28; 20:196, 205, 221
Jonathan, 16:29
Joseph, 16:29; 18:19, 214
Lydia (Farrington), 17:150
Lydia (Johnson), 17:49
Margaret, 18:18
Margaret (___), 18:18
Mary, 18:18, 19
Mary (Alley), 18:15, 18; 20:205
Mary (Breed), 16:29; 17:145
Mary (Ramsdell), 16:29
Naomi, 19:28; 20:103, 205
Nathaniel, 16:83; 18:18
Nehemiah, 16:29
Phebe, 16:45, 109
Ralph, 16:29; 17:145; 18:19; 19:151
Ruth, 16:29
Samuel, 18:18
Sarah, 16:29; 17:99; 18:15, 18, 19
Sarah (Alley), 18:18, 20; 19:144; 20:100
Thomas Andrews, 16:29
Vicki, 16:187
LINFORD
Francis, 19:48
LINSEY see LINDSAY
LINSFORD
Francis, 17:46
LINZEY see LINDSAY
LIPP
Annie, 17:64

Jacob, 17:64
LIPPIATT
Alice D., 16:108
Herbert C., 16:134
LIPPINCOTT
Mary, 18:39
LIPPINGWELL see also LEFFINGWELL
Abigail, 19:38, 39, 98
LISBREL
Sarah, 19:84, 169
LISCOM/LISCOMB/LISCUM/LYSCOM
see also LUSCOM, 16:95; 18:104
Abigail, 19:80; 20:210
Abigail (Brewer), 19:77-79
Bethiah, 19:80
Ebenezer, 19:80
Gideon, 17:119
Hannah, 19:80
Hannah (___), 19:79, 80
John, 19:79, 80
Lucy (Morgan), 17:119
Mary, 19:80
Mary (___), 19:79, 80
Persis, 19:80
Rebecca (Hudson), 19:80
Samuel, 19:79, 80
Sarah, 19:80
LISTERNICK
Julie Evelyn, 17:175
Roselyn, 16:29; 17:148; 18:137, 228; 19:49
Stanley Edwin, 17:175
LISTON
Mary (Gannon), 19:57
William J., 19:57
LITCHMAN
William Morris, 18:136
LITTFOT
William, 20:199
LITTLE
Aileen May (Longfellow), 16:51
Benjamin, 20:82, 83
Ellenor (___), 16:19
Genvieve, 17:170
George, 16:17
Henry, 18:215
Judith, 18:212, 215
Lydia, 18:215
Lydia (Little), 18:215
Sarah (Barnard), 16:17
Wayne, 16:51
LITTLEFIELD
Aaron, 20:13
Anthony, 20:51
Christopher, 19:167
Daniel, 17:102
Edmund, 19:165
Eva/Dora P., 17:167
Evaline P. (Grimes), 17:167
George W., 17:167
Joanna, 20:51
Jonathan, 20:51
Joseph A., 17:102
Josiah, 20:59
Lizzie H. (Friend), 17:102
Lois, 17:199
Mary, 19:165
Mary (Larrabee), 20:51
Persis, 17:201
Priscilla M. (___), 17:102
Rachel, 18:205
Sally (Steele), 17:178
Samuel, 17:178
Stephen, 20:59

Thomas, 19:165
LITTLEHALE
Abraham, 18:239
Mary (Langton), 17:178
Mary (Stearns), 18:239
Richard, 18:140
Sybil, 18:239
LITTLETON
James Rufus, 19:19
Mary King (Marland), 19:19
LITTLEWOOD
Thomas, 19:131
LIVERMORE
Nancy, 16:85
Samuel, 16:105
LLOYD
Sally, 20:222
LOCKE
Abigail, 20:42
Bethia (Blaney), 16:83
Dorothy (Blake), 16:117
Esther (___), 17:43
Hannah, 16:76
John, 20:97
John P., 17:187
Joseph, 16:83
Margaret, 16:229
Mary, 19:170, 172
Mary (Winn), 20:97
Nathaniel, 16:117
Rebeckah, 16:42
Sanborn H., 16:111
Sarah (Osborn), 17:187
Tryphena, 16:116
LOCKER
George, 16:31; 17:196
Lyder, 16:32
LOCKWOOD
Homer, Mrs., 16:111
LOKER/RIDDLESDALE
Bridget, 18:175
Elizabeth (___), 18:175
Henry, 18:175
LOMAX, 16:13
LOMBARD
Abigail, 18:23
Allen, 16:108
Charles, 16:108
Charlotte, 16:108
Sibyl, 16:108
Sibyll Ainger (Farnum), 16:108
LONG
Ann, 16:228
Elizabeth, 16:225
Enoch, 18:236
H. C., 17:38
Robert, 19:30
Samuel, 18:236
LONGBRIDGE
Joseph, 18:169
Olive (Witt), 18:169
LONGFELLOW
Aileen May, 16:51
Alice Arrogina, 16:50
Alice May, 16:52
Allen, 16:51
Amy Alma, 16:52
Arizina, 16:48
Arizina (___), 16:51
Beatrice (Trottier), 16:53
Betsey (Edwards), 16:48
Cora May (Sargent), 16:52
Donald E., 16:52

Donald P., 16:53
E. J. (Sutte), 16:48
Edward, 16:48
Edwina Victoria (Durgin), 16:52
Elizabeth Elaine (Palmer), 16:53
Elwood Dale, 16:51
Elwood Irwin, 16:51
Emily May, 16:53
Emma (Stevens), 16:53
Esther Elvira, 16:52
Etta May, 16:48
Florence Vernabelle (Gove), 16:53
Frances, 16:53
Frances Amelia (Sonneman), 16:51
Frank, 16:48
Frank Davis, 16:48
Franklin Davis, 16:48
Frederick, 16:53
Gardner, 16:52
Gardner Carl, 16:50
Gardner George, 16:52
George, 16:52
George James, 16:53
George Russell, 16:50
Gladys May, 16:51
Glendon Sargent, 16:52
Harold Allen, 16:52
Irene (___), 16:53
Iva Clara, 16:51
Jacqueline Hope (St. John), 16:53
James, 16:53
James Franklin, 16:50
Jeanne Rita, 16:53
John Franklin, 16:48
Jonathan, 16:48
Jonathan P., 16:50
Joyce, 16:52
Judson, 16:48
Judson P., 16:48
Judson Perkins, 16:49
June, 16:53
Lewis Carlton, 16:52
Madeline Mae (Bean), 16:52
Mammie (Fletcher), 16:53
Margaret (___), 16:53
Marion Zepha, 16:52
Martha E., 16:50
Martha E. (Mooney), 16:50
Martha Eulela (Mooney), 16:49
Mary (Pritchet), 20:236
Mary Ellen, 16:52
Mary Margaret, 16:53
Mildred (Keniston), 16:52
Nathan, 16:48
Netta Wier (Dale), 16:51
Pauline, 16:53
Percival, 16:48
Richard George, 16:53
Ruth, 16:51
Ruth Elizabeth, 16:52
Samuel, 16:48
Sarah Elizabeth (Folsom), 16:52
Shirley R. (Laken), 16:53
Stephen, 20:116, 236
Tabitha, 20:116
Thomas, 16:48
William, 16:48; 18:135
Wynneth (Colwell), 16:51
Yvonne K. (Williams), 16:52
LONGLEY
Abigail, 17:83
Anna, 17:82
Anna (Kent), 17:83
Bridget (Melvin), 17:83
Elizabeth, 17:117
Israel, 17:82
James, 17:82
John, 17:83; 18:231
Joshua, 17:82
Lydia, 17:81
Lydia (Wallingford), 17:177
Lydia (Warren), 17:83
Mary, 17:82
Mary (Parker), 17:82
Miriam (Sawtell), 17:83
Molly (Bartlett), 17:83
Nehemiah, 17:82
Richard, 20:189, 195
S., 17:177
Sarah, 17:83
Sarah (Longley), 17:83
Sarah (Prescott), 17:83
William, 17:82; 18:72, 164, 223, 230; 19:142; 20:184, 196
LONGWORTH, 16:13
LONSDALE, 16:13
LOOK/LOOKE
Bethiah (Larrabee), 19:226, 227
Experience, 18:234; 20:133-136, 141
John, 19:227
Jonathan, 19:227
Mary (Curtis), 19:227
Sarah (___), 20:134
Thomas, 20:134
LOOMIS
Ann Livingston, 18:174
Solomon, 19:218
Sophia, 20:147
LOPER
Susanna, 16:41
LORD see also LADD
Abigail, 20:225
Amanda, 20:57
Betty, 18:49
Elias, 18:49
Elizabeth (Kilgon), 18:49
Elizabeth N., 19:19, 20
George, 17:179
Hannah (Kilgon), 18:49
James, 18:106; 20:57, 216
Joseph, 18:49
Lucy, 18:106
Lydia (Buckland), 18:112
Margaret, 18:49
Mary, 17:179
Mary (___), 16:238; 18:106
Mary (Haskell), 20:216
Melinda, 20:57
Miriam, 20:51
Nancy, 18:134
Nathan, 18:49
Nathaniel, 20:226
Nicholas, 18:49
Olive, 20:57
Olive (___), 20:57
Patience (___), 17:179
Philip, 18:134
Robert, 16:196; 20:225
Ruth, 18:49
Ruth (Hart), 18:49
Sabrina, 20:57
Samuel, 18:90, 112; 20:103
Sarah, 18:106-108
Sophronia Ann, 20:57
Susanna (Collins), 18:112
Susannah, 16:238; 17:119
Thomas, 16:238
William, 18:112
LORING
Ellen Mary (Stevens), 19:57
Ellen/Nell Louise (Higgins), 19:57
Gustavus, 19:57
James, 18:50
Lawrence B., 19:57
Nicholas, 20:115
Prudence Clark (Hart), 18:50
LORR
Clarissa (___), 17:35
James, 17:35
Martha Kimball (Friend), 17:35
William W., 17:35
LOTHROP see also LATHROP, 17:173
___, Capt., 16:201; 18:19
Bethiah, 16:137
Melatiah, 17:172
Sarah (Farrar), 17:172
Thomas, 16:137
LOTT
Ballard, 18:163
LOUDER see also LANDER
Benjamin, 16:145
Mary (Kimball), 16:145
LOUFKIN see also LUFKIN, LOVEKIN
Thomas, 20:200
LOUIS
King, XIII, 17:125
King, XIV, 17:125; 20:12
King, XV, 17:125
LOURVE/LURVY
Peter, 16:133
LOVEJOY, 18:163
Abigail, 20:23
Christopher, 16:68
Eben., 16:68
Hannah, 19:97
Isaac, 19:35
Isaac Upton, 20:213
John, 20:23
Jonathan, 20:213
Joseph, 16:68
Mary (Osgood), 20:23
Naomi (Hoyt), 20:20
Nathaniel, 16:68; 19:33, 34
Rebecca, 19:93
Sarah (___), 19:34
Tabitha (Upton), 20:213
William, 16:68; 19:34, 94
LOVEKIN see also LOUFKIN, LUFKIN
Thomas, 17:76
LOVELACE
___, Gov., 16:18
LOVELL see also LOWELL
Thomas, 20:223, 224
LOVERING, 18:68
John, 16:142
Joseph, 16:76
Mary, 16:142
Mary (Kimball), 16:142
LOVETT see also LEAVITT
Benjamin, 20:154
J., 20:157
J. B., 20:159
Joanne, 20:58
John, 20:198
Joseph, 20:198
Mary, 16:137; 19:221
S. P., 20:159
Samuel P., 20:153

LOVEWELL
  Nehemiah, 20:118
LOVISS
  Sarah B., 20:222
LOW/LOWE, 20:17, 18
  "Daughter", 17:110
  Abigail (Fellows), 17:19
  Amanda (Friend), 17:110
  Amanda D., 17:111
  Daniel, 19:127
  David, 17:12
  David W., 17:110
  David Wilbur, 17:111
  Eliza (Davis), 17:111
  Elizabeth, 16:220
  Ellen H., 17:109
  Ellen Pearce, 17:111
  Esther (___), 17:110
  Frank D., 17:110
  Frank Dale, 17:111
  Frederick, 17:111
  Frederick Gilman, 17:111
  George, 17:110
  Jane G., 17:165
  John, 16:147
  Joseph, 20:142
  Julia F., 17:111
  Laura Burbank (Friend), 17:110
  Lucy (Lord), 18:106
  Margaret, 16:177
  Martha, 17:110; 19:179
  Nathan, 18:106, 107
  Ned, 19:185
  Sarah, 19:104
  Susannah (Haddock), 16:147
  Thomas, 17:19
LOWATER
  Elias, 16:118
  Elizabeth (Perkins), 16:118
LOWD
  Dorcas (Hanson), 19:20
  Laura Etta, 19:19, 20
  Sylvester, 19:20
LOWE see LOW
LOWELL see also LOVELL, 18:135
  Abigail, 18:239
  Alexander, 20:225
  Elijah O., 17:187
  Eliza C., 17:187
  Elizabeth (Morss), 18:235-237
  George, 18:235, 236
  John, 18:236; 19:14; 20:224
  Mary, 18:236
  Mehitable (Osborn), 17:184
  Percival, 19:115, 192
  Samuel, 18:236
  Thomas, 20:223
LUCAS see also LUKIS
  Annabella, 17:166
LUCE
  James, 17:59
  Lydia (Nye), 17:59
LUDDEN
  Eunice, 19:46
LUFF
  Bridget, 16:137
  John, 19:191
LUFKIN see also LOUFKIN, LOVEKIN, 17:139; 20:17, 18
  Caleb, 16:176
  Ebenezar, 18:180
  Eliza (Decker), 17:167
  Emma, 17:167
  George, 17:167
  Harriet, 17:108
  Lois, 18:205
  Mary, 16:176
  Moses, 18:135
  Sarah (___), 18:180
  Sarah (Hill), 16:176
  Thomas, 17:240
LUKIS see also LUCAS
  Mary, 17:57
LULL
  Maria (Prince), 18:218
  William, 18:218
LUMMUS/LUMUS
  John, 16:31
  Rebecca, 16:100
LUND
  Betsey, 20:138
LUNSFORD
  ___, Mr., 20:71
LUNT
  Daniel, 19:119
  Elizabeth, 19:119
  Margery (Greenleaf), 19:119
  Samuel, 19:161
LURVEY/LURVY see also LOURVE
  Abraham, 16:133; 20:58
  Anna, 20:58
  Jacob, 18:135
  Lydia, 20:58
  Molly, 20:240
  Peter, 18:200
  Rachel, 20:58
  Ruell (Harraden), 18:200
  Sarah, 20:58
  Sarah (Pulcifer), 20:58
LURVY
  Love, 16:64
LUSCOM/LUSCOMB/LUSCOME see also LISCOM
  Benjamin, 16:102
  George Alfred, 17:33
  John C., 17:33
  John H., 17:33
  Lydia (Richards), 16:102
  Mary, 20:58
  Sarah (Friend), 17:33
  Sarah A., 17:33
  William F., 17:33
LUSHMAN
  Thomas, 18:136
LUSTIG
  Mildred (Keniston), 16:52
LUTON
  Melissa Pope (Garrett), 19:233
  Tanis Monique, 19:233
  Timothy, 19:233
LUX
  William, 18:90
LYE
  Anna (Hart), 18:50
  Hannah (Ingalls), 19:51
  Joseph, 16:102; 18:50; 19:51
LYFORD see also LIFFORD, 19:124
  James O., 16:21
  John, 16:60a
LYMAN
  Benjamin, 18:34
  Mary, 18:34
  Mary (Bassett), 18:34
  Medad, 18:34
  Ruth (Holton), 18:148
  Thankful (Pomeroy), 18:34
  Thomas, 18:148
LYNAN
  Gertrude (Clarke), 20:172
  Joseph, 20:172
  Mary E., 20:172
LYND/LYNDE/LYNE
  Abigail, 19:100
  Amos Porter, 19:177
  Benjamin, 18:208
  Elizabeth, 19:148
  Elizabeth (Mower), 17:43
  Hepsibah (Newhall), 20:42
  Isobell (Potter), 19:153
  Jabez, 20:42
  John, 19:153, 177
  Jonathan, 17:43
  Joseph, 18:158; 19:177
  Louisa Jane, 19:177
  Mary (Porter), 19:177, 178
  Nancy (Jenkins), 19:177
  Nathaniel, 17:213
  Nicholas, 19:102
  Samuel, 20:79
  Sarah, 19:41, 102
  Sarah Ann (Sprague), 19:177
  Simond, 17:213
LYNSEY see LINSEY
LYON
  Elijah, 18:125
  Hannah (Bessom), 19:231
  John, 17:143
  Martha, 16:110
  Mary, 16:210
  Mehitable (___), 18:125
  Nehemiah, 18:125
  Thomas, 19:231
  William, 17:143
LYONARDE see also LEONARD
  John, 20:70
LYONS
  Mary, 18:106, 108
LYSCOM/LYSCOMB see LISCOM

MABER
  Mary, 20:231, 233, 234
  Mary (Allen), 20:233, 234
  Richard, 20:233, 234
MACALLOM
  Macam, 20:197
MacDONALD/MACDONALD
  ___, Mrs., 16:43
  Chris (___), 19:58
  Ella (Amy), 18:239
  John, 18:239
  John R., 19:58
  Lillian (Masse), 19:58
  Marion, 18:133, 135-137
  Marion A., 16:29; 17:40; 20:42, 205
MACE, 17:179
  Isaac, 17:37
  Matilda (Garland), 17:37
  Suzie A., 17:37
MacFARLAND
  Moses, 18:106
MACINNIS
  Karen, 20:16
MacINTIRE/MACINTYRE/MacKINTIRE see also MACKENTIRE
  Betsey/Betty (Aborn), 16:93
  Daniel, 16:89
  David, 20:225, 226
  Ebenezer, 19:217
  Jean, 17:170

John, 16:157
Martha (Graves), 20:225, 226
William, 16:94
MACK see also MURCH
John, 18:204
Ruth (Norwood), 18:204
MacKENNA/MacKENNEY
Ann (Kennan), 17:161
Kenneth, 17:169
Margaret Alice, 17:161
Michael Henry, 17:161
MACKENTIRE see also MacINTIRE
Abigail (Fraile), 17:21
Daniel, 17:21
Jonathan, 20:225
Martha (Kneeland), 20:225
Mary (___), 20:226
Philip, 20:202, 226
Samuel, 20:202
Timothy, 20:202
MacKENZIE
Daniel, 16:36
MACKEY
William Harvey, 17:135
MACKINDIAH
Jonathan, 19:218
MacKINTIRE see MacINTIRE
MACKWORT
Samuel, 16:23
MACKWORTH
Elizabeth, 16:23
Jane (___), 16:23
MACLEAN
Norman, 19:13
MacLEOD
___ (McKenzie), 20:55
Elizabeth, 20:54
Roderick, 20:55
MacLYSACHT
Edward, 17:137
MacMAHON
Elizabeth, 17:235
MACOMBER
Chloe (Smith), 16:239
Elijah, 16:239
Mehitable (Johnson), 16:239
MACY
Thomas, 16:15; 20:80
MADISON
___, Pres., 17:100
MADOX, 17:38
MAHAN
Catherine (McDermot), 17:235
James, 17:235
Mary, 17:235
MAHEW
Benjamin, 17:41
Rebecca (Mower), 17:41
MAHONEY
Huldah (Estes), 18:95, 97
Timothy, 18:97
MAINARD
Mary, 17:82
MAINS
Abiah, 16:63
John, 19:225
MAKIE
John, 16:151
MALL
Elizabeth, 19:83
MALLETT
Margaret, 16:211
Martha, 20:220

MALOON
Anna, 17:199
Daniel, 17:199
Edna Mertelle, 20:239
Elizabeth, 17:119
Eunice, 17:199
Eunice (Osborn), 17:199
Flora Ann (Carleton), 20:239
Oliver Libby, 20:239
Rachel (Adams), 20:239
Sarah Shores (Bragg), 20:239
Solomon, 20:239
Stephen, 20:239
William, 17:199
MANCHESTER
Earl Of, 19:202
Elizabeth (Potter), 19:150
James, 19:150
MANGIONE
Jerre, 16:128
MANN
Carrie, 17:53
Carrie Cutter, 17:177
Charles C., 16:161
Charles E., 16:158
Elizabeth (Emery), 17:54
Elizabeth (Pittman), 17:53
Ezekiel, 17:53
Ezekiel Fitzgerald, 17:177
Harriet (Fitzgerald), 17:53
Joseph, 17:53
Martha (Cutter), 17:53
Martha Wise (Cutter), 17:177
Peter, 17:54
Vashti, 16:81
MANNES
Clara (Damrosch), 17:170
David, 17:170
Marya, 17:170
MANNING, 17:51; 18:135, 136
___, Capt., 18:112
Arthur H., 16:48
Eliphalet, 16:91
Elizabeth, 16:91
Hannah, 16:91
Hannah (Aborn), 16:91
Hannah (Twiss), 16:37
Isaac, 16:91
Jacob, 18:101
James, 18:207
John, 16:91
Lydia (Pike), 16:91
Mary, 18:101
Mehitable (Spalding), 16:91
Nicholas, 18:111
Rebecca, 16:91
Rebeckah (___), 16:91
Samuel, 16:91; 18:240
Sarah (Goodwin), 16:91
Sarah (Pike), 16:91
Sarah (Stone), 18:101
Sophia Wheeler (Norwood), 18:207
Thomas, 16:37
William, 16:91
William H., 16:91; 17:78;
MANSFIELD, 20:36
___, Capt., 20:157
___, Mr., 19:37
Abigail, 17:159
Abigail (Lindsey), 17:159
Amos, 17:27

Andrew, 16:93; 17:46; 18:72-74, 114, 115,
  147, 165, 222, 223; 19:26-28, 47, 137,
  213; 20:39, 132, 184, 195, 205, 215
Ann (Roby), 18:152; 19:101
Anna, 17:159
Anna (___), 19:41
Anna (Johns), 17:159
Bethia, 19:98
Bethia (Gedney), 17:149
Betsey, 18:212
Betsy (Ellerson), 18:212
Charity, 18:23; 19:145
Charity (Payson), 18:212
Daniel, 16:44; 17:46; 18:24, 103, 150, 212,
  213; 19:28, 106, 159, 229; 20:102-105,
  111
David, 18:212; 19:148, 157
Deborah, 18:165
Deborah (Whipple), 17:159
Dolly Carter, 20:41
Ebenezer, 17:99; 18:211; 19:50
Edith G., 17:30
Elizabeth, 17:46; 18:36; 20:104
Elizabeth (___), 16:164
Elizabeth (Burchsted), 16:95
Elizabeth (Stocker), 17:30
Elizabeth (Walton), 16:60a
Elizabeth (Williams), 16:80
Ella Josephine, 17:30, 31
Ephraim Sylvester, 17:30
Hannah, 16:85; 17:159; 18:102; 19:108
Hannah (___), 19:41
Hannah (Browne), 18:226, 227
Hannah (Gibbs), 18:212
Hannah (Williams), 17:113; 18:211; 19:50
Henry, 18:212
Isaac, 16:80; 17:101; 19:41, 42, 53
Israel, 18:212
Jacob, 18:212
James, 16:80; 17:138
James S., 17:149; 18:212
Jane, 18:11
Jane (Goodridge), 20:211
Jno., 16:196
Joanna, 18:212
Joanna (___), 20:103
Joel, 18:212
John, 18:72, 214, 217; 19:100, 108, 145,
  228; 20:112
Jonathan, 16:86; 17:159; 18:22
Joseph, 16:80; 17:18; 18:46, 150, 165, 211,
  225; 19:157, 217, 227; 20:103, 112, 196
Liddy, 17:145
Lois, 18:212
Lucy, 20:42
Lydia, 17:149; 18:212; 19:171
Lydia (___), 18:212
Lydia (Norwood), 18:212
Margaret, 16:238
Margaret (___), 19:28
Martha, 16:27; 18:227, 228
Martha (Johnson), 18:212
Martha (Stocker), 16:167
Mary, 17:148; 18:227; 19:41, 107, 239
Mary (Benighton), 19:145; 20:33, 36
Mary (Brown), 17:159
Mary (Clapp), 19:41
Mary (Gibbs), 18:212
Mary (Hart), 17:159; 18:47
Mary (Hawkes), 18:227
Mary (Ingalls), 19:53
Mary (Newhall), 16:238; 20:33, 35, 39, 41
Mary (Norwood), 17:99; 18:211

Mary (Piper), 18:212
Mary (Rhodes), 18:212
Mary Elizabeth, 17:104
Mary/Polly, 18:212
Matthew, 16:88
Nathaniel, 17:159
Newell, 18:212
Peggy, 17:159
Polly, 18:212
Rebecca, 16:100; 17:159
Rebecca (Alley), 18:22
Relief (Cowan), 18:212
Robert, 16:80; 17:30; 18:22, 28, 148; 19:195
Rufus, 17:160; 19:76
Ruth (Cheever), 19:41, 42
Sally, 18:212
Samuel, 17:46; 18:212, 228; 19:41, 145; 20:36, 133, 196
Sarah, 16:198; 18:16
Sarah (Breed), 17:145
Sarah (Cheever), 19:100
Sarah (Edmands), 17:27
Sarah/Sally (Fuller), 17:160
Susannah (Wilson), 18:212
Thomas, 18:212, 227; 19:101; 20:111
Trevitt, 17:99; 18:212
William, 16:93; 17:159; 18:212
MANSON
Polly (Hart), 18:50
Richard, 18:50
MANSUR
Elizabeth, 18:159
MANWARING
Charles W., 16:186
Charles William, 19:218
MARBLE
Abigail, 18:117
Asenath (___), 20:38
Cyrus, 19:88
Daniel, 17:201
Dorcas, 19:88, 120
Elizabeth, 18:169
Enoch, 19:88
Esther, 17:198
Esther (Putnam), 17:201
Fanny, 19:88
Hannah, 16:214
Hannah (Parker), 19:88
Isaac, 19:88
Jonathan, 18:169
Joseph, 16:68
Louisa, 16:240
Mark, 20:38
Mary, 19:88
Nabby, 19:88
Naoma, 19:88
Perses, 19:88
Phebe, 19:97
Samuel, 16:68; 18:117
Sarah, 19:88-90
Sarah (___), 18:169
MARCH
Nathaniel, 18:24
Tabitha, 19:160
MARCHANT, 17:139; 20:18
Abigail Kimball, 17:35
Albert, 17:34
Benjamin William, 17:35
Charles, 17:34
Daniel, 16:64
Emeline, 17:34
Emeline (Marchant), 17:34

Emily Friend, 17:34
Epes William, 17:34
Frederick Norwood, 17:35
Hannah (___), 17:34
Hannah P. (Shephard), 17:34
James, 17:34
Mary (Friend), 17:34
Mary Friend, 17:34
Rebecca (Haskell), 17:34
Richard Friend, 17:34
Sam'l, 16:64
Sarah E., 17:165
Simeon, 17:34
William, 17:34
MARDEN
Barbara, 19:54
Barbara B., 18:138
John, 20:54
Rachel (Shaw), 20:54
Sarah, 20:54
MARDENBOROUGH
Elizabeth, 17:58
Elizabeth (Martin), 17:58
Giles, 17:58
Sarah, 17:58
MARGERISON, 16:13
MARIE
Martha Celia, 16:149
MARION
Dorothy (Fuller), 17:157
John, 17:157
MARJERISON, 16:13
MARKAM
Irene, 18:86
MARKS
Hezekiah, 18:178
John, 18:178; 20:196
Joseph, 18:178
Joseph Hopkins, 18:179
Mary (___), 18:178
Richard, 18:178
Sarah (Holt), 19:220
MARLAND, 16:66
Abby Billings, 19:19
Abigail Northey, 19:19
Abraham, 19:17-20
Abraham Stewart, 19:19, 20
Albina (Frazier), 19:20
Andrew Stewart, 19:19
Anna Laura (Shattuck), 19:20
Anna Theresa (Rock), 19:20
Anne Brierly, 19:17
Bannie (___), 19:19
Beatrice (Wood), 19:20
Charles Edward, 19:20
Charles Hitchcock, 19:19, 20
Charles Northey, 19:20
Charlotte Amy, 19:20
Christina Evelyn, 19:20
Clifford R., 19:81
Clifford Raymond, 19:20
Dunnie (Taylor), 19:20
Edith (Polis), 19:19
Edna Louise, 19:20
Elizabeth (Carr), 19:17
Elizabeth (Hill), 19:20
Elizabeth (Scanlon), 19:20
Elizabeth Caroline, 19:18
Elizabeth N. (Lord), 19:19, 20
Eva M., 19:19
Frances Anne, 19:18
George Abbott, 19:19
Hannah Jane, 19:18

Harold Webb, 19:20
Harriet Fletcher, 19:18
Harry Freeman, 19:20
Helen, 19:19
Helen (Collins), 19:20
John, 19:17-19
John Thomas, 19:18
Jonathan, 19:17
Joseph Lowd, 19:20
Julia Ann (Nutter), 19:19
Julia Maria, 19:18
Laura Etta (Lowd), 19:19, 20
Laura Northey, 19:20
Lucretia, 19:18
Lucretia (Dorr), 19:17, 18
Margery, 19:20
Martha (Lawton), 19:17
Martha Lawton, 19:17
Martha Punchard, 19:19
Mary (Sykes), 19:17
Mary Bertody, 19:18
Mary King, 19:19
Mary Sykes, 19:17, 19
Roger Freeman, 19:20
Roy John, 19:20
Ruth Anderson (Upton), 19:20
Salome Jane (Abbott), 19:19
Sarah (Northey), 19:17, 19, 171
Sarah Dorothy, 19:20
Sarah Fisher, 19:18
Sarah Helen, 19:19
Thomas, 19:17
William, 19:18, 19
William Sykes, 19:17, 19, 20, 171
MARRETT
Susanna, 20:212
MARRINER
Mary (Graves), 20:220
Samuel, 20:220
MARRIOTT
Abigail, 20:179
MARRONE
Stephen, 18:139
MARROW
Lydia, 16:132
MARS, 19:68
MARSDEN, 18:187
MARSH
Abigail, 18:100
Alice (___), 18:100
Alice (Booth), 18:100
Benjamin, 18:100
Bethia, 18:101, 174
Caleb, 18:75
David, 16:133
Ebenezer, 18:100
Elizabeth, 18:100
Elizabeth (Wheeler), 18:100
Esther (Osborn), 17:198
Ezekiel, 17:20; 18:100
Grace, 18:149
Hannah (Buffington), 18:100
Hannah (King), 18:100
John, 17:193; 18:100, 101, 149, 174
Jonathan, 17:198; 18:100
Joseph, 20:118
Lucius B., 17:92
Mary, 18:100
Mary (Silsbee), 18:100, 101, 174
Mary (Very), 18:100
Onesiphorus, 18:141
Rebecca (Gould), 18:100
Samuel, 18:174

Susanna (___), 18:101
Susanna (Skelton), 18:100, 174
Susanna (Sprague), 18:75
Susanna (Travis), 18:174
Zachariah/Zachery, 18:100, 101, 174
MARSHALL, 17:51; 18:132
   ___, Capt., 17:234; 18:223; 19:25; 20:133
Abiel, 16:159
Abigail, 16:158, 234
Abigail (___), 16:160
Abigail (Barney), 18:165
Abigail (Norwood), 18:203
Alice (___), 16:160
Alice (Potter), 19:153
Alice (Willey), 19:208
Anna, 16:160
Anna (___), 16:159
Anne/Annie, 16:76
Benjamin, 16:159; 17:76; 18:174; 20:224
Bethia (Goodhue), 16:160
Caleb, 18:203
Catherine (Learned), 18:203
Damaris (___), 16:232
Dorcas (___), 16:161
Ebenezer, 16:76; 18:203
Edmond/Edmund, 16:233; 18:174; 19:196
Edward, 16:159; 19:136, 212; 20:197
Eliakim, 16:160
Elizabeth, 16:103, 234; 18:203; 19:82, 142, 153; 20:180
Elizabeth (___), 16:230
Elizabeth A., 16:103
Elizabeth/Betsy (Richards), 16:103
Ellen Frances (Tarbox), 20:147
Ezekiel, 16:234
Frances, 16:160
Francis, 18:203
George, 16:103
Hannah, 16:158; 17:156; 18:149, 180
Hannah (Atkinson), 16:233
Hannah G. (Newhall), 16:103
Hester, 18:166
Isaac, 16:233
J. Craig, 16:230
Joan/Joanna (___), 16:158, 162, 199
Joanna (___), 16:159; 18:136, 174
Johana, 16:233
John, 16:158, 231; 17:85
Jonas, 17:84
Joseph, 16:159
Lucy (Tyler), 18:203
Mary, 16:158, 232; 17:51; 18:149, 151, 152, 199, 201; 19:149
Mary (___), 17:84
Mary (Burrage), 16:233
Mary (Parker), 17:85
Mary (Swain), 16:159
Mehitable (Haven), 16:76
Mehittabel, 16:233
Millicent (___), 18:174
Nicholas, 19:153
Peter, 16:160; 18:165
Prudence, 16:159
Prudence (Woodward), 16:159; 20:224
Rachel, 16:160
Rebecca, 16:158, 233
Rebecca (___), 16:158, 168; 18:151
Robert, 16:103
Ruth, 16:158; 17:85
Samuel, 16:158; 18:203
Sarah, 16:74, 233; 19:207, 208
Sarah (Perkins), 16:160
Sarah J. (Mason), 16:10

Sherry, 18:134, 137, 138
Sherry S., 17:114; 18:137
Sherry Schaller, 16:56; 18:134
Sibyl, 17:85
Susanna, 16:158
Thomas, 16:120, 203; 17:46; 18:72, 99, 111, 114, 115, 136, 148, 151, 166, 167, 174, 222, 230, 231; 19:27, 46, 75, 138, 155, 163, 207, 208, 210, 212; 20:147, 184, 187, 189-192, 194, 196, 206, 207
Unis (Rogers), 16:233
Warren Webster, 16:103
William, 16:103; 20:186
MARSTEN
John, 19:88
Mary, 19:88
MARSTON/MARSTONE
Benjamin, 16:90
Bethia, 16:85
Deborah, 19:238
Deborah (Marston), 19:238
Elizabeth (Jarvis), 16:85
Elizabeth (Richards), 16:101
Ephraim, 18:159, 237
Eunice, 16:85
Hannah, 16:85; 20:167
Hannah (___), 16:132
Hannah (Brown), 17:235
Jacob, 16:68; 18:1159, 161, 162; 19:33
James, 16:85
Jeffs/Jeptha, 16:84
Jeremiah, 19:238
John, 16:68; 17:235; 18:158, 159; 19:34
Jonathan, 16:85
Jonathan Blaney, 16:85
Joseph, 16:68; 17:235; 18:159
Lucinda (Danforth), 16:85
Lucy Ann, 17:188
Martha (___), 18:158
Mary, 16:81; 18:156, 158, 159
Mary (Mason), 19:238
Mary (Osgood), 20:166
Mary (Rowell), 17:235
Mary Jane (Brown), 17:235
Mercy, 16:84
Nathan Washington, 16:84; 18:158
Olive Jane, 19:238
Orrin C., 19:238
Ruth, 16:85
Sarah, 16:84
Sarah (Blaney), 16:83
Susan M., 19:238
Susan M. (Marston), 19:238
Thomas, 17:235
William, 16:101
MARTAIN
Abraham, 18:162
Joseph, 18:162
MARTIN/MARTINE/MARTRY/ MARTYR/MARTYN, 18:133; 20:120
   ___, Mrs., 17:12
Alice (___), 20:21, 23
Ann (___), 16:202, 203
Ann (Graves), 20:224
Ann (Potter), 19:153
Ann/Nancy Larkin, 19:231
Damar (Storey), 19:179
Deborah, 17:148
Elizabeth, 17:54; 18:162; 19:95
George, 16:15; 17:55; 19:238; 20:224
Grace Alice (Farr), 16:151
Hannah, 19:239

John, 16:15; 17:214; 19:81, 82, 88, 237; 20:199
John H., 20:228
Joseph, 18:213; 19:92, 179
Josiah, 18:214, 215; 19:75
Lydia, 19:238
Lydia (___), 17:178
Lydia (Burrage), 18:213, 214
Maggie L. (Mooney), 16:49
Margaretta, 17:53
Maria Preston (Goodale), 20:228
Martha, 17:120
Mary, 16:15; 17:159
Mary (Hoyt), 17:54
Mary (Weed), 16:15
Nancy A. (Rogers), 16:60
Peter, 19:82
Rebekah, 19:231
Richard, 17:54
Robert, 19:82, 231
Samuel, 16:68; 19:82; 20:22
Sarah (Northey), 19:81, 82, 237
Solomon, 17:204
Susanna (North), 16:15; 17:55; 18:136
Susannah, 20:55
Thomas, 17:97; 19:82, 153
William, 17:89
William H., 16:60
William Paul, 16:151
MARTINO
Caroline/Carolyn, 18:133, 137, 138
MARTRY/MARTYR/MARTYN see MARTIN
MARVIN
Lydia, 18:113
Phebe, 18:113
MARYFIELD
Maria, 17:239
MASCOLL/MASKAL see also MASKELL
John, 16:35
Joseph, 17:231
Ruth (Purchase), 17:231
MASCONOMET, 16:193; 17:75
MASE
Enoch, 16:64
MASERVEY
Ephraim, 16:214
Patty/Martha (Friend), 16:214
MASKELL see also MASCOLL
Joseph, 16:133
MASON
   ___ (Heath), 17:235
   ___, Miss, 20:30
Andrea, 19:184
Betty, 18:138
Elias, 19:193
John, 16:103; 17:155
Jonathan, 19:131
Lemuel Bickford, 18:136
Mary, 17:148; 19:238
Nathaniel, 17:235
Sarah J., 16:103
Thomas, 16:98; 18:94
MASQUENOMOIT, 19:203
MASSE
Lillian, 19:58
MASSEY see also MUZZEY, 18:136
Benjamin, 17:158; :217
Hart, 16:113
Jeffry, 19:196
John, 16:136
Lucy (Swain), 16:113
Susanna, 18:217

Susanna (___), 18:217
MASTEN/MASTENS
Jacob, 18:161, 162
MASURVEY
Nathaniel Friend, 16:214
Sarah Berry (Stocker), 16:214
MASURY
Abigail, 16:218
Abigail (___), 16:218
Abigail (Abbott), 16:218
Augusta F., 16:218
Francis Macomber, 16:218
James, 16:218
Joseph, 16:218; 18:210
Lucy Jane, 16:218
Lucy Jane (Masury), 16:218
Lydia Ann, 16:218
Margaret, 16:88
Martha J., 16:218
Mary, 16:218
Nathaniel Friend, 16:218
Polly (Bootman), 16:218
Polly (Friend), 16:220
Sarah, 16:88, 89; 18:58
Sarah B. (Stoker), 16:218
MATHER
Cotton, 17:95; 18:140, 141, 192; 19:16, 37, 240a; 20:46
Frederick G., 18:191
Increase, 19:16, 40, 143
MATHEWS see also MATTHEWS
Eunice, 20:208
Lois Kimball, 18:191
MATHEWSON
Mary (Potter), 19:149, 150
Richard, 19:149, 150
MATOSSIAN
Marian Kilbourne, 20:120a
MATSON see also MATTSON
Thomas, 19:132
MATTHEW/MAYTHAM
Elizabeth, 16:149
Lois Kimball, 18:187
Samuel, 16:41
Sarah (Parker), 16:41
Sarah (Smith), 16:149
Thomas, 16:149
MATTHEWS see also MATHEWS
Angeline, 20:38
G. B., 16:147
Hannah (Knight), 18:77
John, 18:77, 170
Keith, 17:190
Lydia, 18:149, 168, 170
Lydia (___), 18:170
Mary (___), 19:97
MATTOON
Ebenezer, 17:5
MATTSON see also MATSON
Carol W., 19:56
MAUL/MAULE
Elizabeth, 18:19
Hannah (Johnson), 17:49
John, 18:90
Joseph, 17:49
Thomas, 18:90; 19:155, 162
MAVERICK
Anna (___), 20:192
Eunice (___), 20:14
John, 20:14
Mose/Moses, 17:210, 214; 20:14, 15
Remember (Allerton), 20:14
Ruth, 20:192

Samuel, 17:90
Sarah, 20:15
MAWRY
Roger, 18:230
MAXEY
Elizabeth, 20:136, 142
MAXFIELD
Ichabod, 18:81
Mary (Godfrey), 18:81
MAXTIER
Daniel, 16:35
MAXWELL
Richard H., 17:51
MAY
Abigail, 16:39
Abigail (Parker), 16:39
Benjamin, 16:39
Ebenezer, 16:39
Henry, 16:39
Prudence, 16:39
Solomon, 16:39
Susannah, 16:39
Susannah (Parker), 16:39
Thede/Theoda, 16:39
MAYBERRY
Richard, 16:78
MAYFIELD/MAYFIELD-ARMITAGE/ MEFIELD
Benoni, 16:159; 18:232, 234
John, 18:232, 234
Rebecca (Armitage), 18:234
MAYNARD
Deborah (Coates), 19:159
Jane, 20:42
Samuel, 19:159
Simon, 17:82
Susannah, 17:159
MAYO
Hannah, 16:208
MAYOR
Mary, 17:172; 20:92
MAYS
Ebenezer, 20:116
MAYTHAM see MATTHEW
MAZION
Valentine, 16:36
McADAMS
Martha, 19:35
Nellie, 16:149
McALLISTER
Don L., 19:55
McARTHUR
Asenath, 18:96
Asenath (___), 18:96
Joseph, 18:96
Kate, 18:96
McBUNDY
___, Rev., 17:165
McCALL
Clare M., 19:117
James, 19:117
John, 19:117
Rebecca, 19:117
McCARTY
Esther, 17:191
McCAUL
Evelyn, 20:172
McCLEARY
Mary (Lukis), 17:57
Polly, 17:57
Samuel, 17:57
McCLURE
James, 17:129

Jerusha (Hodgkins), 17:129
McCOBB
David, 19:54
McCOLLASTER
Archibald, 16:101
Polly (Fowle), 16:101
McCONAUGHY
Terri, 19:21, 23, 24
McCONICEY
Mary, 18:179
McCONNELL
Laura F. (Sargent), 17:170
McCOY
Elizbeth Virginia, 19:232
Georgiana, 19:17
Grace A., 17:164
John, 17:164
Mary A. (___), 17:164
McCRACKEN, 19:211
George E., 19:176
McDERMOT
Catherine, 17:235
McDONALD
Charles, 17:163
Flora B., 17:104
John, 17:104
Margaret, 17:163
Margaret (McLane), 17:163
Mary, 20:31
Sarah (___), 17:104
McDUFFEE
Franklin, 17:184
McFARLAND
Daniel, 18:202
Esther (Foster), 18:202
John, 18:202
Miriam (Foster), 18:202
McFEDRICK
Neal, 16:133
McGLENNEN
Edward W., 19:134
McGOFF
Hazel W., 20:176
McINTIRE
Maria, 17:106
Phebe, 20:38
Phebe (___), 20:38
Polly, 19:239
Samuel, 20:38, 89
William, 19:239
McINTOSH
Walter, 18:134
Walter E., 18:136
McKEEN/McKEAN, 18:136
Agnes (Clark), 19:55, 59
James, 19:55, 59
Margaret (Alexander), 19:55, 59
Samuel, 19:55, 59
McKENNEY
Hannah, 20:114
Lydia (Rand), 20:239
Samuel, 20:239
McKENZIE, 20:55
McKINNEY
Elizabeth, 20:239
McLANE
Harriet (___), 17:107
Margaret, 17:163
Martha H., 17:107
Murdock, 17:107
McLAUGHLIN
James, 19:57
W. G., 16:189

McLEAN
    Fanny (Friend), 17:162
    John W., 17:162
    Jonathan, 17:162
    Millie (Wright), 17:162
    Virginia Beverly, 19:232

McMANN
    Mary (Mahan), 17:235
    Michael, 17:235

McNAUGHT
    Mary, 19:235

McEVOY
    Catherine (Guilfoyle), 18:58
    Phanton, 18:58

McFARLAND
    James, 17:119
    Margaret (Smith), 17:119
    Sarah, 17:119

McGILL
    Grace, 16:53

McINTIRE
    Aaron, 16:90

McKENNEY
    Henry, 17:238
    Rebecca (___), 17:238
    Robert, 17:238

McKINLEY
    Richard, 16:12

McLEOD
    Elizabeth, 16:86

MEACHAM/MEACHEM
    Isaac, 18:86
    Jeremiah, 20:94, 233
    Jeremy, 19:194
    Margaret (___), 20:94
    Margaret (Prisse), 20:94
    Mary, 18:85, 86
    Rebecca (Hawkins), 20:233
    Sarah, 20:27, 94
    Susanna, 18:26

MEAD/MEADE
    Sarah A., 17:165
    Thomas, 17:213

MEADOWCROFT, 16:10
    Aaron, 16:7
    Elizabeth (___), 16:6
    Elizabeth (Whitehead), 16:7
    Hannah, 16:7
    Harriet, 16:7
    John, 16:6
    Mary (Cheatham), 16:8
    Mary Elizabeth, 16:7
    Thomas, 16:6

MEANS
    J. F., 17:165

MEAR
    John, 20:199

MEARS
    Catherine, 16:86
    Daniel, 17:41
    Elizabeth (Mower), 17:41
    John, 16:132
    Lydia, 16:132
    Mary (___), 16:131
    Robert, 16:131
    Samuel, 16:131
    Sarah (___), 16:131
    Thomas, 16:132

MECOM/MECUM
    Anne, 20:142
    Eben, 17:13

MEESTER
    Betty, 20:126

MEFIELD see MAYFIELD

MEHONEY/MEHONCY
    Sarah, 16:132

MEK
    Richard, 20:199

MELLEN
    Abigail, 17:177
    Abigail (Pratt), 17:177
    Deborah (Sprague), 16:81
    Henry, 17:177
    R. G., 17:110
    Robert, 17:23

MELLENS
    Elizabeth (Bucknam), 16:172

MELNYK
    Marcia, 16:123; 18:68; 19:176; 20:116
    Marcia D., 18:123; 20:3

MELTOS
    John, 20:199

MELVIN
    Bridget, 17:83
    Mary, 17:204

MEMORIE
    Gorg, 20:199

MEMOY
    Anne, 17:239

MENGELE
    ___, Dr., 17:125

MERCHANT
    Elizabeth, 17:219
    Hannah (Wheeler), 18:202
    Martha, 19:119
    Sally (Davis), 19:118
    Samuel P., 19:118
    Sarah Abigail, 19:118
    William, 18:202

MERCY
    Jeffry, 16:136

MERIT see also MERRITT
    Nicholas, 17:214

MEROLLA, 20:82

MERREY
    Mary, 20:210

MERRIAM see also MIRRIAM, 18:136
    ___, Mrs., 17:46
    Abigail, 20:42
    Abigail (Goodwin), 20:42
    Abigail (Locke), 20:42
    Abigail (Mower), 16:167
    Abigail (Ramsdell), 18:92, 228
    Anna, 16:75
    Athelred, 18:19
    Athelred (Berry), 17:172
    Dianna/Dinah (Hudson), 20:42
    Ebenezer, 17:172; 19:100; 20:92
    Elisha, 20:42
    Elizabeth, 16:204
    Elizabeth (Breed), 16:199
    Esther, 18:228
    Ethelred (Berry), 20:92
    James, 20:42
    Jane (Maynard), 20:42
    Jerusha, 18:92
    Jerusha (Berry), 17:172; 20:92
    John, 16:233; 18:150; 20:42
    Jonas, 20:42
    Jonathan, 18:216
    Joseph, 18:226, 228; 20:197
    Lot, 20:42
    Lucy Wilder (Carter), 20:42
    Lydia Woodward, 20:42
    Margaret (Ives), 20:42
    Martha (Berry), 16:75
    Mary, 20:42
    Mary (Bancroft), 20:42
    Nathaniel, 16:75
    Rebecca (Sharp), 16:233
    Samuel, 18:150; 20:42
    Sarah, 18:116; 19:108
    Theophilus, 18:92, 228
    William, 16:164; 17:90; 18:116, 150, 151, 228; 20:42, 92

MERRIE
    Joseph, 18:140

MERRILL see also MORRILL
    Abraham, 20:80
    Abraham Dow, 17:52; 20:178
    Anne, 17:188
    Anne Osborn, 17:188
    Benjamin, 20:45
    Daniel, 16:212; 18:220
    Eliza J., 18:217
    Elizabeth, 19:93
    Elizabeth (Bailey), 19:178
    Esther, 19:17
    Hannah (Graves), 20:212
    Hannah (Kent), 19:178
    Hannah (Osborn), 17:187
    Harry Wilcox, 17:188
    Isaac, 20:80, 81
    Jacob, 20:80
    James, 17:52; 20:178
    Joanna (Kenny), 17:52; 20:178
    John, 16:212; 17:52; 20:178
    Joshua, 17:52; 20:178
    Josiah, 20:212
    Lucy (Webster), 17:52; 20:178
    Madeline Osborn (Curtis), 17:187
    Madeline Osborne, 17:183; 18:136
    Margaret (Harris), 20:45
    Margaret (Osborn), 17:184
    Martha Louise (Richardson), 17:188
    Mehitable (Dow), 17:52; 20:178
    Mehitable (Hale), 16:212
    Molly, 19:178; 20:46
    Molly (Emery), 17:52; 20:178
    Nathan, 19:178
    Nathaniel, 17:52; 20:178
    Orlando Bagley, 17:132
    Peter, 18:161
    Richard, 17:188
    Ruth (Wallingford), 17:52; 20:178
    Samuel, 16:212; 19:96
    Sarah (Friend), 16:212
    Stephen, 19:178
    Susan Batchelder, 17:188
    Susanna, 20:221
    Susanna (Gale), 16:212
    Thomas, 16:212

MERRIMAN
    Nathaniel, 18:41

MERRITT see also MERIT
    Elizabeth, 16:58; 17:118
    James, 19:83
    Mary, 19:53
    Mary (Northey), 19:83
    Susanna, 18:149, 170

MERRY
    Elizabeth (___), 18:173
    Lucy, 18:50
    Mary, 20:208

MESSER
    Abiel, 20:130
    Abigail (Parker), 16:41
    Elizabeth, 18:159
    John, 20:130

Jonathan, 16:40
Nathaniel, 20:130
Richard, 20:130
Thomas, 20:130
METCALF
Addie E. (Edmands), 17:31
Curtis, 17:31
Elizabeth, 19:211, 214, 215, 217; 20:33
Jane/Jennie, 17:238
Martha, 19:212
Michael, 19:211
Sarah (Ellington/Ellwyn), 19:211
METHVEN
Paul, 20:130
MEYERINK
Kory L., 20:11
MICHEL/MICHELL see MITCHEL
MIDDLETON, 17:161
Agnes/Jill Lamar, 17:169
Ann Ethelyn (Friend), 17:169
Evelyn (___), 17:169
John Frazier, 17:169
Lamar, 17:169
Margaret Lamar, 17:169
MIDURA
Stevie, 20:148
MIELZINER
Annie Laurie (Jaques), 17:170
Ella Lane (Friend), 17:169
Jean (Macintyre), 17:170
Jo, 17:170
Leo, 17:169
Levald, 17:169
Mary (Phillips), 17:169
Marya (Mannes), 17:170
Moses, 17:169
Rosette (Levald), 17:169
MIERES
Cumby, 18:57
Rebecca (Cumbey), 18:57
Thomas, 18:57
MIGHILL
Elizabeth (Northend), 18:73
Ezekiel, 18:73
Nathaniel, 18:240
Thomas, 17:140
MIHILL
Mary (Dimon), 19:120
Moses, 19:120
MILAN
John, 18:230
MILBURY
Henry, 19:226
Joanna, 19:225-227
MILES
Ann (___), 19:29
John, 19:29
Joseph, 19:142, 143
Nancy, 17:189
MILIKIN see also MILLIKEN
Elizabeth, 20:139
Sarah, 20:139
MILINTON
Alice, 17:178
MILK
John, 19:143
MILLAGE
John, 17:41
Susannah (Mower), 17:41
MILLAIS
Susanna, 20:212
MILLBANK see also BANKS
Katherine, 19:111, 113

Lucy (Dyer), 19:113
Philip, 19:113
MILLER see also WILLARD
Alice, 19:229
Andrew, 18:39
Arthur, 17:75; 20:100
Bessie (Thompson), 20:172
Dorothy May (Wood), 20:172
Edwina Victoria (Durgin), 16:52
Elmer Thomas, 16:52
Elizabeth, 19:211, 214, 215, 217; 20:33
Florence, 19:21, 24
H. D., 19:24
Henry D., 19:21
John, 20:172
John T., 16:52
June, 19:237
June (Butler), 19:142
Mary, 18:77
Minnie (Plante), 16:52
Myrtle (Farnham), 19:24
Myrtle E. (Farnham), 19:21
Olga K., 18:191
Peter, 17:135
R. G., 17:105
Rachel (___), 17:64
Rachel (Bassett), 18:39
Rachel (Leeds), 18:39
Robert L'hommediue, 20:172
Russell E., 16:189
Samuel, 16:72
MILLET/MILLETT, 20:18
Charles, 20:157
Elizabeth, 16:235
Hannah (Estes), 18:95
Job, 17:240
John, 16:133; 18:240; 20:200
Jonathan, 18:95
Joshua, 19:112
Mary (Greenaway), 18:176
Mehitable, 18:176
Nathaniel, 17:240
Sarah Sprague (Punchard), 18:95
Thomas, 17:240; 18:176
MILLHOUSE
William T., 19:3
MILLIKEN see also MILIKIN
Benjamin, 20:238
Elizabeth, 20:238
Sarah, 20:238
MILLINGTON
Mehitabel, 20:16
MILLS
Anne-Scott (Goldthwaite), 19:56, 59
Deborah, 20:44
Deborah (Larrabee), 18:18; 20:44
Dorrity/Dorothy, 18:18
Edith, 18:134
Edith G., 16:176; 20:141
Elizabeth Shown, 18:66, 68
James, 18:14, 15, 17-20; 20:44
John, 18:236
John Alvey, 17:107
Lucretia, 20:44
Martha, 18:18
Martha (___), 18:18
Martha (Alley), 18:15, 18; 20:44
Mary, 16:199
Mary Mangam (Pool), 16:176
Naomi (Hinkson), 18:18; 20:44
Patience, 20:44
Paul, 19:56, 59
Sarah, 18:18

MINER, 18:136
Camilla Virginia, 20:32
Elizabeth, 18:224
MINKEMA
Kenneth P., 16:35
MINOR
Esther, 17:54
MINOT
Ephraim, 18:106
George, 16:144
Jerusha, 19:157
Stephen, 19:82
MINOTI
Stephen, 17:97
MINZIES
Rebecca, 16:76
MIRICK
Abigail, 20:23
Mary (Bodwell), 18:159
Timothy, 18:159
MIRRIAM see also MERRIAM
William, 19:78
MITCHEL/MITCHELL/MICHEL
___, Col., 18:76
Abigail, 18:158, 160-162; 20:54
Abigail (Atwood), 18:160
Alice (Friend), 17:111
Andrew, 18:160-162
Anne, 20:227
Anne (Foster), 20:225
Christopher, 19:229; 20:44
Deborah (Mills), 20:44
Eleanor (Larrabee), 19:229
Ellenor (___), 19:229
Gorg, 20:199
James, 16:149; 20:54
John, 18:157; 19:229
Joseph, 20:54
Lydia, 20:115
Lydia (Lapham), 20:54
Margery (Bolton), 20:54
Mary, 20:54
Philip, 17:111
Robert, 20:225
Susanna, 20:45
William, 18:157, 162
MIX see DIX, 20:58
MIXER
John, 19:80
Josiah, 19:104
Lois (Cheever), 19:104
Mary (Liscom), 19:80
MOFFORD
Juliet Haines, 16:10
MOKOTOFF
Gary, 17:74
MOLTEN/MOLTON see MOULTON, 18:216
MOLTZEN
Helena L., 17:31
MOLYNEAUX
Chloe, 20:172
MONROE see MUNROE
MONSISE
Cornelius, 19:159
Elizabeth (Coates), 19:159
MONTAGUE
Abigail, 18:169
Abigail (Montague), 18:169
Josiah, 18:169
Lovice, 18:169
MONTENARI, 16:125
___, Mrs., 16:124

MONTGOMERY
  Alexander Charles, 17:135
  Emma Thrasher (Hackett), 19:237
  Fred Elbridge, 19:237
  Mabel Sarah, 19:237
MONTU
  Lena Farr (Carstairs), 16:151
  Mario, 16:151
MOODY
  ___, Capt., 20:44
  Adaline, 19:111
  Caleb, 18:236
  Clarissa, 19:111
  Daniel G., 19:111
  David F., 19:111
  Eliezer, 19:78
  George F., Mrs., 16:152
  Henry, 16:106
  Jane, 19:111
  John, 19:111
  Lucy J., 19:111
  Maria G., 19:111
  Marinda, 19:111
  Rebecca (Chandler), 19:111
  Robert, 19:111
  Rozilla, 19:111
  Sally, 19:111
  Sally (Garcelon), 19:111
  Samuel, 16:104
  Sarah, 16:222
  William, 16:106
MOONEY
  Charles, 18:175
  Charlotte Kendall, 18:175
  Clara (Cousens), 16:49
  Edith, 16:49
  Gina, 16:49
  Ira Ezra, 16:49
  John M., 16:49
  Laura Hannah (Cate), 18:175
  Maggie L., 16:49
  Martha E., 16:50
  Martha Eulela, 16:49
MOOR/MOORE/MOWER see also MORE, 16:195; 17:40
  ___, Mrs., 17:13
  ___ (Kane), 16:50
  Bethiel (Webb), 16:180
  Daniel, 16:180
  Eliza, 19:58
  Elizabeth, 19:140, 141
  Hannah, 17:44
  Hattie (___), 16:51
  Israel, 18:237
  John, 16:167, 197
  Katherine, 18:74
  Lydia (Witt), 18:170
  Martha, 16:65
  Mary (___), 16:131
  Mary (DeJersey), 18:237
  Mary (Hamlin), 17:57
  Richard, 16:196, 197; 19:194
  Rita I. (Dubois), 20:173
  Ruth, 17:58
  Samuel, 16:131, 197
  Thomas, 16:197; 17:57
  Uriah, 18:170
  William, 17:13
MOOREHOUSE see also MOREHOUSE
  James, 18:107
MOORES
  Abigail, 16:148
  Edmund, 19:179

  Sarah (Cooper), 19:179
MORE see also MOOR
  ___, Mrs., 19:201
  "Children", 17:51
  Abraham, 16:68
  Ann (Walker), 17:50
  Asahel, 17:50
  Benjamin, 17:50
  Caleb, 16:201
  Catherine, 16:120a
  Catherine (___), 18:136
  Catherine (More), 16:120a
  Christian, 16:201
  Christian (Hunt/Hunter), 16:200; 17:50
  Ellen, 16:200
  George, 16:36
  Hannah (Conant), 17:50
  Jane (___), 16:200
  Jasper, 16:200
  John, 17:50; 18:57; 19:201
  Joshua, 16:201
  Josiah, 17:50
  Josiah Dodge, 17:50
  Mary, 16:200
  Phoebe, 17:50
  Rebecca (Cumbey), 18:57
  Rhoda, 17:50
  Richard, 16:196; 17:50; 18:136
  Samuel, 16:201
  Sarah, 17:50
  Sarah (___), 16:201
  Susanna, 16:201; 17:50
  Susanna (Knowlton), 17:50
  Tabitha (Perkins), 17:50
  Thomas, 16:201
MOREHOUSE see also MOOREHOUSE
  Anna, 19:180
MORENO
  Edgard, 19:200
MORESE
  Benjamin, 20:81
MOREY
  George, 18:148
  Hannah (Lewis), 18:148
  Roger, 18:79
MORGAN
  Abigail, 17:119
  Aurie Willis, 16:82
  Benjamin, 17:240
  Betsey/Betty, 17:240
  Charity, 20:107
  Deliverance (Bassett), 18:37
  Henry, 17:161
  John, 20:143
  Joseph, 16:111
  Lucy, 17:119
  Luke, 16:63
  Mary, 18:151
  Mary Frederica Rhinelander, 16:189
  Polly (___), 17:240
  Robert, 16:137
  Sally (Tarbox), 20:143
  Samuel, 18:76, 240
  Sarah (___), 18:76
  Thomas, 18:37; 19:220, 223
MORGRIDGE
  Samuel, 16:133
MORIARTY
  G. Andrews, 17:83; 18:154; 20:20
  John, 18:178
MORIN
  ___ (Wescott), 16:240
  Daniel, 16:240

  Martin, 16:240
  Sepherine, 16:52
MORLEY, 16:13
MORRE
  Olive (Tarbox), 20:238
  Wyatt, 20:238
MORREALE
  Ben, 16:128
MORRELL/MORRILL see also MERRILL
  Abner, 19:120
  Archibald, 19:57
  Charles, 17:58
  Eliza, 19:58
  Jeremiah, 16:132
  Jonathan, 20:82
  Latty (Andrews), 19:57
  Lydia (Greeley), 19:120
  Mary, 19:120
  Moses, 20:145
  Ruth, 20:238
MORRIS see also NORRIS
  ___, Mr., 18:50
  Ann, 18:39
  Joan, 20:101
  Lewis, 18:39
  Prudence Clark (Hart), 18:50
  Sarah (___), 18:39
  Thomas, 17:135
MORRISON, 16:141
  L. S., 20:227
  Leonard A., 20:228
  Leonard Allison, 18:165; 20:16, 136
  Willard, Mrs., 16:111
MORSE, 17:139; 20:80
  Abigail, 16:76
  Abner, 17:176
  Betsy, 19:42
  David, 18:156
  Elizabeth (Cook), 16:118
  Elizabeth (Lunt), 19:119
  Ephraim, 19:119
  Experience (Sabin), 18:156
  Hannah, 17:52; 20:178
  Hannah/Joanna (Kimball), 17:52; 20:178
  Harriet E., 17:103
  Humphrey, 19:119
  John, 16:118
  Jonathan, 16:238
  Joshua, 17:52; 20:178
  Katherine, 18:59
  Levi, 19:171
  Mary, 16:38
  Mary (Clark), 16:238
  Mercy Cross (Northey), 19:171
  Rachel (Noyes), 19:119
  Rebecca, 19:48
  Sarah N. (Thomas), 19:119
  Stephen, 19:119
  Theoda Mears, 16:39
MORSS
  Elizabeth, 18:235-237
MORTENSEN
  Louisa Albian (Hanright), 17:178
  Thomas Christian, 17:178
MORTIMER
  Dorothy, 16:56
MORTON, 17:57
  Thomas, 20:180a
  William, 19:45
MOSELEY
  Polly (Tarbox), 20:147
  Samuel, 20:147
MOSES, 18:197

MOSHER
   Ida May, 18:175
   Olive A. (Gardiner), 18:175
   William Fenderson, 18:175
MOTTY
   Joseph, 19:136
MOULD
   Thomas, 16:166; 17:20
MOULTON/MOLTEN/MOLTON, 18:136
   Deborah, 18:212, 216, 218
   Deborah (Palmer), 18:216
   Ebenezer, 16:93
   Elizabeth, 18:59
   Elizabeth (Corey), 16:92
   Elizabeth (Winn), 18:59
   Hannah, 16:36
   Henry W., 16:92
   James, 16:140
   Jeremiah, 16:104; 17:101; 19:165
   John, 16:92; 17:112; 18:216
   Jonathan, 20:141
   Joseph, 19:165
   Josiah, 20:141
   Joy Wade, 16:12
   Lydia, 19:165
   Margaret, 16:37
   Mary, 16:140
   Mary (Tarbox), 20:141
   Moses Benjamin, 18:59
   Rebecca (Tarbox), 20:141
   Robert, 16:92; 17:14; 19:190
   Sarah, 16:110; 17:53
   Thomas, 19:165
MOUNTFORT
   John, 16:111
MOURNEY, 17:97
MOURS
   Joseph, 16:131
MOUSALL
   Sarah (Lynde), 19:41, 102
   Thomas, 19:102
MOWER see also MOORE
   ___ (Hale), 17:44
   ___ (Warner), 17:44
   Aaron, 17:44
   Abigail, 16:82; 17:43; 18:151
   Abigail (Curtis), 17:42
   Alfred, 17:44
   Alice/Alce (___), 16:195
   Ammi, 17:44
   Anna (Brown), 17:44
   Bemis, 17:44
   Calvin, 17:44
   Charles, 17:44
   Comfort (Learned/Larned), 17:43
   Curtis, 17:44
   Cynthia, 17:44
   Cyrus, 17:44
   Dan, 17:44
   Deborah, 17:43
   Diodema, 17:44
   Ebenezer, 16:167; 17:41
   Eleanor, 17:44
   Elizabeth, 17:41
   Elizabeth (___), 16:195
   Elizabeth (Bemis), 17:44
   Elizabeth (Collins), 17:41
   Elizabeth (Devereux), 16:167; 17:42
   Elizabeth (Garfield), 17:44
   Elizabeth (Sprague), 16:167; 17:43
   Ephraim, 16:167; 17:40
   Esther (___), 17:43
   Ezra, 17:41; 19:106, 158, 159
   Hannah, 17:43
   Hannah (___), 16:223; 19:107
   Hannah (Breed), 17:41; 18:36
   Hannah (Moore), 17:44
   Henry, 17:44
   Hiram, 17:44
   Isaac, 17:44
   Jabez, 17:44
   Jemima, 17:44
   Joanna, 16:167; 17:42
   Joanna (Marshall), 16:167
   John, 16:166; 17:40; 18:36; 19:107, 159, 217; 20:196
   John Russell, 17:44
   Jonathan, 17:44
   Josiah, 17:43
   Laura, 17:44
   Leonard, 17:44
   Lewis, 17:44
   Lois, 17:43
   Lois (Lewis), 17:41
   Loring, 17:44
   Lucretia, 17:44
   Lucy, 17:44
   Luther, 17:44
   Lydia, 17:44; 18:93; 19:107
   Lydia (Burrill), 17:41
   Margaret (Case), 17:42
   Marshall, 17:44
   Martha, 17:44
   Martin, 17:44
   Mary, 16:167; 17:41
   Mary (Burrill), 17:41; 18:36
   Mary (Kenney), 17:43
   Mary (Lewis), 16:167; 17:42
   Mary Belcher (Wheeler), 17:44
   Nancy, 17:44
   Nancy Ann (Leach), 17:44
   Nelson, 17:44
   Olive, 17:43
   Oliver, 17:44
   Pamelia, 17:44
   Peter S., 17:44
   Polly, 17:44
   Rachel, 17:44
   Rebecca, 16:167; 17:41
   Richard, 16:166; 17:40; 18:72, 136, 240; 19:158
   Ruth, 17:44
   Sally, 17:44
   Sally (Curtis), 17:44
   Samuel, 16:167; 17:40; 19:157; 20:196
   Sarah, 16:167; 17:42
   Sarah (___), 17:43
   Sewell, 17:44
   Shubel, 17:41
   Shubel Burrill, 17:41
   Sophia, 17:44
   Susanna, 16:167, 198; 17:41
   Susanna (Marshall), 16:166, 197
   Temperance, 17:44
   Thankful, 17:41
   Thankful (___), 17:44
   Thankful (Sever), 16:167; 17:40
   Thomas, 16:166; 17:42
   Timothy, 17:44
   W. L., 17:42
   Walter L., 16:195
   Warren, 17:44
   William, 17:44
MOWRY
   Anna (Appleby), 19:150
   John, 19:150
   Lois (Potter), 19:149, 150
MOY
   Alice, 16:48
   Alice (Atto), 16:48
   Alice Rosina, 16:48
   James Richard, 16:48
MOYSTON
   Agnes/Jill Lamar (Middleton), 17:169
   Guy, 17:169
MUCKFORD
   James, 19:151
   Lydia (Nicholson), 19:151
MUDGE
   ___, Mr., 20:90
   Alfred, 18:25
   Elizabeth (Baker), 18:25
   Ellen (Pike), 20:227
   Enoch, 19:108
   Frank A., 17:174
   Frank Pierce, 20:227
   Hannah (Ingalls), 18:22, 25; 19:107
   Lemuel, 20:227
   Lydia (Ingalls), 19:108
   Nathan, 18:22, 25; 19:107
   Ruth Tapley, 17:174; 20:227
   Sarah Adaline (Tapley), 17:174; 20:227
MULBURY
   Benjamin, 18:78
MULFORD
   David, 19:92
   Phebe, 19:92
   Phebe (___), 19:92
MULLEN
   Pat, 20:125
MULLIKEN
   Lydia (Fuller), 17:160
   Robert, 19:87
   Samuel, 17:160
   Sarah (Newhall), 17:160
MUNGEL
   Lydia (Aborn), 16:94
MUNGER
   Donna Bingham, 18:191
MUNN
   Donald, 20:54
   Elizabeth (MacLeod), 20:54
   Hannah, 18:149
   John, 20:55
   Lavina Jane, 20:54
   Mary (Galbreath), 20:55
   Mary Jane (Smith), 20:54
   Neil, 20:54
MUNROE see also MONROE
   Abigail (Parker), 16:39
   David, 16:39
   Elizabeth, 18:18
   Jedediah, 16:40
   Lydia, 16:42
   Mary (Lindsey), 18:18
   Rebeckah (Locke), 16:42
   Salley (Newhall), 16:47
   Sarah (Parker), 16:40
   Susannah, 19:239
   Timothy, 16:47; 19:135
   William, 16:42; 18:18
MUNSEY
   Nancy, 20:228
MURCH see also MACK, 18:204
   Ann/Anna (Dean), 16:179
   Joanna, 16:179
   John, 16:179
MURGATROYD, 16:13

MURPHY
Andrea (___), 20:77
Esther, 18:206
Hanora, 19:57
J. Frank, 18:177
James, 18:177
John, 18:177; 20:124, 126
Lawrence, 18:177
Mary, 20:125
Patricia, 18:177
Walter, 18:177
Winnifred (O'Connor), 18:177

MURRAY
"Daughter", 17:191
"Son", 17:191
Ann, 17:117
Charles T., 19:170
Isabelle (Northey), 19:170
James, 18:177
John, 17:136
Judith (Sargent), 17:191; 18:70
Judith Sargent, 20:80
Mary, 18:180
Mary F. (O'Connor), 18:177
Nicholas, 16:22
William, 18:136

MURRELL
Peter, 20:198

MURRY
Eunice, 16:238

MUSCHONOMET, 18:9

MUTCHMORE
Mary, 17:103

MUZZEY
Benjamin, 17:90
Sarah, 20:212

MUZZEY see also MASSEY
Jane, 18:49

MYCALL
James, 19:117
Mary (Farr), 19:117

MYERS
Eleanor, 18:191

MYLES
Anne (Humphreys), 17:214
John, 17:214

MYRICK
Anne, 19:119

NADEAU
Charles, 16:178
Mathilda (Pansano), 16:178

NAGELS/NAGLES
Elizabeth (Parker), 16:42
Michael, 16:42

NANCE
Grace (Bessom), 19:230
Joseph, 19:230

NANNY
Robert, 19:190

NARREMORE, 18:226

NASH
Abby (Tarbox), 20:143
Caroline (Gallison), 17:162
David, 17:162
John, 20:143
Lonson, 17:138
Lucretia R., 17:162
William, 16:134

NASON
Abigail (Knight), 18:77
Charity, 20:139
Richard, 18:7; 20:13
Sarah, 20:140
Uriah, 18:77

NASSENBAUM, 17:14

NEAGLES
James C., 17:74
Lila Lee, 17:74

NEAL/NEALE see also NEALL, NEILL, 18:93
Benjamin, 17:231
Jeremiah, 17:231
John, 18:48, 117; 19:158
Samuel, 18:11
Sarah (Coats), 18:48, 117; 19:158

NEALEY
Daniel, 20:237
Dorcus (Tarbox), 20:237

NEALL see also NEAL, NEILL
Arther, 20:199

NECK/NECKS see also NICK
Benjamin, 16:84
Elizabeth, 16:84
Elizabeth (Blaney), 16:83
John, 16:84; 20:196
Jonathan, 20:133
Jonathan Blaney, 16:84
Richard, 16:84
Sarah, 16:84
Sarah (Riddan), 16:84

NEEDAM/NEEDHAM, 18:36
___ (Blaney), 20:26
___, Mr., 16:164; 17:19, 215
Abigail, 20:233
Alice (Blaney), 16:79; 20:26
Ann (Lawson), 20:91
Anna Marie (Spiller), 20:25
Bathsheba, 18:53, 54; 20:24, 25, 27
Caroline, 16:47
Daniel, 16:26; 17:151; 18:53, 136, 216, 232; 20:24-27, 91, 196, 215
Ebenezer, 16:171
Edmond/Edmund, 16:26; 17:172; 18:46, 52-54, 115, 116, 136, 233; 20:24-27, 91, 92, 111
Edward, 17:142; 20:112
Elias, 20:41
Eliza, 16:101
Elizabeth, 20:27, 91
Ezekiel, 16:24; 18:47; 20:91, 93, 133, 196
Francis Drake, 18:136
George, 16:171
Hannah, 18:115, 116, 136, 232, 233; 20:24, 25
Hannah (___), 17:173; 18:52
Hannah (Berry), 16:26; 17:172; 18:53; 20:25, 26, 91, 92
Hannah (Boyce), 20:24-26
Hannah (Buxton), 20:26
Hannah (Hood), 17:216
Hannah (Wilson), 20:25
James, 16:79; 20:25, 26
Joan (Leazing/Leesone), 18:46, 115, 232; 20:91
John, 18:136; 20:91
Judith, 20:91
Keziah (___), 20:91
Lucille, 16:171
Lydia (Skelton), 20:25
Margaret, 20:24, 91
Margaret (Winn), 20:24, 25
Mary, 18:46; 19:48; 20:25, 91
Mary (___), 20:91
Mary (Parkman), 20:91
Mary (Twiss), 16:37
Mehitabel, 17:205
Olive (Wheeler), 20:25
Pamela (Hawkes), 20:41
Priscilla (Halsey), 20:91
Robert F., 18:136
Ruth, 20:91
Ruth (Chadwell), 18:53; 20:26, 91
Sally (Wright), 16:171
Sarah, 16:37; 20:24, 25
Sarah (Buffum), 16:26; 18:53; 20:25, 27
Sarah (Saunders), 20:26
Thomas, 16:37
William, 20:25

NEELAND/NELAND see also KNEELAND, 20:225
Edward, 20:120
Martha (___), 20:120

NEFF
Mary, 18:141

NEILL see also NEAL, NEALL
James, 19:94

NEKOROWSKI
Gail Goodwin, 18:138

NELAND see NEELAND, KNEELAND

NELSON, 17:141
___ (Blaney), 20:26
___, Mr., 16:164; 17:215
Anna (___), 17:201
Catherine E., 19:92
Elizabeth, 16:159
Ellen, 18:145
Florence, 20:117
Henry M., 17:140
Margaret (___), 19:229
Sarah, 17:166; 18:164
Thomas, 16:155

NESBIT
Hannah, 20:58

NESMITH
John, 19:13

NEVERS
Esther (Trull), 16:179
Samuel, 16:120

NEVINS
W. S., 20:230

NEWBEGIN
Ann (Murray), 17:117
Dennis, 17:117
Jean, 19:237
John, 17:117
Lupira Spaulding, 17:117
Sarah (Howland), 17:117

NEWBERRY/NEWBURY
Walter, 20:78, 79

NEWBOLD
___, Mr., 18:31, 52
Sarah (Bassett), 18:31, 52

NEWBURY see NEWBERRY

NEWCOMB/NEWCOMBE
Henry, 17:13
Richard, 16:33, 89
Sarah, 16:201

NEWELL
Anthony, 19:138
Benjamin, 16:208
Hannah, 16:119; 17:25
Hannah (Edmands), 16:208
Isaac, 16:208
Jonathan, 16:208
Mary, 16:208
Philip, 16:208
Thomas, 19:138

NEWHALL/NEWILL, 16:153; 17:45; 18:214, 231; 19:29, 69, 105, 145
___, Capt., 18:44
___, Judge, 20:187
___, Mr., 19:143
"Daughter", 19:218
Aaron, 20:41
Abby, 18:177
Abigail, 16:46; 17:218; 18:21, 150, 151; 20:25, 26, 29
Abigail (Aborn), 16:92; 19:218
Abigail (Baker), 18:150, 151
Abigail (Bassett), 18:36, 55
Abigail (Denmark), 17:172
Abigail (Hanson), 16:47; 20:100
Abigail (Lindsey), 18:19, 21, 23, 24; 19:144; 20:29, 100
Abigail (Newhall), 18:151
Abijah, 18:36, 55
Albert, 17:160
Alice (Breed), 18:36
Allen, 16:29
Amos, 19:218; 20:116
Andrew, 19:148
Anna, 16:80; 18:31, 93, 98; 20:105
Anna (Hitchings), 19:51
Anne, 17:215
Anne (Darby), 17:218
Anthony, 17:19, 215; 18:51-53, 136; 20:194
Asa, 16:92; 19:218; 20:42
Asa T., 16:70; 17:26
Benjamin, 16:43; 17:172; 18:50, 55, 102; 19:148; 20:34
Benjamin F., 17:26
Benjamin Franklin, 18:136
Bethia, 19:148
Betsey (Brown), 16:47
Betsey (Dewey), 16:92
Betsy (Lewis), 16:100
Bridget, 16:43
Charles, 16:92; 20:43
Charles R., 18:28
Clarissa (Day), 16:92
Daniel, 16:16; 17:172; 18:97, 171; 19:137, 217; 20:37, 42, 48, 116, 212
David, 17:218
Deborah, 18:97
Dolly/Dorothy, 16:44
Dorcas, 20:42
Dorcas (Newhall), 20:42
Dorothy (Chamberlain), 16:44
Easter, 16:44
Easter (Newhall), 16:44
Ebenezer, 16:47; 17:145; 18:171; 19:137
Edward, 19:51
Eleazer, 17:218
Elijah, 19:101; 20:38
Elisha, 16:44; 17:145; 19:137, 144, 227; 20:42, 112
Eliza, 19:144
Elizabeth, 16:44; 17:96; 18:21-23, 47, 53, 73, 152, 173, 224; 19:101, 106, 107, 144, 148, 151; 20:100
Elizabeth (___), 17:219; 19:106
Elizabeth (Bancroft), 17:172; 19:217, 218; 20:48
Elizabeth (Breed), 17:145
Elizabeth (Dodge), 18:97
Elizabeth (Fowle), 17:172
Elizabeth (Hodgkins), 18:22
Elizabeth (Hodgman), 19:148
Elizabeth (Johnson), 18:48; 19:158, 218
Elizabeth (Laughton), 17:47
Elizabeth (Merchant), 17:219
Elizabeth (Normanton), 17:99
Elizabeth (Pecks), 16:46
Elizabeth (Potter), 17:172; 19:143, 144, 148; 20:100
Elizabeth (Symonds), 17:160; 19:144
Elizabeth (Townsend), 18:151
Elizabeth Little, 16:110
Ephraim, 16:92; 17:172; 18:151
Estes, 18:11, 97
Esther, 16:92; 17:159; 20:35
Esther (Bartram), 19:144
Eunice, 18:48; 19:158
Eunice (Curtain), 16:46
Ezekiel, 17:218; 19:107
Ezra, 16:46; 17:160; 18:36, 153, 213; 19:76, 150; 20:38
Farrar/Pharoah, 18:36
Frederick, 16:100
Gertrude C., 18:132
Gilbert, 17:160
Hannah, 16:46; 17:149; 20:42, 111, 116
Hannah (Berry), 17:159
Hannah (Chadwell), 17:159
Hannah (Estes), 18:97; 20:212
Hannah (Larrabee), 16:47
Hannah (Newhall), 17:219
Hannah (Peabody), 16:46
Hannah G., 16:103
Hanson, 16:47
Henry, 17:217
Hepzibah, 16:45; 18:21, 22, 53; 20:42, 100
Hepzibah (Breed), 16:47
Huldah, 16:44; 17:145; 18:24, 173; 20:100
Huldah (Breed), 16:29
Increase, 16:70; 17:219; 18:224; 19:76
Isaiah, 17:158
Israel, 18:50
Jacob, 16:92; 17:159; 18:22; 19:75, 100, 158
Jacob Landlord, 18:136
James, 17:218; 18:229
James R., 16:71; 17:87; 18:14, 18, 47, 51, 60a, 109, 230; 19:43, 100, 136, 162; 20:194, 195
Jane, 16:47
Jane (Breed), 17:145; 20:42
Jedediah, 16:70; 19:106, 148; 20:116
Jemima, 17:172
Jerusha, 16:45; 20:100
Joanna, 16:47; 20:116, 117
Joanna (Collins), 20:116, 117
Joanna (Farrington), 16:47
Johanna, 17:160
John, 16:45; 17:19, 158; 18:52, 73, 151, 209, 222, 223, 225; 19:76, 144, 146, 218, 227; 20:111, 112, 132, 135, 196, 214
John Breed, 18:28
Jonathan, 16:46; 17:159; 18:48; 19:158, 218
Joseph, 16:43; 17:160; 18:53, 151, 171; 19:106, 144, 148, 218, 227; 20:42, 100, 196
Josiah, 16:44; 17:219
Judge, 19:145
Katherine/Catarina (Stone), 16:45; 20:26, 29, 100, 101
Keturah (Hitchins), 16:47
Keziah (Breed), 17:172; 18:53, 97, 98
Landlord, 18:214; 229
Lettice (Johnson), 20:116
Lois (Blaney), 16:79
Lois (Hitchins), 16:47
Lois (Howard), 16:46; 20:29
Love, 16:92
Lydia, 16:45; 17:49; 18:97; 19:108; 20:100, 111
Lydia (Bassett), 18:36
Lydia (Scadlet/Scarlet), 17:219; 19:76
Lydia (Williams), 16:46; 17:113; 19:50
Marcy, 17:160
Margaret (Southwick), 19:218
Martha, 16:92; 19:148
Martha (Breed), 16:47
Mary, 16:44; 17:99; 18:11, 12, 20, 30, 51, 52, 150, 151, 208, 209, 211, 222, 223, 224; 19:144, 148, 159, 218; 20:33, 35, 38, 39, 41, 42
Mary (Bligh), 20:100
Mary (Breed), 16:92; 17:172; 20:42
Mary (Burchstead), 17:219
Mary (Cheever), 19:101; 20:38
Mary (Grant), 16:46
Mary (Grice), 17:219
Mary (Hutchinson), 16:44
Mary (Johnson), 16:46; 17:219; 20:100
Mary (Legare), 18:113
Mary (Legree), 16:46
Mary (Newhall), 17:172; 19:218; 20:42
Mary (Papoon), 16:46
Mary (Stone), 16:45
Mary (White), 17:215
Mary (Wood[Ard]), 18:222
Mary (Wyman), 17:158
Matthew, 16:44
Mehitable, 19:100
Mehitable (Cheever), 17:160; 19:102
Mercy, 19:101
Michael, 20:116, 117
Michajah, 16:47
Michal, 16:47
Michal (Newhall), 16:47
Miriam, 18:11
Miriam (Witt), 18:171
Moses, 16:90; 19:159
Nathaniel, 16:44; 17:217; 18:26; 19:144, 148, 217, 218; 20:196
Patty, 18:24
Paul W., 18:11
Peter, 16:79
Pharoah, 16:16; 18:55
Phebe (___), 16:45
Phebe (Hart), 18:50
Phebe (Lindsay), 16:109
Polly, 16:46
Polly (Hawkes), 20:41
Priscilla, 17:218
Rachel (Annis), 17:219
Rachel (Johnson), 17:160
Rebecca, 16:92; 17:16; 18:47, 167, 208; 19:108, 144
Rebecca (Alley), 18:22
Rebecca (Collins), 17:149
Rebecca (Green), 19:144
Rest (___), 17:217
Richard, 16:46; 17:113; 19:50
Rufus, 16:98; 18:173
Ruth, 16:47; 18:36, 55; 20:33, 37, 42
Ruth (Bancroft), 20:42
Ruth (Ingalls), 19:106, 148
Sally, 16:47
Sally (Berry), 20:43
Sally (Dunklee), 20:42
Sally L., 20:143
Sampson, 16:98

Samuel, 16:44; 17:160; 18:14, 19, 21, 23,
   24, 36, 52, 53, 55, 97, 98, 209; 19:137,
   144, 146; 20:26, 29, 37, 100, 101
Sarah, 16:47; 17:149, 219; 18:116, 167;
   19:105, 106
Sarah (___), 19:218
Sarah (Bannister), 18:171
Sarah (Berry), 17:159
Sarah (Flanders), 17:149; 18:151
Sarah (Fuller), 17:160
Sarah (Hart), 18:50
Sarah (Lewis), 17:219
Sarah (Phillips), 16:223; 19:150
Sarah (Sergeant), 17:160
Sarah (Tarbell), 19:218
Sarah (Witt), 18:173
Solomon, 16:45; 17:113; 18:24, 113, 213;
   20:29, 100
Stephen, 16:46
Susan (Raymond), 17:160
Susanna, 17:145; 20:116, 133
Susanna (___), 17:219
Susanna (Farrar), 17:172; 18:53, 151;
   19:144, 148
Susanna (Soudan), 19:76
Susanna (Swift), 17:219
Susannah (Bowden), 19:159
Susannah (Brown), 19:148
Theodate (___), 16:223
Theodate (Breed), 18:36
Thomas, 16:43; 17:17, 160; 18:21, 136,
   151, 164, 171, 222, 225; 19:102, 137,
   144, 145, 215-218; 20:42, 48, 100, 193,
   194, 214
Timothy, 16:46
William, 16:46; 17:219; 18:22, 173
NEWLAND
Mary (___), 16:73
William Henry, 18:239
NEWLIN
Abigail (___), 18:239
Joseph M., 18:239
NEWMAN
Abigail (Ramsdell), 17:157
Alice, 17:139
Antipas, 16:139; 17:195
Elizabeth, 19:229; 20:113
Elizabeth (Winthrop), 16:139
John, 17:157
John J., 16:128; 17:74
Mary (Ramsdell), 17:157
Robert, 17:214
Thomas, 17:157
William, 16:134
NEWMARCH
George, 18:32, 33
NEWMARK
John, 20:139
NEWMARTH
Ann, 18:55
NEWTON
___, Rev., 16:191
Abigail (Parker), 16:38
Deborah, 19:180
Eleanor (Larrabee), 20:111
Isaac, 20:64, 211
Jonas, 16:38
Jonathan, 20:212
Lydia, 20:212
Mary, 20:211, 212
Mary (Witt), 18:170
Sarah (Belknap), 20:211
Stephen, 18:170

Tabitha (___), 20:212
Tirzah, 20:212
Ziras, 20:111
NICHILLS see also NICHOLLS
Edward, 20:202
NICHOLAS
Ann, 19:171
Czar, 17:125
NICHOLLS/NICHOLS, 20:201
___, Mr., 18:30; 20:59
Abel, 20:231
Abigail (Osborn), 17:201
Amos, 20:236
Anna, 19:239
Anna (White), 20:236
Belon, 19:59
Benjamin, 17:116
Caroline, 17:168
David, 18:239; 20:95
David C., 16:134
Dolly (Chase), 18:239
Ebenezer, 17:116
Elizabeth, 17:116; 20:33
Elizabeth (Dix), 17:116
Elizabeth (Pickering), 20:59
Elizabeth (Preston), 20:231
Elizabeth L., 16:11
Gertrude, 17:58
Hannah, 18:98; 20:212
Hannah (___), 18:98
Hannah (Gaskill), 20:95
Hannah Gaskell, 18:136
Harriet, 16:179; 17:119
James P., 17:168
Jane, 16:59
John, 18:136; 19:39, 59
Lewis, 18:106
Lydia, 18:105
Mary, 16:60; 20:208
Mary (Elwell), 18:30
Mary (George), 16:179; 17:119
Mary (Trow), 17:116
Mary (White), 20:236
Mehitable, 20:232
Mercy (Cole), 17:168
Nathaniel, 19:224, 225
Nich., 16:68
Rebecca, 19:215
Samuel, 19:39, 59; 20:236
Sarah/Sally, 17:179
Susanna, 20:35
Thomas, 16:179; 17:119; 18:98; 20:80
William, 17:201; 18:136; 19:193
NICHOLSON
Annice, 19:151
Edmond, 17:212
Elizabeth, 20:208, 213
Lois, 19:151
Lydia, 19:151
Lydia (Potter), 19:150, 151
Mary, 19:151
Ruth (Lee), 19:151
Samuel, 19:150, 151
NICK see also NECK
Cristover, 20:199
John, 20:199
Mary (Aborn), 20:52
Susanna, 20:52
William, 20:52
NICKERSON
___, Capt., 17:134
NICKS
Mary, 18:78

NICOLET
Samuel, 20:162
NIGHT see KNIGHT
NILES
Elizabeth, 19:174
Joseph, 19:117
Mary (Farr), 19:117
NILSSON
Edward, 20:15
Mrs. Edward, 20:15
NISSENBAUM, 19:116, 220
Stephen, 20:168
NITE see KNIGHT
NO-NOSE
"Sagamore", 18:60a
NOBLE
Abigail, 20:13
John, 20:58
Joseph, 20:13
Lydia (Lurvey), 20:58
Mary (Babson), 20:240
Mercy (Brown), 20:240
Molly (Lurvey), 20:240
Philemon, 20:240
NOCKS
Drisco, 18:49
Margaret (Lord), 18:49
NOE/NOOT
Elizabeth, 19:230
NOEL
___ (Haddock), 16:149
___, Mr., 16:149
NOLAN
Edward, 20:126
Julia, 20:126
Mary, 20:126
Michael, 20:126
Thomas, 20:126
NOLEN
Charles, 16:87
Elizabeth (Blaney), 16:87
Elizabeth (Gridley), 16:87
Esther (Langley), 16:87
George, 16:87
Hervet, 16:87
Mary Ann (Haven), 16:87
Mehitable (Pratt), 16:87
Thomas, 16:86
NOLENS
Robert, 18:57
Sarah, 18:57
NONNUPANOHOW
David, 18:60a
NOOTHE
Margery (___), 20:175
Robert, 20:175
Thurston, 20:175
NORCROSS
Betty (Lewis), 18:221
Jane, 17:115
NORDEN
Nathaniel, 19:82
NORDICA
Lilian, 16:140
NORMAN, 19:194
Arabella, 19:203
Arabella (___), 17:139; 19:203
Edward, 17:214
Hannah, 19:203
John, 17:139; 19:154, 201-203; 20:14-16,
   199
Lydia, 17:139
Margaret (Alford), 17:139

Richard, 17:139; 19:124, 197, 201; 20:14, 15
Sarah (Maverick), 20:15
NORMANTON
Abraham, 17:217
Elizabeth, 17:99
NORRIS see also MORRIS
Edward, 17:212; 19:192
Martha (Potter), 19:149
Thomas, 19:149
NORTH
Elizabeth, 16:80
Mary/Marie, 18:83
Richard, 18:83
Susanna, 16:15; 17:55; 18:136
Ursula (___), 18:83
NORTHEND
Elizabeth, 18:73
Ezekiel, 18:73
NORTHEY/NORTHIE/NORTHY
Abigail, 19:170, 172
Abigail (Stodder), 19:85, 170
Abigail (Wood), 18:117; 19:85, 170, 200
Abigail Wood, 19:171
Abijah, 18:35, 117; 19:19, 84, 85, 170, 171, 198, 200
Abraham, 19:85
Alice (Thomas), 19:85, 170
Andrew, 19:172
Ann, 18:35
Ann (Nicholas), 19:171
Anna, 19:83, 85
Anne, 19:84, 85
Arthur P., 19:171
Austin B., 19:172
Betsey, 19:169
Betty (Brown), 19:83, 169
Bithiah, 19:82
Charles W., 19:172
Chloe (Jesseman), 19:170, 171
Chloe W., 19:172
Cynthia (Winslow), 19:171
Cynthia W., 19:171
Darius, 19:170
Darius Clark, 19:172
David, 16:78; 18:35, 117; 19:82-85, 169-172, 198-200
Deborah, 19:83
Deborah Peach, 19:171
Dorothy, 19:81, 82
Dorothy/Demaris (___), 19:81
Ebenezer, 19:83, 169
Edward, 18:35; 19:84, 85, 169, 172, 198-200
Edward A., 19:171
Eleanor, 19:83, 170, 172
Eleanor (Parsons), 19:170, 172
Eleanor (Woodworth), 19:82, 83, 169
Eli, 19:170
Eliphelet, 19:83, 85, 170-172
Elizabeth, 19:83, 84, 169
Elizabeth (Mall), 19:83
Elizabeth (Marshall), 19:82
Elizabeth (Northey), 19:83, 84, 169
Ellen (Harrub), 19:170
Ezra, 19:169, 171, 199
George, 19:172
Hannah, 18:35; 19:85, 169, 170, 172
Hannah (Peach), 19:169
Hannah (Wade), 19:169, 170
Harriet, 19:171
Harriet Newell, 19:172
Harvey, 19:169

Henry B., 19:171
Henry Howard, 19:170
Herbert W., 19:171
Hitte, 19:170
Hooper, 19:171
Isabelle, 19:170
James, 19:82, 83, 85, 170-172
Jane (Price), 19:171
Jane Parsons, 19:172
Janet (___), 19:170, 172
Jesse, 19:83
John, 19:81-85, 169-172, 192, 198, 237
John Holman, 19:171
John Tucker, 19:171
John Westly, 19:171
Joseph, 19:82-85, 169-172
Joshua, 19:170, 172
Joshua L., 19:172
Lang, 19:172
Lucy, 19:172
Lydia (Holman), 18:35; 19:19, 171
Lydia L., 19:172
Lydia Mansfield, 19:171
Margaret (Anthony), 19:171
Mary, 18:35; 19:83, 85, 172
Mary (___), 19:83, 85
Mary (Cross), 19:169, 170
Mary (Locke), 19:170, 172
Mary (Russell), 19:171
Mary (Sanderson), 19:83, 85
Mary (Stockbridge), 19:82, 83
Mary (Symons), 19:82
Mary Alice, 19:170
Mary Ann, 19:172
Mary Ellen, 19:172
Mary King, 19:171
Mary S. (Barker), 19:172
Mary S. (Shreve), 19:171
Mehitable, 19:83
Mercy, 19:85, 169
Mercy (Hildreth), 19:171
Mercy (LeCraw), 19:84, 169
Mercy Celia, 19:172
Mercy Cross, 19:171
Mercy P. (Brown), 19:170, 172
Miriam (___), 18:117
Miriam (Bassett), 18:34, 35; 19:83, 84, 198-200
Moses, 19:172
Moses Hibbard, 19:172
Nehemiah, 18:35; 19:85
Patty, 19:170
Phillip, 19:170, 172
Polly, 19:169
Rebecca, 18:35; 19:84, 85
Rebecca (Collins), 18:35; 19:85, 169, 198, 199
Rebecca Maria, 19:171
Richard P., 19:171
Robert, 19:85, 170, 172
Roger, 19:169
Rosina, 19:172
Ruth, 19:83
Sally, 19:169-172
Sally (Clapp), 19:170, 172
Sally G. (King), 19:170
Sally Gerrish (King), 18:35; 19:171
Samuel, 19:82, 170-172
Samuel Bartol, 19:171
Sarah, 18:35; 19:17, 19, 81-85, 171; 19:237
Sarah (Ewell), 19:82
Sarah (Hill), 19:82, 198

Sarah (Lisbrel), 19:84, 169
Sarah Craw, 19:169
Susanna, 19:169
Susanna (Parsons), 18:35; 19:85, 169, 199
Susanna (Somes), 18:35; 19:85
Susannah (Hines), 19:83, 84
Susannah (Somes), 19:169
Thaddeus, 19:172
Thomas, 20:199
William, 18:35; 19:84, 85, 169, 171, 198-200
William E., 19:171
William Hussey, 19:172
William M., 19:171
NORTHIE see NORTHEY
NORTHLY
Ezra, 16:223
NORTHY see NORTHEY
NORTON
Elizabeth (Brown), 17:238
George, 19:202
Hannah, 18:50
Jane, 17:238; 18:175
Jonathan, 18:192, 194
Joseph, 17:238
Joshua, 17:238
Lydia (Bishop), 17:238
Nicholas, 17:238
Susanna (Getchell), 17:238
NORWELL
Elizabeth (Coldam), 18:198
Francis, 18:198
NORWOOD, 17:139; 20:18, 112
___ (Damon), 18:205
___ (Hassey), 18:205
"Child", 18:205, 207, 211
"Son", 18:201
Aaron, 18:205
Abigail, 18:199-205, 215; 19:54; 20:118
Abigail (___), 18:204
Abigail (Brooks), 18:205
Abigail (Eames), 18:215
Abraham, 18:204, 205
Adaline Augusta (Choate), 18:207
Alice, 18:203
Alice (Donnell), 18:200, 202
Almira E. (Wiley), 18:217
Amos, 18:205
Anna, 18:203, 205, 207
Anna (Andrews), 18:205
Anna (Gill), 18:211
Anna (Lee), 18:203
Anna Smith, 18:207
Anna Smith (Norwood), 18:207
Anner (___), 18:201, 206
Bathsheba, 18:207
Bathsheba (Greenleaf), 18:215
Benjamin, 18:205, 206, 217
Benjamin Massey, 18:217
Benjamin Richardson, 18:204
Betsey/Betsy, 18:204, 206, 216
Betsey (Bray), 18:205
Betsey Warner, 18:204
Betsy (Peabody), 18:217
Betsy (Skinner), 18:217
Betty, 18:205
Betty (Ford), 18:205
Caira, 18:207
Caleb, 18:199, 200, 202, 203, 205-207, 224
Candace, 18:206
Caroline, 18:217
Caroline Parmelia, 18:217
Catherine (Pearson), 18:215

Charles, 18:204-207, 217
Charlotte, 18:204
Clarissa, 18:204
Clarissa (Norwood), 18:204
Daniel, 18:205
David, 18:210, 213, 216-218
Deborah, 18:199, 200, 203, 206, 216
Deborah (Moulton), 18:212, 216, 218
Deborah (Parsons), 18:206
Deborah (Winslow), 18:204
Diana, 18:206
Ebenezer, 17:99; 18:204, 209, 211, 215, 224
Elbridge, 18:207
Elias, 18:204
Elisha, 18:205
Eliza, 18:205, 207
Eliza (Friend), 16:216; 18:207
Eliza (Norwood), 18:205
Eliza J. (Merrill), 18:217
Elizabeth, 18:31, 92, 152, 199, 201, 202, 204, 206, 210, 217, 218; 19:147, 149
Elizabeth (Andrews), 18:200, 201, 205
Elizabeth (Coldam), 18:208, 224; 19:149
Elizabeth (Davis), 18:200, 203, 204
Elizabeth (Grover), 18:202, 206
Elizabeth (Ingollsbee), 18:200
Elizabeth (Quiner), 18:211
Elizabeth (Tarbell), 18:213, 217, 218
Elizabeth Peabody (Thurston), 18:218
Emeline, 18:217
Ephraim, 18:206
Esther, 18:204, 206
Esther (Gott), 18:206
Esther (Grover), 18:205
Esther (Lathrop), 18:199, 200
Esther (Murphy), 18:206
Esther (Norwood), 18:206
Frances (Hall), 18:205
Francis, 17:99; 18:92, 93, 198-204, 206-211, 213, 224, 240; 19:54, 149
Frederick, 16:216; 18:207
George, 18:205, 207, 217
Gorham, 18:206
Gustavus, 18:203, 204
Hamilton, 18:207
Hannah, 18:200, 201, 204, 205, 210, 215-217
Hannah (Brown), 18:206
Hannah (Pierce), 18:210
Harriet, 18:217
Harriet Newhall, 18:205
Harriet Newhall (Norwood), 18:205
Harriott, 18:203
Harry, 18:204, 205, 217
Isaac, 18:205
Jacob, 18:205
James, 18:200, 203-205, 216, 217
Jane, 18:207
Jane (___), 18:205
Jane (Robinson), 18:206
Jane Massey, 18:217
Jerusha, 18:205, 207
Jerusha (___), 18:205
Jerusha (Butman), 18:207
Jerusha (Gross), 17:99; 18:211, 215
Jerusha (Story), 18:202, 206, 207
John, 18:203, 205, 207, 212, 215-218
John Andrews, 18:204
Jonathan, 18:200, 203, 204, 206, 209-211, 213-217, 224
Joseph, 18:204, 206
Joseph Eddes, 18:205

Joseph Thurston, 18:206
Joshua, 16:63; 18:199-201, 204, 206
Judith, 18:203, 204, 215
Judith (Gilbert), 18:217
Judith (Little), 18:212, 215
Judith (Norwood), 18:203, 204
Judith (Woodbury), 18:200, 203, 204
Laura Matilda, 18:207
Lavinia (Knowlton), 18:205
Lemuel, 18:207
Lois (Lufkin), 18:205
Louisa, 18:217
Louisa (Odell), 18:207
Lucinda, 18:206
Lucretia (Edes), 18:205
Lucy, 18:200, 203, 206, 207
Lucy (Norwood), 18:203, 207
Lucy (Pool), 18:207
Lydia, 18:205, 212, 215, 216
Lydia (Barney), 18:206
Lydia (Burrage), 18:211, 213-215
Lydia (Cooper), 18:206
Lydia (Hawkes), 18:209, 212, 224
Lydia (Parsons), 18:206
Lydia M. (Nye), 18:217
Margaret (Davis), 18:206
Marietta, 18:207
Martha Ann (Gilbert), 18:207
Martha/Patty (Brooks), 18:205
Mary, 17:99; 18:199-201, 203, 204, 206, 207, 209, 211, 213, 215, 217, 224; 19:145
Mary (___), 18:203, 205, 210
Mary (Brown), 17:99; 18:199, 208, 223, 224; 19:145
Mary (Newhall), 17:99; 18:209, 211, 223
Mary (Page), 18:204
Mary (Pierce), 18:210
Mary (Pool), 18:204
Mary (Rand), 18:224
Mary (Richards), 18:211, 213
Mary (Rowe), 18:204
Mary (Stevens), 18:199, 200
Mary (Trevitt), 17:99; 18:209, 211, 224
Mary A. (Williams), 18:204
Mary Ann (Rhodes), 18:217
Mary Baker, 18:204
Mary Elizabeth (Wheeler), 18:207
Mary Russell (Calendar), 18:215
Mary S., 18:217
Matilda, 18:206
Mehitable, 18:214, 215
Mercy/Esther (___), 18:203
Micajah, 18:206
Miriam, 18:202
Molly, 18:205
Moses, 18:204, 205, 210
Nancy, 18:204, 217, 218
Nancy (Harwood), 18:217
Nancy (Norwood), 18:204
Nathan, 18:205
Nathaniel, 18:205
Nicholas, 18:203
Otis, 18:217
Patience, 18:202
Philemon, 18:204
Polly, 18:216
Polly (Hart), 18:217
Polly (Nutter), 18:206
Rachel, 18:202, 207
Rebecca, 18:205, 206, 210
Rebecca (Gammage), 18:201, 205
Rebecca (Rumney), 18:205

Rhoda, 18:205
Ruth, 18:204
Ruth (Andrews), 18:204
Sally, 18:205, 206, 216, 218
Sally (Carroll), 18:205
Sally (Fears), 18:204
Sally (Parker), 18:205
Sally Pool, 18:204
Samuel, 18:204, 205, 215
Sarah, 17:217; 18:201, 203-206, 210, 212, 217; 20:103
Sarah (Bulow), 18:201
Sarah (Burlow), 18:210
Sarah (Goodrich), 18:201, 204
Sarah (Goodwin), 18:201
Sarah (Hale), 18:205
Sarah (Hodgdon), 18:206
Sarah (Hudson), 18:209, 211, 224
Sarah (Trevitt), 17:99; 18:92, 209, 210, 224
Sarah Brooks, 18:217
Sarah Ellen, 18:217
Sarah Page (Pool), 18:205
Seth, 18:207
Simon, 18:205
Solomon, 18:201, 205
Sophia, 18:217, 218
Sophia (___), 18:205
Sophia Wheeler, 18:207
Stephen, 18:199-201, 205, 206, 210
Susan, 18:206
Susan Massey, 18:217
Susanna, 18:201-207, 214, 215
Susanna (Dwinel), 18:211, 213
Susanna (Massey), 18:217
Susanna (Norwood), 18:203, 204, 206, 207
Susanna (Presson), 18:205
Susanna (Wheeler), 16:216; 18:207
Susannah (Curran), 18:206
Theodore, 18:206, 207
Thomas, 17:99; 18:199, 208-213, 215-218, 224; 19:145, 228
Thomasine (York), 18:204
William, 18:200, 203-207, 213, 215-218
William Vandecamp, 18:207
Zaccheus, 18:204, 209, 211, 213-215; 19:75; 20:48
Zebulon, 18:211
Zerviah, 18:211; 19:50
NOSQUA
William, 17:135
NOTT
Maria Eleanor (Nutting), 16:115
NOTTINGHAM
Harriet Spady, 19:233
NOURSE/NURST see also NURSE
David, 17:179
John, 17:179
Jonathan, 19:119
Lydia, 17:179
Martha (Twist), 19:119
Mary (Carr), 17:179
Nathaniel, 17:179
NOWELL
Increase, 18:230
Moses, 16:107
NOWERS
Deborah K., 20:106
NOYCE
Samuel, 18:236
NOYES, 16:153; 17:45; 18:49; 19:118; 20:36, 44, 115, 146
___ (Haddock), 16:149
___, Dr., 19:34

Abbie D., 19:238
Abigail Knapp (Hills), 19:238
Abram, 20:108
Anna, 18:43
Anna (___), 19:161
Ariel S., 16:149
Benjamin Lake, 18:219
Daniel, 18:24
Elizabeth (Eaton), 19:91
Follansbee, 19:238
George W., 17:120
Henry E., 19:91
John Follansbee, 19:238
Jonathan, 19:161
Joseph, 19:161
Lucy Ann, 20:107, 108
Marguerite (Goodhue), 17:120
Nicholas, 17:15; 19:34, 94
Phebe, 19:91
Polly, 16:81
Rachel, 19:119
Rebecca (___), 20:108
Rebecca (Haddock), 16:147
Rebecca (Richardson), 19:238
Sarah, 19:234
Sarah A. (Haddock), 16:149
Sibyl, 19:224
Simon, 19:91
Sybil, 16:21; 17:202
William A., 16:147

NURSE see also NOURSE, 17:16
Francis, 17:60, 214; 20:187, 235
George, 16:36; 19:137
Hannah (Wallis), 16:94
Jonathan, 16:89
Lydia, 16:94
Rebecca, 17:15; 18:136; 20:235
Rebecca (Towne), 17:60; 19:221; 20:187
Rebecca Towne, 16:67
Samuel, 17:60

NURST see NOURSE, NURSE

NUTT
John, 17:23
Peter C., 20:174
Sarah, 20:99

NUTTER
Elizabeth, 17:45
Julia Ann, 19:19
Polly, 18:206
Polly (___), 18:206
William, 18:206

NUTTING
Abigail (___), 16:115
Daniel, 16:115
Eleanor Maria (O'Brian), 16:115
Elizabeth (Holden), 16:115
Ezekiel, 16:115
Hannah, 16:115
Hannah (___), 16:115
James, 17:81
John, 16:78; 18:94; 19:35
Luther, 16:115
Lydia, 17:80
Lydia (Longley), 17:81
Maria Eleanor, 16:115
Mary (Lakin), 16:115
Sarah, 19:26, 117
Sarah (Varnum), 19:35
William, 17:85

NUTTON
Jonathan, 17:93

NYE
Lydia, 17:59

Lydia M., 18:217
Nathaniel, 18:170
Sarah (Witt), 18:170

O'BRIAN
Daniel, 16:115
Eleanor Maria, 16:115
Martha (Gay), 16:115

O'BRIEN, 18:63; 20:126
George Edward, 18:239
Nicholas, 18:239
Sarah (Perkins), 18:239

O'CONNELL
Bridgett, 17:179
David, 17:179
George, 17:179
John, 17:179; 20:127
Mary (Horan), 17:179
Mary Jane, 17:179
William, 17:179

O'CONNOR/CONNOR
Abbey (Bradley), 18:177
Ellen/Helen, 18:177
Honora/Nora, 18:177
John F., 18:177
Lawrence M., 18:177
Mary F., 18:177
Michael, 18:177
Winnifred, 18:177

O'KELLY
Joseph, 20:96
Tabitha (Baker), 20:96

O'MALLEY
Patricia, 18:144

O'TOOLE
J. M., 16:189

OAKES see also OAKS
George, 20:197
John, 16:134; 19:118; 20:233
Mary (Goodale), 20:233
Sally/Sarah (Ingersoll), 19:118

OAKLEY
Annie, 20:120
Nathaniel, 17:135

OAKS see also OAKES
Richard, 18:29, 92

OAKUM
Jack, 17:135

OBEAR/OBER, 17:51; 20:150
Abigail, 20:238
Benjamin, 19:167
Edith, 16:143
Elizabeth, 20:150
Fanny, 17:162
Hannah, 16:145; 17:165
Israel, 20:58
James, 18:206; 20:151
Joanne (Lovett/Leavitt), 20:58
Josiah, 16:145; 20:82
Lidea (Cleaves), 20:151
Mary, 16:102; 19:158
Mary (West), 20:58
Priscilla (Woodbury), 16:143
Richard, 16:143; 20:198
Sally (Norwood), 18:206
Sarah, 17:51
Sarah (Kemball), 16:145

ODDING
Sarah, 20:96

ODELL
Charles, 20:154
Louisa, 18:207

ODLIN/ODLINE
James, 17:201
John, 19:132
Martha (Hale), 17:201

OESTRICH
Arthur Conrad, 20:56
Judith A. (Southard), 20:56

OLDPATH
Obadiah, 18:79, 80, 82; 19:75

OLIVER, 19:194
___, Capt., 16:138
Abigail (___), 16:47
Abigail (Farrington), 17:148; 19:49
Ann H., 17:199
Anne (Squire), 17:231
Benjamin, 16:47
Caroline (Needham), 16:47
Daniel, 16:111
David, 16:47
Elisha S., 17:27
Eliza (Brown), 16:47
Elizabeth (Putnam), 16:157
Ephraim, 17:148; 19:49
Hannah, 16:47
Henry, 16:16; 18:11, 105; 19:106
Huldah (Howard), 19:116
Huldah (Rhodes), 16:47
James, 16:47
John, 19:116
Lydia (Batchelder), 16:47
Mary (Dexter), 16:138
Mary (Sweetser), 17:27
Nathan, 19:116
Nathaniel, 16:157; 17:93
Olive, 18:11
Olivia (Cobb), 16:47
Peace (Collins), 16:47
Peter, 18:233
Ruth (Newhall), 16:47
Ruthy, 16:47
Sarah (Newhall), 16:47
Stephen, 16:47
Thomas, 17:231
Thoms, 19:197
William, 16:47

OLMSTEAD
Dorothea, 16:209

OLSON
Margaret J., 19:81
Pamelia, 18:109

OMMER, 16:194

ONIMAL
Stephen, 17:97

ONTHANK
Ruth, 20:137

ONYON see UNYON, 20:73

ORANGE
Hannah (___), 16:78

ORCOTT/ORCUTT
Elisha, 18:179
Samuel, 17:175
Susanna, 16:237

ORDWAY
Anne (Emery), 17:55
Anne (Huntington), 17:54
Elizabeth (Heath), 17:54
James, 17:54
Martha, 17:54
Moses, 17:54
Samuel Blanchard, 18:63
Stephen, 18:240
Titza (Titcomb), 17:54

ORGAN
  Dennis, 17:12
ORMES
  Ann, 17:101
  Mary, 20:235
ORMSBY, 18:132
ORN/ORNE see also HORN, HORNE
  ___, Capt., 20:37
  Aniss, 17:100
  Elizabeth, 17:100
  Elizabeth (Pike), 18:93
  Epithis Smith, 16:60
  Frances Nichols (Whittemore), 16:60
  Jane/Jennie (Metcalf), 17:238
  Joseph, 16:33; 17:238
  Joshua, 17:100; 19:38
  Louise, 16:151
  Mary, 16:78; 18:31, 92, 93
  Richard, 18:93
  Sally, 17:100
  Susanna (Trevitt), 17:100
  Timothy, 19:217; 20:36, 37, 48
ORNES
  Timothy, 19:217
ORR
  Shirley Ann, 19:240
ORVIN
  Thomas, 20:199
OSBORN/OSBORNE see also OSBURN
  ___ (Griffin), 17:187
  "Son", 17:201
  Aaron, 17:199
  Abel, 17:199
  Abigail, 17:184
  Abigail (Chase), 17:199
  Abigail (Lamb), 17:200
  Abigail (Simpson), 16:117; 17:183
  Abigail Simpson, 17:186
  Abraham, 17:198
  Addie M., 17:187
  Almira, 17:187
  Amos, 17:199
  Ann Augusta, 17:187
  Ann H. (Oliver), 17:199
  Ann/Anna, 17:184
  Anna (___), 17:201
  Anna (Fowler), 17:199
  Anna (Purinton), 16:117; 17:186
  Anne (Curtice), 17:201
  Archie, 17:188
  Benjamin, 17:198
  Benjamin E., 17:185
  Betsey, 17:187
  Betsey (Osborn), 17:187
  Bezaliel/Bazaleel, 17:195
  Caleb, 17:200
  Christopher, 17:200
  Clarissa, 17:187
  Damaris, 17:200
  Daniel, 17:199
  Danvers, 17:196
  David, 17:198
  Deborah (Stearns), 17:201
  Deliverance, 17:198
  Desire, 17:199
  Dorcas, 17:199
  Douglas, 17:201
  Effie Gertrude, 17:188
  Eleanor, 17:197; 20:234
  Eleanor (Southwick), 17:197
  Elijah, 16:88; 17:184
  Eliza E., 17:187
  Elizabeth, 17:197
  Elizabeth (Estes), 17:197
  Elizabeth (Flint), 17:198
  Elizabeth (Galucia), 17:200
  Elizabeth (Jones), 18:85
  Elizabeth (Poole), 17:199
  Elizabeth (Shove), 17:197
  Elizabeth (Sprague), 17:201
  Elizabeth (Tucker), 17:198
  Emma F., 17:187
  Esther, 17:198
  Esther (Buxton), 17:198
  Esther (Marble), 17:198
  Eunice, 17:199
  Eunice (Peaseley), 17:199
  Eunice (Very), 17:199
  Ezra, 17:199
  Fannie (Ham), 17:188
  Frank H., 17:187
  Frizwid/Fredisweed (Collicott), 17:195
  George, 17:195, 201
  George Washington, 17:201
  Ginger, 17:199
  Green, 17:184
  Hannah, 17:187
  Hannah (Buffam), 16:117; 17:186; 20:93
  Hannah (Burton), 16:117; 17:186
  Hannah (Clough), 17:187
  Hannah (Poor), 17:201
  Hannah (Trask), 17:200
  Hannah C., 17:187
  Henry, 17:201
  Henry F., 19:210
  Hitty/Mehitable, 17:200
  Isaac, 17:197; 18:85
  Israel, 17:199
  Jacob, 16:117; 17:183
  James, 17:201
  James L., 17:184
  Jemima, 17:184
  John, 16:117, 236; 17:18; 19:105; 20:93
  John H., 17:184
  John Proctor, 17:199
  John Simpson, 17:183
  Jonathan, 16:236; 17:195
  Jonathan P., 17:187
  Joseph, 17:195
  Joseph C., 17:187
  Joshua, 16:117; 17:187
  Judith (Francis), 17:199
  Leah Marie, 17:184
  Lois, 17:199
  Lois (Littlefield), 17:199
  Lucinda, 17:185
  Lucretia, 17:198
  Lucretia (Osborn), 17:198
  Lucy Ann (Marston), 17:188
  Lydia, 17:198
  Lydia (Foster), 17:199
  Lydia (Proctor), 17:199
  Lydia (Southwick), 17:199
  Lydia (Wellman), 16:236; 17:200
  Lyman P., Mrs., 17:196
  Margaret, 17:184
  Margaret (Derby), 17:197
  Margaret (Green), 17:184
  Margaret (Stone), 17:197
  Margaret Derby, 17:201
  Martha, 17:187
  Martha (Jewett), 17:201
  Martha (Osborn), 17:187
  Martha Hale, 17:201
  Mary, 17:197
  Mary (Buxton), 16:236; 17:200
  Mary (Carter), 17:185
  Mary (Clark), 17:198
  Mary (Cook), 17:201
  Mary (Lane), 17:184
  Mary (Osborn), 17:197
  Mary (Proctor), 17:199
  Mary (Shillaber), 17:199
  Mary (Southwick), 17:197
  Mary (Ward), 17:201
  Mary Ann (Allen), 17:201
  Mary Ann (Wiggin), 17:201
  Mary Elizabeth, 16:236
  Mary Esta (Griffin), 17:187
  Mary J., 17:187
  Mehitable, 17:184
  Mercy, 17:200
  Mercy (Southwick), 17:197
  Micajah, 17:187
  Nancy (Lang), 17:201
  Nathan Henry, 17:235
  Nathan Henry Clough, 17:188
  Nathaniel, 17:199
  Oliver W., 17:201
  Patience, 17:198
  Patience (Boyce), 17:198; 20:27
  Paul, 17:197
  Persis, 17:201
  Persis (Littlefield), 17:201
  Phebe, 17:197
  Philadelphia, 17:197
  Rachel, 17:199
  Rachel (Foster), 17:197
  Rebecca, 19:200
  Rebecca (Goldthwait), 17:200
  Recompense, 17:195
  Richard, 17:201
  Robert, 17:198
  Robert W., 17:188
  Ruth, 17:198
  Sally (Sanderson), 17:200
  Samuel, 17:196, 197; 20:27
  Samuel C., 17:187
  Sarah, 17:15
  Sarah (Buxton), 17:198
  Sarah (Clark), 17:197
  Sarah (Douglas), 17:198
  Sarah (Gardner), 17:197
  Sarah Douglas, 17:201
  Sophia, 17:201
  Stephen, 17:198
  Susanna, 17:200
  Susanna (Buffum), 17:200
  Susanna (Codner), 17:200
  Susanna (Smith), 17:199
  Susanna (Southwick), 17:199
  Sylvester, 17:199
  Thomas, 17:197
  William, 16:117; 17:20, 22; 18:136
  William A., 17:185
  William Roberts, 17:200
  Winifred A. (Campbell), 17:188
OSBURN see also OSBORN
  Archie Clifton, 17:188
  Byrle, 19:54
  Edward Clarence, 17:188
  Effie Gertrude, 17:188
  Mattie Augusta, 17:188
  Rebecca, 18:117; 19:170
  Sarah (Swan), 17:200
  William, 16:32
OSGOOD, 18:136, 161
  ___, Dr., 20:90
  ___, Mrs., 16:68

Abiah, 19:35
Abigail, 19:89
Abigail (Day), 19:89
Ann (___), 19:46
Calvin, 20:30, 53
Christopher, 16:68; 18:93; 19:89; 20:165, 168
Desire (___), 18:179
Dyer, 17:187
Elizabeth (Clere/Clare), 19:179
Enoch, 17:240
Esther, 20:165
Esther (Barker), 20:166
Ezekiel, 18:162
Hannah, 16:82
Hannah (Abbott), 20:216
Hannah (Barker), 20:165
Hannah (Dane), 19:115
Hooker, 16:68
Ira, 19:89
J., 19:125
Jane (___), 17:240
Jeremiah, 18:162
Joanna, 16:117
John, 16:65; 18:155, 157; 19:34, 46, 89; 20:164-168, 214, 216
Jonathan, 17:200
Joseph, 20:82
Joshua, 18:45
Josiah, 18:162; 19:89
Lucy (Wiborn), 20:53
Lydia, 19:33
Margery (Fowler), 20:165
Mary, 18:45; 19:46, 216; 20:23, 165, 166
Mary (___), 18:45, 93
Mary (Clement/Clements), 19:115; 20:22, 166
Mary (Osborn), 17:200
Mary J. (Osborn), 17:187
Mehitable, 19:137
Molly, 19:97
Nathaniel, 20:221
Nealand, 17:240
Peter, 18:93
Phineas, 18:179
Priscilla, 16:233; 20:165
Samuel, 18:162; 19:115; 20:165
Sarah, 20:165
Thomas, 16:68; 19:90, 96; 20:168
Tim, 19:90
Timothy, 16:68; 19:88
William, 19:89, 179
OTIS, 20:13
Christine, 18:149
Harrison G., 19:131
OTLEY
Adam, 19:189
OTTEN
Marjorie Wardwell, 18:133, 135; 19:30, 219; 20:19, 119, 164, 216
OTTWAY
John, 17:89
OULTON
John, 20:49
Mary (Elithorpe), 20:49
OVERALL
Mary, 20:132-134
OWEN
Paula F., 18:133, 134
OWENS
Martha Anne, 17:120

PACKER
Elizabeth (Friend), 16:116
John, 16:116
Tamsen, 16:116
PAERS see also PEARSON, PIERSON
John, 20:112
PAGE/PAIGE, 18:206; 20:207
___, Mr., 20:232
Alvira/Elvira, 19:59
Anna (Marshall), 16:160
Cornelia (Breed), 16:224
Daniel, 19:92
Elizabeth, 17:83
Enoch, 16:224
Hannah, 18:11, 39
Hannah (___), 16:131
Hester (Goodale), 20:232
Huldah, 17:206
James, 18:39
Jeremiah, 20:89
John, 18:39
Joseph, 18:156
Lucius C., 16:71
Lucius R., 16:31, 200; 17:45; 18:71, 52, 229; 19:224
Martha (Dow), 18:156
Mary, 16:57; 17:52; 18:39, 204; 20:178
Nicholas, 16:18
Rachel, 18:39
Rebecca (Bassett), 18:39
Rebekah, 18:39
Samuel, 16:160; 17:83
Sarah, 16:147; 18:39
Sarah (Lawrence), 17:83
William, 19:96
PAIN/PAINE see also PAYNE
Amos Martin, 20:54
Elizabeth (Colburn), 16:56
Elizabeth (Pierce), 16:56; 17:115
Huldah (Blaney), 16:82
John, 20:55
Joseph, 16:82
Lavina Jane (Munn), 20:54
Lavinia L. (Stevens), 20:54
Margaret, 19:226; 20:45
Mary, 17:30; 18:101; 20:96, 209
Moses, 16:56; 17:115
Polly, 20:221
Rachel (Hill), 20:54
Rebecca (Bachelder), 16:82
Robert, 18:192, 193
Sarah, 16:56; 17:115
Sarah (Sanford), 16:56
Stephen, 16:82; 17:29
Susannah (Martin), 20:55
Thomas, 16:56; 17:7
Thomas Demint, 20:54
William, 16:56; 18:193; 19:193
Zemira Rita, 20:54
PALFRAY/PALFREY, 19:126
Edith, 17:127
Peter, 16:136; 19:123, 124,127, 189; 20:185, 192
Phebe, 20:97
Richard, 17:12
PALMER
___, Mr., 20:53
Abigail, 16:214; 20:220
Albina, 17:239
Ann (Denison), 16:55
Asenath, 16:55
Charles, 17:239
Comfort (Fairbanks), 17:176
Daniel, 16:214
Deborah, 18:216
Dorothy (Brown), 16:55
Ebenezer, 17:176
Elizabeth, 18:56
Elizabeth Elaine, 16:53
Elizabeth Elaine (Hardy), 16:53
Frances (Prentice), 16:55
Frank W., 18:50; 20:143
George, 16:53; 20:9
George Francis, 16:53
Gershom, 16:55
Hannah, 16:55; 17:176; 20:31, 53
Hannah (___), 16:217
Hannah (Palmer), 16:55; 17:176
Hannah (Stanton), 16:55
Henry, 17:93; 18:140
Horace Wilbur, 17:176
John, 16:213; 17:97
John Friend, 16:214
Joseph, 16:55
Lucy, 17:176
Martha, 16:214
Martha (Friend), 16:214
Mary, 16:55; 18:160
Mary (Gilbert), 16:34
Mary (Hatch), 20:31, 53
Mary (Palmer), 16:55
Mercy, 16:171; 17:51
Naomi, 16:55
Nehemiah, 16:55
Pauline (Longfellow), 16:53
Rebecca (Short), 16:55
Rhoda (Pettingell), 17:239
Richard, 16:34
Sarah, 16:214
Sarah (Friend), 16:213
Susanna, 17:239
Theron, 20:83
Thomas, 17:18
Timothy, 17:141
Walter, 16:55
Zebulon, 17:176
PALMES
Jonathan, 16:165
PAMER
John, 20:199
PANSANO
Mathilda, 16:178
PAPOON
Elizabeth (Ivory), 19:147
Mary, 16:46
Richard, 19:147
PARDEE
Aaron, 17:56
Eveline Blancy (Eyles), 17:56
Harriet E. (Bayley), 17:55
Henry Clay, 17:55
Jessamine, 17:55
PARIS/PARRISH see also PARRIS
___, Mr., 20:235
Susannah, 16:119
PARK/PARKE
Dorothy (Bacon), 16:115
Hannah (___), 16:116
John, 19:132
Martha (Chaplin), 16:116
Phebe, 16:115
Robert, 16:115, 116
Samuel, 16:116
Tamsen (Packer), 16:116
PARKER, 17:140; 19:189, 216
___, Capt., 18:227

___, Goody, 19:30
___, Mr., 17:118
___, Mrs., 17:118
"Child", 18:162; 19:91, 95
"Daughter", 19:87
"Son", 17:85; 18:163; 19:92, 95
A. G., 16:225
Aaron, 16:40; 19:90
Abel, 17:81
Abiel, 17:86
Abigail, 16:38; 17:82; 18:162, 163; 19:89, 93
Abigail (___), 17:84
Abigail (Baker), 16:39
Abigail (Michel/Mitchell), 18:158, 160-162
Abigail (Osgood), 19:89
Abigail (Sawtell), 17:80
Abigail (Wright), 16:38
Abijah, 16:40; 17:83
Abraham, 16:225; 17:78
Alford, 19:91
Alice (Woods), 17:84
Almira, 19:97
Almira Ellis, 19:97
Amasa, 17:84
Anis, 16:38
Ann, 19:91
Anna, 17:47; 19:48, 88
Anna (Errington), 19:48
Anna (Parker), 19:88
Anna (Swain/Swaine), 20:53
Anna/Hannah, 16:227
Anne (___), 16:225; 17:78
Anne (Coker), 18:235, 236
Anne (Newhall), 17:216
Apphia (Spofford), 19:89, 90
Asa, 16:42; 18:178; 19:89, 90
Augusta, 19:97
Azubah, 17:84
Azubah (___), 17:82
Azyba (Farnsworth), 17:83
Baldwin, 17:216
Benjamin, 17:78; 18:235-237; 19:33, 87-90, 92, 93
Benjamin Woods, 17:84
Bethiah, 16:39
Bethiah (Polley), 20:191
Betsey, 18:217; 19:93
Betty, 19:89
Betty/Elizabeth, 16:38
Caleb, 16:38
Calvin, 16:41
Carlton, 18:163
Catharine, 16:38
Chandler, 19:97
Charles, 19:92
Charlotte, 19:89, 97
Clarissa B., 19:97
Dalton/Daalton, 18:163
Daniel, 17:120; 19:48, 180, 214
David, 16:39; 17:120
Deborah, 16:40
Deliverance, 17:81
Didamia, 17:84
Dinah (___), 18:162, 163
Dolly, 19:92
Dolly/Dorothy, 16:38
Dorcas, 19:89, 92, 95
Dorcas (Smith), 16:40
Dorothy Farrington, 17:142
Ebenezer, 16:40; 17:84; 19:87, 144
Eber, 17:85
Edith, 19:97

Edmund, 16:42
Edmund Lawrence, 16:43
Elijah, 17:83
Eliphalet, 18:235-237
Eliza (Whitcomb), 19:180
Elizabeth, 16:39; 17:78; 18:154, 157-159, 236, 238; 19:31, 87, 88
Elizabeth (___), 16:43; 17:79; 19:33, 87-89
Elizabeth (Baker), 18:235, 236
Elizabeth (Batchelder), 16:38
Elizabeth (Brown), 19:144
Elizabeth (Chandler), 19:97
Elizabeth (Cheever), 19:102
Elizabeth (Farley), 17:83
Elizabeth (Gage), 19:33, 87, 88
Elizabeth (Green), 16:42
Elizabeth (Hinckley), 19:96
Elizabeth (Kingsbury), 18:155, 157, 160
Elizabeth (Long), 16:225
Elizabeth (Martin), 18:162; 19:95
Elizabeth (Morss), 18:235-237
Elizabeth (Page), 17:83
Elizabeth (Parker), 17:80; 18:236
Elizabeth (Stevens), 18:238
Elizabeth (Whippo), 18:159, 235
Ellen, 19:180
Enoch, 19:90
Ephraim, 17:82
Esther, 17:85; 19:93
Esther (Daves), 18:162
Esther (Foster), 18:236
Esther (Shattuck), 17:86
Eunice, 16:41; 17:85
Eunice (___), 16:41
Eunice (Brooks), 16:225
Eunice (Lakin), 17:85
Frances, 18:236
Francis (Tew), 18:236
Frederick, 19:88, 95
Frederick D., 19:97
Gideon, 17:86
Grace, 16:41
Hamilton, 19:180
Hannah, 16:39; 17:82; 18:159, 160, 202, 238; 19:31, 33, 88, 89, 93, 95-97; 20:33
Hannah (Abbott), 19:95
Hannah (Blood), 17:79
Hannah (Brooks), 17:84
Hannah (Brown), 19:31, 32
Hannah (Carter), 19:97
Hannah (Chandler), 19:93, 95
Hannah (Frie/Frye), 19:33, 92
Hannah (Jenkins), 17:78
Hannah (Lovejoy), 19:97
Hannah (Robinson), 19:92
Hannah (Stevens), 16:40; 19:33, 87, 88
Hannah (Swan), 19:35, 95, 96
Hannah (Weld), 16:39
Hannah/Joannah (Bailey), 19:93
Hannaniah, 19:144, 212, 216; 20:53, 186, 190
Harriet (Haskell), 19:97
Henry, 17:135
Hepsibah, 18:160
Hester, 18:156
Horatio Newton, 16:38
Imlah, 17:85
Isaac, 19:96, 97
Isaac M., 19:90
Israel, 16:154
Ithamar, 19:180
Jacob, 16:40; 17:78; 19:101, 102, 225
Jacob Lakin, 17:85

James, 16:41; 17:78; 18:136, 161-163; 19:31, 35, 87, 91, 92, 95, 229; 20:52, 53
Jane/Jenny, 19:90
Jebes, 16:38
Jennie (Cochrane), 19:180
Jeremiah, 16:39; 19:90
Jesse, 17:85; 19:89, 91
Joab, 17:82
Joanna, 18:120; 19:97
Joanna (___), 16:41
Joanna (Stephens), 17:81
Joanna/Anna, 17:81
Joel, 16:41
Johan (Coker), 16:227
Johannah (Grout), 17:83
John, 16:39; 17:78; 18:156, 159, 237, 238; 19:31-33, 87-89, 91-93, 95, 215; 20:184, 190
John/Johnston, 19:92
Jonas, 16:42
Jonathan, 16:38; 19:33, 87, 92, 214
Joseph, 16:39; 17:78; 18:136, 154-158, 160-163, 235-238; 19:30, 31, 33-35, 87, 88, 91, 93-97, 174
Joshua, 17:83; 19:96
Josiah, 17:79; 18:162
Judith (Bancroft), 19:214
Junia, 17:85
Katharine, 16:40
L. M., 18:86
L. N., 18:83
Loea Howard, 20:195
Lois (___), 16:40
Lucy, 16:40; 19:90, 93
Lucy (Pushard), 19:90
Luther, 18:178
Lydia, 16:38; 17:81; 19:35, 95-97; 20:33
Lydia (___), 16:42
Lydia (Frye), 19:31, 33
Lydia (Munroe), 16:42
Lydia (Nutting), 17:80
Lydia (Parker), 19:97
Lydia (Vernum), 16:42
Lydia Faulkner (Stephens), 19:97
Marble, 19:97
Margaret, 17:78; 18:235-237
Margaret (___), 16:42; 17:78
Margaret (Clark), 18:159, 235
Margaret (White), 16:40
Martha, 16:39; 17:82; 18:162; 19:34, 35, 95
Martha (___), 16:39
Martha (Barker), 18:161
Martha (Dow), 18:156
Martha (Johnson), 19:35, 93-95
Mary, 16:38; 17:79; 18:155, 156, 159; 19:31-33, 90, 92, 93, 95, 97
Mary (___), 16:228; 17:80; 18:154, 159, 163, 237; 19:97
Mary (Ayer), 19:30, 31, 174, 175, 221; 20:166, 168
Mary (Bradstreet), 17:80
Mary (Brown), 19:31, 32
Mary (Emery), 19:35, 93, 95
Mary (Farnsworth), 16:42
Mary (Friend), 16:217
Mary (Hovey), 19:93
Mary (Lacount/Lavant), 19:87
Mary (Mainard), 17:82
Mary (Marston), 18:156, 158, 159
Mary (Morse), 16:38
Mary (Perkins), 16:41
Mary (Richardson), 16:38

Mary (Sawtell), 17:80
Mary (Scarborough), 16:39
Mary (Stevens), 19:88
Mary (Williams), 16:39, 40
Mary (Wood), 19:96
Mary/Molly, 19:97
Mehitable, 19:89, 90
Mehitable (Bancroft), 19:214
Michael, 17:152; 19:95, 97
Minerva, 19:180
Molley, 16:41; 19:89, 95
Molly (Osgood), 19:97
Moses, 19:90, 97
Nabby, 19:97, 174
Nancy, 18:163; 19:91
Nathan, 18:154, 155, 162; 19:30-34, 87-93, 95-97, 174
Nathaniel, 16:38; 17:80; 19:30, 88, 180; 20:191
Nehemiah, 16:38; 17:83
Obadiah, 16:40; 17:82; 18:162
Olive, 19:90
Oliver, 16:40; 19:239
Patience, 17:84
Peggy/Margaret, 16:40
Peter, 19:31, 34, 35, 94-07, 174
Phebe, 16:38; 19:34, 35, 91, 92, 95, 97
Phebe (Farnam), 19:92
Phebe (Farrington), 17:152; 19:95
Phebe (Ingalls), 19:33, 91
Phebe (Marble), 19:97
Phebe (Mulford), 19:92
Phebe (Noyes), 19:91
Pheihas, 19:93
Phineas, 16:41; 17:81; 19:93, 95
Polly, 17:120; 19:35, 93, 97, 111, 113
Polly/Mary (Barker), 19:97
Rachel, 16:40
Rebecca, 16:40; 19:93
Rebecca (Newhall), 19:144
Robert, 19:31, 96, 97, 174
Ruth, 16:38; 18:155, 156, 160, 238; 19:97
Ruth (Shattuck), 17:81
Ruth (Smith), 16:40
Ruth (Stevens), 16:41
Ruth (Wood), 19:97
Sally, 16:43; 18:205
Sally (Darling), 19:97
Sally B., 19:90
Sam Stevens, 16:41
Samson, 16:41
Samuel, 16:41; 18:154-156, 159-162, 238; 19:88, 97, 217; 20:34, 36
Sarah, 16:40; 17:79;18:155, 156; 19:31, 90, 91, 93, 95, 175, 221, 228, 229; 20:33, 53
Sarah (___), 16:226; 17:82; 19:87, 88; 20:52
Sarah (Chadwick), 19:33, 89
Sarah (Larrabee), 19:228, 229
Sarah (Lawrence), 16:43
Sarah (Marble), 19:89, 90
Sarah (Parker), 17:84
Sarah (Richardson), 17:85
Sarah (Wooster), 16:41
Scarborough, 16:39
Serena, 19:97
Seth, 19:87
Sewall, 17:86
Simeon, 16:41; 19:96, 97
Simon, 19:91
Sophia (Patch), 16:40

Stephen, 16:38; 18:154-156, 158, 159, 162, 235-238
Submit, 17:153
Susanna, 16:39; 19:93, 97
Susanna (Hartshorn), 18:156, 158, 160
Susanna (Loper), 16:41
Susanna (Short), 19:30, 31
Sybil, 16:41
Tabitha, 19:92
Tabitha (Sawyer), 17:82
Thankfull (Pratt), 16:38
Theoda, 16:40
Theodore, 20:184, 190
Thomas, 16:38; 18:71, 136, 154-156, 160, 230; 19:138; 20:183, 184, 186, 188, 190-192, 195
Tilly, 16:41
Timothy, 16:39; 17:82
Trueworthy, 16:41; 18:178
Tryfena, 17:82
Willard, 16:150
William, 17:81; 18:162; 19:93
Winslow, 17:85
Zachariah, 17:84
Zerviah (Lincoln), 18:162
PARKIS/PARKHURST
Elizabeth, 17:35
Joseph, 17:78
Rebecca (Read), 17:78
Samuel, 18:237
PARKMAN, 18:136
Edward Henry, 17:57
Eileen (Allen), 17:180
Elias, 18:230
Georgina, 17:57
Kay, 17:180
Mary, 20:91
Thomas, 17:57
Tyler, 17:180
Waldo A., 17:57
William Gordon, 17:57
PARLEE
Charlotte, 16:178
Henry, 16:178
Mary Jane (Chambers), 16:178
PARLIN
Aaron, 20:41
Lois, 17:116
Martha (Bancroft), 20:41
PARLO
Thomas, 20:198
PARMENTER
Amy (Eames), 17:177
Edmund, 18:168
George, 20:10
H. R., 17:161
Harriet, 20:9, 10
John, 17:177
Lydia, 17:177
Mary (Stewart), 18:168
PARMITER
Benjamin, 19:202
PARNALL/PARNELL
Giles, 20:198
Jonas, 19:29
Martha (Henderson), 19:29
PARRIS, 17:60
___, Rev., 17:15
Samuel, 17:16; 19:15
PARRISH see PARIS, PARRIS
PARROT/PARROTT
Benjamin, 16:102; 19:107, 109
Catherine (___), 16:100

Deborah (Richards), 16:102; 19:107
Elizabeth (___), 16:102
Elizabeth (Ingalls), 19:107
Hannah, 19:107
Hannah (Ingalls), 19:106, 107
Hannah (Swan), 19:107
Hephzibah (Ingalls), 19:107, 109
James, 19:106, 107
Lydia, 16:102
Nathaniel, 19:107
Rufus, 19:107
Sally (Burrell), 19:107
William, 16:102; 19:107
PARSON see also PEARSON
___, Capt., 17:11
"Son", 17:223
Alice, 17:223
Andrew, 17:11
Anne, 16:229
Annie, 17:223
Eben, 20:36
Elizabeth A. (___), 17:223
Gilman Stearns, 17:223
James, 20:34
Katie (___), 17:223
Mary (___), 17:11
Robert, 19:138
PARSONS see also PEARSON, 17:139; 20:41
___, Mrs., 17:12
Abigail, 17:137
Abigail (___), 20:105, 138, 237
Abigail (Robinson), 20:237
Abigail (Smith), 18:45
Abigail (Younglove), 17:58
Andrew, 17:12
Annette, 17:38
Annette Pulcifer, 16:218
Charlotte (Norwood), 18:204
David, 18:201; 19:119; 20:39
Deborah, 18:206
Deborah (___), 18:206
Eben, 17:56
Ebenezer, 16:94; 17:56; 18:45; 20:39
Edward, 17:105
Eleanor, 19:170, 172
Eleazer, 18:240
Eliza Adeline G. (Peel), 17:56
Eliza S. (Friend), 17:105
Elizabeth, 18:173
Emma Marie, 17:55
Esther (Norwood), 18:204
Hannah, 18:173; 20:13
Hannah (Bray), 17:56
Hannah (Harris), 18:201
Israel, 20:39
Jacob, 18:172
James, 18:206
Jeffrey, 17:58
Jeremiah, 17:12
John, 17:13; 18:240
Jonathan, 17:223; 19:169, 199
Joseph, 17:12
Josiah, 18:204
Langdon B., 19:32
Lois (Bancroft), 20:39
Lois Jane, 17:180
Louise Friend, 16:218
Lydia, 17:13; 18:206
Mark, 16:134
Martha Frances, 16:218
Martha Hale (Friend), 16:218
Mary (___), 17:223

Mary A. (Cran), 17:105
Mary E., 17:166
Molly (Winnery), 19:119
Nabby, 20:39
Nabby (Smith), 20:39
Nathaniel, 18:204
Nehemiah, 16:134
Rhoda, 18:88
Robert, 20:195
Samuel, 17:13
Sarah, 17:137; 18:86
Sarah (Sayward), 17:137
Sidney, 17:224
Stephen, 20:237
Susanna, 18:35, 19:85, 169, 199, 235
Susanna (Hadley), 19:169, 199
Susannah (Norwood), 18:204
Theophilus, 18:136
William, 16:218
Zacceus, 17:12
Zebulon, 17:137
PARTRIDGE see also PATRIDGE
Ruth, 20:31
Sarah, 17:55
Sarah (___), 17:94
William, 19:138; 20:195
PASEN
Jacob, 16:27
Sarah (Pix), 16:27
PASLY
William, 20:197
PATASHALL
Jane (Greenleaf), 18:77
Martha, 18:77
Robert, 18:77
PATCH, 16:76
Abraham, 17:18
Amos, 17:238
Asahel Huntington, 17:238
Augustus, 17:238
Benjamin, 17:18
Daniel, 17:238
Edmund, 17:18
Elizabeth, 16:116; 17:32
Elizabeth (Gould), 17:238
Eunice (Fraile), 17:18
H., 16:43
Hannah (Dodge), 18:98
Ira H., 18:98
James, 16:215; 20:198
Jemima, 16:142
Jonathan, 18:136
Lydia (___), 16:215
Martha, 17:238
Mary, 17:22
Mary M., 18:98
Nicholas, 16:137
Sophia, 16:40
PATRICK
Katharine, 18:20
The Scot, 16:111
PATRIDGE see also PARTRIDGE
John, 16:180
Mary (Smith), 16:180
William, 16:180
PATTE/PATTEE
Martha, 17:24
Mary Alice, 20:56
PATTEN
Deborah (Wright), 17:174
Nathaniel, 17:174
Phebe, 17:174
Ruth, 20:81

Sally, 18:169
PATTERSON
Abigail (Cradock), 17:12
James, 17:12
Jane (___), 17:104
Lydia (Larrabee), 20:50
Nancy J. (Dean), 17:104
Nehemiah, 20:50
Sarah A., 17:104
William, 17:104
PATTILLO, 17:139
PAUL
Elizabeth, 19:155
John, 17:88; 18:225, 226
Joseph, 16:203
Katherine Choate, 18:174
Lydia (___), 17:93; 18:225, 226
Mary, 18:225; 20:113
Sarah, 18:225, 226
PAXWELL
William, 20:73, 74
PAYNE see also PAIN/PAINE
Bethyah, 20:145
Ebenezer, 17:29
Fred, 16:232
John, 18:193
Sally (Kirby), 17:29
Sarah A., 17:29
W. P., 17:161
PAYSON
Charity, 18:212
Edward, 20:161
Johanna (Newhall), 17:160
Lemuel, 17:160
PAYTON
Mary, 17:232
William, 20:208
PEABODY, 17:140
Betsey (Russell), 18:217
Betsy, 18:217
Elizabeth, 18:218; 20:142
Ephraim, 17:228
Eunice, 16:194
George, 17:141; 19:15
Hannah, 16:46
Isaac, 20:202
Jacob, 16:217
Jerusha (White), 20:236
John, 16:193; 19:32
Joseph, 16:193
Judith (Dodge), 17:141
Lucy, 16:217; 17:38
Lydia, 16:194
Mary Jane (Derby), 17:228
Priscilla, 18:106
Richard, 18:107
Ruth (___), 17:205
Ruth (Trask), 18:177
Sally/Sarah, 18:177
Samuel, 18:177
Sarah (Potter), 16:217
Thomas, 17:141; 19:89
William, 16:193; 18:217
William, Mrs., 16:111
Zerobabel, 20:236
PEACH
Bethia (Blaney), 16:84
Ebenezer W., 16:84
Hannah, 19:169
John, 16:140; 17:212
Lot, 16:84
Sarah (Blaney), 16:84
Sarah (Elkins), 17:230

William, 17:230; 20:15, 199
PEACOCK/POCOCK
Edward, 18:180
Eunice, 18:171
John, 18:171
Sarah, 16:180
PEAK/PEAKE see also PICKE
Hannah, 16:209
Ralph Frank, 20:148
Shirley Anne (Tarbox), 20:148
PEARCE see also PEARSE, PEIRCE, PIERCE
Abigail (Symonds), 20:224
Anna (Laskin), 16:119
Elizabeth (Merritt), 16:58
Frank C., 17:111
Hannah (Alley), 18:21, 53
Joanna, 16:79; 20:224
John, 16:58; 17:240; 20:200
Jonathan, 18:21
Julia F. (Low), 17:111
Mary, 16:58
Mary/Polly (Doliber), 16:58
Nathaniel, 16:119
Robert, 20:224
Sarah, 18:19
Sarah (___), 16:58
Sarah (Weber), 16:58
Thomas, 18:21, 53
PEARD
Sarah (Bartol), 18:225
William, 18:225
PEARL
Benjamin, 20:83
John, 19:239
Mehitable (Hall), 19:239
Ruth Mehitable, 19:239; 20:120
PEARS
William, 20:199
PEARSE see also PEARCE, PEIRCE, PIERCE
Abigail, 18:33
Deborah, 18:33
Elizabeth (Armitage), 18:232
Hannah, 18:33
Hannah (Bassett), 18:33
John, 18:33, 232
Richard, 18:33
Ruth, 16:238
PEARSON see also PIERSON, PARSON, 20:41
Abigail (Brown), 18:215
Bartholomew, 18:240
Catherine, 18:215
Dorcas (___), 16:178
Ebenezer, 19:136, 137, 216; 20:36
George, 19:226
Hannah, 19:137
Hannah (___), 19:216
Hepsibah (Swayne), 18:43
Hepsibar, 18:43
Hepsibel, 19:137
James, 18:43, 208; 19:136, 137, 216; 20:36, 103
John, 16:178; 17:113; 18:28, 43, 137; 19:105, 135, 136, 212, 214, 216, 217; 20:34
Jonathan, 18:240; 19:137
Kendall, 19:136
Lois, 20:41
Lois (Bancroft), 20:41
Maudlin (___), 19:135, 136
Rebeckah, 17:113

Samuel, 20:41
Sarah, 16:173
Simeon, 18:215
Sophia (Osborn), 17:201
Tabitha, 16:171; 17:113; 19:137
Tabitha (Kendall), 17:113
Timothy, 20:41
William, 17:137, 201
PEARSON/PAERS
John, 20:112
PEARSON/PRESTON
James, 17:48
PEASE, 17:161; 18:157
Abner, 17:152
Anna, 18:87, 89
Bathsheba (Jones), 18:86
Daniel, 18:87
David, 18:86
Elizabeth (Farrington), 17:152
Elizabeth (Thomas), 17:22
Gideon, 18:86
Hannah (Jones), 18:87
Henry, 20:57
Ida Florence (Hutchins), 20:57
Isaac, 17:22
Jerusha (Spencer), 18:86
John, 18:86; 19:189, 193
Josephine (Watson), 20:57
Leola Maud, 20:56
Mabel Josephine, 20:57
Mary, 17:22
Sarah, 18:86
Simeon, 18:86
Thomas, 18:86
Walter Scott, 20:57
PEASELEE/PEASELEY/PEASLEE/ PEASLEY
Alice, 16:27
Alice (Currier), 16:78
E. R., 16:150
Eunice, 17:199
John, 16:15
Joseph, 16:14; 18:137, 141
Mary, 16:15
Mary (Johnson), 16:15
Mary (Martin), 16:15
Nathaniel, 17:198
Robert, 16:78
Ruth (Barnard), 16:15
Ruth (Osborn), 17:198
Sarah, 16:15
Susannah, 20:81
PEAVEY see also **PEVEY**
Sarah, 19:238
PECK
Elizabeth, 18:75
Esther, 19:28
Esther (Knight), 18:75
George, 18:75
Hannah, 16:73; 18:75
Jacob, 18:75
John, 18:75
Priscilla (Kirtland), 18:112
Rebecca, 18:75
Samuel, 18:75, 112, 113
Sarah, 18:75
Sarah (Blaney), 16:26
PECKER
"Daughter", 16:141
Abigail, 16:141
Elizabeth (Friend), 16:140
James, 16:141
Jeremiah, 18:143

Jonathan Eastman, 18:143
Mary, 16:141
Mary Land (Eastman), 18:143
Susanna, 16:141
PECKS see also **PIX**
Elizabeth, 16:46
PEDRICK/PEDRIK, 19:230
Elizabeth, 16:36
John, 16:36; 18:137; 20:199
Lydia (Ricker), 17:103
Lydia Ellen, 17:103
Mary, 16:84
Miriam (___), 16:36
Richard, 17:103
Sarah, 19:231
PEEL
Eliza Adeline G., 17:56
Sarah (___), 17:56
William, 17:56
PEIRCE see also **PEARCE, PEARSE, PIERCE**
Anne Brierly (Marland), 19:17
Elizabeth, 19:18
Hannah, 17:82
John B., 17:57
Mary Alice, 19:18
Mary/Maria, 17:57
Polly (McCleary), 17:57
Ruth, 18:113
Thomas Marland, 19:18
Thomas Sims, 19:17
William, 17:57
PEIRKS
Catharine (Parker), 16:38
David, 16:38
PEIRSON see also **PEARSON**
John, 17:217
PELHAM
Anthony, 20:69
Thomas, 16:134
PELL, 19:138
Joseph, 20:195
PELLETIER
Marie, 20:169
PELLETT
Sarah, 17:79
PELTRO
Mary Caste/Casbe, 16:119
PEMBERTON/PEMERTON
Abel, 19:206
Alice (___), 19:207, 209
Ann (Jewett), 19:208
Bridget, 19:208
Bridget (Wood), 19:208
Deborah, 19:208; 20:119
Deborah (Blake), 19:206, 208, 209
Deborah (Hills), 19:206
Elizabeth, 19:207
Elizabeth (___), 19:207
Ephraim, 19:206, 208, 209
Hannah, 19:208
Hannah (Hadley), 19:208
James, 16:160; 18:58; 19:206-209
Jeremiah, 19:208
John, 19:206-209
Margaret (___), 19:207, 209
Martha (Cheney), 19:208
Matthew/Martha, 19:208
Mary, 19:208, 209
Nathan, 19:208
Rachel (Spalding), 18:58; 19:206
Rebecca, 19:208
Rebecca Jewett (Burpee), 19:208

Sarah, 19:209
Sarah (___), 16:161
Sarah (Dutton), 19:206
Sarah (Marshall), 19:207, 208
Sarah (Willey), 16:160
Thomas, 19:206, 207, 210
William, 19:206
PENCE
Richard, 16:187
PENDEXTER
Alice (Miller), 19:229
Edward, 19:229
Elizabeth, 19:229
Elizabeth (Larrabee), 19:229
John, 19:229
Margaret, 19:229
Mary, 19:229
Philip, 19:229
PENDLEBURY, 16:13
PENDLETON
Ann, 18:224
Mrs. Nathaniel, 20:5
Thankful, 19:164
PENFIELD
Samuel, 19:212; 20:197
PENJON
Nicholas, 18:230
PENN
Hannah, 16:56
William, 18:185, 189
PENNEY/PENNY
Thomas, 16:64; 17:240
William, 20:98
PENROSE
Ann (Dowdin), 18:215
Hannah (Norwood), 18:215
Thomas, 18:215
William, 18:215
PENTZ
Ann (Corkum), 17:53
Conrad, 17:53
Dorothea, 17:53
Elizabeth (Prepper), 17:53
Jacob Ernst, 17:53
Johana (___), 17:54
Rudolph, 17:54
PEORD
Richard, 20:199
PEPPER
Alice, 16:59
Stephen, 19:137
PERADEAU see also **PERODEAU**
Amable (Pluff), 20:170
Jean Baptiste, 20:170
Marie Anne, 20:170
PERHAM
Joseph, 16:179
Patience, 18:239
PERKINS, 18:138; 19:135
Aaron C., 17:170
Abigail (Blake), 16:52
Abraham, 18:178
Albert, 17:27
Alice May (Longfellow), 16:52
Anna (___), 16:113
Anne, 18:153
Arthur Herbert, 16:52
Benjamin, 17:207
Bethia (Johnson), 17:49
C. A., Mrs., 20:77
Charles, 17:27
Chester A., 16:52
Damaris (___), 20:180

Daniel, 16:113
David, 20:198
Dudley D., 17:105
Elisha, 16:113; 20:142
Eliza, 17:120
Elizabeth, 16:3; 18:178
Ella, 17:27
Elmer, 17:27
Emma, 17:27
Esther (___), 18:178
Esther (Russell), 17:207
Eunice (Bancroft), 20:43
Flora Bella (Perkins), 16:52
Flora T. (Friend), 17:105
Frank, 17:27
George, 17:164
Hannah, 17:148; 18:152; 19:101; 20:225, 226
Hannah (Borman), 19:98
Hannah M., 17:170
Isaac, 17:27
Jacob, 19:98, 161, 168; 19:168; 20:180
James, 17:132; 20:218
Jennie, 17:27
John, 16:113; 17:207; 19:137; 20:142, 188
John Webster, 17:105
Jonathan, 16:52; 18:56
Joseph, 16:113
Josiah, 18:204
Leah (Cox), 20:218
Lucellia (Edmands), 17:27
Lucy, 17:105
Lucy (Tarbox), 20:142
Mary, 16:17; 17:205; 18:56, 113
Mary (___), 17:207; 20:142
Mary (Edmands), 17:27
Mary (Norwood), 18:204
Mary A. (Elliott), 17:105
Mehitable (Hood), 18:56
Nathaniel, 17:49; 18:178
Nellie A. (Jones), 20:147
Owen A., 16:26; 20:25
Priscilla, 16:113
Rebecca, 17:27
Ruth, 17:240; 19:98
Samuel, 17:132
Sarah, 16:160; 18:239; 20:217, 218, 238
Sarah (___), 20:224
Sarah (Denison), 16:113
Sybell B. (Cole), 17:170
Tabitha, 17:50
Thomas H., 17:132
Tobijah, 16:113
Wilbur, 17:27
William, 16:113; 17:232; 18:137; 19:137
Zacheus, 20:43
Zenus, 17:27
PERLEY, 19:118
Alice, 16:193
Allen, 16:193
Asa K., 16:234
Deborah (___), 16:194
Eunice, 20:142
Eunice (Hood), 18:57
Eunice (Peabody), 16:194
Francis, 16:194
Hannah (Coker), 16:194
Harriet (Spofford), 16:194
Henry, 18:57
Hepzibah, 16:194
Humphrey, 16:194
Isaac, 16:193
Jacob, 16:194

Jeremiah, 16:193
John, 16:193
Lydia, 16:194
Lydia (Peabody), 16:194
M., 16:219
M. V. B., 20:17
M. V. P., 16:193
Martha, 16:193
Martha (Fowler), 16:194
Mary, 16:193
Mary (Howlett), 16:193
Mehitable (Dwinnell), 16:194
Nathaniel, 16:193
Samuel, 16:193
Sarah, 16:193
Sidney, 16:30, 201; 17:18, 202; 18:42, 71, 99, 106, 137, 165, 222, 225; 19:25, 32, 98, 210, 230, 233; 20:26, 42, 99, 180a
Stephen, 16:194
Susanna (Bokeson), 16:193
Thomas, 16:193
Thomas P., 16:234
Timothy, 16:194
William, 16:234
PERODEAU see also PERADEAU
Marie Anne, 20:170
PERRAS
J. A., 16:50
PERRING
___, Mrs., 17:11
PERRY
___, Cmdr., 17:131
Abigail (Friend), 16:215
Adeline, 17:33
Ebenezer, 18:175
Emeline, 17:33
Francis, 19:195, 197
Horace Derby, 17:33
James, 17:33
James Albert, 17:33
Jefferson, 16:215
Jonathan, 20:229
Maria (Friend), 17:33
Maria Adelaide, 17:33
Mary, 17:240; 18:175
Mehitable White (Goodale), 20:229
Mercy (Brigham), 18:175
Ruth (___), 17:33
William, 17:33
William Francis, 17:33
PERS see PIERCE
PERSON
John, 20:191
PERSONS
James, 20:200
Jeffry, 20:200
Robert, 18:230
PERTHEL
Donald Frederick, 16:52
Gothold F., 16:52
Mary Ellen (Longfellow), 16:52
Wenda (Hadley), 16:52
PESTER
William, 19:188
PETAGHUNCKSQ
Cicely, 18:60a
PETENGIL
Benjamin, 19:208
Marthew/Martha (Pemberton), 19:208
PETER
___, Mr., 18:17
PETERS
Andrew, 16:68; 19:223; 20:202

Eleanor Bradley, 19:234
Elizabeth, 20:119
Franklin Demetrius, 19:139
Helen Elizabeth, 19:139
Helen Pleasants (Corr), 19:139
John, 19:94
Mary Ann, 18:96
Mercy, 19:115, 116, 220, 223
Mercy (Beamsley), 19:223
Samuel, 18:162
Sunda Anderson, 19:240
PETERSON
Judy, 18:146
Willit, 18:236
PETTEN
Sarah, 16:37
PETTINGELL/PETTINGILL
Elizabeth (Moulton), 18:59
Hannah (___), 19:112
Harriet Moulton, 18:59
Hugh, 19:112
Jacob, 19:160
Jennet, 19:111, 112
Joseph, 17:152
Martha, 19:160; 20:55
Martha (Coates), 19:160
Mathew, 19:160
Nicholas, 19:160
Rhoda, 17:239
Sarah (Farrington), 17:152
Tabitha (March), 19:160
William Fisher, 18:59
PETTIT
Bessie Martina, 20:32
Joseph, 18:39
Sarah (Bassett), 18:39
PEVEY see also PEAVEY
Edward, 20:119
Esther (Barker), 20:119
Mary, 20:119
Peter, 20:119
Rachel (___), 20:119
PEW
Richard G., 16:134
PFEIFFER
Ella, 19:56
PHANEUF
Matthias, 18:7; 20:13
Wilfred, 19:26
PHAROAH see FARRAR
PHELPS
___, Mrs., 16:68
Asenath, 17:49; 20:141
Edward, 16:68
Elizabeth, 16:67; 20:22, 23
Elizabeth (Abbott), 20:216
Grace, 20:230
Hannah, 16:98
Hannah (Tarbox), 17:49; 20:141
Henry, 17:138; 20:82
Israel, 18:87
Joseph, 20:216
Joshua, 17:49; 20:141
Pricilla (Jones), 18:87
Samuel, 16:68
PHILBRICK
Hannah, 17:57; 18:177; 19:240; 20:240
Sally, 20:239
PHILIP see also PHILLIP
King, 20:12, 189
Prince, 17:125
PHILIPS see also PHILLIPS
Benja, 16:173

Dina, 18:88
PHILLIP see also PHILIP
Elizabeth (___), 19:92
PHILLIPS see also PHILIPS, 20:84
___, Mrs., 16:32; 20:78
Abigail, 16:59
Abigail (___), 16:59
Abigail (Allen), 16:27; 18:31
Abigail (Curtin), 16:224
Albert M., 16:153
Alice, 16:224
Alice (___), 16:224
Amos, 16:224
Anna (Brown), 16:221
Anna (Sargent), 16:223
Anne/Anna, 16:223
Augustus Orvis, 16:224
Beniah, 16:224
Benjamin, 16:223
Benjamin H., 16:223
Bethia, 16:157
Charles S., 16:151
Charlotte, 17:139
Content, 16:221
Content (Hood), 16:27; 18:35, 36, 54, 55, 104
Ebenezer, 19:80
Elizabeth, 16:97; 18:36, 105, 238
Elizabeth (Blaney), 16:26
Elizabeth (Taylor), 16:157
Esther Amelia (Ready), 16:224
Eunice, 16:223
George, 16:223; 18:160; 19:57
Gideon, 16:222; 18:35, 55
Hannah, 16:153; 18:36; 19:39, 99
Hannah (___), 16:153
Hannah (Graves), 16:85; 20:212
Hannah (Liscom), 19:80
Helen Burton (Carstairs), 16:151
Hepsibah (Parker), 18:160
Hepzibah, 18:159, 160
Jacob, 16:85
James, 16:97
James Duncan, 17:225; 18:160
Jane, 16:154
Jeremiah, 16:210
John, 16:27, 221; 18:36, 54; 20:197
John Marshall, 19:200
Jonathan, 16:155; 18:36, 55, 159, 160, 238; 19:102
Judith (Dow), 16:223
Katherine (Burchstead), 16:221
Lydia, 16:27; 18:26, 160
Lydia (Howland), 16:27
Lydia/Elizabeth (Blaney), 16:27
Margaret, 16:154; 17:203
Margaret (___), 16:153; 17:204
Mary, 16:222; 17:169; 18:160; 19:37
Mary (Brown), 16:156; 18:36, 55
Mary (Burrill), 16:224
Mary (Dow), 16:223
Mary (Mower), 16:223
Miriam, 20:56
Nabby (Ingalls), 16:224
Patience, 16:222
Rachel (Stacey), 19:57
Rebecca, 16:16; 18:35, 53
Rebecca (Hood), 16:222; 18:35, 55
Rebecca (Snelling), 16:156
Richard, 16:27; 18:55
Ruth, 16:86; 18:31, 36, 97, 160; 20:208, 212
Ruth (Purchase), 16:27; 18:31; 20:212

Sadie Myrtle (Senter), 16:224
Samuel, 16:67; 18:160, 161, 163; 19:133
Sarah, 16:85, 223; 18:104, 172; 19:102
Sarah (___), 16:221
Sarah (Glover), 16:223
Sarah (Ingalls), 16:224
Sarah (Lynde), 19:102
Sarah (Stevens), 16:155, 157
Sewall Augustus, 16:224
Silence, 16:154
Stephen, 18:160, 238
Susannah, 18:160
Tabitha, 16:154, 155
Thankful, 16:96
Walter, 16:27, 153; 17:204; 18:29, 31, 35, 54, 55, 92, 104, 137; 20:197, 212
William, 16:27; 18:31
Zaccheus, 16:100
PHINNEY
Ed, 20:116
Elizabeth (Kinney), 18:67
G. A., 17:104
Isaac, 18:67
PHIPPEN
Abigail, 17:98
Atwater, 16:96
Dorcas (Wood), 16:177
Elizabeth (___), 18:137
Gamaliel, 17:230
John, 18:137
John S., 18:137
Joseph, 16:177
Mary, 16:177; 17:236; 19:171
Sarah (Purchase), 17:230
PHIPPS/PHIPS
___, Gov., 16:194
John, 20:220
William, 19:219
PICK see PICKE, PEAKE
PICKARD
Samuel, 18:239
Sarah (___), 18:239
PICKE/PICK/PICKLE see also PIKE, PEAK, 17:96
George, 17:96; 20:199
Hannah (Trevitt), 17:96
PICKERING
Alice, 18:96; 20:95
Alice (Flint), 20:60a
Anna Dane (Varney), 20:60a
Benjamin, 16:88
Elizabeth, 16:76; 18:100, 101; 20:59
Elizabeth (___), 20:60a
Elizabeth (Alderman), 16:118
Eunice, 16:88
George, 17:138
Hannah, 18:101; 19:59
Hannah (Browne), 17:41
James, 17:41
Jane, 16:88
Jane (Cromwell), 16:118; 18:101
Jane (Hobby), 16:88
John, 16:78; 18:71; 19:84, 196, 229; 20:60a
Jonathan, 16:118; 18:101; 19:213
Mary, 16:101
Mary (Wingate), 20:60a
Mehitable S. (Cox), 20:60a
Ruth (Benson), 20:60a
Sally, 18:220
Sarah (Burrill), 20:60a
Sarah (Coughlan), 20:60a
Sarah (White), 20:60a

Thankful (Mower), 17:41
Timothy, 17:7; 19:84; 20:137; 20:60a, 230
William, 17:41
PICKET/PICKETT
Clay, 19:232
Dorcas (Bennett), 18:180
Dorothy (Northey), 19:81, 82
Hepsibah A., 17:104
John, 16:119; 19:81, 82
Josiah, 17:104
Judith (Sewall), 18:180
Mary (___), 17:104
Meriam/Miriam (Allen), 16:119
Nicholas, 19:82; 20:199
Richard, 20:153
Robert, 18:180
Sarah (Trevitt), 17:101; 19:52
Saydee Jefferson (Harwood), 19:232
Thomas, 17:101; 19:52
William, 18:180
PICKLE see PICKE
PICKMAN
Anstis (Derby), 17:227
Benjamin, 17:227; 18:94
Clark Gayton, 18:94
Elizabeth (___), 18:94
John, 18:93
Tabitha, 18:101
William, 18:94
PICKNEY
Deborah, 16:238
PICKUP, 16:13
PICKWORTH
John, 19:202
PIEMONTE
Kurt M., 17:135
PIERCE/PERS see also PEARCE, PEARSE, PEIRCE, 18:137
___, Dea., 16:76
Abigail, 19:240a
Abigail (Browne), 19:48
Calvin P., 16:139; 17:102
Cynthia (Hall), 19:120
Elizabeth, 16:56; 17:115; 18:76
Elizabeth (Brown), 17:139
Elizabeth (Cheever), 17:226
Emma Florence, 17:30
Emmaline Hadin (Cooley), 17:30
F. C., 18:175
Francis, 17:139
Hannah, 16:76; 18:210
Hannah (___), 18:210
Hannah (Bassett), 18:32
Hannah (Locke), 16:76
Jane (Bessom), 19:230
John, 16:57
Joseph, 16:56
Joshua, 18:95
Lydia (Bishop), 17:139
Lydia (Fernside), 16:56
Martha S., 17:39
Mary, 18:198, 208, 210
Mary/Polly, 19:240
Molly, 17:12
Molly (Ballard), 16:76
Moses, 19:48
Nathaniel, 17:226
Polly (Estes), 18:95
Richard, 17:139; 18:210
Richard D., 16:200
Robert, 19:230
Ruel, 19:120
Samuel, 18:170

Sarah, 20:209
Susanna (Merritt), 18:149, 170
Thomas, 16:76; 17:30
William, 17:240
William Henry Harrison, 17:30
PIERPOINT/PIERPONT
Hannah, 18:202
Joseph, 16:88
Mary, 20:33
Sarah, 16:106
PIERSON see also PEARSON, 17:154, 20:41
Elizabeth, 16:56; 17:115
Elizabeth (Hammond), 16:56
Elizabeth (Wheelwright), 16:56
George, 16:56
John, 16:163
Sarah, 20:33
Thomas, 16:56
PIGDEN, 19:143
Thomas, 19:143
PIGEON
Sarah, 20:58
PIGNON see PINION, 20:71
PIKE see also PICKE
___, Maj., 17:193
Alice, 17:208
Allen R., 20:101
Benjamin S., 20:89
Dorothy, 19:48
Dorothy (Day/Daye), 20:101
Elizabeth, 18:93
Elizabeth (Andrews), 17:229
Elizabeth (Mackworth), 16:23
Ellen, 20:227
Hannah (Newell), 16:119
Joannah, 17:58
John, 20:101, 143
Lydia, 16:91
Margaret, 18:93
Martha, 20:56
Mary (___), 18:93
Mary (Tarbox), 20:143
Mary (Wallis), 17:233
Richard, 16:23; 17:229; 18:93, 94
Robert, 19:179
Samuel, 16:23; 17:229; 20:197
Sarah, 16:91; 17:22
Simon Mellen, 16:119
PILLSBURY/PILSBURY, 19:141
Amos, 18:240
Charles S., 19:115
Daniel, 17:179
Job, 17:179
Katherine (Gavet), 17:179
Parker, 19:16
Sarah (Allen), 17:179
Susannah, 16:146
PILLTAILE
Humphrey, 20:215
PILSBURY see PILLSBURY
PIMENTAL
Cecile (___), 19:176
Jerry, 19:176
PINCHON
Wm, 16:88
PINDAR/PINDER
John, 20:223
S., 20:90
Samuel D., 20:89
PINET
Claudia, 17:239
PINGREE, 17:141

PINION/PINNION/PIGNON see also
  PYNION, SPRAYE, 20:63, 71
Elizabeth, 16:112
Elizabeth (___), 16:175
Nicholas, 16:175; 20:67, 71, 72, 76
PINKHAM, 18:133, 137
Isaac, 18:98
Lydia (Estes), 18:98
PINNION see PINION, 20:77
PINSON
Mary, 19:156, 157
Mary (___), 19:157
Thomas, 19:157
PIPER
Mary, 18:212
PITCHER
Mary (Clapp), 20:179
Mary/Moll (Diamond), 18:105
Molly Diamond, 18:137
Nathaniel, 20:179
Robert, 18:105
Sarah, 20:179
PITKIN
Victor, 16:240
PITMAN see also PITTMAN
Abigail, 19:229; 20:114
Bethia, 18:101
Elizabeth, 16:71; 18:73, 75
Emma, 17:102
George, 17:102
Joseph, 17:102
Mark, 20:15
Mary, 18:46
Mary (Smith), 17:203
Mary Ellen, 17:102
Nathaniel, 18:101
Sarah Elliot (Friend), 17:102
Sarah Trask, 17:102
Sarah/Mary (Dennis), 17:204
Tabitha (Pickman), 18:101
Thomas, 17:203; 18:75
PITT
___, Mr., 17:96
William, 16:30; 17:211; 19:193
PITTMAN see also PITMAN
Elizabeth, 17:53
Jaems, 20:199
Mosis, 20:199
Nicholas, 20:199
Thomas, 17:214; 20:199
PIX see also PECKS
Benjamin, 16:27
Sarah, 16:27
Sarah (Blaney), 16:27
PLAISTED
Ichabod, 16:95; 18:101
PLANTE
Minnie, 16:52
PLASSE
Alice, 19:142
PLATTS
Eleanor, 19:104
Joseph, 20:49
Mary, 20:216
Sarah, 18:201
Sarah (Larrabee), 20:49
PLOVER
Ellenor, 20:94
PLUFF
Amable, 20:170
PLUMB
Volney A., 18:132, 137

PLUMER/PLUMMER, 17:141; 20:18
___, Dr., 18:203
Anna (Barber), 18:203
David, 18:203, 240
Elizabeth (Marshall), 18:203
John, 20:174
Judith (Norwood), 18:203
Judith Norwood, 18:203
Mary, 16:107
POCOCK see PEACOCK, 18:180
POKE
Joseph, 20:146
POLAND
Bethiah (Friend), 16:141
Elizabeth, 16:63
Hannah, 16:141
Harriet, 20:25
James, 16:141
John, 16:141
Joseph, 16:141; 18:70
Lloyd Orville, 16:141
Mary, 20:46
Samuel, 16:141
Thomas, 16:64
POLIS
Edith, 19:19
POLLARD
Elizabeth Moore (Clemens), 19:139, 141
George, 19:81
John Nichols, 19:139, 141
Mary, 20:98
Peter, 20:221
Sarah Pleasant, 19:139
POLLEY/POLLY
Bethia, 20:191
Elizabeth (Kellogg), 16:178
Miriam E., 16:178
POMEROY/POMROY, 16:240
Martha, 18:94
Mary, 20:46
Thankful, 18:34
POND
Joseph, 18:170
Margaret (___), 18:170
Nancy, 18:170
POOKE
Mary, 16:117
POOL see also POOLE, 20:18
Abigail Patch (Choate), 18:205
Abraham, 16:176
Caleb, 16:176; 18:207
Calvin W., 16:176
Ebenezer, 17:233; 18:137, 198, 201, 205, 207
Eliza (Norwood), 18:207
Elizabeth, 18:201
Elizabeth (Norwood), 18:201
Ellen Elizabeth (Tarr), 16:176
Francis, 18:201, 204
Jerusha (Norwood), 18:207
John, 16:176; 17:240; 18:201; 19:216;
  20:48, 113, 183, 184, 186, 190, 191, 194
Judith (Grover), 18:201
Lois (Story), 18:201
Lucy, 18:201, 207
Lucy (Haskell), 18:207
Margaret (Somes), 18:201
Martha (Tarr), 18:201
Mary, 18:201, 204
Mary (Lufkin), 16:176
Mary (Pool), 18:204
Mary Mangam, 16:176
Miriam, 18:201

Moses, 18:201
Nathan, 18:207
Rachel (Norwood), 18:207
Sally (Norwood), 18:205
Sarah (Haskell), 16:176; 18:201
Sarah (Howe), 16:176
Sarah Page, 18:205
Sophia (Tarr), 16:176
Stephen, 18:201
Timothy, 20:48
William, 16:176; 18:205
Winthrop, 18:207; 20:83
POOLE see also POOL, 17:217; 20:118
   ___, Capt., 20:207
   Archibald, 16:149
   Elizabeth, 17:199
   Harriet (Hardy), 16:149
   Harriet Jane, 16:149
   John, 16:163; 19:136-138, 214; 20:190, 192
   Jonathan, 19:214; 20:189
   Judith (Jacobs), 19:214
   Mary, 19:239
   Rebecca (Williams), 17:113
   Samuel, 17:113
   Sarah, 19:214; 20:33
   Sarah (___), 20:189
   Thomas, 19:137; 20:189
   Timothy, 19:137, 218
   William, 16:88
POOR/POORE, 18:163
   ___, Mrs., 16:68
   "Child", 19:161
   Abigail M. (___), 17:38
   Alfred, 19:210
   Amelia Titcomb, 19:160, 161
   Benjamin, 19:35
   Daniel, 16:68; 19:34, 160, 161
   David, 19:161
   David Coates, 19:161
   Dorothy, 17:208
   Eben, 17:33
   Ebenezer, 19:13, 35
   Frank W., 17:38
   George Horace, 19:19
   Georgiana Maria (Friend), 17:38
   Hannah, 17:201; 19:45, 115, 116, 222
   Jeanette (Tenney), 19:210
   Jonathan, 19:35
   Joseph, 17:201; 19:93, 94
   Martha, 16:20
   Mary (___), 19:160
   Mary (Coates), 19:161
   Nathan H., 17:38
   Phebe, 17:153
   Phebe (Varnum), 19:35
   Robert, 19:161
   Samuel, 19:94
   Sarah Helen (Marland), 19:19
   Silvanus, 20:85
   Susannah (Varnum), 19:35
   Thomas, 19:88, 94
   Tristam, 19:161
POPE, 19:118, 206, 216
   ___, Mrs., 16:89
   Abi (Preston), 20:230
   Amos, 20:229
   Benjamin, 16:34; 17:204; 19:137
   C. H., 16:153
   Charles H., 19:210
   Charles Henry, 16:22; 17:45; 18:82; 19:142
   Damaris (___), 16:117
   Damaris (Shattuck), 17:204

   Ebenezer, 20:27
   Edward, 16:76
   Elizabeth (Ballard), 16:76
   Elizabeth (Buffum), 20:27
   Enos, 16:88; 18:21
   Gertrude (___), 20:92, 93
   Hannah, 16:16; 20:27, 92, 93
   Henry, 18:234; 19:43
   John, 16:16; 17:204; 18:11; 20:42
   Joseph, 16:117; 17:16; 20:92, 93
   Mary, 17:204
   Mary (Eaton), 17:204
   Nathaniel, 20:230
   Phebe, 16:94
   Ruth (Newhall), 20:42
   Samuel, 16:34; 18:21, 91, 103; 19:137; 20:78, 79
   Sarah (Goodale), 20:229
   Sarah (Smith), 17:204
POPLE
   Elizabeth, 20:97
PORTER, 19:16
   Alice (Fornis), 17:102
   Ann Maria (Friend), 17:32
   Billy, 16:212
   Elijah, 19:98
   Emma E., 17:102
   Ezra, 17:199
   George, 20:89
   Hannah (___), 17:32
   Hannah (Smith), 17:203
   Hathorne, 20:89, 90
   Israel, 16:154; 18:60a, 240
   John, 17:14; 18:78, 240; 19:190, 191, 195; 20:140
   John A. P., 20:108
   John B., 16:218
   John Edwin, 17:32
   Jonathan, 19:101
   Joseph, 17:14; 20:89, 90
   Joseph W., 19:97
   Lucy, 20:147
   Lucy (Boynton), 20:108
   Lydia (Tarbox), 17:49; 20:140
   Martha J. (Masury), 16:218
   Mary, 16:179; 17:240; 19:177, 178; 20:141
   Mary (Tardy), 16:83
   Matthew, 20:46
   Mehitable (Osborn), 17:199
   Nehemiah, 16:83; 17:203
   Rebecca, 19:179; 20:180
   Samuel, 20:154
   Sarah, 17:226
   Thomas, 16:88
PORTERFIELD
   Lettice, 20:50
POSSANTE
   Antonio, 17:31
   Florence (Edmands), 17:31
POST
   Hannah, 19:221
   Jeremiah, 18:125
   John, 16:68
   Mary, 19:221
   Mary (Tyler), 19:221
   Susanna, 19:221
POTE
   Cyndi, 16:188
   William, 18:137
POTTER, 17:89
   ___, Capt., 17:147
   ___, Mrs., 19:153
   Abigail, 18:56, 152; 19:149

   Abigail (Dunwell), 19:150
   Agnes (___), 19:153
   Agnes (Beard), 19:153
   Ales/Alice, 19:152, 153
   Alice (Cyckins), 19:153
   Alice (Plasse), 19:142
   Ann, 19:142, 152, 153
   Ann (Beomont), 19:153
   Anna, 16:29; 17:100; 19:150-152
   Anthony, 18:120; 19:152, 153
   Barnard, 19:152, 153
   Benjamin, 16:25; 17:100; 18:208; 19:100, 143, 145-147, 150, 151, 155, 161, 163, 237; 20:89, 90
   Bernard, 19:153
   Bethiah, 18:166, 168; 19:143-145
   Bridget (Brounaff), 19:153
   Catherine, 19:153; 20:221
   Christopher, 20:223
   Clark, 19:153
   Clemens, 19:152
   D. Howland, 20:162
   Daniel, 16:142; 19:153
   David, 19:149, 150
   Deliverance, 18:199; 19:150
   Dorothy (___), 19:153
   Dorotjy (Gray), 19:153
   Dwight E., 20:162
   Elijah, 19:150
   Elisabeth (Stone), 18:120
   Elizabeth, 16:238; 17:146; 18:43, 73, 152, 168, 199; 19:143, 144, 147-150, 152, 153; 20:100
   Elizabeth (___), 19:153, 217
   Elizabeth (Ashby), 19:153
   Elizabeth (Barnes), 19:153
   Elizabeth (Earle), 18:199; 19:149, 150
   Elizabeth (Hart), 18:43; 19:147, 151
   Elizabeth (Kimball), 16:142
   Elizabeth (Marshall), 19:142, 153
   Elizabeth (Norwood), 18:152, 199; 19:147, 149
   Elizabeth (Richardson), 19:153
   Elizabeth (Whipple), 18:120
   Eme/Emma (Carter), 18:71; 19:142, 144, 153
   Eme/Emma (Knight), 19:142, 144
   Ephraim, 18:149, 168; 19:147-149
   Esther (___), 18:168; 19:148
   Eunice/Eunis, 17:156; 18:49; 19:150, 237
   Ezra, 19:149
   Frank Elwood, 18:152; 19:152
   Hannah, 19:143-145, 149-151, 236; 20:136
   Hannah (Brown), 19:151, 161
   Henry, 20:83
   Isobell, 19:153
   Isobell (Sumner), 19:153
   Jane (Rhoads), 19:149
   Jeffery/Geffray, 19:152153
   Joan, 19:152
   Joan (Leach), 19:153
   John, 18:26, 152, 153, 199; 19:142, 146, 147, 149, 150, 152, 153
   Joseph, 18:168, 200; 19:145, 147-150, 152
   Judyth, 19:152
   Katherine, 19:152
   Katherine (___), 19:153
   Lodwick, 19:153
   Lois, 19:149, 150, 236, 237
   Lois (Walker), 18:168; 19:148
   Lucy, 19:150
   Lucy (Ward), 19:150
   Luke, 19:152

Lydia, 19:144, 145, 150, 151
Lydia (Lamb), 18:199; 19:149
Margaret, 19:152, 153
Margaret (Whyte), 19:153
Martha, 18:168; 19:147-149, 152
Martha (___), 19:153
Martha (Hall/Halle), 18:168; 19:147
Mary, 18:168; 19:142-145, 147, 149-153
Mary (Baker), 18:153
Mary (Breed), 17:151
Mary (Burlingame), 19:150
Mary (Carter), 19:153
Mary (Gedney), 18:168; 19:142, 144, 145
Mary (Steere), 19:150
Mary (Thompson), 18:152; 19:149
Mehitable, 19:150
Mehitable (Smith), 18:200; 19:150
Mercy, 19:149
Mercy (___), 17:151
Mercy (Breed), 17:145; 19:148
Miriam (Aldrich), 19:150
Nathaniel, 18:152, 199; 19:147, 149, 150; 20:226
Nicholas, 16:196; 17:89; 18:71, 72, 74, 147, 164, 168; 19:136, 138, 142, 143, 145, 147, 149-153, 236; 20:194
Persis, 18:168; 19:148
Peter, 19:152
Phebe, 19:150
Phineas, 19:150
Rebecca, 18:152; 19:149
Rebecca (Baker), 18:152, 199; 19:149
Rebecca (Trask), 19:145
Rhoda, 19:150
Richard, 19:152, 153
Robert, 16:206; 17:46; 18:29, 43, 60a, 168, 199, 222, 223; 19:142-153; 20:105, 196, 214, 215
Ruth, 16:25; 18:152, 171, 208; 19:100, 147-151, 161
Ruth (Burrill), 16:25; 17:100; 19:147, 150
Ruth (Driver), 18:43, 199; 19:144, 145
Samuel, 18:43; 19:137, 143-145, 147, 151-153, 217; 20:37
Sarah, 16:217; 17:145; 18:43, 168; 19:143, 144, 148-151
Sarah (Gardner), 19:150
Sarah (Graves), 20:226
Sarah (Hart), 18:43; 19:151
Sarah (Witt), 18:149, 168; 19:147
Susan Emiline (Burlingame), 20:162
Susann, 19:142, 152
Susannah, 19:151
Theophilus, 18:168; 19:148
Thomas, 18:43; 19:142, 151, 153
Thoms, 19:152
Tibudah (Hayden), 18:168; 19:148
William, 19:149, 150, 152, 153
Wyllya, 19:153
Zerviah (Chapman), 19:150

POTTLE
Christopher, 20:224
Hannah (Bodwell), 18:159; 20:207
Hannah (Graves), 20:224
Samuel, 18:159

POULTER
John, 16:228
Mary (___), 16:228

POUSLAND/ROWSLAND see also RUSSELL
Betsy (Friend), 16:215
Mary, 16:119
William, 16:215

POW
Bruce, 16:53
Emily May (Longfellow), 16:53
William, 20:199

POWELL
Thomas, 17:213

POWERS
Grace F., 17:166
John, 17:166; 20:172
Sarah (Nelson), 17:166
Virginia (Wood), 20:172

POWSLAND see also POUSLAND
Thomas, 20:199

PRAEY see PRAY, 20:71

PRANCE
Rachel (Rowland), 17:212

PRASHER see PRESHER

PRATT/PRATTE
Abby W., 18:11
Abigail, 17:177; 18:151
Abigail (Bancroft), 20:35
Abigail (Phillips), 16:59
Abigail (Tarbox), 20:138
Amos, 20:138
Anna, 16:144; 17:33
Anna (Cheever), 19:104
Anne (Ballard), 16:76
Benjamin, 17:240
David, 19:107
Dolly/Dorothy (Parker), 16:38
Dorcas (Folger), 16:208
Edward, 20:35
Elizabeth, 19:107
Elizabeth (Clark), 18:112, 113
Elizabeth (Pratt), 19:107
Ephraim, 16:76
Grace, 16:201
Grover, 18:31, 213, 214; 19:107; 20:210, 218
Hannah, 19:239
Hannah (___), 19:107
Hannah (Kirtland), 18:111, 112
Henry, 16:210
Hephzibah (Bancroft), 20:41
James, 19:107
John, 16:99; 19:107; 20:41
Jonathan, 16:59
Joseph, 16:208; 19:107, 147, 158, 239
Joshua, 17:149
Lewis, 19:107
Lydia, 18:113
Lydia (Mower), 19:107
Lydia (Parmenter), 17:177
Margery, 20:54
Mary, 16:206
Mary (Keppel/Rappel), 19:107
Mary (Mansfield), 19:107, 239
Mary (Turner), 17:240
Mehitable, 16:87
Mercy/Marcy, 19:107
Mercy (Upham), 19:107
Micajah, 18:11, 12
Nathan, 16:38; 20:38
Nathan Grover, 19:107
Nathaniel, 19:107
Polly (Bancroft), 20:38
Prudence (Farrington), 17:149
Rebecca (___), 19:107; 20:210
Rebecca (Ingalls), 19:107
Rebekah, 19:107
Richard, 16:16; 17:93; 18:23, 50, 153, 208, 224; 19:29, 106, 107, 160, 227; 20:105, 112, 137, 138
Ruth, 19:151, 161
Ruth (Floyd), 19:147
Samuel, 19:103
Susannah (Quiner), 19:107
Tabitha, 20:35
Tabothy, 19:107
Thankfull, 16:38
Thomas, 17:93; 18:232; 19:40, 104
William, 18:112, 113

PRAY/PRAEY/PRAYE see also PREY, SPRAYE, 18:137, 138; 20:63, 73, 77
___, Goodman, 16:175
Agnes, 20:71
Alias Pynyon, 20:71
Donald Everett, 20:72
Dorothy, 16:112
Joan (Valliance), 20:71
John H., 17:30
Quentin, 16:175; 20:67, 70-72, 76
Richard, 20:67
Robert, 20:71
Sarah Anne, 18:58
Thomas, 20:71

PREBLE
Bethiah, 20:145
Ebenezer, 17:132
Jemima, 19:155

PREDIES
Adam, 20:199

PRENDERGAST
Anna Josephine, 20:149

PRENTICE/PRENTISS
Elizabeth (Orne), 17:100
Frances, 16:55
Grace Bubier, 20:221
Rebecca (Jackson), 16:55
Thomas, 16:55

PREPPER
Elizabeth, 17:53

PRESBURY
John, 18:56
Sarah (Hood), 18:56

PRESCOTT
___, Gov., 18:143
Benjamin, 17:199
Dorothy, 19:35
Leah, 17:184
O., 16:43
Sarah, 17:83

PRESHER/PRASHER
Abigail (Graves), 16:85
Henry, 16:85

PRESSER
Mary Elizabeth, 17:166

PRESSEY
John, 20:80

PRESSON
Susanna, 18:205

PRESTON see also PEARSON
"Daughter", 20:230
Aaron, 20:232
Abi, 20:230
Asenath, 20:230
Betsey, 20:230
Betsy (Morse), 19:42
Charles Henry, 20:228
Daniel, 20:232
David, 20:230, 231
Diggery, 16:134
Elizabeth, 20:179, 231
Elizabeth (Voden), 20:231, 235
Etta (Faxon), 17:208
Frederick G., 17:208

Hannah, 16:218; 20:230, 231
Hannah (Putnam), 20:229, 231, 235
Hitty, 20:228-230
Ira, 20:230
James, 20:40
Jane (Whitmore), 20:230
John, 16:68; 20:228-232, 235
Joseph, 18:201
Joshua, 20:230, 231
Levi, 20:232
Marion W., 17:207
Marion Webster, 17:208
Mary, 16:233
Mary (Harris), 18:201
Mary (Leach), 20:235
Mehitable (Nichols), 20:232
Mehitable (White), 20:228-232
Moses, 20:232, 235
Philip, 20:231, 235
Randall, 16:179
Rebecca (Nurse), 20:235
Rebecca (Upton), 20:230
Roger, 20:228, 230
Ruth (Putnam), 20:235
Sally, 20:40
Sally (___), 20:40
Samuel, 16:68
Sarah (Berry), 20:232
Susannah (Stone), 16:179
Thomas, 20:235
PREY see also PRAY
Richard, 18:79
PRICE
Anne, 18:235
Jane, 19:171
John, 17:226
Martha (Derby), 17:226
Mary (Phippen), 19:171
Matthew, 16:203
Richard, 19:171
Sabra, 16:58; 17:58
Walter, 16:164; 17:20
PRICHARD/PRITCHETT
William, 18:79
PRIDE
Amy, 20:44, 115, 116, 176
Elizabeth (Bond), 20:216
Hannah (Smith), 20:59, 180
John, 19:188; 20:198
Joseph, 20:216
Peter, 20:59, 180
PRIEST
John, 17:83
Mary (Longley), 17:83
PRIMROSE
Eliza (Tarbox), 20:147
John, 20:147
PRINCE, 18:195
Benjamin, 20:45
Betsy, 18:218
Elizabeth (Norwood), 18:218
Hannah, 17:156
Hannah (Harris), 20:45
John, 17:103
Jonathan, 18:90, 218
Joseph, 19:175
Maria, 18:218
Martha (Derby), 17:226
Mary (Allen), 18:218
Mary (Charnock), 16:25
Mary (Putnam), 20:235
Mary (Townsend), 19:175
Robert, 17:14

Samuel, 18:218
Thomas, 17:240; 20:200
Timothy, 20:235
Warren, 20:154
PRINDLE
Daniel Smith, 17:120
Mary (Burnham), 17:120
PRINGLE
Elizabeth (Young), 17:32
Hannah Elizabeth (Friend), 17:32
James, 17:32
James R., 17:111
James R., Mrs., 18:145
PRIOR
Ann, 18:85, 86
John, 18:86
PRISBURY
Dorcas, 18:225, 227, 228
PRISSE
Margaret, 20:94
PRITCHET/PRITCHETT, 17:217
David, 20:236
Dorothy (Averill), 20:236
Eunice, 20:236
Hannah, 20:236
Huldah, 20:236
John, 18:56; 20:232, 236
Lydia, 20:236
Martha, 20:229, 232, 236
Martha (Gould), 20:232, 236
Mary, 20:236
Patience, 20:236
Priscilla, 20:236
Ruth, 20:236
Sarah, 20:236
Sarah (Harris), 20:236
PROCTER/PROCTOR, 18:137; 20:17
Abigail, 17:75, 76
Abigail (Wilson), 20:99
Agnes (Stacey), 17:98
Benjamin, 18:41, 42; 20:29, 99, 100
David R., 17:37
Deborah (Hart), 18:41, 42
Denmark, 17:35
Ebenezer, 18:93
Eliza (Friend), 17:37
Eliza Ann (___), 17:37
Eliza Ann (Gilbert), 17:111
Elizabeth, 18:72
Elizabeth (Bassett), 17:76; 18:29
Elizabeth (Friend), 17:35
Elizabeth (Thorndike), 18:29
Hannah, 17:109
Hannah (Larrabee), 18:226
Hannah (Mansfield), 17:159
Isaac, 17:159
Jemima (___), 18:103
Joanna, 18:25
John, 17:75; 18:29, 42, 240; 20:99, 100
Jonathan, 19:42; 20:219
Joseph, 17:37
Joseph A., 16:100
Joseph J., 17:111
Lavinia (___), 17:35
Leland H., 18:137
Lucy Ann (Lewis), 16:100
Lucy E., 17:168
Lucy Elizabeth, 17:111
Lydia, 17:199
Lydia (Waters), 20:100
Martha, 17:161
Martha (___), 17:76; 18:42; 20:99
Martha (Graves), 20:219

Martha (Harper), 18:29
Mary, 17:199; 18:38; 20:26, 29, 99, 100
Mary (___), 19:42
Mary (Bassett), 18:38, 55
Mary (Buckley), 20:29, 99, 100
Michael, 18:38
Olive, 18:120
Priscilla, 20:100
Robert W., 17:51
Samuel, 18:38, 55; 20:44
Sarah, 18:32; 20:100
Sarah (Larrabee), 20:44
Sarah A., 17:36
Sarah Elizabeth, 17:167
Simon, 18:32
Tabitha, 17:100
Thomas, 18:38
Thorndike, 16:78; 17:196; 20:99
William, 17:35; 18:103, 104, 226
PROUDLOVE, 16:13
PROUTE
Eunice, 17:232
PROVENDER
Mary, 18:24
PROWS
John, 20:199
PRUITT, 20:118
PUCKETT
Edwin M., 20:101
PUDNEY
Johanna, 17:18
Jonathan, 17:22
PUFFER
Abigail (Vose), 20:179
Hannah, 20:179
John, 20:179
Mary (Holbrook), 20:179
PULCIFER/PULCIFUR/PULSIFER,
17:51; 18:137
Abel A., 16:239
Abigail, 17:118
Alcy, 16:239
Benjamin, 17:51
Betsy (Fish), 16:239; 17:51
Deborah (___), 16:239
Elizabeth, 16:239
Gerrish, 16:238; 17:51
James D., 16:218
John, 16:239; 17:51
John H., 16:239
Jon., 16:239
Lucinda, 16:239
Mary (Marshall), 16:239; 17:51
Mary E., 17:109
Nathan, 16:239
Nelson, 16:239
Richard, 16:239; 17:51
Sally, 16:239
Sarah, 16:239; 17:51; 20:58
Sarah (Gerrish), 17:51
Sarah (Ober), 17:51
Sarah Hovey (Friend), 16:218
Sebrina, 16:239
PUNCHARD
Benjamin Hanover, 19:17
Dorcas, 19:173
Ellen, 19:17
Martha Lawton (Marland), 19:17
Sarah Elizabeth, 19:17
Sarah Sprague, 18:95
PUNCHIR
William, 20:199

**PURCHAS/PURCHASE/PURCHES/
PURCHIS**
   ___ (Williams), 17:229
   Abigail, 17:232
   Abraham, 17:230
   Anne (Squire), 17:231
   Aquilla, 17:229; 18:137
   Benjamin, 17:231
   Elizabeth, 16:25; 17:229; 19:147; 20:93
   Elizabeth (___), 17:229
   Elizabeth (Andrews), 17:229
   Elizabeth (Mackworth), 16:23
   Elizabeth (Williams), 17:230
   Hannah, 17:230
   Hannah (Cook), 17:230
   Jane, 17:230
   Joan, 17:229, 230
   Jonathan, 17:230
   Lydia, 17:230
   Margaret (Worthington), 17:230
   Mary, 17:230
   Mary (Grove/Gove), 17:229
   Mary (Perkins), 17:232
   Oliver, 16:164, 196; 17:46, 91; 18:29, 30, 60a, 110, 114, 166, 231; 19:145
   Priscilla, 17:232
   Ruth, 16:27; 17:231; 18:31; 20:212
   Ruth (Williams), 17:230
   Sarah, 17:230
   Sarah (___), 17:232
   Sarah (Parsons), 17:230
   Thomas, 16:23; 17:202; 18:137; 20:197

PURINGTON/PURINTON
   Amos, 18:34
   Anna, 16:117; 17:186
   Anna (Breed), 18:31
   Anne (___), 18:25
   Betsey (___), 18:11
   Content (Alley), 18:22, 25
   Damaris (___), 17:186
   Damaris (Jones), 16:117
   Daniel, 17:197; 18:34, 53
   George, 16:117
   Huldah, 16:16; 18:25
   James, 16:96; 18:11, 25, 26, 31
   John, 16:117
   Joshua, 16:117; 17:186
   Mary (Pooke), 16:117
   Matthew, 18:11
   Mary (Barton), 16:117
   Mercy (Bassett), 18:34
   Miriam, 16:16
   Moses, 18:22, 25
   Peace (___), 18:22, 25
   Pelatiah, 18:22, 25
   Ruth (Breed), 18:53
   Sarah (Osborn), 17:197
   Stephen, 16:90

PUSHARD
   Lucy, 19:90

PUSHEE
   Elizabeth (___), 20:226

PUTMAN
   Augusta (Friend), 16:215
   Thomas, 19:215
   William, 16:215

PUTNAM, 18:137, 189; 19:16; 20:202
   ___, Gen., 17:120
   Abigail (Bomer/Brown), 16:144
   Amos, 16:157; 18:218; 20:235
   Andrew, 18:218
   Ann, 16:66; 17:171
   Ann (Carr), 19:178
   Ann (Holyoke), 19:178
   Anna, 18:94
   Anne, 20:92, 98
   Anne (___), 20:98
   Anne (Holyoke), 20:97
   Archelaus, 18:238
   Augustus, 20:89
   Benjamin, 16:154
   Betsey (Preston), 20:230
   Cornelius, 16:155
   David, 16:156
   Eben, 16:157; 20:97
   Edward, 17:60; 19:39
   Elizabeth, 16:157; 17:152; 20:234
   Elizabeth (Leach), 18:101, 112
   Esther, 17:201
   Experience, 19:178
   Ezra, 18:169
   Hannah, 16:157; 20:229, 231, 235
   Hannah (Cutler), 20:235
   Hannah (Phillips), 16:157
   Hannah (Putnam), 16:157
   Henry, 18:240
   Israel, 16:234; 19:15; 20:98
   J. W., 17:162
   James Phillips, 16:157
   Jane Phillips, 16:88
   Jeremiah, 20:89
   John, 16:154; 17:14; 20:132, 235
   Jonathan, 16:35; 17:60
   Joseph, 19:39
   Joseph C., 20:235
   Joshua, 20:231, 234, 235
   Lincoln I., 20:89
   Mary, 20:235
   Mary (Gott), 16:157
   Mary (Herrick), 16:157
   Mary (Ingersoll), 16:179
   Nathan, 16:157
   Nathaniel, 17:14; 19:193; 20:224
   Perley, 20:230
   Prudence, 20:28, 97, 98
   Rachel, 20:235
   Rachel (Goodale), 20:231, 234, 235
   Rebecah (Dike), 18:169
   Ruth, 20:235
   Sally, 20:25
   Samuel, 16:93; 18:112
   Sarah, 16:79
   Sarah (Hutchinson), 16:155
   Thomas, 16:71; 17:15; 18:231; 19:39, 178, 212, 231; 20:97, 98, 132
   William, 16:220

PUTNEY
   Annie Rogers Cross (Fennell), 16:236
   Barbara Breed, 16:236
   Enoch, 16:236
   Evelyn Augusta (Breed), 16:236
   Francis S., 16:236
   Fred Willard, 16:236
   Luther Roy, 16:236
   Nancy Willard (Sibley), 16:236
   Ruth, 16:209
   Sally (Carleton), 16:236
   Sally (Eastmen), 16:236
   Stephen, 16:236

PYBOT
   Anne Medico, 17:224

PYNCHON
   ___, Gov., 20:188

PYNION/PYNYON see also PINION
   Everod, 20:71
   John, 20:71
   Robert, 20:71

PYTHARCH
   Richard, 17:211

**QUANOPHKOWNATT/
QUANOPLIKOWNATT**
   James, 18:60a
   Joan (___), 18:60a
   John, 18:60a

QUARLES
   Anne, 18:166
   Eleanor (Dennis), 19:232
   John, 19:232

QUIGG
   Marjorie Marsh, 18:132

QUILTER
   Joseph, 20:223, 225

QUIMBY
   Lydia, 16:56

QUIN
   ___, Capt., 20:159

QUINBY
   Martha (Eastman), 16:59
   William, 16:59

QUINCY
   Josiah, 19:37
   Mary, 18:149

QUINER
   Abner, 18:218
   Elizabeth, 18:211
   Elizabeth (Fuller), 16:74; 17:157; 18:211
   Hannah (___), 19:107
   John, 16:74; 17:113; 18:211, 214; 19:50
   Priscilla (Williams), 17:113; 19:50
   Susannah, 19:107

QUITERFIELD
   Clement, 16:109
   Priscilla (Collins), 16:109

QUONOPOHIT
   James/Natick, 18:60a
   Mary (___), 18:60a

RACKLEY
   Benjamin, 20:46
   Mary (Larrabee), 20:46

RADCLIFFE, 16:13

RADDIN
   John P., 17:27
   Sarah (Sweetser), 17:27
   Thomas, 18:105

RADMAN
   John, 18:230

RAE see also RAY
   Agnes, 17:56
   Elizabeth (Deyarmond), 17:55
   Elizabeth Jane (Garthet), 17:56
   James, 17:56
   John, 17:56
   Margaret Annie, 17:55
   Mary (Young), 17:56
   Mary Bell, 17:55
   William, 17:55

RAFUSE
   Catharine Eliz. (Clattenburg), 19:238
   Eberhard, 19:238
   Sophia Elizabeth, 19:238

RAIMENT/RAYMOND
   John, 16:140

RAINER
   Humphrey, 17:140

RAINS
   ___, Mrs., 17:11

RAINSFORD
 Ranis, 17:157
RAIRDEN
 See Reardon, 20:145
RAMEZAY
 Catherine (Charpentier), 19:26
 Claude De, 19:26
RAMSDALLE
 John, 18:230
RAMSDELL
 Abednego, 16:69
 Abigail, 17:157; 18:92, 228
 Abigail (___), 18:167
 Abigail (Fuller), 16:74; 17:157
 Anna (Chadwell), 19:164
 Aquilla, 17:149; 18:222; 20:140, 196
 Benjamin, 16:74; 17:157
 Bethiah, 18:25, 26
 Beulah (Brown), 16:83
 Bill, 18:132, 135, 137
 Elizabeth, 17:157
 Elizabeth (Collins), 18:26
 George, 16:236
 Hannah, 18:228; 19:177
 Hathorn, 18:215
 Isaac, 17:147; 18:167; 20:137, 196
 Jacob, 18:25, 26
 James, 16:236
 Joanna (Downing), 17:148; 19:49
 John, 17:148; 18:72, 137, 228; 19:49
 Jonathan, 18:167; 19:164
 Joseph, 18:137
 Kimball, 16:83
 Lydia (Hudson), 17:149
 Margaret (Riddan), 16:236
 Margarit, 19:164
 Mary, 16:29; 17:157
 Mary (Batten), 19:177
 Mary (Teale), 16:83
 Mary (Wares), 17:157
 Mary Susan, 16:236
 Moses, 17:157
 Nathaniel, 17:148; 19:49
 Noah, 19:177
 Sarah (Bowden), 16:236
 Sarah (Hathorn), 18:167
RAND, 19:236
 Daniel, 20:38
 Elizabeth (___), 18:75
 Elizabeth (Richardson), 16:79; 18:209
 Florence Osgood, 16:79; 20:138
 Hannah, 16:27; 18:73, 75; 20:210
 Hannah/Anna (Ivory), 20:138
 Isabella (Tilly), 18:232
 Jemima, 16:102
 Joshua, 16:198; 17:40; 18:54, 150; 20:103
 Lydia, 20:239
 Mary, 16:80; 18:112, 209, 224; 20:138, 205
 Matilda, 20:38
 Remembrance, 20:13
 Robert, 16:79; 17:89; 18:75, 99, 112; 19:154; 20:104, 138, 140, 196, 204, 205
 Sarah, 19:47
 Susannah (___), 20:140
 Susannah (Hemenway), 20:38
 Thomas, 17:13
 William, 18:232
 Zachariah, 16:79; 18:209; 19:106, 155; 20:112, 138
 Zachary, 20:196
RANDALL/RANDELL, 18:157
 ___, Goody, 17:212

 Catherine, 19:167
 Charles, 17:208
 Charles Albert, 17:117
 Elizabeth (Witt), 18:171
 Helen May (Smith), 17:208
 Isaac, 19:146
 Lillian Alberta, 17:117
 Nathan, 17:117
 Robert, 17:213
 Samuel, 17:13; 18:158
 Sarah, 17:212
 Sarah Wooldridge (Trefry), 17:117
 Silas, 18:171
 Susan Ann (Tupper), 17:117
 Susanna (Gates), 17:117
 William Henry, 17:117
RANDOLF/RANDOLPH
 Edward, 18:14, 232
RANKIN
 Elsie Jane, 17:164
 Joseph, 16:18
 Sarah (Hackett), 16:18
RANKS
 Dorothea Marion, 17:176
 John, 17:176
 Mildred Louise (Ellis), 17:176
RANUFF/RENOIR see also RENEW
 Mary, 17:206
RAOULT
 Alexandre, 20:169
 Jeanne, 20:169
 Marie (Des Rosiers), 20:169
RAPPEL
 Mary, 19:107
RASLE
 ___, Fr., 20:114
RATCLIFF
 Elsie Lucille (Smith), 17:175
 John Moses, 17:175
 Roselyn, 17:175
RAWDEN/RAWDIN/REDDEN/RODDEN
 Hepzibah (Bancroft), 19:218
 Samuel, 19:218; 20:36
RAWS
 Daniel, 19:29
 Mary (Farr), 19:29
RAWSON
 Ann M. (___), 20:142
 Edward, 18:42; 19:28, 129
RAY see also RAE, REA, 18:184
 Aaron, 17:12
 Abigail (Herrick), 16:55
 Asenath (Palmer), 16:55
 Fabius M., 20:176
 Gideon, 16:55
 Hannah (York), 17:176
 Jabesh, 16:55; 17:176
 John, 16:55
 Naomi (Palmer), 16:55
 Sally Burton, 17:176
 Staphen, 16:55
RAYMENT
 John, 20:198
 William, 20:198
RAYMOND
 ___ (Patch), 16:76
 Anna, 16:76
 Edward, 16:76
 Eunice (Tarbox), 20:141
 George, 20:141
 Hannah (Gaskill), 18:97
 John, 16:136; 19:127
 M. D., 20:102

 Margaret, 16:95
 Mary Ann, 20:24
 Rachel (Scruggs), 16:136
 Richard, 19:193, 195
 Samuel, 16:142; 20:141
 Sarah (Dodge), 16:142
 Stephen, 18:97
 Susan, 17:160
 Susannah (Tarbox), 20:141
 Thomas, 20:141
RAYNER
 Elizabeth, 20:225, 226
RAYNES
 John, 18:220
 Sarah (Eaton), 18:220
RAYNOR
 Polly (Parker), 17:120
 Thomas, 17:120
REA see also RAY, RAE
 ___, Dr., 17:114
 Caleb, 18:218
 Daniel, 17:114; 18:75
 Elizabeth (Leach), 16:55
 Joshua, 16:55; 17:14; 20:224
 Margaret (Rogers), 17:114
 Rebecca, 16:157; 18-73, 75; 19:27, 28, 175
 Sarah (Waters), 16:55
 Zorobabel, 17:114
READ see also REED, REID
 Abigail, 18:179; 19:35
 Abigail (Rowland), 17:212
 Bartholomew, 20:45
 Clarissa, 16:179
 Elizabeth (Phillips), 16:223
 Hannah (___), 16:59
 Hannah Ford (Foster), 16:239
 Isaac, 16:32
 John, 18:94
 Joseph, 19:35
 Kezia, 19:35
 Leonard, 16:239
 Lydia, 19:35
 Lydia (Nourse/Nurse), 17:179
 Lydia (Parker), 19:35
 Mary, 16:116
 Mary (Harris), 20:45
 Obediah, 16:59
 Rebecca, 17:78
 Samuel, 17:212
 Sarah, 19:35
 Sarah (Fletcher), 16:59
 Thomas, 16:59; 19:35
 William, 17:179
READING
 John, 16:156; 17:94
READY
 Esther Amelia, 16:224
REANEY
 Percy H., 16:12
REARDON
 Abigail (Tarbox), 20:145
 James, 20:145
RECORD
 Olive D. (Edson), 20:55
 Salmon (Ricard), 20:55
 Susan P., 20:54
REDDEN see RAWDEN
REDDING
 Mary, 20:145
REDDINGTON
 Abraham, 16:178, 193
 Elizabeth, 18:57
 Isaac, 18:159

John, 18:164
Margaret (___), 16:178
Mary (Gould), 18:164
Ruth (Bodwell), 18:159
Sarah (___), 18:164
REDFERN, 16:4
Lydia, 20:143
Lydia (Tarbox), 20:143
William, 20:143
REDFORD, 16:13
REDIAT
Deborah, 18:168
REDINGTON see REDDINGTON
REDKNAP/REDNAP
Benjamin, 17:47; 20:134, 196
Joseph, 16:196; 17:19; 19:138; 20:195
Sarah, 17:47; 18:102
REDMONDS
George, 16:12
REDNAP see REDKNAP
REED see also READ, REID, 18:175
___ (Madox), 17:38
Abigail, 19:119; 20:97
Abigail Hinds, 17:38
Anna, 17:159
Benjamin, 16:27
Benjamin Tyler, 17:100
Bethia L., 17:59
Deliverance (Potter), 18:199; 19:150
Ebenezer, 18:37
Elizabeth, 18:221
Elizabeth (Norwood), 18:217
Hannah (Blaney), 16:26
Hannah (Wyman), 20:99
Israel, 20:99
Jacob Whittemore, 20:97
James, 18:217
Jason, 19:160
John, 16:27
Joseph, 17:38
Joseph Hinds, 17:180
Joshua, 18:199; 19:150
Kezia, 19:177
Lois Jane (Parsons), 17:180
Lydia, 19:34
Mary, 16:27
Nancy Elizabeth (Coates), 19:160
Remember, 20:235
Sampson, 19:131
Sarah (Harris), 18:37
Sarah (Kimball), 18:179; 20:16
Thomas, 19:34
William, 16:27; 20:97
REEVES/REVIS
Anna, 17:119
Elizabeth (Dearing), 17:119
Samuel, 17:119
REGAN
Mary Louise, 17:174; 20:227
REID see also READ, REED
Henry, 20:40
Lucy (Bancroft), 20:40
REILLY
___, Mr., 16:53
Beatrice (Trottier), 16:53
John, 17:137
John C., 16:63; 17:11; 18:135, 137
REINER
Elizabeth (___), 16:34
William, 16:34
REITH
Ann (Ormes), 17:101
Ann/Anna, 17:98

Emeline (Friend), 16:216
Joseph, 16:216
Richard, 17:101; 19:38; 20:15
REMEMBER
W. A., 16:48
REMINGTON
Gordon, 20:73, 74, 77
RENAR, 16:194
RENEW see also RANUFF
Abigail, 20:240
RENOIR see RANUFF, RENEW
REVERE/RIVOIRE, 18:137
Paul, 18:50; 19:110, 200
REVIS see REEVES
REXFORD
Benajah, 18:180
Roxana (Ayer), 18:180
REYNOLDS
Abigail, 20:52
Mary (Chapell), 16:84
Nathaniel, 16:84
RHOADES/RHOADS see also RHODES, ROADES, RODES
Abigail (Reynolds), 20:52
Charles Casper, 17:117
Chester, 20:52
Dorothy (Johnson), 17:118
Elizabeth (Pedrick), 16:36
Elizabeth A. (Goldthwaite), 17:117
Ephraim, 19:100
Henry, 16:36
Hezekiah, 19:100
Jane, 19:149
Jerusha (Graves), 20:210
John, 18:26
John Caspar J., 17:118
John W., 17:117
Jonathan, 20:210
Joseph, 17:158
Josiah, 19:100, 228, 229
Levi, 20:52
Mary, 16:36; 18:228
Nancy (Harwood), 18:217
Reuben, 20:52
Rufus Benfur, 20:52
Sarah, 17:117
Sarah Elizabeth (Brown), 17:117
Thomas, 16:36
RHODE
___, Mr., 16:164
RHODES see also RHOADES, ROADES, 18:134; 19:154, 162
Abigail, 17:157; 19:162
Abigail (Coates), 17:157; 18:30, 102; 19:162
Abigail (Graves), 20:209
Ann (Graves), 19:229; 20:205
Anna (Ireson), 19:108
Athelred (Merriam), 18:19
Benjamin, 18:30, 102; 19:162
Bethia (Marston), 16:85
Charles F. H., 18:217
Eleazer, 16:196; 19:155, 162; 20:52, 209
Elizabeth, 16:92; 18:226; 19:155; 20:205
Elizabeth (Burrage), 20:205
Elizabeth (Coates), 16:207; 19:155
Elizabeth (Estes), 18:19
Elizabeth (Paul), 19:155
Ely, 20:196
Emma (Chapman), 17:157
Ephraim, 16:74
Hannah, 20:205

Henry, 16:72; 17:18; 18:19, 137, 226, 231; 19:47, 154, 155, 158, 162, 205, 206, 229; 20:52, 135
Huldah, 16:47; 19:116
Huldah (Howard), 19:116
Ignatius, 19:108
Jane, 19:155; 20:205
Jane (Coates), 19:154
Jeane, 19:162
Jemima (Preble), 19:155
Joanna (Alley), 19:155
Joanna (Larrabee), 19:229; 20:205
Joanna/Hanna (Alley), 18:19
John, 17:96; 18:19; 19:155
Jonathan, 19:155, 157, 163; 20:210
Joseph, 16:74; 17:157; 18:19; 19:154, 155, 162; 20:111, 196, 205
Joshua, 16:196; 19:229; 20:196, 205
Josiah, 16:207; 18:103; 19:155; 20:52, 197, 205
Lydia, 17:157
Martha (Coates), 19:155
Martha (Stanbury), 19:155
Mary, 17:157; 18:212; 19:155; 20:205
Mary (Ballard), 16:75
Mary (Fuller), 16:74; 17:157
Mary (Rand), 20:205
Mary Ann, 18:217
Obadiah, 19:162
Patience (Fletcher), 17:157
Priscilla (Smith), 19:155; 20:205
Rachel, 18:102
Rachel (Silsbee), 18:30, 102
Ruth, 17:157
Ruth (Marston), 16:85
Samuel, 17:157; 18:30, 102; 19:106, 155, 162, 163; 20:52, 196, 207
Sarah, 17:157; 18:19, 227; 19:155, 162
Sarah (Frothingham), 17:157
Sarah (Merriam), 19:108
Solomon, 20:52
Susannah, 19:155
Thomas, 16:85; 19:108, 157, 229; 20:205
RICE, 20:13
Jason, 17:23
Jesse, 18:15
John, 18:106
Joyce, 20:23
Louise, 19:55, 56
Mary (Tarbox), 20:138
William, 20:138
RICH, 19:205
___, Rev., 20:155, 162
Alice (Pike), 17:208
Beth, 18:135
Dan, 17:208
Della A., 17:207
Della Alice, 17:208
Elizabeth (Phillips), 16:224
Elizabeth Lewis, 18:137
Hannah (___), 16:223
Hannah (Holder), 20:240
James, 16:223; 20:240
Louisa, 19:57
Mary, 18:178
Mary (Phillips), 16:223
Mary (Upton), 20:234
Robert, 16:224
Sally, 18:177
Thomas, 16:33; 20:234
RICHARD
Daniel, 20:208

RICHARDS, 16:46; 18:133, 139
___, Capt., 16:90
"Child", 18:72
Abigail, 16:103; 17:29; 18:72; 20:211
Abigail (Breed), 16:96
Alexander, 16:107
Ann (Knight), 18:72, 73; 19:27
Anna, 16:99
Anna Louise (Smith), 17:207
Anne (Bare), 16:99
Benjamin, 16:98; 18:26; 19:229
Benjamin F., 16:103
Benjamin H., 16:103
Benjamin Newhall Hallowell, 16:103
Benjamin T., 16:102
Betsy, 16:70
Betsy (Danford), 16:99
Bridget, 16:103
Charles, 18:107
Crispus, 16:27, 221; 17:173; 18:36, 100, 103; 19:77, 78
Daniel, 18:29, 72; 19:228; 20:206
Deborah, 16:70; 18:72; 19:107
Edward, 16:24, 101; 17:216; 18:72, 74, 79, 137, 231; 19:27, 189
Elisabeth (Newhall), 16:99
Elizabeth, 16:70; 19:78
Elizabeth (Alley), 16:96; 18:24, 26
Elizabeth (Bassett), 18:29
Elizabeth (Burchsted), 16:95
Elizabeth (Proctor), 18:72
Elizabeth Ann, 16:99
Elizabeth Tweed (Currier), 16:102
Everett B., 17:207
Hannah, 16:95; 17:113; 19:50
Hannah (Cox), 16:96
Hannah (Graves), 16:221
Hannah (Hilton), 16:99
Hannah (Johnson), 16:101
Hannah (Larrabee), 19:229
Hannah (Newhall), 16:46
Hannah (Phelps), 16:98
Hannah Leach, 16:99
Henry, 16:99; 19:105, 106, 109
Henry Burchstead, 16:95
Jacob, 16:221
James, 16:69
Jane, 16:103
Janney, 16:100
Jeremiah, 16:209
Jerusha, 16:98
Jerusha (Alley), 16:97; 18:24
Jerusha (Newhall), 16:46
John, 16:27, 171; 17:113; 18:24, 26, 137, 211, 213; 19:77-79; 20:140, 196
Joseph, 16:69; 18:29, 92, 103, 173; 19:77, 79
Joseph Warren, 16:103
Katherine, 16:96, 97
Katherine (Burchsted), 16:95, 96
Lidia (Phillips), 18:26
Lydia, 16:69; 18:26
Lydia (Ingalls), 16:97; 19:105, 106, 109
Lydia (Parker), 16:102
Lydia (Phillips), 16:27
Lydia (Witt), 16:69
Lydia Mariah, 16:103
Martha, 16:69
Martha (Burrill), 16:69
Martha Ellen, 16:103
Mary, 16:98; 18:72, 211, 213; 19:39, 98
Mary (___), 18:213
Mary (Brewer), 19:79

Mary (Ober), 16:102
Mary Eliza, 16:102
Mary Jane, 16:103
Nabby D. (Haskel), 16:103
Naby/Abigail, 16:103
Patty (Newhall), 18:24
Polly, 16:98
Polly (Fowle), 16:101
Rebecca, 16:70
Richard, 16:70, 221
Sally, 16:102
Sarah, 16:69; 19:50, 109
Sarah (Collins), 16:27; 18:100
Sibyl Sawyer (Smith), 16:107
Stephen, 16:98
Susan (Whitney), 16:103
Susan Maria, 16:103
Tabitha, 16:98
Tabitha (Williams), 16:96; 17:113; 19:50
Walter, 16:95
William, 16:46; 17:113; 18:24, 72; 19:50
RICHARDSON, 20:68
"Child", 19:31
Abijah, 17:119
Addison, 16:101; 19:199
Albert, 18:207
Amos, 17:119
Amy (Graves), 18:18; 19:28; 20:205
Andrew, 20:28
Ann (Potter), 19:153
Anna, 16:59; 17:179
Anna (Norwood), 18:207
Annah (Jones), 18:89
Aquillar, 17:179
Bernice Lucretia (Franklin), 18:176
Betsey, 16:42
Caleb, 18:159
Chloe (Bancroft), 20:40
Constance Franklin, 18:176
Daniel, 17:179
David, 17:119
Deborah, 18:205
Edward, 19:31
Elizabeth, 16:79; 18:205, 209; 19:45, 153, 223; 20:119, 218, 222
Elizabeth (Winn), 20:28
Elizabeth A., 17:222
Esther, 19:31
Francis, 19:47
Hannah, 17:16; 20:228
Jabez, 16:64
Jane, 17:119
Jane (___), 19:31
Jedediah, 17:119
Jesse, 18:89
Joanna, 18:232
John, 17:179; 20:112, 228
Jonas, 16:42
Jonathan, 18:212
Joseph, 18:236; 19:120; 20:119
Joshua, 19:31
Louisa, 17:179
Lucy, 16:42
Lydia, 17:179
Lyman, 17:119
Margaret (Godfrey), 19:120; 20:119
Martha, 16:42
Martha (Parker), 16:42
Martha (Wyman), 16:42
Martha Louise, 17:188
Mary, 16:38; 19:31
Mary (Parker), 19:31
Moses, 17:179

Oliver, 20:40
Philip, 16:209
Rebecca, 19:238
Richard, 17:89; 18:232; 20:196, 205
Richard Heber, 18:176
Robort, 16:131
Sally, 17:119
Sally (Mansfield), 18:212
Samuel, 17:179
Sarah, 17:85; 20:41
Sarah (McFarland), 17:119
Stephen, 17:179
Susanna (Gardner), 17:179
Susannah, 17:179
Thomas, 20:78, 79, 205
Tiffen (Bodwell), 18:159
Wesley, 17:119
William, 19:153; 20:113
RICHESSON
George, 19:189
RICHMOND
Betsey, 20:118
Ebenezer, 20:118
Edward, 18:81; 20:118
Elizabeth, 18:81
John, 20:118
Joshua Bailey, 18:82
Josiah, 20:118
Lemuel, 20:118
Molly (Richmond), 20:118
RICHTER
Paula, 18:139
RICKER
Lydia, 17:103
RIDDAN, 16:96
Elizabeth, 16:25; 17:101
Jerusha, 19:49
Jerusha (Collins), 17:218
Joanna, 17:159
John, 16:79; 18:103; 19:49; 20:211
Margaret, 16:236
Sarah, 16:84
Thaddeus, 17:213; 18:137
Thomas, 17:158; 18:226; 19:49, 228, 229; 20:48, 113, 226
RIDDELL
___, Mr., 20:171
Emma Frances (Wood), 20:171
RIDDEN
Ebenezer, 20:211
Joseph, 20:211
RIDDLESDALE see LOKER, 18:175
RIDENOUR
Blanche, 16:111
RIDER
Ester, 20:56
Experience (Atwood), 18:178
Lydia, 20:55
Rebecca (Winslow), 20:55
Samuel, 18:178; 20:55
W. H., 17:110
William H., 17:111
RIDGWAY
Daniel, 18:38
Rachel (Fogg), 18:38
RIDLAN, 20:44
G. T., 19:224; 20:36
RIGGS
Aaron, 16:64
Joseph, 17:42
Judith, 18:203
Martha, 17:42
Mary (Mower), 17:42

Moses, 16:134
Ruth, 18:204, 205
Sarah, 17:42; 18:76
Thomas, 17:240
RINES
Dennis, 16:134
RING
Abigail (Graves), 20:219
Benjamin, 20:44
Elizabeth, 18:31
Hannah, 16:19
Lucretia (Mills), 20:44
Mary, 16:63
William, 20:219
RIPLEY
Donald, 18:83, 135
Ezra, 16:107
Gulielma Maria (Estes), 18:98
John, 20:50
Mary (Larrabee), 20:50
Thomas, 18:98
RISBY
Robert, 19:132
RISING
Josiah, 20:13
RISTINE
Mary C., 19:21
RITCHOT
Jacques, 18:7
Suzanne (Calquette), 18:7
RITEWEISNER
William Adams, 17:125
RITH
Richard, 20:199
RIVARD
Francoise, 20:169
RIVOIRE see REVERE
RIX
Susanna (Skelton), 18:174
Thomas, 18:174; 19:143
ROACH/ROTCH
Benighton, 19:236
Benjamin, 19:236
Elizabeth, 19:144, 238
Elizabeth (Sadler), 19:236
Hannah, 19:144, 236
Hannah (Green), 19:236
Hannah (Potter), 19:143-145, 236
Joseph, 19:144, 236
Mary, 19:144
Mary (Kingman), 19:236
Nicholas, 19:236
William, 19:143-145, 236
ROADES/ROADS/RODES see also RHOADES, RHODES
Charity (Lewis), 18:37
Elizabeth, 16:239
Henry, 16:207
Joanna (Larrabee), 19:228
John, 20:199
Josiah, 16:206, 207
Stephen, 18:37
ROBBINS
Thomas, 18:90
William, 19:135
William A., 20:100
ROBBINSON see ROBINSON
John, 19:136
Mary, 17:171
ROBERT
Abraham, 20:133
ROBERTS, 17:115
Abigail, 20:140

Abraham, 19:135; 20:196
Elizabeth, 18:159, 164
Elizabeth (Richardson), 20:119
Ephraim, 18:160; 20:218
Eunice (___), 20:14
Gary Boyd, 16:174; 17:125; 18:63
Hannah (Bassett), 18:39
Hannah (Bray), 20:119
Hannah (Smith), 20:218
Job, 20:140
John, 16:64; 18:39, 164; 20:119, 200
Lemuel, 17:230
Lydia (Purchase), 17:230
Mary (___), 18:178
Mary (Rich), 18:178
Oliver, 17:115
Oliver A., 16:230
Rachel, 16:97
Rebecca (Goldthwait), 17:200
Sarah, 20:119, 218
Sarah (Tarbox), 20:140
Susannah, 20:118
Theophilus, 20:103
Thomas, 20:15, 119
William, 18:178
ROBERTSON
Alexander, 20:41
Elizabeth/Eliza, 16:120, 178; 17:81
Irene P., 19:75
James, 20:40
Lucinda (Bancroft), 20:41
Mary, 16:53
Sarah (Bancroft), 20:40
Timothy, 20:41
ROBICHAUD, 18:6
ROBIE
Henry, 17:58
Mary (Page), 16:57
Ruth (Moore), 17:58
Samuel, 16:57
Theodate, 16:57
Thomas, 18:238
ROBIN, 17:42
ROBINS
William, 16:64
ROBINSON see also ROBBINSON, 20:18
Abigail, 18:76; 20:237
Abigail (Worden), 16:77
Abraham, 17:240; 20:200
Alexander P., 16:151
Andrew, 17:191; 20:237
Benjamin, 16:240
Catharine Lucy (Farr), 16:151
Damaris (___), 20:180
Dane, 19:33
Daniel, 19:239
Daniel A., 19:119
Dean, 19:33, 90
Dorothy, 20:23
Elizabeth, 20:180
Elizabeth (Grindle), 19:239
Elizabeth (Pemberton), 19:207
Ephraim, 19:90
George, 16:208
Hannah, 18:202; 19:92
Isaac, 19:90
James, 16:4; 19:239; 20:83, 196
Jane, 18:206
Jeremiah, 16:64
John, 17:240; 18:140, 179; 19:207, 210, 212, 239
Jonathan, 16:32
Joseph, 16:68; 19:88, 90, 115

Judith (Dodd), 19:119
Lewis, 16:77
Mary (___), 19:33
Mary (Kimball), 20:16
Mary (Parker), 19:33
Mehitable, 18:81
Micajah, 16:77
Nancy (___), 16:240
Nathaniel, 20:180
Peter, 20:16
Phebe (Dane), 19:115
Rachel (Lurvey), 20:58
Rebecca, 19:59
Samuel, 18:179; 20:16
Sarah, 19:119; 20:16
Sarah (___), 20:16
Sarah (Ballard), 16:77
Sarah (Kimball), 18:179
Sarah (Norwood), 18:205
Sarah (Tucker), 18:179
Stephen, 20:58
Susanna, 18:202
ROBY
Ann, 18:152; 19:101
Sarah (Cheever), 18:152; 19:101
Thomas, 16:29
William, 18:152; 19:101
ROCK
Anna Theresa, 19:20
Joseph, 16:23
ROCKWOOD
John, 19:53
Ruth (Farrington), 17:152
Samuel, 17:152
Sarah (Ingalls), 19:53
Tabitha, 19:169
ROD
Elizabeth (Purchase), 17:230
Peter, 17:230
Thomas, 17:230
RODDEN see RAWDEN
RODER
Elizabeth (Potter), 19:153
Thomas, 19:153
RODERICK
Thomas H., 17:123
RODES see also ROADES, RHOADES
Henery, 18:230
RODGERS see also ROGERS
Elizabeth, 17:114
Silvanus, 16:155
RODICK
Abigail (Stover), 18:176
George, 18:176
Mary, 18:176
RODMAN
David, 18:11
ROE
Rebecca (Rowland), 20:180
Sarah (Graves), 20:224
William, 20:224
ROFF
Betsy, 16:148
ROGERS see also RODGERS, 17:135
___, Capt., 19:217
___, Mr., 17:11
Aaron, 19:180
Abigail, 16:174; 17:114; 19:177
Abigail (Chisemore), 19:180
Abigail (Trescott), 17:114
Alexander, 20:50
Ann (Dennis), 19:53
Ann S. (Collins), 17:38

Anna (Turner), 18:59; 19:180
Arthur G., 17:165
Betsy (Stoodley), 16:60
Charles, 17:38
Daniel, 16:63; 17:114; 20:225
Dorcas, 17:114
Dorcas (___), 17:114
Elizabeth, 17:114; 18:137
Elizabeth (Hemingway), 17:114
Elizabeth (Witt), 18:169
Emeline, 17:163
Ezekiel, 16:73; 17:140; 18:9, 193; 20:224
Frederick, 18:169
George, 17:59
George M., 16:60
Hannah, 17:59; 18:239
Hannah (Larrabee), 20:50
Hannah (Sinclair), 17:59
Hannah/Annie, 16:236
Hiram, 17:59
Jane, 20:50
Jehosophat, 17:114
Jeremiah, 17:114
John, 16:134; 17:114; 18:194; 19:53
John Gorham, 17:138
Lois, 18:29; 19:180
Lois (Rogers), 19:180
Love, 17:114
Margaret, 17:114
Mary, 16:174; 17:11; 18:59
Mary (Wade), 16:174
Mehitable, 17:59
Mercy, 17:114
Miriam, 18:59
Miriam (Rogers), 18:59
Nancy A., 16:60
Nathan, 20:180
Nathaniel, 16:174; 18:192-194
Paul, 18:59
Pheobe, 18:137
Richard, 20:225
Robert, 20:180
Robert P., 17:38
Samuel, 16:174; 17:59
Sarah, 16:97
Sarah (Bailey), 20:180
Sarah Clementina (Friend), 17:38
Sarah Ellen (Derby), 17:228
Silas, 19:180
Simeon, 18:59; 19:180
Susanna (Lewis), 20:180
Unis, 16:233
William E., 17:38
ROLES see also ROLLS
Charity (Bassett), 18:37
John, 18:37
ROLFE
Ezra, 16:178
Sarah (Jackson), 16:178
ROLLAND
___, Capt., 19:110
Rebecca, 18:88
ROLLINS
Abbott W., 17:167
Abigail (Osborn), 17:184
Ebenezer, 17:179
Eliphalet, 17:179
Gertrude (Friend), 17:167
Ichabod, 17:179
John, 17:179
John A., 17:167
Josiah, 17:179
Louisa A., 16:118

Lydia, 17:179
Lydia (Clark), 17:179
Nathaniel, 17:179
Patience, 17:179
Rebecca, 20:13
Sarah, 17:179
Stephen, 17:179
Susan E. (___), 17:167
Susanna, 17:179
William, 20:13
ROLLS see also ROLES
Anna, 17:218
ROMER
Annie Stewart, 17:31
ROMULUS, 19:68
ROOD
Amanda, 19:180
Anna (Morehouse), 19:180
Aurelia, 19:180
Lewis, 19:180
Mary Celina, 19:180
Sarah, 19:180
ROOLS
Samuel, 19:84
ROOLTON
Richard, 20:190, 192, 194
ROOT
Jonathan, 20:141
Joseph, 19:197
Mary (Tarbox), 20:141
Nathaniel, 20:141
Sarah (Tarbox), 20:141
Thomas, 19:197
ROOTEN
Anna (___), 18:20
Richard, 18:20, 99; 19:47, 138, 196
ROOTES/ROOTS
Alfred B., 17:29
Josiah, 16:137
Sarah (Edmands), 17:29
ROPER
Betsy (___), 17:108
Betsy D., 17:108
John, 17:108; 20:223
ROPES
"Child", 17:231
Abraham, 17:231
Anna, 19:42
Benjamin, 18:93
Daniel, 17:231
David, 17:231; 18:94; 19:199
Elizabeth, 17:231
Elizabeth (___), 17:231
Elizabeth (Felt), 16:26
Elizabeth (Purchase), 17:231
George, 17:231; 19:195
Joseph, 16:26; 17:231
Ruth, 17:231
Sarah, 17:231
ROSE
Antone, 19:176
Christine, 20:11
Gregory S., 18:191
Margaret, 18:132
ROSENCRANTZ
Bessie Grove (Tyler), 19:232
William Dayton, 19:232
ROSEWELL
Elizabeth (Coffin), 16:238
Joseph, 16:238
Ruth, 16:238
ROSS
Abigail (Goodhue), 16:178

Abigail (Tarbox), 20:141
Anna (Larrabee), 20:115
David, 20:115
Elizabeth, 19:111, 113, 114
Frances Ellen (Woodman), 16:220
Hannah (Staniford), 16:178
Hugh, 20:239
Mary (Libby), 20:239
Mary Ann, 20:239
Nancy (Gilman), 20:239
Samuel, 20:141
Thomas, 16:178
Wentworth, 20:239
ROSSELL see also RUSSELL
Myntan, 20:74
ROTCH see ROACH, 19:236
ROUND
Mary, 20:58
ROUNDAY
Sarah, 16:218
ROUNDS
Joseph, 20:6
Spencer, 20:6
ROUNDY
C., 19:231
Emma, 16:79
John, 19:151
Mary Susan (Savory), 19:184, 185
Ruth (Devereux), 19:151
Tabitha Lewis (Bessom), 19:231
William, 20:198
ROUS
Mary, 17:204
ROUSAMIERE, 19:174
ROUX
Aimee, 20:169
ROW
___, Mrs., 17:12
Charles, 17:240
Eliza, 17:11
Hugh, 17:240; 20:200
Jabez L., 16:134
James, 17:240
James P., 17:34
Jonathan, 17:12
Joseph, 16:134
Martha Ann (Friend), 17:34
Timothy S., 17:34
ROWDEN
Elizabeth (___), 17:202
John, 17:202
ROWE
___, Mrs., 17:11
Anthony, 19:229
Benjamin, 17:103
Betsy (Bowdy), 19:238
Clara Eve (Friend), 17:106
Elizabeth, 19:226, 229; 20:114
Ida M., 17:103
James, 19:238
John, 16:64; 17:240; 18:204
John S., 17:106
Louise (White), 17:106
Mary, 18:204
Mary (Mutchmore), 17:103
Mary C., 17:165
Minnie, 17:106
Sarah, 19:238
Sarah (Harris), 18:201
Sarah A. (Brown), 19:238
Sarah E. (Marchant), 17:165
Solomon, 17:165
Thomas, 18:201

Washington, 19:238
William N., 17:106
ROWELL
Hannah (Winslow), 17:235
John, 17:235
Mary, 17:235
Miriam, 16:223
Molly, 18:180
Moses, 16:173
Philip, 17:193
ROWLAND/ROWLING
___ (Smith), 16:30
Abigail, 17:211
Abigail (Trask), 17:212
Elizabeth, 19:150
Elizabeth (Lindsey), 18:19
James, 19:150
John, 17:211
Joseph, 16:30; 17:211
Lois (Potter), 19:150, 236, 237
Lucy (Band), 17:212
Mary, 16:30; 17:212; 18:169
Mary (Smith), 17:210, 212, 213
Philip, 17:210
Rachel, 17:212
Rebecca, 19:179; 20:180
Richard, 16:31; 17:210; 20:199
Samuel, 16:30; 17:210
William, 18:19
ROWLING see ROWLAND, 19:237
ROWSELL see RUSSELL, 20:74
ROWSLAND see POUSLAND, RUSSELL
ROYAL/ROYALL see also RYALL
Bethyah (Payne), 20:145
Joseph, 20:145
Phebe, 20:145
Susan (Tarbox), 20:143
William, 20:143
ROYLS, 16:13
RUCK see also DeRICH, DERICK, 18:30
___, Mr., 19:188
Elizabeth (Tawley), 19:39
John, 18:60a; 19:39
Margaret, 17:159
Mary (Bassett), 16:232; 18:29
Samuel, 19:39, 216
Sarah (Cheever), 19:38, 39
Thomas, 16:166; 18:231; 19:39
RUDDOCK
John, 19:131
RUMNEY
Rebecca, 18:205
RUMNEY MARSH
James, 18:60a
RUNDLET/RUNDLETT
Jane, 16:86
Lizzie, 20:228
RUNKLE
Priscilla D., 16:63
Priscilla Davis, 18:137
RUNNO
Peeter, 20:197
RUSHWORTH, 16:13
RUSKOSKY
Beverly Harwood (Wescoat), 19:232
Debbie, 19:232
Richard, 19:232
Ricky, 19:232
RUSS
John, 16:68; 17:55
Margaret (___), 17:55
Mary, 17:54

**RUSSEL/RUSSELL/ROSSELL/
ROWSELL/ROWSLAND**, 20:63, 74
___, Mrs., 19:34
Abigail, 17:207
Abigail (Flint), 16:233
Abre, 20:73
Albert William, 20:24
Anthonie, 20:74
Aubrey, 20:73, 74
Augusta M. (Tibbetts), 20:24
Benjamin, 16:233; 18:57; 20:24
Benjamin F., 20:24
Betsey, 17:16; 18:57, 217
Betsy (Norwood), 18:216
Caroline, 18:216
Charles Warren, 20:24
Clara Anna (Withey), 20:24
Clement, 20:74
Donna Valley, 19:116
Edmund Needham, 20:24
Edward Needham, 20:24
Elbridge, 18:216
Eliza, 18:216
Elizabeth, 16:233; 17:98
Elizabeth (Belnap), 18:57
Elizabeth (Henley), 19:103
Elizabeth (Pitman), 16:71; 18:73, 75
Elizabeth (Russell), 17:100
Enoch, 18:216
Esther, 17:207
Esther (Smith), 17:207
Eunice (Warren), 20:24
Ezekiel, 18:57; 19:37, 38
Ezekiel Cheever, 18:57
George Ely, 18:191
George Warren, 20:24
Giles, 17:100
Hannah, 16:233
Henry, 18:75; 20:199
James, 16:97; 17:23; 19:87, 212, 216, 217; 20:188
James Needham, 20:24
Jason, 17:4
Joanna (Winn), 20:97
John, 16:233; 20:74, 97
Jordan, 20:75
Joseph, 16:233; 19:38
Judith Cooper, 18:57
Katharine, 19:103
Levi, 17:207
Mabel, 19:178
Margaret (Needham), 20:24
Martha (Johnson), 19:93
Mary, 16:159, 233; 19:171
Mary (Marshall), 16:159, 232
Mary (Preston), 16:233
Mary Ann (Raymond), 20:24
Mary Jane (___), 20:24
Maryan, 18:216
Moses P., 17:207
Nathaniel Pope, 18:57
Nicholas, 20:74, 75
Nycho, 20:75
Onyon, 20:74, 75
Peter, 18:216; 20:74, 75
Peter Orin, 17:207
Phebe (___), 16:233
Priscilla (Kimball), 16:145
Priscilla (Osgood), 16:233
R. G., 17:167
Ralph, 18:114; 20:67, 73, 74, 76
Richard, 18:230; 19:188; 20:199
Robert, 16:68, 159; 19:93

Ruth, 16:131
Salley Belknap, 18:57
Sally, 18:216
Samuel, 20:199
Sarah, 16:233; 19:46; 20:234
Sarah (Barrett), 20:217
Sarah (Chandler), 16:233
Sarah (Hood), 18:57
Sarah Jane, 20:24
Susanna (Cheever), 19:38
Tabitha, 19:230
Thomas, 16:68; 19:103
William, 16:145; 19:94; 20:75, 199, 217
Zebiah, 20:43
RUSSELLS
Skinner, 20:221
RUST
Abigail, 16:102; 18:173
Daniel, 18:173
Elizabeth, 17:19
John, 18:172
Samuel, 18:172
RYALL see also ROYAL
Ann, 18:100
John, 16:111
RYAN
Ambrose, 16:134
Daniel, 16:94
Rebecca (Bancroft), 16:94
RYDER
Ester (Hall), 20:56
John, 20:56
Patience, 20:95
Winona, 17:75
RYERSON
Abigail (Ellery), 17:37
John, 17:37
Lucy Ellery, 17:37
RYNN
Anna, 16:132
Daniel, 16:132
James, 16:132
John, 16:132
Lucy, 16:132
Nathaniel, 16:132
Samuel, 16:132

SABENS/SABIN
Benjamin, 18:155, 156
Dorothy, 16:209
Experience, 18:156
Jeremiah, 18:156
Nehemiah, 18:156
Patience, 18:156
Ruth (Cooper), 18:156
Sarah, 18:156
Sarah (Parker), 18:155, 156
Stephen, 18:156
Timothy, 18:156
SACK
Sallyann Amdur, 17:74
SACKETT
Elizabeth (Kirtland), 18:112
Richard, 18:112
SADIE
John, 19:221
SADLER
___, Mr., 19:138
Elizabeth, 19:236
Richard, 16:161; 20:183, 187, 191, 194
SADLEY, 20:191
SAFFORD
Charlotte, 20:153

Deborah, 20:226
Ebenezer, 17:201
Hannah (Osborn), 17:201
Jesse, 20:118
Mary, 16:34
Mary (Hood), 18:56
Moses, 18:56
SAGAMORE
George, 18:60a
SAGAMORE JOHN, 19:203
SAGE
Abigail, 17:127
Allen, 17:127
Comfort, 17:127
Elizabeth Westbrook (Becroft), 17:127
SAKAMAKI
Shunzo, 17:132
SALESBURY see also SALSBURY
Hannah (Potter), 19:150
Jonathan, 19:149, 150
SALIS see also SALLOWS, SOLLAS
John, 20:198
SALK, 17:64
Bluma/Florence (___), 17:65
Charlotte/Solit, 17:65
Eli, 17:65
Robert, 17:65
Solomon, 17:65
SALLOWS/SALIS see also SOLLAS
Abigail (___), 16:177
Elizabeth, 18:137, 138
Freeborn (Wolfe), 16:177
Hannah, 16:137
Joseph, 16:177
Michael, 16:177
Rebecca (Groves), 16:177
Robert, 16:177
Thomas, 16:177
SALMON
Daniel, 17:88; 18:147, 164; 20:132
Sarah, 19:179
SALSBURY see also SALESBURY
Hannah (Potter), 19:149
SALT, 20:18
SALTER
Benjamin, 16:83
Eunice (Tardy), 16:83
Francis, 19:83
Hannah, 18:224
Henry, 18:224
John, 18:224
Mary, 18:224
Mary (Adams), 18:224
SALTONSTALL, 16:4
___, Col., 18:69
Nathaniel, 18:193
Richard, 18:193, 240a; 20:190
SALVATORE, 17:211
SAMERSET
John, 18:76
SAMMONS
Elizabeth, 19:47
SAMPSON, 16:35
Andrew, 17:232
Benjamin H., 19:172
Harriet Newell (Northey), 19:172
John, 17:88; 20:198
Rachel (Codner), 17:232
SAMUELS
Eleanor (Smith), 17:208
Thomas A., 17:208
SANBORN, 18:187
Alice, 20:180

Benjamin, 20:180
Eleanor (Chandler), 16:118
George, 18:5
George F., 17:177; 18:139
Hannah, 20:180
Hannah (Thorne), 20:180
James, 16:118; 18:178; 20:180
Jonathan, 16:118
Melinde, 16:22
Melinde Lutz, 18:67; 19:87, 116
Rachel (Fifield), 16:179
Sarah (Shaw), 16:178
Sarah Dimond, 19:239
Sarah/Sally (Avery), 16:118; 18:178
V. C., 18:109
SANDERS see also SAUNDERS, 20:18
"Child", 17:13
Abigail, 19:118
Abigail (Corney), 19:118
Amos, 16:132
Ann (___), 16:179
Elizabeth (Norwood), 18:202
John, 16:134; 18:202
Joseph, 16:134; 18:202
Martha (Henderson), 18:202
Mary (___), 16:179
Pardon, 17:50
Phoebe (More), 17:50
Sarah, 18:39
Thomas, 17:13; 19:118
SANDERSON see also SAUNDERSON, 20:113
Elijah, 17:200
H. K., 17:113
Howard K., 18:44
Howard Kendall, 16:69; 18:153, 214, 217; 19:75, 161; 20:38
Mary, 19:83, 85
Sally, 17:200
Samuel Allen, 18:137
Sarah, 18:120
SANDIN
Ephraim, 18:30
Merriam (Gale), 18:30
SANDY
Miriam/Merriam (Bassett), 18:29, 30
SANFORD see also STANFORD
___, Mr., 16:160
Adaline (Tarbox), 20:147
Bathsheba, 16:206
Charles W., 20:147
Christian (___), 16:208
Elizabeth (Skelton), 16:57
Florence (Friend), 17:37
Harriet E. (___), 17:37
Horatio Frank, 17:37
Horatio G., 17:37
John, 16:163
Robert, 16:56; 17:115
Sarah, 16:56
Thomas, 16:208
SANGER
George J., 17:110
Richard, 17:23
SARGANT/SARGEANT/SARGENT see also SEAGEANT, SERGANT, 18:132; 20:17, 18
"Child", 17:12
Aaron, 16:82
Abigail, 17:236; 18:48, 200; 19:157
Abigail (Clark), 17:236; 18:200
Abigail (Mower), 16:82; 17:43
Abigial (Blaney), 16:82

Albert, 16:149
Amos, 16:223
Ann (___), 16:223
Anna/Anne, 16:173
Benjamin, 19:161
Charles, 20:80, 81
Christopher, 20:81, 131
Cora May, 16:52
Daniel, 16:134; 20:80, 81
David, 19:118; 20:80, 81
Deborah, 17:179
Ebenezer, 16:223
Edmund, 20:83
Elias, 20:81
Elizabeth, 16:223; 17:53
Emily (___), 16:149
Epes, 17:191
Ephraim, 20:81
Esther, 17:191
Esther (McCarty), 17:191
Fitz William, 17:191
Francis, 18:200
Frank Wendell, 17:170
H. Marion, 17:170
Hannah, 17:52; 20:178
Harriet Kimball (Friend), 17:170
Ichabod Barnard, 20:81
Ignatius, 19:14
Jabez, 16:82; 17:43
Jacob, 20:80, 81
James, 20:81
James M., 16:102
John, 17:12; 18:240; 20:80, 131
John Singer, 17:192
Jonathan, 20:80
Joseph, 20:80
Joshua, 18:200; 20:81
Josiah, 16:223
Judith, 17:191; 18:70
Judith (Saunders), 17:191
Laura Adeline (Hardy), 17:170
Laura F., 17:170
Lois (Waite), 16:82
Lucy, 18:179
Lydia, 16:82; 18:200
Lydia (Parrott), 16:102
Mary, 16:223; 17:236; 18:132, 137, 200
Mary (Duncan), 17:191
Mary (Emerson), 18:200
Mary (Norwood), 18:199, 200
Mary (Sargent), 17:236
Mary (York), 18:200
Mehitabel, 18:213
Miriam, 16:173
Miriam (Rowell), 16:223
Moses, 20:81
Nathan, 17:170
Nathaniel, 17:11
Nathaniel Peaslee, 20:81
Oliver, 20:82
Orlando, 20:81
Patience (Phillips), 16:222
Patten, 20:81
Peter, 16:134; 18:204
Philip, 20:80, :81
Rachel, 18:200
Rachel (Barnes), 17:52; 20:178
Robert, 20:81
Ruth (Flood), 16:223
Ruth (Patten), 20:81
Ruth E., 17:170
Sally, 20:41
Sally Pool (Norwood), 18:204

Sally/Sarah (Ingersoll), 19:118
Samuel, 16:82; 18:199, 200; 19:104; 20:81, 200
Sarah, 19:108
Sarah (Coates), 19:161
Sarah (Somes), 18:200
Solomon, 18:200
Stephen, 18:200; 20:81
Susanna (Harraden), 18:200
Susannah (Peaslee), 20:81
Thomas, 17:52; 20:80, 81, 178
Timothy, 20:80, 81
Trueworthy, 20:81
William, 16:82; 17:191; 18:200; 20:80, 81, 139, 200
William M., 17:229
William Philip, 20:81
Winthrop, 17:12; 18:70

SARNA
Jonathan, 16:189

SATCHWELL, 20:224

SAULER
Abigail (Pulsifer), 17:118
Davis, 17:118
Mary Ann, 17:117

SAUNDERS see also SANDERS
Caleb, 19:14
Daniel, 19:13, 14
Elizabeth (Estes), 16:78; 18:93, 94
Esther, 19:178
Henry, 20:131
Judith, 17:191
Mary, 19:38, 41
Mary (Elkins), 18:94
Paul, 16:175
Philip, 18:94
Sarah, 20:26
Sarah (Lane), 19:119
Simeon, 19:119
Thomas, 17:191
Tobias, 16:112

SAUNDERSON see also SANDERSON
David, 19:158
Lucy (Coates), 19:158

SAVAGE, 18:233; 19:80, 116
James, 16:17; 17:18; 18:18, 71, 82, 83, 110, 154; 19:27, 30, 43, 116; 20:102
Sarah (Cheever), 19:103
Thomas, 18:230; 19:103, 191, 193, 194

SAVELL
Jane (___), 18:235

SAVILLE
Clara P., 17:164
Jesse, 17:135
Martha (Babson), 17:135
Oliver, 17:135
Richard, 18:138
Thomas, 17:138

SAVORY
Anne, 18:10
John, 16:154; 17:152
Mary Susan, 19:183, 185
Sarah (Wood), 17:152

SAWIN
Eunice (Gilbert), 16:240
Jonathan, 16:240
Luther, 16:240
Mary (Whitney), 16:240

SAWTELL/SAWTELLE
Abigail, 17:80
Anna (Parker), 17:79
Elizabeth (___), 20:97
Ephraim, 16:40
Hannah, 18:169; 20:28, 97
Hannah (Lawrence), 17:82
Hannah (Stevens), 16:40
Josiah, 17:81
Lydia (Nutting), 17:81
Margaret, 17:79
Mary, 17:80
Miriam, 17:83
Obadiah, 17:82
Richard, 17:78; 20:97
Zachariah, 17:79

SAWYARDS
Bettie, 17:13
Joseph, 17:13

SAWYER
Abiel, 16:173
Abraham, 17:236; 20:143
Alan, 17:187
Amos, 19:120
Ann (Osborn), 17:187
Ann/Anna (Osborn), 17:184
Anna, 16:173
Charles, 17:236
Daniel, 16:222
David, 17:12
Eleanor Grace, 16:222
Elijah, 16:173
Elizabeth, 18:55; 19:169, 198
Elizabeth A., 17:166
Enoch, 16:106
Ezra, 16:222
Fred E., 16:173
Hannah, 16:173; 17:237
Hannah (___), 16:173
Hannah (Babson), 17:236
Hannah (Phillips), 16:222; 18:36
Hepsibah, 20:207
Humphrey, 16:173; 17:187; 18:36
Isaac, 20:216
Jacob, 17:204
James, 16:134; 17:11; 18:138; 20:89
John, 18:199
Judetha, 16:173
Martha, 16:235
Martha (___), 16:222
Martha (Bond), 20:216
Mary, 16:222; 17:11
Mary (___), 17:187
Mary (Breed), 16:222; 18:36
Mary (Eaton), 17:204
Mary (Hoag), 16:222
Mary (Morrill), 19:120
Mary (Sayward), 17:236
Micajah, 16:104
Miriam (Brown), 16:222
Philips, 16:173; 18:36
Rachel (Dolliver), 17:236
Reuben, 19:120
Ruth, 16:222
Sally, 20:219
Samuel Elwell, 17:236
Sarah, 16:222
Sarah (Bailey), 19:120
Sarah (Bray), 17:236
Sarah (Brown), 16:222
Sarah (Moody), 16:222
Sarah (Pierpoint), 16:106
Sybil (Farnum), 16:104
Tabitha, 17:82
William, 16:146; 17:12

SAY AND SELE
___, Viscount, 20:187

SAYRE
Job, 19:44; 20:194
Thomas, 19:44; 20:194

SAYWARD
Abigail (Sargent), 17:236
Abigail (Smith), 17:35
Alice T., 17:110
Caroline (Friend), 17:110
Caroline Dolliver, 17:36
Carrie E., 17:111
Charles A., 17:36
Daniel, 18:200
Deborah, 20:143
Deborah (Stover), 17:236
Elizabeth, 20:226
Epes, 17:110
George, 17:110
Henry, 17:110
James, 18:200
Joseph, 16:177
Judith, 18:200
Lucy, 16:176; 19:235
Lucy (Norwood), 18:200
Mary, 17:236
Mary Ann (Story), 17:110
Mary Ingersoll, 17:35
Mary Story, 17:111
Samuel, 18:200
Sarah, 17:137
Sarah (Giddings), 16:177
Steven, 16:134
William, 17:35

SCADLET see also SCARLET
Lydia, 17:219

SCADLOCK
Elizabeth, 16:86

SCALES
Abraham, 17:235
Hannah, 17:187
Sarah, 20:138
Sarah (Thompson), 17:235

SCAMMON
Dominicus, 20:139
Elizabeth, 20:139
Hannah (Tarbox), 20:139
Humphry, 20:139
James, 20:144

SCANLON
Elizabeth, 19:20

SCARBOROUGH
Bethiah (Wise), 16:39
Mary, 16:39
Samuel, 16:39

SCARLET/SCARLETT see also SCADLET
Anne (___), 16:34
Elizabeth, 16:86
Hannah, 16:85
Lydia, 19:76
Molly (Merrill), 19:178
Nancy, 19:178
Newman, 19:178
Samuel, 20:199

SCHAFFNER
Lillian, 18:138

SCHAUFELE
Elaine Collins, 18:133

SCHERER
Heinrich, 18:138

SCHINDLER
Solomon, 16:189

SCHMID
Jean Parker, 16:225; 17:78; 18:133, 135
John Carolus, 16:225; 17:78; 18:133, 136

SCHOENBURG
  Nancy, 17:74
  Stuart, 17:74
SCHOFIELD, 16:13
  Paul, 17:75
SCHUKNECHT
  Patti (Gottscholl), 16:115; 18:137
SCHWARZ
  Sonja, 17:169
SCOTT
  Abijah, 16:209
  Addie, 17:187
  Alice C., 17:187
  Asa, 16:209
  Craig, 17:10
  Daniel, 19:102
  Deborah (Richards), 16:101
  Dorothea (Olmstead), 16:209
  Elizabeth, 17:140; 19:102
  Elizabeth (Tackless), 16:209
  Ephraim, 16:209
  George, 16:101
  Hannah, 16:209; 18:39
  Harriet B., 19:56
  Harriett Grace, 16:202
  Hester/Esther, 18:39
  Joanna (Jenks), 16:72
  John, 19:51
  Joseph, 16:101
  Lemuel, 16:209
  Mary, 16:209
  Mary (Edmands), 16:209
  Nellie (Hodgedon), 17:187
  Polly, 16:87
  Rebecca, 18:39
  Rebecca (___), 16:209
  Robert, 20:200
  Sarah, 16:209
  Sarah (Cutting), 16:209
  Sylvanus, 16:72
  Thomas, 17:140
  Walter, 17:187
  William, 16:209
SCRIBNER
  Edward, 16:120
  Olive, 20:54
  Samuel, 16:120
  Sarah (Bucknell), 16:120
SCRUGGS
  Rachel, 16:136
  Thomas, 16:136; 19:127
SCUDDER
  Thomas, 19:191
SEABERG see also SIEBERG
  Alma Matilda Josephine, 19:235
SEABURY
  Barnabas, 20:45
  Margaret (Pain), 20:45
  Samuel, 20:45
SEAGEANT see also SARGANT
  Sarah, 17:160
SEALE
  Marjorie May (Farnham), 16:48
SEARS
  Anthony, 20:91
  Daniel, 16:76
  Elizabeth (Needham), 20:91
  Fear (Freeman), 16:76
  Mary, 16:57
  Robert, 19:40
  Sarah, 16:76
  Sarah (Jenkins), 19:40

SEARY
  E. R., 17:189
SEAVER
  Hannah (Wilson), 17:40
  Mary (Ballard), 16:76
  Richard, 16:76
  Shubael, 17:40
SEAVEY
  Betsey (___), 17:178
  James, 17:178
  John, 17:178
SEBRILL
  Edword, 20:199
SECCOMB
  Ebenezer, 19:231
  Hannah Phillips (Bessom), 19:231
  Joseph, 16:83
  Mary/Polly, 16:83
  Ruth (Brooks), 16:83
SEDDON, 16:13
SEEGER see also SEGAR
  Ferdinand, 16:17
SEELEY
  Abigail, 16:63
SEETE see SUEETT
SEGAR see also SEEGER
  Ephraim, 16:87
  Eunice, 16:87
  Priscilla (Harrington), 16:87
  Rebeckah (Lewis), 18:37
  William, 18:37
SEGARS
  William, 17:137
SELLECK
  George A., 16:189; 19:71
SELMAN
  Abigail, 16:236
SENDALL
  Samuel, 17:213
SENTER see also CENTER
  Elizabeth, 19:38, 39
  John, 19:39; 20:98
  Sadie Myrtle, 16:224
  Sarah (Weeden), 20:98
SERGANT/SERGEANT see also SARGANT
  Daniel, 20:13
  Sarah, 20:13
  Stephen, 16:203
SETTES
  Adeline, 18:239
  Mary Caroline, 18:239
  Patience (Perham), 18:239
  William, 18:239
SEVER
  Thankful, 16:167; 17:40
SEVERIE
  Andrew, 20:199
  Petter, 20:199
SEVERN/SEVERNE
  John, 16:165; 20:197
SEVERUS/SEVERY/SEVVERNS
  Abigail (Rhodes), 17:157
  Edward, 17:156
  Elizabeth (Fuller), 17:144, 156
  Jacob, 17:157
  John, 17:144, 156
  Joseph, 17:156
  Mary, 18:38
  Pat, 17:11
  William, 17:156
SEWALL see also SEWELL
  Abigail (___), 17:100
  Jane, 16:89

Joseph, 17:100; 18:236
  Judith, 18:180
  Mary, 17:100
  Mehitabel, 16:89
  Samuel, 16:72; 17:100; 18:36, 37, 210
  Stephen, 16:90; 19:49; 20:103
SEWARD
  George, 19:229
  Lydia, 20:112
  Margaret (Pendexter), 19:229
SEWELL see also SEWALL
  ___, Judge, 20:192
  Jane, 16:35
SEXTON
  Abigail, 17:152
  Asahel, 17:152
  Mehetable, 17:152
  Patience (Farrington), 17:152
SEYBOLT
  R. F., 16:172
SEYERS
  Job, 19:138
  Thomas, 19:138
SHACKLEY
  Richard, 18:49
SHAFFER
  Kathryn Johnson, 16:198; 18:135
SHAFFLIN
  Michael, 19:190
  Sarah, 20:100
SHAPLIE
  David, 20:199
SHARMAN
  Nathaniel, 18:216; 19:137
SHARP/SHARPE, 16:231
  ___, Lt., 17:141
  Abigail, 16:75, 86
  Deborah (Thayer), 16:56
  Elizabeth, 16:233
  Elizabeth (Gibbons), 16:56
  John, 16:56
  Jonathan, 16:56
  Mercy, 16:56
  Nathaniel, 16:231, 233; 17:90
  Rebecca, 16:233
  Rebecca (Marshall), 16:231, 233
  Ruth, 16:233
  Samuel, 16:233; 18:99; 19:190
SHARPLES, 16:141
  S. P., 20:227
  Stephen, 20:228
  Stephen Paschall, 20:16, 136
SHATSWELL
  Johanna (___), 16:59
  John, 16:59
  Margaret, 16:59
  Mary, 17:56
SHATTUCK
  Anna Laura, 19:20
  Charles H., 17:102
  Deborah, 17:204
  Emily May, 17:102
  Esther, 17:86
  J., 16:43
  James, 16:43
  Jeremiah, 17:81
  Lemuel, 16:5
  Louisa M. (Hayes), 17:102
  Lydia, 16:43; 20:54
  Lydia (Parker), 16:42
  Moses, 17:82
  P., 18:158
  Phillip, 18:158

Reuben, 16:43
Ruth, 17:81
Sally (Parker), 16:43
Sarah, 16:43
Sarah (Parker), 17:81
Tryfena (Parker), 17:84
SHAW, 16:4
Abigail (Haddock), 16:148
Abigail (Marshall), 16:160
Abigail (Smith), 20:54
Abigail Smith, 20:54
Anna, 18:200
Benjamin, 17:18
Daniel, 16:157; 17:18
David, 20:54
Ebenezer, 17:18
Edward, 16:160; 18:207
Elizabeth, 17:18
Elizabeth (Booth), 17:18
Elizabeth (Fraile), 17:18
Ellen, 17:109
Ellen H. (Low), 17:109
Henry, 17:51
Israel, 17:18
James, 16:148; 17:51
Jane (Norwood), 18:207
Johanna (Pudney), 17:18
Keziah (Crane), 17:51
Mary (___), 17:18
Moses H., 17:109
Rachel, 20:54
Richard, 17:51
Robert, 19:53
Roger, 18:51
Samuel, 17:18
Sarah, 16:178
Sarah (Breed), 17:51
Sarah (Glasey), 19:53
Sarah (Knight), 18:77
Sarah (Marden), 20:54
Sarah Miner, 17:51
Sarah Miner (Shaw), 17:51
Sargent, 18:77
Thomas, 17:51; 19:163
William, 17:18
SHEA
Jonathan D., 16:128
SHEDD
Emeline, 19:178
Esther (Saunders), 19:178
Isaac, 19:178
Nancy (Scarlett), 19:178
Nathan, 19:178
Sybil (Bullard), 16:236
SHEHAN
Arlene M., 18:138
SHELDON
Asa, 17:118; 18:138
Elizabeth (Goodell), 17:120
Francis, 16:94
Godfrey, 17:120
Jeremiah, 17:120
Lydia, 16:93
Mary, 16:93
Phebe (Pope), 16:94
Samuel, 17:120
Skelton, 17:120
Susan (___), 17:31
SHELLEY
Mehitable (Godfrey), 18:81
SHEPARD/SHEPHARD/SHEPHERD/ SHEPPARD
___, Mr., 16:166; 18:223

___, Rev., 18:30, 54
Alexander, 19:157
Calvin, 18:138
Elizabeth, 17:53
Hannah P., 17:34
Isabella, 18:88
Jeremiah, 16:156; 17:47, 155; 18:93, 111, 148, 167, 223
John, 17:16
Jonathan, 20:219
Lucinda (Burdick), 20:219
Margaret, 16:212
Mary, 17:47; 18:178, 223; 20:219
Mary (Graves), 20:219
Mehitable, 20:219
Patricia Susan, 17:208
Robert A., 18:138
Ruth, 17:159
Sally (Sawyer), 20:219
Samuel, 17:47
Sarah, 20:219
SHEPLE
Joseph, 17:82
SHEPPARD see SHEPARD
SHEPPERSON
Wilbur S., 16:10
SHERBURN/SHERBURNE
Henry, 19:229
Joseph, 16:96
Mary (Larrabee), 19:229
Sarah (Wiggin), 19:229
SHERIDAN
Elizabeth (MacMahon), 17:235
Henry, 17:235
Mary Ann, 17:188
SHERLOCK
Eunice (Blaney), 16:85
John, 16:85
SHERMAN
Abigail, 20:179
Betty, 17:116
David, 20:28, 96
Ebenezer, 20:96
Elizabeth (Havens), 20:96
Grizell (Fish), 20:96
Harold B., 17:111
Isabel, 20:95
John, 20:96
John H., 20:28, 96
Martha, 20:96
Martha (Knowles), 20:96
Martha (Tripp), 20:28, 96
Mehitable, 20:26, 28, 96
Nathaniel, 17:116
Othniel, 20:96
Phillip, 20:96
Rebecca, 20:96
Rebecca (Lawton), 20:96
Robert M., 19:176
Ruth (Friend), 17:111
Ruth Wilder, 19:176
Samuel, 20:28, 96
Sarah, 16:111; 20:96
Sarah (Odding), 20:96
Susanna (Burnap), 17:116
William, 16:238
SHERRATT
Hugh, 18:140, 141
SHERWIN
Ebenezer, 16:193
SHERWOOD
Lucy, 17:175
Lucy (Hollister), 17:175

Nathaniel, 17:175
SHID
Jonathan, 16:132
SHIFOLD
William, 19:43
SHILDEN
Elisabeth, 16:132
SHILLABER see also SHULLABER
John, 20:112
Mary, 17:199
Robert, 16:88
William, 16:88
SHILLIS
Hannah, 18:38
SHILLITO
George, 19:231
Sarah E., 19:233
Sarah E. (Bessom), 19:231
SHINN
Catherine Lucy Stevenson, 16:148
John, 16:150
Mary (White), 16:150
SHIPMAN
Elizabeth (Kirtland), 18:113
John, 18:113
SHIPP/SKIPPER/SKEPER
Katherine, 19:44
SHORE/SHORES
Abigail, 17:232
Abigail (Benson), 17:232
Abigail (Purchase), 17:232
Anne, 17:232
Elizabeth, 17:232
Eunice (Proute), 17:232
George, 17:232
Hannah, 17:232
James, 17:232
John, 17:232
Jonathan, 17:232
Jonathan Lynn, 17:232
Mary (Payton), 17:232
Priscilla (Hathorne), 17:232
Rachel (Codner), 17:232
Sampson, 17:232
Sampson Hull, 17:232
Sarah, 20:239
Susanna/Susanne, 17:98
SHOREY
Abby (Newhall), 18:177
Alfred, 20:58
B. E., 17:232
Charles, 17:120; 19:58
Charles Osborne, 17:120
Delmar, 17:120
Delmer A., 17:238
Eliza (Moore), 19:58
Eliza (Morrell), 19:58
Emma, 19:58
Eugene, 17:120
Frederick, 17:238
George, 17:120
Georgie, 17:238
Harriett, 19:120
Hattie (Boulder), 17:238
Henrietta (Hopke), 18:177
Herbert Lewis, 18:177
Herbert S., 17:238
Jemima (___), 19:58
John, 19:58
Joseph, 17:120; 18:177
Laura, 19:120
Levi, 20:58
Lorenzo, 19:58

Maria (Luscome), 20:58
Martha (Hamlin), 19:58
Martha (Martin), 17:120
Mary Jane (Brackett), 17:120
Melville, 19:58
Nellie (Kinsley), 19:120
Wilbur, 19:120
SHORT
Elizabeth, 17:55
Henry, 19:30
Rebecca, 16:55
Sarah, 19:30
Susanna, 19:30, 31
SHOVE
Asa, 17:197
Edward, 17:197
Elizabeth, 17:197
Lydia, 17:197
Lydia (___), 17:197
Nancy, 18:98
Phebe, 17:197
Phebe (Osborn), 17:197
Philadelphia (Osborn), 17:197
Samuel, 17:197
Squiers, 16:90
Theophilus, 17:197
SHREVE
Isaac, 20:160
Mary S., 19:171
Octavius, 19:171
Sarah (Daland), 19:171
SHRIMPTON
___, Col., 16:230
SHULLABER see also SHILLABER
Mary, 20:29
SHULTY, 20:160
Charles F., 20:159
SHURE
Bluma/Bloomer (Creeger), 17:64
Charlotte, 17:64
Eli, 17:64
Robert, 17:64
SHURTLEFF
Joseph, 20:42
Mary (Merriam), 20:42
Nathaniel, 19:210
Nathaniel B., 16:226
SHUTE
Abigail (Russell), 17:207
Ada Marian, 19:118
James Lovell, 19:118
John, 18:105
Jonathan B., 17:207
Richard, 19:104
Sarah Abigail (Merchant), 19:118
SIAS
Mary P., 16:53
SIBBALDS
Mary, 17:135; 18:134, 145; 20:17
SIBLE
John, 20:197
SIBLEY, 19:40
Elizabeth (Comins), 16:236
John, 19:201, 202
John Langdon, 16:104
Mary (Barstow), 16:236
Nancy Willard, 16:236
Samuel, 17:16
Timothy, 16:236
Timothy Willard, 16:236
SIBSON
Joseph, 18:162; 19:94
SIDEBOTTOM, 16:4

SIEBERG see also SEABERG
Johannes, 17:132
SIGOURNEY
Henry, 18:16
SILLOWAY
Thomas, 20:81
SILLSBE/SILLSBEE/SILSBE/ SILSBY
"Child", 18:101
Abigail, 18:101, 104, 105
Abigail (Collins), 18:30, 102-105
Abigail (White), 18:101
Abner, 18:104
Ann Livingston (Loomis), 18:174
Anna, 18:101
Benjamin, 18:101
Bethia (Marsh), 18:101, 174
Bethia (Pitman), 18:101
Bethiah, 18:101
Content, 16:223
Daniel, 18:54, 104, 105
David Gillis, 18:174
Deborah (Tomkins), 18:100, 101
Dorothy (___), 18:99
Douglas Wheeler, 18:174
Edwin, 18:174
Elizabeth, 18:101
Elizabeth (Breed), 18:105
Elizabeth (Collins), 18:101
Elizabeth (Pickering), 18:100, 101
Ephraim, 16:156; 18:30, 100, 102, 103, 105, 138; 19:49, 216; 20:196
Esther (Southwick), 18:30, 102
Grace (___), 18:99
Hannah, 17:47; 18:101, 102, 104, 105
Hannah (Bassett), 18:37, 55, 105
Hannah (Pickering), 18:101
Henry, 16:95; 17:47; 18:30, 37, 55, 99-105, 138, 222; 19:25-27, 46, 47, 154, 163; 20:104, 196, 206, 207
Jane, 18:101
John, 18:101
Jonathan, 18:100, 101, 174; 20:196
Joseph, 18:101
Lydia, 18:104, 105
Lydia (Curtin), 18:105
Lydia (Nichols), 18:105
Margaret, 18:101
Margaret (Abbott), 18:101
Martha (___), 18:101
Mary, 18:30, 100-102, 104, 174
Mary (Briscoe), 18:101
Mary (Chase), 18:105
Mary (Manning), 18:101
Mary (Pain), 18:101
Miriam, 18:92; 104, 105; 19:148
Miriam (Gould), 18:105
Nathaniel, 18:100, 101
Nehemiah, 16:96; 18:105
Patience, 16:16
Patience (Hood), 18:54, 104
Rachel, 18:30, 102
Rachel (Bassett), 18:29, 30, 102
Robert H., 18:174
Sally (Curtin), 18:105
Sampson, 16:98; 18:104, 105
Samuel, 16:95; 18:32, 99, 101, 104, 105, 174, 239; 20:196
Samuel P., 18:239
Sarah, 18:100, 102, 104; 20:102
Sarah (Breed), 18:32, 104, 105
Sarah (Phillips), 16:223; 18:104
Sarah L. (___), 18:239

Susanna, 18:174
William, 18:101
SILVER
Eunice, 16:235
Rebecca (Bassett), 18:39
Sarah, 16:94; 18:17
William, 18:39
SIM
Evelyn (Goldthwaite), 19:56
Peter A., 19:56
SIMMONS
Jean, 18:46
SIMON
William, 20:198
SIMOND
Francis, 19:165, 166
John, 19:212
SIMONDS/SIMONS, see also SYMONDS
___, Mr., 16:202
Abigail (Larrabee), 20:49
Benjamin, 17:172
Elizabeth (___), 19:212
Elizabeth (Webster), 17:56
Jane, 19:212
John, 19:212
Judith (Hayward), 16:59
Mary, 16:59; 17:56; 19:226; 20:48, 49
Mary (Roach), 19:144
Nathaniel, 18:218
Polly, 17:238
Ruth, 16:119
Samuel, 17:56; 19:144
Sarah, 20:101
Susanne (Farrar), 17:172
William, 16:59; 20:49
SIMPSON/SIMSON
Abigail, 16:117; 17:183
Abigail (York), 16:117; 17:235
Andrew, 16:117; 17:183
Archie P., 19:58
Dave, 19:58
Eleanor, 17:129
Frances, 17:212
Joseph, 20:149, 238
Laomie, 20:199
Louise (Tiel/Tiele), 19:58
Sarah, 18:151
Savil, 16:75
Thomas, 20:125
SINCLAIR
Abigail, 19:238
Alexander, 17:135
Arthur Henry, 17:117
Barbara, 17:117
Edward Manning, 17:117
Hannah, 17:59
John Caspar, 17:117
Mary Ann (Sauler), 17:117
Mary Ellen (Tuttle), 17:117
Sarah (Rhoades), 17:117
SINECROSS/SIGNCROSS
Elizabeth, 20:221
SINGER
Faithful, 18:77
Susanna (Knight), 18:77
SINGLETARY
Benjamin, 16:68
Eunice, 17:56
Richard, 17:56
Susanna (Cook), 17:56
SINNET/SINNETT
___, Mr., 17:97
Charles N., 20:220

SIP, 17:12
SISSON
    Elizabeth (Newhall), 16:46
    Francis, 16:46
SKAMP
    Robert, 17:240; 20:200
SKEATH
    Hannah, 18:25
SKELTON see also SKILTON
    ___, Mr., 19:190
    Elizabeth, 16:57
    Lydia, 20:25
    Samuel, 19:188, 195
    Susanna, 18:100, 174
SKEPER see also SHIP
    Katherine, 19:45
SKERRY
    Ephraim, 18:101
    Francis, 17:231; 19:191, 214; 20:189
    Henry, 16:31; 18:231; 19:213
    Margaret (Silsbee), 18:101
SKILLING
    Abigail, 19:118
    Mary, 16:119
    Thomas, 17:209
SKILLINGS
    Deborah (___), 19:118
    Hannah H., 20:115
    Thomas, 19:118
SKILTON see also SKELTON
    Jaems, 20:199
SKINNER/SKINER
    Allen, 20:134
    Betsy, 18:217
    Charles D., 16:119
    Deborah, 17:49; 20:140, 146
    George W., 17:107
    Jams, 20:199
    Joseph, 18:217
    Julius Goodrich, 16:119; 17:59
    Louisa G. (Lewis), 16:119; 17:59
    Martha (Burrill), 17:148
    Nancy (Woodhouse), 16:119
    Richard, 17:148
    Sarah (___), 18:217
    Walter, 19:143
SKIPPER see SHIP, SKEPER
SLADE
    Hannah (___), 17:89
    Henry, 20:83
    John, 17:89
SLATE
    Elizabeth (Abbe), 16:119
    William, 16:119
SLATER, 16:4
SLEEPER
    Ann, 20:239
SLOAN/SLOANE
    Charles St. John, 20:177
    Elmira, 20:177
    Hannah (___), 20:176, 77
    John, 20:176, 177
    Robert, 17:115
    Sarah (Whitman), 17:115
SLOWMAN
    Thomas, 16:58
SMALL
    Benjamin, 17:196
    John Wells, 18:138
    Lucretia R. (Nash), 17:162
    Mary, 20:234
    Thomas, 17:14

SMALLIDGE see also SMELLAGE
    Martha, 16:207
SMALLWOOD
    Grahame, 18:64, 67
    Grahame Thomas, 18:65
SMELLAGE see also SMALLIDGE
    John, 17:41
SMETHURST
    Michael, 18:38
    Tabitha, 18:38, 55
SMIT
    Ditmar, 17:133
SMITH, 16:13; 17:139; 18:184; 20:53, 240a
    ___ (Palfrey), 20:192
    ___, Goody, 17:96
    ___, Mr., 16:17
    ___, Rev., 16:105
    "Child", 17:204
    "Daughter", 17:204
    "Son", 17:204
    Abigail, 17:35; 18:45; 20:54
    Abigail (___), 20:42
    Abigail (Hart), 17:205; 18:44, 45
    Abigail (Kilburn), 17:205
    Ada Marian (Shute), 19:118
    Adeline Florella (Dempster), 20:32
    Agnes Spears, 17:56
    Albert, 17:86
    Alexander James, 19:118
    Alice, 16:72
    Alice (___), 19:120
    Alpha, 16:240
    Amos, 16:93; 17:205; 18:44, 45, 226; 19:120
    Andrew John Eyring, 20:32
    Angeline, 17:37
    Ann, 17:213; 19:120
    Ann (___), 18:104
    Ann Louise, 17:208
    Anna, 17:204; 18:105
    Anna (Woodbery), 17:203
    Anna Louise, 17:207
    Annabelle (___), 17:208
    Annie E., 17:207
    Arthur Warren, 17:208
    Asa, 17:206; 18:45
    Barbara (Tedford), 17:208
    Bartholomew, 17:205; 18:45
    Benjamin, 16:17; 17:52; 20:58, 178, 192
    Benjamin Alexander, 20:32
    Bernice Sophronia (Will), 18:175
    Bertha S. (Bailey), 17:207
    Bessie Martina (Pettit), 20:32
    Betty (Sherman), 17:116
    Caleb, 17:179
    Camilla Virginia (Miner), 20:32
    Carole, 20:201
    Caroline, 16:107
    Caroline B., 17:207
    Caroline Colburn (Ladd), 17:175
    Cassa Adelaide, 17:207
    Cassandra (Hart), 17:206
    Catherine, 16:30; 17:211
    Ceplae, 17:37
    Charles F., 17:32
    Charles L., 20:31
    Charles Martin, 17:207
    Chloe, 16:239
    Clifton, 17:188
    Daniel, 16:101; 20:139
    Danny D., 18:139
    David, 17:204; 18:38; 19:150
    Dean Crawford, 18:63

    Deane, 20:56
    Della A. (Rich), 17:207
    Della Alice (Rich), 17:208
    Dorcas, 16:40
    Dorothy (Farnum), 16:104
    Dorothy (Poor), 17:208
    Douglas A., 17:188
    Easter/Esther, 17:205
    Easter/Esther (Smith), 17:205
    Ebenezer, 16:214; 17:116
    Edward James, 17:208
    Edward L., 16:195
    Elbridge, 16:240
    Eleanor, 17:208
    Elias, 18:138; 20:203
    Elias Hasket, 17:206
    Elice (Brockway), 17:116
    Eliza (Robertson), 16:178
    Eliza Ann, 17:207
    Elizabeth, 16:64; 17:150; 20:205
    Elizabeth (___), 17:103
    Elizabeth (Bassett), 18:39
    Elizabeth (Hayward), 17:203
    Elizabeth (Lynde), 19:148
    Elizabeth (Marshall), 16:234
    Elizabeth (Osborn), 17:201
    Elizabeth C. (Emro), 17:208
    Ellen, 16:189
    Elsie Lucille, 17:175
    Elvira, 16:240
    Emeline, 20:32
    Emma E., 17:103
    Endicott, 17:207
    Ester (Rider), 20:56
    Esther, 17:206; 18:45; 20:42
    Esther (Smith), 17:206; 18:45
    Ethel Farrington, 17:47; 18:27, 31, 40, 212, 224; 20:41, 212
    Fannie B., 20:32
    Fannie B. (Smith), 20:32
    Francis, 16:162; 19:120; 20:185, 192
    Francis A. (Eastman), 18:178
    Frank, 16:11
    Franklin B., 20:32
    Gardner, 16:5
    Geoffrey Bryant, 20:32
    George, 16:240; 19:196; 20:54
    George Dempster, 20:32
    George Washington, 20:32
    Gertrude (Fifield), 20:32
    Grace L. (Griffith), 17:208
    Hannah, 17:203; 20:59, 139, 180, 205, 218
    Hannah (___), 20:139
    Hannah (Cheney), 17:119
    Hannah (Graves), 20:205
    Hannah (Grover), 17:202
    Hannah (Marble), 16:214
    Hannah (Potter), 19:149, 150
    Hannah (Sargent), 17:52; 20:178
    Hannah (Shillis), 18:38
    Hannah (Wiborn), 20:32
    Hannah V. (Wiborn), 20:53
    Harediah, 17:202
    Harriet B., 17:116
    Hazadiah, 17:202
    Hazel Adeline, 20:32
    Helen May, 17:208
    Helen N. (Barr), 17:208
    Heman, 20:55
    Henry, 16:178; 19:120
    Henry E., 18:44
    Henry Endicott, 17:207
    Henry F., 17:208

Hepzibeth (Damon), 17:116
Hezekiah, 17:204
Huldah (Page), 17:206
Humphrie, 19:72
Ida, 18:135, 175
Ida Louise, 18:176
Ina Georgia (Harvey), 17:208
Isaac, 20:160
Isabell (Drake), 19:120
Jacob, 17:204
James, 16:30; 17:52; 18:45, 57, 138, 230; 19:231; 20:42, 83, 139, 178
Jean Cora, 17:208
Jean Cora (Smith), 17:208
Job, 20:30
Job A., 20:31
Job Alexander, 20:32, 53
John, 16:163; 17:14; 18:72, 74, 81, 138, 178; 19:69, 120, 138, 148, 194, 239; 20:31, 183, 184, 191, 192, 194, 219
John Calvin, 17:208
Jonathan, 17:203; 18:45; 19:49
Jonathan Hammond, 17:204
Jonathan Hart, 17:206
Jonathan Henry, 17:207
Jonathan Warren, 17:207
Joseph, 16:234; 17:208; 18:38, 138
Joseph F., 17:202
Joseph Franklin, 17:207
Joseph Warren, 17:208
Josiah, 16:104; 17:203; 20:209
Josiah G., 18:178
Judith (Blyth), 17:32
Juliana Leadd, 20:31
Katharine Grover, 19:118
Kathren, 17:210
L. H., 20:230
Leonard H., 20:95
Leonard Preston, 17:208
Lizzie/Elizabeth O., 17:104
Lorenzo, 16:240
Lorna R., 16:149
Louisa (Marble), 16:240
Lucy, 17:226
Lucy Ann (Friend), 17:32
Lucy (Blanchard), 17:205; 18:45
Lucy Marie, 17:208
Lydia, 17:204; 18:98; 19:177
Lydia (Graves), 20:219
Lydia (Norwood), 18:205
Marcy (Hood), 18:57
Margaret, 17:119; 18:212, 225, 228; 19:177; 20:58, 139
Margaret (___), 16:17
Margaret (Buffum), 16:155
Margaret (Phillips), 16:155; 17:203
Margaret (Staniford), 16:107
Maria, 20:211
Mariah, 20:208
Marilyn Libbie, 20:32
Marion W. (Preston), 17:207
Marion Webster (Preston), 17:208
Martha (___), 20:167
Martha (Ellenwood), 17:203
Martha (Trenance), 17:203
Martha/Patty, 17:179
Mary, 16:180; 17:48; 18:45; 20:31, 59, 139, 205, 207, 209
Mary (___), 16:30; 17:205; 18:45
Mary (Bill), 19:120
Mary (Brattle), 17:214
Mary (Chambless), 18:38
Mary (Flint), 17:206; 18:45

Mary (Giles), 17:205; 18:45
Mary (Godfrey), 18:81
Mary (Ingalls), 19:49
Mary (Lincoln), 20:55
Mary (McDonald), 20:31
Mary (Mitchell), 20:54
Mary (Paine), 20:209
Mary (Perkins), 17:205
Mary (Plummer), 16:107
Mary (Ranuff/Renew/Renoir), 17:206
Mary (Round), 20:58
Mary (Smith), 17:206; 18:45
Mary (Tarbell), 16:59
Mary (Tarbox), 20:139
Mary Elizabeth, 20:31
Mary Emeline, 17:207
Mary Jane, 20:54
Mary Louisa (Bassett), 17:207
Mattie Augusta (Osborn), 17:188
Mehitable, 18:200; 19:150
Mehitable (Needham), 17:205
Miriam, 20:55
Molly, 17:205; 18:45; 20:139
Moris, 20:200
Myron, 17:136
Myron C., 17:131
Myron H., 20:31
Nabby, 20:39
Nancy Jane, 20:31
Nathan, 17:206; 18:45
Nathaniel, 17:116
Nehemiah, 17:203
Patience, 16:59
Patricia Susan (Sheppard), 17:208
Peter, 16:96
Phebe, 17:116
Phebe (Potter), 19:150
Philip, 20:89
Phoebe, 18:34
Polly, 17:206; 18:44, 45
Polly (Hart), 17:206; 18:45
Priscilla, 17:204; 18:85, 87; 19:155; 20:205
Rebecca, 17:207
Rebecca (___), 17:100; 18:149
Rebecca Cleaves, 19:230, 231
Rebekah (Wood), 17:203
Rhoda, 18:81
Richard, 16:111; 17:119; 19:119, 191; 20:199
Robert, 16:193
Robert Faxon, 17:208
Ruth, 16:40; 17:205; 20:31
Ruth (Burnap), 19:148
Ruth (Fuller), 17:204; 18:45
Ruth (Maverick), 20:192
Ruth Allen, 17:207
Ruth M., 17:208
Rutherford Endicott, 17:207
Sally, 16:171; 20:114
Samuel, 16:155; 17:135; 18:39; 19:150, 200; 20:130, 139, 223
Samuel Ralph, 18:175
Sarah, 16:149; 17:27, 205, 213, 214; 18:45; 20:100, 139, 178, 205
Sarah (___), 16:17
Sarah (Bassett), 18:38
Sarah (Chambless), 18:38
Sarah (Chandler), 19:119
Sarah (Coker), 17:52; 20:178
Sarah (Cresy), 17:203
Sarah (Curtis), 17:204
Sarah (Hart), 17:205; 18:45
Sarah (Hidden), 18:178

Sarah (Kingsley), 19:120
Sarah (Pedrick), 19:231
Sarah (Silsbee), 18:104
Sarah Ann, 20:32
Sarah Leonise, 20:31
Shirley (Kent), 17:208
Shirley D., 17:208
Sibyl Sawyer, 16:107
Stephen, 16:16; 18:104
Sumner Theodore, 17:208
Susanna/Susanne, 16:155; 17:199; 19:119
Tabitha (___), 17:37
Thelma (Currell), 17:208
Thomas, 17:32; 18:38, 79, 223; 20:15, 45, 116, 205, 223
Titus (Howell), 17:208
Virginia, 17:188
Walter, 16:155; 17:204; 18:45
Warren Job, 20:32
Wendell W., 17:208
Willard Earl, 17:175
William, 17:103; 18:38, 103, 205; 20:196, 204, 205
William F., 20:31
William H., 20:31
SMOOLT
Richard, 19:36
SNELL
Anna, 18:178
Hannah (___), 19:112
SNELLING
Abigail, 16:236
Rebecca, 16:156
SNIFFEN
Arthur F., 19:176
SNODGRASS
Andrew, 18:107
SNOW, 19:102
Agnes, 18:54
Constance (Hopkins), 17:57
Daniel, 18:170
Elizabeth (Wyman), 20:99
Hannah (Storrs), 20:56
Henry, 18:54
Jabez, 20:96
Jane (Collins), 20:55
Lucy (Hart), 18:50
Lydia (Witt), 18:170
Nicholas, 17:57
Prince, 18:50; 20:55, 56
Sarah, 20:55
Sarah (___), 18:54
Sarah (Atwood), 20:55
Thankful (Baker), 20:96
Walter A., 16:41
Zerrubbabel, 20:99
SNOWDEN
Isaac, 18:39
Mary (Bassett), 18:39
SOAMES see also SOMES
Hannah (Sargent), 17:52; 20:178
Morris, 17:127
SOLARIS
"Daughter", 16:219
Adeline Augustus, 16:219
Charles Albert, 16:219
Ellen Maria, 16:219
Ephraim Masury, 16:219
Frances Ellen, 16:219
Francis, 16:219
Francis Edward, 16:219
Francis William, 16:219
George Augustus, 16:219

Nancy (Friend), 16:219
Nancy Jane, 16:219
SOLAS/SOLLIS/SOLLACE see also
SALLOWS, SALIS
Hannah (Wolfe), 16:177
John, 16:177
Joseph, 16:177
Rebecca, 16:177
Susanna (Johnson), 16:177
SOLOMON
King, 17:120
SOMERS
Jane, 18:79
SOMERVILLE
___, Lt., 20:160
SOMES see also SOAMES
___, Capt., 17:12
___, Mrs., 17:12
"Son", 17:12
Abraham, 16:179
Benjamin, 17:13
Isaac, 17:138
John, 17:138
Jonathan, 17:137
Margaret, 16:176; 18:201
Margaret (Gidding), 16:176
Martha, 16:63
Martha (Emerson), 16:179
Morris, 17:240
Nathaniel, 20:200
Rachel (Brown), 16:176
Sarah, 18:200
Sarah (Parsons), 17:137
Stephen, 16:176
Susanna, 19:85, 169
Susanna (___), 20:138
Susanne, 18:35
Thomas, 17:240
William, 16:176
Williams, 17:12
SONNEMAN
Frances Amelia, 16:51
SOUDAN
Susanna, 17:219; 19:76
SOULE
George, 19:116
Huldah, 20:145
John, 20:145
Patience, 20:145, 149
Patience (Wormall), 20:145
SOUTH, 19:138
___, Mr., 20:194
SOUTHARD
Abraham, 16:119
Amos, 16:119
Charles Harold, 20:56
Earnest George, 20:56
Geraldine Agnes (Akeley), 20:56
Jenny (Lambert), 16:119
Judith A., 20:56
Mary Alice (Pattee), 20:56
Phyllis Ann, 20:56
Susannah (Paris/Parrish), 16:119
SOUTHER
___, Mr., 18:233
Eunice, 17:218
SOUTHGATE
Elizabeth (Potter), 18:152; 19:149
Elizabeth (Steward), 18:152; 19:149
Richard, 18:152; 19:149
Steward, 18:152; 19:149
SOUTHWICK, 17:195
Abraham, 16:89

Betty, 19:99
Caleb, 16:88
Cassandra, 16:15
Cassandra (___), 18:184
Cassandra (Burnell), 20:94
Clarissa (Sweetser), 17:27
Daniel, 16:31; 17:197; 18:102
Ebenezer, 20:100
Edward, 17:198
Eleanor, 17:197
Elizabeth, 17:198
Elizabeth (Southwick), 17:198
Enoch, 17:198
Esther, 17:198; 18:30, 102
Esther (Boyce), 17:197
George, 16:88
Hannah, 17:198
Hannah (Osborn), 17:198
Hannah (Southwick), 17:198
Isaac, 18:42
John, 16:89; 17:198; 18:230, 231; 19:216; 20:95
Jonathan, 17:198
Joseph, 16:26; 17:196
Josiah, 18:21
Lawrence, 16:15; 17:183; 18:30, 102, 184; 20:93, 94
Lydia, 17:199
Margaret, 19:218
Mary, 17:197
Mary (Aborn), 16:89
Mary (Gaskill), 20:95
Mercy, 17:197
Provided, 20:94
Samuel, 16:31; 20:94
Sarah (___), 16:89
Sarah (Proctor), 20:100
Susanna, 16:26; 17:199; 20:93
Tamoson (Buffum), 20:93
Tamson (___), 18:102
William, 17:27
Zaccheus, 17:198
SOUTHWORTH
Constant, 18:113
Elizabeth, 18:129
Elizabeth (___), 18:129
Elizabeth (Collier), 18:113
Lemuel, 18:129
Martha (Kirtland), 18:113
William, 18:113
SPALDING see also SPAULDING
Mehitable, 16:91
Rachel, 18:58
Sampson, 16:91
SPARHAWK
___, Rev., 16:35
Abigail, 17:113
Edward, 20:39
Elizabeth, 19:137
Nathaniel, 16:34; 19:137
SPARKS
Caroline, 18:136
Caroline Massey, 18:137
Rebecca (___), 17:238
Thomas, 17:238
SPARROW
Rebecca, 20:56
SPAULDING see also SPALDING
Ezekiel, 20:59
Hannah (Ballard), 16:67
John, 16:67
Leonard, 19:206
Martha (Kimbel/Kimball), 20:16, 59

Rachel, 19:206
SPEAR see also SPEER, 19:135
SPEARIN
John, 16:180
Rachel (Curtis), 16:180
SPEER see also SPEAR
Sarah, 16:86
SPEISS
Sophia Catherine, 17:53
SPENCER/SPENSER, 17:12
Elizabeth, 20:120
Gerard, 16:71
Irene, 19:232
Irene (Markam), 18:86
Israel, 18:86
Jarrett, 18:72; 19:138; 20:194
Jehiel, 18:86
Jerusha, 18:86
Jerusha (Jones), 18:86
Jonathan, 18:86
Joseph, 20:218
Michael, 19:138; 20:194
Obadiah, 18:86
Ruth, 18:86
Wilbur Daniel, 17:202
Zachariah, 18:86
SPILLER, 18:138
Anna Marie, 20:25
Eleanor V., 17:112; 18:133
SPINCKES
Edmund, 17:87
SPINNER
Allen, 20:134
SPOFFORD, 18:138
Abner, 17:141
Apphia, 19:89, 90
Apphia (Spofford), 19:89
Daniel, 17:141
Eliphalet, 19:89
Elizabeth (Scott), 17:140
Francis, 17:141
Harriet, 16:194
Jeremiah, 17:140; 19:89; 20:82
John, 17:140; 19:90
Judith, 16:213; 17:141
Moody, 17:141
Nathaniel, 19:89
Parker, 20:82
Samuel, 17:141
Sarah, 20:59
Sarah (___), 19:89
Thomas, 17:141
SPOKES
Alfred E., 19:235
Amy Lois (Tarr), 19:235
SPOONER
Thomas, 19:194
SPRAGUE, 17:25; 20:240a
Abiah, 19:100, 147
Ann, 20:43
Anna, 16:75
Catherine, 19:93
Deborah, 16:81
Dorothy, 18:75
Dorothy (Floyd), 19:147
Elizabeth, 16:167; 17:43; 18:75
Elizabeth (Green), 17:43
Emma Merriam, 16:171
Jacob, 18:75
Jemima (Burditt), 19:178
Jeremiah, 18:75
Joanna, 18:75
John, 18:75

Knight, 18:75
Lawrence, 16:107
Mary, 18:75
Mary (___), 18:75
Mary (Lewis), 18:75
Nehemiah, 18:75
Patience, 16:72
Phineas, 17:43; 19:177, 178
Priscilla, 18:75
Priscilla (Knight), 18:75
Rebecca, 18:216
Sally/Sarah (Fuller), 19:177
Samuel, 19:104
Sarah Ann, 19:177
Susanna, 18:75
Waldo Chamberlain, 20:74
William, 19:147
SPRAYE see PRAY, PINION, 20:72
SPRING
Henry, 18:158, 237
SPRINGER
Henery, 17:58
Joannah (Pike), 17:58
SPURR
Caroline (Corbitt), 19:238
Catherine Matilda, 19:238
Elizabeth (Roach), 19:238
John M., 19:238
Michael, 19:238
SQUIRE
Anne/Ann, 17:231
Henry, 17:231
ST. CLARI
Mike, 16:187
ST. JOHN
Jacqueline Hope, 16:53
STACEY see also STACY
Agnes, 17:98
Alice (Norwood), 18:203
Benjamin, 17:97
Ebenezer, 19:47, 53
Edward, 19:198
Elizabeth (Sammons), 19:47
Ephraim, 18:103; 19:47
Hannah, 18:25; 20:234
Hannah (Ingalls), 19:47
Hannah (Skeath), 18:25
Henry, 17:143; 19:47; 20:196
John, 17:98; 19:47
Joseph, 16:88; 18:25
Martha (Trevitt), 17:98
Nymphas, 18:203
Rachel, 19:39, 57, 99
Richard, 17:97
Ruth (Cheever), 19:38
Sarah, 19:47
Tabitha (___), 19:47
William, 19:47
STACK
Mary, 18:58
STACKHOUSE
Richard, 16:136
STACKPOLE
Everett, 18:49
Everett S., 18:160
Phebe, 20:139
Richard, 20:198
Sarah, 20:144
STACY see also STACEY, 18:104
Benjamin, 18:210; 20:221
Betsy, 17:120
Ebenezer, 18:210
Henry, 17:214; 18:231

John, 18:210
Samuel, 16:33; 18:160
Sarah, 18:133
Susannah (Phillips), 18:160
STAFFORD
Linda Berg, 17:114
STAINWOOD see also STANWOOD, STAYNWOOD
John, 20:200
Jonathan, 20:200
Phillip, 20:200
Samuel, 20:200
STALLWORTHY
Mary, 16:177
STAMFORD
Robert, 20:198
Thomas, 20:198
STANBOROUGH
Josiah, 19:138
STANBURY
Josias, 20:194
Martha, 19:155
STANDISH
James, 19:202
Miles, 18:196; 19:124; 20:180a
STANDLEY see also STANLEY, STANLEE
Andrew, 20:155
Benjamin Franklin, 20:109
Mary, 20:222
Sarah Elizabeth (Boynton), 20:109
Thomas, 16:223
STANFORD see also SANFORD, STANIFORD
Esther (Lane), 19:57
Thomas, 20:199
William, 19:57
STANHOPE
___, Capt., 20:126
STANIFORD see also STANFORD
Hannah, 16:178
John, 20:223
Margaret, 16:107; 20:223
Samuel, 20:225
Thomas, 20:223
STANLEE see also STANDLEY, STANLEY
George, 20:198
STANLEY see also STANDLEY, STANLEE
Daniel, 17:220
Mathew, 20:132
Rebecca, 16:235
STANSFIELD, 16:13
STANTON
Hannah, 16:55
Lydia, 18:203
STANWOOD see also STAINWOOD
___, Mrs., 17:13
Amanda, 17:108
David, 18:240
Hannah (Harrenden), 17:108
James, 18:240
Joel, 16:134
John, 16:64
Lucy, 17:58
Mary, 16:64
Mary (___), 17:221
Philip, 17:240
Richard Goss, 17:108
Susan Roberts, 17:56
William, 16:134
Zebulon, 17:221
STAPLES
Andrew, 20:139
Elizabeth (___), 20:220

James, 20:139
Mary (Gray), 20:139
Ruth (Tarbox), 20:139
Samuel, 20:220
Sarah, 20:220, 221
Stephen, 20:220
Susanna (Hobbs), 20:220
STAPPS
John, 16:155
STARR
Comfort, 16:203
Elizabeth, 16:57
Hana, 16:32
Mary, 16:32
Mary (Aborn), 16:32; 17:211; 20:52
Robert, 16:32; 17:211; 20:52
Sara, 16:32
Susanna (Hollingworth), 16:32
STARRATT
Eleanor (Armstrong), 19:239
Hannah (Bancroft), 19:239
John, 19:239
Peter, 19:239
START
Betsey (Mansfield), 18:212
Ebenezer, 18:212
STASEY
Ephraim, 19:105
STATEN
Betsey/Betty (Morgan), 17:240
Charles Albert, 17:39
Daniel Friend, 17:39
Edward A., 17:39
Edward Henry, 17:39
Elias, 19:113
Henry, 17:39
Keziah, 19:113
Louisiana, 19:113
Lucy Ann (Friend), 17:39
Lucy Ann Knight, 17:39
Polly (Parker), 19:113
Sally, 19:113
Samuel Cheaver, 17:39
Samuel W., 19:113
Susan Alinda, 17:39
STATTLER
Richard, 19:63
STAYNWOOD see also STAINWOOD
Philip, 18:84
STEAD, 16:13
STEADMAN see STEDMAN
STEARNS see also STERNS, 17:161; 20:38
___, Mr., 17:224
___, Mrs., 17:224
Ann E. (Cross), 17:167
Charles Theodore, 17:169
Deborah, 17:201
Ezra S., 17:82
George W., 17:167
Gloria Pease, 17:169
Marcia Ellen Bush, 17:169
Margaret Lamar (Middleton), 17:169
Martha, 17:47
Martha Ann, 17:167
Mary, 18:239
Peter Pindar, 16:138; 17:32; 18:134
Samuel, 19:137
Shubael, 16:44; 19:136, 137
Sonja (Schwarz), 17:169
Theodore, 17:169
STEBBENS/STEBBINS, 20:13
Sarah, 18:21

STEDMAN/STEADMAN
    Bethiah (Parker), 16:39
    Caleb, 16:39
    Hannah, 16:39
    Jonathan, 18:44
    Tabitha (Hart), 18:44

STEEL/STEELE
    Frederick Morgan, 17:229
    John, 17:219
    Sally, 17:178
    Stephen, 19:218

STEERE
    Mary, 19:150

STEPHENS see also STEVENS
    ___ (Sherman), 16:238
    Edward, 16:238
    Joanna, 17:81
    Lydia Faulkner, 19:97
    Mary, 17:152
    Rebecca, 19:175
    Rebecca (Rea), 18:75; 19:27
    Rebecca (Waldron), 19:175
    Samuel, 18:75; 19:27, 175
    Sarah, 19:175
    Sarah (___), 18:238
    Thomas, 18:238; 19:175
    William, 16:200

STEREUX
    Shubael, 20:140

STERLING see also STIRLING
    John, 18:124

STERNS see also STEARNS
    Abigail, 20:98
    John, 19:218
    Shubael, 18:26; 19:216

STETSER
    William, 19:229

STETSON
    Esther, 17:59
    Phebe (Parker), 19:97
    Samuel, 19:97

STEVEN, 18:161

STEVENS see also STEPHENS, 20:17
    ___, Capt., 17:13
    ___, Mr., 17:224
    ___, Mrs., 16:68
    Abigail, 20:237
    Abigail J., 16:100
    Abijah, 17:239
    Abraham, 19:55
    Alexander, 17:129
    Anna, 17:129
    Benjamin, 16:68; 19:33-35
    Caroline A. (Friend), 16:220
    Cornet Nathan, 16:68
    David, 19:234
    Dorothy (___), 19:34
    Eleanor (Simpson), 17:129
    Elijah, 17:239
    Elisabeth (Parker), 17:81
    Elizabeth, 17:239; 18:238; 20:222
    Elizabeth (___), 20:21
    Elizabeth (Abbot), 20:21
    Elizabeth (Parker?), 18:154
    Ellen Mary, 19:57
    Emma, 16:53
    Ephraim, 16:68; 19:96, 221; 20:19, 21
    Esther (Barker), 20:165
    Hannah, 16:40; 17:239; 19:33, 87, 88, 95, 96
    Hannah (Abbot), 16:220
    Hannah (Bernard), 20:21
    Hannah (Heald), 16:40
    Hannah (Varnum), 19:35
    J. P., 17:129
    Jacob, 20:54, 55
    James, 16:220; 17:240; 19:34, 93, 94; 20:83
    James F., 16:220
    Jerusha, 18:202
    John, 16:68; 17:191; 18:154; 19:46; 20:21, 165
    John Harrington, 18:175
    Jonathan, 16:19; 17:81
    Joseph, 16:68; 19:13, 32, 46
    Joshua, 16:68; 20:130
    Judith (Bradley), 19:234
    Judith (Sargent), 17:191
    Ken, 16:82
    Lavinia L., 20:54
    Martha (___), 17:239
    Martha (Pettingill), 20:55
    Mary, 17:239; 18:199, 200; 19:55, 88; 20:111, 112, 120, 167, 217, 222
    Mary (Ellery), 20:237
    Mary (Ingalls), 19:46
    Mary (Parker), 17:117
    Mary (Sargent), 17:236
    Nathan, 16:68; 19:91; 20:21
    Olive, 17:239
    Patience, 17:116
    Peter, 16:238; 19:92
    Philippa (___), 17:191
    Rachel, 16:64
    Rebecca, 16:71
    Rebecca (Rea), 16:157; 18:73
    Richard, 16:40
    Ruth, 16:41
    Ruth (Rosewell), 16:238
    Ruth (Wright), 16:41
    Samuel, 16:41; 17:12, 239; 19:92; 20:237
    Sarah, 16:155
    Sarah (Abbot), 20:21
    Sarah (Blaisdell), 16:238
    Susan P. (Record), 20:54
    Susanna, 20:136, 143
    Thomas, 17:239
    Timothy, 17:117
    William, 17:12; 20:200
    William A., 18:133, 139

STEVENSON
    Noel C., 17:74

STEWARD see also STEWART, 18:168
    Benjamin, 20:57
    Elizabeth, 18:152; 19:149
    Emma (Roundy), 16:79
    Melinda (Lord), 20:57

STEWART see also STEWARD, 17:133
    Alexander, 18:168
    Antipas, 18:168
    Benjamin, 17:152
    Daniel, 18:149, 168
    Deborah, 18:168, 171
    Deborah (Rediat), 18:168
    Ebenezer, 18:168
    Eleanor, 17:19
    George Robert, 16:53
    Jeanne Rita (Longfellow), 16:53
    John, 18:168
    Lucy (Adams), 18:168
    Lydia (Cutting), 18:168
    Martha (Farrington), 17:152
    Mary, 18:168
    Persis, 18:168
    Persis (Witt), 18:149, 168
    Phineas, 17:152
    Rachel (Haley), 18:168
    Rediat, 18:168
    Robert, 17:13
    Solomon, 17:152
    William, 19:163
    William Robert, 17:132

STICKNEY, 17:141
    Abbie Davis (Friend), 17:168
    Alfred Clifton, 17:168
    Alfred Fitz, 17:168
    Bessie Savory, 17:168
    Betsy, 17:168
    Betsy (Stickney), 17:168
    David, 19:161
    Dorothy, 19:161
    Helen Palmer, 17:168
    John, 17:168
    Jonathan, 19:161
    Marion Friend, 17:168
    Mary, 16:81
    Mary (Duley), 17:168
    Moses, 20:226
    Richard Carlton, 17:168
    Sarah (___), 20:226
    William, 19:160, 161

STILEMAN
    Elias, 17:209; 19:190, 191
    Richard, 19:190
    Samuel, 19:190

STILES
    David, 20:203
    G., 17:132
    Henry, 16:92
    Robert, 16:193

STILSON
    Agnes, 20:233
    Jaems, 20:199
    Vinson, 20:199

STILWELL
    Lewis D., 18:191

STIMPSON/STIMSON
    Edward, 20:89
    Hepsibah, 17:49
    James, 19:227
    Margaret Derby (Osborn), 17:201
    William, 17:201

STINCHFIELD
    Rebecca, 20:143

STINNIS
    Ruthy (Bessom), 19:231
    Samuel, 19:231

STIRLING see also STERLING
    ___, Lord, 17:142
    Hannah (Norwood), 18:205
    John, 18:205

STITCH
    Richard, 18:230

STOCKBRIDGE
    Charles, 16:134
    John, 19:83
    Mary, 19:82, 83
    Mary (Godfrey), 19:83
    Samuel, 16:134

STOCKER, 18:138
    Abigail, 16:86; 19:108
    Abigail (Lewis), 16:167
    Ebenezer, 16:74; 17:132; 19:108; 20:49, 197
    Ebenezer Bancroft, 20:43
    Elizabeth, 17:30
    Elizabeth (Griffin), 18:215
    Elizabeth (Mansfield), 17:150
    Ephraim, 16:45; 19:108; 20:100

Hanna (Lewis), 16:167
Hannah (___), 20:210
Jane, 18:227
John, 16:167; 18:227; 20:43
Joseph, 18:215
Lydia, 18:215
Lydia (___), 16:45
Lydia (Newhall), 19:108; 20:100
Martha, 16:167; 18:114, 115, 166
Martha (___), 16:167; 18:115
Mary, 17:145
Mary (Divan), 18:115, 166
Mehitable (Norwood), 18:215
Rebecca, 16:167; 18:167
Ruth (Breed), 18:227
Ruth (Hitching), 18:215
Samuel, 16:167; 18:114, 115, 150, 166, 167, 215; 19:158, 159, 212; 20:197, 210
Sarah, 16:73; 17:150; 18:228
Sarah (Ballard), 20:43
Sarah (Berry), 16:167; 17:172; 20:92
Sarah (Marshall), 16:74
Sarah Berry, 16:214
Thomas, 16:75; 17:41; 18:115, 150, 224; 19:78, 106, 108, 158; 20:92
Zacheus Norwood, 18:215
STOCKEWELL
Elizabeth (Shaw), 17:18
William, 17:18
STODDARD
___, Mayor, 18:145
David F., 19:176
Margaret Lillian (Edmands), 17:31
Morris F., 17:31
William, 18:210; 18:240a
STODDER
Abigail, 19:85, 170
Elizabeth (Sprague), 18:75
Nathaniel, 18:75
STOKER
Sarah B., 16:218
STONE, 17:139
___, Mr., 17:118
Daniel, 18:120
Eliab, 16:90
Elizabeth, 17:120; 18:77, 120; 20:101
Elizabeth (Hardy), 20:101
Elizabeth Gooch (Ballard), 16:77
Emma, 18:77
Ester, 16:45
Esther (Haskell), 18:77
Francis, 18:169
Gregory, 18:120
Hannah, 16:45; 18:77, 202; 20:177
Henry, 20:177
Hezekiah, 16:77
James B., 18:138
Jean, 18:77
Joanna (Parker), 18:120
John, 16:68; 18:138; 20:198
Jonathan, 18:237
Joseph, 18:168; 19:148
Josiah, 17:24
Katherine, 16:45; 20:26, 29, 100, 101
Lucy, 20:115
Lydia (___), 18:120
Margaret, 17:197
Mary, 16:31; 18:77; 19:148; 20:99, 101
Mary (Haven), 16:74
Mary (Treadwell), 16:45; 20:29, 100, 101
Mercy, 16:45
Meriam, 20:227
Newell, 17:24

Patty (Frail), 17:24
Robert, 16:45; 20:100, 101
Ruth, 18:77
Ruth (Knight), 18:77
Samuel, 16:45; 18:77; 20:29, 100, 101
Sarah, 16:45; 17:233; 18:101; 19:161; 20:101
Sarah (Aborn), 16:88
Sarah (Potter), 18:168; 19:148
Sarah (Shafflin), 20:100
Sarah (Simonds), 20:101
Sarah (Wheeler), 18:120
Sarah (Witt), 18:169
Simon, 16:68
Susannah, 16:179
William, 18:77
STONEMAN
Elizabeth, 16:75
STONES
Mary, 16:9
STONINGS, 19:70
STOODLEY
Betsy, 16:60
STORER
"Child", 20:221
Charlotte (Knight), 20:221
Elizabeth, 20:221
Joanna, 20:221
Joanna (Graves), 20:221
John, 18:34
Joseph, 18:34; 20:221
Mary (Griffin), 18:34
STOREY see also STORY
Damar, 19:179
Elizabeth, 19:179
Elizabeth (___), 19:179
Elizabeth (Robinson), 20:180
Martha, 19:179
Martha (Low), 19:179
Rachel (Andrews), 19:179
Sarah, 19:179
Seth, 19:179; 20:180
Zechariah, 19:179
STORROW
Charles, 19:14
STORRS
Hannah, 20:56
STORY see also STOREY
Abigail, 17:139
Amos, 18:204
Elizabeth, 17:139
Elizabeth (Norwood), 18:204
Henry E., 17:32
Jerusha, 18:202, 206, 207
Lois, 18:201
Marie R. (___), 17:32
Mary Ann, 17:110
Mary E. (Friend), 17:32
Mary/Polly (Pierce), 19:240
Parker, 19:240
Polly (___), 19:240
Sarah, 16:176
Stephen, 17:32
Susanna, 16:72
William, 17:76
STOTT, 16:13
STOUGHTON
___, Mr., 17:193
Daniel, 20:59
Sarah (___), 20:59
STOVER
Abigail, 18:176
Abigail (Elwell), 18:176

Amos G., 16:58
Anna, 17:178
Charles Albert, 16:58
Deborah, 17:236
George, 18:176
Jonathan, 16:180
Lydia (Coombs), 17:178
Nathaniel, 16:180; 17:178
STOW
Anna, 16:74
Mary, 16:114
Mary (___), 16:113
Nathaniel, 16:113
STOWER
Nicholas, 19:25
Richard, 19:25, 29
STOWERS
Anna (Cheever), 19:104
Elizabeth, 19:25, 26
Hannah, 19:82
Joseph, 19:104
Mary, 17:159
Richard, 19:26, 27
Susannah, 16:118
STRAIGHT
Thomas, 18:158
STRATTON see also STRETTON
Caleb, 16:172
Elizabeth, 16:172
H. R., 16:172
John, 18:158, 237
Mary (Adams), 16:172
William, 19:194
STREETER
Elizabeth, 20:216
STRETTON see also STRATTON
Elizabeth, 20:217
Elizabeth (___), 20:217
William, 20:217
STRICKER
Samuel, 19:157
STRICKLAND
Alian, 20:120, 152
Elizabeth (Spencer), 20:120
Sally (Woodbury), 20:152
Sarah, 20:151, 152, 157
Sarah (Woodbury), 20:120
STRONG
Caroline (Baldwin), 16:238
Joseph, 16:238
Susannah (Bessom), 19:230
William, 19:230
STROPLE
Mary, 20:17
STROUTHERS
Elizabeth, 19:50
Hannah, 18:211
STUART see also STEWART
Abigail (___), 19:59
Charles, 19:59
Ellenor, 20:233
Leah, 19:115
William, 19:212
STUBBLEFIELD
Virginia A., 19:232
STURGIS
William, 19:14
STURTEVANT
Amasa (Clarke), 19:18
Francis, 19:18
STYRE
Betty M., 18:138

135

SU GEORGE
   Cicely, 18:60a
SUEET/SUEETT/SUTTE/SEETE/SWETE
   ___ (Blanchard), 16:48
   Daniel, 16:48
SUGARS
   Esther, 16:172
   Gregory, 16:172
   Jane (___), 16:172
   Mary, 16:172
SUGDEN, 16:13
SULLIVAN, 18:8; 20:126
   "Baby", 20:124
   Bridget (___), 20:124
   Emily Hannah Purdy, 20:228
   Jane, 17:120
   Thomas, 20:124
SULTER
   ___, Mr., 20:215
SUMMER
   Sarah, 19:45
SUMNER
   Ann (Tucker), 18:148
   Benjamin, 18:148
   Ebenezer, 18:148
   Edward, 18:148
   Elizabeth (Clement), 18:148
   George, 18:147, 148; 19:162
   Isobell, 19:153
   Jane, 19:162
   Jemima (Tarbox), 20:146
   Joseph, 18:148
   Mary, 18:148
   Mary (Baker), 18:147, 148
   Sally, 17:115
   Samuel, 18:148
   Thomas, 19:162
   William, 18:148; 20:146
SUNDERLAND
   Elizabeth, 18:53
   John, 18:53
   Mary (___), 18:53
SUTHERLAND
   Catherine, 20:220
SUTTE see SUEETT
SUTTON
   John, 16:237
   Julian (___), 16:237
   Margaret, 16:237
   Thomas, 20:143
SWAIN/SWAINE see also SWAYNE/
   SWEYNE, 18:138
   Abigail (Aborn), 16:93
   Anna, 20:53
   Betsey, 16:114
   Charlotte, 16:114
   Elizabeth, 16:114
   Hannah, 16:114
   Jeremiah, 18:60a; 20:189
   John, 16:113; 18:226; 20:48, 113
   Jonathan, 16:114
   Joseph, 16:114
   Lewis, 16:114
   Lucy, 16:113
   Marcus, 16:114
   Marion, 16:114
   Mary, 16:114; 20:36
   Mary (___), 16:113
   Mary (Perkins), 16:113
   Mary (Stow), 16:114
   Nathaniel, 16:113
   Oliver, 16:114
   Thomas, 16:94; 18:226; 20:113

SWALLOW
   Phebe, 20:234
SWAN
   Aphia (Farrington), 17:152
   Asa, 19:96
   Asie, 20:130
   Christiana (___), 17:33
   Christiana M., 17:33
   Ebenezer, 20:41, 221
   Elizabeth, 17:53
   Ephraim, 17:152
   Hannah, 19:35, 95, 96, 107
   Hannah (Stevens), 19:95, 96
   John, 17:33
   Joshua, 19:46; 20:130
   Martha (Farrington), 17:152
   Mary (Bancroft), 20:41
   Molly, 17:152
   Richard, 20:130, 131
   Robert, 16:68; 17:152; 19:92, 95, 96;
     20:130, 131
   Samuel, 16:68
   Sarah, 17:200; 18:170
   Sarah (Ingalls), 19:46
   Thomas, 20:128
   Timothy, 16:68
SWANSBURY
   Richard, 19:131
SWAYNE see also SWAIN, SWEYNE
   Benjamin, 19:216
   Hepsibah, 18:43
   Jeremiah, 19:213; 20:185, 186
   Jeremy, 17:48
   Mary (Smith), 17:48
   Sarah, 17:48
SWEAT see also SWETT
   Hannah (Knott), 17:98
   Joseph, 17:97
SWEATLAND see also SWEETLAND,
   SWETLAND
   William, 17:171
SWEET
   Joseph, 18:159
   Ruth, 18:159
SWEETLAND see also SWEATLAND,
   SWETLAND
   Elizabeth (Grant), 20:222
   John, 20:222
   Rebecca, 20:222
SWEETSER, 18:45
   Clarissa, 17:27
   Cornelius, 17:27
   Dana, 17:202
   Daniel, 20:41
   George, 16:238; 17:26
   George Washington, 17:27
   Lois (Pearson/Pierson), 20:41
   Lucy (Danforth), 19:177
   Lydia (Smith), 19:177
   Mary, 17:27
   Mary/Polly (Edmands), 16:238; 17:26
   Sally, 19:177
   Samuel, 18:228
   Sarah, 17:27
   Sarah (Smith), 17:27
   Seth, 17:27; 19:157
   William, 19:177; 20:113
SWETE see SUEETT
SWETLAND see also SWEETLAND,
   SWEATLAND
   Ruth, 20:147
SWETT see also SWEAT
   Hannah, 18:160

   Hannah (Devereux), 18:160
   Henry, 17:98
   John, 17:98
   Joseph, 17:98; 18:160, 238
   Martha, 17:98
   Martha (Trevitt), 17:98
   Mary (Palmer), 18:160
   Ruth, 18:160
   Ruth (Parker), 18:160
   Samuel, 17:98; 20:221
   Stephen, 18:160
SWEYNE see also SWAIN, SWAYNE
   ___ (Smith), 20:192
   Jeremiah, 20:192
SWIFT
   Betsey, 17:179
   Charles, 17:34
   Charles Frederic, 20:32
   Dean, 17:179
   Elnathan, 17:179
   Emily Friend (Marchant), 17:34
   Enoch, 17:179
   Hasadiah, 17:179
   James Lynn, 20:32
   John Frederic, 20:32
   Marilyn Libbie (Smith), 20:32
   Mary, 17:179
   Mary (Lord), 17:179
   Nancy Elizabeth, 20:32
   Peter DeMott, 20:32
   Rebecca, 17:179
   Rufus, 17:179
   Sadie (Dennen), 17:222
   Sarah, 17:179
   Seddie, 17:222
   Susanna, 17:219
SWINDELL, 16:13
SWINERTON/SWINNERTON
   Amos Putnam, 20:229
   Elizabeth, 17:16
   Hannah, 17:205
   Job, 17:14, 16
   Mary (Sumner), 18:148
   Sally Bodge (Goodale), 20:229
SWINNELL, 18:107
SWINNERTON see SWINERTON
SWORTON
   John, 20:198
SYKES
   Bryan, 17:123
   Mary, 19:17
SYLVAN, 18:8
SYLVESTER
   Eva F. (Friend), 17:165
   Frederick W., 17:165
   Jane G. (Low), 17:165
   Samuel, 17:165
SYMMES
   Elizabeth, 17:118
   Zachariah, 18:9
SYMONDS/SYMONS see also SIMONDS
   Abigail, 20:224
   Benjamin, 19:144
   Elizabeth, 19:144
   Elizabeth (___), 16:45
   Elizabeth (Andrews), 19:144
   Elizabeth (Baker), 17:118
   Frances, 16:88
   Grace, 18:44
   Mary, 19:82
   Nathaniel, 17:118
   Rebecca Elizabeth, 17:117
   Samuel, 16:193; 18:192, 193; 19:144

Sarah/Sally, 17:179
Susanna (Farrar), 19:144
Thomas, 16:45

TACKLESS
Elizabeth, 16:209
TAFT see also TUFT, DEFT
Benjamin, 18:94
TAGNEY
Brooke (___), 17:8
Ronald, 17:3
TAINER
Thomas, 20:199
TAIT
Jennie (Wilson), 19:58
Robert Y., 19:58
TALBOT
George, 20:179
Hannah (___), 20:179
Mary (Turrel), 20:179
Peter/George, 20:179
Sarah, 20:179
TALMAGE
___, Goodman, 18:74
Thomas, 19:138; 20:191, 194, 195
TANGUAY
Cyprian, 18:4
TAPLEY, 19:135
Alexander, 18:56
Amos, 20:232
Amos Lawrence, 20:227
Ann (Lewis), 20:59
Charles S., 17:60
George Somerville, 17:174; 20:227
Hannah (Preston), 20:232
Harriet Sylvester, 17:202
John, 20:59
Joseph, 18:216
Mary, 20:140
Mary Ann (Graves), 17:174; 20:227
Phillip Preston, 20:227
Sarah (Hood), 18:56
Sarah Adaline, 17:174; 20:227
William, 20:59
TAPPAN
George, 17:12
Nabby, 19:42
TARBEL/TARBELL/TARBLE, 16:157
Cornelius, 17:199; 18:217, 218
Elizabeth, 18:213, 217, 218
Elizabeth (Giles), 17:199; 18:217, 218
John, 16:100
Lydia (Tufts), 16:100
Mary, 16:59
Nathaniel, 17:199
Rachel, 17:199
Rachel (Osborn), 17:199
Sarah, 16:155; 19:218
Thomas, 17:85
William, 17:199
**TARBOX/TARBOCK/TARBOCKE/
TARBACK/TORBOCK/TORBOCKE**,
18:138; 20:143
"Child", 20:139
___ (Andrews), 20:132, 133, 146, 148
___, Mrs., 17:12
Aaron Donelson, 20:147
Abby, 20:143
Abigail, 20:138, 139, 141, 143-145, 238
Abigail (___), 20:105, 139, 237
Abigail (Bartholomew), 17:49; 20:140
Abigail (Baxter), 20:137
Abigail (Cox), 20:137
Abigail (Emery), 20:139
Abigail (Taylor), 17:49; 20:141
Abigail (Webber), 20:139, 140, 144, 145, 148
Abigail/Nabby, 20:147
Abijah, 20:140
Abner, 17:21; 20:137, 138
Adaline, 20:147
Agnes (Hooper), 20:139
Alfred Rowley, 20:148
Amasa Soule, 20:149
Amelia/Milly, 20:147
Andrew, 20:105, 138, 144
Ann, 20:136
Anna, 20:141, 143
Anna Josephine (Prendergast), 20:149
Anne (Cox), 20:138
Arthur Roland, 20:149
Asenath (Phelps), 17:49; 20:141
Baxter, 20:137
Benjamin, 16:90; 20:105, 136, 138, 139, 141, 142, 144, 146, 147, 237, 238
Bethiah, 20:145
Bethiah (Tyler), 20:144, 145, 149
Betsey, 18:23; 20:138
Betsey (Lund), 20:138
Betty, 20:140
Bill Augustus, 20:147
Caleb, 20:136
Cara, 20:149
Caryl/Carroll, 20:139, 238
Charity, 20:238
Charles, 20:147, 148
Charles Henry, 20:147, 148
Clarissa (Collins), 20:147
Cora, 20:237
Cornelius, 20:144, 145, 149, 237
Daniel, 18:172; 20:105, 137, 139
David, 17:49; 20:140
Deborah, 20:105, 138, 143, 146
Deborah (Gray), 20:105, 138, 237
Deborah (Sayward), 20:143
Deborah (Skinner), 17:49; 20:140, 146
Deliverance, 20:143
Dolly R. (Hill), 20:143
Dorcas, 20:144, 237
Dorothy (Blayney), 20:148
Dorothy (DeCumbermere), 20:238
Dorothy (Gray), 20:105, 137
Eben, 17:12
Ebenezer, 17:20; 18:172; 20:105, 133, 134, 136-138, 142, 237
Edward, 20:238
Elaine (Baldwin), 20:148
Eleanor, 16:115; 20:140
Eleanor (___), 17:49; 18:234; 20:135, 140, 146
Eliakim, 20:139
Eliezer, 20:139
Eliza, 20:147
Eliza Ellen, 20:147
Eliza/Betsy (Crane), 20:147
Elizabeth, 17:21; 20:136, 137, 140, 142, 144
Elizabeth (___), 20:134, 136
Elizabeth (Emery), 20:138, 139, 144, 148
Elizabeth (Hodgdon), 20:139
Elizabeth (Maxey), 20:136, 142
Elizabeth (Milikin), 20:139, 238
Elizabeth Jane (Thompson), 20:149
Elizabeth Jane Thompson (Ellingwood), 20:238
Ellen Frances, 20:147
Emma Frances, 20:148
Esther, 20:141, 238
Esther (Edwards), 20:136, 141
Eunice, 20:141, 142, 144
Experience, 20:136, 137, 141-143
Experience (___), 19:227
Experience (Look), 18:234; 20:133-136, 141
Ezekial, 20:144, 237
Ezekiel Jordan, 20:145, 149
Fanny, 20:147
Frederick, 20:149, 238
Frederick S., 20:149, 237
George Edward, 20:132, 140, 146, 148
Godfrey, 17:49; 18:23, 234; 20:135, 140, 146-148
Hannah, 17:49; 20:134, 136, 139, 141
Hannah (___), 20:139
Hannah (Burrows), 20:138
Hannah (Laughton), 17:49; 20:140, 146
Hannah (Smith), 20:139
Harey, 20:147
Haven, 20:139, 140, 144
Helen (Askling), 20:148
Henry, 20:138
Henry Edgar, 20:147
Hepzibah, 18:23
Huldah, 20:140
Increase N., 17:21; 18:234; 20:132
Isaac, 20:142
Jacob, 20:137, 138
James, 20:138, 141, 144
Jane (Gilpatrick), 20:139
Jemima, 20:137, 146, 238
Jeremiah, 20:138
Jeremy, 20:138
Jerusha, 20:144
Joan (Hunt), 20:238
Joanna (___), 20:147
Joanna (Cook), 20:138
John, 16:165; 17:17; 18:234; 20:105, 132-148, 196, 237, 238
Jonathan, 17:49; 18:234; 20:133-135, 137, 139-141, 146-148
Jordan, 20:237
Joseph, 17:11; 20:134, 136, 139, 143, 144, 237, 238
Judith (Haskell), 20:143
Kate A. (Curtin), 20:147
Keziah, 20:137
Lemuel, 20:139
Lois Mae Van Winkle, 20:148
Loring, 20:144
Lucy, 18:57; 20:142, 144, 145, 238
Lucy (Card), 20:145
Lucy (Porter), 20:147
Lund, 20:138
Lydia, 17:21; 18:57; 20:137, 140, 142, 143, 147
Lydia (Atwell), 20:143
Lydia (Bill), 20:146, 147
Lydia (Brookings), 20:145, 149
Margaret, 20:137
Margaret (___), 20:136
Margaret (Fletcher), 20:139
Marie Augusta, 20:148
Mary, 16:36; 18:234; 20:134, 136, 138-143
Mary (___), 20:145, 237
Mary (Baker), 20:138, 142
Mary (Belcher), 20:139
Mary (Bell), 20:143
Mary (Brean/Breen), 17:21; 20:105, 134, 137, 237

Mary (Clough), 20:141
Mary (Cue), 20:141
Mary (Haley), 20:139
Mary (Haven), 20:133, 148
Mary (Knight), 20:145
Mary (Overall), 20:132-134
Mary (Rand), 20:138
Mary (Wheeler), 20:137
Mary Elizabeth (Flynn), 20:148
Mary/Polly (Brown), 20:145
Mehitable, 20:136
Miriam, 20:140
Miriam (Dempsey), 20:140
Molly, 20:144
Nabby, 20:144
Nahun, 20:144
Nancy Maria, 20:147, 149
Nathan, 20:140
Nathaniel, 17:21; 19:155; 20:134, 137-140, 144, 145, 148
Nellie A. (Jones), 20:147
Noah, 20:138
Olive, 20:144
Olive Hodgdon (Brooks), 20:149
Patience (Soule), 20:145, 149
Phebe (Stackpole), 20:139
Phoebe A. (Davidson), 20:147
Polly, 20:147
Rebecca, 18:234; 20:132, 135, 140-143
Rebecca (___), 18:234
Rebecca (Armitage), 18:233, 234; 20:133-135, 146
Rebecca (Stinchfield), 20:143
Rebekah (Dow), 20:141
Robert Cue, 20:141
Ron, 20:149
Ronald, 20:237
Rose (___), 20:148
Royal, 20:145
Ruth, 20:139
Ruth (___), 20:138
Ruth (Fraile), 17:21; 20:137
Ruth (Swetland), 20:147
Ruth Riggs (Jewett), 20:145
Sally, 20:143, 144
Sally L. (Newhall), 20:143
Samuel, 17:19; 18:223, 234; 20:133-137, 140-143, 145-148, 196
Sarah, 18:172, 234; 20:134, 135, 137, 138, 140-142, 144
Sarah (Bill), 20:147
Sarah (Gilpatrick), 20:139, 140
Sarah (Hall), 20:136, 142
Sarah (Hill), 18:172
Sarah (Hull), 20:237
Sarah (Milikin), 20:139, 238
Sarah (Nason), 20:140
Sarah (Smith), 20:139
Sarah (Stackpole), 20:144
Sarah (Wright), 20:138
Sarah Adaline (Bodge), 20:147
Shirley Anne, 20:148
Shuah, 20:144
Shuah (Libby), 20:144
Simon, 20:238
Solomon, 17:49; 20:141
Sophia, 20:139
Sophia (Loomis), 20:147
Stephen, 20:140, 144
Stevie (Midura), 20:148
Susan, 20:143
Susanna, 20:134, 141, 143, 144
Susanna (___), 17:11; 20:237

Susanna (Stevens), 20:136, 143
Temperance (Baker), 20:146, 147
Thomas, 17:49; 20:133-136, 140-143, 146, 147, 238
Tristram, 20:139
Wilbert Irving, 20:148
William, 20:105, 137, 141, 143
William Francis, 20:148
Zachariah, 20:139, 238
TARDAY/TARDY
Eunice, 16:83
John, 16:83; 17:57
Mary, 16:83
Ruth Catherine, 16:83
Ruth (Blaney), 16:83
Ruth M. (Blaney), 17:57
TARPY
Florence May (Haddock), 16:149
TARR, 17:139; 20:17
A. Augusta, 17:109
Alma Matilda Jos. (Seaberg), 19:235
Amy Lois, 19:235
Anna (Norwood), 18:203
Arthur Myron, 17:168
Asa, 16:176
Benjamin, 16:176; 19:235
Betsy (Gott), 16:176
Caleb, 18:206; 19:235
Charles, 16:176
Charlotte (Thurston), 19:235
Daniel, 17:12
David, 16:134
Deborah (Norwood), 18:206
Ebenezer, 19:235
Edith Mae (Craig), 19:235
Elizabeth (Dicer), 19:235
Elizabeth (Holland), 16:176
Ellen Elizabeth, 16:176
Eunice (Collins), 19:235
Francis, 18:207
George Washington, 19:235
Grace (Hodgkins), 20:44
Harriet, 17:162
Helen Palmer (Stickney), 17:168
Henry, 18:203
Honor, 19:235
Jabez, 16:176
James, 18:201
James H., 17:167
Jennie, 17:169
Joshua, 19:235
Louis Elmer, 19:235
Lucy (Norwood), 18:207
Lucy (Pool), 18:201
Lucy (Sayward), 16:176; 19:235
Margaret (Somes), 16:176
Martha, 18:201
Martha (Wallis), 19:235
Mary, 16:177
Mary (Barber), 16:176
Mary (McNaught), 19:235
Mercy/Esther (___), 18:203
Mollie (Barber), 19:235
Nancy (Lane), 16:176
Oliver, 19:57
Polly, 19:235
Rebecca (Wallis), 16:176
Rebecca Wallis (Card), 19:235
Richard, 17:240; 19:235
Richard Craig, 19:235
Robert, 18:204
Ruth (Gammage), 18:201
Sally, 16:176

Sally (Davis), 19:57
Samuel, 18:201
Shirley Alma, 19:235
Sophia, 16:176
Susannah (Jumper), 19:235
William, 19:235
TARRIS
Andrew, 20:198
TARTE
Robert, 19:54
TATE
W. E., 16:12
TAWLEY
Elizabeth, 19:39
TAYLOR see also TILER, TYLER, 16:13; 17:159
___, Goodman, 18:41
Abigail, 17:49; 20:33, 41, 141
Abigail (Drake), 16:57
Anne, 16:57
D., 20:90
David, 20:89
Deborah (Godfrey), 16:57
Dunnie, 19:20
Ebe, 18:86
Edward, 18:42; 20:190, 191
Elizabeth, 16:157
Elizabeth (___), 19:28
Elizabeth (Blaney), 16:26; 20:94
George, 18:72; 19:28, 138; 20:184, 186, 189, 195
James, 20:198
John, 16:26; 20:94
Joseph, 16:41
Margaret (Locke), 16:229
Martha (Graves), 20:212
Mary, 16:26; 20:33, 37, 43
Mary (___), 17:205; 18:45
Mathew, 20:198
Othniel, 20:212
Priscilla Moore, 16:151
Rebecca, 16:119
Richard, 16:57
Richard H., 16:189
Robert, 16:81
Robert L., 20:132, 140, 144, 145
Ruth, 20:208, 211, 219
Ruth (Spencer), 18:86
Sarah, 20:41
Sarah (Burrill), 18:153
Sarah (Carr), 16:57
Sarah (Cheever), 19:103
Sarah (Fuller), 17:159
Thomas, 20:185, 190
William, 16:26; 18:150, 153; 10:103, 157; 20:103, 104
TEAGUE
Emeline Augusta, 16:216
William, 16:216
TEAL/TEALE
John, 19:215
Mary, 16:83
Mary (Woodward), 19:215
TEDFORD
Barbara, 17:208
TELBE/TEALBY
Annis/Ann, 19:173
TEMPLE
Elizabeth (Henley), 19:103
Grenville, 19:103
Sarah, 20:33
TENNEY, 17:140
Hannah, 18:156

Jeanette, 19:210
TENNITY
Marilyn Libbie (Smith), 20:32
William P., 20:32
TERRY, 17:229
Elizabeth, 19:232
Phebe, 17:29
Roberd, 17:143
Sarah (Farrington), 17:143
TESSIER
Michelle, 20:169
TETLOW
Edwin, 17:176
Emeline Augusta (Eccleston), 17:176
Mary, 17:176
TEW
Francis, 18:236
TEWKSBURY
Hannah, 18:218
Hannah (___), 19:41
Samuel, 16:89
Susanna (Aborn), 16:89
THACHER/THATCHER
Ebenezer, 17:135
Elizabeth (Blaney), 16:82
J. C., 17:163
L. C., 17:110
Thomas Cushing, 16:82
THAYER, 18:137, 138
Deborah, 16:56
Deborah (Townsend), 16:56
Dorothy (Mortimer), 16:56
Dorothy (Pray), 16:175
Edward Davis, 16:110
Ellen (Darling), 16:110
Ernest L., 16:110
Ernest Lawrence, 16:110
Nathaniel, 16:56
Richard, 16:56
Rosaling Hannett (Buel), 16:110
Sally, 18:96
THERNSTROM
Stephan, 16:10
THIRSTLE
Richard, 20:198
THIRSTON see also THURSTON
Mehitable, 19:160
THISTLETHWAITE
Frank, 17:229
THOMAS
Alice, 19:85, 170
Alice (___), 18:110
Betsy, 17:33
Edward, 16:40
Elizabeth, 17:22; 18:23
Emeline, 17:37
Evan, 18:110
James, 17:95; 20:145
James W., 17:30
Jane (___), 18:110
Jane (Downs), 16:239
Jeremiah, 18:81
Keysar, 18:231
Lewis, 17:135
Lydia, 18:81
Margaret Ellen (Edmands), 17:30
Mary, 19:37, 45
Mary (___), 18:81; 19:219, 222
Mary (Parker), 16:40
Mary S., 18:221
Nancy, 17:36
Nancy (Berry), 17:36
Nancy (Currie), 17:37
Nathaniel, 16:239; 17:33
Samuel, 17:36
Samuel R., 17:37
Sarah N., 19:119
Susannah, 18:179
Susannah (Hawkes), 17:30
Walter, 20:221
THOMASON
Joseph, 16:94
Mary (Aborn), 16:94
THOMPSON/THOMSON/TOMSON/
TOMSONN, 19:156
___, Gen., 20:50
"Daughter", 20:40
Abigail (Bancroft), 20:40
Amy, 18:202
Ann, 18:92
Asa, 18:96
Bessie, 20:172
Betsey Warner (Norwood), 18:204
David, 18:200
Dorcas (___), 19:58
Edward, 16:33; 17:20, 194; 19:119; 20:103
Elizabeth, 17:235; 19:158
Elizabeth (Bancroft), 20:40
Elizabeth Jane, 20:149
Ezra, 20:40
Jane, 19:155
Jane (Coates), 19:156
Joanna, 19:58
Jonathan, 19:156
Libby, 20:9, 10
Marjorie Barnes, 18:137
Mary, 17:76; 18:152; 19:149
Mary Holmes, 19:232
Maurice, 17:240
Patience (Harraden), 18:200
Rebecca, 18:39
Rebecca (Sweetland), 20:222
Rhoda (Norwood), 18:205
Sally (Estes), 18:96
Sarah, 17:235; 19:46
Sarah (Webster), 19:119
Sarah D., 20:108
Silas, 20:40
Thomas, 18:205
Waldo, 20:83
William, 17:76; 18:204
William S., 19:165
THORN/THORNE
Barnard, 20:240
Elizabeth, 19:167
Hannah, 20:180
Martha (Brown), 20:240
William, 20:195
THORNDALE
William, 20:11
THORNDIKE
Elizabeth, 17:22; 18:29
Jeremiah, 20:157
Larkin, 19:167
Mary (Patch), 17:22
Paul, 17:22; 20:198
THORNE see THORN, 19:138
THORNTON
Larkin, 20:150
THORP see also THROOP, 16:13
Daniel, 18:165
Dorcas (Barney), 18:165
Mary, 18:165
THRASHER
John, 20:177
Mercy, 20:93

THRELFALL
John B., 17:78
John Brooks, 19:173
M. B., 19:116
THRESHER
Francis, 20:78
Mary G., 17:52; 20:178
THROOP/THROOPE see also THORPE
Billings, 20:118
Mary, 16:237
Mary (Chapman), 16:237
William, 16:237
THURBER
Hepsebah (Lewis), 18:148
James, 18:148
THURSTON see also THIRSTON
Charlotte, 19:235
Elizabeth (Peabody), 18:218
Elizabeth Peabody, 18:218
James, 18:218
John, 19:160
Lois Ware, 18:134
Mehitable, 19:160, 161
Polly (Tarr), 19:235
William, 19:235
TIBBETS/TIBBETTS see also TYBBOT
Augusta M., 20:24
Catherine, 20:115, 116, 177
Catherine (___), 20:115
Charles S., 18:71, 135; 19:27
Dorothy (Tuttle), 16:117
Emma, 16:51
James, 17:120
Jane, 16:220
Joel P., 17:120
Joseph, 20:115
Martha Anne (Owens), 17:120
Mary, 16:117
Mary (Pendexter), 19:229
Nancy (Allen), 17:120
Richard, 19:229
Samuel, 16:117
Sarah (Emery), 17:120
TIDD
Ebenezer, 18:171
Mary (Witt), 18:171
TIEL/TIELE
Louise, 19:58
William, 19:58
TIFFANY
Nathaniel, 18:87
Zerviah (Jones), 18:87
TILER/TIJLER see also TYLER, 20:72
John, 16:68
Moses, 16:68
TILLINGHAST
Nicholas, 18:160
Ruth (Phillips), 18:160
TILLY
Elizabeth, 18:138
Isabella, 18:232
TILTON
___, Mrs., 18:51
Abraham, 18:51
Annie M. (True), 18:59
Bertram Moses, 19:165
Daniel, 17:234; 18:138
Lucy, 17:223
Mary Elizabeth, 19:165
Oskar Kipp, 18:59
William, 17:234; 18:99, 138; 19:154
TINGLE
William, 20:132

TINK
Elizabeth (Thompson), 19:158
John, 19:158
Margaret, 19:158
TINKER
Abigail, 19:119
David, 19:119
Elizabeth (Henville), 19:59; 20:59
John, 19:59, 119; 20:59
Rebecca, 19:119
Rebecca (Robinson), 19:59
TINKHAM
Mary, 20:55
TINON
Aimee (Roux), 20:169
Emard, 20:169
Genevieve, 20:169
TITCOMB/TITCOMBE
Ann, 19:156, 160
E., 19:210
Elizabeth (Bitfield), 17:55
Mary (Dam), 19:160
Oliver, 16:106
Thomas, 19:160
Titza, 17:54
William, 17:55
TITUBA, 17:15
TITUS
Anson, 18:156
Isaac, 18:107
Jonathan, 16:91
Rebecca (Wellman), 16:91
TOBEY
Deborah, 16:75; 18:169
TOD/TODD
___, Goodman, 19:30
Barbara Breed (Putney), 16:236
Edith May, 17:161
Edith May (Todd), 17:161
Elizabeth (Breckenbank), 20:212
Emily (Friend), 17:161
Emma, 17:161
George, 17:161
Hannah, 20:208, 212
John, 19:30; 20:98, 212
Lucy F., 17:161
Mary Ann (___), 17:161
Mary Jane, 16:100
Michael T., 17:161
Ruth, 20:28, 98
Susannah (___), 20:98
TOLMAN
Hannah, 18:225
Mary, 17:218
Mary Turner, 18:50
TOMKINS
Deborah, 18:100, 101
Hannah (Aborn), 16:30
John, 18:100
Mary (___), 20:44
Mary/Margaret (Goodman), 18:100
Ralph, 16:30; 20:44
TOMLIN/TOMLINS
___, Lt., 18:147
Edward, 16:164; 18:40, 41, 72, 230; 19:138; 20:188, 194
Timothy, 16:71, 165; 18:71, 72, 230; 19:138; 20:194
TOMLINSON, 16:4
TOMSON/TOMPSON see also THOMPSON
Alice (Freeman), 17:177
Benjamin, 19:156

Cornelius, 19:156
George, 19:156
John, 17:177; 19:156
Jonathan, 19:156
Martha, 19:156
Mary, 17:177
Mary (Graves), 20:224
Samuel, 19:156
William, 19:156; 20:224
TONER
Annie, 16:120
Annie (Carr/Corr), 16:120
Arthur, 16:120
Arthur James, 16:120
Evelyn, 16:120
Gertrude Mary, 16:120
James, 16:120
Joseph, 16:120
Louis J., 16:120
Peter F., 16:120
Rosella, 16:120
TONGES
Joseph, 19:193
TONOHQUNNE
John, 18:60a
TOOGOOD
Mary, 18:165
TOOTHAKER
___, Mr., 19:45
Allen, 16:68
Margaret, 19:220, 221, 223
Margaret (___), 19:223
Martha, 19:220, 221, 223
Mary (Allen), 19:45, 115, 116, 220, 221, 223; 20:166
Mary (Dane), 19:116
Roger, 19:115, 116, 220, 221, 223
TOPPAN
Elizabeth (___), 16:104
Jacob, 16:104
Richard, 18:236
TOPPINS
Thomas, 18:235
TORREY, 17:45; 19:45, 116, 118
Almon, 18:148; 19:142
Clarence A., 16:21; 19:210, 223
Clarence Almon, 18:67; 19:173
William, 19:129
TOWN/TOWNE, 16:65
Abigail, 17:43
Abigail (Curtis), 17:43
Archeleaus, 17:43
Charles A., 17:60
David, 17:43
Dinah (Hobbs), 20:141
Edmund, 20:141
Edwin Eugene, 17:43; 20:141
Elijah, 16:76
Elizabeth (Knight), 20:141
Esther (Tarbox), 20:141
Eunice, 17:43
Gardner, 20:40
Hannah, 20:40
Hannah (Ballard), 16:67
Israel, 16:74
Joseph, 17:42; 19:91; 20:202
Lucy (Ballard), 16:67
Lucy (Bancroft), 20:40
Martha, 19:229; 20:111
Mary, 19:221
Mary (Lewis), 17:42
Mary (Mower), 17:43
Mary (Poole), 19:239

Molly (Ballard), 16:76
Nathan, 19:239
Nathaniel, 20:202
Philip, 20:141
Rebecca, 17:60; 19:221; 20:187
Ruth, 18:56; 20:142
Samuel, 20:141
Sarah, 19:221
Susannah (Haven), 16:74
Thomas, 16:67; 17:43
William, 17:43; 20:141
TOWNS
Richard, 18:240
TOWNSEND, 18:23, 99
___, Capt., 19:133
___, Mr., 18:216
Andrew, 16:172; 19:28; 20:196
Charles Delmar, 16:173
Daniel, 16:238; 19:137
David, 18:209, 210, 240; 19:228
Deborah, 16:56
Deborah (Pickney), 16:238
Dodivah, 16:58; 17:58
Elias, 16:172
Elizabeth, 18:47, 151; 19:157; 20:209-211
Elizabeth (Berry), 17:172; 20:92
Elizabeth (Bucknam), 16:172
Elizabeth (Stratton), 16:172
Esther (Sugars), 16:172
George, 16:173
Gregory, 16:172
Hannah (Penn), 16:56
Harry Wallace, 16:172
Jacob, 17:178
John, 16:173; 19:136, 216
Jonathan, 16:232
Joseph, 17:172; 20:92
Lucretia (Hubbard), 16:172
Lydia, 19:58
Margaret (Phillips), 16:238
Margaret (West), 17:178
Martha (Bourne), 16:172
Mary, 17:228; 19:175
Mary Jane, 17:58
Moses, 16:238
Nathaniel Church, 16:172
Peter, 16:172
Polly (Norwood), 18:216
Priscilla, 19:229; 20:111
Rebecca (Baker), 16:172
Robert, 17:58
Robert W., 18:138
Robert Wallace, 16:172
Sabra (Price), 16:58; 17:58
Samuel, 16:172
Samuel James, 16:172
Sarah, 18:28
Sarah (Hancock), 16:172
Sarah (Pearson), 16:173
Sarah/Sally (Symonds), 17:179
Solomon, 16:172
Thomas, 16:172; 18:41, 72, 138, 166, 230, 231; 19:138, 175; 20:132, 193, 195
Timothy, 17:23
William, 16:56
TRACY
Alden, 19:172
Mary (Northey), 19:172
TRAFT
Abigail, 18:96
TRASK
___, Capt., 16:136; 19:191
___, Mr., 20:232

Abigail, 17:212
Abigail (Foster), 17:197
Amos, 17:200
Ann Maria, 17:38
Anna Maria, 16:217
Bartholomew, 20:231
Edward, 17:197
Elizabeth, 16:55; 17:197; 20:112
Elizabeth (___), 17:38
Elizabeth (Gally), 16:55
Elizabeth (Pool), 18:201
Elizabeth (Preston), 20:231
Elizabeth (Sallows), 18:137, 138
Elizabeth K., 16:84
George, 17:197
Hannah, 17:197
Hannah (Goldthwaite), 17:200
Hannah (Osborn), 17:196
Hester (Goodale), 20:232
Israel, 17:38
James, 17:197
John, 16:33; 17:197; 19:145; 20:198
Jonathan, 17:196
Joseph, 16:90; 18:137, 138
Mary, 17:197
Osmund, 16:55
Rebecca, 19:145; 20:94
Rebecca (Tarbox), 20:143
Richard, 17:60; 18:139
Richard B., 19:15
Ruth, 18:177; 19:168
Samuel, 17:197
Samuel P., 20:89
Sarah, 17:197
Sarah (___), 16:32
Susan M., 17:110
Susanna, 16:31; 17:211
William, 16:32; 17:197; 19:123, 126, 127; 20:143
William B., 17:40
TRAUTVETTER see TROPHITER
TRAVERS
Sarah, 17:52; 20:178
TRAVIS/TRAVICE
___, Mrs., 16:64
Nathaniel, 16:134
Susanna, 18:174
TRAVITT see also TREVITT
Elizabeth (___), 19:51
Richard, 19:51
TREADWELL
___, Rev., 16:69
Abigail, 16:45
Abigail (Wells), 20:100
Elizabeth (White), 16:79
Jacob, 16:79
Mary, 16:45; 20:29, 100, 101, 238
Mercy, 18:202
Nathaniel, 20:100
Thomas, 20:100, 101
TREETHY
Joanna, 20:220
TREFREY/TREFRY
Elizabeth (Humphreys), 20:233
James, 16:84
Sally (___), 17:117
Sarah Hanover (Wooldridge), 17:117
Sarah Wooldridge, 17:117
Susannah M. (Blaney), 16:84
Thomas, 17:117; 20:233
TREMERE
Charles, 16:118
Charles A., 16:119

Eleanor, 16:119
Eleanor (Booth), 16:119
Frances, 16:119
Harriet Booth, 16:118
John, 16:119
John Ernest, 16:119
Violette Ernestine, 16:119
William Thomas, 16:119
TRENANCE
Martha, 17:203
TRESCOTT
Abigail, 17:114
Lemuel, 20:47
Mary, 17:114
Rebecca (Edes), 20:47
TREVARD
___, Capt., 17:94
TREVETT/TREVITT see also TRAVITT, 18:138; 20:104
Ann, 17:101
Ann/Anna (Reith), 17:98
Anna, 17:101; 19:53
Anna (Potter), 17:100
Benjamin, 17:97
Benjamin George, 17:100
Edmund, 17:98
Eleazer, 17:97; 19:52
Elizabeth, 17:9, 100
Elizabeth (___), 17:96
Elizabeth (Bowden), 19:52
Elizabeth (Ingalls), 16:80; 17:98; 19:52
Elizabeth (Newhall), 17:96; 18:224
Elizabeth (North), 16:80
Elizabeth (Riddan), 17:101
Elizabeth (Russell), 17:98
Elizabeth Ann, 17:101
Hannah, 17:96
Henry, 16:80; 17:96; 18:211, 224; 19:52; 20:196
John, 17:98; 19:52
John Eldrige, 17:100
Lydia (Henchman), 17:100
Martha, 17:97; 19:52
Martha (Chadwick), 17:96
Martha (Jackson), 17:96; 19:52, 53
Mary, 17:96; 18:209, 211, 224; 19:52, 53
Mary (___), 17:96; 19:28
Mary (Blaney), 16:80; 17:101; 19:52
Mary (Hitchings), 17:96
Mary (Holloway/Halloway), 18:211, 224
Mary Leary/Seaver, 17:101
Rebecca, 17:100
Richard, 16:80; 17:96; 19:52, 53
Robert, 17:96
Robert Wormstead, 17:100
Russell, 17:97
Sally, 17:100
Samuel, 17:96
Samuel Russell, 17:100
Sarah, 17:98; 18:92, 209, 210, 224; 19:52
Sarah (Gale), 17:100; 19:52
Sarah (Ingalls), 17:98; 19:52
Sarah (Wormstead), 17:100
Soloman, 17:96
Susanna, 17:100
Susanna (Ellis), 17:100
TRICKER
Marks, 20:198
TRICKETT, 16:13
TRIPP
James, 20:96
John, 20:96
Martha, 20:28, 96

Mary (Paine), 20:96
TROPHITER/TRAUTVETTER
John George, 16:89
Susanna (Aborn), 16:88
TROTT
Preserved, 20:179
TROTTIER
Beatrice, 16:53
Caroline (Lepage), 16:53
Peter, 16:53
TROW
Joseph, 20:35
Mary, 17:116; 20:35
Mary (Greene), 16:238
Sarah, 20:35
Sarah (Bancroft), 20:35
Susanna (___), 16:144
Tobias, 16:238
TROWBRIDGE
James, 17:44
John, 17:82
Lydia (Mower), 17:44
TRUE
___, Mr., 20:220
Rebecca (Graves), 20:220
Richard, 16:134
TRUEBODY
Lydia, 17:106
TRUESDALE
Mary (Hood), 18:51
Richard, 18:51
TRULE
David, 16:132
TRULL
Esther, 16:179
Esther (Wyman), 16:179
John, 16:179
TRUSDALE
Mehitable, 16:209
TRUSSELL
Henry, 20:54
Sarah, 18:133; 20:54
Sarah (Foot), 20:54
TUCK
___, Mrs., 19:35
John, 20:198
Joseph, 19:34, 35
Love, 18:178
Lydia, 19:34, 35
Martha, 19:34, 35
Martha (Parker), 19:34, 35
Sarah, 19:34, 35
Sarah D., 16:220
TUCKER, 17:139; 19:183
Abigail, 17:85
Alice (___), 18:179
Amos Dennis, 20:222
Andrew, 17:97; 18:210
Ann, 18:148
Eleanor, 17:158; 18:41, 43, 134, 135, 137, 212; 19:136, 147
Elizabeth, 17:198
Elizabeth (Mower), 17:43
Grace, 18:76
James, 18:149
Jedediah, 17:43
John, 18:76; 19:231
Martha (Bessom), 19:231
Mary, 18:179; 19:51, 53, 109
Mary (Graves), 20:222
Oliver, 19:157
Rufus Stickney, 18:191
Sarah, 18:179

Sarah (Baker), 18:149
Sarah (Riggs), 18:76
William, 18:179
TUCKERMAN
Isaac, 19:150
John, 20:199
Rhoda (Potter), 19:150
TUCKFIELD
Mary (Larrabee), 20:115
Thomas, 20:115
TUDOR
Frederic, 18:16
William, 19:131
TUFT see also DEFT, TAFT
Samuel, 16:72
TUFTS, 18:138
Abigail J. (Stevens), 16:100
Ammi, 16:100
Barbara S., 18:136
Betsey Daniels, 16:101
David, 18:50
Elisebeth, 16:100
Eliza (Needham), 16:101
Elizabeth (Holden), 16:100
Elizabeth A. (Marshall), 16:103
Eunice (Hart), 18:50
Frederick, 20:89
Grimes, 18:172
Hannah (Farrington), 17:205
Huldah (Lee), 16:100
Jane, 16:100
Janney (Richards), 16:100
John, 16:100
Jonathan, 16:100
Lydia, 16:100
Martha, 16:199; 17:113; 19:50
Mary (Witt), 18:172
Moses, 16:100
Oliver H. Perry, 16:101
Pamelia, 16:100
Peter, 20:98
Prudence (Putnam), 20:98
Robert Daniels, 16:101
Samuel, 16:103; 19:160
Stephen, 17:206
Susan Ingraham, 16:101
TULLY
John, 18:113
Parnell (Kirtland), 18:113
TUOHY
Ann Dobbs, 18:133
TUPPER, 16:175
___, Col., 19:166
Elizabeth (Longley), 17:117
John, 17:117
Susan Ann, 17:117
TURE
Annie M., 18:59
TURELL
Daniel, 20:179
Hannah (Barrell), 20:179
TURFERY
___, Mr., 19:133
TURNER
___, Capt., 16:71
___, Mrs., 19:36
Addie M., 17:239
Alexander, 18:179
Anna, 18:59; 19:180
Benjamin, 17:179
Daniel, 17:179
David, 17:179
Elisha, 20:59

Elizabeth (Wilson), 18:179
Eunice, 17:179
Fanny, 17:179
Hollis, 17:179
Ignatius, 18:179
Isaac, 18:77
James, 17:179; 18:179
Joanna (Goodridge), 18:59; 19:180
Job, 18:179
John, 18:92, 179; 19:132, 197; 20:67
Jonas, 18:179
Joseph, 17:179
Joshua, 17:240
Lawrence, 16:112
Lois, 17:179
Lucy (Sargent), 18:179
Mary, 17:179; 18:179
Mary (Arnold), 17:179
Mary (McConicey), 18:179
Mary (Perry), 17:240
Mercy, 18:179
Micah, 18:179
Nehemiah, 17:179
Rachel (Bray), 20:59
Ralph, 20:200
Robert, 19:132
Sarah, 16:112; 17:179
Solomon/Solon/Salmon P., 18:58
Susannah (Thomas), 18:179
Thomas, 18:230
William, 18:59; 19:162, 180
TURREL
Mary, 20:179
TURTON
F. T., 20:143
TUTTLE, 18:135, 138
___, Gov., 18:143
Abigail (Floyd), 19:104
Ann (Smith), 19:120
Dorothy, 16:117
Elizabeth, 16:174; 19:104
Elizabeth (Merritt), 17:118
James, 20:45
John, 16:174
Jonathan, 19:120
Lydia, 20:45
Mary, 18:151
Mary (Cogswell), 16:174
Mary (Rogers), 16:174
Mary Elizabeth (Willis), 17:117
Mary Ellen, 17:117
Nathaniel, 17:118
Samuel, 17:94; 19:104
Sarah (___), 16:81
Simon, 16:174
Steven, 17:117
Thomas, 16:102
TUXBURY
Henry, 20:80
TWAIN
Mark, 19:139, 140
TWING
C. H., 17:95
TWINING
Isabel, 20:95
Thomas Jefferson, 20:26
William, 20:26
TWISS
Anna, 18:226
Anne (Callum), 16:37
Daniel, 16:35
Ebenezer, 16:37
Edward, 16:37

Hannah, 16:37
Hannah (Aborn), 16:36
Hannah (Harwood), 16:37
Hannah (Wyman), 16:37
James, 16:37
John, 16:37; 17:231
Lydia (Callum), 16:37
Lydia (Farley), 16:37
Mary, 16:37
Mary (___), 16:89
Mary (Aborn), 16:36
Peter, 16:34; 18:138
Sarah (Hopkins), 16:37
Sarah (Petten), 16:37
TWIST
Benjamin, 16:44
Martha, 19:119
Peter, 20:197
TWORGY
Judith, 20:238
TYBBOT see also TIBBETTS, 20:18
Agnes, 17:139
Mary, 20:216
Mary (___), 17:139
Walter, 17:137
TYLER see also TAYLOR, TILER, 20:63
Abraham, 18:140
Ann, 17:30
Anne (Gotier), 20:73
Anthony, 20:72, 73
Arthur Melborn, 19:232
Benjamin Maury, 19:232
Bessie Grove, 19:232
Bethia, 19:31; 20:144, 145, 149
Bethiah (Preble), 20:145
Catherine (Bragg), 19:150
Charlotte Woodruff, 19:232, 233
David, 16:115; 19:31; 20:140
Dorothea, 20:73
Ebenezer, 16:115; 19:150
Elizabeth (Walker), 16:115
Ellen (___), 20:73
Florence Maury, 19:232
Hannah, 19:221
Hannah (Parker), 19:31
Helen Dearborn, 19:233
Henry, 20:89
Hope, 19:30, 33
Hopestil, 16:68
Hostill, 19:34
Irene (Spencer), 19:232
Jacob, 19:35
James, 20:72, 73, 145
Jane (___), 18:109
Jenyns, 20:72
Joanna, 19:221
Job, 19:30; 20:214
John, 19:31; 20:64, 67, 72, 73
Joseph, 16:39; 18:79; 19:31
L. G., 19:233
Lillian Janette (Bass), 19:232
Linda A., 20:109
Lucy, 18:203
Lucy (Parker), 16:40
Lydia, 16:115
Lydia (Varnum), 19:35
Marah, 19:31
Marietta Jane (Dennis), 19:231, 232
Marion Gregg, 19:232
Martha, 19:221
Martha (Howard), 16:115; 20:140
Mary, 19:221
Mary (Lovett), 19:221

Mary (Parker), 16:39
Mary Holmes (Thompson), 19:232
Mehitable (Potter), 19:150
Mercy, 19:31
Moses, 16:193; 19:30
Nathan, 19:31
Nathaniel, 17:142; 18:79, 109
Nicholas, 20:72, 73
Phebe (Royall), 20:145
Quintin, 20:72, 73
Robert, 19:31; 20:72, 73
Roger, 20:64, 67, 72, 73, 76
Royal, 20:145
Samuel, 20:79
Simon, 20:72
Simond, 20:72
Solomon, 16:39
Virginia Beverly (McLean), 19:232
William, 19:150; 20:73
William Henry, 19:231, 232

TYNG
D., 16:189
Edward, 17:213

ULLMAN
Helen S., 18:132
ULRICH
Laurel Thatcher, 16:65
UMPEE
John, 19:202
UNDERHILL
___, Capt., 18:195
John, 19:60a
UNDERWOOD
Adrian, 19:20
Aquila, 17:79
John, 18:158
Joseph, 17:79
Lucien M., 17:79
Margery (Marland), 19:20
Martha, 18:40
Samuel, 17:79
Sarah, 17:85
Sarah (Parker), 17:79
Sarah (Pellett), 17:79
William, 17:79
UNOGOET, 18:76
UNYON/ONYON
Nicholas, 20:73
UPHAM, 19:16
Asa, 17:26
Charles, 20:93, 100
Charles Wentworth, 19:219
George, 17:26
Harriet, 17:28
Helen M., 17:163
Jacob, 19:148
Mary, 18:34; 19:158
Mary (Cheever), 18:152; 19:101
Mary P. (Wonson), 17:163
Mercy, 19:107
Phineas, 19:148
Rebekah (Burnap), 19:148
Sarah, 17:206
Simeon, 17:163
Tamzen (Hill), 19:148
Timothy, 18:152; 19:101
William P., 19:204, 205
UPSON
Hannah, 17:126
Katherine (___), 17:126
UPTON
Abigail (Frost), 17:119

Abigail (Gray), 20:213
Amos, 20:43
Ann, 17:19
Caleb, 20:234
Daniel, 20:213
David, 16:90; 20:231
Dorcas, 20:234
Ebenezer, 20:213
Edith (Herrick), 20:234
Edward, 17:197; 20:234
Eleanor (Osborn), 17:197; 20:233, 234
Eleanor (Stewart/Stuart), 17:19
Eli, 18:44
Elizabeth (Carlton), 20:213
Elizabeth (Putnam), 20:234
Emma Belle, 16:110
Eunis, 20:231
Eunis (Upton), 20:231
Ezekial, 20:226
Ezra, 16:93; 20:231
Francis, 20:234
George, 17:205; 20:231
Guy, 19:120
Hannah, 20:228, 229, 231
Hannah (Felton), 20:234
Hannah (Goodale), 20:231
Hannah (Stacey), 20:234
Hezekiah, 18:43
Isaac, 19:156; 20:213
James, 20:234
Jeremiah, 20:213
John, 16:70; 17:16; 20:233
Joseph, 20:213
Laura (Shorey), 19:120
Lydia (Bernap), 20:234
Lydia (Flint), 18:43
Mary, 20:234
Mary (Maber), 20:231, 233, 234
Mehitable (Goodale), 20:231
Patty, 20:213
Paul, 20:229, 231, 234
Phebe, 20:231
Phebe (Goodale), 20:229, 231, 234
Phebe (Swallow), 20:234
Rebecca, 20:230
Richard, 20:234
Ruth (Whipple), 17:120
Ruth Anderson, 19:20
Samuel, 17:119; 20:233
Sarah, 19:156; 20:43, 213
Sarah (Bickford), 20:43
Sarah (Goodale), 20:231
Sarah (Goodell), 20:213
Stephen, 19:120; 20:231
Susanna (Daggitt), 20:234
Susanna (Whipple), 20:231, 234
Tabitha, 20:213
Tabitha (Graves), 19:156; 20:213
Timothy, 20:234
William, 17:197; 20:231, 233, 234
URBAIN
Marguerite, 20:170
USHER
___, Gov., 19:226
Daniel, 20:90
Landon, 19:131
UYNTAM see VINTON, 20:69

VADNAIS
Agathe, 20:170
Louis, 20:170
Marguerite, 20:170

VAILE
Jeremy, 19:195
VALENTINE
Betsey, 16:77
Elizabeth, 16:77
Elizabeth (Gooch), 16:77
Thomas, 16:77
VALYANTS/VALLIANCE
George, 20:72
Joan, 20:71
John, 20:72
Richard, 20:72
VAN HORN
Charity (Ehrle), 17:120
Richard, 17:120
VAN NESS
Henry, 18:217
Sarah Ellen (Norwood), 18:217
VAN WINKLE
Lois May, 20:148
VANDER HILL
C. Warren, 18:191
VANNAN
Mary (Marshall), 16:239
VANNAS
Mary (Marshall), 17:51
VARIL/VARILL
Thomas, 16:64
VARNEY
Abigail (Proctor), 17:75
Alma, 18:125
Anna Dane, 20:60a
Content (Gaskill), 20:95
Mary, 17:75; 19:41
Nathaniel, 20:95
Sarah, 20:95
Thomas, 17:75
VARNUM
___, Gen., 19:35
Abiah (Osgood), 19:35
Dolly, 19:35
Dorcas, 19:35
Dorcas (Brown), 19:35
Dorothy (Prescott), 19:35
Eleanor (Bridges), 19:35
Hannah, 19:35
James, 19:35
John, 19:34, 35, 94
John Marshall, 19:35
Jonas, 19:35
Lydia, 19:35
Martha (McAdams), 19:35
Parker, 19:35
Peter, 19:35
Phebe, 19:35
Phebe (Parker), 19:34, 35
Polly (Parker), 19:35
Prudence (Hildreth), 19:35
Sarah, 19:35
Susannah, 19:35
VARY/VERY
John, 20:46
Lydia (Larrabee), 20:46
VELKE
Bob, 16:184
VENIN
Jane, 20:211
VENINE
William, 20:199
VENN
John, 20:240a
VEREN/VERIN see also WREN
Dorcas, 19:195-197

Hilliard, 16:32; 19:143, 197
Mary (Conant), 16:180
Mary (Ingersoll), 16:179
Nathaniel, 16:179
VERNUM
Jonas, 16:42
Lydia, 16:42
Lydia (___), 16:42
VERRY/VERY
Abigail, 16:180
Benjamin, 17:172
Daniel, 17:199; 20:113
Edward D., 20:89
Eunice, 17:199
Hannah (Larrabee), 20:113
Jemima (Newhall), 17:172
Mary, 18:100
Samuel, 20:196
Sarah (Osborn), 17:199
Thomas, 17:240
VIAL/VIALL
Elizabeth, 17:94
John, 17:94
Mary, 17:94
Mary (___), 17:94
Nathaniel, 17:93, 94
Samuel, 17:93, 94; 18:153
Sarah (Bennett), 17:89, 94
VICKERY/VICKORIE
Elizabeth, 16:81
Hannah, 17:225
Mary, 19:51
Rebecca (Norwood), 18:210
Roger, 18:210; 19:83; 20:199
Susannah (Hines), 19:83
VICTORIA
Queen, 17:125
VINCENT see also VINSON
William, 17:240
VINING
Anna (Nichols), 19:239
Thomas, 16:96; 18:22, 49
William, 19:239
VINSON see also VINCENT
Abigail, 17:237
Nicholas, 20:197
Rachel (___), 17:237
William, 17:132
VINTOME
Blase, 20:69
Sibella, 20:69
VINTON/WYNTYM/WYNTYN/WINTON
see also VYNTON, UYNTAM, 16:175; 20:63, 70
Ann (___), 20:75, 76
Eleanor, 20:75, 76
Eleanor (Knolles), 20:76
Elinor (___), 20:75
John, 16:208; 18:230; 20:67, 68, 75, 76
John Adams, 16:42; 17:19; 19:31; 20:213, 233
Joseph, 16:210
Joshua, 16:209
Mehitable (Trusdale), 16:209
Peter, 20:69
VIRGIL, 18:240a
VKQUENKUFSENNUM
Thomas, 18:60a
VODEN
Elizabeth, 20:231, 235
Mary (Ormes), 20:235
Moses, 20:235

VOSE
Abigail, 20:179
John, 20:179
Sarah (Clapp), 20:179
VYNTAM see also VINTON
Alice, 20:69
Blasius, 20:69
Eleanor (Knolles), 20:69
William, 20:69
VYNTON/VYNTEN see also VINTON
John, 20:69
Peter, 20:68

WADE, 20:165
Hannah, 19:169, 170
Jonathan, 18:194
Mary, 16:174; 17:27
WADLEIGH/WADLIGH
Joseph, 20:83
Ruth, 20:219
WADSWORTH
___, Capt., 17:141
Ebenezer, 20:179
George, 20:179
Lois, 18:88
Mary (___), 20:179
Sarah (Pitcher), 20:179
Susannah, 20:179
WAGER
Deborah, 18:113
WAGGETT, 18:138
WAGNER
Anthony R., 16:195
WAHLE
William, 19:81
WAIEMOTH
Thomas, 20:199
WAINWRIGHT
___, Gen., 17:21
Francis, 20:223
John, 16:72
WAIT/WAITE/WAITT/WAYTE, 18:138
Abigail, 16:82
Abigail (Lynde), 19:100
Alexander, 19:226
Benjamin, 20:118
Damaris (___), 16:233
Elizabeth, 16:82
Elizabeth (Blaney), 16:82
Enoch, 18:77
Hannah (Graves), 20:211
Huldah, 16:82
Isaac, 19:103
Jabez, 20:211
John, 16:227; 17:166; 20:211
Jonathan, 18:105, 150
Joseph, 20:37
Lois, 16:82
Mary, 19:161
Mary (Knight), 18:77
Mary Elizabeth (Presser), 17:166
Mary Philbrooks, 17:166
Nehemiah, 16:82
Richard, 17:91
Ruth, 17:159
Ruth (Fellows), 17:19
Samuel, 17:19
Sarah, 19:100
Sarah (Collins), 20:211
Susan, 16:227
Susanna (Bancroft), 20:37
Thomas, 19:40
William, 16:82, 96; 19:100; 20:221

William H., 18:137, 138
William, Mrs., 20:143
WAKEFIELD, 20:183
___, Dea., 20:189
Deliverance, 16:146
Elizabeth, 20:51
Homer, 16:146
John, 16:146
Lydia, 20:51
Robert, 16:195
Robert Sidney, 16:200
WALCOTT
Ebenezer, 18:240
Jonathan, 17:14
WALDEN see also WALKER
Edward, 19:27
Elizabeth, 17:144
Hannah, 19:27, 28; 20:205
Ruth, 20:207
WALDO
Esther, 16:106
George, 20:83
Jonathan, 16:35
Samuel, 17:231
WALDREN
John, 17:213
WALDRON
Dorothy (Dolliver), 19:175
Hannah (___), 16:25
Joanna, 19:175
John, 19:175
Joseph, 16:25; 19:175
Michael, 20:127
Rebecca, 19:175
Samuel, 19:175
Sarah, 19:175
Thomas, 19:175
WALES
Asenath (Frail), 17:24
Elijah, 17:24
Mary, 18:178
WALFORD, 20:240a
WALKER see also WALDEN
___, Capt., 16:164; 20:187, 191
Ann, 17:50
Elizabeth, 16:115
Elizabeth (Fraile), 17:21
George D., 19:19
Hannah, 16:74
Hannah (___), 19:148
Henry, 17:21; 18:84
Katherine, 16:27
Lois, 18:168; 19:148
Lois (Bancroft), 20:40
Louise Laggup, 18:107
Martha, 16:74
Martha Punchard (Marland), 19:19
Nathaniel Kennard, 18:58
Richard, 16:161; 17:46; 18:230; 19:138, 212; 20:183, 184, 186, 187, 190-193, 195
Samuel, 20:40, 190-192
Sarah, 17:24; 18:10
Sarah Anne (Pray), 18:58
Temperance, 20:51
Thomas, 19:148
WALKUP
Elizabeth (Potter), 18:168; 19:148
Thomas, 18:168; 19:148
WALLACE see also WALLIS
Douglas C., 17:130
Grace E. (Dunn), 19:23
Howard, 19:23
Joshua, 18:138

Marietta (Kelley), 20:228
Nora E., 18:180
Sarah, 16:212
Wesley G., 20:228
WALLERS, 19:191
WALLES see also WALLIS, WALLACE
John, 20:200
Josiah, 20:200
WALLING
Hannah, 18:96
Sarah (Elwell), 18:30
Thomas, 18:30
WALLINGFORD
Deborah, 18:10
Deborah (Haseltine), 17:52; 20:178
Ezekiel, 17:177
James, 17:52; 20:178
Lydia, 17:177
Lydia (Brown), 17:177
Nicholas, 17:52; 20:178
Ruth, 17:52; 20:178
Sarah (Travers), 17:52; 20:178
WALLIS/WALLES see also WALLACE, 19:205; 20:18
Abial (Conant), 17:233
Caleb, 17:233
Dennison, 16:90
Ebenezer, 17:233
Elizabeth (___), 17:236
Hannah, 16:94; 17:233
Hannah (___), 16:212; 17:233
Hannah (Fuller), 17:159
John, 16:177; 17:233
Joshua, 17:233
Josiah, 17:236
Lydea (English), 20:151
Lydia, 17:233; 20:208, 213
Martha, 19:235
Mary, 17:233
Mary (Phippen), 16:177; 17:236
Mary A., 17:103
Nathaniel, 17:233
Rebecca, 16:176
Robert, 16:212; 17:159
Sarah, 20:47
Sarah (Devereux), 16:25
Sophia Mary, 19:179
Thomas, 20:47
William, 16:25; 20:83
WALLS
Abigail (___), 19:120
John, 19:120
WALMESLEY, 16:13
WALSH see also WELCH, WELSH, 20:46
Janie, 18:145
WALTER
Elizabeth (Mower), 17:42
William, 17:42
WALTHAM
William, 19:188
WALTON, 19:138
___, Mr., 17:209
Elizabeth, 16:60a
Isaac, 17:92
John, 16:134
Mary, 20:43
Samuel, 20:199
Sarah (Marston), 16:84
William, 16:84; 19:202; 20:193, 194
WALTOWN
John, 20:199
WANSON
Elizabeth, 16:58

Elizabeth (Wanson), 16:58
Lois (Gott), 16:58
Samuel, 16:58
WANTON
Edward, 18:90
WARD
Abigail, 17:44
Abigail (Phippen), 17:98
Alice Standley, 17:164
Andrew H., 16:38; 17:82
Azubah, 17:44
Barbara McLean, 19:200
Benjamin, 19:132
Cora M., 16:49
Cordelia A., 20:57
Daniel, 17:98
Delphina M., 20:57
Elizabeth, 17:44
Ephraim, 16:74
Francina, 20:57
Gerald W. R., 19:200
Henry, 17:44
Henry B., 16:49
Irena (Jones), 18:86
Ithamar, 16:38
Jacob, 18:86
James, 18:107; 20:57
Jane, 18:139
Jane E., 19:80
John, 17:98; 18:140, 141, 193; 20:57
Joshua, 17:97
Julia A., 20:57
Laura A. (Wells), 17:164
Lucretia, 17:44
Lucy, 19:150
Lydia, 17:44
Lydia (Burrill), 17:98
Lydia (Mower), 17:44
Martha, 17:98
Mary, 17:44
Mary (Booker), 20:57
Mary (Haven), 16:74
Mehitable (Curwen), 17:98
Miles, 17:98; 18:101
Nathaniel, 18:140, 141, 193, 196
Olive A., 20:57
Phebe (Parker), 16:38
Richard, 17:98
Ruth (Woodward), 17:98
Sabrina (Lord), 20:57
Samuel, 17:44; 19:81
Sarah, 17:21
Sarah (Trevitt), 17:98
Susanna (Shores), 17:98
Thankful, 19:174
Thomasine, 16:117; 20:92
William, 17:164
WARDENAAR
Willem, 17:133
WARDWELL
Abigail Smith (Shaw), 20:54
Asa Kimball, 20:54
Claire Marjorie, 20:54
Clarence Milton, 20:54
Dorothy (Wright), 20:119
Eliakim, 20:119
Flora Etta (Keyser), 20:54
Herbert K., 20:54
John, 20:54
Jonathan, 19:34
Joseph, 19:120
Lydia (Hardy), 20:54
Margaret (Barker), 20:119

Mary (Pevey), 20:119
Mary Saunders, 19:120
Ruth (Church), 20:119
Samuel, 16:68; 19:34; 20:119, 166-168
Sarah (___), 19:120
Sarah (Hooper), 20:119
Sarah (Trussell), 20:54
Simon, 20:119
Simon Willard, 20:119
William, 19:34; 20:23, 119
Zemira Rita (Paine), 20:54
WARE/WEARE
Abel, 17:82
Emma F., 17:83
Ephraim, 17:82
Hannah (Parker), 17:83
John, 17:82
Martha (Parker), 17:83
Mary (Benner), 17:59
Nathan, 17:59
Robert, 17:83
Ruth, 17:58
Sarah, 17:82
WARES
Hannah, 18:96
Mary, 17:157
WARFIELD
Eliphelet, 20:27
Lydia (Boyce), 20:27
WARNER, 17:158; 18:157
Alice (Fuller), 17:159
F. C., 19:176
WARREN
Abigail, 17:174
Arthur, 17:174
Elizabeth (Senter), 19:38, 39
Ephraim, 19:39
Ester, 18:171
Eunice, 20:24
Humphrey, 16:203
Isaac, 17:41
John, 16:180; 19:131
Jonathon, 18:179
Lydia, 17:83
Lydia (Burrill), 17:41
Lydia (Coates), 19:160
Margaret (___), 16:180
Marshall, 18:120
Mary (___), 17:174
Mary/Polly (Cooper), 18:120
Sarah, 19:40
Sarah (Parker), 19:90
Sarah (Whitney), 18:179
William, 19:160
WARROMBY, 19:224
WARTON
Edward, 17:93
WASGATT
Davis, 17:178
Rachel, 17:178
Sally (___), 17:178
Susan G., 17:178
WASHBURN
Barbara, 20:120a
Hannah Jane (Marland), 19:18
Joanna, 18:82
Samuel, 19:18
WASHINGTON, 17:5; 19:166
___, Gen., 19:161, 199; 20:222
___, Pres., 19:75
George, 16:136; 17:192; 19:67, 168; 20:60a

WASSON
  Elisabeth (Parker), 16:41
  Eunice (Parker), 16:41
  John, 16:41
  Samuel, 16:41; 19:137
WATERS, 17:51; 20:190
  Amy, 16:77
  B., 16:136
  Daniel, 16:177
  Harriet Ruth, 19:145
  Henry F., 16:34; 17:87; 18:17, 223; 19:159; 20:26, 100
  James, 16:177
  John, 17:20, 199
  Lydia, 20:100
  Mary (Cloyes), 16:177
  Mary (Stallworthy), 16:177
  Rachel (Osborn), 17:199
  Richard, 16:177; 17:196
  Samuel, 17:231
  Sarah, 16:55
  Sarah (Purchase), 17:231
  Susanna, 16:177
  T. Frank, 17:18
  Thomas Franklin, 16:159
  Wilson, 16:225
WATHIN, 19:138
  ___, Goodman, 20:195
WATKINS
  Amelia, 16:151
  Joseph, 19:198
  Lura, 17:187
  Lura Woodside, 19:98; 20:203
  Walter K., 19:206, 207, 210
WATLY
  William, 19:82
WATSON, 16:111; 18:132
  Abigail (White), 16:79
  Abner, 18:101
  Adeline, 17:34
  Benjamin, 17:34
  Bessie K. (Friend), 17:106
  Christopher, 18:132, 133, 138
  D. Somers, 17:106
  Daniel Somes, 17:34
  Edward, 17:34
  Eleanor Friend, 17:34
  Elizabeth (Larrabee), 20:115
  Frances A. (Knowlton), 17:106
  Frank S., 17:106
  George, 17:34
  Hannah (Darling), 18:132, 133, 138
  Hannah Friend, 17:34
  John, 16:79; 20:115
  Josephine, 20:57
  Knowlton F., 17:106
  Lydia (___), 17:34
  Lydia Ann, 17:34
  Martha, 17:34
  Martha (Friend), 17:34
  Martha (Mower), 17:44
  Nathaniel Kimball, 17:34
  Samuel, 17:44
WATTAWTINNUSK
  John Oonsumug, 18:60a
  Yawatan (___), 18:60a
WATTS
  Abigail (Blaney), 16:85
  Abigail (Ingalls), 19:109
  Hannah (Lewis), 16:100
  Jaems, 20:199
  John, 16:85; 19:109
  Jonathan, 16:29

  Margaret, 18:21
  Nancy, 18:26
  Richard, 18:153
  Samuel, 18:210; 20:215; 18:240a
  Tabitha (James), 16:29
  William, 16:95
WAVE see also WAY
  Aaron, 20:201
WAWA, 20:51
WAY see also WAVE
  ___ (Purchase), 17:229
  George, 17:229
  Hannah, 16:59
  Richard, 19:197
WAYT/WAYTE/WAITS see also WAIT
  Ezra, 16:211
  Hannah, 19:215
  John, 19:164, 215
  Jonathan, 16:211; 18:240
  Mary (Hills), 19:215
WEAD
  Frederick N., 18:109
  Frederick W., 17:47
WEARE
  Elias, 18:106
  Elizabeth, 18:106, 108
  Peter, 18:21
  Ruth (Banks), 18:106
  Sarah (___), 18:21
WEATHERBEE see LARRABEE
WEAVER
  Bill, 20:27
  Richard, 20:198
  Sarah, 17:180; 19:102
WEBB see also EVERED, 19:30, 31
  Benjamin, 20:89
  Bethiel, 16:180
  Daniel, 17:231
  David, 19:144
  Elizabeth (Larrabee), 20:177
  Elizabeth (Roach), 19:144
  Harriet (Northey), 19:171
  John, 19:174, 175; 20:116, 139, 177
  Jonathan, 19:171
  Margaret (___), 18:50
  Rebecca, 18:234
  Rebecca (___), 18:233, 234
  Sally, 18:50
  Samuel, 18:50
  Sarah, 18:233, 234; 20:134
  Thomas, 17:93
  William, 18:233, 234
WEBBER see also WEBER, 20:18
  A., 20:238
  Abigail, 20:139, 140, 144, 145, 148
  Abigail (___), 20:238
  Abigail (Harding), 20:139, 144
  C. H., 20:230
  Damaris (Bowden), 20:145, 238
  Deborah (Bedford), 17:237; 20:146
  Deborah (Bowden), 20:146
  Hannah (Hood), 18:54
  Hannah (Sawyer), 17:237
  Henrietta, 17:139
  Ignatius, 17:135
  Israel, 20:238
  John, 20:139, 144-146, 238
  Joseph, 16:58
  Lucy (Tarbox), 20:145
  Mary, 20:145, 146
  Mary (Lewis), 16:58
  Mary (Parker), 16:58
  Mary (Redding), 20:145

  Michael, 17:12; 20:146
  Paulina, 19:180; 20:120
  Rebecca, 17:237
  Richard, 20:145, 146, 238
  Samuel, 18:54
  Sarah, 18:25; 20:146
  Sarah (Green), 17:237
  Stephen, 20:145
  Thomas, 16:58; 20:146
  William, 20:146
WEBER see also WEBBER
  Gertrude, 17:169
  Jennie (Tarr), 17:169
  Sarah, 16:58
  William T., 17:169
WEBSTER, 16:111; 19:210
  Abigail, 16:147
  Abigail (Eastman), 16:147
  Abigail (Potter), 18:152; 19:149
  Ann (Batt), 17:52; 20:178
  Daniel, 16:147
  Ebenezer, 16:147
  Elizabeth, 17:56
  Israel, 18:240
  James Henry, 19:239; 20:120
  John, 17:52; 18:152; 19:149; 20:278
  Lucy, 17:52; 20:178
  Martha (Ward), 17:98
  Mary, 19:46, 214; 20:33
  Mary (Shatswell), 17:56
  Ruth Mehitable (Pearl), 19:239; 20:120
  Sarah, 19:119
  Sarah Dimond (Sanborn), 19:239
  Stephen/Steven, 18:240; 19:30
  Thomas, 16:134; 19:88
  William, 17:98
  William W., 19:239
WEDE
  Edward, 20:199
WEED
  Deborah (Winsley), 16:15
  John, 16:15
  Mary, 16:15
WEEDEN
  Sarah, 20:98
WEEKS see also WICKES
  Abial, 17:114
  Abigail (Trescott), 17:114
  Alice (Plasse), 19:142
  Amanda (Lord), 20:57
  Bethiah, 19:142
  Ethel Jean (Edmands), 17:31
  Hannah, 19:142
  John, 20:57
  Roland, 17:31
  Thomas, 19:142
WEENWRIGHT
  Francis, 20:197
WEETHEE
  James, 17:81
  Sarah (Parker), 17:81
WEIGHTMAN
  Aubrey, 16:150
  Lucy Haddock (Carstairs), 16:150
WEIK
  Frances, 18:174
WEINBERG
  Simon, 19:186
WEINER
  Miriam, 17:74
WEIS/WEISS
  Frederick Lewis, 16:189
  Kristin, 20:162

WELBY/WELBYE
  George, 19:138; 20:195
WELCH see also WALSH, WELSH
  Deborah, 18:48
  John, 17:106
  Mary, 17:106
  Mary (___), 17:106
  Phillip, 20:199
  Sarah, 16:132
WELD
  Elizabeth, 17:226
  Esther (Waldo), 16:106
  Ezra, 16:104
  Hannah, 16:39
  Hannah (Farnum), 16:104
  John, 16:106
  Katherine (Farnum), 16:106
WELLERS
  Benjamin, 20:143
WELLINGTON
  Ebenezer, 18:158, 237
  Margaret, 20:115
  Thomas W., 20:115
WELLIOR
  John, 20:198
WELLMAN, 19:47
  Abraham, 19:136, 137, 216, 217; 20:35, 37, 39
  David, 20:35, 37
  Elizabeth, 20:41
  Elizabeth (Ellingwood), 16:236
  Elkanah, 20:35
  Emma/Eme, 18:72, 74
  Esther, 20:39
  Esther (Eaton), 20:37
  Esther (Newhall), 20:35
  Ezekiel, 16:236
  Hannah, 16:91; 19:58
  Isaac, 19:136, 216, 217; 20:207
  Jacob, 16:91
  Jedediah, 20:37
  John, 16:91; 19:137; 20:48
  Jonathan, 19:137; 20:35, 39
  Joshua Wyman, 16:91; 18:74; 19:136; 20:35, 37
  Lydia, 16:236; 17:200; 20:35
  Mary, 16:91; 19:137
  Mary (Bancroft), 20:37
  Mehitable, 19:137; 20:35
  Mehitable (Bancroft), 20:35
  Mehitable (Gowing), 20:35
  Mehitable (Wellman), 20:35
  Rebecca, 16:91
  Rebecca (Chase), 16:91
  Sarah, 16:91
  Sarah (Brown), 20:35
  Stephen, 19:137
  Susan/Sukey, 16:110
  Thomas, 16:91; 18:41, 74, 218, 222; 19:136, 137; 20:35, 37
  Thomas B., 16:35; 18:42; 19:136; 20:39
  Union (Aborn), 16:91
WELLS
  Abigail, 20:100
  Elizabeth (Larrabee), 20:115
  Hannah, 16:212
  John, 20:115, 177
  John A., 17:20
  Laura A., 17:164
  Lydia, 16:237
  Mary, 18:180
  Mary (Pecker), 16:141
  Nathaniel, 19:166

  Peter, 18:59
  Richard, 19:138; 20:195
  Saloame (Dustin), 18:59
  Thomas, 16:19; 18:138
WELSH see also WALSH, WELCH, 20:46
  Benjamin, 20:46
  Hannah (___), 16:24
  John, 19:198
  Margaret (Larrabee), 20:45, 46
WELSTED
  ___, Rev. Mr., 20:47
WENDALL/WENDELL
  ___, Col., 19:159
  Abigail (___), 19:106
  Elizabeth (Trevitt), 17:100
  Thomas, 17:100
WENEPAWWEEKIN
  "Sagamore", 18:60a
WENGATE
  John, 20:83
WENMARR
  Thomas, 18:231
WENTWORTH
  Jane, 19:238
  Mary, 16:142
  Sally, 16:219
WESCOAT see also WESCOTT, WESTCOAT
  Beverly Harwood, 19:232
  Elizabeth Lucia, 19:232
  Elizabeth Virginia (Harwood), 19:232
  Harriet Spady (Nottingham), 19:233
  Lucius Nottingham, 19:232
  Nancy Goffigon, 19:233
  William Henry, 19:233
WESCOTT see also WESCOAT, WESTCOAT
  Agnes (___), 19:239
  Annie, 19:239
  Arthur, 19:240
  Charles, 19:240
  Eliakim, 18:77
  Elizabeth, 19:239
  Esther, 16:240
  Eunice (Cole), 19:240
  Joanna (Knight), 18:77
  Laura, 19:239
  Mary, 19:239
  William, 19:239
WESSON/WESTON
  Ebenezer, 20:47
  Elizabeth, 20:47
  Ellen, 17:126
  Mehitable (___), 20:47
WEST, 16:111
  ___, Goodman, 19:45
  Bethia (___), 18:159
  Elisha, 19:83
  Elizabeth (Derby), 17:227
  George, 19:158
  Henry, 16:32; 17:20
  John, 16:12; 18:54
  Joseph, 18:159; 19:218
  Margaret, 17:178
  Margaret (Tink), 19:158
  Mary, 20:58
  Mary (Tucker), 19:53
  Mathew, 19:138; 20:194
  Mehitable (Northey), 19:83
  Molly, 17:12
  Nathaniel, 17:227
  Robert, 17:135
  Ruth (Perkins), 17:240

  Samuel, 18:90, 91; 19:53
  Sarah, 18:54
  Sarah (___), 18:54
  Thomas, 18:60a; 19:202
  Timothy, 17:240
  Zebulon, 19:218
WESTALL
  John, 18:110-113
  Sarah (Kirtland), 18:111
  Susanna (Kirtland), 18:109-113
WESTBROOK
  Thomas, 20:49
WESTCOAT see also WESCOAT, WESCOTT
  Nancy, 19:230
WESTON see also WESSON
  Costelle, 17:168
  Ebenezer, 19:101
  Frances, 19:189
  Rebecca, 18:152; 19:101
WEYLEY
  John, 20:190
WHARF/WHARFE see also WHORF
  Isaac, 16:134
  James, 16:63
  Nathaniel, 18:138, 199
WHARFIELD
  Eleanor, 16:119
  Ernest Chester, 16:119
  Frances, 16:119
  Wilfred Marc, 16:119
WHARTON
  Rebecca, 18:74
  William, 19:133
WHEAT
  Joshua, 20:196
WHEELER, 18:231
  ___, Miss, 16:211
  ___, Mr., 19:158
  ___, Mrs., 17:13
  Aaron, 16:38; 18:202
  Abigail, 20:166-168
  Anne, 17:13
  Deborah (Whitney), 17:116
  Elizabeth, 16:173; 18:100
  Elizabeth (Knight), 18:77
  Elizabeth (Nichols), 17:116
  Esther, 18:202
  Fortunatus, 17:116
  Fred O., 17:116
  Hannah, 18:202; 19:58
  Hannah (Baker), 20:28
  Harriet B. (Smith), 17:116
  James, 18:120
  John, 18:77
  Jonathan, 20:28
  Joseph, 17:116; 18:202
  Katherine (Morse), 18:59
  Laura (___), 18:59
  Laura Ann, 18:59
  Lois, 20:41
  Lydia, 20:168
  Mary, 18:201; 20:137
  Mary (___), 17:17
  Mary (Finson), 18:202
  Mary Belcher, 17:44
  Mary Elizabeth, 18:207
  Medora E. (Bailey), 17:116
  Mehitable, 18:202
  Moses, 16:63; 18:202
  Obadiah, 20:28
  Olive, 20:25
  Paran, 17:116

Persis (Howe), 17:116
R. D., 18:120
Ralph B., 17:116
Richard Anson, 17:176
Richard L., 17:116
Richard S., 18:138
Ruel F., 17:116
Ruth (Parker), 16:38
Samuel, 18:202
Sarah, 18:120
Silias, 18:59
Susanna, 16:118; 18:202, 207
Susanna (Davis), 18:202
Susanna (Woodbury), 18:202
Susannah (Norwood), 18:202
Thaddeus, 18:59
Thankful (Baker), 20:28
Thomas, 16:72; 17:17; 18:231; 19:193
William, 19:93
WHEELWRIGHT, 16:160
___, Capt., 19:166
Elizabeth, 16:56
John, 16:230
Katherine, 19:165
WHIDDEN/WHITTEN
Jonathan, 16:18
Rebecca (Hackett), 16:18
Sarah, 16:120
WHIET
Elias, 20:199
WHIPPLE see also WHIPPO, 20:53
___, Mr., 20:226
Aaron, 18:97
Abigail (Jenks), 16:72
Abraham, 18:86
Anna, 18:86; 20:30
Bathsheba, 18:86
Calvin, 18:86
Cornet, 18:69
Daniel, 18:86
Deborah, 16:86; 17:159; 18:86
Elizabeth, 18:120
Jacob, 19:174
James, 17:135
Jerusha (Leland), 19:174
John, 18:69, 120, 193, 240; 20:92, 224
Joseph, 17:120; 18:69, 86, 153; 19:42
Keziah (Cass), 18:97
Luther, 18:86
Mary, 18:86
Mary (Jones), 18:86
Matthew, 18:69
Nathaniel, 18:70
Ruth, 17:120
Samuel, 18:86
Sarah, 17:16
Sarah (___), 18:120
Susanna, 19:174; 20:231, 234
Thomas, 16:72
William, 20:30
WHIPPO see also WHIPPLE
Abigail (Hammond), 16:230; 18:235
Elizabeth, 18:159, 235
James, 16:230; 18:235
WHITAKER
___, Dr., 18:93
WHITCHEARE
John, 20:198
WHITCHEY
John, 16:173
WHITCOMB
Eliza, 19:180
Francis, 19:172

Rosina (Northey), 19:172
Sarah, 16:87
Sheldon, 19:172
William, 17:157
WHITE see also WHYTE
___, Goodman, 17:209
___, Miss, 16:237
___, Rev., 19:125
Abel, 16:177
Abigail, 16:79; 18:101
Abigail (Blaney), 16:78
Alice (___), 17:13
Andrew, 18:120
Anna, 20:232, 236
Benjamin, 20:179
Deborah, 20:179
Deborah (Fuller), 20:179
Dinah (Kenney), 20:232, 235, 236
Domingo, 20:134, 135, 196
Ebenezer, 20:179
Elizabeth, 16:79
Elizabeth P., 18:191
Eunice, 20:236
Hannah, 19:238; 20:136, 221
Hannah (Hutchinson), 20:232
James, 17:76; 18:237
Jerusha, 20:236
John, 16:68; 17:91; 18:44, 101, 240; 19:13, 124, 138; 20:130, 195, 232
Joseph, 20:232
Josiah, 20:235
Louise, 17:106
Lucretia (Derby), 20:232
Lydia, 18:44; 20:232
Lydia (___), 16:146
Lydia (Wiborn), 20:53
Margaret, 16:40
Martha (___), 16:39
Martha (Pritchet), 20:229, 232, 236
Mary, 16:150; 20:236
Mary (___), 20:179
Mary/Marcy, 17:27
Mehitable, 20:228-232
Moses, 16:40
Polly, 20:25
Rachel (Davis), 16:40
Rand, 20:30, 53
Rebecca (Sollis), 16:177
Rebeckah, 16:79
Rebekah (Curtice), 20:232
Remember (Reed), 20:235
Samuel, 20:229, 232, 235, 236
Sarah, 19:39, 98; 20:60a
Sarah (Sanderson), 18:120
Sarah (Talbot), 20:179
Steve, 18:6
Thomas, 20:15
Victoria, 17:9
William, 16:134; 18:140, 141; 20:224
WHITEFOOT
John, 20:198
WHITEHEAD
Aaron, 16:9
Elizabeth, 16:7
Mary (Stones), 16:9
WHITEMORE see also WHITMORE, WHITTEMORE
Suanna, 16:178
WHITERIDGE/WHITERIGE see also WHITREDGE, WHITTREDGE
Mary, 18:46
Nathaniel, 19:138; 20:195

WHITFIELD
Eleanor, 17:234
Sarah, 17:236
WHITFORD
Elizabeth, 19:137
Mary, 18:212, 224
WHITING/WHITTING
___, Mr., 19:45
David, 17:234
Eleanor (Whitfield), 17:234
Jack, 18:138
James, 17:234
John, 17:234; 18:138
Mary, 18:46
Sa., 18:230
Samuel, 18:147, 148; 19:43, 138; 20:193, 195
Sanders, 17:234; 18:138
Sarah, 16:146; 18:149
Timothy, 18:149
WHITINGS
___, Mr., 19:217
WHITMAN
Abigail, 17:115
Elizabeth, 17:115
Elizabeth (Pierson), 16:56; 17:115
Ezekiel Cheever, 19:102
Francis, 16:56; 17:115
Grace (Cheever), 19:102
Jane (Norcross), 17:115
Mary/Polly, 17:115
Sally (Sumner), 17:115
Samuel, 19:102
Sarah, 16:56; 17:115
Sarah (Paine), 16:56; 17:115
Thomas, 17:115
William, 17:115
WHITMARK
Sarah, 16:85
WHITMORE see also WHITEMORE, WHITTEMORE
Abigail (Babbidge), 18:221
Jane, 20:230
John, 18:77
Joseph, 18:221
Mary, 18:221
Ruhama (Knight), 18:77
W. H., 16:161
William, 18:77
William H., 16:202; 17:42; 18:195
WHITNEY
Amanda Louise, 18:176
Amos Newhall, 20:116, 117
Aura, 20:117
Cephas, 20:117
Cynthia, 20:117
Deborah, 17:116
Francis, 18:138
Hannah, 16:115
Joanna (Newhall), 20:116, 117
Jonas, 16:240
Jonathan, 16:120
Julia Ann, 20:117
Keziah (Farnsworth), 16:120
Lucy, 20:33, 40
Lydia, 16:74
M., 16:150
Mary, 16:120
Mary (Perry), 18:175
Mary Farnsworth, 20:117
Peter, 20:116, 117
Phineas, 16:120
Randi Susan (Kretschmar), 18:176

Richard, 18:175
Sarah, 18:175, 179
Sarah (Holt), 16:120
Sarah (Whittemore), 16:240
Sarah Ellen, 16:150
Submit (Parker), 17:153
Susan, 16:103
Warren Williams, 18:176
WHITREDGE see also WHITERIDGE, WHITTREDGE
A., 19:239
WHITT
Thomas, 20:199
WHITTAKER
Elizabeth, 16:81
Nathaniel, 18:94
WHITTEMORE see also WHITEMORE, WHITMORE
Daniel, 17:198
David, 16:60
Eleanor (Osborn), 17:198
Elizabeth, 16:37
Elizabeth (Rhodes), 16:92
Frances Nichols, 16:60
Hannah, 18:226
James, 18:226
Mary, 16:89
Mary (Nichols), 16:60
Nathaniel, 16:92
Rebeckah, 18:170
Sarah, 16:240
WHITTEN see WHIDDEN
WHITTER
David, 17:133, 135
WHITTIER
___, Mr., 16:15
Abigail, 20:207
Charles Collyer, 16:22
Eleanor (Emery), 16:178
Elizabeth (Bodwell), 18:159
Hannah, 16:19
Ida C., 20:171
John, 16:178
John Greenleaf, 16:15; 18;144; 19:15, 65; 20:94
Joseph, 16:15
Mary (Barnard), 16:15
Richard, 18:159
Thomas, 16:22; 20:130
William, 20:130
WHITTINGTON
Edward, 20:167
WHITTLESEY
Martha, 18:113
WHITTREDGE
Hannah (Osborn), 17:201
Sarah, 20:229, 230
Thomas, 17:201
WHITTSEDGE
George, 20:83
WHORF see also WHARF
Mary A., 20:171
WHYTE see also WHITE
Margaret, 19:153
WIBIRD
John, 16:57
Sarah, 16:57
WIBORN see also WYBORN, 20:53
___, (Mason), 20:30
Anna (Whipple), 20:30
Auburn M., 20:30
Bevil, 20:30
Gershom, 20:30, 53

Hannah, 20:32
Hannah (Breed), 20:30
Hannah V., 20:53
Isaac, 20:30
James, 20:30, 31
John, 20:30, 31, 53
Lucy, 20:53
Lydia, 20:53
Mason, 20:30, 53
Ruth (Partridge), 20:31
William, 20:30
WICKES see WEEKS, 19:142
WIDDOP, 16:13
WIDGER
James, 20:198
WIGGIN
Mary Ann, 17:201
Sarah, 19:229
Thomas, 18:231; 20:67
WIGGLESWORTH
Martha, 18:152; 19:101
Michael, 19:40
Samuel, 18:69
WIGHT
Karen L., 19:200
WIGHTMAN
William, 20:186
WILBORE
___, Ms., 19:60a
Hannah/Anna (Hackett), 18:82
Mary M. (Dean), 18:79
Samuel, 18:79, 82
Shadrach, 18:79, 82
WILBOURNE
Mercy (Beamsley), 19:223
WILBUR, 19:116
Susan, 17:120
WILCOX
Gulielma (Estes), 18:96
William, 18:96
WILD/WILDE, 16:13
Anna, 19:238
Elizabeth, 18:85
John, 18:85
William, 16:195; 18:9
WILDER
Theophilus, 18:138
WILDES
Dudley, 16:195
Elizabeth (___), 16:195
Sarah, 18:138
WILEY
Alfred, 18:217
Almira E., 18:217
Benjamin, 18:217, 240
Betsey (Parker), 18:217
Caroline Augusta (Boynton), 20:108
Ebenezer, 20:39
Elizabeth, 16:27
Harriet (Norwood), 18:217
Israel Augustus, 20:39
Jacob, 20:39
James, 20:37, 39
Lois (Bancroft), 20:39
Lois (Parsons), 20:39
Lydia, 20:41
Margaret (Parsons), 20:39
Nabby (Parsons), 20:39
Ruth, 17:27
Tabitha (___), 20:39
Thomas, 20:39
Timothy, 20:49
William S., 20:108

WILKIE
Walker, 17:170
WILKINS
Betty (Southwick), 19:99
Bray, 16:59; 17:16; 18-17; 20:201
Clarissa, 19:56
David, 18:240
Elijah, 20:203
Elizabeth Virginia (McCoy), 19:232
Hannah (Way), 16:59
John, 19:99
Mary, 18:239; 19:56
Mercy, 19:39, 99
Sarah/Sadie Jefferson, 19:232
Thomas Jefferson, 19:232
WILKINSON
Elizabeth, 19:224
Isaac, 17:93
John, 17:25
WILKOT
John, 20:199
WILL
Adelbert, 18:175
Bernice Sophronia, 18:175
Black, 19:26
Ida May (Mosher), 18:175
WILLARD see also MILLER
Betsey (Gibbs), 18:179
Elijah, 18:179
Esther (Jenks), 16:72
James, 17:83
Josiah, 17:231
Samuel, 16:72
Sarah (Longley), 17:83
WILLER
Mary, 20:225
WILLES
Thomas, 20:132
WILLET/WILLETT
Abigail (Collins), 16:229
Elthea Prince, 18:139
John, 16:229
WILLEY
Alice, 19:208
Alice (___), 16:160
Kenneth L., 18:236
WILLIAM
"Black", 18:180a
Conqueror, 16:240
Duke, 19:26
George, 19:201
King, II, 17:125
Yvonne K., 16:52
WILLIAMS, 17:229; 20:13
___, Goodman, 19:194
___, Mr., 17:102; 19:196
"Child", 18:23
Abigail, 20:211
Abigail (Collins), 17:113; 19:50; 20:211
Abigail (Sparhawk), 17:113
Abraham, 16:64
Addie M. (Turner), 17:239
Alice, 16:118
Alicia Crane, 18:17, 51
Ann, 18:136
Ann (___), 16:64
Ann (Alley), 18:16
Anna, 17:113; 18:23; 19:50
Anna (Alley), 18:22, 23
Anstis, 17:226
Anthony, 20:198
Benjamin Salt, 19:159
Bethia, 16:39

Bethiah (Parker), 16:39
Betsey Elizabeth (Libbey), 20:239
Betsy (Richards), 16:99
Caroline, 16:39
Charles, 16:109
Cora E. (Wright), 18:180
Cornelia Bartow, 16:171
Daniel, 16:134
David, 18:74
Ebenezer, 18:203
Elizabeth, 16:39; 17:230; 18:74
Elizabeth (___), 16:180
Elizabeth (Smith), 17:230
Evan, 17:13
Evelyn, 20:55
Frank, 16:188
George, 16:180; 17:113; 18:137, 139; 20:199
George E., 17:113
Hannah, 17:113; 18:211; 19:50
Hannah (Dunton), 17:113
Hannah (Pratt), 19:239
Hannah (Richards), 16:97; 17:113; 19:50
Helen Dearborn (Tyler), 19:233
Hiram, 18:217
Isaac, 16:146; 19:143
James, 16:98; 17:113; 19:50; 20:211
Jane Massey (Norwood), 18:217
Jenkin, 18:74; 20:197
Joanna, 17:202
Joanna (Marshall), 16:167
John, 16:39; 17:19; 18:52, 74, 140; 19:50, 137, 216; 20:199
Lawrence, 16:171
Lucretia, 16:39
Lydia, 16:46; 17:113; 19:50
Lydia (Coates), 19:159
Mae C., 18:180
Marie (___), 16:180
Martha (___), 18:78
Martha (Comee), 16:171; 17:25
Martha (Knight), 18:74
Martha (Tufts), 16:199; 17:113; 19-50
Mary, 16:39; 17:55; 18:74; 20:210
Mary (Mills), 16:199
Mary (Norwood), 18:203
Mary A., 18:204
Nancy (Breed), 16:171
Nathaniel, 16:167
Nicholas, 18:74
Priscilla, 17:113; 19:50
Priscilla (Collins), 16:109
R. Evelyn, 18:134
Rebecca, 17:113; 19:137
Rebeckah (Pearson), 17:113
Richard, 16:180
Roger, 18:195, 197; 20:96
Ruth, 17:231
Sally, 19:102
Samuel, 18:180
Sarah, 16:64; 17:25; 18:202
Seth W., 19:239
Simeon Breed, 16:171
Simon, 16:168
Stedman, 16:39
Stephen, 16:40
Susanna (Knight), 18:77
Susannah, 17:113; 20:106
Tabitha, 16:96; 17:113; 19:50
Tabitha (Ingalls), 16:199; 17:113; 19:50
Tabitha (Pearson), 16:171; 17:113
Thomas, 16:99; 17:113; 18:16, 23
Umpherie, 20:199

William, 16:167; 17:25; 19:50
Zerviah, 20:212
WILLIAMSON
Anna, 20:49
John, 20:49
Margaret, 20:49
Margaret (___), 20:49
WILLIS, 19:216, 217; 20:187
___, Mr., 17:88; 18:230, 231; 20:183
Abigail (Blaney), 16:82
George, 17:89
Hannah, 16:82
Jirah, 16:82
John, 17:118
Mary (Gale), 17:118
Mary Elizabeth, 17:117
Mehitable (Gifford), 16:82
Samuel, 16:82
Thomas, 19:138; 20:187, 188, 194
William, 20:176
WILLISTON
David Howe, 20:40
Nancy, 16:84
Susannah (Bancroft), 20:40
WILLOUGHBIE/WILLOUGHBY
Elizabeth (___), 16:229
Francis, 16:229; 19:132
Margaret (Locke), 16:229
WILLOW
Moses, 17:8
WILLS
Arline K., 18:138; 20:180a
Eldridge, 18:139
Elthea Prince (Willett), 18:139
George, 18:37
Henry, 18:113
Martha (Kirtland), 18:113
Mary (___), 18:37
WILLSON see WILSON, 16:88
WILLY
Edward, 20:9
WILSON/WILLSON, 17:22; 20:153
___, Aunt, 20:152, 157
Abigail, 20:99
Abigail (Newhall), 16:46; 20:25, 29
Addie L. (Friend), 17:103
Alfred Clare, 16:49
Amelia/Milly (Tarbox), 20:147
Ann, 17:105
Anna (___), 17:105
Annie H. (___), 17:168
Belle Wolfe, 16:151
Benjamin, 16:209; 20:29;42
Benjamin B., 17:104
Betsey, 20:42
Betsey (Briant), 20:151
Charles Everett, 17:103
Clara P., 16:149
Clark, 20:42
Daniel, 17:29
Deborah, 19:64
Deborah (Buffum), 20:99
Dimock, 20:147
Donald, 16:188
Elisha, 20:42
Elizabeth, 18:179; 20:29, 99
Elizabeth (Cook), 20:29, 99
Eric, 17:30
Esther (Edmands), 17:29
Ethel May, 17:103
Everett Carroll, 17:103
Ezekiel, 16:178
Florance S., 17:168

Fred A., 18:14, 17
George, 20:24
Hannah, 17:40; 20:24-26
Harrison, 17:29
Huldah (Blaney), 16:82
Irving Harrison, 17:174
Isaac, 16:46; 20:25, 26, 29, 99, 101
James, 16:209; 17:105; 19:58; 20:42
Jennie, 19:58
Jerome, 17:29
John, 18:163, 233; 19:93; 20:42, 151
John F., 17:168
Jonathan, 16:149; 20:29
Joseph, 16:68; 17:171; 18:114; 20:29
Lydia, 20:42
Lydia (Bancroft), 20:29, 42
Marcia, 17:174; 20:227
Margaret (Mansfield), 16:238
Margaret M., 17:29
Martha, 20:29
Mary, 17:236; 20:29
Mary (___), 16:45
Mary (Proctor), 20:26, 29, 99, 100
Mary (Shullaber), 20:29
Mary (Stone), 20:99, 101
Mary A. (Wallis), 17:103
Mehitable, 16:209
Moses E., 17:103
Nancy (Fisk), 17:29
Nancy M., 20:132, 148
Nancy Marie (Tarbox), 20:149
Nellie M., 17:29
Oliver, 17:232
Peggy, 20:42
Polly, 20:42
Priscilla, 16:165
Priscilla (Purchase), 17:232
Rachel (___), 16:82
Robert, 17:29; 20:26, 29, 99, 100
Rosalinda, 17:29
Ruth, 20:42
Ruth (Edmands), 17:30
Ruth (Jaquish), 16:178
Ruth Tapley (Mudge), 17:174; 20:227
Samuel, 19:100
Sarah, 17:153; 20:29, 42
Sarah Jane (Russell), 20:24
Susanna, 16:82; 18:212
Ursilla, 20:217, 219
William, 16:196; 17:232
WINBORN
Elizabeth (Hart), 18:42
John Rossiter, 18:42
William, 18:42
WINCH
Samuel, 16:131
WINDER
Nancy (___), 20:59
Sarah D., 20:59
Thomas, 20:59
WINDOW, 20:18
WING
Deborah, 18:97
Hannah, 16:224
John, 20:78
WINGATE
Mary, 20:60a
Paine, 20:80
WINKLEY
S. W., 17:37
WINN
Abigail, 20:28, 97
Belcher, 20:25

David, 20:25
Edward, 20:97
Elizabeth, 18:59; 20:28
Elizabeth (Knight), 20:28
Hannah, 20:28, 97
Hannah (Sawtelle), 20:28, 97
Hannah (Wilson), 20:24, 26
Harriet (Poland), 20:25
Increase, 20:28, 97
Jacob, 20:26, 28, 97, 98
James, 20:25, 26
Jeremiah, 20:26
Joanna, 20:97
Joanna (___), 20:97
Jonathan, 20:26
Joshua, 20:24-26, 28
Margaret, 20:24, 25
Mary, 20:97
Mary (___), 20:97
Mary (Center), 20:25, 26, 28
Mary (Rogers), 18:59
Mehitable (Buck), 20:26
Molly, 20:26
Moses, 18:59
Nehemiah, 20:25
Phebe (Palfray), 20:97
Polly (White), 20:25
Prudence, 20:28
Prudence (Wyman), 20:26, 28, 97, 98
Rebecca, 20:97
Sally (Putnam), 20:25
Sarah, 20:97
WINNERY
Molly, 19:119
WINNICK
Rachel, 18:20
WINSHIP
Hannah, 16:83
Mary (Newhall), 16:47
Samuel, 16:47
WINSLOW/WINSLEY
Barnabas, 20:45
Cynthia, 19:171
Deborah, 1615; 18:204
Edward, 16:120a
Gilbert, 20:45
Hannah, 17:235
John, 17:135; 19:171
Josiah, 18:204
Lydia (Hacker), 19:171
Mary, 18:77
Mary (Jones), 18:84
Nathaniel, 18:84
Penelope (Kent), 18:204
Rebecca, 20:55
WINSOR
Brigitte, 20:77
WINTER see also WITTER
___, Goodman, 19:25
___, Mrs., 17:13
Abigail (___), 20:119
Elizabeth, 20:114
Eunice, 20:119
John, 20:119
Wm., 16:64
WINTERTON
Thomas, 18:79
WINTHROP, 16:67; 20:68
___, Col., 20:49
___, Gov., 16:200; 18:140, 141; 20:96, 183, 189
___, Mr., 17:240
___, Mrs., 16:139

Adam, 19:132
Catharine, 16:81
Elizabeth, 16:139
John, 16:138; 17:75; 18:80, 158, 192, 195, 196; 19:123, 127, 201, 202; 20:64, 76, 132, 188
Stephen, 19:132
WINTON see also VINTON
Blase, 20:69
James, 20:69
Joane (___), 20:69
WISE
Abigail, 19:235
Ami Ruhannah, 18:240
Bethiah, 16:39
Daniel, 18:240
Honor (Tarr), 19:235
John, 16:159; 17:75; 18:139; 19:235
Joseph, 17:75
Mary (Thompson), 17:76
William G., 18:139
WISWALL, 16:109; 18:139
Carol Tapley, 17:174
Clare, 16:240
Clarence A., 16:240
Marcia, 18:47
Marcia (Wilson), 17:174; 20:227
Marcia W., 18:133, 172; 20:91
Marcia Wilson, 19:136
William Cobb, 17:174
WITHAM
Abigail (Harris), 18:201
Andrew, 19:97
Elmira Prindall (Ingalls), 19:115
Frank H., 19:115
Henry, 17:240; 20:200
John Emery, 19:115
Joseph, 18:201
Karl Ingalls, 19:115
Mary/Molly (Parker), 19:97
Patience (Harris), 18:201
Rebecca (Harris), 18:201
Sanders, 18:201
Zebulon, 18:201
WITHERDIN/WITHERINGTON
Mary, 19:155
WITHERS
Grace (Bassett), 18:39
Samuel, 18:39
WITHEY
"Female", 20:109
"Male", 20:109
Ann B. (Chapin), 20:109
Caroline D., 20:109
Clara Anna, 20:24
George S., 20:109
Hannah Ellen, 20:109
John, 20:106, 107, 109
John P., 20:109
Linda A. (Tyler), 20:109
Louise (Groom), 20:109
Mary Ellen, 20:109
Richard B., 20:109
Sally (Boynton), 20:106, 107, 109
Sally (Ingalls), 20:109
Samuel P., 20:109
Sarah Elizabeth, 20:109
WITHINGTON
Elizabeth (Preston), 20:179
Hannah, 20:179
John, 20:179
WITT/DeWITT, 18:116, 169
Abigail, 16:46; 18:24, 149, 168, 170, 173

Abigail (Killum), 18:169
Abigail (Montague), 18:169
Abigail (Rust), 16:102; 18:173
Abner, 18:169
Alpheus, 18:169
Ann, 16:237; 18:164, 165
Anna (Bailey), 18:171
Artemus, 18:171
Azubah (Bartlett), 18:171
Benjamin, 16:102; 18:169, 172, 173
Bertha, 18:169
Bethia (___), 18:169
Bethia (Potter), 18:166, 168; 19:143-145
Betsy, 18:24
Catherine (___), 18:169
Catherine (Dexter), 18:170
Daniel, 18:170, 171, 173
Daniel Rust, 18:173
David, 18:169
Deborah, 18:169
Deborah (Stewart), 18:168, 171
Dinah (Brigham), 18:170
Ebenezer, 18:149, 166, 168-171
Elias, 18:169
Elizabeth, 18:149, 164-167, 169, 171
Elizabeth (___), 18:115, 164, 173
Elizabeth (Baker), 18:149, 166, 167; 19:147
Elizabeth (Breed), 18:149, 168, 170
Elizabeth (Cheever), 18:173
Elizabeth (Eames), 18:170
Elizabeth (Marble), 18:169
Elizabeth (Newhall), 18:173
Elizabeth (Parsons), 18:173
Ester, 17:158
Ester (Warren), 18:171
Esther, 18:166
Eunice (Flint), 18:170
Eunice (Peacock), 18:171
Gedney, 18:172, 173
Hannah, 18:171
Hannah (Hawkes), 18:173
Hannah (Parsons), 18:173
Hannah (Sawtell), 18:169
Henry, 18:173
Hester, 18:115, 164, 165, 167
Isaiah, 18:168, 171
Ivory, 18:169, 172
John, 16:102; 17:13; 18:72, 115, 139, 149, 164-173; 19:144, 147; 20:135, 142, 196
Jonas, 18:171
Jonathan, 18:115, 149, 165-170, 231
Joseph, 18:169, 171
Josiah, 18:170
Lovice (Montague), 18:169
Lucy (Adams), 18:170
Lucy (Cobb), 18:173
Lucy (Holmes), 18:170
Lydia, 16:69; 18:170, 172, 173; 20:142
Lydia (Matthews), 18:149, 168, 170
Lydia (Woodbury), 18:169
Margaret (Brewer), 18:173
Martha, 18:164, 166, 171
Martha (Wood), 18:149, 168, 171
Mary, 18:149, 164, 165, 168-173; 19:144; 20:142
Mary (Breed), 18:173
Mary (Dane), 18:149, 167, 168
Mary (Divan), 18:115, 165-167
Mary (Ivory), 16:102; 18:168, 171-173; 19:144, 147
Mary (Rowland), 18:169
Miriam, 18:171

Molly, 18:173
Nancy (Pond), 18:170
Naomi, 18:170
Olive, 18:169
Oliver, 18:170
Olivia (Campbell), 18:169
Patty (Hathaway), 18:173
Persis, 18:149, 168
Phoebe, 18:170
Rebecca, 18:169, 172; 20:142
Rebecca (Breed), 18:149, 168, 171
Rebeckah (Whittemore), 18:170
Ruth, 18:172
Ruth (Breed), 18:172
Ruth (Wright), 18:171
Sally (Blake), 18:171
Sally (Patten), 18:169
Samuel, 18:149, 168, 170, 171
Sarah, 17:146; 18:149, 164, 165, 168-170, 172, 173; 19:147; 20:142
Sarah (___), 16:237; 18:164-166, 169; 19:144
Sarah (Dorr), 18:171
Sarah (Goodnow), 18:170
Sarah (Hudson), 18:170
Sarah (Ivory), 18:169
Sarah (Swan), 18:170
Sarah (Tarbox), 18:172; 20:142
Sibbel, 18:169
Silas, 18:170
Stephen, 18:169
Susanna, 18:171
Susanna (Merritt), 18:149, 170
Thomas, 16:102; 18:149, 164, 166, 168, 169, 171-173; 19:144, 147
Wealthy (Cobb), 18:170
William, 18:169
Zaccheus, 18:169
WITTER see also WINTER
Ebenezer, 19:78
Josiah, 16:165
William, 18:99
WIXON
Hannah (Baker), 20:96
Joshua, 20:96
WOAKER
John, 20:198
WOLCOT
Coram, 20:103
WOLF/WOLFE see also WOOLFE
Freeborn, 16:177\
Georgie (Shorey), 17:238
Hannah, 16:177
Peter, 16:177; 18:132, 139
Sargent, 19:201
William, 17:238
WOLFENDEN, 16:13
WOLFMAN
Ira, 17:74
WOLLASTON
___, Capt., 20:180a
WOLSTENCROFT, 16:13
WOLSTENHOLME, 16:13
WOLTON/WOOLTON
John, 16:134
Richard, 20:199
WONSON
Anna (Lurvey), 20:58
Belinda Richmond (Friend), 17:166
Charles, 18:202
Elizabeth A. (Sawyer), 17:166
Frederick F., 17:166
George, 18:202

John, 18:202
Lydia (Gott), 18:202
Mary P., 17:163
Patience (Norwood), 18:202
Samuel, 18:202; 20:58
Samuel G., 17:166
Samuel R., 17:166
WOOD see also DUBOIS, 20:170
Aaron, 18:107
Abial, 18:81
Abigail, 18:117; 19:85, 170, 200
Alice A. (Clark), 20:171
Alice M. (___), 20:171
Allison C. (Davis), 20:172
Amos, 16:132
Anthony, 20:198
Asa, 16:132
Barnabas, 18:82
Beatrice, 19:20
Beatrice Allison, 20:172
Bridget, 19:208
Carolyn Ruth, 20:172
Charles Brewster, 20:172
Charles Sumner, 20:171
Clarissa (Osborn), 17:200
Cora, 20:171
Daniel, 16:193; 18:74; 20:176
David, 16:194; 17:152
Deborah Jean, 20:172
Donald Yates, 20:172
Dorcas, 16:177
Dorothy, 20:169
Dorothy May, 20:172, 173
Ebenezer, 16:132
Elesibeth, 17:152
Elisabeth (Campbel), 17:152
Elizabeth (Farrington), 17:152
Elizabeth (Williams), 18:74
Elizabeth (Yates), 20:172
Emma Frances, 20:171
Eugene, 20:170, 171, 173
Fannie B. (Adams), 20:171
Florence I. (Joselyn), 20:171
Frank, 20:171
Frederick Warren, 20:171-173
George Eugene, 20:171
Gladys (Holmes), 20:171
Harold Davies, 20:172
Henry Eugene, 20:171
Ida C. (Whittier), 20:171
Israel, 19:97
Jacob, 17:200
Jean Marie, 20:172
Joanna, 20:38
Joanna (Parker), 19:97
John, 18:72, 230; 19:75, 138; 20:194
Jonathan, 17:152
Joseph, 16:132; 19:97
Joshua, 17:152
Katherine (Janes), 16:58
Lavinia, 18:96
Leslie A., 20:169
Leslie Ann, 20:173
Leslie Arnold, 20:172, 173
Leslie Warren, 20:172, 173
Lewis Daigneau, 20:170, 171, 173
Marjorie E. (Brown), 20:171, 172
Martha, 17:152; 18-149, 168, 171
Martha (Farrington), 17:152
Mary, 16:131; 17:152; 19:96, 168
Mary (___), 17:152
Mary A. (Whorf), 20:171
Mary Barry (Cheever), 20:170, 171

Mary E. (Lynan), 20:172
Mary Ellen, 20:173
Mary Frances (Dickason), 20:170, 171
Mehitabell, 16:132
Mercy (Hackett), 18:81
Nabby (Parker), 19:97
Napoleon, 20:170
Nathan, 17:152
Phillip Allen, 20:171
Rebecca, 17:203; 19:179
Rebecca (Osburn), 18:117; 19:170, 200
Richard, 19:84
Robert A., 20:169
Robert Allen, 20:172, 173
Robert Haskell, 19:97
Robert Many, 20:171-173
Roland Lewis, 20:171
Ruth, 19:97
Ruth (Allen), 20:171
Ruth (Haskell), 19:97
Samuel A., 16:58
Sarah, 16:132; 17:152; 18:86, 88; 19:168
Sarah (___), 16:132
Sarah (Northey), 19:84
Sarah Weeks (Brackett), 20:176
Solomon, 17:152
Susannah (___), 20:98
Thomas, 16:132; 18:117; 119:170, 200
Virginia, 20:172
Wilbur Fisk, 20:171
William, 18:180a; 19:75
William Allen, 20:172
William Henry, 20:171-173
WOODALL
___, Mr., 19:158
WOODARD see also WOODWARD
Elizabeth (Aborn), 16:92
Mary, 18:222
WOODART
Deliverance (Potter), 19:150
Elizabeth (Potter), 18:199
Robert, 18:199; 19:150
WOODBERRY/WOODBERRE/ WOODBERY see also WOODBURY
Anna, 17:203
Humphrey, 18:240; 20:198
Isaac, 20:198
Jno., 16:136
John, 16:136; 20:198
Richard, 20:198
Thomas, 20:198
William, 18:60a
WOODBRIDGE, 19:125
___, Rev., 16:67
WOODBURY see also WOODBERRY, 17:51; 18:139; 19:126; 20:18
Abigail, 16:137
Agnes (___), 19:125, 127
Anna, 16:137
Benjamin, 16:134
C.J.H., 19:75
Charles, 16:220
Charles D., 16:220
Deborah (Tarbox), 20:143
Ebenezer, 18:178
Elizabeth, 16:137
Elizabeth (Patch), 16:116
Elizabeth Low, 16:220
Hannah, 16:137; 17:236
Hannah (Dodge), 18:178
Hannah (Tarbox), 20:136
Harry, 20:27
Helen Augusta (Friend), 16:220

Henry, 16:220
Hepsibah A. (Pickett), 17:104
Humphrey, 16:137; 19:125
John, 16:137; 19:119, 123-125, 127, 128
Joseph, 20:143
Josiah, 16:101
Judith, 16:116; 18:200, 202-204
Judith (___), 16:116
Judith (Riggs), 18:203
L. A., 19:210
Laura Goodwin, 16:220
Lydia, 18:169; 20:120
Mary, 16:137
Peter, 16:137; 20:136
Priscilla, 16:143
Ruth Gaskill, 20:27
Sally, 20:152
Sarah, 20:120
Sarah D. (Tuck), 16:220
Susanna (Lane), 19:119
Susannah, 18:202
William, 16:116; 18:203
WOODHEAD, 16:13
WOODHOUSE
Nancy, 16:119
WOODIN
Bethiah, 20:27, 94, 95
John, 20:94
Mary (Johnson), 20:94
WOODIS
Henry, 16:168
WOODLIE
William, 20:199
WOODMAN
Adeline, 16:220
Clarence Flaig, 19:118
Daniel, 16:219
Edwin Wentworth, 16:219
Fanny (Friend), 16:219
Frances Ellen, 16:220
Frederick Augustus, 16:219
Hannah (Nesbit), 20:58
Jonathan, 20:58
Joseph, 20:144
Joseph Warren, 16:220
Katharine Grover (Smith), 19:118
Mary, 17:52; 20:178
Mira (Green), 16:220
Miriam, 16:120
Nathan, 20:139
Olive (Gray), 20:139
Paul, 16:219
Richard, 16:195; 19:142
Sally (Wentworth), 16:219
Sarah Elizabeth, 16:220
Virginia, 19:118
William, 18:133, 139
WOODNUTT
Joseph, 18:39
Mary, 18:39
WOODROE
Benjamin, 17:14
WOODS, 17:140
Aaron, 18:169
Abigail, 16:41; 17:82
Alice, 17:84
Amos, 16:115
Betsey, 17:153
Caira (Norwood), 18:207
Ebenezer, 16:131
Elizabeth, 16:87
Hannah, 16:115
Hannah (Nutting), 16:115

Hannah (Whitney), 16:115
Imri, 18:207
Isaac, 17:82
J., 16:43
Mary, 17:212
Reuben, 17:153
Sarah (Witt), 18:169
Submit (Parker), 17:153
Thomas, 16:115
Tryfena (Parker), 17:82
WOODSUM
Abner, 20:239
Elizabeth (Dyer), 20:239
Emily, 20:239
Michael, 20:239
Sarah/Betsey (Berry), 20:239
WOODWARD see also WOODARD, 19:16
Elizabeth (Aborn), 19:218
Ezekiel, 18:240
George, 19:215
James, 19:215
John, 19:213-215, 217; 20:48
Lydia, 20:42
Margaret, 18:201
Mary, 19:215
Mary (___), 19:215
Nathaniel, 17:218
Prudence, 16:159; 20:224
Rebecca, 17:84
Ruth, 17:98
Samuel, 17:218
Sarah, 19:215
Sarah (Bancroft), 19:213, 215
WOODWELL
Tamison, 16:59
WOODWORTH
Eleanor, 19:82, 83, 169
WOOLDRIDGE
Elizabeth (Symmes), 17:118
Sarah Hanover, 17:117
William, 17:118
WOOLFE see also WOLF
Martha, 16:137
Peter, 16:137
WOOLTON see WOLTON
WOOSTER
Ebenezer, 17:79
Francis, 18:10
Hannah, 18:10
Joseph, 18:10
Margaret (Sawtell), 17:79
Moses, 18:10
Sarah, 16:41
WORCESTER
___, Mr., 16:14
Abigail, 17:85
Anna, 17:85
Anna (Parker), 17:84
Asa, 17:84
Levi, 18:175
Martha (Cheney), 19:208
Mary, 17:85
Polly, 18:175
Samuel T., 17:84
Sarah (Whitney), 18:175
Susanna (___), 17:53
William, 17:154; 19:208
WORDEN
Abigail, 16:77
Amy (Waters), 16:77
Nathan, 16:77
WORK
Elizabeth (Deer), 16:75

John, 16:75
Martha (Ballard), 16:75
Mary (Ballard), 16:75
WORLEY
Mary (Foster), 20:240
Thomas, 20:240
WORMALL/WORMALLY see also WORMWOOD
Patience, 20:145
Tabitha, 17:47
William, 18:223
WORMSTEAD
Michael, 18:55
Sarah, 17:100
WORMWELL
Hester, 20:55
WORMWOOD see also WORMALL
Daniel, 18:73
Elizabeth, 18:73
Henry, 16:71; 17:143; 18:73; 20:196
Jean, 16:73
Mary (Knight), 16:71; 18:73, 174; 19:27
Mehitable, 16:73
Sarah, 16:73
Sarah (Ballard), 16:73; 18:73
Thomas, 19:226
William, 16:73; 18:73, 174
WORTH
Esther Ross, 17:59
WORTHINGTON
Margaret, 17:230
Orrin Shaler, 16:178
Suanna (Whitemore), 16:178
WORTHLEY
Harold Field, 16:189; 19:120a
WOSTER
Rachel (Wasgatt), 17:178
William, 17:178
WREN see also VEREN
Christopher, 20:64
WRIGHT
Abigail, 16:38
Abigail (Warren), 17:174
Carroll D., 16:189
Cora E., 18:180
David, 16:42
Deborah, 17:174
Dorothy, 20:119
Edward, 17:126
Elizabeth (Center), 20:98
Elizabeth (Peters), 20:119
George, 18:180
Hannah, 16:171
Hannah (___), 17:81
Hannah (Upson), 17:126
Ira, 18:180
Jacob, 16:171; 20:98
Joanna/Anna (Parker), 17:81
John, 17:174
Jonas, 17:81
Katherine, 17:126
Louisa (Ayer), 18:180
Martha (___), 18:180
Mehetabel (Center), 20:98
Millie, 17:162
Phebe, 16:179
Ruth, 16:41; 18:171; 20:98
Sally, 16:171
Sally (Smith), 16:171
Samuel, 17:81
Sarah, 16:120; 20:138
Sylvia, 18:180
Walter, 16:68; 20:119, 167

Zacheus, 20:40
WUTTAANOH
Sam, 18:60a
WUTTAQUATIMNUSK
Sarah, 18:60a
WYATT
Chas., 20:158
WYBORN see also WIBORN, 20:53
Hannah (Breed), 20:53
John, 20:53
WYER
Robert, 18:158
William, 16:106
WYLAND
Florence E. Bates, 19:162
WYLEY
Palfrew, 17:145
William, 17:145
WYMAN, 17:113; 18:224
Abigail, 20:99
Abigail (Reed), 20:97
Abigail (Sterns), 20:98
Deliverance, 18:212; 20:98
Edward, 20:98
Elizabeth, 20:98, 99
Esther, 16:179
Francis, 16:240; 20:97-99
Hannah, 16:37; 18:202; 20:99
Hannah (Fowle), 20:28, 99
Harriette C., 18:135
James, 20:98
John, 20:99
Jonathan, 20:28, 99
Joshua, 20:98
Martha, 16:42
Mary, 17:158; 20:26, 28, 98, 99
Mary (Green), 20:98
Mary (Pollard), 20:98
Mary (Winn), 20:97
Nathaniel, 20:97
Prudence, 20:26, 28, 97, 98
Prudence (Putnam), 20:28, 97, 98
Relief, 16:240
Sarah, 20:99
Sarah (Nutt), 20:99
Soloman, 16:179
T. B., 19:170
Thomas, 17:204; 19:207; 20:47, 98
Thomas B., 16:230
Thomas Bellows, 17:17; 18:21, 160; 19:25, 48, 102, 266
William, 20:28, 97, 98
Zachariah, 20:99
WYNTYM see VINTON, 20:68
WYZANSKI
Ernestina (Gutteman/Goodman), 19:186
Solomon, 19:185, 186

YALE
Mary (Clark), 18:116
Rebecca, 18:116
YATAN see YATTEN, YEATON
YATES
Elizabeth, 20:172
Frank, 20:172
Irene (Cobb), 20:172
James, 18:96
Lemuel, 18:206
Lucinda (Norwood), 18:206
Nancy, 16:235
Naomi (Estes), 18:96
YATTEN/YATAN see also YEATON
Jacob, 19:167

Margaret (___), 19:167
Richard, 19:167
YEATON/YEATTEN/YEATTON see also YATAN
Abigail (Bourne), 19:168
Betsey, 19:167
Catherine (Randall), 19:167
Daniel, 19:168
Elizabeth (___), 19:167
Elizabeth (Collier), 19:167
Hophni, 19:168
Hopley, 19:168
Jacob, 19:165, 166, 168
John, 19:167
Lydia, 19:168
Nancy, 19:168
Nathaniel, 19:168
Olive, 19:168
Polly (Chamberlain), 19:167
Samuel, 19:167, 168
YEBORNE see also EBORNE
George, 17:91
YEOMAN
Abigail, 16:85
YONGES
Joseph, 19:193
YORK, 20:18
Abigail, 16:117; 17:235
Abigail (Robinson), 18:76
Deborah, 19:163
Dolly (Haddock), 16:147
George Norton, 16:147
Hannah, 17:176; 18:76
James, 17:176; 19:163
Joseph, 18:76
Lucy (Palmer), 17:176
Mary, 18:200
Mary (Alley), 19:163
Sumner, 17:223
Sumner D., 17:222
Thomas, 18:240; 19:163
Thomasine, 18:204
William, 19:163
YOUNG
"Daughter", 19:18
Abigail, 19:177
Agnes Spears (Smith), 17:56
Alexander, 20:240a
Caroline (Kimball), 16:148
Daniel, 18:202
David, 16:27; 17:54
David C., 19:97
E. Harold, 17:183
Edward, 16:19
Elizabeth, 17:32; 18:228
Elizabeth (Dampney), 16:27
Elizabeth Keene, 19:97
Francis, 20:226
Francis Cogswell, 19:18
George Washburn, 19:18
Hannah, 16:19
Hannah (Whittier), 16:19
Harriet Fletcher (Marland), 19:18
Harriet Marland, 19:18
Jeremiah Smith, 19:18
Joseph, 16:134
Louise, 20:228
Louise Ryder, 17:177
Mary, 17:56; 19:18
Mehitable (Wheeler), 18:202
Sally (Eastman), 17:54
Sarah, 17:53
William, 16:134; 17:56

YOUNGLOVE
Abigail, 17:58
Samuel, 17:58

ZACHARY
Daniel, 18:90
ZARELLA, 16:124
ZECCHINI
Augusto, 19:178
Francis, 19:178
Generosa (Balugani), 19:178
Mary Eleanor (Holt), 19:178
Mary Frances, 19:178
ZEIGLER/ZIEGLER
George, 16:86
George William, 20:32
Mary (Blaney), 16:86
Virginia Adeline (Hunt), 20:32
ZORELLA, 16:123
ZOVAGLIA, 16:123
ZUBRINSKY
Eugene Cole, 17:59

www.ingramcontent.com/pod-product-compliance
Lightning Source LLC
Chambersburg PA
CBHW081132170426
43197CB00017B/2840